HISTORY
OF
BRITISH INDIA

HISTORY

OF

BRITISH INDIA.

HUGH MURRAY, ESQ., F.R.S.E.

WITH CONTINUATION

COMPRISING

THE AFGHAN WAR-THE CONQUEST OF SINDE AND GWALIOR-

WAR IN THE PUNJAUB.

GYAN

Published by

GYAN

Gyan Publishing House
5, Ansari Road
Daryaganj, New Delhi-110002
Phone: 011-47034999, 9811692060
E-mail: books@gyanbooks.com

Distribution Network
gyanbooks.com
India, USA, Canada, UK, Australia, France

ISBN : 978-81-212-9594-9 (PB)
First Published, 1853

2nd Impression 2023

Printed at: Gyan Press, Delhi.

HISTORY OF BRITISH INDIA
Author: HUGH MURRAY

History of British India

The Khyber Pass

Page 645

T. NELSON & SONS, LONDON & EDINBURGH.

HISTORY

OF

BRITISH INDIA.

BY

HUGH MURRAY, Esq., F.R.S.E.

WITH CONTINUATION

COMPRISING

THE AFGHAN WAR—THE CONQUEST OF SINDE AND GWALIOR—

WAR IN THE PUNJAUB.

&c. &c.

Is India free? and does she wear her plumed
And jewelled turban with a smile of peace,
Or do we grind her still?

THE TASK.

MDCCCLIII.

ADVERTISEMENT TO THE FIFTH EDITION.

THE first edition of this History of British India brought down the narrative of events in our great Eastern empire to the close of the Pindaree war, and the conquest of the Mahrattas. Since then, events of the utmost magnitude have transpired, sufficient to cast into the shade the older history of the Peninsula in the estimation of its British rulers. The war in Afghanistan was marked by circumstances at once glorious and tragical beyond perhaps any which distinguished former periods of our history, sufficing for a time to fill the minds of the most sanguine with apprehensions for our whole Indian empire. A fruitless triumph restored confidence and honour; but peace had not long given repose to our arms, ere the war in Sinde called for new exertions, and excited fresh anxiety. To this succeeded the eventful campaigns in the Punjaub and Moultan, where British arms achieved triumphs against braver and more daring enemies than ever before threatened our progress, if not even our very existence, in the East. The chapters in which these eventful incidents of Indian history are narrated have accordingly been added to Mr Murray's original work. They have been compiled with the utmost care from official documents and the narratives of individuals who bore a part in the scenes they have described. They furnish to the reader a concise and comprehensive narrative of the most important wars in which British arms have been engaged since the peace of 1815, and of the most critical struggle which has chequered the later history of our Indian empire.

EDINBURGH, September 1849.

PREFACE TO THE FIRST EDITION.

In addition to a succinct account of the grand natural features of India, contained in the following work, it exhibits that splendid series of discovery and triumph by which the maritime passage to India was achieved, and the Portuguese first established European sway on its shores. These events, which, to the importance of truth, add the interest of romance, being narrated only in voluminous foreign works, have never before been combined in a form suited to general perusal. The early voyages and settlements of the English also include many incidents characteristic of the enterprise that paved the way for the amazing power which the nation has achieved.

Next to the discovery and early trade with India is its history. This commences with the Mohammedan invasion, the remotest period concerning which authentic records exist. A comprehensive view is taken of the revolutions of the Patan and Mogul dynasties, the most splendid in the East, and the story of which is diversified with striking vicissitudes of grandeur and humiliation—of cruel and benevolent exercise of power. Particular care has been taken to exhibit the internal economy of this powerful court; a subject hitherto much overlooked, yet for which ample materials are afforded both by Oriental records and by the observations of intelligent European travellers.

Attention is next invited to a train of events which are at once memorable in the military annals of the world, and deeply interesting to this country. The first of these is the conquest of British India; when a few merchants, with a handful of troops, and struggling against European and native rivalry, subverted all the states which had sprung from the ruins of the Mogul empire, and became arbiters of the destiny of upwards of One Hundred Millions of human beings placed at the opposite extremity of the globe. In this important recital, the incidents which distinguished the several contests are exhibited in one view, instead of passing repeatedly from one to another, and carrying all forward with a regard to nothing but the order of time. This plan, which is followed with such success by Mr. Hallam in his History of the Middle Ages, renders the narrative more perspicuous as well as more interesting.

EDINBURGH, March 1832.

CONTENTS.

CHAPTER I.

GENERAL VIEW OF THE NATURAL FEATURES OF INDIA.

CHAPTER II.

KNOWLEDGE OF INDIA AMONG THE ANCIENTS.

CHAPTER III.

PORTUGUESE DISCOVERY OF THE PASSAGE TO INDIA.

CHAPTER IV.

PORTUGUESE SETTLEMENTS AND CONQUESTS IN INDIA.

CHAPTER V.

EARLY ENGLISH VOYAGES AND SETTLEMENTS.

CHAPTER VI.

EARLY MOHAMMEDAN CONQUESTS IN INDIA.

CHAPTER VII.

THE PATAN OR AFGHAN DYNASTY.

CHAPTER VIII.

THE MOGUL DYNASTY TO AURENGZEBE.

CHAPTER IX.

AURENGZEBE—DECLINE OF THE MOGUL DYNASTY.

CHAPTER X.

BRITISH CONQUEST OF THE CARNATIC.

CHAPTER XI.

BRITISH CONQUEST OF BENGAL.

CHAPTER XII.

WAR WITH MYSORE.

CHAPTER XIII.

CONQUEST OF MYSORE.

CHAPTER XIV.

MAHRATTA WAR, AND CONQUEST OF CENTRAL HINDOSTAN.

CHAPTER XV.

PINDAREE WAR—CONQUEST OF THE MAHRATTAS, &c.

CHAPTER XVI.

THE AFGHAN WAR.

CHAPTER XVII.

THE WAR IN SINDE AND GWALIOR.

CONTENTS.

CHAPTER XVIII.

WAR IN THE PUNJAUB.

CHAPTER XIX.

WAR IN MOULTAN AND THE PUNJAUB.

HISTORY

OF

BRITISH INDIA.

CHAPTER I.

General View of the Natural Features of India.

Great Importance always attached to India—Its Outline and Boundaries—General Aspect—The Great Central Plain—Provinces of which it is composed—Vegetable and Animal Productions—The Great Desert—Mountain-region of the Himmaleh—Belt or Border of thick Jungle—Tract of lower Hills—Elevated Ranges—Their steep and rugged Character—Change in Vegetable and Animal Nature—Three Zones of Vegetation—Central Region — The different River-glens — Valleys — Cashmere—Dangerous Passes—Difficulty of Respiration—Sources of the Jumna and Ganges—Pilgrimage—The Deccan—Vyndhya Range—The Ghauts—Nhilgerries—Opposite Coasts—Central Table-plains—Scenery—Influence of the physical Character upon the political State of these different Regions.

CHAP. I

Of all the countries on the Asiatic continent, India, from the earliest ages, has excited the greatest interest, and enjoyed the highest celebrity. The exploits of the conquerors who made it the object of their warlike expeditions, as also the splendid productions of nature

CHAP. I.

Magnificent associations.

and art which were thence imported, procured for it a great name even in the remotest eras of classical antiquity. It has all along appeared to the imagination of the Western World as adorned with whatever is most splendid and gorgeous; glittering as it were with gold and gems, and redolent of fragrant and delicious odours. Though there be, in these magnificent conceptions, something romantic and illusory, still India forms unquestionably one of the most remarkable regions that exist on the surface of the globe. The varied grandeur of its scenery, and the rich productions of its soil, are scarcely equalled in any other country. It is also extremely probable that it was, if not the first, at least one of the earliest seats of civilisation, laws, arts, and of all the improvements of social life. These, it is true, have at no period attained to the same pitch of advancement as among Europeans; but they have, nevertheless, been developed in very original forms, displaying human nature under the most striking and singular aspects.

Interest as a British province.

The strong interest which India in itself is thus calculated to excite, must to us be greatly heightened by the consideration of its having become so completely a province of the British Empire. The government of this country now directs the fortunes of a hundred millions of human beings placed at the opposite extremity of the earth; and hence the welfare of the state is intimately suspended on that of this vast dependency. This connexion, too, is peculiarly strengthened by the great number of our countrymen who are constantly going out to administer the affairs of that important colony. Closer personal ties, in many instances, are thereby formed with our eastern settlements, than with the different provinces of Britain itself. Thousands, to whom Cornwall and Devonshire are almost strange lands, are connected by the most intimate social relations with Madras and Calcutta. For such persons the history and description of our Indian possessions, independently of the grandeur of the subject and its union with national wealth and power, must have a peculiar interest, as being closely associated with the pursuits and prospects of their dearest friends.

Boundaries of India.

India is enclosed by grand natural boundaries. Its whole northern frontier is separated from the high table-land of Thibet by the chain of the Himmaleh Mountains, which, according to recent observation, appears to reach at least as great a height as any other ridge by which the globe is traversed. The western and eastern limits are formed by the lower course of two great rivers, —the Indus on one side, and the Brahmapoutra on the other. The southern portion consists of a very extensive peninsula bounded by the ocean. Other countries have often been comprehended under the general appellation of India,—particularly Cabul and Candahar, which ranked long as provinces belonging to the Mogul emperors; but this was merely in consequence of those warlike rulers having conquered India, and transferred thither the seat of their empire. These districts, it is manifest, bear a much closer relation to Persia and Tartary; and, when they are included in Hindostan, they necessarily extend that country beyond its great river-line on the north-west, where it has no decided or natural boundaries. But within the limits we have indicated there is found a religion, languages, manners, and institutions, characteristic of this region, and distinguishing it from all the other countries of Asia.

India, thus defined, though some of its extremities have not been very precisely determined, may be suitably described as lying between the 8th and 34th degrees of north latitude, and the 68th and 92d of east longitude. It thus extends somewhat above 1800 miles from north to south, and, at its greatest breadth, nearly 1500 from east to west.

Its geographical features.

In treating of this important country, it will be useful to begin with a general survey of its geographical features; and these, it will soon appear, are distinguished at once by their grandeur and their variety. India is, as it were, an epitome of the whole world. It has regions that bask beneath the brightest rays of a tropical

CHAP. I.

The varieties of its climate.

sun, and others, than which the most awful depths of the polar world are not more dreary. The varying degrees of elevation produce here the same changes that arise elsewhere from the greatest difference of position on the earth's surface. Its vast plains present the double harvests, the luxuriant foliage, and even the burning deserts of the torrid zone; the lower heights are enriched by the fruits and grains of the temperate climates; the upper steeps are clothed with the vast pine forests of the north; while the highest pinnacles are buried beneath the perpetual snows of the arctic zone. We do not here, as in Africa and the polar regions, see nature under one uniform aspect; on the contrary, we have to trace gradual yet complete transitions between the most opposite extremes that can exist on the surface of the same planet.

The Indian plain.

The main body, as it were, of India, the chief scene of her matchless fertility and the seat of her great empires, is composed of a plain extending along the entire breadth from east to west, between the Brahmapoutra and the Indus; and reaching, in point of latitude, from the great chain of mountains to the high table-land of the Southern Peninsula. It may thus possess a length of 1500 miles, with an average breadth of from 300 to 400. The line of direction is generally from south-east to north-west, following that of the vast mountain-range which

Its fertility.

bounds it on the north, and from whose copious streams its fruitfulness is derived. With the exception, perhaps, of the country watered by the great river of China, it may be considered the finest and most fertile on the face of the earth. The whole of its immense superficies, if we leave out an extensive desert-tract to be presently noticed, forms one continuous level of unvaried richness, and over which majestic rivers, with slow and almost insensible course, diffuse their sea-like expanse.

Province of Bengal.

Of this general character of the Indian plain, the province of Bengal presents the most complete and striking example; no part of it being diversified with a single rock, or even a hillock. The Ganges pours through it a continually widening stream, which, during the rainy season, covers a great extent with its fertilizing inundation. From this deep, rich, well-watered soil, the sun, beating with direct and intense rays, awakens an almost unrivalled power of vegetation, and makes it one entire field of waving grain. Bahar, farther up the current, has the same general aspect, though its surface is varied by some slight elevations; but Allahabad, higher still, is mostly low, warm, and fruitful, exactly like Bengal. North of the river the provinces of Oude and Rohilcund, sloping gradually upwards to the mountains, enjoy a more cool and salubrious climate, and display in profusion the most valuable products both of Asia and Europe. Here the valley of the Ganges terminates, and is succeeded by that of the Jumna, more elevated, and neither so well watered nor quite so fertile. The Doab, or territory between the two rivers, requires in many places artificial irrigation. Its woods, however, are more luxuriant, while the moderate cold of its winter permits a crop of wheat or other European grain to be raised, and the summer is sufficient to ripen one of rice. To the south of the Jumna, and along the course of its tributary the Chumbul, the ground is broken by eminences extending from the hills of Malwah and Ajmere; while, even amid its most level tracts, insulated rocks, with perpendicular sides and level summits, form those almost impregnable hill-forts so much celebrated in Indian history. Westward of Delhi begins the Great Desert, which we shall at present pass over to notice the plain of the Punjaub, where the five tributaries of the Indus, rolling their ample streams, produce a degree of fertility equal to that of the region watered by the Ganges. High cultivation, too frequently obstructed by public disorders and the ruder character of the people, is alone wanting to make it rival the finest portions of the more eastern territory.

Source of its fertility. *Provinces of Oude and Rohilcund.* *The Punjaub.*

Artificial changes.

Throughout the whole of this vast plain, the wants of the population and the demands of commerce have entirely superseded the original productions of nature, and

CHAP. I.

substituted plants and grains better fitted for human use. Even under the most careful management, few of those exquisite shrubs are now reared which have given such celebrity to the vegetable kingdom of the East. Here are quite unknown those aromatic gales which perfume the hilly shores of Malabar and the oriental islands. Its staples consist of solid, rich, useful articles, produced by strong heat acting on a deep, moist, and fertile soil,—rice, the eastern staff of life,—sugar, the most generally used of dietetic luxuries,—opium, whose narcotic qualities have made it every where so highly prized,—indigo, the most valuable substance used in dyeing,—and, in the drier tracts, cotton, which clothes the inhabitants of the East, and affords the material of the most delicate and beautiful fabrics. Such an entire subjection to the plough and the spade, joined to the want of variety in the surface, gives to this great central region a tame and monotonous aspect. Baber, its Afghan conqueror, complains, in his Memoirs, of the uniform and uninteresting scenery which every where met his eye, and looks back with regret to the lofty cliffs, the green slopes, and murmuring streams of his native land.

Products of the Punjaub.

Its monotonous aspect.

Counteracting effects.

In spite, however, of every human effort, some tracts are left uncultivated in consequence of political disorder and misrule; while, in others, nature, under the combined influence of heat and moisture, makes efforts so powerful as to baffle all attempts to modify or control her. She then riots in unbounded luxuriance, and covers large tracts with that dense, dark, impenetrable mass of foliage, crowded and twined together, called *jungle*, which opposes an almost impassable barrier even to an army. Trees spreading on every side their gigantic arms,—thorny and prickly shrubs of every size and shape,—canes shooting in a few months to the height of sixty feet,—compose the chief materials of those natural palisades. Even in the open plain, the banian and other single trees, when full scope is given to their growth, spread out into the dimensions of a considerable forest.

Jungles.

From the cultivated regions the various classes of wild

TIGER HUNTING

Page 25.

BOAR HUNTING.

beasts are excluded with the utmost solicitude. Even the domestic species are not reared in great numbers, nor to any remarkable size or strength. There is a small cow with a hump, fit only for draught, but which the Hindoo regards as a sacred object. Light active steeds are bred by the natives for predatory excursions; though, for regular military service, the large Turkish horse is decidedly preferred. But the wooded tracts, where nature revels uncontrolled, are filled with huge and sometimes destructive animals, of which the two most remarkable are the elephant and the tiger. The former, of a species distinct from that of Africa, is here not merely pursued as game, but, being caught alive, is trained for the various purposes of state, hunting, and war. The tiger, the most formidable tenant of the Bengal jungle, supplies the absence of the lion, and, though not quite equal in strength and majesty, is still more fierce and dangerous. These two mighty quadrupeds are brought into conflict in the Indian hunts, when the elephant is used as an instrument for attacking his fiercer but less vigorous rival. The hunter, well armed, is seated on the back of his huge ally; and, in the first advance, the whole body of the assailants are ranged in a line. When the combat commences, the elephant endeavours either to tread down the tiger with his hoof, crushing him with the whole weight of his immense body, or to assail him with his long and powerful tusks. Whenever either of these movements can be fully accomplished, the effect is irresistible; but the tiger, by his agility, and especially by his rapid spring resembling the flight of an arrow, often succeeds in fastening upon the legs and sides of his unwieldy adversary, and inflicts deep wounds, while the latter is unable either to resist or to retaliate. Even the rider, notwithstanding his exalted seat and the use of fire-arms, is not on such occasions wholly exempt from danger.

Domestic animals. *Wild animals.* *Tiger hunts.*

To complete the survey of the great Indian plain, there remains to be described, as already hinted, one feature wholly dissimilar to all the rest. Immediately

The Great Desert.

CHAP. I.

westward of the Jumna, the general level of the country attains a point of elevation, whence it descends on both sides; and all the torrents, falling from this high mountain-range, roll either eastward and become tributary to the Ganges, or westward to pour their waters into the Indus. Between these two rivers and their respective branches there intervenes a considerable space, which is refreshed only by a few small rivulets that spring up and disappear amid the waste. In this manner is formed a desert, of extent sufficient to compose a mighty kingdom, and occupying in that direction the whole breadth, from the mountains to the ocean. This entire region, about 600 miles long and 300 broad, presents an aspect nearly similar to the most dreary tracts of Arabia and Africa. Its surface, scarcely raised above the sea, is covered with saline incrustations and marine exuviæ, and hence bears every appearance of having been at one time a portion of the ocean-bed, which the waters have deserted. According to the observations of Mr Elphinstone, who crossed it in his way to Cabul, the eastern division consists of sand often rising into hills of surprising height, and so loose that, whenever the horses quitted the path hardened by beating, they sunk above the knee. Over this wilderness, however, is scattered some coarse grass, with stunted and prickly shrubs; while, in the midst of the sand, there grow large water-melons, affording the most delicious refreshment to the thirsty traveller. At wide intervals are found villages, or rather clusters of mud huts, round which are reared crops of coarse grain and pulse, whose stalks, like shrubs, stand distinctly separate from each other. Yet a considerable population must be sprinkled over this immense desert, since Bikaneer, in its centre, presents, though on a small scale, the aspect of a city adorned with palaces, temples, and other spacious edifices. Westward of that town the soil is generally a hard clay, variegated only by mounds of sand. Poogul, a village of straw huts defended by a ruinous mud fort, encompassed with naked hills and amid a sea of sand without a trace of vegetation, ap-

Extent and character of the Desert.

Population.

Poogul and its fort.

peared a spot so desolate that it seemed astonishing how any human beings could make it their abode. On the more smooth and level portions of this dreary tract the traveller is tantalized by the phenomenon of *mirage*, producing before him the appearance of immense lakes that even reflect the surrounding objects; and the illusion continues till he has almost touched the watery semblance, and finds it to consist of the same arid soil as the rest of the desert.

The mirage.

Northward of this great plain, and along its whole extent, towers the sublime mountain-region of the Himmaleh, ascending gradually till it terminates in a long range of summits wrapped in perpetual snow. According to Mr Calder, there may be traced, for the space of 1000 miles, a continuous line 21,000 feet above the sea, from which, as a base, detached peaks ascend to the additional height of 5000 or 6000 feet. The inhabitant of the burning plains contemplates, not without wonder, this long array of white pinnacles forming the boundary of the distant horizon. In this progressive ascent nature assumes a continually changing aspect; and hence it will be necessary to view in succession the different stages through which she passes.

Himmaleh Mountains.

The Himmaleh range, where it touches on the champaign country, is almost every where girt with a peculiar belt or border, called the Tarryani. This term is applied to a plain about twenty miles broad, upon which the waters from the higher regions are poured down in such profusion that the river-beds are unable to contain them. They accordingly overflow, and convert the ground into a species of swamp, which, acted on by the burning rays of a tropical sun, throws up an excessively rank vegetation, whereby the earth is choked rather than covered. The soil is concealed beneath a mass of dark and dismal foliage, while long grass and prickly shrubs shoot up so densely and so close as to form an almost impenetrable barrier. It is still more awfully guarded by the pestilential vapours exhaling from those dark recesses, which make it at certain seasons a region of death.

The Tarryani.

Pestilent swamps.

CHAP. I. Hence the destruction which overtakes an army that encamps for any length of time near this valley,—an effect fatally experienced by the British detachments which were stationed on the frontiers of Bootan and Nepaul. Beneath these melancholy shades, too, the elephant, the tiger, and other wild animals, prowl unmolested; while the few human beings who occupy the vicinity present a meagre, dwarfish, and most sickly aspect.

Lower mountain-stages. In emerging from this dark and deadly plain, and beginning to ascend the lower mountain-stages, the visiter enjoys a much more pleasing scene. He passes now through smiling and fruitful valleys, overhung by the most romantic steeps, and covered to a great extent with the noblest forests. Amid trees similar to those which spread their majestic foliage on the banks of the Ganges, various species of the more hardy oak and the pine begin to appear. Some possess rich juices and aromatic odours not found among the lower woods; such as that peculiar mimosa, the fluid extracted from which yields the medical substance called catechu, and a species of cinnamon or rather cassia, the virtue of which resides in its root. The prospects obtained from commanding points in these regions, consisting in a foreground of smiling and cultured vales, hills behind crowned with natural plantations, steeper and loftier ranges beyond, and in the distance the snow-clad tops of the highest mountain-chain, form a combination of the most sublime and enchanting scenery.

Natural productions.

Character of higher ranges. The Himmaleh, as it ascends above the picturesque slopes which diversify its lower border, assumes a much bolder and severer aspect. The lofty ridge, the deep valley, the dashing torrent, produce a resemblance to the most elevated portions of our own central Highlands; and Scottish officers, accordingly, who happened to serve in that remote province, have fancied themselves wandering amid the romantic glens of their native country. Generally speaking, the character of this mountain-chain is rugged and stern; its ridges rise behind each

CHAP. I.

other in awful array; but they enclose no rural scenes, nor present any gentle undulations. Their steep sides, sometimes wooded, sometimes presenting vast faces of naked rock, dip down abruptly, forming dark chasms and ravines, at the bottom of which there is only room for the torrent to force its way through rude fragments fallen from the cliffs above. A laborious task is imposed on the traveller, who has successively to mount and descend this series of lofty terraces, along rough and narrow paths that often skirt the most tremendous precipices. The expedients, too, provided for the passage of the rivers which dash through these gloomy hollows, are of the most slender and imperfect description. Two planks fastened to the point of opposite cliffs, called a *sanga* or *sankha*, are, in many cases, considered amply sufficient; others, called *jhulas*, are formed by ropes stretched across, making a species of loose parapet, and supporting a light ladder for the feet to rest upon. Captain Webb met with an instance where there were merely stretched from bank to bank two or three ropes, round which the passenger was expected to coil himself, and work his way across, having a hoop for the back to rest upon; those who could not effect this movement were pulled across by a cord.

Their stern and gloomy character

Rude bridges.

So irregular is the surface of this territory that great difficulty occurs in finding a level space on which to build their towns. It is supposed that, in the whole extent of country surrounding Serinagur, there could not have been discovered another place on which to have erected that small city; and there is no spot between it and the great plain where a thousand men could encamp. At Nahn the passenger mounts through the principal street by a stair cut in the rock. Rampore, the chief town in the valley of the Upper Sutledge, is reached only over ledges of rocks and flights of steps; its houses rise in tiers above each other along the face of the steep, while the river tumbles beneath, and awful crags overhang it from above.

Extreme irregularity of surface.

In consequence of this peculiar structure, these loftier

CHAP. I.

Monotony.

regions of the Himmaleh do not present that tranquil grandeur, and those picturesque views, which render the mountain-scenery of Europe so enchanting. They are rugged, gloomy, and monotonous. The mighty summits overhang no soft pastoral valleys, nor wave with varied foliage, nor are reflected in the bosom of still and transparent lakes. The traveller, hemmed in between their steep precipices, sees only the dark grandeur of the chasm through which he winds. Sometimes, however, on reaching a clear point, he finds himself in possession of a prospect bearing a character of the most awful sublimity. A spot, raised almost to an immeasurable height above the plain beneath, proves only the base, whence seven or eight successive ranges rise towards heaven, and terminate at length in a line of snowy pinnacles.

Different temperatures.

Mr Royle, in his elegant and instructive work on the botany of the Himmaleh, divides that region, in respect to vegetation, into three zones or belts. The first he considers as rising to the height of 5000 feet. The general temperature is here lowered, as usual, in proportion to the elevation, yet without the disappearance, to the extent that might be expected, of tropical plants. The southern exposure, the intense force of the sun's rays during the hot season, and the tropical rains falling in undiminished abundance, enable these to be brought to almost equal maturity as in the upper part of the central plain. In Nepaul, and other favourable situations, rice as a summer, and wheat as a winter crop, form the regular course of cultivation. But some of the more delicate plants are unable to resist exposure to the keen atmosphere and the nightly breezes; among which are the choicest of fruits, the mango and the pine apple. At the same time, in the colder season, on elevated peaks, the plants of Europe and other temperate climates, are seen springing contiguously to those of the tropic. Snow is scarcely ever observed on this lower stage of the mountain territory.

Tropical and temperate crops at Nepaul.

The second belt is considered as reaching to the height

of 9000 feet. Snow here falls constantly in winter, often to a great depth, but melts in early spring. Although the vegetation becomes more and more that of the temperate zone, yet the causes already stated enable tropical plants to climb beyond their natural height, and to mingle with those of a very different clime. In sheltered well-watered valleys, crops of rice are still successfully raised, while wheat grows on the heights above. But though the herbaceous plants are able to mount thus high, it is otherwise with trees, exposed to every vicissitude of the seasons. The palms and other Indian species are seen no longer, and the foliage appears exclusively European. CHAP. I. Second belt.

Third belt Arctic climate. The third and most elevated belt reaches from the border of the latter to the summit of the Himmaleh. The climate here is that of the more northern part of Europe and America, terminating in the perpetual snows of the arctic world. These, even in the lower districts, do not melt till May or June, when the extreme cold of winter is suddenly succeeded by the most intense heat. The rays of the sun, indeed, beat fiercely and painfully, even when the atmosphere is so little affected by them that the thermometer stands many degrees below the freezing point; and hence the traveller is scorched amidst almost unbearable cold,—extremes which always prove distressing and sometimes fatal. Bhot territory. The territory called Bhot, constituting the most elevated portion, has the severity of the climate aggravated by its rocky surface, so that not above a sixteenth part of it is fit for cultivation; yet, even here, under circumstances not at all favourable, vegetation displays a luxuriance which could little be expected at so great a height. Buckwheat and barley are generally raised with success. At 12,000 feet, Captain Webb saw the finest grain, and at 11,680, he observed forests of oak, and beds of strawberries and currants in full blossom. The pasturage, in consequence probably of copious moisture, combined with the power of the sun's rays, grows with a luxuriance almost unequalled. The natives, prone to exaggeration, assert it

CHAP. I

to be inexhaustible, so that whatever has been cropt during the day is restored in the following night. A productive field, however, is occasionally ruined by the descent of glaciers, or beds of snow, which do not melt for several years. It is alleged, indeed, by the inhabitants, that there is a gradual lowering of the frozen line, and that the snow covers woods and fields which were once entirely free from it.

Glaciers.

Vast forest.

Notwithstanding the shattered and rocky aspect of those precipices, they are yet covered with vast masses of hanging wood. Amidst the wilds, tall and majestic forests of pine, larch, spruce, and silver fir, sometimes even of cypress and cedar, grow, flourish, and decay; for there are no means of conveying the timber to any spot where it might be subservient to human use or ornament. With these trees are intermingled numerous bushes loaded with the fruits which form the luxury of the northern regions of Europe; gooseberry, raspberry, strawberry, all unknown to the plains below. In sheltered spots, the wild rose, the lily of the valley, cowslip, dandelion, and various other flowers, are seen bursting through the green carpet. The trees and rocks in the higher districts are richly clothed with moss and lichen, the vegetation of the countries bordering on the arctic circle; a specimen of the latter has even been observed resembling that which flourishes in Iceland, and which is imported for medicinal purposes under the name of Iceland moss.

Fruits and flowers.

Northern side of the Himmaleh.

After passing the crest of the Himmaleh, and descending the northern side, quite a different scene opens to the view. The periodical rains, which plentifully water all the opposite face, cannot pass that tremendous barrier. Snow also falls in much smaller quantity, and is more easily melted. The same luxuriant verdure and vegetation no longer clothe those remote heights, which are described by Jacquemont as steep and naked, covered with shrubs, parched grass, and debris washed down by the waters. Yet it is remarkable that a mild climate, fit for the production of valuable grain, reaches

Mild climate

to a considerably greater elevation here than even on the southern face. In the Tartar pergunnah of Hungarung, the village of Nako, 12,000 feet high, was seen surrounded by the most luxuriant crops of wheat and barley. A hamlet, in the north-east of Kunawur, at 14,900 feet, is described by Dr Gerard as being encompassed with the finest fields of the latter; and it appeared to him that culture might be carried to the height of 16,000 or 17,000 feet. Even the grasses, though having a withered appearance, are of a nutritious species, and afford subsistence to numerous flocks and herds. Passes 20,000 feet high have, in this region, been found clear of snow. It is remarkable that, on coming to the outer face of one of these mountains, even with a southern exposure, the temperature is greatly diminished. The case is the same with peaks projected into the air, like promontories into the ocean; though the cause of the peculiar mildness in this enclosed part of the great range seems not to be fully understood. Mr Royle suggests the reflection of the sun's rays from opposite mountains, and the warm vapours ascending from the sheltered valleys which lie between them.

Animal life.

The animal world in this higher region undergoes a change equally striking with the vegetable. The elephant and tiger, kings of the forests beneath, disappear, or are very seldom seen. Depredations are chiefly committed by the wild cat, the bear, and the hog. The chamois bounds from rock to rock, and the forests are filled with deer of various species; of which the most rare and precious is that producing the musk. It is found only in the loftiest heights, amid rocks which the human foot scarcely dares to tread. The most intense cold is so essential to its life, that the young, on being brought down to a warm situation, usually perish in a few days. The forests at all the more moderate elevations are filled with flocks of such fowls as are elsewhere domesticated, here running about wild, tempting the pursuit of the sportsman; but, as they very seldom take wing, they are with difficulty reached by the gun. The peacock

Wild fowls.

CHAP. I.

Birds of prey game, &c.

displays his glittering plumage only on the lower hills. The sovereign eagle is seldom descried amid the cliffs, which are inhabited by kites, hawks, and others of the minor predatory birds. Partridges and pheasants are numerous and of various species; the latter are even seen flying amid the snows at a great elevation. Bees swarm in all the lower districts, making their hives in the hollows of trees; these the natives plunder by merely raising a loud noise, which causes the swarm to issue forth and leave the honey unprotected.

Domestic animals.

The domestic animals, fed by the natives on their rich pastures, are the common black cattle of India, combined with the yak of Thibet. A mule bred between the two is also very common. The latter produces with either of the pure species, and even with its own kind, though in this last case it soon degenerates. Sheep and goats are also reared in large numbers, not only for the ordinary purposes of food and clothing, but for the conveyance of merchandise, which they alone are fitted to transport over the steep mountain-passes. Besides the common sheep, there is another breed, powerful, and long-legged, and able to bear more than double the burden of the other; its wool is also very fine.

The greatest elevations.

The most elevated part of this stupendous range is that to the north of Bengal, along the heads of the Gogra, the Ganges, and the Jumna, and westward as far as the Sutledge. In this line there are supposed to be at least twenty-eight peaks higher than Chimborazo; and several appear, upon strict measurement, to reach 25,000 feet. Three, farther to the north, seen at different times, but at some distance, by Moorcroft, Gerard, and a government surveyor, could not, it was thought by these gentlemen, fall short of 29,000 or even 30,000 feet. This sublime formation, supposed to be 1000 miles in length and eighty in breadth, does not enclose any thing that can properly be called a table-land, for though, from the plain it appears like a succession of ridges, in the interior it is found composed of arms, radiating in every direction, intersected by deep ravines, through

Their immense extent.

which the waters struggle, and are often turned in opposite directions. Their line is so winding and irregular, that the traveller is usually obliged to cross the summit of the ridge, as if no openings existed. It is observed, too, that the north-western face is always rugged, while that to the north-east is shelving. The declivity towards Thibet is small, when compared to the descent on the southern side; indicating the great elevation of that country, which is estimated not to fall short of 15,000 feet.

The frontier of Thibet.

Westward of the Sutledge, the Himmaleh greatly declines, or rather, according to Baron Hügel, it stretches in a northern direction, along the frontier of Thibet, detaching only an inferior branch along the Indian border. The white summits are no longer seen in a continuous line, but appear only singly, and at some distance. The most western is Tricota Devi, a beautiful three-peaked mountain, and beyond it a break occurs, which, however, to an eye looking from India is filled up by more distant masses. Southward of Cashmere, the Peer Pandjahl, as it is called, rears its snowy head, though not altogether to the same stupendous height; and it is continued to the Hindoo Coosh, which separates Cabul from Tartary.

Tricota Devi, and Peer Pandjahl.

Valleys of the great rivers.

A natural division of this high country is formed by the narrow valleys, or rather ravines, furrowed out by those mighty rivers which descend from the heights to water the plains of Hindostan. These glens, all deep, dark, and enclosed by precipitous walls, have each, besides, its own peculiar aspect; and a late traveller has enabled us to form some idea of the leading features which distinguish those of the Sutledge, the Pabur, the Jumna, and the Bagiruttee, or principal head of the Ganges.

The Sutledge.

The glen of the Sutledge is little more than a profound and gloomy chasm, without the romantic beauty produced by swelling banks or fringing woods. Cultivation appears only on a few scattered patches; no villages smile along its border, though numerous forts frown over its steeps. —The Pabur, a tributary of the Jumna, presents a pleas-

CHAP I. The Pabur. ing variety compared to this or to any other ravine of the Himmaleh. It rolls through a vale of moderate breadth; its banks and the slopes above are beautifully studded with fields, woods, and villages; while brown hills, tipped with rocks and snow, tower in the background. The Jumna. The Jumna, again, has its borders generally bold and savage; all its higher tracts, too, consist of mighty rocks and precipices buried under huge masses of snow. Yet the lower grounds are wooded; and along the river are seen some narrow vales, rising into slopes covered with cultivation and verdure, which diversify even its wildest scenes with a mixture of softness and elegance. The Bagiruttee. The banks of the Bagiruttee, a broader stream, which has worn a still deeper bed through the mountain-strata, are beyond all others repulsive, and equally destitute of beauty and life. These solitary steeps, too, are only scantily clothed with the foliage of the sombre fir; the cliffs, shattered and splintered, are not even tinted with moss or lichen, but, bearing the dusky colours of their natural fracture, shoot up on every side into pinnacles of amazing height.

The Happy Valley. But, notwithstanding the gloomy aspect of these mountain-scenes, there are a few places in which they open out into smiling plains of considerable extent. The valleys of Nepaul, indeed, besides being very narrow, belong rather to the region of the lower hills. Considerably higher is found the Rama Serai, or the Happy Valley, where little eminences, villages, and richly cultivated fields, combine to form a delightful scene. The most extensive opening however takes place at its western extremity, where these great ridges enclose the little Cashmere. kingdom of Cashmere, which, beyond any other spot on earth, seems to merit the appellation of a terrestrial paradise. Numerous rivulets flowing down the mountain-sides diffuse verdure and beauty over the hills and vales, and in the plains expand into an extensive lake, profusely adorned with all the pomp of art and nature. The Mogul sovereigns had erected on the banks of this sheet of water gay palaces and pavilions, to which they were wont to repair as their most pleasing retreat from the toils of empire. The poets vie with each other in celebrating the delights of this enchanting valley. They extol particularly the rose of Cashmere as possessing beauty without a rival, the opening of whose buds is held by their countrymen as a national festival. M. Jacquemont, a very recent traveller, considers these descriptions of the country as exaggerated; though Baron Hügel, who visited it in 1835, thinks that none can be too flattering. The flora is entirely that of Europe, and particularly of Lombardy; the gigantic plane tree, the vine, the poplar, cover the lower grounds; while on the heights hang majestic forests of cedar and pine. The level part of the valley, nearly 5000 feet above the sea, is about eighty miles long and from six to thirty broad; but between the eternal snows of the opposite Pandjahls, or mountain-ridges, from fifty to sixty miles intervene. Shalimar alone, of the gay palaces erected by the Mogul, is still standing. The beauty of the Cashmerian maidens has also been highly celebrated throughout the East; and though M. Jacquemont professes scepticism upon this point, he gives a solution of his doubt, by mentioning the painful circumstance that almost all who possess good looks are in early life sold and carried away as slaves.

Celebrity of the vale of Cashmere.

Its flora.

Beauty of the maidens.

The passes which extend across this tremendous ridge into Thibet are of extreme and peculiar difficulty. From the structure of the mountains the roads must generally be carried nearly over their summits rising sometimes as high as 20,000 feet. They are in most cases formed by a precarious track along the alpine torrent, which dashes in an unbroken sheet of foam, through dark ravines bordered by precipitous mountain-walls ascending above the clouds. Down the perpendicular faces of these stupendous avenues descend almost continual showers of stony fragments, broken off from the cliffs above. Occasionally large portions of rock are detached, and roll down in heaps, effacing every path which has been formed beneath, filling the beds of the rivers, and converting

Difficult passes into Thibet.

CHAP. I. them into cataracts. The whole side of a mountain has been seen thus parted, and spread in fragments at its base. Trees torn up, and precipitated into the abyss, lie stretched with their branches on the earth, and their roots turned up to the sky. Yet through these tremendous passes, and across all these mighty obstructions, the daring industry of mortals has contrived to form tracks, narrow indeed, as well as fearful and perilous, but by means of which Thibet and India find it possible to exchange their respective commodities. Nothing, it is true, resembling a wagon, not even the ordinary beasts of burden, can pass this way. The goods, as already suggested, are placed on the backs of goats and sheep, which alone can scramble along these precipitous routes, though, in other respects, these animals are ill-fitted for such a laborious employment. Goats, in descending, are often pressed down by the load, while sheep, if at all urged, are very apt to run,—a movement which is here attended with the utmost peril. In some cases human aid is required, and these patient quadrupeds are raised and lowered by slings. The principal passes are those of Niti and Mana, by the heads of the Ganges; Juwar, Darma, and Byanse, by those of the Gogra. They are connected by a few cross-paths; but these are uncertain, and passable only in the very height of summer.

Tracks through the passes.

Sensations in traversing the passes.

In proceeding along these stupendous heights, the traveller occasionally experiences a distressing sensation. The atmosphere, rarefied to excess, becomes nearly unfit for supporting respiration,—the action of the lungs being impeded, the slightest fatigue overpowers him,—he stops at every three or four steps, gasping for breath,—the skin is painful, and blood bursts from the lips,—sometimes he is affected by giddiness in the head and a tendency to vertigo. The natives, who are also seized with these symptoms without being able to divine the physical cause, ascribe them to *bis*, or *bish*, meaning air poisoned, as they imagine, by the deleterious odour of certain flowers. A little observation would have shown them that the flowers in these regions have scarcely any scent; while

SOURCE OF THE JUMNA.

Page 41.

CHAP. I.

it is in the most elevated tracts, where all vegetation has ceased, that the feelings in question become the most severe and oppressive.

Rock staircases.

The arrangements for facilitating a passage over these frightful cliffs are still more perilous than those employed on the lower declivities. Rude staircases are constructed along the precipices, by which the traveller is invited to make his way. The road in some places is formed merely by posts driven into the side of the steep, over which branches of trees and earth are spread, affording a narrow footpath, suspended at a fearful height above the torrent, and shaking beneath the tread of the passenger.

Sources of the Jumna and the Ganges.

Amid these awful scenes there are two spots peculiarly sacred and sublime; those, namely, where the Jumna and the Ganges, the two rivers which give grandeur and fertility to the plain of Hindostan, burst from beneath the eternal snows. No mortal foot has yet ascended to their original springs, situated in the most elevated recesses of the mountains. There they issue forth as torrents, amid broken masses of granite, to force their way through the deep glens of the middle Himmaleh. Above them, huge piles of rock and heaps of snow rise higher and higher, till they shoot up into the two amazing peaks of Roodroo Himala and Jumnavatari.

Jumnotree

Jumnotree is situated at the foot of the immense mountain-mass of Bunderpouch, the upper section of which is entirely buried in snow; but the brow which overhangs the village is rendered green by the trickling of numberless rills that fall down and unite in a broad basin, the fountain of the Jumna. The highest peak that towers above is estimated by Mr Colebrooke at 25,500 feet, which, however, Mr Fraser suspects to be considerably overrated. The river is here swelled by numerous hot springs issuing from the rocky banks, or from pools in its own current. Captain Hodgson penetrated to several of these fountains that lay concealed beneath vast beds of snow, which, being melted by the

Hot springs

CHAP. I. exhalations, were formed into spacious halls resembling vaulted roofs of marble.

Gangoutrie. The mountain-scenery which surrounds Gangoutri, where the infant Ganges bursts into view, is still more sublime and amazing. The traveller winds his way to this place, clambering over steep rocks, or creeping along the face of precipices, where flights of steps are formed by posts driven into the crevices. At length he reaches the village, consisting only of a few huts and the temple dedicated to Mahadeo. Here the naked and pointed cliffs, shooting up to the skies, with confused masses of rock lying at their feet, and only a few trees rooting themselves in the deep chasms, make the spectator feel as if he trode on the ruins of a former world. Shattered precipices, which frown over the temple, have strown the vicinity with enormous fragments of granite, destined probably one day to overwhelm the edifice itself. A few old pines throw a dark shade over the troubled waters, whose roar is heard beneath, mingled with the stifled but fearful sound of the stones borne down by the current. Rocky heights shut in the prospect on every side except towards the east, where, behind a crowd of naked spires, the view is bounded by the four snowy peaks of Roodroo Himala.

Higher rise of the Ganges. Mr Fraser attempted to trace the Ganges above Gangoutri to a spot famous in India under the appellation of "The Cow's Mouth," the river being represented as rushing there from beneath the snows through an aperture bearing that particular form. The ruggedness of the banks and other obstacles obliged him to return; but Captain Hodgson, after three days of severe toil, reached this memorable spot, and saw the stream issuing from under a perpendicular wall of frozen snow, with numerous depending icicles, in a manner not very dissimilar to that which Indian report had led him to expect.

Sacredness of the region. The two places above mentioned, with the lower shrines of Bhadrinath and Kedarnath, and indeed the whole of this region, possess a peculiarly sacred character in the eyes of the Hindoo, and are the scene of many of

GANGOUTRI—SHRINE OF MAHADEO—SOURCE OF THE GANGES.

Page 42.

the most remarkable fictions in his poetical mythology. They are esteemed the chosen dwelling of Siva or Mahadeo, the third person in the Hindoo trinity, who, in withdrawing from Lunka or Ceylon, threw up, it is pretended, the Himmalch as his place of retreat. Dewtas, or spirits, are imagined to haunt the inaccessible glens, and by feigned sounds to allure the unfortunate passenger into their recesses, whence he never returns to the living world. Pilgrimage, the favourite form of Hindoo devotion, is most frequently performed into these mysterious solitudes, where many, however, in attempting to penetrate by the rugged paths buried in snow, either perish, or lose partially the use of their limbs. The perils which bar the approach to Gangoutri deter the greater number of the devotees, who ascend from the great fair at Hurdwar, from proceeding beyond the lower shrine of Bhadrinath; which, in the year when Captain Webb was there, had been visited by between 45,000 and 50,000 pilgrims.

Mythological fictions.

Pilgrimages.

The Deccan.

The Deccan or Southern Peninsula, which alone remains to be described, presents none of those singular features that distinguish the great central plain and its northern boundary. Hills occasionally rising to the rank of mountains, and enclosing table-lands of various elevation, diversify its surface, and procure for it at once the climate and vegetation of the tropical and of the temperate zones. But the most prominent feature is a range of heights corresponding to the triangular form of this part of the continent. The northern border consists in a tract of high country stretching from the Gulf of Cambay to the Bay of Bengal, chiefly along both banks of the Nerbudda, and composing the provinces of Malwah, Candeish, and Gundwana, to which has been given the appellation of Central India. It is known by the name of the Vyndhya chain; yet it is so widely extended and of such moderate height, seldom exceeding 2000 feet, that it seems rather a very rough and broken table-land than a regular mountain-range. Various local names are given to its branches. In some of the districts rise per-

Central India.

CHAP. I. pendicular heights, with a plain at the top, on which, as already mentioned, are constructed those strong hill-forts peculiar to that part of the world. From its extremities extend southward two parallel chains, called the Gates or Ghauts, which, at a greater or less distance, girdle the whole of the opposite coasts of Malabar and Coromandel.

Western Ghauts.

The Western Ghauts, which range along the Indian Ocean, stand generally at a small distance from the sea, and sometimes approach so close that their cliffs are washed by its waves. More commonly at ten or twelve miles from the shore, they rear their peaks, crowned, not like those of the Himmaleh with the trees of the temperate or arctic zones, but with the stately palms and aromatic shrubs which form the pride of tropical groves.

Tropical forests.

The most valuable of these productions are the plant bearing the pepper,—the betel, whose leaves are the universal masticatory in India,—the areca-palm, the nut of which is chewed along with the betel,—the sago-palm, whence flows a rich and nourishing juice,—and the cocoa-palm, so famed for its numerous and important uses. Higher than all towers the teak-tree, whose timber, stronger and more durable than that of the British oak, forms the material of oriental navies. This chain does not in the northern part reach above 3000 feet. Near Bombay, the Peak of Mahabuleshwar, 5000 feet high, affords a convenient station for invalids from that city. But it is on the coasts of Canara and Malabar, southward of the fifteenth degree of latitude, that this range attains its greatest height, shooting up pinnacles of granite 6000 feet. At the boundary of Mysore there crosses the continent a

The Nhilgerries.

ridge called the Nhilgerries, the highest in all this part of India, having one peak estimated at 8700 feet, which has lately become a most important sanitary retreat. Mr Royle conceives this group as joining together and closing the parallel chain of the two Ghauts, so that from thence only a single arm stretches southward to Cape Comorin. The western coast is in general very low, and traversed by numerous rivers flowing parallel to the shore, thus affording great convenience for inland navigation. CHAP. I.

The Eastern Ghauts, rising behind the Coromandel coast, are generally less lofty, but spread into more numerous branches, and over a wider surface. They leave also a broader plain between them and the sea; yet, unless in the deltas of the great rivers, which from the west cross the Ghauts and fall into the Bay of Bengal, this space bears somewhat of a naked and arid character. There occur even extensive tracts of sandy soil impregnated with saline substances, which in some degree taint the atmosphere. More to the north, in Orissa and the Circars, the high grounds often advance close to the sea, and consist to a great extent of mountain and jungle, continuing in a more uncultivated state, and peopled by more uncivilized races, than almost any other part of India. Cuttack, again, a district approaching the Ganges, is so low as to be liable to frequent inundations from the sea, which, in 1830, 1831, 1832, and 1833, broke the bunds or barriers, and overflowed numerous fields. Eastern Ghauts.

These three ranges enclose a table-land, elevated nearly two thousand feet above the level of the ocean, and comprising the main body of Southern India. The south-western tract, the original seat of Mahratta power, forms a hilly country, not extremely rugged, but interspersed with deep valleys. In its aspect it is decidedly highland, and is a fit residence for a pastoral people of predatory habits. The central region, composing the once powerful kingdoms of Golconda and Bejapore, comprehends extensive plains, secured by their elevation from the scorching heats which afflict the territory along the coast. The surface is generally level, and possesses much fertility, though diversified by those insulated steeps which supply a position for the almost impregnable hill-forts. The extreme southern district, called the Carnatic, is divided into two table-lands, the Balaghaut and the Mysore, considerably higher than those of the Deccan, and on that account including a greater variety of climate, soil, and production. Southern India.

Character of the scenery.

The mountain-scenery of Southern India in general, though wanting those features which invest the Himmaleh with so sublime a character, is beautiful, striking, and picturesque. It assimilates more to that of Wales and Scotland,—with this peculiarity, that it never rises above the limit of the richest vegetation, and has its highest summits crowned with woods and verdure. The greater part is under cultivation; though there is distributed over it a considerable portion of jungle, rock, forest, and even of sandy waste.

Political condition.

The political condition of the different regions of India varies strikingly according to the peculiarities in their physical circumstances. The great central plain, for example, has generally, from the earliest ages, been the seat of an empire whose greatness and splendour have eclipsed those of almost every other country. Some detached portions, as Bengal in the east, and the Punjaub in the west, have been frequently divided from the main body; but, under a vigorous and warlike dynasty, they have been as often reunited. It might have been expected that India, separated from other countries by a vast ocean and the loftiest mountain-barrier on earth, would have been secured from foreign aggression; but nothing could check the avarice and ambition which were attracted by the fame of her great wealth. That ocean has been passed,—those mountain-barriers have been scaled,—and during many generations she has groaned, and continues to groan without hope of deliverance, under the yoke of strangers.

Divisions of the country.

The power which bears rule over this central empire has usually aspired to the dominion of the whole; but the success of such undertakings has been only partial and temporary. They have been chiefly directed towards the extensive plains of the Deccan, which have in fact for ages been under foreign sway,—composed of branches broken off from the great trunk of Mogul dominion. In the most southern quarter, the table-lands and coasts have been shared among a number of little kingdoms, wealthy, populous, and civilized. These have often owned allegiance, and even paid tribute, to the Mogul, or more frequently to the Deccan rulers; but in all essential respects they have ranked as independent states.

Races of Northern India.

The mountain-regions of Northern India have enjoyed a happier lot, and been inhabited generally by races different from those which occupy the lower parts of the peninsula. The rugged tracts of the higher Himmaleh are possessed by bold, fierce, semi-Tartar tribes, who scarcely acknowledge the supremacy of the several powers which govern the adjacent plains. They have even from time to time harassed their neighbours by predatory inroads; but their small number, and the strong barriers by which they are separated, have prevented them from forming any extensive schemes of conquest.

Since the war with Nepaul, a considerable tract has been annexed to the British dominion; to which officers of the Bengal presidency are now in the habit of resorting with a view to the restoration of health. At Simla and Landour, government have formed stations for invalids; and in the vicinity of those places, villas built by opulent Europeans stud the summit of hills rising 7000 or 8000 feet above the sea, and commanding extensive views into the regions of perpetual snow.

CHAPTER II.

Knowledge of India among the Ancients.

India early known to the Ancients—Accounts in Scripture of its Trade—Bacchus—Sesostris—Expedition of Semiramis—Conquest by Darius—Accounts by Herodotus and Ctesias—Expedition of Alexander—He is obliged to return—Voyage down the Indus—Voyage of Nearchus—Alexander's March through Gedrosia—Accounts of India obtained by this Channel—Kingdoms of Syria and of Bactria—Its Numismatic Remains—Mercantile Voyage from Egypt to India—Coasts which were then visited.

CHAP. II.

Ancient writers on India.

INDIA, in the view of the earliest Greek and Roman writers, appeared an almost inaccessible region; the extensive seas which intervene being in the infancy of navigation considered quite impassable. The inland route, besides its very great length and the imperfect means of conveyance, lay partly across the loftiest ridge of mountains in the world, partly through deserts as dreary as those of Arabia. Yet the country had features which, seen even at this mysterious distance, strongly attracted attention among the civilized nations of antiquity. Its wealth and large population made it one of the principal objects of ambition to those great conquerors who aimed at universal empire; its fabrics, the most beautiful that human art has any where produced, were sought by merchants at the expense of the greatest toils and dangers; and the manners of its people, as well as the maxims of its sages, had something original and peculiar, which strongly excited philosophical inquiry. For these reasons, from the first moment that its existence became known down to the present-day, Hindostan has continued to hold a conspicuous name in the Western world.

Silence of the sacred writers.

In the sacred volume, which contains the earliest of our historical records, no statement is made whence we might conclude that the Jews had arrived at any knowledge of India. The Great River (Euphrates), and the territory immediately beyond it, appeared to them the most remote objects to the eastward, and are described under the appellation of the "ends of the earth." Yet those writings make a direct allusion to the extensive caravan routes, formed at an early period for conveying the manufactures of that opulent region into the kingdoms of the West. We cannot hesitate to believe, with Dr Vincent, that the embroidered work, and chests of rich apparel bound with cords, mentioned by Ezekiel (xxvii. 23) as brought from Haran, Canneh, and other towns on the Euphrates, were not produced by the ingenuity of the nations on that river, but drawn from the more distant countries of Eastern Asia We have little doubt also, that the trade across Arabia, by way of Dedan and Idumea, and of which "precious cloths" are mentioned as the staple, was an Indian trade.

Classic mythology.

Bacchus, in the classic mythology, is named as the conqueror of India; but this tradition, though probably not destitute of some foundation, is so enveloped in fable that we can attach to it little historical importance. Whether that country was at all included in the wide career of invasion, rather than of conquest, pursued by Sesostris, seems extremely doubtful; though some light may perhaps be thrown upon the subject by the researches now in progress for the interpretation of Egyptian hieroglyphics.

Semiramis.

The next expedition into the East, which is described in more ample detail, was that accomplished by Semiramis, the celebrated queen of Assyria. Although the knowledge possessed by the Greeks respecting the early Asiatic empires is exceedingly imperfect, yet the great fame of this enterprise, and the various shapes in which it has been reported, leave little room to doubt that it was actually undertaken. In the absence of a narrative on which a fuller dependence might be placed, recourse must be had to the account given by Diodorus. The Assyrian queen, it is said, having extended her dominion widely over Western Asia, till even Bactria was comprehended within it, and having been informed that India was the most populous, the most wealthy, and the most beautiful of kingdoms, determined to employ all the resources of her empire in attempting its conquest. Only two circumstances made this great exploit appear impracticable. One was the broad and rapid stream of the Indus, with the entire want of vessels fitted for its passage; the other was the strength and formidable character of the war-elephants, the very aspect of which struck terror into troops unaccustomed to their presence. To supply these deficiencies, the queen engaged naval architects from Phenicia, Cyprus, and other maritime districts; and, as proper materials were not to be found on the banks of the river, she caused vessels suited to its navigation to be constructed at Bactra, and conveyed thence overland. For supplying the want of elephants a still more singular plan was devised. Three hundred thousand oxen were slain, and their hides formed into the shape of the huge animals to be represented, within which camels and men were introduced as the moving power. After three years spent in these extraordinary preparations, she sent forward her armies, which some writers describe as amounting to several millions of combatants; but the narrative of Ctesias, itself much exaggerated, estimates them at three hundred thousand foot, five hundred thousand horse, while two thousand boats and the mock-elephants were conveyed on the backs of camels. Stabrobates, the Indian king, was ready to meet them on the eastern bank, with four thousand boats framed out of the reeds (canes) which grew in abundance on its marshy borders. At the same time he collected, from the various districts of India, an army even greater than that of Semiramis, supported by a numerous body of elephants. The two powers first encountered each other in the river-stream, where the queen gained a decided advantage, sinking many of the enemy's barks, and obtaining posses-

Assyrian preparations for conquest.

Preparations to oppose the invaders.

sion of both shores. She then constructed a spacious bridge, by which the whole army passed, and advanced against her adversaries. In front the pretended elephants, ranged in order of battle, somewhat surprised and appalled the native troops; but Stabrobates, having learned by means of deserters the real composition of these fictitious quadrupeds, prepared without apprehension to encounter them. As long as the contest was confined to the cavalry, victory inclined to the side of Assyria; but as soon as the real and mighty war-elephants, on the most powerful of which the king himself was mounted, rushed to the attack, the artificial semblances opposed to them, wholly unable to sustain the shock, were soon resolved into their constituent elements, who fled in dismay, and, being pursued, were many of them trampled under foot. The whole army was completely routed, and Semiramis brought back scarcely a third of her host; some authors even maintain that she herself perished in the expedition. At all events, the conquest of India appears not to have been again attempted by any of the Assyrian or Babylonian monarchs.

Passage of the Indus.

Rout of the Assyrians.

Invasion of Darius.

Darius, the Persian, is mentioned as the next who undertook to explore and to conquer that vast country. Having reached the Indus, he determined to trace its course till it should fall into the ocean. In this important service he employed Scylax the Caryandean, the most distinguished naval commander of that early age, who sailed down the stream, and, after a navigation of two years and a half, arrived in Egypt,—a most extensive, and at that period most arduous voyage, of which, unfortunately, no detailed account has been preserved. The historian then simply informs us, that "Darius subdued the Indians;" and it appears that he drew from their country a more ample tribute than from any other province of his wide dominions,—paid too in gold, the most valuable of commodities. Yet the description of Herodotus, brief and indistinct as it is, shows that the power of the conqueror extended over only a very small portion of India. The simple statement that this

CHAP. II.

Narrative of Herodotus.

country was bounded on the east by vast sandy deserts, forming on that side the limit of the known world, renders it manifest that *his* India included nothing beyond the western provinces of Moultan, Lahore, and possibly Guzerat. His details, which are truly defective, seem applicable to some rude mountain-tribe rather than to the inhabitants of a great and civilized empire; yet the particulars, when narrowly examined, indicate the early existence of the same features by which the land of the Hindoos is still distinguished. The wool growing on trees like fruit, more beautiful and valuable than that produced from sheep, and like it used for clothing, is evidently cotton, a substance then unknown in the West.

Characteristic Indian manners.

The statement, too, that some natives kill no living thing, but subsist wholly on herbs, points out a characteristic fact in Indian manners; while the assertion that others of them neither cultivate the ground nor inhabit houses, clearly applies to the superstitious practices of the yogues or fakirs. The Padaei, probably a mountain-horde, are described as living on raw flesh, while the people bordering on the river are said to subsist on raw fish. The singular statement that when any one, male or female, falls sick, his relations kill him, and feed upon the body, as well as another passage asserting that those who feel themselves indisposed go out into the desert, and die without any one caring for them, may have been suggested by the various forms of self-immolation, which, if not urged, are at least permitted, by the nearest kindred. A remarkable notice is conveyed respecting the great quantity of gold found in mines and in the beds of rivers; to which is appended an odd story respecting huge ants that defend this treasure, and often give chase to those who attempt to collect it.

Account by Ctesias.

The work of Ctesias, who, after the time of Herodotus, communicated the information collected during a long residence in Persia, is known to us only through the medium of some fragments preserved by Photius and other authors. The knowledge of India in his time does not appear to have been any farther extended. He mentions no river except the Indus, yet says that the inhabitants in its neighbourhood are the remotest people known to the eastward; so that his intelligence evidently terminated with the western desert, and did not include the vast regions which compose the proper Hindostan. Yet, even under this limited view, he relates that it surpassed in number all other nations; and hence it may be inferred, that the country, even in that early age, was populous and highly cultivated. His descriptions of the animals and vegetables, though bearing some traces of truth, are greatly mixed with fable. Some light, however, is thrown on the reports of Herodotus concerning the gold of India, which is here stated to be found, not like that of Pactolus in the beds of rivers, but in extensive and rugged mountains, haunted by wild beasts of peculiar form and fierceness. For this reason, it is added, only a small quantity of the precious metal could be extracted from the mines; and it is probable that their remote and difficult situation led to an exaggerated idea of their real importance.

Very partial knowledge of India.

Much more ample information respecting this quarter of the globe was obtained from the expedition of Alexander, though that great conqueror did not pass or perhaps even reach the limit which had arrested the progress of Darius. Having overrun the whole Persian empire as far as Bactra (Balkh), the capital of Bactria, and finding it every where subdued and submissive, he determined to cross the mountains, and complete the subjugation of the known world by conquering India. He cleared the ridge of Paropamisus, probably by the great caravan-route between Balkh and Candahar, without having suffered any serious loss, though it is admitted that the reduction of the strongholds by which the passes of the mountains were guarded gave occasion to several arduous conflicts. He then marched eastward, and reached the Indus at or near Attock, where its breadth is considerably less than in most other parts of its lower course; and he crossed it without encountering any obstacles, but such as arose from the rapidity of the current.

Alexander's expedition.

CHAP. II.

Persian claims on India

Although this hero founded his claim to India on its being a province of the Persian empire, transferred to him by right of conquest, the truth appears to be, that during the weak reigns of the successors of Darius, every trace of their dominion had been entirely obliterated; the country not being even united under one sovereign, but parcelled out among numerous independent chiefs. The first whose territories the Macedonian entered was named Taxiles, or Tacshailas, who, either considering resistance hopeless or expecting to derive advantage from the Greek alliance, immediately joined him with all his forces. But when the conqueror reached the Hydaspes, he found its opposite bank occupied by Porus, or Phoor, with a very numerous army, composed of stronger men and braver troops than those whom he had so easily vanquished in Persia, and selected, it is probable, from the Rajputs and mountain-tribes, the most warlike part of the Hindoo population. The difficulties of the invading army were increased by the rainy season, which had swelled the river to a height that made it impossible for the soldiers to ford it. Alexander however displayed his generalship by taking advantage of a wooded island at some distance below; to which, while making a feigned attempt in another quarter, he transported the flower of his phalanx as well as the best of his cavalry. These, having easily defeated the small force which hastened to oppose their landing, were soon drawn up in order of battle. Porus without delay attacked the strangers; and his defeat, his noble bearing in captivity, and the generous treatment bestowed upon him, are well-known events in the history of the Grecian prince.

Alexander's generalship.

Causes of the celebrated mutiny.

Alexander having overcome this formidable enemy, pressed onward, and soon arrived on the banks of the Hyphasis, the modern Sutledge, and the last of that series of rivers which water the Punjaub. But here his progress was arrested by the celebrated mutiny, which seems to have originated in the opinion of his followers, from the highest to the lowest, that no farther advance could be made with advantage or safety. The extensive desert which it was necessary to pass, joined to the great magnitude and populousness of the eastern regions, rendered the attempt at invasion most hazardous, and precluded almost every hope of being able to preserve any conquests which they might make in so remote a quarter. Their leader was therefore obliged to set bounds to his vast ambition, and to resign the fondly cherished hope of reaching the Ganges, and the supposed extremity of the world.

Alexander's return.

It behoved Alexander to commence the disagreeable task of returning towards Assyria; but he resolved at least to vary his route, and thereby to extend his acquaintance with the country which he had overrun. Among his other great qualities he was animated with an ardent thirst for knowledge, and particularly for geographical discovery. In retracing his steps towards Babylon, therefore, which he made his Asiatic capital, it appeared to him that he might have an opportunity of determining the course of the Indus and the southern limits of Asia.

Singular geographical fancies.

He was encouraged by an idea, and even belief, which to us it appears astonishing he could even for a moment have cherished, that the Indus and the Nile were the same river. But we must not, from the full light we now enjoy, denounce too severely the imperfect steps by which the ancients groped their way in that twilight of science. The voyage of Scylax being probably forgotten or doubted, and the shores of Asia as well as the situation of the Arabian and Persian Gulfs continuing still very imperfectly known, the imagined circuit uniting the two rivers might appear by no means impossible.

Voyage on the Indus.

Having formed this resolution, he proceeded to execute it with his characteristic activity. Having found on the banks of the Hydaspes an ample store of excellent timber, he employed the Phenicians and other maritime people belonging to his army to construct out of it a fleet of more than two thousand vessels, of which eighty had three banks of oars. He put some of his troops on board, while strong detachments encamped on either

CHAP II.

side of the stream. After solemn sacrifices, celebrated both in the Grecian and Indian manner, this great armament began its movement. The varied and imposing spectacle,—the shouting of the troops,—the brandishing of so many thousand oars, as the flotilla dropped down the majestic river,—struck with admiration even the natives, who watched its progress to a considerable distance. Some time was spent in attacking certain strong places of the Malli (people of Moultan), who are accused by the Greek historians of a hostile disposition, although their whole conduct seems to have been strictly defensive; and Alexander appears to have rashly sacrificed many of his soldiers, and even endangered his own life, in making conquests which he could never hope to retain. After the voyage down the Indus, which from various causes was protracted to nine months, he found, enclosed by the branches of that river, the large insular territory of Pattala. On his approach the inhabitants fled, and allowed him to occupy their capital without resistance. Farther down, the stream divided itself into two spacious channels; in descending one of which his followers were much surprised and alarmed, when the water, suddenly receding, left a great part of the ships on dry land. Next day it rose again and floated the vessels; and hence it was soon perceived that these alternations were occasioned by the tide, and that the Indus, once supposed to reach the plain of Egypt, was already approaching its termination. The king then put a stop to the progress of the main fleet, and sailed down with a few vessels to the mouth of the river, where he beheld, spreading before him as far as the eye could reach, the magnificent expanse of the ocean. Exulting to have thus, as he conceived, reached one of the grand boundaries of the earth, he formed the idea of turning his discovery to the advantage of science, and perhaps of commerce. He proposed to employ a small squadron in surveying the coast, from this point to the entrance of the Euphrates, where the expedition might join the army which he was now preparing to lead back to Babylon.

Novel phenomena of tides.

Alexander reaches the ocean.

The enterprise, however, appeared so very hazardous that none of the naval chiefs were willing to undertake it except Nearchus, the most distinguished of their number and admiral of the fleet. Alexander hesitated much before he would consent to expose so precious a life; but finding that no other would volunteer he at length yielded his concurrence.

Voyage of Nearchus.

Nearchus accordingly performed his celebrated voyage along the coast; during which he suffered very severely, chiefly from the great scarcity of provisions, as a large extent of the land was completely desert, and the rest inhabited by rude tribes, from whom no supplies could be obtained except by violence. At length he entered the Persian Gulf, where he found a fertile and friendly shore, in which all the wants of the fleet were supplied, and where his crews soon recruited their strength. Here, with great joy, he learned that the Grecian camp was pitched at the distance of only a few days' journey in the interior. He accordingly set out with five of his officers, who received the most hearty congratulations from their sovereign and countrymen, who by that time had almost resigned every hope of their return. Alexander himself, in marching through Gedrosia, the modern Mekran and Beloochistan, saw his army exposed to miseries and dangers, greater, if possible, than the sailors had encountered. Their route lay through immense deserts of moving sand, exactly corresponding to the description recently given by Mr Pottinger, rising into steep hillocks, into which the feet sunk as in mire or in the sea. Water occurred only at long intervals, when they reached the banks of rapid streams; and so eager were the men to quench their thirst, that some of them plunged into the current and lost their lives. Indeed, of all the rash enterprises which have been laid to the charge of that conqueror, this march was perhaps the most foolhardy. However, by that energy which he always displayed in the hour of danger, and by sharing the toils and privations of the meanest soldier, he at length conducted his army to the capital of Gedrosia,

His success.

Sufferings of the army.

CHAP. II.

and thence to Carmania (Kerman), where their difficulties terminated. He then gave a loose to rejoicing, and converted the rest of his march into a kind of festive procession.

Historic notices by Alexander's biographer

The biographers of Alexander, and other writers using their materials, have transmitted a pretty full account of the state in which he found India; and their narratives, in the absence of native records, still possess a great degree of historical value. The result, brought out still more fully than in the Persian annals collected by Herodotus and Ctesias, appears to be, that this region was as populous and as highly cultivated at a very remote age as in the present, and that it exhibited manners and customs almost precisely similar. That characteristic institution, the division into castes, according to which, dignities and employments are transmitted from father to son by hereditary succession, was already established.

Learning and philosophy of the East.

The same may be said of the pre-eminence enjoyed among these orders by the priesthood, who were understood to inherit all the learning and philosophy of the Eastern world. The prince and several of his officers, imbued with Grecian literature and curiosity, felt an unusual interest respecting the doctrines of these oriental sages. The self-denial and studied austerity, which had astonished them in Diogenes and others of the Cynic school, were carried here to a much more unnatural and extravagant pitch. The men whom India held in veneration were seen withholding from themselves all the enjoyments and comforts of life, subjecting their persons to the most unheard-of tortures and penances, lying naked, in the woods and fields, exposed to the burning rays of the sun. The Macedonian chief does not seem to have been himself inclined to enter into conversation with these uncouth sophists; but he sent Onesicritus to endeavour to obtain some idea of their principles. This envoy was accordingly guided to a solitary spot, about two miles from the city, where a group of fifteen, braving the noonday heat, had placed themselves in the most painful and fantastic attitudes. The Greek accosted them, and made known the object of his visit, when one of their number, named Calanus, observed, that it little became them to reveal the mysteries of philosophy to one arrayed in the costume of a courtier and warrior; and required, as an indispensable preliminary to all communication, that he should throw himself naked on the same stones where they lay extended. As Onesicritus seemed to pause, Mandanis, another of the Indian group, condemned this harsh reply to the representative of a sovereign and conqueror who deserved praise for such enlightened curiosity; and then through the medium of an interpreter, he gave a summary of the tenets held by his fraternity, and inquired if they bore any resemblance to the doctrines professed in Greece. Onesicritus assured him that Pythagoras, Socrates, and above all Diogenes, entertained opinions very similar. Mandanis admitted this to be in so far satisfactory, yet conceived that no one who wore clothes, or mingled in human society could attain to that mysterious height of wisdom which distinguished the Indian philosophers. The conversation continued till evening, when the learned men rose and accompanied their new companion to the city. It then appeared that this ostentatious self-denial was far from being unrewarded. If any one carrying fruit or provisions met them, they were invited to partake; and they were readily received into the greatest houses, where they were privileged to enter apartments whence all others were excluded. Calanus, notwithstanding the stern pride which he had displayed, was prevailed upon to accompany Alexander into Western Asia, a proposal rejected by his milder companion; but he always preserved the manners and demeanour of a Hindoo philosopher, and, at a very advanced age, exhibited to the Greeks an example of religious suicide, by mounting a funeral-pile, on which he was consumed to ashes.

Singular reception of Onesicritus.

Eastern and Greek asceticism.

Calanus accompanies Alexander

The other castes appear to have been more numerous than they are at the present day, and to have been distinguished on grounds somewhat different from those which are recognised in modern times.

Castes.

CHAP. II.

The following is the enumeration given by the several authors who derived their information from the source now pointed out:—1. Priests; 2. Husbandmen; 3. Shepherds and Hunters; 4. Manufacturers; 5. Military; 6. Inspectors employed in the service of the sovereign; 7. Royal Councillors and Magistrates. The last two orders, with their functions, must in a great measure have ceased during the long subjection of Hindostan to foreign sway; probably they have merged into that of Kuttri or Chittry, which at present includes the most distinguished civil members of Indian society. The ranking of Shepherds as a distinct order was, we may conjecture, founded rather upon observations made on the bordering Afghan and other mountain-tribes, than on the inhabitants of the plain, where the more general pursuit of agriculture must have superseded the habits of pastoral life. Much is said of the honours paid to the class of husbandmen, who were seen ploughing in the midst of hostile armies,—a happy arrangement, not always observed during the evil days which the same country has lately been doomed to experience. Other statements made by the ancients, respecting the early marriage of females,—the worship of the Ganges,—the mode of catching elephants,—the burning of widows on the funeral-pile of their husbands,—confirm the belief that the Greeks beheld the very same race who now inhabit that interesting land.

Shepherds and Husbandmen

Silencus and Sandracottus.

Seleucus, the general who, on the partition of the Macedonian empire, obtained Syria for his share, claimed as its appendage all the vast regions of the East. He undertook an expedition to secure, or more properly to regain, those distant possessions, which, after Alexander's retreat, had probably shaken off entirely the slight yoke imposed upon them. The very imperfect accounts of this enterprise represent it as having been successful, though the invader had to encounter the force of Sandracottus (Chadragupta), who had already established on the banks of the Ganges a sovereignty embracing almost the whole of India. But much doubt will rest on this brilliant result, when we find it to have issued in a treaty by which he resigned all the provinces *eastward* of the Indus. This amity, however, was cemented by intermarriage and mutual presents. Seleucus, moreover, sent Megasthenes on an embassy to Palibothra, the metropolis of this powerful monarch, whence he returned with the most splendid account both of his kingdom and his residence. Sandracottus is said to have possessed an army of 400,000 men, including 20,000 cavalry and 2000 chariots. His chief city was ten miles in length and two in breadth, defended by 574 towers and a ditch thirty cubits deep, and entered by sixty gates. The site of this celebrated capital has been the subject of much controversy. The most precise statement is that made by Arrian after Megasthenes, placing it at the junction of the Ganges with another river (the Erranoboas), considered the third in India as to magnitude. Relying on this indication, D'Anville has fixed upon Allahabad, a great, ancient, and holy city, standing at the junction with the Jumna, a river certainly not ill entitled to the distinction just stated. But this conclusion is positively contradicted by the narrative of Pliny and Ptolemy, the two highest authorities in ancient geography, both of whom place the city a great way farther down,—the former about 400 miles, the latter still more distant. Major Rennell next suggests Patna, likewise a large town, and considerably below the confluence in question; while the Soane, a stream certainly of great magnitude, which at present falls into the Ganges about thirty miles above, is supposed anciently to have followed a different channel, and to have flowed close by Patna. Still that city is not so far down the Ganges as Palibothra is described both by Ptolemy and Pliny; the latter of whom, in enumerating the tributaries of the great river, mentions both the Soane and the Erranoboas as perfectly distinct. Colonel Franklin, by a series of learned researches, has lately endeavoured to fix the position at Rajemahl, which, though still liable to some objections, certainly agrees better than any other with the ancient authorities. The

Army of Sandracottus

Controversies concerning his capital.

Modern conjectures.

CHAP. II.

Boglipoor.

present writer, in a former work, has mentioned Boglipoor, a town not far distant from Rajemahl, but somewhat nearer to the position described by Ptolemy, and still more so to that assigned by Pliny as the site of Palibothra. The name exactly coincides; for, in the European orthography of oriental sounds, *b* and *p*, *a* and *o*, are always used indiscriminately, while the other alterations are manifestly adopted for the sake of euphony in the Greek language. A name is nothing where there is no agreement as to position; but where the coincidence in that respect is so great as in the present instance, it is of much importance, because ancient appellations often remain long attached to the same localities. After being obliged to give up the Jumna, we cannot hope for a river which shall actually be the "third in India." The Ganges, not far from Boglipoor, receives the Coosy, or river of Nepaul,—a large stream, which flows nearly 500 miles, and drains a vast extent of mountain-territory.

Subdivisions of the kingdom of Syria.

As the kingdom of Syria declined in strength, it submitted to the separation of its eastern territories. Bactria was erected into an independent state, which, during several ages, seems to have been both powerful and enlightened; and its dominion appears to have extended even over parts of India that had not been reached by the arms of Darius and Alexander. According to the conclusions of Bayer, it was founded in 256 B.C. by Theodotus, who threw off the Syrian yoke, and was crushed in 125 B.C. by an irruption of a Scythian or Getic nation from the north; but this last date is by some esteemed doubtful. No part of ancient history has been involved in deeper obscurity, on which, however, some rays of light have recently been thrown by a learned examination of coins and medals.

Numismatic evidence.

Major Tod, author of the valuable history of Rajastan, was the first who drew attention to the number of such relics, with inscriptions wholly or partially Greek, which are scattered through the western provinces. They are found in the *topes* or sepulchral tumuli which mark the site of decayed towns; and their profusion is such as to prove both the ancient wealth of the country and the custom of burying treasure. The first great discovery was at Manikyala, a city in the Punjaub, erected upon ruins which appear to have belonged to the capital of a kingdom and the chief seat of the national religion. A very spacious tope had been observed here by Mr Elphinstone; and General Ventura, when encamped in the neighbourhood, succeeded in penetrating its recesses, where he discovered a great variety of interesting coins. Another was opened by M. A. Court with still more important results, westward of the Indus; and at Peshawer and Jellalabad in Afghanistan, M. Hönigberger made similar discoveries. About twenty-five miles from Cabul, M. Masson explored with success the remains of a large town, called by the natives Beghram, which he endeavours to identify with that named Alexandria ad calcem Caucasi; but this hypothesis, even from his own statements, must be pronounced somewhat doubtful.

CHAP. II.

Discoveries in the Punjaub.

The greater proportion of these coins are called Græco-Indian or Græco-Scythic. The oldest, which appear to have been purely Greek, and are of fine workmanship, are succeeded by others of the same country, with an Indian, Scythic, and sometimes Pehlevi, or Persian obverse. There is, moreover, a considerable number of Roman pieces, bearing the impress of Antony, Cæsar, and Agrippa; but these, we think, were probably introduced by commerce, which was always carried on with India in metallic currency.

Character of the coins

No specimens have been found of the two earliest kings, Theodotus I. and II., whence, and from other circumstances, it has been inferred that they ruled only over Bactriana Proper, and never crossed the Indian Caucasus. The next name is Euthydemus, who is even suspected of having usurped the throne. From the places where his coins are found, it may be certainly inferred that he pushed his conquests into the kingdom of Cabul. He was succeeded by Apollodotus, the wide diffusion of whose money proves, not only that he reigned there and in India, but that these were the chief seats of his

Negative evidence.

CHAP. II.

Syrian dynasty.

dominion. Menander, who succeeded him on the throne, is celebrated as a powerful monarch even by the classic writers, whose report is strongly confirmed by the species of evidence now described. India appears even to have been the main theatre of his power; and to conciliate his new subjects he was probably induced to combine a native reverse with the Greek legend. Demetrius, whose name is also mentioned by the ancients, is supposed to have been a brother, and to have reigned in a different quarter. Eucratides I., who assumed the title of Great, is understood, on similar grounds, to have held sway only over Bactriana and Western Afghanistan, his coins not being found so far east as Jellalabad. There are many bearing the impress of Hermæus I. and II., sovereigns who are referred to nearly the same era. These researches have moreover brought to our knowledge a number of princes whose very names had never before reached Europe. Among these is Antimachus, the purity and beauty of whose silver pieces might seem to place him in the age of Apollodotus, though it is difficult to find an interval for him in the succession. From the same source we derive Agathocles, Antilakides, Lysius, Matius or Megas, Unadpherros. M. Hōnigberger brought to light Kadphises, whose coins are as rude as his name, and who is conjectured either to be the prince in whom this remarkable dynasty terminated, or one of the barbarous race that immediately succeeded. There has also been revealed to the knowledge of modern times a mighty and mysterious potentate, "Azos the Great, king of kings," whose titles and the numerous relics of his mint unite in attesting his wide dominion. Mr Prinsep is of opinion that the character of these remains marks them as belonging to the age of the Roman emperor Gallienus; but if a Greek monarchy existed in India at that era, it is a circumstance altogether new to history.

Names of unknown princes.

Strabo's account of Porus.

Strabo relates that Augustus, when at Antioch, received an embassy with letters from an Indian sovereign who called himself Porus, and boasted that he held sway over six hundred kings; but it is not said whether any additional information was ever obtained through this unwonted channel.

Commercial intercourse with the East

Commerce ultimately afforded the means of enabling the ancients to obtain a great accession to their knowledge respecting India. The navigation from Egypt, though it appears, as already observed, to have been performed at a very early date by Scylax under the direction of Darius, did not for a very long period become the regular channel of conveyance. Alexander, by the voyage of Nearchus, connected the mouth of the Indus with the Persian Gulf; but the communication between the latter and the Red Sea, round the peninsula of Arabia, was regarded by him as a discovery yet to be made. It was still considered a novel enterprise when performed by Eudoxus, in the reign of Ptolemy Euergetes, about the year 130 B.C. A powerful impulse was however given by the wealth and unbounded luxury of Rome towards creating an ample market for the beautiful productions of India. In the first century a regular intercourse was established between the Red Sea and Musiris on the coast of Malabar; and in a treatise, entitled the Periplus of the Erythræan Sea, by a writer whose supposed name is Arrian, the details of this voyage are given at considerable length. In conformity to the limited resources of the ancient mariner, who always kept close to the land, it comprised an immense circuit of very dangerous coast.

Navigation of the Red Sea.

Any details as to the voyage down the Red Sea, and along the coasts of Arabia and Persia, do not properly come within the compass of the present undertaking. Suffice it to remark, that in due time the navigators reached the mouth of the Indus, which, in the "Periplus," is called Scynthus, and justly said to be the greatest that enters the Indian Ocean. It has seven mouths, but all narrow and shallow except one, by which alone large vessels could ascend. They soon came to Barbariké (*Barbaricum Emporium*), where they unloaded their ships and received fresh cargoes; but it was necessary to proceed upwards to Minnagara, the principal city of

CHAP. II. this region (which is called by the author Scythia), and where the king, who was subject to the Parthian empire, resided. The commerce appears to have been very considerable, consisting in the exchange of silk and silk stuffs, bdellium, spikenard, sapphires, and indigo, for cloth, coral, incense, vessels of glass and silver, money, and a little wine.

Coasts of the Indian peninsula.

Beyond the Indus the merchantmen passed another more northerly gulf, which they called Eirin (the modern Cutch). The waves, however, were so high and tempestuous, the current so rapid, while the bottom, rough and rocky, destroyed so many of their anchors, that, in order to sail with safety, it was necessary to keep considerably out to sea. They came then to a coast (that of the modern Guzerat), which is accurately described as very fertile in grain, rice, and above all in *carbasus* (cotton), from which was manufactured an immense quantity of clothing. Turning a promontory (Diuhead) they soon entered a third gulf, deriving its name from Barugaza (Baroache), which appears to have been then the emporium of Western India. The navigation of this inlet required great caution, on account of the extraordinary violence of the tide, by which, at its periodical ebb, a great extent of land, before covered with the sea, was suddenly left dry; and the cautious sailor, anticipating this phenomenon, was admonished by the sound as of a great army advancing, which was that of the waves, rushing on with such fury as threatened to drive him ashore. The mouth also of the great river (the Nerbudda) upon which Barugaza was situated, could not be found without difficulty, owing to the flat shore and the numerous shoals. The object of the merchants was to arrive in the month of July, when a great fair was held in that city. The imports were nearly the same as at Barbariké, except that wine is mentioned as a leading article, to which was added a great quantity of gold and silver money. The exports consisted in a variety of cotton cloths and finer muslins, *vasa murrhina* (supposed to be porcelain), and onyx stones, which were brought down chiefly from

Great river at Barugaza.

Ozene (Ougein), a great city, and the capital of an extensive kingdom. Beyond Barugaza, India extended from north to south, and was called Dakinabades (the Deccan or South Country). It is described as comprising regions of vast extent, mountains and deserts filled with wild animals, particularly elephants, tigers, leopards, and serpents of enormous size. In the interior were two great capitals, Plithana and Tagara. The former is supposed to be Piltanah, on the Godavery,—the latter Deoghir, the modern Dowlatabad, in whose vicinity the splendid excavated temples of Ellora still indicate its former greatness.

Description of the coast.

The coast, extending southward from the Gulf of Barugaza, or Cambay, presented the ports of Akabaros, Oopara, and Kalliena, the last of which is easily identified with Kalliana opposite to Bombay. It had once been open to Grecian enterprise, and was a place of considerable resort; but the prince to whom it was then subject rigorously excluded vessels of that nation, which could not even safely pass without a convoy. A line of shore is delineated with a considerable number of ports, which cannot now be very easily ascertained; but when we find them described as the seat of some trade, and infested by pirates, we recognise at once the Concan, which still bears the same character. Having reached the island of Leuke (Angedive), they approached the fertile shores of Limurike, comprising Canara, with part of Malabar Proper, and which seems to have formed the centre of their commerce with India. The three great emporia of this coast were Tyndis, Musiris, and Nelkunda, which Dr Vincent thinks may still be traced in Barcelore, Mangalore, and Nelisuram. Although the second of these was a place of extensive resort, yet Nelkunda is described as the principal emporium. There even appears much reason to conclude that the Egyptian navigators proceeded no farther, but found there an assortment of all the goods produced on the eastern shores of India, and even in the regions beyond. These were, pepper in great abundance, pearls, silk, ivory, spikenard,

Nelkunda the principal emporium.

CHAP. II.

diamonds, amethysts, other precious stones, and tortoise-shell. The imports were nearly the same as elsewhere, except that money was in very particular request.

Observation of the monsoon by Hippalus

The voyage to this part of India, after being for some time pursued by the tedious and circuitous line of the Arabian and Persian coasts, was greatly improved by an accident of which there is perhaps no other example in ancient navigation. Hippalus, having observed the steady course of the monsoon at fixed periods in a certain direction, taught the mariners to steer, under its influence, from the mouth of the Red Sea directly across the ocean; and thus a voyage, which according to the ordinary method usually lasted two months, was often completed in a few days.

Slight notices of the remoter coast.

Beyond Nelkunda, where, as already observed, there is reason to think that the navigation of the Greeks terminated, the description of the shores of India becomes much more meagre and imperfect. The next city mentioned is Colchi, probably Cochin, represented as part of the kingdom of Pandion, which at that time extended over all this part of the continent, and included even Nelkunda. This is followed by Comar, a town evidently adjoining to Cape Comorin, the most southern point of the land, and said to possess a species of convent where persons of both sexes, devoting themselves to celibacy, engaged in the performance of certain religious rites in honour of a goddess whom they imagined to haunt the neighbouring waters. Ceylon is next described under the appellation of Palesimonda, or the more ancient one of Taprobana, and particular mention is made of the extensive pearl-fishery carried on both there and on the opposite coast. The author now proceeds to Coromandel, respecting which he can give only some imperfect notices.

Extravagant accounts of remoter regions

Mesolia, mentioned as an extensive district distinguished for the manufacture of very fine cloths, seems clearly to be Masulipatam and the surrounding country. He came afterwards to a region of terrors and prodigies,—one people with flat noses, and another with horses' heads, reported to feed on human flesh. These wonders unequivocally prove that the narrator had attained the boundary of accurate knowledge; yet the wild tract of mountain and jungle, which composes so large a proportion of Orissa, afforded considerable room for these imaginations. Then, however, he reaches the mouth of the Ganges, where he finds a great commercial city called by the name of the river, an appellation which it no longer bears. Its trade consisted chiefly in cloths of the most delicate texture and extreme beauty,—a description under which it is impossible not to recognise the superb muslins fabricated at Dacca and other districts of Bengal. Beyond the Ganges was the golden country, doubtless the Aurea Chersonesus of Ptolemy, which must be placed on some part of the long range of coast intermediate between India and China.

The Ganges.

The weakness and distractions of the Roman empire, and subsequently the rise of the Mohammedan power, cut off the nations of Europe from all direct communication with India. The rich productions of that country were, during a considerable period, conveyed by Arabian navigators or by inland caravans, and sold to the Venetians and Genoese on the shores of the Mediterranean or of the Black Sea; but these traders themselves, so distinguished in the Middle Ages by their maritime enterprise, made no attempt to open a direct commerce with the distant regions whence those precious commodities were imported.

Cessation of European intercourse with India.

CHAPTER III.

Portuguese Discovery of the Passage to India.

Maritime Power of Portugal—Voyages along the Coast of Africa—Discovery of the Senegal and Gambia—Of the Gold Coast—Of Congo—Bartholomew Diaz discovers the Cape of Good Hope—Mission of Covilham and De Payva—Expedition of Vasco de Gama—He passes the Cape—Touches at Mozambique, Mombaza, and Melinda—Arrives at Calicut—Visit to the Zamorin—Differences with him and the Moors—Departure—Voyage round Africa—Return to Portugal.

CHAP. III.

Maritime power of Portugal.

PORTUGAL, a small kingdom, of little fertility, placed at one of the extremities of Europe, appeared ill fitted for acting any great part in the affairs of that continent. A long period of her history, accordingly, has been obscure and inglorious. Under the Roman government the Lusitanians were only remarkable for their extreme barbarism; and during the Middle Ages they were crushed beneath the yoke of the Moors, who, after having overrun nearly the whole peninsula, erected the western portion into a kingdom under the name of Algarve. In more recent times, oppressed by tyranny and fanaticism, and holding little communication with more enlightened nations, she was kept in every respect very far behind the other countries of Europe. Yet there was an interval between the Middle Ages and the present period, when this monarchy held the foremost place, not only in arms and power, but in all those arts and liberal pursuits which have given lustre to the modern world. But it was in the stern school of adversity that those energies were unfolded. The Portuguese, like the Spaniards their

Moslem wars.

neighbours, had to fight a battle of many hundred years, ere they could drive from their native land the numerous, warlike, and fanatical hosts, united under the standard of Mohammed, by whom it had been subdued. Religious zeal, the blind exercise of which has since degraded Portugal, was then the inspiring principle of her heroic exploits. The kingdom, according to De Barros, was founded in the blood of martyrs, and by martyrs was spread over the globe; for that name he conceives himself entitled to confer on those who fought and fell in her glorious conflicts with infidel nations. After expelling the Moors from Europe they pursued them into Africa, seeking to avenge that long series of outrage and thraldom to which the peninsula had been subjected, and claiming an undoubted right to every territory that might be conquered from the enemies of the faith. This enterprise, as it necessarily involved some degree of maritime skill, attracted the attention of their monarchs towards the ocean, as the scene in which they might find greatness, wealth, and renown. This circumstance, combined with the favourable situation of their country, having a long range of coast bordered by the yet unmeasured expanse of the Atlantic, paved the way for the distinction which Portugal obtained in the career of maritime discovery.*

Influence of the first maritime adventure.

John I.

The first attempt was made by John I. on a limited scale, and in connexion with an expedition to the shores of Barbary. He detached on this occasion a small squa-

* This historical account of Portuguese Discovery and Conquest is derived from the Asia of Juan de Barros (4 tom. folio, 15 tom. 12mo); Asia Portuguesa of Faria y Sousa (3 tom. 4to); History of the Discovery and Conquest of the East Indies, by Hernan Lopez de Castenheda; and History of the Portuguese during the Reign of Emanuel, by Osorio; the first two of which were consulted in the original, and the last two in translations. Although these authors agree in the general tenor of the narrative, there occur various discrepancies in the details, which we have endeavoured to reconcile as we best could, without in general troubling our readers by noticing them. We have considered chiefly the probability and consistency of the events related, giving also a certain preference to the authority of De Barros.

CHAP. III.

A. D. 1418.

First voyage of discovery.

dron to survey the coast of Morocco, and even to trace the whole outline of the African continent. The mariners succeeded in passing Cape Nun (then the limit of European knowledge), and in exploring to a great extent the boundaries of Western Africa. At length, accustomed only to hold a timid course along the shore, they were repelled by the view of those formidable cliffs which compose Cape Bojador, and the tempestuous waves that dash around them. But this voyage upon the whole gave animation and encouragement to farther discovery, which was likewise greatly promoted by an individual of royal race, who devoted all his exertions, and attached the glory of his name, to the cause of maritime enterprise. Prince Henry, a younger son of John, by Philippa of Lancaster, sister to Henry IV. king of England, after having acted a distinguished part in the expeditions against Barbary, directed all his attention to this new object. He fixed his residence at Sagres, near Cape St Vincent, where his eye rested continually on the vast ocean; and there collected every information and every aid which the infant sciences of geography and navigation could then furnish. He afforded to successive adventurers the means of prosecuting their discoveries; while the deep interest he took in their various attempts threw a peculiar lustre around this hazardous pursuit.

Prince Henry.

Discovery of Porto Santo and Madeira.

The first expedition fitted out by Henry, in 1418 consisted of only a single vessel under two officers of his household, Juan Gonzales and Tristram Vaz, who, being driven out to sea by a tempest, made the discovery first of Porto Santo, and afterwards of Madeira. These two beautiful islands, being found very productive in several valuable commodities, were considered as a promising commencement. Yet it was not till 1433, fifteen years after, that Gilianez, steering a bolder course through the open sea, passed Cape Bojador, and thereby proved that the fears which this celebrated promontory had inspired must have been in a great measure chimerical. The success of the Portuguese in tracing the line of the African continent was now rapid; yet for a considerable time it was only rewarded by the sight of a barren and desolate coast, "a dread expanse of lifeless sand and sky." At length they reached the verdant shores of the Senegal and Gambia, where nature assumes a grand and romantic form; and to which gold, ivory, and other precious commodities were brought down from the interior.

The Gold Coast

The progress of discovery was somewhat checked by the death of King John in 1433, and still more by that of Prince Henry in 1463; yet it still advanced. Alphonso, John's successor, granted to Fernand Gomez an exclusive right of navigation for five years, on condition of discovering during that time five hundred leagues of coast. Gomez, accordingly, in 1471, succeeded in exploring the Gold Coast, which, corresponding in some degree to its name, afforded a brilliant promise of wealth. The king no longer hesitated to assume the title of Lord of Guinea; and the castle of Elmina, or the Mine, being erected on this shore, was made the capital of all the Portuguese possessions.

John II.

John II., who succeeded Alphonso, pressed discovery with augmented zeal. In 1484, Diego Cam sailed from Elmina, and proceeded along Africa till he found himself, though considerably out at sea, involved in a powerful current of fresh water. Concluding hence that some mighty stream in this latitude must empty itself into the ocean, he made his way towards land, and discovered the mouth of the Congo. He opened a communication with the natives, and the Portuguese afterwards formed very extensive settlements in the country situated on the banks of that river.

Expedition for circumnavigating Africa.

Discovery had advanced thus far in 1486, when John II. determined to make a grand effort to complete the circuit of the African coast. He placed three vessels under the command of Bartholomew Diaz, whom he strictly enjoined if possible to pass the southern boundary of that continent; and this officer, having arrived at the mouth of the Congo by a course now easy and ascertained, began from that point his career of discovery. He

CHAP. III.

A. D. 1486.

Singular contrivance of Diaz.

adopted the odd contrivance of carrying with him four negro damsels well clothed, and furnished with gold and silver ornaments, toys, and spices, whom he landed at different points of the coast, that they might spread brilliant reports of the wealth and power of the Portuguese. He gave names, as he went along, to remarkable bays and capes; and at St Jago, 120 leagues beyond the Congo, erected a pillar of stone to denote at once the dominion of the king and of the Cross. He passed successively the Bays of the Landing, of Isles, and of Windings; the last name being given on account of the many changes of course which, during five days, the sinuosities of the coast, and adverse gales, obliged him to make. The weather continuing stormy drove him from the land in a southern direction, where his frail barks seemed scarcely fitted to live amid the tempestuous billows by which they were surrounded. After a voyage too along the burning shores of Guinea, the Portuguese felt intensely the cold blasts of the antarctic seas. They considered themselves as lost; when after thirteen days, the tempest having abated, they sought by steering eastward to regain the land; but they were already beyond the farthest point of Africa, and saw nothing before them except the unbounded ocean. Surprised and bewildered they turned towards the north, and at length reached the coast at a point which proved to be beyond the Cape of Good Hope. They called it "the Bay of Cows," from the large herds seen feeding, but which the natives immediately drove into the interior. Diaz steered onwards till he came to a small island, where he planted another pillar or ensign of dominion. A general murmur, however, now arose among his exhausted and dispirited crew. They urged, that they had already discovered enough of land for one voyage, having sailed over more sea than had been traversed by any former expedition; that their vessel was shattered, and their provisions drawing to a close; and, finally, that the coast having been left running north and south, and now found running west and east there must intervene some

Difficulties of Diaz.

remarkable cape, the discovery of which would give lustre to their voyage homeward. Diaz then called a council of his principal officers, who all agreed in the necessity of returning. The commander yielded, it is said, with deep reluctance, and parted from the island where he had planted his last ensign "as a father parts from an exiled son." The Portuguese had not sailed far westward, when they came in view of that mighty promontory which had been vainly sought for so many ages, constituting, as it were, the boundary between two worlds. The commodore, from the storms he had endured in doubling it, named it the Cape of Tempests; but on his return the king, animated by a more sanguine spirit, bestowed the appellation, which it has ever since retained, of the Cape of Good Hope.

CHAP. III. — A.D. 1486. Cape of Good Hope.

At the time when Diaz sailed, the king had also sent Pedro Covilham and Alonzo de Payva, by way of the Red Sea, to gain through that channel every possible information respecting India. The latter died in Egypt; but his colleague, in two successive voyages, visited Cananor, Calicut, and Goa, the three principal cities o Malabar; also Sofala, on the coast of Eastern Africa, and Ormuz, the splendid emporium of the Persian Gulf. On his return through the Red Sea he visited the Emperor of Abyssinia, venerated by the Portuguese under the character of Prester John. Covilham was well received, but, according to a custom prevalent at that court, was never permitted to quit the country. He transmitted to his sovereign accounts which were never made public, but were understood to favour the most sanguine expectations as to the advantages to be derived from opening a passage into the seas of India.

Portuguese expedition to the Red Sea.

John did not immediately follow up the discovery of Diaz. He was at this time much engrossed by the arrival of a negro prince from the Senegal, and in fitting out an expedition to reinstate him in his dominions. He suffered also a deep mortification from having been induced, by unenlightened advisers, to reject the application of Christopher Columbus, which was made in the

Various projects of John II.

CHAP. III. A.D. 1495.

first instance to the Portuguese monarch as the chief patron of naval discovery. This navigator having performed his grand expedition, was obliged, in returning home, to put into the river of Lisbon. He brought with him trophies of the newly-discovered world, which the king could not view without the deepest agitation. He even held several councils, and sought to advance untenable claims to those new regions. There were not even wanting at court certain base instruments who tendered their services to assassinate the great discoverer; but the king was of a character that raised him far above sanctioning so dreadful a crime.

Emanuel of Portugal.

John died in 1495, before a new expedition could be fitted out; but his cousin Emanuel, who succeeded him, displayed an ardour in this cause surpassing even that of all his predecessors. There were indeed not a few counsellors who represented, that he would thus waste the resources of his kingdom in undertakings every way uncertain, and the happiest results of which might be snatched away by foreign aggression. The king, however, buoyed up by sanguine hope, and calculating that the task of penetrating to India descended to him by inheritance, applied himself with the utmost diligence to the fitting out of a grand expedition. Diaz was instructed to superintend the building of the ships, that they might be made of such size and strength as to be fit for traversing the stormy seas which he had experienced.

Vasco de Gama.

The command, however, was bestowed not upon him, but upon Vasco de Gama, a member of the royal household, who had acquired a reputation for nautical skill and talent which his subsequent conduct fully confirmed. The preparations being completed, Gama was called before the king in presence of some of the most distinguished lords of the court, and presented with a silk banner, having attached to it the cross of the order of the knighthood of Christ, of which his majesty was perpetual master. On this token he was made to swear that he would, to the very utmost of his power, accomplish the voyage, and fulfil its objects. The banner was then delivered to him, with a list of instructions, and a letter to the mysterious prince called Prester John of India, with whom it was not doubted that he would open some channel of intercourse. That he might depart under favourable auspices, various solemnities were observed, inspired by the religious and somewhat superstitious spirit of the age. On the day of embarkation, the captains and mariners repaired to the convent of Our Lady of Bethlehem, where the sacrament was administered to them; the monks walked to the ships in devout procession, bearing wax tapers, and uttering a prayer, echoed by the whole population of Lisbon, who flocked behind to witness the scene. The sailors then went through the ceremonies of confession and absolution, according to a form prepared by Prince Henry for those who should perish in these distant expeditions. This was a somewhat gloomy preparation for the parting. They hastened on board, and began to unfurl the sails; but when they saw the shore lined with their relations and dearest friends dissolved in grief, and felt themselves entering on a voyage so full of doubt and peril,—while they looked alternately to the land that they were quitting, and on the ocean into which they were advancing,—they could not restrain a few natural tears.

Preparation for the expedition to India.

Gama sailed on the 8th July 1497, with three good vessels,—the St Gabriel and St Raphael, commanded by himself and his brother Paulo, and the Berio, a caravel, under Nicolas Coelho. Castanheda describes them as encountering in the early part of their voyage severe tempests, and even repeated alarms; and though this is not mentioned by De Barros, it seems probable, since after sailing four months they had not yet reached the Cape. Vasco landed in a bay, which he called St Helena, to obtain water and to make astronomical observations. Here having espied two negroes, he caused them to be waylaid and brought before him; but they could hold no communication by words, and were, besides, in such agitation and alarm as to be unable to comprehend the

Voyage of Gama.

CHAP III.
A.D. 1497.

signs of friendship which were liberally tendered. Gama hereupon desired two of his grumettas, or negro-servants, to take them apart and give them abundance of food, of which when they had partaken, their minds apparently underwent a happy change, and they pointed to a village two or three miles distant belonging to their countrymen. Fernando Veloso, a Portuguese, obtained permission to repair thither and make observations on the natives. Not long after his departure, however, he was seen running back full speed, pursued by a large party of negroes. He found refuge in the boat, but several of the sailors were wounded with spears and assagaies thrown by the savage assailants. Veloso then related that he had been at first well received, but observing some suspicious symptoms he took to flight, and found his alarm fully justified by the event.

Passage of the Cape.

De Gama, quitting this inhospitable shore, steered directly towards that grand promontory which he was now closely approaching, and the passing of which was to decide the fate of his voyage. Deep and solemn emotions filled the minds of the sailors, as on the 18th November they came near to the southern extremity of the African continent. They roused their courage to the highest pitch, in order to face the tempests which they had been taught to expect in making the circuit of this formidable cape. But as they proceeded, a moderate breeze from the south-west filled the sails; and, keeping well out to sea, they rounded without danger, and almost without effort, that mighty and dreaded barrier. With the sound of trumpets and loud acclamations they celebrated this memorable event, which was to give a new character to the commercial policy of Europe. The shore itself showed nothing of that forbidding aspect which rumour had announced: it was lofty indeed, but green and wooded, with numerous flocks feeding on the hills; though the deep recess which it enclosed on the eastern side could not be safely entered. Before them lay the unbounded expanse of the Indian Ocean; and Gama did not pause till he reached the Bay of San Blas, called

Enter the Indian Ocean.

afterwards by the Dutch Mossel Bay, where he landed to obtain water and refreshments. Scarcely had the boats touched the shore, when on the top of the neighbouring heights ninety natives appeared, similar in aspect to those in the Bay of St Helena. The Portuguese commander desired his men to approach cautiously and well armed, throwing to the savages a few bells and toys; upon which the latter came forward in the most familiar manner, and offered to exchange their cattle for such European commodities as attracted their eyes. Three days were employed in carrying on this barter, and also in various scenes of mirth and frolic,—the inhabitants performing on a species of pastoral flute, to the sound of which both parties danced. Yet towards the close of the visit suspicious symptoms began to appear. The people increased in number, and parties of them were seen lying in ambush; their attitude became more and more hostile, and they were observed closely watching every movement of the Portuguese. Gama, humanely and wisely desiring to avoid any hostile collision, dispersed them by merely firing a few balls over their heads, and proceeded on his voyage.

Traffic with the natives.

The navigators were soon after overtaken by a violent storm, the first they had encountered in those unknown seas. It was truly terrible; and in their despair they sought relief, according to De Barros, too exclusively in religious exercises, without employing sufficiently their own exertions to escape the pressing danger; however, the tempest having abated, the two ships rejoined each other, and proceeded cheerfully onwards. Having passed the coast, called Natal from the day on which it was discovered, they were tempted to land at the mouth of a fine river, where they were soon surrounded by a numerous band of natives, chiefly composed of females; whose comfortable clothing of skins indicated, in comparison of the former parties, both a colder country and a higher degree of industry and civilisation. The latter inference was not belied by their demeanour. Martin Alonzo, one of the sailors, having succeeded in making himself understood, received an

First storm

CHAP. III. A. D. 1497. invitation to their village, which, notwithstanding the alarm sustained by Fernando Veloso, he did not hesitate to accept. The huts of which it consisted were rudely built of straw, but comfortably fitted up; he was treated with the greatest respect and kindness, and sent back next day under an escort of two hundred men. The chief came afterwards with a large retinue to take a view of the ships, and harmony continued uninterrupted during the five days that the voyagers remained on the coast. Gama, delighted with this people, who belong to the comparatively improved race of the Caffres, distinguished their inlet as the River of Peace.

Progress of the voyage. In navigating this coast, the admiral found the sea agitated by violent currents coming down the Mozambique Channel, which greatly impeded the progress of his ship. Having passed a bold cape, to which, in allusion to this fact, he gave the name of Corrientes, and seeing the land now trending rapidly to the westward, which made him afraid of being involved in a deep gulf, he steered out into the ocean. Thus he failed to discover Sofala, then the chief emporium of this part of Africa, enriched by the commerce of gold and ivory brought down the Zambeze. He came, however, to a river on whose banks were persons dressed in silk and blue cotton vestments, some of whom understood Martins, the Arabic interpreter. They gave information that, towards the rising sun, there was a white nation Cheering prospects. who sailed in ships resembling those of the Portuguese, and were often seen passing and repassing. These symptoms of an approach to the civilized countries of the East greatly cheered Gama; and his vessels having been considerably shattered, he determined to spend some time here in refitting and preparing them for their arduous Crew attacked by disease. voyage across the Indian Ocean. His joy was damped by an unexpected calamity; the crews were attacked by a disease of unknown and terrible symptoms, —putrid spots overspreading the body,—the mouth filled with flesh which did not seem to belong to it,—the limbs unable to move,—exhaustion and debility of the whole frame. This appears to be the first mention of scurvy, since so fatally known to mariners. Several fell victims to it, the others were cured by means, as was supposed, of medicines brought from Lisbon, but more probably by the use of the fresh meat and vegetables with which they were supplied from the shore.

Mozambique.

The armament again set sail from this river, to which the admiral gave the name of "Good Signs," on the 24th February 1498, and in five days came to a port formed by two small islands, about a league from the mainland. This he learned was called Mozambique, a place of considerable trade, then subject to Quiloa, but since distinguished as the capital of the Portuguese settlements in Eastern Africa. Here the ships were visited by some boats, having on board people well clothed in cotton, and wearing silk turbans like those of Barbary, a circumstance which delighted the eye of the navigators from the assurance it conveyed that they had completely passed the domain of barbarism; not being aware that a more deadly enmity, arising from religious antipathies, was now to be encountered. Gama being asked who he was and what he wanted, replied, that he was a subject of the King of Portugal, who had despatched him on a mission to India, and particularly to the King of Calicut, and that he wanted only water, provisions, and two pilots. Unfortunately the person addressed was a native of Fez, in whom the prejudices of a different faith were heightened by the deadly wars waged between his nation and the Portuguese. Yet, though some change was observable in his countenance, he maintained a friendly demeanour, assuring the admiral that these moderate demands would be most cheerfully complied with. An unrestrained intercourse was immediately opened between the Europeans and the natives; and, a few days afterwards, the governor, or *xeque*, came himself on board, wearing robes of fine linen and rich velvet, and on his head a silk turban trimmed with gold. The interview passed most amicably; though, amid all this show of kindness, there were not wanting slight grounds of suspicion. There came on board, among others, three

Religious antipathies.

CHAP. III. A.D. 1498.

individuals, who proved to be subjects of the King of Abyssinia, a monarch whom the Portuguese had almost deified under the appellation of Prester John. Though these visiters had become converts to the Moslem creed, yet, on seeing a painting of the angel Gabriel on the stern of one of the vessels, they were so far moved by old recollections as to bend down on their knees, and do reverence to it. This movement, which betrayed their secret and ancient faith, led to an eager inquiry and a more intimate communication; which the Moors no sooner remarked, than they drove the Abyssinians out of the ship, and carefully prevented the voyagers from holding any farther intercourse with these strangers. Notwithstanding these unfavourable symptoms, the necessity of procuring wood and water induced Gama to send two boats' crews daily on shore, where they obtained an ample supply at a moderate rate. One day these boats, having gone beyond the range of the ships, were suddenly attacked by seven large barks, whence was discharged a cloud of darts, spears, and javelins. The natives were soon driven off by a volley of fire-arms, and their conduct was disavowed by the xeque. Sundry transactions followed, and promises were alternately made and broken, till Vasco, by the terror of his artillery, and the threat of reducing Mozambique to ashes, compelled the governor to allow him to complete his supplies, and also to grant him a pilot for Mombaza, where he was assured that he would find a more skilful one to conduct him to India.

Moors and Abyssinians.

Treachery of the Moors.

Voyage along the coast.

Gama sailed from St George, an island near Mozambique, on the 1st April, and continued to steer close to the coast of Africa. A strong current carried him past Quiloa, for which he felt deep but ill-founded regret, having been treacherously assured by his guide that this was a Christian city. In a few days the armament reached Mombaza, which, on the same authority, was asserted to contain at least a large proportion of Christians. This town, situated on an elevated point of land resembling an island, and seen from a great distance at sea, delighted the eyes of the mariners; the houses built of good stone, with terraces and windows like those of Portugal, inspired a pleasing illusion, as if they were approaching their native shore. They soon saw a boat coming out with four persons apparently of consequence, who, on making the usual inquiries, and learning the object of the adventurers, assured them that their arrival would afford the greatest pleasure to themselves and to the king, and that all their wants would be supplied. Much care, though probably without success, was taken to prevent intercourse between them and the trusty pilot from Mozambique. The admiral was urged to land immediately, and this request was reiterated next day by another party; but he chose previously to send two sailors on shore to make observations. These last were entirely pleased with every thing they saw, having been received by the king without much pomp, but with great kindness; and having been introduced to merchants from Guzerat, who professed themselves Christians, were assured by them that Gama, on landing, would meet with many of the same faith. The admiral no longer hesitated; and next day the vessels began to move into the harbour. Providentially, while that of the commander was near the beach it seemed in danger of striking a sandbank, to avert which an anchor was let down. This operation gave occasion to violent running to and fro, and to those loud clamours which European mariners are wont to raise in such emergencies. Hereupon the Moors on board were seized with such a panic that they, along with the Mozambique pilot, leaped into the sea, and swam full speed to the shore. This alarm, though groundless, disclosed to Gama the deep treason to which he had nearly fallen a victim. He immediately resumed his former station, where it required the greatest vigilance to defeat the repeated attempts which were made by the enemy to surprise his ships or cut the cables. He pursued and took one boat, having on board thirteen men, whom he treated well, but compelled them to show him the way to Melinda, a town which was at no great

CHAP. III.
A. D. 1498.

Appearance of Mombaza

Providential warnings.

Treachery of the natives.

CHAP. III. A.D. 1498. distance, and where he hoped at last to obtain a pilot for the Indian Sea.

Melinda. Melinda proved a large, well-built, beautiful city, surrounded by numerous gardens and forests of palm-trees crowned with perpetual verdure. The king, though a Mohammedan, and imbued with the usual bigotry of that faith, appears to have been otherwise a prince of liberal and enlightened views, who saw all the advantages which his subjects might derive from intercourse with an opulent and powerful people. The Moors, therefore, being sent on shore, returned with assurances which bore a greater air of sincerity than any received in the cities hitherto visited. Gama, however, was still too prudent to accept the invitation to visit Melinda, pretending that his master had strictly prohibited him from landing; but he proposed a meeting in boats between his vessels and the shore. His majesty, accordingly, was soon seen approaching in a spacious silk pavilion open in front, where he appeared seated in a chair supported on the shoulders of four men. Vasco then manned his boats, having his officers and sailors dressed in their gayest attire, and sounding trumpets; and, that some fear might mingle with the joy of the Africans, he gave orders to fire a round of artillery. This salute produced an effect beyond expectation; the natives, with every mark of alarm, were hastening back to the shore, when he made a signal to conclude this warlike compliment. He then rowed up to the royal barge, and had a most satisfactory interview. The king was even inspired with such confidence that he sailed round the ships, examining their structure, and putting various questions respecting the nature and uses of the artillery. He inquired about the King of Portugal, his power, the number of his armed vessels, and various other particulars. After this friendly communication, the adventurers received on board many distinguished visiters, among whom were several Banian merchants from Guzerat, "Pythagorean philosophers," who held it a crime to kill or eat any living thing. An image of the Virgin being presented to those sages, they

Vasco's interview with the king.

worshipped her with much more profound adoration than the Europeans themselves, presenting her with pepper, cloves, and other precious spices. This complaisance probably originated in the common usage of venerating images, or from some resemblance to the objects of their own adoration; but the Portuguese were willing to regard their conduct as indicating some tincture of Christianity, which might, they supposed, have been introduced by the missionaries of St Thomas. Amid this increasing familiarity, Gama no longer hesitated to sail along the coast, viewing as he proceeded the skilful manœuvres of the Arab cavalry. The king came down to the shore, and urged him to land; but the admiral still thought it prudent, under pretext of strict injunctions from his master, to decline this invitation.

Image of the Virgin.

Crossing the Indian Ocean.

The Portuguese commander being now supplied with a trusty pilot, Malemo Cana, a native of Guzerat, quitted on the 26th April the African coast, to which his own progress and that of his countrymen had hitherto been confined, and launched into the vast expanse of the Indian Ocean. They could now see at once the northern and southern polar constellations, the former of which had long been invisible. As yet it was a new thing for European mariners to steer three thousand miles through a waste of water where nothing appeared except sea and sky. But at length, being wafted by favouring breezes, they happily performed this voyage, and in twenty-three days beheld a high and bold coast, which the pilot declared to be India. It was not, however, contiguous to Calicut; but a change of course brought them in four days to a station whence Gama descried that large city stretching far along the shore, having behind it a fertile and beautiful plain terminated by a distant range of lofty mountains. The object of his adventurous voyage, and that of Portuguese ambition and enterprise during successive ages, was now attained; he was on the shores of Hindostan. A solemn thanksgiving to Heaven was mingled with loud acclamations of joy at having brought this high adventure to so glorious an issue.

Calicut.

CHAP. III.

A.D. 1498.

Communication with Calicut.

Gama had now to consider in what manner a communication might be opened with the court of Calicut, and such privileges obtained as would enable his countrymen to carry on an advantageous commerce on this opulent shore. The Mohammedans under Secunder had already established their empire over the northern plain of Hindostan; but the Southern Peninsula, and even the Deccan, were still in possession of numerous native princes with various degrees of power. Among these, on the coast of Malabar, a great pre-eminence was held by the

Sovereign of Calicut.

sovereign of Calicut, bearing the title of Zamorin, or "King of Kings." He was a Hindoo, superstitious but tolerant, and opened his ports to merchants of every religion. The commercial world, however, at that period consisted entirely of Moors from Egypt and Arabia, who, by their numbers and influence, possessed extensive means of rendering a residence at Calicut dangerous to their enemies or rivals. The commander, that he might proceed with all due caution, began by sending ashore his pilot, along with a condemned criminal who had been brought out expressly to meet the hazard of such perilous missions. Considerable anxiety was felt, after a whole day and night had elapsed without any tidings, and when all their barks were observed carefully shunning the Portuguese as if they had been an infected race. At length the boat appeared with the two messengers and a third person on board. The former reported, that, on their first landing, they had drawn round them an immense crowd, astonished at the appearance of the European sailor, and eager to ascertain what sort of

Moorish hospitality.

being he was. In this somewhat awkward situation, they were accosted by a Moor calling himself Monzaide,* who stated that he had come originally from Tunis, where he had formed an acquaintance with the Portuguese, and had even embraced the Christian faith. He invited them to his house, entertained them with savoury

* In Castanheda the name is Bontaybo. However unlike, the two words are probably corruptions of the same oriental sound.

cates and honey, and on learning the object of their mission, professed his resolution to act as their friend. In pursuance of his kind intentions he accompanied them to the ship; on entering which he immediately addressed Gama with the frankest cordiality, bidding him welcome to a country where he would find in abundance emeralds, rubies, spices, and all other valuable commodities. The king, he mentioned, was then at Panane, a smaller town about five leagues distant, whither he advised the admiral to send messengers requesting permission to land and engage in traffic. Vasco despatched two of his men along with Monzaide, by whom they were introduced to the monarch, who gave them the most gracious reception. That prince, having inquired whence they came and the particulars of their voyage, declared they were heartily welcome to his dominions, and invited them to come round to the port of Pandarane as more secure than that of Calicut, which was merely an open roadstead. This recommendation, being entirely in unison with Gama's own views of the two nautical positions, inspired him with additional confidence. He allowed himself, without hesitation, to be guided to Pandarane, though he declined to go altogether so far into the harbour as the pilot appeared to wish. Here he received a message requesting that he would visit the king, into whose presence the cutwal or principal officer was appointed to conduct him. The leading men among his crew now besought the admiral to pause before placing his person in the power of this unknown potentate, surrounded with such a host of his mortal enemies; but he magnanimously replied, that he could not otherwise fulfil his duty to his sovereign and his country, which he was determined on no account to postpone to his own personal safety. Leaving therefore directions for their conduct, in case of his being detained or suffering any violence, he put himself with twelve men under the guidance of the cutwal.

Messengers sent to the king.

Gama sails to Pandarane.

Gama, in landing for the first time on the shores of India, endeavoured to make a somewhat brilliant appearance. His sailors, in their best attire, moved in re-

First landing in India.

CHAP. III.
A.D. 1498.

Reception of Gama.

gular order, with trumpets sounding. He was immediately elevated into a palanquin, and carried forward on the shoulders of four men with such rapidity that his attendants, who were on foot, were soon left behind. Thus he found himself entirely in the power of the Hindoos; but they made no improper use of their advantage. On reaching the banks of a river, the bearers waited for the remainder of the party, whom they embarked in two almadias or country-boats. There now appeared in view a splendid pagoda with lofty pillars of brass, where the Portuguese were invited to land. They chose, on very slender grounds, to conclude that this must be a Christian temple,—because the half-naked ministers wore strings of beads like those of the Romish priests, sprinkled the company with water which might be consecrated, and presented sandal-wood powdered, as the Catholics do ashes. The Europeans, being ushered into the grand apartment, found the walls covered with images, which being willing to identify with those of the Madonna and saints, they threw themselves prostrate on the ground. Juan de la Sala, however, chancing to look up and observe the strange and uncouth aspect of these imaginary apostles, some of whom brandished four or five arms and had enormous teeth projecting out of their mouths, judged it advisable to guard himself by the exclamation,—"If these be devils, it is God whom I worship." The others laughed; and soon verifying with their own eyes the just grounds of his apprehension, started up and regained the boats.

Visit a pagoda.

Arrival at Calicut.

On the arrival of the party at Călicut, to which the zamorin had now returned, they were joined by several friends of the cutwal, and other nobles or *nayrs*, who escorted them to the palace in great state, with sound of trumpet. This royal residence, though built only of earth, was of large extent, delightfully situated amid gardens and pleasure-grounds. They were received at the gate by a venerable old man, the chief Bramin, dressed in white robes emblematic of purity. He took Gama by the hand, and led him through long halls into the presence-chamber, where the sovereign was found reclining in all the luxurious pomp of the East. The couch was spread on a sort of platform or stage raised above the general level of the apartment; his robe of the finest cotton, and his silk turban, were both richly embroidered with gold; from his ears depended rings adorned with the finest brilliants; and his naked legs and arms were covered with bracelets of gold and precious stones. On one side an old man held a golden plate, on which was the betel-leaf and areca, the chewing of which is esteemed a great luxury among oriental nations; while on the other side was a golden vase to receive it when chewed. This lofty potentate, on the approach of the Portuguese, merely raised his head from the embroidered pillow on which it rested, and made a sign to an attendant to seat Gama on one of the steps leading to the throne. He, however, received graciously the admiral's credentials, and promised to examine them at leisure,—meantime recommending that he should retire to rest, and appointing for that purpose a place where he would be secure against any annoyance from his Moorish adversaries.

Presentation to the sovereign.

Quarters assigned to him.

The admiral proposed to wait next day upon the zamorin, but was informed that he must abide the prince's commands; and also, that this second interview must be accompanied with a present, by the value of which the greatness of his royal master, and the importance of his own mission, would be measured. Gama, according to De Barros, had been fully aware that every thing in the East must begin and end with gifts; yet his appointments did not indicate any consciousness of this important truth. He had been provided with no royal robe or precious stone, and his only resource was to select from his stores something which might make an appearance not wholly unsuitable. He produced, therefore, some scarlet cloth, six hats, a few pieces of brass and coral, with a little sugar and honey. On viewing this intended donation, the cutwal and his attendants burst into a fit of immoderate laughter, declaring that, so far from becoming so powerful a sovereign as his

Difficulties about a suitable gift.

CHAP. III. A.D. 1498.

master was represented, it was such as the meanest merchant who entered the port would have been ashamed to offer to the great zamorin. They thought it would be better to send no present at all than one of so little value. Gama, however, after serious meditation, determined, wisely it should seem, that the gift, such as it was, should be sent, accompanied by an explanation that, having left Lisbon under much uncertainty, and with scarcely a hope of reaching Calicut, he came unprovided with any present from his royal master, and could only select from his own stores what might seem least unworthy of his majesty's acceptance; but that, in his next voyage, this failure would be amply compensated. The king, apparently satisfied with this apology, admitted the admiral to an interview, at which, if we may believe the historians, he assigned, as the chief motive of his voyage, the belief of the zamorin being a Christian prince,—and received even on that head a satisfactory answer. But, in regard to this point, there must have been on the one side or the other a complete misapprehension.

Gama's wise policy.

Jealousies of the Moors.

Hitherto, it appears that the king, actuated by motives of the soundest policy, had shown a decided disposition to favour the Portuguese. The Moors, however, who saw in these amicable feelings their own worst fears confirmed, determined to leave no means untried for the destruction of their rivals. Their leading men held a meeting, and represented to each other, in exaggerated colours, the ruin with which they were threatened from this western people. The astrologers announced visions which had appeared to them of fleets destroyed or sunk in consequence of the entrance of these detested strangers into the Indian Seas; and the conclusion was, that no exertion should be omitted by which they might destroy their vessels. As, however, their direct interference, would be justly imputed to motives of rivalry, they adopted a circuitous course. Having subscribed a large sum, they bribed the cutwal, who possessed the intimate confidence of his master, and who could not be supposed to be actuated but by a view to his welfare. This officer

Plots for their destruction.

represented that all the accounts from the West described those strangers as persons of a very different class from what they had described themselves; that, instead of being merchants or ambassadors from any king, they were pirates, who, having by their crimes rendered the European seas unsafe for them, had unhappily sought in the East an escape from justice, and a sphere in which to exercise their criminal vocation. He added, that, in their passage along the coast of Africa, they had committed the most dreadful outrages, firing upon the towns, and carrying off the inhabitants; of which they were so conscious, that, though received at Melinda in the most friendly manner, they could by no entreaty be prevailed upon to land. It was manifest that had they come, as they pretended, under the commission of a great monarch, they would have brought some present corresponding to his dignity, instead of offering one of which the meanest trading captain would be ashamed.

Misrepresentation to the king

The king, considerably moved by these representations, sent for Gama, who possessed no means of directly refuting the charges; but he entered into very full explanations, with which his majesty appeared satisfied, and allowed him to depart unmolested. The admiral, who did not quite admire the aspect of affairs, had no sooner left the palace than he got into his palanquin, and set off full speed for the ships. The cutwal, however, using great diligence, overtook him with a body of his nayrs, and politely rallied Vasco on his extreme haste, which, he said, had nearly deprived him of the pleasure of being his escort. It behoved the commander to frame some apology, and express a satisfaction which he was far from feeling. Late in the evening he reached Pandarane, and eagerly inquired for a boat; but none, he was assured, could be found at the moment; and he was, with some difficulty, prevailed upon to spend the night in a spacious mansion fitted up for his reception. In the morning he was early prepared for departure; when, in confirmation of his secret fears, he found all the avenues strictly guarded by nayrs, and his egress politely but

Gama's explanations.

Attempted return to his ship.

CHAP. III. A. D. 1498. His arrest. firmly resisted. He was a prisoner. The cutwal was inflexible as to his detention, yet treated him with the utmost politeness and respect, and even exhausted every form of courteous importunity to prevail upon him to send out an order for bringing the ships close to the shore. He represented the many dangers they incurred as long as they were kept tossing in an open roadstead, while the position which he recommended would at once place them in safety, and secure the confidence of the zamorin, who could not but interpret their present shyness into a proof of guilt and fear. Gama, fully aware that this proposal was urged solely in the hope of obtaining an opportunity of burning or otherwise destroying his vessels, chose to dissemble his conviction, and merely replied that his ships, from their large dimensions, could not without hazard be drawn on shore, like the flat-bottomed barks of India. Obtains his freedom. Seeing clearly that the zamorin's officers were acting without any authority from him, he assumed a high tone, and resolutely declared that, by some channel or other, he would bring his grievances under the view of their monarch. At length he was allowed to go on board, after having landed part of his cargo, which he left under charge of his factor Diego Diaz, and Alvaro de Braga his secretary.

Prevented from trading. The cutwal and the Moors, since they could not keep Gama in confinement, studied to spoil his market; and they had influence sufficient to prevent almost every purchaser from repairing to Pandarane. He sent Diaz to complain of this conduct to the zamorin, who appeared always disposed to favour traffic, and allowed the cargo to be brought to Calicut, where it was advantageously disposed of. These transactions led to considerable intimacy with the natives, many of whom went familiarly on board the ships. Success of the moors. Yet the Moors abated nothing of their enmity; and Monzaide sent advice, that they had at length completely gained over the king to their hostile views. Of this Diaz was soon made sensible, when he waited on his majesty to take leave, and to request that he would sanction the continuance of the trade, and fulfil the intention formerly expressed of sending an ambassador to Portugal. His hopes were at once chilled by the cold and frowning looks of the prince,—an effect which he had it not in his power to remove by the presentation of a suitable gift. On his return he found himself escorted by a large body of nayrs, in token as he at first hoped of respect; but when he reached the factory they immediately placed him under close confinement. Gama being, through his steady friend Monzaide, duly apprized of this outrage, felt his situation somewhat embarrassing. Judging it necessary to dissemble, he received successive parties of the natives with his accustomed cordiality, and even wrote a letter to the king betraying no consciousness of any injurious conduct. The Indians accordingly resumed their intercourse with the same confidence as formerly, and he had at length the satisfaction to see the approach of a boat, having on board six nayrs and fifteen other distinguished personages. These had no sooner entered the vessel than they were arrested and placed in close custody. The admiral then wrote to the king, informing him of this step, and adding, that as soon as his majesty should be pleased to release the factor and secretary he would receive his own subjects in return. The zamorin pretended ignorance of the factor's detention, yet appeared little disposed to yield to this compulsory mode of redress. Gama, determining then to take summary measures, weighed anchor, and set sail. Presently seven boats were seen pulling out from the shore with the utmost speed; in one of which were discerned the factor and secretary. They were cautiously sent forward in a boat by themselves, in which Vasco returned the principal captives. He nevertheless detained several of his prisoners, who he hoped might be gained over by good treatment, and, after seeing the splendour of the realm of Portugal and the honour in which the members of the expedition were held, might return next year with a report calculated to dispel the injurious suspicions instilled into their sovereign.

Change of the king.

Arrest of Diaz

Reprisals of Gama.

Their success

This conduct was manifestly unjust and unwise, con-

CHAP. III.

A.D. 1499.

firming for the present all the suspicions of the prince, and inspiring him with irreconcilable enmity. He immediately despatched a squadron of boats, which closely followed the Portuguese, watching every opportunity of attack;—he succeeded even in arming against them the whole coast of India. A spy who came out from Goa, being discovered and tortured, confessed that the zabaio, or sovereign of that territory, was busily equipping an armament destined for their destruction; and that every bay, creek, and river, were filled with boats ready, at a moment's warning, to co-operate in the same undertaking. Under such circumstances, the European chief, though somewhat unprepared for the voyage, could no longer delay his departure, and accordingly resolved to steer across that formidable ocean which separated him from the African coast. He had a tedious passage of four months, delayed alternately by storms and calms, while the scurvy renewed its terrible ravages among his several crews.

Impolicy of his last step.

Recrosses the Indian Ocean.

In a most exhausted state he reached Magadoxo, a more northerly port than any he had formerly visited; but, learning that it was entirely in possession of a bigoted tribe of Moors, he chose rather to proceed to the friendly harbour of Melinda. There he was received with the wonted cordiality, and amply supplied with fresh provisions, which could not, however, arrest the mortality that had begun to rage on board. The sailors were so reduced in strength and number that they could not undertake to navigate all the three vessels round the Cape; and hence he judged it necessary to burn the St Raphael, and convey her stores on board of the two other ships. In his progress along the coast of Africa, he touched at the islands of Zanzibar, Pemba, and Monfia, and met a good reception; but avoided having any communication with Mozambique. Being regularly supplied with fresh provisions, all his men, at the time of passing the Cape, were fit for duty, and they met with no farther obstruction in making the circuit of the continent. The admiral, however, had to sustain at Terceira the

Reach Magadoxo.

Exhausted state of the crew.

CHAP. III. A.D. 1499

deep affliction occasioned by the death of his brother Paulo, who had rendered the ties of kindred closer by being an able and faithful coadjutor in this grand expedition. On the 29th August 1499 he entered the Tagus, after a voyage of two years and two months, in which he had fully explored a new path to the commerce and empire of India. But of the hundred and eight mariners who had originally manned the vessels, only fifty-five returned to their native country.

Return to the Tagus.

Gama's reception and reward.

Gama, according to the devotional and somewhat superstitious spirit of the age, repaired first to the convent of Bethlehem, and spent eight days in paying homage at the shrine of Our Lady. He then made his entry into Lisbon with a pomp resembling that of a royal conqueror. The king celebrated his arrival with bull-fights, puppet-shows, dog-feats, and other entertainments suited to the taste of that rude age. He bestowed upon him and his posterity the titles of Don, and of Conde de Vidigueira; assigned him a liberal pension, to be commuted as soon as possible into a landed estate; and finally granted the still more valuable privilege of importing, to a considerable amount, Indian spices free of duty. That Our Lady also might obtain her reward, he raised a splendid temple to her honour, which was afterwards converted into a royal palace.

CHAPTER IV.

Portuguese Settlements and Conquests in India.

Expedition of Cabral—Discovery of Brazil—Passage of the Cape—Arrival at Calicut—Friendly Reception—Quarrels with the Moors—Factory destroyed—Hostile Proceedings—Establishment at Cochin—Return—Juan de Nueva—Second Voyage of Gama—His severe Proceedings at Calicut—Visits Cochin—Wars between Calicut and Cochin—Exploits of Pacheco—Lope Soarez—Almeyda—Maritime War in Guzerat—Albuquerque—Unsuccessful Attempt on Calicut—Reduction of Goa—Expulsion from that City—Its Recovery—Means employed for cementing the Portuguese Power—Conquest of Malacca—Of Ormuz—Albuquerque is superseded—Dies—Extent of Portuguese Dominion—Remarkable Sieges of Diu—General Confederacy against the Portuguese—Defeated—Their Decline—Wars with the Dutch—With the English—Low State of their Power.

CHAP. IV.

A. D. 1500.

Portuguese armament.

NOT a moment was lost by the Portuguese in following out the grand objects of naval and commercial enterprise. An armament was immediately equipped, at that time considered truly formidable, and which, consisting of thirteen ships and twelve hundred men, was indeed sufficient to keep the sea against all the navies of the East. The command was not bestowed upon Gama; whether it was that an opposite interest had begun to prevail at court, or that his conduct in the former expedition was not considered as altogether discreet and conciliatory. On this, as on every other subject which might affect the reputation of their sovereign, the national writers maintain a profound silence. The new admiral was Alvarez Cabral, a person perfectly qualified for this important undertaking. He was accompanied by eight

Admiral Alvarez Cabral

Franciscan friars, and, according to De Barros, was instructed to carry fire and sword into every country which should refuse to listen to their preaching.

Departure of the fleet.

On the 8th March 1500, the king repaired to the convent of Bethlehem, heard mass, and delivered a consecrated banner to Cabral, who then kissed his majesty's hand and embarked. The assembled multitude beheld the fleet depart next day with sensations of joy, much more general and unmixed than those with which they had seen Gama set forth on his bolder and more doubtful adventure. The passage through the Atlantic was distinguished by a brilliant discovery. Standing westward to avoid Africa, the admiral found himself unexpectedly in sight of another shore, extensive, fertile, finely wooded, and evidently forming part of the continent recently made known by Columbus. This coast was that of Brazil, which proved afterwards the brightest jewel in the crown of Portugal, continuing to shine after all the others were dimmed. From thence he steered direct for the Cape of Good Hope, where, during more than two months, he was involved in the most frightful tempests, in which he lost four of his ships. In one of them was the renowned Bartholomew Diaz, who thus perished in those stormy seas which he had been the first to brave. Cabral had only three vessels with him when he doubled the Cape, which he passed without having seen it. Like his predecessor, he missed Sofala, though in its vicinity he detained a vessel which had been richly laden with gold; but the crew, prepossessed with the idea that they were about to be attacked by pirates, had thrown the greater part of it overboard. On being assured that no injury would be done to them, nor to any other friendly ship, they expressed the deepest regret, and vainly implored the Portuguese to use the magical powers which they were understood to possess, to bring up the treasure again from the bottom. The discoverer scarcely stepped at Mozambique, but remained some days off Quiloa, which he found a large and flourishing port, situated, too, in a very fertile country. The king behaved

Discovery of Brazil.

Passage of the Cape.

CHAP IV.
A.D. 1500.

at first with the utmost cordiality, and consented to hold an interview with the stranger on the water; though he was more alarmed than flattered by being saluted with a general discharge of artillery. But there soon appeared symptoms of that jealousy which arises from the difference of religious creeds; and hence it became manifest that commerce could not be transacted upon any liberal or advantageous footing. He therefore set sail for Melinda, where he met with the same agreeable reception which his countrymen had twice before experienced. The king rode over the bowels of a sheep newly killed to the edge of the water, and earnestly solicited a visit from the European captain, who, however, firmly declined the proffered honour. The latter then left the African coast, and, after touching at the island of Angedive, came, on the 13th September, in view of the city of Calicut.

Reception at Quiloa.

Arrival at Calicut.

He is said to have entertained considerable anxiety in regard to the reception that he was likely to experience, after the abrupt and somewhat uncourteous close of the transactions with Gama in the former expedition. First appearances, however, were very promising. Some of the principal people came out in almadias, or country-boats, with assurances from the zamorin of the most friendly disposition. Cabral then restored the captives carried off by his predecessor, handsomely dressed, and ready to bear testimony to their good treatment. Having received an invitation to land and visit the prince, he expressed an earnest wish to comply and also to negotiate a treaty of amity and alliance, only soliciting that four persons of distinction, whom he named, should be sent as hostages. To this proposal the king very strongly objected, as these were Bramins of high and holy character, who could not, without profanation, enter a ship, or perform there any of their sacred ceremonies and ablutions. The Portuguese commander however stood firm, and carried his point. Preparations were forthwith made on shore for his reception, by erecting a gallery, which, though not very spacious, was richly hung with carpets and curtains

Friendly invitations.

Royal reception.

of crimson velvet fancifully embroidered. Here Cabral, having equipped his attendants in the most handsome manner, found the monarch ready to receive him. The sole clothing of his majesty was a richly-embroidered cloth round the middle; but his person presented a most dazzling spectacle, being adorned with girdle, bracelets, rings of gold, diamonds, rubies, sapphires, and very large pearls. The interview was amicable; the present, consisting of several vessels of gold and silver, and cloths ingeniously wrought, was graciously accepted, and, in return, full liberty was conceded to establish a factory in Calicut. Meantime the hostages, who on their passage to the ship had shown the deepest alarm and horror, were struck, on entering, with such dismay that they threw themselves into the sea, and endeavoured to swim to the boats; but two of them were brought back and thrust into close confinement. This caused such a panic on shore, that, even after the admiral's return, no vessel would venture out to receive them; and these unfortunate chiefs remained three days on board without tasting a morsel, and in a state of the most deadly consternation, when at length, compassionating their sufferings, and even dreading fatal consequences from their agitated feelings, he contrived to land them on an unfrequented part of the coast.

Fears of the hostages

Promising commencement of intercourse.

The intercourse with the city was opened in a very promising manner, and even some of the Moors assumed outwardly the character of friends. It was intimated to Cabral that a very large vessel was passing from Cochin, a hostile city, having on board a rich cargo, part of which consisted of seven elephants, one of them peculiarly desired by the zamorin, to whom, therefore, he could not do a more acceptable service than to capture this foreigner. The European sailor, with less regard to justice than expediency, directed Duarte Pacheco to perform the exploit with a single caravel. This lieutenant, by means of his cannon, drove the ship before him till it was taken, or, according to Osorio, forced into the harbour of Calicut, where it became the prize of the sovereign.

CHAP. IV

A. D. 1500.

Jealousies of the natives.

But the pleasure derived from this acquisition did not compensate for the alarm inspired by such a display of Portuguese prowess. The first good understanding, accordingly, was soon clouded; the Moors used all their influence with the native merchants to prevent any goods from being sent to the adventurers, who constantly saw numerous vessels richly laden taking their departure, while they, after a delay of two or three months, had made no progress towards obtaining a cargo. They therefore laid their complaints before the king, whom they seem to have held responsible for the conduct of his mercantile subjects. He declared that he could not prevent such disappointments; that the Moors were too shrewd both for him and his people; and one day hastily observed, that they had better take forcible possession of one of their cargoes, provided they paid for it an equitable price. This hint was very probably thrown out in a fit of impatience, in order to get rid of their remonstrances, without any idea of its being practically adopted. However, Aires Correa, the factor, a man of a warm and eager temper, was disposed to receive it in its literal sense; while his pretended friends among the Moors eagerly urged him not to neglect the royal permission. Cabral, on this information being transmitted to him, felt it to be a matter of extreme delicacy, and was by no means forward to engage in the transaction. Correa, however, sent repeated and urgent representations to him, upbraiding his supineness, and almost threatening mutiny.

Disappointments of the Portuguese.

Novel mode of trading.

Plots of the Moors.

The Moors, meantime, began ostentatiously to lade a vessel with the richest spices, and fixed an hour for her departure, of which they took special care to apprize the Portuguese. The admiral, on seeing the ship leave the harbour, allowed himself to be overcome by the urgency of his factor and agents, and sent his boats, which captured it, and proceeded to transfer its precious contents to their own ships. The Moslems, who had long watched for this crisis, ran instantly to the king, representing that the band of pirates were now seen in their true colours, having, in defiance of his royal power, commenced their system of robbery. His majesty, who had either forgotten his alleged permission, or never meant it to be seriously taken, entered into their views, and allowed them to seek redress as they chose. The nayrs, and other inhabitants of Calicut, having joined them, they proceeded in a united body against the factory. The Portuguese felt so perfectly secure that they at first supposed the tumult to be raised only in jest, and hence, on ascertaining its hostile purpose, found great difficulty in shutting the gates. Correa, with his slender troop, forthwith manned the roof of the edifice; but it was a contest of seventy individuals against thousands, who rent the air with their cries, and poured in a thick cloud of darts and javelins. Signals of distress were raised to inform Cabral of their situation, who at first sent two boats to reconnoitre, and then all his strength, with orders to push full speed to the shore. Meantime the Moors, unable to effect an entrance, brought a large battering engine, which overthrew part of the wall and afforded an inlet to the infuriated multitude. The little band of Europeans were completely overpowered. Aires Correa and fifty men were killed; the remainder leaped into the sea and swam to the boats.

Assault on the factories.

Cabral having witnessed this dreadful catastrophe, called together his officers, and in the heat of the moment determined by the most decisive measures to avenge their wrongs. Yet, according to Castanheda, a short pause was allowed to give room to the zamorin to offer an explanation; but when, instead of this, tidings were brought that he was employed in sharing the plunder of the factory, it was resolved no longer to delay a severe retaliation. Ten Moorish ships were attacked and taken, their cargoes emptied into those of the Portuguese, and their crews made prisoners; the captured vessels were then ranged in a row, set on fire, and exhibited in full blaze to the citizens of Calicut. The assailants next drew their squadron as close as possible to the shore, and began a furious discharge of artillery, when they had the

Cabral's reprisals.

CHAP. IV.
A. D. 1501.

satisfaction to see the city on fire in several places, and of being assured that a ball had nearly struck the king, who hastily fled into the country.

Proceeds to Cochin.

Having thus gratified his resentment, Cabral set sail, and proceeded southward to Cochin, the second city on this coast as well for extent as for commercial importance. In those days the preliminary step necessary in all oriental traffic was a negotiation with the sovereign. He happened at that juncture to be in the interior, but the admiral had secured as a mediator one Michael, a yogue or fakir, one of those eastern sages who wander over the country half-naked, smeared with cow-dung, and abjuring all the decencies and accommodations of social life. This holy but uncouth messenger proved completely successful. The king, an oppressed and reluctant vassal of Calicut, saw, in the commerce and alliance of these powerful strangers, the means of deliverance from this yoke, and of raising himself to an equality of splendour and independence. He even hastened to the city, and gave them an audience, which passed most satisfactorily, though the Portuguese saw nothing of that profuse wealth which had dazzled them in the person and court of the zamorin. The city, compared to Calicut, did not exhibit the same busy and crowded scene: there was, however, a great abundance of pepper, the commodity chiefly valued by the Europeans, and a cargo was obtained with the utmost facility. When they were ready for sea, tidings came that the ruler of Calicut had sent against them sixty sail, of which eighteen were very large vessels. Cabral went out with the resolution to give them battle, without much dread of the result; but, as a favourable wind sprung up, he considered that even a victory could be of no benefit to his country, and that he should more completely realize the object of his expedition by carrying home the cargoes with which he had laden his vessels. He touched at Cananor, and met a reception, if possible, still more friendly than at Cochin; afterwards, steering round the Cape, he reached Lisbon on the 31st July 1501.

Reception by the king

Obtains a cargo.

Arrives at Lisbon.

But, before his arrival, the king had sent out three additional ships and a caravel, under Juan de Nueva, to reinforce his squadron. This officer was steering directly for Calicut, but fortunately found at San Blas, on the coast of Africa, a letter detailing the tragic and hostile proceedings which had taken place, and advising him to proceed at once to Cochin. He followed this course, and was well received, though the Moors here also succeeded in raising some obstacles to European traffic. The zamorin, on learning the arrival of the new admiral, sent a fleet to attack him; but it was beaten off with such vigour as induced the Indian monarch to make overtures for accommodation, to which Nueva did not, in the first instance, think fit to listen.

Second expedition.

Meantime Cabral had entered the capital, where the narrative of his disasters, and of the deadly hostility which he had encountered, excited a deep interest. Not only the individuals who from the first had opposed those distant and perilous enterprises, but even some who had supported Gama in his early career, considered the undertaking as having now assumed a very critical aspect. As long as the object was confined to establishing factories, forming alliances, and purchasing valuable cargoes, such expeditions had promised to augment without hazard the splendour of the monarchy and the national wealth; but now when a mighty war was to be waged against a monarch situated at the opposite extremity of the globe, in a burning and pestilential climate, the resources of a small kingdom would too probably, they thought, be vainly exhausted in the attempt. The king, however, remained unmoved by these arguments. Inspired, as usual in that age, by a mixture of religious and ambitious motives, he trusted in the papal grant which had conferred on Portugal the dominion of all the eastern regions discovered by her fleets, and deemed it both a right and a duty to take possession of the inheritance of these proscribed nations. Descending to views of a more ordinary policy, he reflected, that against the hostile disposition of Calicut the friendship of the potent

Reception of Cabral on his return.

Apprehension of the courtiers.

Resolute conduct of the king.

CHAP. IV.

A. D. 1501.

kings of Cochin and Cananor would be a powerful counterpoise. In short, he was fired with the ambition of founding an eastern empire; and, accordingly, instead of being intimidated by these tidings of temporary reverse, chose at this very moment to assume the lofty title of "Lord of the Navigation, Conquest, and Commerce of Ethiopia, Arabia, Persia, and India." To make good such high pretensions an armament was fitted out, much larger than had yet been sent into the Eastern Seas. The main fleet, amounting to fifteen sail, was ordered to support the factories of Cochin and Cananor; while another squadron of five vessels was directed to assume a station at the mouth of the Red Sea, with the view of excluding the hostile Moors from any communication with the coast of Malabar. The command of the fleet was offered to Cabral, and that of the squadron to Vicente Sodre; but the former not brooking a divided power, Vasco de Gama was again invested with the direction of the expedition.

New Indian armament.

Vasco de Gama invested with the command.

This officer, in his progress round Africa, touched for the first time at Sofala, where he formed a treaty of alliance and commerce. At Quiloa he assumed a higher tone, and, in resentment of the inhospitable treatment inflicted on Cabral, extorted from the king a promise of submission and tribute. Approaching the coast of Arabia, he captured a large Moorish vessel; when, we regret to add, he stained all the glory of his discoveries by the most savage cruelty, and in the excess of his anger outdid the crimes which he came to avenge. Having first plundered the vessel, and shut up all the crew in the hold, he set it on fire. He then made for the coast of India, touched at Cananor, and thence proceeded to Calicut. Here a negotiation was opened, to demand redress for the injuries sustained by his predecessor. Conceiving that the transaction was studiously protracted by the authorities, he collected fifty natives from the several vessels which he had captured, and, with an hour-glass in his hand, assured the messenger, that unless he received satisfaction before the sand was run, all

Cruelties practised on the Moors.

their lives would be forfeited. The time having elapsed without obtaining a reply, he fulfilled his savage threat; adding to its horror by cutting off the hands and feet of the victims, which he sent on shore. Having then for some time poured a destructive fire upon the city, he sailed to Cochin, where he was received with the accustomed cordiality. Soon afterwards, however, a message was brought from the zamorin, by a Bramin of venerable age and aspect, as well as of the most consummate address, who began by making inquiries respecting the Christian religion, for which he professed great admiration, and even feigned a disposition to embrace it. He then assured Gama of his master's anxious wish to renew his friendship with the Portuguese, and to make ample reparation for the wrongs they had suffered; in short, he wrought so artfully upon the admiral, as to prevail upon him to go to Calicut in a single ship to confer with the zamorin. But when he arrived at that port, instead of being admitted to the expected meeting, he found himself, as might have been anticipated, surrounded by thirty-four proas of the enemy, who considered him their certain victim. In this extremity, however, he acted with the utmost promptitude and vigour; for, having cut his cable, he made full sail, and being supported by Vicente Sodre, extricated himself without loss from this imminent peril. He then set out upon a cruise, in the course of which he captured several valuable ships, particularly one in which was a most magnificent idol, adorned with a vesture of beaten gold and eyes of emerald. After touching at Cananor, and leaving Sodre with his squadron to blockade the Red Sea, the admiral took his departure for Portugal.

CHAP. IV. A. D. 1501.

Plots for his apprehension.

Vigour and courage of Gama.

In this last step Gama does not seem to have duly considered the interests and safety of his Indian ally. The zamorin, as soon as he saw the Portuguese force removed, thought the time was come for avenging himself on his refractory vassal the King of Cochin, through whom this foreign enemy had obtained a fixed establishment on the coast of Malabar. He at first represented

Neglect of his Indian ally.

CHAP. IV. A.D. 1501.

his preparations as intended only against the Europeans; but, having mustered a large army, he directed his march upon Cochin, with a peremptory demand that the sovereign should at once dissolve connexion with this new people, and deliver up all the members of their factory left in his capital. Considerable agitation pervaded the royal councils; a general alarm was spread among the people; and many of his majesty's steadiest advisers were of opinion, that he would in vain attempt to make head against so mighty an invader. But he himself remained firm, determining to brave every peril in maintenance of the Portuguese alliance. His troops, however, unable to withstand the immense force of the enemy, were driven from post to post; his allies, and even his great lords, deserted him; and at length he had no hope left but that of being able, with a chosen band, to defend a strong passage leading to his chief city. The zamorin, flushed with victory, rushed on to the assault; and the Cochinian troops, after a very gallant resistance, in which three princes of the blood fell, were forced to give way. The death of Narmuhin, next heir to the crown and a youth of distinguished gallantry, struck the deepest despondence into the minds of the people; inspiring them at the same time with unbounded rage against the strangers, who, through the king's obstinate attachment to them, had involved the nation in such dreadful calamities. But the monarch still adhered to his allies; and to prevent them from being torn to pieces, he conducted them every where in his own train. Being at length obliged to abandon Cochin he took refuge in the island of Vipeen, which, from its natural strength as well as from being invested with a sacred character, afforded a temporary security. It would not, however, have long availed, had he not been relieved by the arrival of ample succours from Europe.

Assault of the zamorin on Cochin.

Defeat of the Cochinians.

Arrival of succour from Europe.

Emanuel was determined to maintain the footing which he had acquired in the eastern world; and having secured at Cochin a fixed point where he might land and concentrate his troops, he despatched his reinforcements, no longer in one united fleet, but by successive detachments. Three expeditions were equipped, one under Alphonso Albuquerque, the future conqueror of the East; another under Francisco Albuquerque; and a third under Antonio Saldanha. Francisco arrived first on the coast of Arabia, and collected there the remains of the squadron formerly commanded by Vicente Sodre, who, neglecting the safety of the King of Cochin, had engaged in a general piracy, and at length perished in a violent storm. The Portuguese admiral then sailed to the succour of that resolute monarch, whom, as we have already suggested, he found in the Isle of Vipeen, reduced to the last extremity. He was hailed as a deliverer, and the troops of the zamorin almost immediately evacuated the city. Having reinstated the king, he farther undertook, on the arrival of Alphonso, expeditions into the interior, and even into the dominions of the enemy. On several occasions, however, they were surrounded by greatly superior numbers, and with difficulty escaped. The sovereign of Calicut then made overtures for peace, which was granted on condition that full satisfaction should be given for the previous outrages; that a large quantity of pepper should be delivered; and that the city should be completely opened to Portuguese commerce. Soon after Fernando Correa had an unfornate encounter with one of his ships, which he took and carried into Cochin. Osorio represents Alphonso as acting in the most unjust manner, by refusing all redress or compensation; while, according to De Barros, the zamorin merely caught at this incident as a pretext for dissolving a treaty concluded with the mere view of gaining time. The two Albuquerques, on perceiving this hostile disposition, sailed to Calicut, and endeavoured to intimidate the monarch into a renewal of the engagement, but without success. They then, very unaccountably it should seem, set sail for Europe, leaving the capital of their ally guarded only by a few hundred men under Duarte Pacheco.

Three expiditions equipped.

Sovereign of Cochin reinstated.

Portuguese return to Europe.

The zamorin, seeing Cochin left thus defenceless, de-

CHAP. IV.

A.D. 1502.

termined to make a grand effort to crush his rebellious vassal and extirpate that hated race, who, through him, were every day obtaining a firmer footing on the Indian shores. All his nayrs were summoned; his allies and dependent princes were called into the field; the Moors eagerly forwarded the equipment of the expedition; while two Milanese deserters taught him to cast brass cannon, and to introduce other European improvements. According to report fifty thousand men assembled, and began their march upon Cochin. The rumour of these mighty preparations shook the fidelity of many of the chiefs. Several stole off to join the invader; others, especially the Moslems, formed plots to aid him when he should arrive; and a general panic spread even among the well-affected. Attached as the king was to the Portuguese, his courage failed; he expressed to Pacheco his fear that every attempt at resistance was now vain, and that no choice was left but of unconditional submission; yet assuring him that care would be taken to secure his safe retreat. The European replied in a tone of lofty indignation, giving vent to his astonishment that the king should doubt whether his countrymen would fulfil their promise of defending him; and declaring, at the same time, with the fullest confidence, that his little band, aided by the forces of Cochin, would bring the war to a triumphant issue. The monarch's spirits revived; and, confiding in these assurances, he placed all his resources, and the whole conduct of the campaign, in the hands of Pacheco. That chief, perhaps the ablest and wisest of the Portuguese officers, began to prepare with the utmost activity to meet this imminent danger. He proclaimed the severest penalties against deserters, guarded all the passages by which they might escape, and having detected five Moors while making the attempt, he carried them on board with the avowed intention of putting them to death. The king made earnest intercession for their deliverance, which Pacheco resolutely refused, and even announced their doom as fixed; yet he only kept them in close and secret custody, that, after

Immense preparations of the King of Calicut.

Dismay of his rival.

Courage of the Portuguese.

Preparations of Pacheco.

the crisis should have passed, he might agreeably surprise the sovereign and their friends by their re-appearance. He began also to act on the offensive, making various incursions into the enemy's territory; and his return from thence laden with booty wonderfully revived the spirits of his adherents.

Defence of Cochin.

The zamorin, meantime, with his mighty host in full array, was bearing down upon Cochin. That city possessed a very defensible position, as it could only be approached across a number of islands separated from the continent by narrow channels. But these channels were passable by fords, to defend which became the main object of the Portuguese. The invader, supported by a fleet of 160 vessels, marched towards one of these shallows, at a place where his squadron had room to act. They immediately began an attack upon four European barks, and at the same time the whole army attempted to pass over. Pacheco awaited the onset with 400 of his countrymen and 500 chosen troops of Cochin. The latter, however, as soon as they saw the mighty host in glittering armour advancing with loud shouts into the water, fled at full speed, leaving only their two chiefs, whom Pacheco detained, that they might be witnesses of European valour. The first attack was made by the fleet, of which the proas covered the sea; yet his little squadron kept up a fire so well directed, that all the ships which approached were either sunk or dispersed. The hardest conflict was with twenty, which were bound together by an iron chain; but Pacheco, by a well-aimed discharge from a large cannon, cut the chain in two, and they were scattered like the others. The land-army, meantime, were making furious efforts to pass the ford, darkening the air with their javelins, which they discharged from a huge turret with powerful effect. The attack was continued so long, that the Portuguese were nearly overpowered with fatigue; yet their little band maintained their ground so firmly, and kept up so destructive a fire, that the enemy was finally beaten off. Of the defenders a few were wounded, but not a single

Assault of the fleet.

CHAP. IV.

A. D. 1513.

man killed; while more than a thousand of their opponents were believed to have fallen.

Increased preparations of the zamorin and their failure.

The zamorin, most deeply mortified by this issue, determined to make another grand effort. He augmented his fleet to upwards of two hundred vessels, and put 15,000 troops on board, designing to make a combined naval and military attack. Pacheco, on seeing this armament approach, ordered his men not to move till the enemy should come up, when he opened a tremendous fire, which struck them with such amazement, that, in spite of the utmost exertions on the part of their leaders, the whole betook themselves to a shameful flight. Repeated attempts, always with the same result, were made on successive days by the Indian sovereign. On the last occasion the Portuguese were rather hard pressed, and suffered some loss; but the casualties on the other side were also greater than ever, and sickness having broken out in his army, he renounced all hopes of success, and returned to Calicut.

Foundation of European empire in India.

These advantages may be considered as having laid the foundation of European empire in India. It hence became manifest, that the innumerable multitude of the native people, and the vast armies which they brought into the field, would not avail either for conquest or defence, and that a handful of disciplined warriors possessed an irresistible superiority over the countless hosts of Asia. Pacheco pointed out the road of victory to Albuquerque, by the brilliancy and extent of whose exploits his own name was afterwards eclipsed; yet, with inferior means, he commanded more uniform success, and was perhaps superior to him in wisdom and talent, as well as in humanity. He was at length superseded by

Arrival of a fleet and army from Portugal.

Lope Soarez, who arrived with a fleet and army from Portugal, but who treated him with merited distinction, and on their return home loaded his character with the highest commendations. In his zeal for the public service he had neglected his private fortune, which the king gave him an opportunity of retrieving by appointing him Governor of El Mina, the chief settlement on

CHAP. IV
A. D. 1505.

the coast of Africa. Here, however, a violent faction was raised against him; he was sent home in chains, and kept long in confinement; and though at last honourably acquitted, died without receiving the rewards due to his signal merits.

Wrongs of Pacheco.

Overtures of peace.

Soarez, on reaching the coast of India, was immediately waited on by a Moor called Coje Bequi, accompanied by a Portuguese boy who had been a captive at Calicut. They brought overtures of peace from the zamorin, who offered to release all the prisoners, and to grant every commercial privilege the admiral could desire. This chief appears to have been now in earnest, and Lope agreed to steer for Calicut, whence a ship brought out to him a supply of provisions with several of the principal captives, who were delivered unconditionally. The treaty seemed to be proceeding in the most favourable train, when the Europeans added a condition, that the Milanese who had assisted the zamorin in the late war should be delivered up. The Moorish negotiator replied, that an article which so deeply affected his master's honour could not be concluded without special reference to himself; for which purpose a certain delay was craved, as he was then at some distance in the interior. But Soarez, with that overbearing temper to which his countrymen were too prone, demanded immediate assent; and this being withheld, he opened a fire upon the city, and reduced a great part of it to ashes. He then sailed for Cochin, the king of which earnestly pressed him to destroy Cranganor, a frontier town strongly attached to the zamorin. He found this a somewhat difficult task; however, after an obstinate contest, he took the place, burned it, and carried the fleet in triumph to his head establishment. Having afterwards destroyed a considerable squadron stationed at Panane, he returned to Europe.

Terms proposed by Soarez.

His cruel reprisals.

First Viceroy of India.

In 1505, the King of Portugal sent out a large fleet under Francisco Almeyda, who bore for the first time the pompous title of Viceroy of India. Having spent some time in establishing the dominion of his flag over

CHAP. IV. A.D. 1505. Eastern Africa, he sailed across to Malabar. In resentment for some acts of piracy, he attacked Onor, and obtained temporary possession of that place; but the enemy came down in such vast numbers, that he was soon obliged to re-embark. However, as they had suffered severely, and as his strength was still formidable, they were induced to grant his demands. He was soon afterwards flattered by the arrival of an embassy from the King of Narsinga, a mighty Mohammedan potentate, whose capital, Bisnagar, was justly described as far surpassing in magnificence the greatest of the maritime cities. The unrivalled splendour of the gems which they brought as presents bore ample testimony to the wealth of their master. They carried a most courteous message from this great sovereign, who even offered to bestow in marriage on John, the young prince of Portugal, his daughter, a virgin of exquisite beauty. What reply was made respecting the lady historians have not recorded; but Almeyda's answer showed a disposition to cultivate a friendly intercourse with the monarch himself.

Embassy from the King of Narsinga.

Changes at Cochin.

On repairing to Cochin he found a remarkable change. Triumpara, the old and faithful friend of the Portuguese, was now a fakir, living on herbs, clothed in tatters, renouncing the world, and entirely absorbed in the contemplation of the mysterious essence of Brahma,—a transformation of which the West has presented only one signal example, but which is much less foreign to oriental ideas. Anxious as he was to show every mark of respect to this benevolent devotee, it would have been superfluous to bestow his rich presents on one who had bidden adieu for ever to the earth and all its concerns. He tendered them to his nephew, Nambeadim, who, by the law of nayr succession, had already ascended his uncle's throne. Meantime Coulan, a port frequented on account of the abundance of excellent pepper which it afforded, had become the scene of a dreadful tragedy. Homo, whom Almeyda had stationed there, finding it difficult to make up his cargo, determined upon using the most violent means for effecting his ob-

Rash proceedings of the Portuguese agent.

ject. He caused all the Moorish ships to be dismantled, and would not allow them to take on board a pound of the spice till the Portuguese had completed their lading. This outrageous prohibition was as annoying to the natives as to the Moors; and the former were easily induced to join in a scheme of revenge. They assembled in vast numbers, and attacked the aggressors, who, amounting to no more than thirteen, fled to a chapel dedicated to the Virgin. The mob soon surrounded this sanctuary; but not being able to force an entrance, they brought a quantity of wood, and succeeding in setting fire to it, they destroyed the edifice with all who were in it. Almeyda censured and even degraded Homo, who, however, had left the place before this crisis; yet, deeming it not the less necessary to inflict a memorable chastisement on the Coulanites, he sent an armament under his son Lorenzo, who destroyed a part of their fleet.

Indignation of the natives.

The viceroy now found himself exposed to a danger of the first magnitude, and which threatened to shake the very foundation of Portuguese ascendency. The Sultan of Cairo, inflamed at once by that bigoted zeal with which the Mohammedan creed inspires its votaries, and by the injuries which his vessels had sustained from European pirates, fitted out a large fleet, and sent it, under the command of Mir Hocem, to the coast of India, to extirpate that infidel race who were extending conquest and devastation over all the Eastern Seas. At the time he received intelligence that this flotilla was under sail, a considerable part of his squadron was still out under Lorenzo, to whom he sent instructions to attack the enemy before they could arrive on the coast and be joined by any of the native princes. The young admiral, who had anchored off the port of Chaul, was busily preparing to execute his father's directions when the Egyptians were seen approaching the harbour. The enemy, having a favourable wind and tide, entered the river, and at once drew up their ships in order of battle. The Portuguese fought for two days with the most desperate valour, not only keeping up a constant

Moorish armament sent against the Portuguese.

Preparations to oppose it.

CHAP. IV. A.D. 1505.

cannonade, but boarding and capturing several of the sultan's galleys; and Lorenzo was only prevented by an adverse current from taking the commander's ship. But on the second morning Mir Hocem was reinforced by Melique Az, the viceroy of Diu. At the end of that bloody day the squadron under the son of Almeyda was dreadfully shattered; the principal officers, including the gallant leader himself, were wounded; and the force of the enemy was so immensely superior, as to leave no hope of a successful resistance. It was determined, in a council of war, to take advantage of a favourable tide, and proceed out to sea. This movement having been commenced at midnight, was going on successfully, when, by a fearful mischance, the ship in which Lorenzo himself sailed ran foul of some fishing-stakes. Pelagio Sousa, who commanded the nearest galley, fastened a rope, and, plying all his oars, endeavoured to tow her off, but in vain. Meantime the whole of the enemy's fleet, having discovered what was going on, pressed close behind. Sousa's men, apprehending that they would be involved in the fate of the vessel to which they were attached, basely cut the rope, when their ship was irresistibly borne out to sea by the current, leaving the admiral to contend alone with his numerous pursuers. He was now entreated to enter a boat, in which he might still have easily regained the fleet; that brave and high-spirited youth, however, declared his fixed determination not to abandon his crew in this extremity, but to share their fate whatever it might be. He had not yet lost all hope that, by prodigious exertions of valour, he might hold out till the advancing tide should float his ship. He drew up his hundred men, of whom seventy were wounded, with such skill, that the enemy durst not attempt to board. They merely collected their vessels round him, and opened a tremendous fire, which wrapped the combatants in a cloud of flame and smoke. Lorenzo having received a ball in the thigh, which rendered him unable to move, caused himself to be lashed to the mast, whence he continued to direct and cheer

Overpowering force of the Moorish fleet.

Perilous position and fate of the admiral.

Bravery of Lorenzo.

his men. At length another ball struck him in the breast; he fell down and expired. Still the crew resisted three successive attempts to board, till Melique Az, a prince equally distinguished for bravery and humanity, prevailed on the twenty survivors, all of whom were wounded, to surrender, and treated them with the most tender care and sympathy. De Barros adds, that he wrote a letter to Almeyda, deeply condoling with him on the death of his son, whose valour had commanded his warmest admiration.

Magnanimity of the Moorish leader.

It was a most painful task to communicate to the governor the loss of his only son, cut off in the midst of such a high and hopeful career. He received the tidings with fortitude and piety, declaring that he had much less desired for the youth long life than a distinguished character. Gratified in this point, and trusting that he was now enjoying the reward of his excellent conduct, he did not feel any cause to mourn. Meantime, however, he was eagerly preparing to avenge his death, and that too, we are sorry to add, in a temper ill accordant with the meek spirit of the faith which he had just professed. He had got ready a fleet of nineteen ships, having on board an army partly Portuguese, partly natives of Cochin, and was about to sail, when his path was crossed by a most unexpected event.

Conduct of the viceroy.

In the year 1506, Alphonso Albuquerque was despatched with a large reinforcement to the fleet now in India. He went out burning with hope, and big with vast schemes of ambition, aspiring to the reputation of spreading the Portuguese sway over all the East. Having sailed first to Arabia, he reduced Curiat, Mascat, and other important cities on that coast. He then attacked the celebrated kingdom of Ormuz, and, after several dreadful combats by sea and land, had so far succeeded as to impose a treaty which rendered its king tributary, and was erecting a fort that would have commanded the city, when the treacherous desertion of three of his officers compelled him for the present to relinquish the fruit of his victories. Almeyda, who was friendly to moderate

Despatch of reinforcements.

Proceedings of Alphonso.

CHAP. IV. — A. D. 1506.

Almeyda superseded.

measures, and averse to schemes of conquest, had sent a disavowal of these violent and ambitious assaults. But what was his astonishment when Albuquerque arrived at Cochin, and presented a commission constituting himself Governor-general of India. To be thus checked in an undertaking to which he was impelled by such powerful motives was more than he could endure. Finding that his principal officers, by whom he was idolized, were ready to support him even in resistance to the royal will, he told his successor that, under present circumstances, it was impossible to carry the order into effect, and more especially until, by vanquishing the Egyptian fleet, he had avenged his son's death. The other replied indignantly, and not without reason, that the king's mandate was imperative and unconditional, and that any delay in obeying it was equivalent to setting the royal authority at open defiance. The former adhered to his resolution, and even, on polite pretences, declined allowing to his successor any share in the expedition, who retired in disgust to Cochin.

Almeyda sails against the enemy

Almeyda now sailed to attack the enemy; but on his way having learned that Dabul, one of the greatest commercial establishments on this coast, had embraced with zeal the Egyptian cause, he determined to turn aside and reduce it. This station was very strongly defended, not only by a trench and palisade, but by a fort with powerful batteries, to disembark in the face of which appeared a very perilous enterprise. The Portuguese commander, however, caused the ships to be drawn up in a line facing the shore, then ordered his troops to enter the boats, and push full speed towards the land. They followed his directions with enthusiasm, and even with rapture leaped on shore, striving which should be foremost, and pressed on to the rampart. By this rapid and skilful movement the artillery pointed against the ships, having a somewhat high range, passed over the heads of the advancing soldiers, who without any annoyance reached the gates. They could then advance only by three narrow passages between the city and the beach, each stoutly defended

Assault of Dabul.

by large bands of armed citizens. The contest was dreadful; the piles of dead formed a barrier more formidable than even the palisade; and the assailants thronging behind impeded each other. Almeyda, perceiving these obstacles, ordered Vasco Pereyra to penetrate by another passage less open but also less diligently guarded, by which he entered the city, and soon placed it in possession of the Portuguese. The conqueror gave it up to plunder; and his followers, it is reluctantly admitted, stained their glory by inexpressible cruelties. The streets streamed with blood, and the parent besought in vain for the life of his child. The distracted multitudes fled in crowds to the great mosque, but soon finding that no place was sacred in the eyes of their enemies, hastened through the opposite gates, and sought refuge in the caves of the neighbouring mountain. The commander took up his quarters in the holy edifice; but confusion still reigned through the city, and in the morning an alarm was given that a fire had broken out in the eastern quarter. The flames spread rapidly through the light fabrics of timber; and the sparks flying from roof to roof, street after street was enveloped in the conflagration. Almeyda and his officers fled before it; and in a few hours there remained of this magnificent city only a pile of smoking wood and ashes. The fire also reached the shipping, which was entirely consumed, and even the Portuguese vessels were in danger. According to Osorio and other historians, this conflagration was ordered by the admiral himself, as the only means of withdrawing his men from plunder, and preventing an entire loss of discipline; but De Barros mentions this only as a rumour, and it certainly appears somewhat improbable.

Capture of Dabul.

Cruelties of the conquerors.

Conflagration of the city.

From this disgraceful triumph the victor hastened to his main object of attacking the combined fleets in the Gulf of Cambay. Overtures of peace were received, but being considered, apparently with little reason, as insidious, they obtained no notice. The enemy's squadrons were strongly posted in the harbour of Diu, where Melique Az advised his ally to await the onset;

Sail for Cambay.

CHAP. IV. — A.D 1508

but the impetuous spirit of Mir Hocem impelled him to leave the harbour, keeping, however, so near the shore as to be supported by a chain of batteries. The large vessels were linked two and two, and defended against boarding by a sloping network of strong rope. The Portuguese, notwithstanding, advanced to the attack with the utmost intrepidity; and Vasco Pereyra, the hero of the fleet, undertook to bear down upon the emir himself. The enemy opened a terrible fire, one discharge of which killed ten of his men. Undismayed by this loss, he was soon on board of their ship; where, having for a moment lifted his helmet, a ball pierçed his throat and he expired. Tavora with his followers had mounted the network, when, part of it breaking, they fell down upon the deck: still, notwithstanding this accident, the Egyptians were at length all either killed or forced to quit the vessel. Pedro Cam also attacked another ship, and before the grappling-irons could be fixed, thirty-eight of his sailors were on the network; but while they were unfortunately entangled in it, his head was struck off, and they themselves could not use their weapons with freedom; yet, being seasonably supported by another party, they rallied and in the end subdued the crew. In fine, all the large vessels were either sunk or taken; the remainder, discomfited and shattered, retreated far up the river, where the victors could not follow. The captured ships were found to contain ample booty, the whole of which Almeyda divided among his people.

Assault of the fleet.

Bravery of the Portuguese leaders.

Their complete success.

Treaty of peace.

After this signal defeat, Melique Az sent to treat for peace. The conqueror assumed at first a very high tone, demanding that Mir Hocem, the inveterate enemy of the Christian name, should be delivered into his hands. The Cambayan prince, with that lofty sense of honour which had always distinguished him, declared that such treatment of a firm and faithful ally was altogether inadmissible, and he could only engage to restore unconditionally all the European captives. With this Almeyda, after such a dear-bought victory, thought it expedient to be satisfied. We grieve to add that, inspired by a

CHAP. IV
A. D. 1509.

feeling very different from that of his antagonist, on arriving off the port of Cananor, he disgraced his cause by a general massacre of the prisoners. It is lamentable to reflect that a commander, who had previously gained some reputation for clemency, should have been stimulated to such actions by grief for the death of a son, who had fallen in open and honourable battle against a generous foe.

Excessive cruelty of the victors.

On his return to Cochin, he was again summoned by Albuquerque to yield up the command assigned by the sovereign to himself; but, encouraged by his partisans, he still held the reins of power, and even went so far as to place his rival under a nominal arrest. At this juncture, however, arrived Fernando Coutinho, a nobleman of high character, with fifteen ships and a considerable body of troops. This officer immediately undertook to mediate between the contending parties, and by representing to Almeyda how very irregular the course was into which he had been betrayed, persuaded him amicably to resign the viceroyalty. Having made this sacrifice to duty, he set sail for Portugal. In passing along the southern coast of Africa his men involved themselves in a scuffle with a band of Hottentots, when he hastened to their aid with a party nearly unarmed, and full of contempt for this rude and almost savage enemy. These barbarians, however, swift and fearless, made so terrible an onset, that Almeyda, deserted by his troops, was mortally wounded with a javelin in the neck and fell. The Portuguese writers lament it as a singular caprice of fate, that this illustrious commander, who had fought in all the Indian Seas, and had vanquished the mightiest warriors of the East, should perish thus miserably on an unknown shore, in a contest with a handful of naked and deformed wretches scarcely entitled to the name of men.

Almeyda summoned to resign the vice-royalty.

His fate.

Albuquerque now determined not to lose a moment in entering on his vast schemes of conquest. The first object of attack was Calicut, the chief seat of a power which had the most resolutely opposed his countrymen.

Vast scheme of Alberquerque.

CHAP. IV

A. D. 1510.

Assault of Calicut.

Coutinho, who was about to return to Portugal, insisted upon being allowed to take the lead upon this occasion, which his rank and the friendship that subsisted between them made it impossible for him to refuse. The fleet arrived on the 2d January 1510 in front of Calicut; but as the city could only be approached by narrow avenues through thick woods, in which the whole army had not room to act, it was arranged that the two commanders should advance in separate divisions. Albuquerque's party scarcely slept, so much were they excited by the joyful and eager anticipation of landing; and as soon as day dawned, they could no longer be restrained, but sprung on shore and rushed against a fortified palace, which was to be the first object of assault. A few minutes placed it in their possession; and Coutinho, whose march had been delayed by several accidents, came up and found the prize won. He burst into a torrent of invective against the viceroy, for having anticipated him contrary to faith and agreement, declaring that he should not be so cheated in regard to the attack on the principal palace, which stood on the other side of the city. Albuquerque attempted to explain, and besought him not to advance without having secured a retreat; but the other would not listen either to advice or remonstrance. He forced his way with impetuous valour through the streets of Calicut, and reached the royal residence, which, as is common in the East, formed a little town surrounded by a wall, and was the only regular fortification in the city. It was, besides, defended by the main strength of the army; but nothing could arrest Coutinho, who soon forced open the gates, and rendered himself master of the whole enclosure. Deeming his victory already complete and secure, he allowed his men full license to plunder, and, repairing himself to the regal halls, sought rest and refreshment after the toils of the battle. The Indians had been surprised, but were not dismayed; perhaps they had allowed Coutinho to advance so far, with the view of drawing him into a trap. The chief nayr uttered a cry which, repeated from mouth to

First success.

Impetuous rashness of Coutinho.

CHAP. IV.

A.D. 1510.

mouth to the distance of several miles, drew quickly around him thirty thousand men well armed, and determined to conquer or die. They fell first upon Albuquerque, who with his troops occupied the city, maintaining a communication with the fleet. He found himself wholly unprepared to sustain this attack. The Indians, occupying the roofs and all the most advantageous coverts, poured upon the Portuguese a continued shower of darts; while they, entangled in narrow lanes and avenues, could neither advance nor recede. Their chief, after seeing some of his bravest men fall, had no resource but to set fire to this part of the city; when the enemy, being dispersed by the flames, the Europeans, taking advantage of the confusion, made a rapid retreat, and reached the ships. Coutinho meantime received repeated warnings of the alarming state of affairs; but secure in fancied triumph, and viewing the natives with fixed contempt, he shut his ears to all intimations of peril. Soon, however, when his colleague had given way, and the whole force of the enemy was turned against himself, the danger became too pressing to be any longer overlooked. He then sprung to the head of his troops, and fought like a lion. The palace was set on fire; and his men, completely surrounded by a vast army, in a disadvantageous position, sought only to cut their way through to the ships. In this disastrous day Coutinho himself fell; and, in endeavouring to defend him, Vasco Sylveira and other chiefs of the noblest families in Portugal shared his fate. De Barros reckons that, out of 1600, eighty were killed and 300 wounded. Albuquerque, stunned by repeated blows, remained for some time apparently dead; but he was carried off by his followers, and conveyed to Cochin, where he slowly gained strength.

Muster of the native forces.

Fate of Coutinho.

This inauspicious commencement in no degree cooled the ardour of the viceroy. Scarcely had he recovered from his wounds, when he resumed his boldest schemes of conquest; and though he no longer ventured to attack the metropolis of the zamorin, he still wished to gain some great city which his countrymen might establish as their

Ardour of the viceroy.

CHAP. IV. — A.D. 1510.

capital, where he might safely moor his fleets, and thence realize his plans of victory and colonization. Timoia, an Indian pirate, the trusty friend of the Portuguese, drew his attention to Goa. This town is situated upon an island twenty-three miles in circuit, if island it may be called, which is separated from the land only by a salt-marsh fordable in many places. The surface is fertile, diversified by little hills and valleys, and almost sufficient of itself to supply a great city with every necessary of life. The adjoining territory, called Canara, forms the seacoast of the Deccan. It had been conquered by the Mogul, and annexed to the dominions of Delhi; but, in the distracted state of that empire, several independent kingdoms had arisen in the south, among which Narsinga, with its capital of Bisnagar, set the example. Of these rulers the sovereign of Goa, called the zabaim, was the most powerful. Timoia, however, gave notice that this prince, being occupied in war with several states of the interior, had left his own almost unprotected. Albuquerque, readily embracing this suggestion, hastily assembled an expedition, and, in conjunction with his guide, arrived off Goa on the 25th February 1510. Several of the forts which defended the approaches having been taken, and the fleet of the besiegers brought up close to the walls, the citizens, who were chiefly persons connected with trade, began seriously to ponder the consequences likely to ensue were the place to be taken by storm, especially by an enemy whose mercy had never been conspicuous. They sent, therefore, a deputation, composed principally of merchants, who privately intimated that the Portuguese commander might obtain admission on certain conditions, including full protection to commerce and private property. Albuquerque granted these terms, and was immediately put in possession of the town. He fulfilled his stipulations in the strictest manner, adopting every measure calculated to preserve order and prosperity, and even continuing many of the natives in their civil employments. Having occupied the palace of the zabaim, he assumed

Goa.

Expedition against Goa.

Submission of the citizens.

at once the character of a great eastern potentate; sending an embassy to the King of Narsinga, and receiving, in the most gracious manner, those of Persia and Ormuz, who were then on a mission to the sovereign of Goa. But he soon found himself by no means in the secure and agreeable position he at first imagined. The zabaim, on hearing that his capital was in the possession of those hated foreigners, roused all his energies, and disregarded every object in comparison with their immediate expulsion. He at once concluded peace with his enemies, several of whom made common cause with him against this powerful adversary; and an army of upwards of 40,000 men began its march under his direction. Albuquerque undauntedly viewed its advance, though threatened with an internal danger perhaps still more formidable. In this distant service, the spirit of discipline was not easily maintained, and both men and officers had acquired a habit of criticising the proceedings of their general. There arose a numerous party, who argued, that with so small a number of troops, and without any prospect of reinforcement, it was madness to attempt making head against the numerous host now approaching, surrounded by a population generally hostile, and in the heart of an immense city, whose inhabitants only watched for an opportunity to aid in their destruction. These fears and reasonings were by no means without foundation; but the lofty spirit of Albuquerque indignantly repelled the idea of tamely relinquishing so magnificent a prize. The faction, amounting to nine hundred, insisted that so brave an army ought not to be sacrificed to the obstinacy of one man, and began to form a scheme for wresting the power from their commander, and carrying into effect their own counsels. But having traced this plot to its origin, he surprised the conspirators at a secret meeting, and threw the ringleaders into prison. The remainder sued for pardon, which he could not well refuse, being unable to want the services of any of his small number of troops; they were therefore, with a very few exceptions, restored to their employments.

Assumption of the viceroy.

His difficulties and dangers.

Conspiracy among the Portuguese.

The ringleaders seized.

CHAP. IV.

A.D. 1510

Advance of the zabaim.

The zabaim meantime was advancing upon the city. The chief hope of Albuquerque depended upon his success in defending the approaches to the island; but the channel separating it from the mainland was so narrow, and in many places so shallow, that it presented by no means an insuperable obstacle. He stationed chosen troops at all the exposed points, covering them with walls and intrenchments. The native prince, completely baffled in his first attempts, had almost resigned himself to despair; but at length he bethought himself of a nocturnal attack, favoured by the monsoon. The night of the 17th May being dark and stormy, two large bodies advanced at different points, and though unable to surprise the Portuguese, succeeded in forcing their way into the island. The whole army was soon transported over, and commenced operations against the city. The viceroy stood his ground with his characteristic firmness; but as the enemy was aided by repeated risings within the walls, while his own officers took occasion to renew their remonstrances as to the untenable nature of the place, he found at last that no alternative remained but to retire into the fort, whence, by means of the river on which it was situated, he could still communicate with the fleet. But the zabaim, having taken possession of the town, immediately commenced operations for reducing this stronghold. By sinking large ships in the stream, he endeavoured to interrupt the communication, and at the same time provided pitch, sulphur, and other combustibles, for the purpose of setting fire to the Portuguese squadron. Albuquerque, unable to obstruct the progress of these fatal measures, at last felt that he must evacuate the fortress. Even this was become difficult; but he executed his resolution with vigour and success. Having conveyed privately on board all the guns, ammunition, and provisions, and seen the troops embark in profound silence, he himself went last into the flag-ship. He might have reached the fleet unnoticed and unmolested, had not the explosion of a magazine, which roused the enemy, given rise to a severe encounter.

Viceroy's firmness.

Retires to the fort.

Compelled to evacuate the fortress.

Surprise of Pangin.

Being in this manner compelled to move out to sea, he was anxious to do something which might redeem the honour lost in his late undertaking, and revive the spirits of his men. At Pangin, near Goa, the enemy had formed a strongly intrenched camp, and frequently sent out vessels to annoy the Portuguese. He therefore fitted out an expedition, which, approaching in deep silence, reached the shore at the first dawn, suddenly landed, and having sounded the drums and trumpets, and raised loud shouts, the Indians awoke in such a panic, that they ran off without once facing their assailants; upon which the latter, at their leisure, carried off a great quantity of artillery and stores, as well as a large supply of provisions. Learning soon after that a squadron was preparing to attack him, he anticipated the movement by sending a number of ships, under his nephew, Antony Noronha, who was met by the Indian chief at the head of thirty paraos; but, after an obstinate conflict, the zabaim was compelled to retreat full speed to the shore. The conquerors followed, when Peter and Ferdinand Andrade, with five men, boarded the principal vessel; but their captain, mounting behind them, was severely wounded, and fell into the boat. Amid the general anxiety, and while all efforts were employed to remove their leader out of danger, the Andrades and their party were forgotten; the ship, by the receding of the tide, was left on dry land; and they were attacked by greatly superior numbers, against whom they could only defend themselves by prodigies of valour. When their condition was observed, it was for some time doubtful how to reach them; at length eight bold mariners pushing on shore in the long-boat, attacked and made themselves masters of the ship; but, being unable to tow it off, were obliged to content themselves with the feat of rescuing their comrades. It is pleasing, amid the ferocity of this war, to find an exchange of chivalrous courtesy. The zabaim sent messengers, expressing his admiration of the valour of the Portuguese; and a polite answer was returned. Even a negotiation for peace was opened, though without success.

Bravery of the Andrades.

Mutual courtesies of the rivals.

CHAP. IV.

A. D. 1510.

Second attempt on Goa projected.

The pride of the enemy being humbled, and the spirits and courage of the Portuguese revived by these exploits, Albuquerque sailed to Cananor, where he refitted his fleet, and received considerable reinforcements; resolving, as soon as the season allowed, to make a second attempt upon Goa. His confidence of a happier issue on this occasion seems to have been founded chiefly on the fact that the zabaim was involved in war with the kingdom of Narsinga, which was likely for some time to occupy the greater part of his forces. Unable, however, to muster more than 1500 European and 300 native troops, it was a very serious undertaking to attack a large and strong capital, garrisoned by upwards of 9000 men. It had been farther strengthened by a new wall and ditch, and by a stockade drawn through the water, behind which the ships were moored in security, and stood like so many towers. However, having arrived in front of the city, he determined not to delay the assault, though there was no appearance of his ally Timoia. In the morning, accordingly, he opened with his cannon a tremendous fire, and the whole shore was wrapt in a cloud of smoke, illumined only by the flashes. He landed and divided his troops into two parts, one of which was led by himself, and attacked the northern quarter; the other, in three separate bands, proceeded in an opposite direction. One division, led by the Limas and other chosen heroes, having anticipated their commander, drove the enemy within the walls; and as they were shutting the gate, Fernando Melos thrust in a large spear, which prevented it from closing. Several others following this example, it was, after a most desperate struggle, forced open, and the assailants entered along with the fugitives. These, however, still made a resolute stand in the houses and corners of the streets, particularly in the palace of the zabaim. Here a strong body had taken post, and twenty Portuguese, who rashly advanced, were almost entirely cut to pieces. John de Lima, on forcing a passage, found his brother Jeronymo, with several of his comrades, lying in the agonies of

Great disparity of the forces.

Assault of the town.

Gain an entrance.

CHAP. IV.

A.D. 1510.

death; but the fallen chief professed perfect resignation to his fate, and entreated that there might not, on his account, be a moment's delay. The enemy, driven from the palace, rallied on a neighbouring hill. The commander, who had been extremely surprised to find the battle raging in the city, now entered, but had still to wage a hard contest of six hours' duration before it was completely in his power.

The city taken.

Albuquerque, being left for some time in the undisturbed possession of this capital, applied himself to secure it as a permanent acquisition to his country. His views on this subject materially differed from those of Almeyda, who conceived it wisest to keep their fleets united and at sea, only touching occasionally at friendly ports. So combined, they appeared to him more formidable than when dispersed over different stations and settlements, while they could at the same time overawe the native powers without giving any reasonable ground of jealousy. Albuquerque's opinion, on the contrary, was, that a large city and a spacious port, which they could call their own, were essential to the maintenance of Portuguese supremacy. They would then have a secure station for their fleets, a fixed point for receiving reinforcements, and a retreat in case of disaster, without depending on the precarious friendship of their allies. He studied, therefore, to render Goa a suitable capital for an eastern empire. He sent and received ambassadors, whom he astonished by the display of a pomp surpassing even that of India; and he surprised them still more by the extensive fortifications and useful works which he had already constructed. He viewed it also as an essential object to attach the natives to his government, for which purpose he adopted a somewhat singular expedient. Having numerous female captives, some belonging to the first families in the country, he treated them in the most honourable manner; but, not satisfied with this, he proceeded to arrange matrimonial connexions between them and his European followers, without leaving much choice on either side. Some such

Plans of Albuquerque for securing Portuguese supremacy.

His extensive fortifications.

Singular expedients.

CHAP. IV. — A. D. 1512. procedure is at least alluded to by De Barros, when he compares his mode of cementing the Portuguese power to that employed by Romulus for peopling his infant state of Rome. It was made an absolute condition with the brides that they should embrace Christianity; an obstacle which was not found insurmountable, the prejudices of caste and religion being less deeply rooted there than in other parts of the East. A few such marriages being formed, the viceroy showed the parties peculiar favour, and bestowed on the husbands some of

Success of his scheme.

his best appointments. The principal families, finding themselves aggrandized by these connexions, so far from objecting to them, gave their countenance to new matches. An odd story is told of a great number of weddings being celebrated at once with a splendid festival, when the lights being prematurely extinguished, it became difficult for the parties to recognise each

Curious dilemma.

other, and they fell into many mistakes. Next morning an investigation was proposed; but, on mature reflection, it was judged best, that each should remain content with the wife who had accidentally fallen to his lot, though different from the one to whom the church had united him; and the affair furnished to the army only an occasion of mirth.

Plans of conquest.

Having thus settled the government, the viceroy resumed the consideration of his more distant schemes of conquest. Two objects engrossed his mind,—Ormuz, the splendid emporium of the Persian Gulf, which had been snatched from him almost in the moment of victory; and Malacca, a native kingdom, considered then as the key to the remotest regions and islands of Asia. The latter obtained the preference. The capital, though situated upon the coast of a barren peninsula, was enriched in an extraordinary degree by being the centre of the commerce carried on between Hindostan, China, and the eastern islands,—a trade which now gives prosperity to Singapore. Albuquerque sailed thither with a force of eight hundred Portuguese and six hundred Indians; to oppose which the king had mustered a garrison that has been represented as exceeding 30,000. Negotiations were opened, and professions made on both sides of a desire for peace; but it was obvious that such an expedition could terminate only in an appeal to arms. A vigorous resistance was made by means of wooden machines, cannon, and a species of artificial fire peculiar to the East; but the intrepidity of Albuquerque and his followers finally triumphed. Having expelled all the native troops, and become complete master of the city he immediately began to erect a strong fort out of the materials of the shattered palaces; he settled the government on that firm yet conciliatory principle which distinguished his policy; and opened negotiations with Siam, Java, and Sumatra, from which countries it is even asserted that he received friendly embassies.

Capital of Malacca taken.

During his absence on this expedition, the zabaim again mustered his forces, and sent a powerful army under successive commanders, who forced their way into the island of Goa, erected there a strong fort called Benaster, and pressed the city very closely. Having, after some delay, arrived with a considerable reinforcement, he obliged the enemy to raise the siege, but was completely repulsed in an attack on the garrison; and it was not till after repeated assaults that he was able to drive them from their fortress, and finally establish the Portuguese supremacy.

Attempt of the zabaim to recover Goa.

The viceroy again resumed his plans of distant conquest, but was baffled in two successive attempts upon Aden, then the chief emporium of the Red Sea. At length he equipped a great armament to achieve the most favourite object of his ambition. With 1500 European and 600 Asiatic troops he sailed against Ormuz, where his strength was considered so formidable, that the king did not venture to oppose his demand for permission to erect a fort. Having performed this task with his usual diligence, he forthwith suggested the great convenience of transporting to this station all the cannon in the city. The unfortunate monarch, conscious of the state to which he was reduced, felt it no longer

Expedition against Ormuz.

CHAP. IV.

A. D. 1513.

possible to refuse even this request, and the celebrated Ormuz became completely a Portuguese establishment; a triumph which left the ambitious commander hardly any thing to wish in that part of the world, where he had firmly established the flag of his country.

Close of Albuquerque's career.

But this brilliant career was approaching to its close. Albuquerque was now somewhat advanced in years, and his constitution, exhausted by so many toils, began to exhibit symptoms of decay. Finding his health in an infirm state, he became anxious to revisit Goa; and as he passed along the coast of Cambay, tidings arrived which struck him to the heart. A new fleet had been sent out, and Lope Soarez, the name of all others which he most detested, not only commanded it, but was appointed to supersede him as Governor of India. New officers were nominated to the principal vessels and forts, —all of them known to be most hostile to his interest. His power and influence, he felt, were at an end. The Portuguese writers, always silent on every thing which might affect the credit of their sovereign, give no hint of the motives that induced him to cast off so suddenly the man who had conquered for him a great empire. European counsellors, it may be presumed, possessed the ear of the monarch, and might whisper that the viceroy was becoming too great to continue a subject. There was not even a letter or any other mark of honour to soften this deep disgrace.

Lope Soarez appointed viceroy.

Despair of Albuquerque.

A death-blow was now given to this great leader, who no longer wished to live. Amid his agonies, it was suggested to him that the attachment of his adherents was so devoted as might enable him to defy the mandate of an ungrateful master, and still remain ruler of the Indian Seas. His mind seems to have opened for a moment to the temptation; but he finally repelled it, and sought only in the grave a refuge for his wounded pride and honour. Violently agitated, refusing food and refreshment, and calling every hour for death, he could not be long of finding it. As his end approached, he was persuaded to write a short letter to the king in favour of his son, expressed in the following proud but pathetic terms:—"Senor,—This is the last letter which, in the agonies of death, I write to your Highness, of the many which I have written during the long period of my life, when I had the satisfaction of serving you. In your kingdom I have a son, by name Braz de Albuquerque, whom I entreat your Highness to favour as my services may merit. As for the affairs of India, they will speak for themselves and for me." Feeling that he must die before reaching Goa, his mind became tranquillized; he ascribed the present change to the ordination of Providence, and turned all his thoughts to that other world on which he was about to enter. A light barge sent before him brought out the vicar-general, who administered to him the sacraments of the church; and on the morning of the 16th December 1515 he expired. He was carried in pomp to the shore, where his funeral was celebrated by the tears both of his own countrymen and of the natives, whose hearts he had completely attached to him. Thus died Alphonso d'Albuquerque, who stood foremost among his countrymen, and ranks with the greatest navel commanders of modern Europe.

Letter to the king.

His death.

At his death the Portuguese empire in the East, so recently founded, had reached its utmost limits. Only a few points on the remoter coast of Africa, and two or three settlements on the shore of Coromandel, were afterwards added to it. Their dominion, according to the boast of their historian Faria y Sousa, stretched from the Cape of Good Hope to the frontier of China, and comprehended a coast 12,000 miles in extent. It is impossible however not to observe that this is somewhat of an empty boast, since over this immense space there were not perhaps more than thirty factories established,—and the nearest of them separated by upwards of a thousand miles. In many, perhaps in most cases, they possessed not a spot of ground beyond the walls of the fortress. Their real sovereignty was on the ocean, where their ships, armed and manned in a manner superior to those of the native powers, were victorious in almost every encounter.

Extent of Portuguese empire in the East.

Its very partial possession.

CHAP. IV.

A. D. 1536.

Influence of Portuguese supremacy.

This species of government, with the exclusive commerce between Europe and India, they retained for upwards of a century. Their history, during this period, consists chiefly of the struggles to maintain their ground against the natives, whom their domineering, bigoted, and persecuting spirit, soon inspired with the bitterest enmity. These contests, which usually ended in the repulse of the latter, and in the two parties being replaced in their wonted position, are too monotonous to justify a detailed narrative. One or two of them, however, were so memorable as to deserve to be here recorded.

Nuno da Cunha.

In 1536, Nuno da Cunha, then governor-general, obtained permission to erect a fort at the important city of Diu, in a situation highly favourable for trade, but which brought his people in contact with the powerful kingdoms of Cambay and Guzerat. Badur, ruler of the former of these nations, who at first welcomed their approach, soon began to view them with jealousy. In a visit that he paid to the settlement a scuffle ensued, in which he himself was killed, while the commandant and several other European chiefs shared the same fate. Sylveira, who succeeded to the charge, made the greatest efforts to justify the conduct of his countrymen in the eyes of the natives, and appeared at first to have succeeded; yet there still remained a leaven of discord. This was strongly fomented by Khojah Zofar, a Moorish chief, who had at first embraced with apparent zeal the cause of the Portuguese, but afterwards became their bitterest enemy.

Immense force levied against him.

Through him a great force was levied in Guzerat, with which Solyman Pasha, the governor of Cairo, was ordered by the Grand Seignior to co-operate. This officer sailed from Suez with seventy galleys, having on board 7000 of the best Turkish soldiers, and a superb train of artillery. He was joined on his arrival by upwards of 20,000 troops of Guzerat, and early in September 1538 laid close siege to the Portuguese fort. Sylveira had only 600 men, many of whom were sickly; and in consequence of an interregnum in the general government, occasioned by the appointment of Garcia de Noronha to supersede

Nuno da Cunha, no succours were received from Goa. He, however, prepared for resistance with the utmost vigour; and the siege which he sustained is considered one of the most memorable in the annals of Portuguese domination in Asia. Exploits of the most daring valour were achieved, the women vying with the other sex in courage and enthusiasm. Donna Isabella de Vega assembled the females within the fort, and, representing that all the men were required to bear arms against the enemy, induced them to undertake the laborious task of repairing the works shattered by the incessant fire of the batteries. Ann Fernandez, lady to a physician, ran from post to post, even while the assault was hottest, cheering and encouraging the soldiers; and her son falling in one of the attacks, she carried away his body, then returned to the scene of combat, and remained till the close, when she went to perform his obsequies.

CHAP. IV.
—
A. D. 1538.

Isabella de Vega.

Under the impulse of this high feeling, the enemy were defeated in successive attempts, made during several weeks, to carry the fortress by storm. The garrison, however, who suffered in each attack, were at length reduced to less than half their original number, and these so exhausted that they could ill continue such severe exertions. The besiegers, wearied out and exasperated with the length and obstinacy of the defence, determined to make one grand and desperate effort. They first began by withdrawing their galleys, as if intending to raise the siege, then at midnight suddenly returned, and immediately applied scaling-ladders to the sea-wall. The garrison were instantly roused, and hastened to meet the attack; but the others persevered with such fury, that they at length forced an entrance into one of the principal bulwarks. They were repulsed by an almost preternatural valour, and are reported to have had 1500 men killed and wounded in the assault. But after so long and desperate a conflict, the Portuguese had not above forty soldiers fit for duty; Sylveira was already oppressed by the most gloomy apprehensions, when, to his joyful surprise, he found that the besiegers had made their

Defeat of the assailants.

Immense losses on both sides.

CHAP. IV — A. D. 1545.

last effort. Solyman, not aware, it may be presumed, of the desperate situation of his adversary, weighed anchor on the 5th November, and set sail for Egypt with all his fleet.

Khojah Zofar invests the Castle of Diu.

Khojah Zofar, who continued to retain the supreme sway in Guzerat, still cherished the most inveterate rancour against the Portuguese. Seven years after the period now mentioned, he assembled an army nearly as large as the former, and invested the castle of Diu, defended by Don Juan Mascarenhas with a garrison of only 210 men. With this slender force the governor most stoutly and gallantly maintained his post, keeping up a very destructive fire on the besiegers. The King of Cambay, who had come in the firm expectation of witnessing the fall of the castle, was so alarmed by a ball which penetrated his tent and killed an officer at his side, that he departed, leaving his generals to prosecute the siege. Zofar, soon after, had his head carried off by a cannon-shot; but his son, Rumi Khan, inherited his daring spirit as well as his enmity to Christians. Notwithstanding the valour with which the besieged repulsed every assault, their numbers were gradually thinned, and they began to suffer the extremities of famine. At length Alvaro de Castro brought a reinforcement of 400 men; but these troops, having insisted on being led out against the enemy, were driven back after suffering great loss. In October 1545, however, the new viceroy, Don Juan de Castro, one of the ablest and most distinguished of the Portuguese officers, arrived; and having a powerful armament, he considered himself in a condition immediately to commence offensive operations. He broke through the enemy's intrenchments, obliged them to give battle, and drove them, with prodigious slaughter, into the city. Thence they again sallied to the amount of 8000, whom De Castro totally routed, and entering along with them, was soon master of Diu; but he stained his glory by giving it up to indiscriminate plunder and massacre. Returning to Goa on the 11th April 1546, he made a most splendid triumphal entry,

Don Juan de Castro, the new viceroy.

with bands of music, his head crowned with laurel, and the royal standard of Cambay dragged behind him. The streets were hung with silk, and resounded with acclamations. Queen Catherine, however, on receiving the account of this ostentatious procession, is said to have remarked, that the governor had indeed conquered like a Christian, but had triumphed like a pagan.

Death of De Castro.

De Castro held the office of viceroy only from 1545 to 1548, during which time he established a high reputation, and made the Portuguese name dreaded on all the coasts of India. He appears to have been zealous in the service of his country, and singularly disinterested; since, after holding the government during the period we have mentioned over this rich province, he died in extreme poverty. But the dreadful barbarities of which he was guilty, though they do not seem to have shocked the historians of his own country, must tarnish his fame in the view of all nations possessing more humane feelings.

Critical situation of the Portuguese.

The most critical situation in which the Portuguese settlements were ever placed was in 1570, during the government of Don Luis de Ataide. Adel Khan and Nizam-ul-Mulk, two distinguished officers under the Mogul, formed an alliance with the zamorin; uniting with the firm resolution to expel this foreign people from the shores of India. The siege of Goa, considered the most important enterprise, was undertaken by the former, who collected for this purpose his whole force, estimated at 100,000 men, and commanded it in person. His army spent eight days in defiling through the Ghauts; after which, being encamped in tents ranged in straight lines, in that regular and magnificent order observed by the Mogul soldiers, it presented the appearance of a handsome and spacious city. The viceroy was apparently taken by surprise, not having in Goa above 700 troops, with 1300 monks and armed slaves. By stopping a fleet about to sail for Europe, he might have obtained a reinforcement of 400 men; but he intrepidly rejected this resource, on account of the inconvenience

Siege of Goa.

Intrepidity of Don Luis de Ataide.

CHAP IV.

A. D. 1570.

which would be occasioned at home by the vessels not arriving; he was also, perhaps, ambitious to show that he could defend the town with only its own garrison, and such soldiers as might be obtained from the neighbouring settlements. The enemy began a series of most formidable attacks, attempting to cross into the island. Don Luis, however, not only repulsed them with success, but, on receiving some reinforcements, made repeated sallies into their quarters, on which occasions his troops acted with their usual courage and barbarity. Having killed numbers of the natives, the soldiers sent into the city cart-loads of heads, to afford to the people the savage encouragement derived from this spectacle. At the end of two months Adel Khan began to despair, and even opened a correspondence with the governor; but as each party not only concealed his wish for a termination of the siege, but assumed an air of haughty defiance, the negotiation made very slow progress. Ataide received various accessions, particularly one of 1500 men from the Moluccas, and was thereby rendered so strong, that the enemy could scarcely cherish any hope of success. The Mongolian general, however, observing a point which, from confidence in its natural strength, had been less carefully fortified, resolved on a desperate attempt to effect a passage. On the 13th April, Solyman Aga, captain of the guards, made an attack so sudden and vigorous, that, in spite of the most resolute resistance, part of his troops forced their way into the island; but the Portuguese soon mustered their forces, and, after a brisk conflict, drove back or cut in pieces the whole of the assailants. Adel Khan, who viewed from the opposite bank this obstinate engagement and the discomfiture of his troops, was equally enraged and disheartened. From this time all his operations were conducted in a languishing manner; yet his pride induced him to persevere several months longer, till, about the end of August, he struck his tents, and withdrew from before the city, after sustaining during the siege a loss of 12,000 men.

Courage and barbarity of the Portuguese.

Accessions to the garrison

Discomfiture of Adel Khan

Meantime Nizam-ul-Mulk, in fulfilment of his part

CHAP. IV.

A. D. 1570.

of the stipulation, advanced with an army equally formidable against Chaul, then a settlement of considerable importance near Bombay. The defence of this place appeared still more hopeless, it being situated entirely on the continent, and defended only by a single wall, with a fort little superior to a common house. The governor-general was therefore advised to withdraw his troops without any attempt at resistance; but he formed a resolution more worthy of him, and Luis Freyre d'Andrada the commander of the town, having had his garrison augmented to 2000 men, undertook to supply all deficiencies by his valour and genius. After some unsuccessful attempts to carry the place by a *coup de main*, the enemy opened a regular battery of not less than seventy cannon. At the end of a month the town had suffered considerable injury, the wall was entirely beaten down, and the assailants were attacking house after house. Each mansion, however, was in its turn converted into a species of fortress, and defended with the utmost obstinacy. The Moors, attempting a general assault, penetrated the city at different points, but were every where completely driven out. In one house that the Portuguese found themselves obliged to evacuate, they lodged a mine, which unfortunately springing before they left it, killed forty-two of their number. Another dwelling was defended six weeks, and a third during a whole month. In the beginning of June, after the siege had continued nearly half a year, and many thousands of the natives had perished, some overtures were made for an accommodation, but without any result. The nizam then renewed the attack with greater vigour than ever, and carried successively the monastery of St Dominic, the houses of Nuno Alvarez and of Gonzalo Menesez. But this progress was too slow to fulfil his object, though it encouraged him to attempt one desperate assault. On the 20th June, the whole army rushed forward with barbarous shouts against the ruined works, on which the small body of Portuguese had taken their stand. The artillery in full play alternately illumined

Assault of Chaul.

Courage of the governor.

Determined assault by the Moors.

CHAP. IV

A. D. 1570

Defeat of the Moors.

the sky and wrapped it in darkness. The shock was terrible; the enemy planted their colours on several of the remaining bulwarks, and seemed repeatedly on the eve of obtaining full possession of the city; but the valour and discipline of the Europeans were in the end triumphant. The Mongolian general, after continuing the attack till night, drew off his army, and soon after opened a negotiation, which terminated in a league offensive and defensive.

Total dissolution of the native league.

The zamorin manifested little zeal to fulfil his part in the grand alliance. Indeed, on seeing the Portuguese hard pressed by the two other confederates, he offered, on certain conditions, to withdraw from it altogether, and conclude a separate treaty. But the pride of Ataide disdained, even in this extreme peril, to purchase peace by any humiliating concession; he defied the monarch's power; trusting to his own talent, and the bravery of his countrymen, to extricate him from every difficulty The zamorin then sent some small aid to the nizam, and afterwards laid siege to Chale, a fort about two miles from Calicut. But this place being defended with the usual vigour, and its garrison reinforced, he was obliged to withdraw; hence this formidable combination, which had comprehended the greatest powers of Southern India, was, by the conduct of the governor and the courage of his troops, entirely dissolved.

Supremacy secured.

By these and other achievements, the subjects of Portugal, during the whole of the sixteenth century, maintained their possessions on the coasts, and their supremacy in the seas of India. Even after their military enterprise relaxed, the high name which they had established deterred the natives from any attempt to shake off the yoke. But about the year 1600 a new enemy appeared, much more formidable than any power which they had yet encountered in that quarter of the globe.

Dutch republic.

The Dutch, driven to desperation by the tyranny of Philip II., had revolted against Spain, and after a long, hard, and glorious struggle, raised themselves to the rank of an independent republic. Even before the neighbouring

CHAP. IV

A. D. 1600

states fully recognised them in this character, they had gained the reputation of being the first naval power in Europe. Owing to the narrow extent of their territory, they themselves, as well as the multitude of refugees who found among them the enjoyment of civil and religious liberty, were induced to seek on the ocean the means of subsistence and wealth. The happy situation of their coasts, both for commerce and fishery, had already led to considerable progress in these branches of industry, which now attained a magnitude before unexampled in modern times. After embarking so deeply in these pursuits, their attention could not fail to be attracted by the trade of India, to which has always been assigned an overrated importance. They were not, however, yet prepared to encounter the naval armaments of Spain and Portugal, which guarded with the most jealous care all the approaches to the Eastern Seas. They were hence induced to attempt a passage by the north of Asia, which the imperfect knowledge then possessed respecting the extent of that continent, and the character of its Arctic shores, led mariners to regard as not impracticable. Three successive expeditions were accordingly sent, chiefly under the command of Barentz; in the last of which the people were obliged to winter on the dreary shores of Nova Zembla; but they failed altogether in their hope of discovering a north-east passage, which, if it does at all exist, must, it was found, be too difficult to be ever productive of any practical utility.

Dutch turn their attention to India.

Attempt to discover the north-east passage.

They now felt the impossibility of rivalling the Portuguese by any other route than that round the Cape of Good Hope; and their courage and resources having been augmented in the course of a successful struggle for liberty, they no longer hesitated to brave all the dangers of this undertaking. The necessary information was obtained through Cornelius Houtman, who collected it during a long residence at Lisbon. The jealous government there, displeased with his active and diligent inquiries, threw him into prison, whence he was liberated only on the payment of a considerable ransom. But by

Resolved to follow the route of the Portuguese.

CHAP. IV.

A. D. 1596.

Houtman's voyage to Java.

his instructions the Dutch in three months equipped a squadron of four vessels, well armed and provided with the materials of trade. Houtman set out in the autumn of 1596, and after a tedious voyage, without however encountering any important opposition or obstruction, arrived off Bantam in the island of Java. He was at first extremely well treated, but afterwards, seemingly through his own rashness and violence, became involved in a quarrel with the king, was thrown into prison, and obtained release only by sacrificing part of his investment. He then effected a safe return to Europe, where he was received with the highest exultation, having evinced the practicability of a fleet finding its way without molestation from the enemy, to those remote and opulent shores. The original company, augmented by one more recently formed, sent out early in 1599 no fewer than eight ships under the joint command of Houtman and Van Neck. They reached the coasts of Sumatra and Java, where they carried on a successful traffic; and at length the second of these officers returned to Amsterdam with four of the vessels laden with spices and other valuable commodities.

Return to Europe.

Companies established in Holland.

This favourable beginning encouraged the Hollanders to prosecute the Indian trade with the utmost activity. Several new companies were established, without being invested with any exclusive privileges, or apparently actuated by any hostile rivalry: and thus mutually aiding and co-operating with each other, they soon raised this branch of commerce to the highest prosperity. In 1600, not five years after the first of their squadrons had sailed round the Cape, they sent out forty vessels bearing from 400 to 600 tons; and, by their superior diligence and punctuality, had almost completely supplanted the Portuguese in the spice-market. Hitherto they had studiously shunned any interference with that people, selecting the spots not occupied by them; while the latter seem not to have ventured on any violent measures to enforce their monopoly. However, as they became stronger, they began to form schemes for the

Large squadrons sent out to India.

expulsion of their rivals. They studied by every art to foment the discontent of the natives, who had themselves begun to observe that the Portuguese were more intent on conquest than commerce, and who were besides disgusted with the harsh means employed for inducing them to renounce the Mohammedan faith. Impelled by these motives, the Malays at Acheen, aided by some Dutch volunteers, surprised the fort which the subjects of Portugal had erected in the bay, and made a general massacre of the garrison. They were deprived in a similar manner of several stations on the Molucca Islands; losing in this way some important seats of trade, while those of the Hollanders were continually extended.

League with the natives.

Philip II. of Portugal.

Philip II., who, on the death of Don Sebastian, had seized the crown of Portugal, felt highly indignant at finding his people expelled from those valuable possessions by the arms of a rebellious province, which his own oppression had driven into resistance, and in fact raised to its present maritime greatness. Having learned that the Dutch East Indiamen were expected home, he fitted out an armament of thirty ships, mostly of a large size, and sent them to intercept the fleet. Near the Cape de Verde Islands, this squadron met eight of their vessels going out under the command of Spilbergen; but the latter, by their bravery and skilful manœuvres, succeeded in beating off the assailants, and made their way to India without any serious loss. From this time Philip seems to have given up every attempt to contend at sea with this rising people, and directed all his efforts, though without effect, to subjugate them by military force. He satisfied himself with issuing proclamations, prohibiting them, under the severest penalties, from trading in any of the Spanish possessions. The Portuguese in India, aided by his subjects from the Philippines, still kept up a harassing piratical warfare, to which the Dutch determined to put a stop by wresting from their antagonists all the remaining settlements in the Spice Islands. In 1605 they reinforced their fleets with nineteen fresh vessels, having on board two thou-

Unsuccessful attempt to intercept the Dutch fleet

Piratical warfare.

CHAP. IV. A. D. 1605.

sand veteran soldiers. They then invested, and successively reduced, all the forts which their opponents had erected in the islands of Amboyna and Tidor, capturing the shipping which lay under their protection, and finally lading their own with valuable spices. The supremacy of the Dutch in the Indian Seas was thus fully established.

The Dutch establish supremacy in the Indian seas

To complete this triumph, the Admiral Matelief sailed against Malacca, which the Portuguese had made the capital of their possessions in the more eastern parts. The place, however, was so well prepared for defence, that, after several weeks spent in the most vigorous efforts, he gave up the attempt. But what was his surprise, when on reaching Amboyna he was saluted with a heavy fire, and saw the Spanish flag flying on the walls of the castle! This revolution had been effected by a naval force from the Philippines, which, taking advantage of his absence, had sailed to those important islands, and finding them almost defenceless, completely reduced them. Matelief was at first a little disconcerted; but, encouraged by the valour of his men, he landed, attacked the fortress, and carried it by storm, making, as was too common, a general massacre of the unfortunate garrison. Inspirited by this success, he proceeded against the other settlements, and in two months brought all of them again under the dominion of the United Provinces.

Settlement of Ceylon.

The Dutch were soon afterwards induced to form a settlement in the island of Ceylon; an expedition was sent thither in 1605, under the command of De Weert, who was at first favourably received. Having, however, not only violated a solemn engagement in the first instance, but afterwards, when he went to court, conducted himself with the *hauteur* which his countrymen had now generally assumed, he was seized, and struck dead with a scimitar. His brave companions, who attempted with unequal strength to avenge his loss, only shared his fate. The tragical issue of this adventure did not discourage Borth the governor-general, who imputed the disaster of De Weert solely to his rash and culpable violence, from sending a fresh armament under Marcellus Boschkouveur, an officer of distinguished talent and address. He arrived at the critical moment when the Portuguese were advancing from their principal settlement at Columbo in such force against Candy, that the rajah scarcely hoped to be able to resist them. The Dutch commander, however, both by directing the operations of the Candians, and by affording to them the aid of his own troops, gained for them a complete victory. The power of their rivals was thus humbled, while they themselves obtained from the grateful monarch ample liberty to form an establishment on the most advantageous footing. But it was not till 1656, after a long and bloody struggle, that they gained the complete mastery over their competitors. In that year Columbo surrendered, after a siege of seven months, and the Portuguese were completely expelled from Ceylon. We reserve for the chapter on the English Settlements in India an account of the contest in which the Hollanders were involved with our countrymen, and the means that they used to thwart their success. Having obtained the complete command of the Oriental Islands, they determined to build a city which might become the capital of their Asiatic conquests, and the centre of all their political and commercial transactions. They fixed upon a spot near the western extremity of the north coast of Java,—a very happy situation, commanding the route to the Spice Islands, and enjoying an easy communication with Sumatra, Borneo, and Celebes. Having overcome the resistance of the native powers, they founded a city which, being named Batavia, from the ancient appellation of their country, was subsequently rendered by them a great and flourishing station. Europeans, however, suffer severely from its climate, the evils of which are increased by canals drawn round the place and even through its very streets, exhaling in that tropical climate the most pernicious vapours.

Dutch alliance with the Candians.

The capital of Batavia.

The Dutch made repeated efforts to drive the Portuguese from Malacca, the capital of their possessions in

Obtain possession of Malacca.

CHAP. IV.

A. D. 1640.

that quarter of India. At length, in 1640, after encountering an obstinate resistance, they effected their object, and they then became complete masters of the Eastern Islands and Seas, with the exception of some settlements made by the English on the coast of Sumatra. But as they never formed any important or extensive establishment on the continent of India, to which this volume specially relates, we have not thought it necessary to give more than a short summary of their oriental career.

First appearance of the English.

In the western provinces the Portuguese found themselves chiefly opposed by the English, and they soon, as will hereafter appear, found the contest very unequal. Notwithstanding their influence with the Mogul, they were gradually supplanted at Surat and the other ports of Guzerat by the superior power and policy of their new rivals. An expedition, jointly undertaken by our countrymen and Shah Abbas, king of Persia, deprived them of Ormuz; while the Imam of Mascat, seconded by the natives, expelled them from most of their possessions on the coast of Africa. They were thus stripped of their vast dominions almost as rapidly as they had acquired them; and now Goa and Mozambique, in a very decayed condition, form nearly the sole remnant of that proud empire which formerly extended over so great a part of the eastern world.

CHAPTER V.

Early English Voyages and Settlements.

Importance always attached to Indian Trade—Mission by Alfred—The English attempt to penetrate to India by the North-East, and through Russia—By the North-West—Voyage of Drake—Of Cavendish—Newbery and Fitch, by way of Aleppo and Ormuz—Fitch visits many Parts of India—First English Voyage by the Cape—Its Disasters—An Association formed—Voyage of Lancaster—Middleton—Michelborne—Keeling and Others—Sharpey—Loss of his Vessel—Sir Henry Middleton—His Adventures at Surat—Hippon—Settlements on Coromandel—Saris—Profits of the Trade—Quarrels with the Dutch—Massacre at Amboyna—Acquisition of Bombay—Settlements on the Coromandel Coast—In Bengal—Disputes with the Mogul—Company begin to form Plans of Conquest.

CHAP. V

British Enterprises.

From the first dawn of maritime enterprise and adventure in Britain, the trade of India was contemplated as its grandest object,—the chief fountain of commercial wealth. Into the sanguine conceptions formed on this subject there entered, no doubt, a considerable degree of illusion. A more enlightened school of political economy seems to have demonstrated, that agriculture and manufactures open more copious sources of prosperity than traffic of any description; that the home trade, from its quick returns, is more productive than the foreign; and the intercourse between closely contiguous countries more valuable than that with distant regions. A commerce, therefore, of which the market is at the opposite extremity of the globe, can never do more than employ the surplus capital of a community already wealthy. Yet there were circumstances which, even at

CHAP. V.

A. D. 883.

that early stage of mercantile speculation, threw a peculiar lustre on the trade of India. The staple articles consisted of finer and richer fabrics than any that had yet been produced in the West; and, besides, there were diamonds, pearls, jewels the most beautiful and brilliant, and spices the most fragrant and grateful to the senses. The great scale, too, on which operations were conducted, and the large fortunes occasionally made, gave to this traffic a character of grandeur not belonging to the smaller transactions which took place within the limits of Europe. Even the mysterious remoteness of the regions that were to be the theatre of this intercourse,—the train of adventure and uncertainty through which they were to be reached,—heightened their attraction, and were altogether congenial to the spirit of that bold and enterprising age.

Products of India.

Records of an early voyage to India.

It may be proper here to observe, that some record exists of a voyage from England to India at a much earlier period. Hakluyt has quoted two passages from different chronicles by William of Malmesbury, in which it is asserted that King Alfred, in the year 883, sent Sighelmus, bishop of Sherburn, into the East, that he might present gifts at the shrine of St Thomas. He is said to have happily performed this great undertaking, and to have returned laden with gems and rich spices, the produce of that celebrated region. It is added that, at the time the chronicle was written, some of these commodities were still preserved in the church of Sherburn. Such a mission was worthy of that great monarch, whose views, far in advance of his age, were doubtless more enlightened than those which the annalist here ascribes to him. But it must be very difficult, from such meagre notices, to determine whether so very distant a pilgrimage could at that period have been really performed. Without pronouncing it absolutely impossible, we may be allowed to suspect that he merely reached those eastern shores of the Mediterranean, to which Indian commodities have always, by some channel or other, been conveyed in large quantities.

Its doubtfulness.

CHAP. V.

A.D. 1550.

Era of English naval enterprise.

The reign of Edward VI., and more especially that of Elizabeth, formed the era at which industry and naval enterprise received that impulse which has since carried them to so unprecedented a magnitude. Prior to this period Britain was surpassed in manufactures by the Flemings, in navigation by the Italians, and still more by the Spaniards and Portuguese. These last, then her bitterest enemies, she had seen, with grief and humiliation, gain unrivalled glory by discovering a new passage to the East, and a new world in the West. They had thus almost completely preoccupied the ground of discovery and settlement, and were, moreover, prepared to defend it in the most vigorous manner against all who should attempt any encroachment. The English, therefore, in the new career on which they were ambitious to enter, had to encounter not only the disadvantages of a long voyage, but the active opposition of the two greatest powers who at that time claimed the dominion of the ocean.

Ardour of all classes for discovery.

But the nation was not to be deterred by such considerations. Nor was the ardour of discovery confined to merchants, whose estimates might have been more cautious and professional; it was fully shared by courtiers, statesmen, and warriors. Under the auspices of Elizabeth there arose a brighter galaxy of great men, than had adorned any former period of English history. They began, however, by attempting to reach India by some new path undiscovered by the Portuguese, and where there was no chance of coming in contact with those formidable rivals. The first effort was made on the northern coast of Asia; but, like that of the Dutch in an earlier age, it was founded on a most imperfect knowledge both of the great extent of that continent and of its dreary and frozen boundaries. This expedition, fitted out by a company of merchant-adventurers, and commanded by the gallant Sir Hugh Willoughby, with three well-appointed vessels, had a most disastrous issue. He was driven upon the coast of Lapland, where, in the course of the ensuing winter, he and his crew perished by cold

North-east passage attempted.

CHAP. V. A. D. 1553.

and famine. Richard Chancelor, however, with one of the vessels, reached the White Sea, and proceeded to Moscow, where he opened a communication with the court of Russia, then almost unknown in Western Europe. The adventurers having made several other unsuccessful attempts by water in those high latitudes, conceived the idea of opening an intercourse with India across the Russian and Persian empires. They expended in vain much capital and enterprise in this arduous undertaking. Several of their agents penetrated across the Caspian into Persia, and even reached Bokhara, the capital of Independent Tartary. But at length they became sensible that no commodities could pay the cost of such an immense circuit, both by land and sea, besides the hazards attendant on the conveyance through the territory of so many barbarous nations. Even when this journey should prove the most prosperous, the goods could not be so cheaply carried as by the direct route across Persia and Syria to Aleppo.

Attempts to establish an overland trade.

North-west passage attempted.

The next attempt was made by the north-west passage, round the Arctic shores of America. This continent was, at that early era, imagined to terminate, at a high latitude, in a point or cape, the passing of which would enable the mariner to enter the South Sea, and reach by a direct course the wealthy shores of India and Eastern Asia. Most intrepid, energetic, and persevering efforts to effect this object were made by a succession of illustrious navigators,—Cabot, Frobisher, Davis, Hudson,—and the pursuit has been continued down to the present time. But though brilliant displays have been exhibited of courage and heroism, and striking views obtained of the shores and their rude inhabitants, every attempt to find a practicable passage to India by this route has ended in disappointment.

Failure of these attempts.

The abortive and even calamitous result of successive efforts to penetrate by the northern extremity of the great continents, or by journeys overland, at length turned the attention of the English nation to the passage by the Cape of Good Hope, as that from which alone

CHAP. V.

A.D. 1577.

any positive benefit could be derived. The exclusive right, however, to this line of navigation was claimed by Philip II., who had now succeeded as King of Portugal; and the claim was somewhat in unison with the laws generally admitted in that age respecting distant discovery. The government was afraid of bringing itself into premature collision with the greatest monarch of the time; while private and unarmed vessels, obliged to pass near the coasts of Portugal as well as of her numerous settlements in Africa and India, and exposed to meet her ships continually passing and repassing, could scarcely hope to escape her hostile attacks.

Exclusive claims of Portugal.

But as the views of British navigators expanded, and their country began to rise to the first rank among maritime nations, a new path suggested itself, from which their haughty rivals would in vain seek to exclude them. Drake, after having served with distinction in the West Indies and on the coast of America, conceived the design of penetrating into the South Sea. The wealth acquired in his former expeditions was expended in fitting out five vessels, the largest not exceeding 100, and the smallest only 12 tons. He equipped them very completely, taking on board rich furniture, fine specimens of British manufacture, and even a band of expert musicians. He prepared every means, in short, by which he might dazzle and conciliate the natives of the unknown regions which he was about to explore. He sailed from Plymouth on the 13th December 1577, and in August the following year he accomplished a passage through the Straits of Magellan. He then cruised for some months along the western coast of Spanish America, not hesitating to appropriate some rich prizes that presented themselves in the course of his voyage. Having obtained great wealth, though his fleet was reduced to a single vessel, he determined to attempt a return homeward by the north-west passage. He sailed to the coast of California, of which he claimed the discovery, and called it New Albion; but finding his main object impracticable, he resolved to cross the Pacific, and proceed to Europe by

Plans of Drake.

Passage of Magellan Straits.

Discovery of California.

CHAP. V.

A. D. 1580.

the Moluccas. He steered directly through the ocean, pausing nowhere till he found himself among the Spice Islands, the valuable productions of which were then the subject of general interest in the West. The King of Ternate, who was in a state of hostility with the Portuguese, gave a friendly reception to the English navigator, who first began that commerce with India which has since been carried to so immense an extent. Having coasted along Java, he proceeded to the Cape without touching at any part of the Asiatic continent. He took in supplies at Sierra Leone, and arrived at Plymouth on the 26th September 1580, after a voyage of two years and ten months. His arrival was hailed with the utmost exultation by his countrymen, who regarded so successful a voyage as having raised to the highest pitch the naval glory of the realm. The queen, after some cautious delays, visited him on board his vessel, and conferred on him the honour of knighthood.

Friendly reception by the King of Ternate.

Return to England.

Cavendish.

This brilliant career of Drake encouraged other commanders to tread in his footsteps. Thomas Cavendish, a gentleman of extensive property in Suffolk, after having served his naval apprenticeship under Sir Richard Grenville, determined to sell his estate, and embark the produce in a voyage to the South Sea, and round the world. Having left Plymouth on the 21st July 1586, he reached, early next year, the western coast of South America, and, being restrained by no very nice scruples, made a number of valuable prizes. Stretching thence across the Pacific he touched at Guahan, one of the group to which the Spaniards give the appellation of Ladrones. He passed afterwards through the Philippines, observing with surprise their extent and fertility, and holding communication with the natives, who expressed a decided preference of the English to the Spaniards, by whom these islands had been occupied. Sailing next through the Moluccas, and along the coasts of Floris and Sumbawa, he opened a friendly correspondence with some of the princes of Java; and, following the course of Drake, reached England in September 1588, by the Cape of Good Hope.

His unscrupulous proceedings.

Return to England.

Notwithstanding the admiration excited by so many successful voyages, they were on too large a scale to be considered as models for commercial enterprise. Yet, invention being now employed to discover some more suitable channel of intercourse, a body of adventurers resolved upon attempting one hitherto untried by Britons. They proposed to proceed up the Mediterranean,—land on the coast of Syria,—travel by way of Aleppo and Bagdad to the Persian Gulf,—and to sail thence by Ormuz, in order to reach the shores of Malabar. Mr Stevens, who had made a voyage in a Portuguese vessel to Goa, sent home a most favourable report of the fertility of the region in which that city is placed, the opportunities it afforded for trade, and the liberality with which the port was opened to vessels of every nation. John Newbery and Ralph Fitch, the leading parties in this undertaking, were furnished with two letters, the first to the Mogul emperor Akbar, under the title of "Zelabdim Echebar, king of Cambaya." It solicited his kind offices to men who had come from a remote part of the world to trade in his dominions, promising reciprocal aid and kindness to his subjects. The other, to the King of China, was expressed in nearly the same terms. The travellers set out early in 1583.

Novel scheme of English adventurers.

Letters furnished to the leaders.

Newbery's letters from Aleppo and Bagdad relate almost entirely to commercial subjects. In regard to the latter place, he complains that the sale of goods was very slow and difficult; though, had he been well provided with money, he might have obtained abundance of valuable spices at very reasonable rates. From Bagdad he proceeded to Bassora, and thence to Ormuz, where he was allowed at first to carry on business without molestation. In six days, however, a charge was raised against the adventurers by Michael Stropene, an Italian, jealous of rivals in a trade which he himself had found very lucrative; whereupon both Newbery and his companion Fitch were arrested and thrown into prison. The former writes in considerable dismay to his associates at Bassora, saying—"It may be that they will cut our

Newbery's letters.

Rival jealousy.

CHAP. V. A. D. 1583.

throats, or keep us long in prison,—God's will be done." They were soon sent to Goa; but immediately upon their arrival, after a tedious voyage, they found themselves again in confinement. The principal charge related to Captain (Sir Francis) Drake, who was stated to have fired two shots at a Portuguese galleon near Malacca. Newbery professed total ignorance as to this transaction, which in fact could in no shape be brought home to him. He represented how unjust it was, that while French, Flemings, Germans, Turks, Persians, Moscovites,—all the nations of Europe and Asia,—were allowed freely to reside and traffic at Goa, Englishmen alone should be thus barbarously treated. He was, however, remanded to prison; but, after being kept in durance for about a month, was set at liberty, having been required to sign a bond, amounting to 2000 pardaos, not to quit the town without permission. At the time of writing he had no inclination to leave it, having taken a house in one of the principal streets, and finding his mercantile transactions very advantageous. He met with much friendship from Stevens, who had formerly been a student at New College, Oxford, and had entered the service of the Archbishop of Goa; also from John Linscot or Linschoten, an intelligent Dutch navigator.

Imprisoned at Goa.

His release.

Threatened dangers and flight.

According to the accounts given afterwards by Fitch, these favourable appearances proved delusive. They had many of their articles purloined, were obliged to give large presents, and to spend much money in procuring sureties. Having, after a residence of five months, made an appeal to the governor, they received a very sharp answer; being told that they would be better sifted erelong, and that there was further matter against them. This reply gave occasion to a very serious alarm lest they should be made slaves, or, according to some hints that were dropped, be exposed to the *strapado*. They determined, while they yet enjoyed any measure of liberty, to effect their escape, and on the 5th April 1585 fled out of the town. Proceeding into the interior of India they passed through Belgaum, where there was a great market for diamonds and other precious stones; and afterwards they arrived at the royal city of Bejapore. Here they saw all the pomp of Hindoo idolatry, the neighbouring woods being filled with numberless temples and idols. "Some be like a cow, some like a monkey, some like peacocks, and some like the devil." Fitch, who is now the narrator, was struck with the majesty of the war-elephants, and the abundance of gold and silver. He proceeded to Golconda, which he describes as a fair and pleasant city, the houses well built of brick and timber, in a country abounding with delicious fruits, and having in its vicinity rich diamond-mines. He heard of Masulipatam as a great port enjoying a very extensive traffic. From Golconda he struck northward through the Deccan till he reached Burhampoor, the capital of Candeish. He represents the country as surprisingly fertile and populous, though the houses were built only of earth and thatch; and in the rainy season, which now prevailed, the streets were rendered almost impassable by streams of water. He viewed with much surprise the matrimonial arrangements of the Hindoos, seeing boys of eight or ten married to girls of five or six; and these unseemly unions being celebrated with extraordinary pomp, the two parties riding through the streets "very trimly decked, with great piping and playing." He passed next through Mandoo, the former capital of Malwa, which he describes as a very strong town built on a high rock, which it had cost Akbar twelve years to reduce. Thence he proceeded to Agra, a great and populous city, superior to London, well built of stone, and having fair and large streets. The emperor, however, then resided at Fatepoor, which, according to him, was still larger though less handsome than the other. Being a place of decidedly inferior importance, it must have derived this temporary greatness from being the residence of the court and camp of Akbar. The whole way between these great cities resembled a market, "as full as though a man were still in a town." He was struck by seeing the grandees conveyed in little

Hindoo idols.

Fitch's account of Candeish.

Visits Mandoo the capital of Malwa.

CHAP. V.

A.D. 1585.

carts, carved and gilded, covered with silk or very fine cloth, and drawn by two little bulls of the size of dogs. On the banks of the Jumna he had an opportunity of witnessing the various ceremonies and ablutions performed by the Bramins. "They come to the water, and have a string about their necks made with great ceremonies, and lave up water with both their hands. Though it be never so cold, they will wash themselves in cold water. They pray in the water naked, and dress their meat and eat it naked, and for their penance they lie flat upon the earth, and rise up and turn themselves about thirty or forty times, and use to heave up their hands to the sun, and to kiss the earth with their arms and legs stretched along out. Their wives do come by ten, twenty, and thirty together, to the water-side singing, and there do wash themselves, and then use their ceremonies." He saw also a number of naked beggars, of whom great account was made. One in particular appeared "a monster among the rest;"—his beard of enormous growth, his hair hanging more than half down his body, his nails two inches long; "he would cut nothing from him, neither would he speak; he would not speak to the king." The Bramins are represented by Fitch, as also indeed by modern writers, to be "a crafty people, worse than the Jews."

The Bramins.

Indian devotees.

William Leader's experience at Agra.

On the departure of the fugitives from Agra, William Leader, the jeweller of the party, remained in the service of Akbar, who allowed him a house, a horse, five slaves, and a regular pension. There must, therefore, have been some communication held with that great monarch, of which it is to be regretted the narrator has omitted all the particulars.

Allahabad.

From Agra the traveller went to Allahabad, which he calls Prage, a corruption of the name Prayaga, signifying the junction of rivers, and therefore specially applied to the union of the Ganges and Jumna. He descended the former of these streams to Benares, and viewed with wonder that grand seat of Hindoo commerce and superstition, and the numerous and splendid temples with

GROUP OF FIGURES—BRAMINS, CSHATRYA AND RAJPOOT PRINCE.

Page 134

CHAP. V.

A. D. 1585.

which it was filled. He beheld the idolatries of this country on a still greater scale than before; almost every place was filled with idols of various shapes and sizes, but none worthy of admiration. "Many of them are black and have claws of brass with long nails, and some ride upon peacocks and other fowls which be evil favoured, with long hawk's bills, some with one thing and some with another, but none with a good face. They be black and evil favoured, their mouths monstrous, their ears gilded and full of jewels; their teeth and eyes of gold, silver, and glass." The observances in honour of these uncouth deities were also very various and fantastic,—particularly the modes of ablution in the Ganges. "They never pray but in the water, and they wash themselves over-head, and lave up water with both their hands. Some of them will make their ceremonies with fifteen or sixteen pots, little and great, and ring a little bell when they make their mixtures; and they say divers things over their pots many times, and when they have done they go to their gods, and strowe their sacrifices, which they think are very holy." He was witness also to the burning of women on the death of their husbands, in failure of which "their heads be shaven, and never any account is made of them afterwards." When a person is sick, they are said to lay him all night before the idol, and if next morning there be no signs of recovery, "his friends will come and sit a little with him and cry, and afterwards will carry him to the water's side, and set him upon a little raft made of reeds, and so let him go down the river." A very odd picture is also drawn of some marriage-ceremonies to which the traveller was witness. The two parties are represented going into the water along with a priest, a cow, and a calf; "and the man doth hold his hand by the old man's hand, and the wife's hand by her husband's, and all have the cow by the tail, and they pour water out of a brass pot upon the cow's tail, and then the old man doth tie him and her together by their clothes. Then they give somewhat to the poor, and to the Bramane or priest they give the

Native idols.

Burning of widows.

Marriage ceremonies.

CHAP. V. — A.D. 1585.

cow and calf, and afterwards go to divers of their idols and offer money, and lie down flat upon the ground, and kiss it divers times, and then go their way."

Patna.

From Benares he proceeded to Patna, once the capital of a kingdom, but at that time subject to Akbar; and though a large city, it contained only houses of earth and straw. The country was much infested by robbers, wandering like the Arabians from place to place; whence we may conclude, that the system of *decoit*-gangs was already in full force. The people were greatly imposed upon by idle persons assuming the appearance of sanctity. One of these sat asleep on horseback in the market-place, while the crowd came and reverentially touched his feet. "They thought him a great man, but sure he was a lazy lubber,—I left him there sleeping." Fitch went next to Tanda in Bengal, also belonging to Akbar, and thence made an excursion northward to Couche, which appears to be the country situated along the foot of the mountains of Bootan; being described as so moist, that every district could be easily inundated knee-deep, and rendered impassable. The people, who appear attached to the religion of Boodh, showed the usual fantastic reverence for animal life, keeping hospitals for lame or aged creatures, and giving food to ants. Four days' journey beyond was the country now called Bootan, said to be of great extent, and filled with mountains so lofty that they could be seen at the distance of six days' travel,—a report which was so far correct; but imagination only could have induced the inhabitants to assert that from the top of those eminences the sea could be descried. It was frequented by merchants from cold regions in the north, dressed in woollen cloths, hats, white hose, and boots (the Tartars); and by others without beards from a warm land in the east (Chinese). The former reported that their country contains a numerous breed of small but active horses, whose long tails, covered with a luxuriant growth of hair, formed an article of import into India, where they were greatly valued.

Native Devotees.

Boodhists.

CITY OF BENARES.

Page 136.

Hoogley.

Fitch now went southward to Hoogley, "the chief keep of the Portuguese," and then undertook a journey through Orissa, the borders of which he found almost a wilderness, with few villages, "grass longer than a man, and very many tygers." The haven of Angeli, which we know not how to identify, was found the seat of a very great trade, frequented by vessels from Sumatra, Malacca, and various quarters of India. Returning to the Ganges, he made an excursion also into the eastern district of Tippara, whose inhabitants were engaged in almost continual warfare with the Mogen (Mugs), occupying the kingdom of Arracan. Again reaching the banks of the river, he notices Serampore, and several other towns situated on its lower branches. The people of this part of India, he observes, were in a state of regular rebellion against the Emperor Akbar, being favoured by the numerous islands and river-channels, and especially by the facility of retreat from one to another. He justly characterizes the cotton fabrics in this district as of superior quality to those made in any other part of the empire.

Serampore.

Negrais in the kingdom of Pegu.

From Serampore our traveller obtained a passage in a vessel to Negrais in the kingdom of Pegu, and had an opportunity of visiting that capital as well as Malacca, then a great Portuguese emporium, where he learned some particulars respecting China and Japan. Returning to Bengal, he "shipped himself" for Cochin, and in his way touched at Ceylon, which he found "a brave island, very fruitful and fair." The Portuguese also held a fort at Columbo, which the king often attacked with a hundred thousand men, "but naked people all of them," though partially armed with muskets. Having doubled Cape Comorin, and observed the extensive pearl-fishery upon this coast, he passed by Coulan, and reached Cochin, which he found by no means a desirable residence; the water was bad, and victuals very scarce, the surrounding country producing neither corn nor rice; yet the want of a conveyance obliged him to remain there for eight months. The Zamorin of Calicut, he understood

CHAP. V

A.D. 1589.

continued still hostile to the Portuguese, and carried on a species of piratical war, sending out numerous proas with fifty or sixty men in each, which swept the whole coast, boarding and plundering every vessel which they encountered.

Close of Fitch's expedition.

Leaving Cochin, Mr Fitch sailed successively to Goa and Chaul, whence he obtained a passage to Ormuz, after having achieved the most extensive journey that had yet been performed in India by any European.*

Impracticable nature of the overland traffic.

Although this expedition was executed in a manner creditable to the adventurers, and much information collected respecting the trade and commodities of the country, still it was evident that commerce, carried on by a tract so circuitous, and exposed to so many perils, could neither be safe nor profitable. It was in fact one of the channels by which that traffic had been conducted by the Venetians, who were much better situated for it than the English, and who had yet been unable, ever since the discovery of the passage by the Cape, to sustain the rivalry of the Portuguese. The mercantile interest began now to contemplate the last-mentioned route, as alone affording the prospect of a secure and

Jealousy of the Spaniards and Portuguese.

advantageous intercourse. It was guarded, however, with the most jealous care by the Spaniards and Portuguese; and the government of Elizabeth, though then at war with these nations, hesitated to sanction arrangements which would shut the door against accommodation. Mr Bruce found in the State-paper office a petition, presented in 1589 from sundry merchants, requesting to be allowed to send to India three ships and three pinnaces.

First English ships pass the Cape.

The answer does not appear; but in 1591 three ships were actually sent out under Captains Raymond, Kendal, and Lancaster, who sailed from Plymouth on the 10th April. In August, when they reached the Cape,

* An ingenious writer, Maritime and Inland Discovery, vol. iii. p. 191, expresses a doubt as to the authenticity of this statement. I cannot perceive on what his scepticism is founded. The voyage is inserted in the standard collection of Hakluyt, and the narrative appears to me to bear every mark of truth.

the crews had already suffered so much from sickness that it was found necessary to send Captain Kendal home with the invalids. The two others proceeded on their voyage; but near Cape Corrientes they were overtaken by a most tremendous tempest, in which the Raymond, the admiral's ship, was separated from its companion, and appears to have perished. Lancaster's vessel alone remained; but a few days after there occurred such a dreadful thunder-storm, that four men were killed on the spot, and all the others either struck blind, severely bruised, or stretched out as on the rack. Having in some degree recovered, they sailed onwards, and reached the island of Comoro, where they took in a supply of water. The natives at first gave them no annoyance; but, after confidence had been fully established, two parties of sixteen each, when busily employed on shore, were suddenly surrounded by a vast troop of these treacherous people; and Lancaster had the distress of seeing his men almost entirely cut in pieces, without the possibility of affording them any aid. Sailing thence with a heavy heart, he touched at Zanzibar, where he found good anchorage, and put his vessel into tolerable repair; but though not openly opposed by the Portuguese, he learned that they had formed a scheme to attack his boat. Adverse gales now carried him out of his course, till he approached the island of Socotora, when the wind becoming favourable he stood directly for Cape Comorin. He doubled it in May 1592, and having missed the Nicobar group, proceeded to Sumatra, and thence to the uninhabited islands of Pulo Penang, where he spent what he calls the winter, being the season distinguished by the heavy storms to which those seas are exposed in July and August. Sailing along the coast of Malacca he fell in with three vessels of 65 or 70 tons, one of which struck to his boat alone; and, as it was found to belong to a certain body of Jesuits, he felt no scruple in making it a prize. Determined to persevere in this practice, he stationed himself off the Straits of Malacca, through which the Portuguese vessels were obliged to

Disasters of the voyagers

Treachery of the natives of Comoro.

Lawless mode of proceeding.

CHAP. V. A. D. 1592. pass in their way to China and the Moluccas. He soon took one of 250 tons, from Negapatnam, laden with rice. A fine ship of 400 tons from St Thomas escaped; but a short time afterwards he fell in with a splendid galleon of 700 tons from Goa, which almost immediately surrendered. She was found richly laden with all the commodities fitted for the Indian market. The captain and crew contrived by a stratagem to effect their escape, when Lancaster, displeased with the disorderly conduct of his own men, took out the most valuable articles, and allowed her to drive to sea. He then sailed for the Bay of Junkseylon, where he obtained some pitch to refit his vessels, and from thence he made for the Point de Galle in Ceylon. There he took his station to wait for the Bengal and Pegu fleets, which were under the necessity of passing this way; but the seamen, satisfied with their previous success, and fatigued with so hard a voyage, insisted upon forthwith returning home. They reached the Cape in the beginning of 1593, and, after a tedious passage round Africa, were obliged by the scarcity of provisions, especially of bread, to make for Trinidad. They entered by mistake the Gulf of Paria; whence they found their way through the whole group of the West Indies, till they reached the Bermudas. In this quarter they were assailed by a violent tempest, and driven back. The ship was finally carried out to sea, leaving the captain and crew on a desolate island, where they must have perished but for some French vessels, which took them up and conveyed them to Dieppe. They arrived there on the 19th May 1594, after a voyage of three years and two months, being double the time usually spent by the Portuguese in this navigation.

Visits Ceylon.

Return to the Cape.

Lose their ship.

New English expedition.

The ardour of the English seems to have been for some time chilled by the unfortunate issue of this expedition. On learning, however, that the Dutch, in 1595, had sent out four vessels, they were inspired with a sentiment of emulation; and an association, formed in 1599, subscribed £30,000, to be employed in fitting out three ships for the Indian trade. The queen not only gave full sanction to the undertaking, but even sent out John Mildenhall as ambassador to the Great Mogul, to solicit the necessary privileges. Of this mission some account will be given in treating of the reign of the celebrated Akbar, who at that time occupied the throne of Hindostan; but the envoy having died in Persia on his way home, his journey led to no practical result. Before, however, he could have returned, the adventurers had entered on their project. The first association merged, in 1600, into one on a greater scale, having at its head George, earl of Cumberland, with 215 knights, aldermen, and merchants, who were constituted the "Governor and Company of Merchants trading to the East Indies." They were invested with the too ample privileges which it was then customary to bestow on mercantile corporations, being not only allowed to export bullion to the amount of £30,000, and English goods for the four first voyages without duty, but obtaining the right of exclusive trade in all the countries beyond the Cape. The charter was granted for fifteen years, but liable to be annulled at any time on two years' notice. They began on the footing of a joint-stock company; though, as the subscribers were slow in paying up their shares, a certain number of the more zealous took the concern altogether into their own hands, supplying the funds on condition of reaping the profits. They expended £75,373, of which £39,771 was invested in shipping, £28,742 in bullion, and £6860 in goods. It was the wish of the court that Sir Edward Michelborne should be nominated to a command; but the merchants expressed their resolution not to employ *gentlemen*, "but to sort their business with men of their own quality." They therefore appointed Lancaster, whose conduct in his former bold though unfortunate expedition was considered highly creditable to his spirit and talents.

Foundation of the East India Company.

Mercantile spirit.

On the 2d of April 1601, this navigator sailed, having the command of five ships, varying from 600 to 130 tons. He passed the Cape of Good Hope without encountering any unusual difficulty. The almost exclusive objects of

Lancaster passes the Cape.

CHAP. V. A.D. 1601.

the Indian trade, at that era, were spices, pepper, cloves, and nutmegs; commodities found in Sumatra, Java, the Molucca and Banda Islands, without landing on any part of the continent. These first voyages, therefore, do not come within the proper limits of our present subject, and will demand only a cursory notice. After touching at Madagascar and the Nicobar Islands, merely for the purpose of taking in refreshments, the commodore proceeded direct to Acheen, the principal port of Sumatra. Notwithstanding the intrigues of the Portuguese, he concluded a commercial treaty with the king on favourable terms, and proceeded to lade his ships with pepper; which, however, proved so scarce and dear, that he became apprehensive of incurring the loss, and, what he seems to have dreaded still more, the disgrace of returning home without a cargo. From this anxiety he was relieved by meeting a Portuguese vessel of 900 tons, of which he made a prize, and found it so richly laden with calicoes and other valuable goods, that he not only occupied all his tonnage, but could have filled more ships if he had had them. He did not, however, return immediately, but sailed to Bantam, where also he found the utmost facility in negotiating a commercial treaty on satisfactory terms. Having sent forward a pinnace of 40 tons to the Moluccas, with instructions to prepare a lading of spices for a future expedition, he sailed for England.

Trade at Sumatra.

Portuguese prize.

Negotiates a commercial treaty and returns home.

New fleet under Middleton.

The next fleet, equipped in 1604, was commanded by Captain Middleton, who afterwards, under the title of Sir Henry, acquired the reputation of being one of the most enterprising and successful of eastern navigators. He sailed on the 25th March from Gravesend, with the Red Dragon and three other ships, and an invested capital of £60,450. After a favourable voyage, having stopped nowhere but at Saldanha, near the Cape, he arrived in the end of December in the road of Bantam. Here the vessels separated; two remaining to take in a cargo of pepper, one going to Banda, while Middleton himself proceeded to the Moluccas. He found these islands the seat of a most furious war, which the Dutch, in conjunction with the King of Ternate, were waging against the Portuguese and the King of Tidore. The former nation, from whom the English commander considered himself entitled to expect a friendly reception, afforded subject, on the contrary, for his most bitter complaints. They represented our countrymen as a band of mere pirates, and boasted that the King of Holland was more powerful at sea than all Europe besides. Thus, partly by fear, partly by persuasion, they dissuaded his majesty of Ternate from allowing any commercial intercourse; and the Portuguese being masters at Tidore, Middleton does not appear to have attempted any trade there, though he received a letter from the king imploring his aid and that of the English monarch against the Dutch. Captain Colthurst, who commanded the other ship, reached Banda, where he spent twenty-two weeks, without suffering any inconvenience except from the difficult navigation of those seas.

Unfriendly conduct of the Dutch

The Company were now threatened with a formidable rivalry. Sir Edward Michelborne, whom they had rejected as the commander of their first expedition, obtained a license from government to undertake a voyage to various parts of the East. He carried with him only a ship and a pinnace, called the Tiger and the Tiger's Whelp. This navigator, however, did not confer any distinction upon his voyage, either by discovery or commercial transactions of the slightest importance. He did not even reach the Moluccas; but while in the Indian Seas employed himself chiefly in piratical practices, not against the Portuguese, for which the hostility between the two nations might have afforded some pretext, but against all native vessels. He captured a Japanese junk, the crew of which first lulled the suspicions of the visiters by courtesy and apparent cordiality, then suddenly rose and made a most desperate attempt to possess themselves of the vessel. Captain Davis was killed, and Michelborne escaped only by leaping into the hold, where, with his boatswain, carpenter, and a few seamen,

A rival English expedition.

Lawless proceedings of Michelborne.

CHAP. V. — A. D. 1607.

he kept the assailants at bay, till he opened upon them such a fire as killed a part, and compelled the rest to retreat. Their leader was taken; and being asked his reason for making this furious onset, replied, he wished to take the ship and cut all their throats; then coolly desired them to hew himself in pieces. Michelborne afterwards captured two Chinese vessels laden with silk, and returned to England with his ill-gotten spoil.

Second expedition of the East India Company.

Meantime the Company sent out another expedition of three ships and 310 men, commanded by Captains Keeling, Hawkins, and David Middleton. The first two sailed in April 1607, entered Bantam road on the 18th October, and immediately pushed forward to the Molucca and Banda Islands. A great change had taken place during the few years that had elapsed since the voyage of Henry Middleton. The Portuguese were no longer heard of in those seas, whence they appear to have been expelled by the Dutch, who were now completing the subjection of the native princes. Keeling, on his arrival, found them engaged in hot warfare, which they justified by stating that the natives had ensnared and murdered forty of their countrymen. Notice was therefore given to him, that he should instantly withdraw his ship from the island which they had now conquered by force of arms. Keeling replied, "that till he was commanded otherwise than by words, he would ride there till he was laden;" but finding soon after that a treaty had been concluded between the Dutch and Bandanese, amounting to the entire submission of the latter, he consented to retire. Middleton, who had sailed on the 12th March, did not meet with the two others, but followed nearly the same course without any remarkable adventure.

Supremacy of the Dutch.

Expedition under Sharpey.

A fourth expedition, consisting of two large ships, the Ascension and the Union, was fitted out in 1607, with an invested capital of £33,000, and the command intrusted to Captain Alexander Sharpey. His object appears to have been to reach the coast of Cambay, and particularly Surat, understood at that time to be the most extensive emporium of Western India. He sailed in March, but experienced throughout a series of misfortunes. The two vessels were separated in doubling the Cape of Good Hope, and never met again. The Ascension proceeded along the eastern coast of Africa to Pemba, but was twice attacked by the treacherous Moors, and several of the crew cut off. In the prosecution of their voyage the English, when greatly exhausted, fortunately lighted on a cluster of uninhabited islands, which apparently were the Sechelles, where they obtained an abundant supply of turtles and cocoa-nuts. Proceeding to the Red Sea they touched at Aden and Mocha, where they met with a favourable reception. They descended that inlet, and having touched at Socotora and obtained some supplies, steered for India. They reached Diu, and prepared to cross the Gulf of Cambay for Surat, but were warned that a pilot, who could be procured on easy terms, was necessary to conduct the vessel in this dangerous passage. The master, however, full of obstinacy and self-conceit, judged himself, without any such aid, quite competent to guide her course. She was soon entangled in the shoals that abound in that sea, and struck repeatedly with such violence that she became a total wreck. "Thus," says the narrator, "was this tall ship lost, to the great injury of the worshipful Company and the utter undoing of all us the poor mariners." They betook themselves to their boats, and attempted to reach the River Surat, but were compelled to enter that of Gondevee,—a change of direction which proved to be almost providential, for the Portuguese had a force prepared at the former place to intercept and capture them. Some of the crew went up to Agra, where Hawkins then resided as ambassador to the Great Mogul, and contrived to find their way home overland through Persia, while several obtained a passage to Europe from Goa.

CHAP. V.

A.D. 1607.

The ship Ascension.

Obstinacy of the master, and wreck of the vessel

The Union, meantime, had not, as was supposed by the crew of the Ascension, suffered shipwreck. Her mainmast had sprung, but the men contrived to recover it, and to reach the coast of St Augustin in Madagascar.

The ship Union.

CHAP. V.

A. D. 1609.

Thence they sailed for Zanzibar; but being involved in a quarrel with the natives, lost several of their number, and were obliged to return to that island; but there, too, fresh disasters were sustained, both from the climate and the treacherous hostility of the people. They then proceeded northwards to Arabia, but being at a loss how to find their way to the Indian coast, determined to steer direct for Sumatra; and having reached Acheen and Priaman, they obtained, on advantageous terms, an abundant cargo of pepper. The voyage homeward is very indistinctly related; but it is clear that it was accompanied with many delays and some damage; and, in February 1611, the vessel was run ashore on the coast of Brittany, near Morlaix, where great depredation was committed by the inhabitants. The Company, on being apprized of her situation, sent a skilful shipwright, with other persons, who reported the vessel to be wholly unserviceable, but saved two hundred tons of pepper, with the anchors, ordnance, and other equipments. Of seventy-five seamen, who went out from England, only nine survived.

Obtains a cargo.

Fate of the Expedition.

The ship Expedition.

In 1609, Captain David Middleton again sailed with only a single ship, the Expedition, which, with its lading, was valued at £13,700. He proceeded directly for the Spice Islands, and found the Dutch, as before, in great force, and claiming the entire sovereignty; yet, by his address and activity, he contrived to obtain a good investment. Hereupon their indignation was such, that they formed several plans for destroying him and his vessel, and he was in a great measure indebted to chance for his escape. However, he was fortunate enough to reach Bantam without encountering any serious disaster.

Enmity of the Dutch.

Large expedition.

In 1609-10, the Company sent out a larger expedition than ever, consisting of three vessels, one called the Trade's Increase, of a thousand tons; while a capital of £82,000 was invested in the shipping and cargoes. The commander was Sir Henry Middleton, who, in a former voyage, had obtained a character for courage and enterprise, which in the present he fully maintained. The

Red Sea and Surat, in preference to the Spice Islands, hitherto the favourite object, were the points of his destination. Having effected his passage round the Cape, he proceeded direct to the Arabian Gulf and the port of Mocha, where he at first flattered himself with having obtained a most cordial reception: but being inveigled on shore by the treacherous and bigoted Turks, he was seized, treated with the utmost indignity, and carried a prisoner to Sana, the capital of Yemen. He contrived, however, to obtain his liberation, and afterwards to avenge severely this ungenerous usage.

Descends the Red Sea.

Middleton now descended the Red Sea, whence he sailed directly to Surat, with the view of opening a mercantile intercourse with that great emporium of India. He arrived on the coast of Cambay in October 1611, though he had considerable difficulty in finding the river on which the city is built. He at length procured a pilot; but soon thereafter learned that his entrance, as well as his scheme of commercial transactions, would be opposed by a still more serious obstacle. A Portuguese squadron, represented by some accounts as amounting to twenty armed vessels, had stationed itself at the mouth of the river, for the express purpose of preventing the entrance of ships belonging to any other European state. The commander, Don Francisco de Soto Mayor, sent a messenger to state that, if the English brought a letter from the King of Spain or the viceroy, authorizing them to trade in these parts, they might depend on every attention; otherwise, his instructions were to interdict the port to the people of all countries except his own. Sir Henry very promptly replied, that he had no letter either from king or viceroy; that he came with credentials and rich presents from his own sovereign, to open a traffic with the Great Mogul, who was under no vassalage to the Portuguese, but whose territory was free to all nations; that he wished no harm to Don Francisco or his countrymen, though he considered himself to have quite as good a title as they had to the commercial advantages of Cambay. The other, however, deter-

Opposition of the Portuguese.

Spirited conduct of Middleton.

CHAP. V. A.D. 1611.

mined to refuse the slightest concession, immediately began to intercept the supply of provisions from the town —causing thereby a most serious privation to the English, among whom, from having been so long at sea, symptoms of scurvy began to be severely felt. At the same time, accounts were received that Sharpey, after losing his vessel in the manner already described, was now at Surat. He had received communications from Hawkins, still at the court of the Mogul, and from Fitch at Lahore, by which it appeared that the Indian rulers were so fickle and easily swayed by opposite influences, while the Portuguese and native merchants were so closely combined against him, that there could be little or no hope of establishing any secure or beneficial intercourse. Middleton now paused, and was advised to try his fortune on another division of the coast; but having obtained from some of the higher authorities in the city an assurance that, were it not for their fear of the Portuguese, they would be very willing to trade with him, he resolved that nothing on his part should be wanting to fulfil the views of his employers. The Trade's Increase was too large to approach the shore; but the Peppercorn, with two smaller vessels, began to move towards the harbour. During their progress, the Portuguese armada kept abreast of them, between their line and the land, in order of battle, with colours flying, and raising loud shouts, yet without showing any disposition to an actual engagement. At length, one of Middleton's boats having been sent forward to take soundings, two of the enemy's barks rowed out, and openly attempted to capture it. A brisk fire, however, being directed against them, they lost no time in commencing their retreat; and one was so hotly pursued, that the crew leaped overboard, and struggled through the deep mud to the shore. The vessel became a prize to the English, which proved of some value, as it contained a tolerable assortment of Indian goods. The rest of the fleet made a movement in aid of their distressed comrades, but received such entertainment as induced them quickly to retire. The two

Fickleness of the native rulers.

Resolute conduct of the English.

Their complete success.

CHAP. V.

A. D. 1611.

merchantmen were then anchored in seven fathoms water, at the mouth of the river; and every subsequent attempt which the Portuguese made to annoy them, or prevent their landing, was defeated with great loss.

Native intercourse with the English.

The authorities of Surat, on seeing such determined resolution displayed by the English, no longer hesitated to enter into treaty with them. Mocrib Khan, the governor, with sixteen leading mercantile characters, spent a night on board, accepting with readiness the viands and delicacies presented to them, as well as various little ornamental articles which they were allowed to select as presents. At last the strangers landed, and the parties began to negotiate about the exchange of their respective commodities. Khojah Nassan and the other merchants produced an ample assortment of calicoes; but Downton complains that they both bought and sold at rates most unsatisfactory, expecting very exorbitant profits, not less than fifty per cent. on merchandise purchased at their own doors, while for the goods which had been brought from a great distance, they would scarcely allow enough to pay the freight. We cannot, however, forbear taking some exceptions to the mode in which our countrymen, according to their own report, conducted their transactions. The native merchants very reasonably wished to select commodities suited to their trade, and for which they could find a demand; but the English, having burdened themselves with other articles, particularly a large stock of lead, which proved exceedingly unsaleable in this market, insisted on forcing these upon the reluctant purchasers. At length the Indians, seeing they could do no better, agreed to take the lead along with the other goods; but, after these had been landed, Sir Henry learned that Khojah Nassan was expressing the utmost discontent at the assortment thus obtruded on him, raving like a madman, and even countermanding the wagons which were to carry away the obnoxious article. It was added that, according to the custom of the country, any bargain could be annulled, on notice to that effect being given within twenty-four hours. To

Mode of conducting transactions with the natives.

CHAP. V.

A. D. 1611.

Violent proceedings of Middleton.

avert this peril, Middleton had recourse to a step, the expediency of which appears exceedingly questionable. The governor and several other official persons happening to be on board his vessel, he placed them under arrest, to be liberated only when the transactions should be closed by the delivery of the Indian goods. The option, however, was given to the merchant to relieve the governor by supplying his place,—a proposal to which, with many wry faces, he was at last induced to consent. By this step the English gained, indeed, their immediate object; yet it probably contributed, in no small degree, to the resolution which was soon afterwards made known to them, that they must forthwith depart from Surat, without establishing a factory or even collecting their debts. This inhospitable proceeding was imputed to the intrigues of the Portuguese and Jesuits; but, whether it were so or not, Sir Henry was obliged to retire with a very unsatisfactory cargo, and no favourable prospect as to the future reception of his countrymen.

Return to the Red Sea.

From Surat he sailed along the coast, and touched at Dabul, where he was at first very heartily welcomed, but soon found or suspected that the governor secretly counteracted all his measures, so that he could form no advantageous arrangement. He returned to the Red Sea, and extorted from the citizens of Mocha farther compensation for the wrongs he had formerly suffered there. He moreover stopped every Indian vessel he met, and obliged her to agree to an exchange of goods, the conditions of which he himself dictated,—a course which he justifies on grounds that seem rather untenable. He next sailed across the Indian Ocean for Bantam; but in the course of the voyage the Trade's Increase struck upon a rock, and sustained considerable damage. While it was under repair he sent Downton home in the Peppercorn, intending himself to follow; but he was seized with a violent illness, and died in Java.

Death of Middleton.

In 1611, the Company sent out the Globe, under Captain Hippon, to endeavour to open a trade on the Coromandel coast; and Floris, a Dutchman, accompanied him as factor. They departed in January, and at the end of July doubled the Point de Galle in Ceylon, whence they ran along the coast to Negapatam. Without stopping there, they proceeded to Pulicat, where they hoped to traffic with some advantage. The day after their arrival, however, Van Wersicke, president of the Dutch settlements on this coast, waited upon them, and gave notice that his countrymen had obtained a *kaul* from the King of Narsinga, in whose territory that city stood, prohibiting all Europeans from trading, unless under patent from Prince Maurice. The captain replied that he held the patent of the King of England, which he deemed quite sufficient; and high words arose. But the Shah Bandur, or governor, persuaded them to suspend the dispute till the expected arrival of the Princess Konda Maa, who held the sovereignty of the city. Her royal highness came; but when Hippon applied for an audience, she returned for answer that she was not then at leisure, promising, however, to send for him next day. Considering this reply evasive, he went to the minister, and was assured that the Dutch had in fact obtained the exclusive right which they asserted; and he was advised to apply to them for permission to trade. But Hippon, calculating that this expedient would occupy two months, and being almost certain, besides, that he would be refused, proceeded to Petapoli, where he left a small factory, and then to Masulipatam, the great market for the beautiful fabrics produced upon this coast. The governor there readily entered into treaty, but pursued, at the same time, a complete system of fraud and chicanery. He told the most palpable lies, and insisted that he, as a Mir, or descendant of Mohammed, was to be believed before Christians. The English, therefore, had determined upon "foul means" to obtain redress; but, through some of the merchants, an accommodation was effected. They sailed next to Bantam, and thence to Patane, where, in June 1612, they landed in great state, with minstrels playing and flags flying, bearing the king's letter in a golden basin on the back of an elephant. This they

Trade to the Coromandel coast.

Disputes between the Dutch and English.

Proceedings at Masulipatam.

CHAP V.

A.D. 1612.

presented to the queen, who received them graciously, and finally gave the desired permission to erect a warehouse. At Patane the captain died, upon which the others proceeded to Siam. Floris, who had visited this part of India four years before, probably in a Dutch vessel, found such a demand for goods as the whole world, it appeared to him, was insufficient to satisfy; but now there had ensued such a glut, as to leave room only for very limited sales. They afterwards returned to Masulipatam, and met with a better reception, but without being able to carry their transactions to any great extent.

Second Expedition to the Coromandel coast.

In 1611 also, the Company sent out a much larger expedition, of three ships,—the Clove, Hector, and Thomas,—under Captain John Saris. This was an active and adventurous voyage, but does not come within our immediate sphere; the vessels not having touched at any part of the continent of India. Saris sailed first to the Red Sea, where he met Sir Henry Middleton on his second visit there; and the parties for some time acted in concert both for trade and piracy. In August 1612, he steered for Bantam, still considered as the chief English factory in the East, where he arrived in the end of October, but learned that the number of vessels belonging to different countries, assembled and expected, had caused a very inconvenient rise in the price of cloves, pepper, and the other staple commodities. He sailed, therefore, to the Moluccas, which were found to have been cruelly desolated by civil wars between the native princes, as well as by the contests for pre-eminence between the Dutch and Portuguese, supported by the Spaniards from the Philippines.

Supremacy of the Dutch.

The Hollanders had now nearly expelled the other nations, and were using their utmost efforts, by threats and misrepresentations, to deter the several chiefs from holding any intercourse with the English.

Success of the English

Saris, however, by his activity and address, contrived to collect a suitable cargo of cloves. He then sailed for Firando, in Japan, in the hope of opening a communication with that celebrated empire, where the rigid exclusion of Europeans, which has been since

CHAP. V
A.D. 1612

so strictly enforced, did not yet prevail. Being waited on by the governor, who is here called king, they made arrangements for visiting the emperor at Surunga, where they met with a good reception, and entertained hopes of establishing a profitable factory at Firando; which, however, proved ultimately fallacious.

Profits of the company.

The Company had now sent eight expeditions, the result of which was judged on the whole to be extremely advantageous. Leaving out of the account the unfortunate voyage of Sharpey, they had derived an average profit of not less than 171 per cent. Mr Mill hence draws the natural inference, that these had been conducted in a manner decidedly more judicious than subsequent adventures that yielded a very different return. Yet we cannot forbear observing, that many of the cargoes were made up on such very easy terms as their successors could not expect to command. Independently of the fact that whole fleets were sometimes laden with captured goods, trade was often carried on by compulsory means, calculated to ensure a profitable return only to the stronger party. These first voyages, in short, exhibit the profits of trade combined with the produce of piracy.

Questionable sources.

New scheme of the Indian company.

The commerce of India, according to the original plan, was to be conducted on the principle of a joint-stock company, in which the transactions were to be managed by a governor and directors, and a dividend made to the subscribers in proportion to the number of shares. But as the paying up of the instalments upon this principle proceeded very slowly, another arrangement was made, by which each individual furnished a certain proportion of the outlay, and received the entire profit arising from its investment. Though the affairs of the Company prospered under this system, it was necessarily attended with a good deal of confusion and difficulty, which suggested to the governor and Company the expediency of returning to the old method of conducting affairs on the regular joint-stock system. This plan was accordingly adopted in 1612, and on those terms a capital of £429,000 was subscribed, with which the directors undertook, during

CHAP. V.

A. D. 1614.

the next four years, to build twenty-nine vessels, at an expense of £272,000, and to employ the rest of the sum in the investment.

Royal patronage.

The commerce of India being considered more and more a national object, King James, in 1614, sent out Sir Thomas Roe as ambassador to the Great Mogul, with the view of obtaining permission to trade on reasonable terms in the principal ports of his dominions. The details of this embassy, which remarkably illustrate the manners and arrangements of the Mogul court, will be introduced in our account of that dynasty. The result could not be considered as a total failure; yet the influence exercised against the English by the Portuguese and native merchants was so powerful,—the views of this splendid but barbarous court were so vacillating and capricious,—that, though Sir Thomas did at last extract a species of firman in favour of his countrymen, he could give them little encouragement to place any reliance upon it; assuring them that their actual success must ever depend mainly upon arrangements with the local merchants and magistrates.

Very partial success of the English embassy.

General view of the English trade to India.

A regular intercourse being now formed with India, and all the maritime paths to that region fully explored, the particular voyages cease to possess much interest, and have therefore been seldom recorded. The situation of the English was sometimes rendered critical by the rivalry of the other European powers who had formed establishments previously, and continued as long as possible to treat them as interlopers. The Portuguese from the first manifested the loftiest pretensions, aggravated by the most imbittered feelings; but their naval power had now become so feeble in comparison with the fleets of Britain, that they scarcely ever encountered her vessels without signal defeat.

Formidable navy of the Dutch.

It was much otherwise with the Dutch, whose extensive marine rendered their hostility truly formidable. They had already completely driven the Portuguese from the Molucca and Banda Islands, which they claimed in complete sovereignty. The English did not attempt to interfere with the Hollanders in those settlements where the right of prior occupation could be urged; but the small islands of Pularoon and Rosengin, forming part indeed of a group occupied by that people, though containing no actual settlement, were considered as open territory, and forts were erected on them. This seems sufficiently conformable to Indian practice, where the factories of different nations are often found in the closest contiguity. The Dutch, however, chose to understand it otherwise; and, after having in vain endeavoured to expel their rivals from these strongholds, seized two of their vessels, announcing their determination not to release them till England should have withdrawn her pretensions to the trade of the Spice Islands. The demand was strenuously resisted, and hostilities ensued, which were attended with disastrous consequences to both nations, and particularly to our countrymen. Pring, when he was on the coast of Coromandel in 1619, heard the doleful tale that four ships, the Dragon, Bear, Expedition, and Rose, were captured near the Isles of Tecoo; that the Star was taken in the Straits of Sunda, and that two other vessels were in great peril. The Companies now presented heavy complaints against each other to their respective governments; negotiations were opened, and in order to prevent these partial hostilities from terminating in a general war, a treaty of a very singular complexion was concluded. The English and Dutch agreed to become, as it were copartners in the Indian traffic; the former to have half the trade in pepper, and a third of that in the finer spices; and each of the nations to keep ten ships in common for the purpose of protection, as well as for conveying goods from one port of India to another. There was also to be formed a "Council of Defence," consisting of four members of each Company, who were to be intrusted with the duty of enforcing the provisions of this extraordinary treaty.

Disputes with the Dutch.

Losses of the English.

Alliance between the Dutch and English.

It was obvious that these stipulations were of such a nature, and involved so constant an interference in private transactions, as could not fail to lead to the most

Impracticable nature of this union.

CHAP. V
A.D. 1620.

serious differences. The Dutch, who maintained larger fleets among the islands, interpreted every question in their own favour, and refused to admit the others to the stipulated share of the trade, till they had paid their proportion of all the sums which they themselves, with or without necessity, had expended on fortifications. The enmity between the two parties became always more rancorous, till the Hollanders, availing themselves of superior strength, proceeded to that dreadful outrage called the "Massacre of Amboyna." The island of that name is well known as the richest of the group of the Moluccas, and the one which affords the most copious supply of cloves. The principal settlement of both companies was at the capital, where the Dutch had a strong castle with a garrison of about two hundred men; while the English, eighteen in number, occupied merely a house in the town, where, however, they thought themselves in safety under the faith of treaties. The former, conceiving suspicions of a Japanese soldier who was in their service, arrested and put him to the torture. By that barbarous mode of extracting evidence, they brought him to confess that he and several of his countrymen had entered into a conspiracy to seize the fortress; and upon the information thus obtained, others of the same nation were apprehended and tortured. The English, while this transaction was going on, went back and forward to the castle as business led them, inquiring about it as an ordinary affair, in no shape affecting themselves. Abel Price, the surgeon, however, having been confined in that building on account of some excesses committed through intoxication, was one morning assured that his countrymen also were engaged in this nefarious plot. He professed utter ignorance on the subject; but the rack was applied to him with such severity as made him soon confess whatever his tormentors were pleased to direct. At the same time a message was sent to Captain Towerson, and the other members of the English factory, requesting that they would visit the governor. On their arrival, they were much surprised at being arrested, all

Massacre of Amboyna.

Reliance of the English.

Price put to the torture.

their property seized, and themselves called upon to acknowledge their share in the alleged conspiracy. Notwithstanding the most solemn denial, they underwent separate and successive examinations, enforced by the most cruel torture, their cries being heard by their companions without, even at a great distance. Agony, indeed, at length extorted their assent to every thing which their accusers chose to suggest. The confessions evidently appear to have been given in a manner which renders it quite manifest that they were wrung from the unhappy victims by the extremity of suffering. On being released, they repeated their denials in the most impressive manner; two, in particular, being adjured by Towerson, retracted altogether the testimony they had borne against him. But they were impelled by the renewed application of torture to return to their accusation both of themselves and of him. One desired to be told at once what he was required to own; but this being treated as contumacy, torture was again applied till he invented such a story as was likely to satisfy his persecutors. In general, however, leading questions were put, intimating the charges made against the individual; and the judges contented themselves with his passive admission. The issue was, that Captain Towerson and nine others were condemned to die, the remaining eight being pardoned. They were allowed to see each other, and had the sacrament administered by the Dutch clergyman, when they declared in the most solemn manner their perfect innocence. Samuel Colson said aloud:—"O Lord, as I am innocent of this treason, do thou pardon all my other sins; and if in the smallest degree guilty thereof may I never be a partaker of the joys of thy heavenly kingdom." The rest answered, "Amen! amen!" They then earnestly asked and cordially received forgiveness from each other for their mutual accusations,—John Clark saying, "How shall I look to be forgiven of God if I do not forgive you." They were then executed by having their heads cut off with a scimitar. A black pall was provided for the captain, the

Cruel treatment of the English.

Confessions under torture.

Nine of them condemned to death.

Their execution.

CHAP. V. — A. D. 1620.

expense of which his enemies had the effrontery to charge on the English Company. One Portuguese, and nine natives of Japan, who suffered at the same time, made equally strong protestations of innocence.

Indignation of the English.

The indignation of the English people, always easily roused, never mounted to a higher pitch than when tidings arrived of this cruel and bloody transaction. The nation was in a ferment, and a universal cry arose for redress and vengeance. The Court of Directors prepared and distributed a picture, in which the tortures of the unhappy sufferers were represented with every feature of aggravation. The press was actively employed in inflaming still farther the indignation of the multitude, and the excitement was such that the Dutch residents made an application to the Privy Council for the protection of their persons. Mr Mill, always studious to guard against national partiality, is willing to suppose that this matter had been viewed at home through a somewhat exaggerating medium. Reluctant to ascribe to the actors the malignant spirit of demons, he thinks it more probable that, biassed and embittered by the violent opposition of interests, they may have believed their rivals really guilty, have rashly brought them to trial, decided with minds too much blinded to discern the truth, and then put them to death without remorse. The torture, however unjustifiable, was still employed in Holland and other European kingdoms as an instrument for extorting evidence. Both nations, he observes, in those distant seas, where they were beyond the reach of regular government and legal restraint, were guilty of many cruel and violent actions. Admitting to a certain extent the force of these observations, we cannot yet refrain from condemning the transaction as one of deliberate and cold-blooded ferocity.

Evasive defence of the Dutch.

The Dutch, on being called upon for satisfaction, returned at first very evasive answers; but when the English began to detain their vessels, they found the matter assuming a more serious aspect, and authorized an investigation. The negotiations were very long protracted, and no final adjustment took place till 1654, during the government of Cromwell, when eight commissioners, four on each side, awarded a compensation of £3615 to the heirs and representatives of those who had suffered. At the same time, each party brought forward a statement of the amount of injury alleged to have been sustained from the other during the forty years which elapsed from the time they began their abortive attempt at a joint trade, down to 1652. The English raised their estimate to no less than £2,695,999; while the Dutch chose to fix theirs at the still more enormous amount of £2,919,861. These excessively-exaggerated demands were cut down by the commissioners, who in the end awarded the sum of £85,000 to be paid to our countrymen.

Dissolution of the system of united traffic.

The catastrophe of Amboyna broke up entirely that system of united traffic, which indeed from the first might easily have been foreseen to be impracticable. Yet the English maintained for some time longer their settlement at Bantam, which they had even made the capital of their eastern possessions. But the greater force maintained by the enemy in those islands, and which they always increased, rendered the tenure by which our people held a footing there difficult and precarious; and the greater attractions presented on the continent of India induced them gradually to relinquish their insular stations, with the exception of a few on the coast of Sumatra .

Establishment on the Persian Gulf.

Considerable expectations were at one period entertained from an establishment on the Persian Gulf. An English naval force, as formerly mentioned, co-operating with the army of the Shah of Persia, drove the Portuguese in 1622 from their once opulent settlement at Ormuz, which has since sunk into total insignificance. In return for their services, our adventurers received not only a share of the booty, but also liberty to establish a factory at the fort of Gombroon, the transactions at which appeared at first to wear a promising aspect.

Surat for a considerable time was the principal seat of

CHAP. V.

A. D. 1625.

Settlement at Surat.

British settlement in India, and annual investments to a large amount were sent to the factory in that city. Being exposed, however, to the arbitrary exactions of the Mogul and his officers, and also to the incessant incursions of the Mahrattas, the government felt it very desirable to obtain some place entirely their own, and which they could fortify against external aggression. An opportunity was offered in 1662, on occasion of the marriage of the Infanta Catherine to Charles II., when the island of Bombay was ceded as part of her dowry.

Cession of the Island of Bombay.

Some misunderstanding arose as to the extent of this grant, the English conceiving it to include Salsette and other dependencies; while the Portuguese chose to view it as not extending beyond the bare precincts of the island,—in which last interpretation Britain was finally obliged to acquiesce. Thus the crown acquired for the first time a territorial possession in India; which, however, did not yield revenue sufficient to defray its expenses. In 1668, therefore, the entire sovereignty was made over to the Company, who, in 1687, transferred thither from Surat the presidency over their other settlements; and Bombay has ever since continued the capital of their dominions in Western India.

Coromandel stations.

Meantime, the establishments on the eastern coast were gradually rising into their present importance. For some time, the Coromandel stations were considered secondary, shifted from place to place, and held subordinate to Bantam. In the voyage of Hippon we have traced the first foundation of the important settlements of Masulipatam and Pulicat; but the latter was soon relinquished, in consequence of Dutch rivalry. To escape the hostility of that people and the oppressions of the native government, the English, in 1625, procured a spot of ground at Armegum, a little south of Nellore, where they stationed a factory. This place, however, viewed as an emporium of the fine cotton manufactures which gave the chief value to that coast, was not found equal to Masulipatam; and accordingly the trade of this last was soon revived. Valuable privileges in its favour were obtained

Factory at Armegum.

CHAP. V.

A. D. 1640.

from the King of Golconda; while the Mogul emperor sanctioned an establishment at Pipley in Orissa. It being still considered important to have a place of strength for the security of the Company's trade, permission was obtained, in 1640, from a native chief to erect a fort at Madraspatam. The Directors, actuated by a spirit of economy which has not always ruled their counsels, objected to this erection, and limited very strictly the sums to be expended on it. However, they called it Fort St George, and made it afterwards the capital of their settlements on the coast of Coromandel.

Establishment at Bengal.

The establishment in Bengal, which has since risen to such unrivalled prosperity, was formed somewhat later than either of the others. An English medical gentleman of the name of Boughton, resident at Surat, having visited Agra in 1651, was fortunate enough to remove a dangerous illness which had affected the daughter of the Emperor Shah Jehan. The gratitude felt by the monarch was, with a laudable patriotism, employed by the physician to obtain for his countrymen some commercial privileges. From Agra he proceeded to the court of the Nabob of Bengal, where his skill, exerted with equal success, was rewarded by a grant to the English of very extensive local advantages and immunities. The merchants of Surat, on payment of 3000 rupees, procured full freedom of trade, exempt from customs; and in 1656 they erected a factory at Hoogley, situated on that branch of the river which has always been considered the principal channel for the trade of the Ganges. From this time ships and investments were sent to Bengal every year. Several other factories were subsequently formed; but its commerce was still considered secondary to that of Coromandel, and made subject to the superintendence of the authorities at Fort St George.

First establishment of political and military power

It was in Bengal, however, that the English first attempted to establish political and military power. The agents of the Company transmitted a detail of various wrongs sustained from the native rulers, and suggested the expediency of seeking redress by force of arms. The

CHAP. V.

A. D. 1686.

Directors sent out, in 1686, Captain Nicholson, with ten armed vessels and six companies of soldiers, destined to a service of no less magnitude than that of levying war against the Great Mogul and the Nabob of Bengal. The plan of the campaign was in the first instance to seize and fortify Chittagong, a point rather remote from the scene of commercial activity, but which they meant to make the centre of their military movements. Hence they were not fortunate in the execution of this grand scheme; the different parts of the armament arriving separately, and acting, too, with little concert. The fleet sailed up to Hoogley, and commenced a cannonade, but being completely repulsed, was obliged to seek shelter in a port which occupied the present site of Calcutta. Factories that had been formed at Patna and Cossimbuzar were taken and plundered. The nabob, after a deceitful truce, assembled his whole army to attack the discomfited English, who at that crisis, however, under the command of the Company's agent, made a brilliant display of valour. They not only checked the Mogul forces, but entered the harbour of Balasore, and burnt forty sail of their ships. An accommodation was then agreed to, by which they were permitted to re-establish their factory at Hoogley; and affairs were on the point of being replaced on their former footing, when two British ships of war, under an officer named Heath, entered the river. That commander immediately disallowed the treaty, and commenced warlike operations, which he conducted very unfortunately; and the invaders were soon obliged to evacuate Bengal. Aurengzebe, at that time seated on the Mogul throne, was so exasperated at these proceedings, and other violent steps taken by Sir John Child, governor of Bombay, that he ordered a general attack on the Company's factories. Those at Surat, Masulipatam, and Vizigapatam, were reduced, the last not without some bloodshed; and Bombay was very closely pressed. Our countrymen were compelled to have recourse to the most humble submission; when that politic sovereign, weighing the benefit

Plan for seizing Chittagong.

Destruction of the Mogul fleet.

Violent and impolitic proceedings of the English

which his people derived from foreign commerce, gradually relaxed, and allowed the traffic to resume its usual channels.

Commencement of English ascendency in Asia.

From this time, however, the Company began openly to aspire to independent authority in the East. In 1689, as Mr Mill observes, "it was laid down as a determinate object of policy, that independence was to be established in India, and dominion acquired." At that date they wrote to their agents,—"The increase of our revenue is the subject of our care, as much as our trade." Henceforth, then, the English may be considered as having commenced their system of political ascendency in that part of Asia; but before following them through the various steps of this arduous undertaking, it will be advantageous to turn back and take a survey of the fortunes of that great empire, whose place they were destined to occupy.

CHAPTER VI.

Early Mohammedan Conquests in India.

Rise of the Mohammedan Power—Conquests in Central Asia—The Samanian Dynasty—Abistagi—Subuktagi—Mahmoud the Ghizneride—His Twelve Expeditions into India—Victory in Lahore—Successive Conquests of Bimé; Tanassar; Kanouge; Muttra; Sumnaut—His Death—Character—Anecdotes—Literature of the Court of Ghizni—Ferdusi—Oonsuri—Abu Rihan—Decline of the Ghiznian House—Subverted by that of Ghori—Mohammed Ghori—His Conquests in India—Cuttub conquers Delhi and makes it his Capital.

CHAP. VI.

A. D. 640.

Rise of the Mohammedan power.

THE ARABS OR SARACENS, in spreading by their arms the religion of Mohammed, effected a most astonishing revolution in the eastern world, and penetrated to more remote parts of Asia than were ever reached by the Roman eagle. After the death of their prophet, a short interval only had elapsed when their victorious cavalry drank at once the waters of the Tagus, the Niger, and the Jaxartes. Bagdad became the capital of the greatest empire then on the face of the earth; its court was the most splendid and the most polished, and the seat of all the learning by which that dark age was illumined.

Advantages to Central Asia.

No region derived such advantages from this triumph of the Moslem arms and faith as the country called Mavar-ul-Nahar, being that extensive tract of Independent Tartary which is watered by the great rivers Oxus and Jaxartes. Though blessed with a fertile soil, and one of the finest climates of Asia, it is represented in all the ancient records as entirely Scythian, covered with roaming hordes of shepherds and warriors, who lived in tents, and subsisted on the milk of their flocks. Under the Arab sway, it acquired and has ever since retained regular government, improved cultivation, large and populous cities; and yet this province was one of the first which were severed from the Caliphate. Its governors, distant from the seat of empire, began gradually to assume the character of independent princes; they extended their power first over Khorasan; then over the interior provinces of Persia; and finally hemmed in Bagdad itself more and more closely, till the name of Caliph, which had caused the extremities of the earth to tremble, became little more than an empty sound.

Ismael Samani.

It was in the year 873, the 258th of the Hegira, that Ismael Samani of Bochara assumed the title of king; and his posterity in the family of Samania reigned nearly a hundred years over those vast regions, with a high reputation for justice and beneficence. At length his house felt that decline to which despotic power in all countries is ultimately liable. Its weakness was further increased by a disputed succession; while Abistagi, governor of the vast semi-Tartar province of Khorasan, successfully raised the standard of insurrection. Having become an independent sovereign, he added to his domain the high mountain-territory of Cabul and Candahar. This region, situated on the crest or in the declivities and deep valleys of the Indian Caucasus and of its numerous tributary branches, is inhabited by the Afghans, a race of hardy husbandmen, shepherds, and warriors, who have often extended the authority of their princes over the surrounding countries. Here Abistagi selected Ghizni as the capital of an empire which long ruled over Asia.

Independent sovereignty established at Cabul.

Successor of Samani.

In the year 977 he was succeeded, not by his son, who died young, but by Subuktagi his general, who had been saluted sovereign by the voice of the troops. This prince consolidated the new kingdom, and became the real founder of a mighty dynasty. He bears a high reputation for probity, simplicity, and mildness. The Orientals fondly relate a little incident that at least expresses their

CHAP. VI. A.D. 997.

Humanity of the king.

ideas respecting his temper, and forms a pleasing contrast with the hardihood of his character and the rough scenes in which he acted. Hunting one day in the forest, he espied a fawn with its mother bounding over the plain. He caught the animal, tied its feet, and threw it over his saddle; but on looking back, he beheld the mother following with so piteous an aspect that his soul was melted. He released the fawn, and allowed it to rejoin its parent, who, as she turned into the wilderness, looked back with eyes streaming tears of gratitude. Subuktagi's pleasing reflections upon this scene, and his own share in it, suggested at night a dream or vision, where, in reward for his humanity, a kingdom was promised to him. As a proof of his simplicity of taste, we are informed that, on being introduced to a splendid pavilion erected by his son Mahmoud, he told the prince that this object was to be despised as a perishing bauble, and that he ought to make it his study to obtain a good name, which would last for ever.

His successor Mahmoud.

This youth, after a short usurpation by his brother Ishmael, whom, after vanquishing, he merely imprisoned for life, succeeded in the year 997 to Subuktagi, and proved one of the greatest princes that ever ruled in Asia. Being attacked by the Emperor of Bokhara, he felt or professed great reluctance to engage in war with the representative of the venerated dynasty of Samania; but his scruples were overcome when that prince was murdered, and his throne seized by two of his generals. Mahmoud then joined the King of the Uzbecks in extinguishing the empire of Bokhara; and the fine territory of Mavar-ul-Nahar was added to his dominion, which then comprehended all Asia from the Caspian to the Indus.

Mixed character of Mahmoud.

There is not a more chequered fame in oriental history than that of Mahmoud. His justice has been so much celebrated that, according to eastern writers, the wolf and the lamb in his reign drank at the same fountain; yet instances are not wanting in which his conduct appears marked by the grossest iniquity and extortion.

His piety, which is as much celebrated, is equally problematical. According to Ferishta, he was in early life prone to scepticism. His mind was agitated with doubt on two very different points,—whether there be a future world, and whether he was the son of Subuktagi; for the general deportment of his mother, it seems, left this last question open to controversy. A vision appeared to him, when the Prophet in person removed both these subjects of inquietude; and the emperor then commenced a high religious profession. His zeal, however, brought such an accession of power and wealth, as made it be doubted whether his devotions to heaven were not chiefly valued as they tended to make him lord of the earth. His fervour was especially inflamed by reports of the boundless wealth accumulated in the holy shrines of Hindostan, and his conscience incessantly reproached him, till he used means to have these profane treasures transported to adorn the palaces of Ghizni.

CHAP. VI.

A. D. 1000.

His religion.

Influence of Mohammedanism on India.

The rise of the Mohammedan power was pregnant with events to India, over which its princes were destined to rule for ages; yet their dominion had endured four centuries without finding its way into that extensive region. But this security was necessarily impaired, when so formidable a kingdom was erected on its frontier. Subuktagi had already made two inroads into Moultan and Lahore, in which he was successful, having in both completely defeated Jeipal, prince of the latter country. He annexed to Ghizni the fine province of Peshawer, and extended his authority to the Indus. Mahmoud, who, in these invasions, had given early proofs of personal bravery, soon made the country beyond that river the grand theatre of his military exploits, from which he was diverted only by some insurrections in his more distant dependencies, and by occasional alarms of Tartar invasion. Historians record twelve expeditions by this great potentate, from all of which he returned triumphant, and laden with booty.

In the first he merely crossed the Indus; but the second was against Jeipal of Lahore, who had again reared

CHAP. VI. — A. D. 1009.

Jeipal of Lahore.

the standard of independence. This country, in which mountains and deserts are intermingled with tracts of luxuriant fertility, has, from the days of Alexander to the present, nurtured a warlike people, who have formed a bulwark against western invasion. Jeipal had mustered another formidable army, but was vanquished and made prisoner; his neck, as well as those of fifteen chiefs, being encircled with jewels of immense value. This unfortunate prince, after being twice a captive, considered his honour as irretrievably tarnished: for which reason, and actuated by the barbarous pride of his countrymen, he prepared a funeral-pile, and threw himself into the flames. Annindpal, his son, acknowledged his kingdom tributary to Ghizni.

Immense expeditions beyond the Indus.

The three next expeditions of Mahmoud were made with the view of collecting imposts and suppressing partial rebellions. The fifth, in 1009, commenced by an attack on the part of Annindpal. Having formed alliances with all the great kings of the interior,—Delhi, Kanouge, Ougein, Gwalior, Callinger, and Ajmere,—he assembled the largest army that had been seen in that region for hundreds of years. They crossed the Indus, and entered the Plains of Peshawer, where the Moslems, afraid to encounter in the open field an enemy so immensely superior, began to intrench their forces. The two armies remained forty days in presence of each other, when at length a battle was begun on the side of the natives by the Gickers or Gwickwars, a race almost entirely savage, inhabiting the mountainous tracts north of Lahore. Their arrows did considerable execution; yet the main body were unable to make any impression on the brave and strongly intrenched army of Mahmoud.

Panic among the native army.

Many fell on the part of the assailants, when at length the elephant on which the Prince of Lahore rode, frightened by a fire-ball, ran off, and carried his master out of the field. At that moment the troops, thinking themselves deserted by their commander, were struck with panic; and the whole of that mighty host fled in complete and irretrievable confusion. An alarm so sudden and so slightly raised, may lead us to conclude that, instead of hardy and veteran warriors, Mahmoud had encountered only an effeminate and tumultuary militia, like that which Xerxes led into Greece. Twenty thousand were slain in the pursuit; and numerous elephants laden with treasure were captured. The conqueror, finding no longer an army to oppose him, marched directly upon the fort of Bimé, or Bheemghur, considered almost impregnable, and which had therefore been made a general depository for all the sacred wealth of the surrounding temples. The Indian princes having marched forward with a full assurance of victory, and without ever dreading attack, had withdrawn the garrison to reinforce their ranks, leaving only priests to guard the shrine and treasures. These defenders soon opened the gates and fell flat on their faces before the victorious prince. The gold, silver, and precious stones found in Bimé are declared by Ferishta to have exceeded all similar possessions of any other prince on earth; yet Major Price's authorities, and even his own, when carefully analyzed by Colonel Briggs, fix the amount at little more than £300,000 in specie, with perhaps a somewhat larger value in diamonds and other jewels. These acquisitions, on Mahmoud's return, were displayed several days to the admiring gaze of the Ghizni mountaineers; and the exhibition was closed by liberal donations to the poor and the ministers of religion.

Dreadful slaughter.

Treasures at Bimé.

The sovereigns of India, by this abortive expedition, had revealed to Mahmoud the fatal secret of their weakness and the valuable treasures which their kingdoms contained,—lessons by which he was not slow to profit. He had obtained intelligence respecting Tanassar, a shrine of singular opulence and sanctity, situated near the theatre of the great war recorded in the Mahabarat. As he passed on his march the territories of Lahore, Anindpal addressed an earnest supplication that he would remain content with having swept away at Bimé the riches of so many temples, and would spare this peculiar object of Hindoo veneration; but Mahmoud announced

Further Moslem aggressions.

CHAP. VI. A.D. 1017. his firm purpose to obliterate from India every vestige of idolatry. He reached the place before it could receive even the feeble aid of the King of Delhi, and became possessed, without resistance, of the accumulated treasure of ages. All the idols were broken in pieces and thrown on the highway, except one of stupendous dimensions, called Jug Soom, which was carried to Ghizni and reduced to fragments. The conqueror took possession of Delhi, and even formed the design of annexing this fine region to his dominions; but on farther reflection he considered it impossible, so long as the brave and well-defended province of Lahore intervened, that a regular communication could be maintained between that capital and Ghizni. To subdue Annindpal would therefore have been a requisite preliminary; but that prince acted with such prudence, and so carefully avoided all occasion of offence, that Mahmoud found neither pretext nor temptation to renew the war. He therefore never attempted to conquer India; he merely pounced, from time to time, like an eagle, from his tremendous eyry amid the snows of Caucasus, snatched his prey, and flew back to his mountain-domain.

Treasures of Tanassar

Conquest of Cashmere.

This prince spent a summer in conquering the beautiful Valley of Cashmere, the possession of which opened to him a way into the interior of Hindostan, without the reluctant consent of the Prince of Lahore. In the year 1017 he assembled all his troops from the Tartar provinces, and at the head of a hundred thousand horse and thirty thousand foot, marched along the sources of the great rivers against Kanouge, the proudest of all the Indian capitals. The oriental writers represent, in the most magnificent terms, its pomp and greatness. The towers are described as reaching the skies; while the city is said at one time to have contained 30,000 shops for the sale of betel, and 60,000 performers on musical instruments. A state thus dissolved in ease and luxury was ill prepared to encounter the hardy bands who poured down from Afghanistan. The king did not even attempt resistance; he advanced and tendered his submission to

CHAP. VI. A.D. 1017.

the invader. Kanouge was consequently treated with lenity, and the conqueror remained only three days. After reducing several other places, he received intelligence of a city which afforded the means of gratifying to the utmost his rapacious piety. Muttra or Mathura, sacred to Krishna, contained shrines eclipsing all others even in this most wealthy region. The Mohammedan prince entered it with little opposition, and found its temples the most splendid he had yet seen, filled with gigantic idols of pure gold, having eyes of rubies; in one was stuck a sapphire of extraordinary magnitude. The conqueror lost no time in decomposing these rich objects of pagan homage, and, having reduced them to their constituent elements of gold and jewels, loaded with them a long train of camels. He is said to have once formed the design of demolishing the temples; but being dazzled with their beauty, he desisted, and left that task to the bigoted zeal of Aurengzebe. The reduction of some other cities was attended with hard fighting and comparatively little spoil. He marched by way of Lahore to Ghizni, and made a display of booty eclipsing even that brought from the plunder of Tanassar. It has been estimated at half a million in specie, with jewels and pearls beyond all calculation; to which were added fifty-three thousand captives, whose price, however, was so much reduced by the immense supply, that they scarcely brought five shillings a-head. The wealth obtained by the private chiefs and soldiers was supposed to equal that of the sovereign.

Shrines of Krishna spoiled.

Immense treasures.

Ghizni hitherto, notwithstanding the riches conveyed to it, had been little more in itself than an encampment of migratory shepherds; but Mahmoud, smitten with the magnificence of Kanouge and Mathura, determined now to erect edifices which might render his capital an object of admiration to the world. A mosque was built of granite and marble, on which the richest materials were profusely lavished, and new ornaments continually added, till it became celebrated over Asia under the title of the "Celestial Bride." The nobles, imitating the

Ghizni adorned as the Moslem capital.

CHAP. VI. A.D. 1024.

taste of their sovereign, vied with each other in costly structures, till Ghizni acquired a magnificence surpassing that of the greatest cities of India.

Mahmoud's defence of his allies.

Meantime Mahmoud received the mortifying intelligence that the submission and alliance of the King of Kanouge had proved fatal to that prince. Indignant at his desertion of the general cause, Nunda, king of Callinger, seconded by the neighbouring monarchs, commenced a furious war, which ended in his defeat and death, and the surrender of his capital. The Ghiznian ruler made all the despatch which his distance admitted. After forcing the passage of the Jumna, he advanced and found the victor strongly intrenched, and apparently waiting his attack; but, after due consideration, the Indian prince retreated, leaving the country to be laid waste by the invader. The kingdom and city of Kanouge, however, were never able to regain their ancient splendour.

Subjugation of Lahore.

Lahore, though so closely contiguous to the Ghiznian territory, had continued independent during thirty years of Mahmoud's reign; but on the death of Annindpal, he determined upon a vigorous effort to obtain possession of this important key of India. Accordingly, having assembled an immense force, he marched towards the metropolis; when the young prince, unable to face so great an armament, abandoned the city and neighbouring territory, and sought refuge in Ajmere. Lahore was thus attached to the Ghiznian monarchy.

Last expedition of Mahmoud.

After some minor inroads, the conqueror, in the year 1024, undertook his last and greatest expedition into India; his arms being then turned somewhat in a new direction. In the province of Guzerat, on the shore of the Indian Ocean, stood Sumnaut, a shrine higher and holier than any yet devoted to spoliation. Two thousand villages were assigned for its support, besides presents poured in from all the surrounding regions. Sumnaut himself was esteemed the general judge of the dead, and his statue of pure gold was washed every morning with water brought from the Ganges, a thousand miles dis-

Fanatic zeal of the Moslems.

tant. The attendants consisted of two thousand Brahmins, five hundred dancing-girls, three hundred musicians, and three hundred barbers. The king was farther incited by learning that the priests of Sumnaut considered themselves secure from his utmost power. According to them, the sins of Delhi and Kanouge had been the sole cause of the downfal of those cities; while they themselves, high in purity and sanctity, might bid defiance to the impious fury of the Moslem invader. Eager to undeceive them, this monarch, having mustered his troops, led them into Moultan; employing twenty thousand camels to convey provisions across the great western desert. The city of Ajmere was found abandoned, and its fort too strong to be attacked. Nahrwalla, capital of Guzerat, had been left in the same state. After passing another desert, the Ghiznevide sovereign came in view of Sumnaut, a lofty castle on a peninsula completely enclosed by the sea, except at one point, which was defended by strong walls, on whose battlements stood an innumerable multitude of combatants. They announced by a herald that their great god had drawn the Moslems hither, in order that the destruction of so many divinities, who had fallen under their axe, might now be avenged. The invaders, however, advanced with a despatch which amazed the Hindoos, and caused them to fall down in tears before their idol; though, on seeing the scaling-ladders applied, they drew strength from despair, and rushed forward to the defence with the utmost fury. The dreadful contest was prolonged a whole day, at the end of which the assailants, overpowered with fatigue, were obliged to retire. On the following morning the attack was renewed, but with no better success.

Boast of the Indian natives.

Succour to the besieged.

On the third day, an immense army was seen advancing to the relief of Sumnaut. Mahmoud instantly led his troops to battle; but, as this quarter of India has always supplied a race of brave and hardy warriors, the contest was severe. Fortune still wavered, when the Indian host was strengthened by a powerful reinforce-

CHAP. VI. A.D. 1024.

ment under Byram Deo and Dabissalima, two of the principal chiefs of Guzerat. The battle then became more doubtful and truly terrible, and Mahmoud, for the first time on the soil of India, saw himself in danger of being vanquished. He appealed to the religious zeal of his troops; he prostrated himself on the ground, imploring the aid of Heaven in this holy conflict, and earnestly called on his chiefs to advance either to conquest or the crown of martyrdom. He at length gained a complete victory; and the garrison, on seeing the flight of the great army to which they had trusted for deliverance, were seized with panic, and abandoned the place. The conqueror entered, and was led to the temple, a spacious and antique structure, the interior of which consisted of a majestic hall supported by fifty-six columns, and entirely encircled with golden images of Hindoo deities. Sumnaut himself, whose gigantic dimensions are variously reported, towered high over all. On first beholding this idol, Mahmoud, fired with wrathful zeal, struck off its nose, and gave orders that the whole figure should forthwith be reduced into fragments. When the attendant Brahmins saw the downfal of this object of their profoundest veneration, they fell on their knees, and offered an immense sum to save what remained; and the omrahs advised, even as a matter of prudence, the acceptance of the ransom: but the king indignantly rejected the idea of becoming a "seller of idols." The work of demolition proceeded; and, on its reaching the interior of the image, there was disclosed a treasure in pearls, rubies, and diamonds, almost beyond conception, and far surpassing the immense sum tendered for its redemption. It is somewhat difficult to ascertain the amount; but it is generally admitted to have greatly exceeded that of any of the former captures.

Victory of Mahmoud. *Destruction of the idols.* *Immense treasure.*

Adiration of Guzerat.

Mahmoud was so much pleased with Guzerat, that he deliberated whether he should not make it the principal seat of his government, or at least annex it permanently to his dominions; but he became satisfied, that the distance from Ghizni was too great, and the communications too difficult. He attempted, however, to retain a control over this fine country, by raising to the sovereignty a Brahmin of humble birth; but he had not long departed when the people again transferred their allegiance to their ancient race of kings. Some romantic and rather absurd details are given with relation to this occurrence, which we pass by, as they were probably invented to supply an excuse to Mahmoud for superseding the sovereign whom he had chosen to impose upon Guzerat.

Attack on the Jauts.

The victor, while on his return to Ghizni, suffered considerably in passing through the vast deserts; and was greatly annoyed also by the Jits or Jauts, a tribe inhabiting Moultan, who, by their strong force of war-boats, commanded the navigation of the Indus. The indignant monarch undertook next year an expedition against this people, and having prepared a vast number of small vessels fortified with iron spikes, encountered, and, after an obstinate conflict, defeated them so completely, that almost the whole nation were slain or taken prisoners.

Death of Mahmoud.

The following season he was employed in an expedition into Khorasan, on his return from which, in 1030, he was taken ill, and died at the age of 63.

His remarkable character.

There are few characters, we have remarked, in oriental history more doubtful than that of this great conqueror. By some he is extolled as the model of a perfect prince, while others brand him as a monster of avarice, injustice, and rapacity. There seems to have been in his nature a strange combination of opposite qualities, his best actions being alloyed by a mixture of wild caprice. He carefully discharged many of his duties as a sovereign, and made great exertions to secure the husbandman and merchant against the inroad of the predatory bands who occupied the mountain-fastnesses. He was accessible to complaints from every quarter. A woman from a remote Persian province came to his audience, and complained that her son had been killed and her property carried off by a gang of plunderers. The king replied

CHAP. VI.
A.D. 1030.

that this was a distant conquest, in which it was impossible for him to prevent some disorders. The woman warmly rejoined "Why then do you conquer kingdoms which you cannot protect, and for which you will not be able to answer in the day of judgment?" That this rebuke could be addressed to the king was no small honour to his character, and still more when we find that it roused him to establish order in those remote parts of his dominions. A still more signal act of justice is recorded. A citizen of Ghizni represented that a powerful lord of the court, having become enamoured of his wife, arrived nightly, thrust him out of his own dwelling, and forcibly supplied his place. Mahmoud, with the deepest indignation, desired that information should be given to him the first time that this outrage was repeated. The injured person came three nights after with the expected notice, and the monarch, attended by a guard of soldiers, hastened to the house. Having ordered all the lights to be extinguished, he advanced in the dark with a weapon, and, seizing the offender, with one blow severed his head from his body. He then caused a light to be brought, and having seen the victim, fell on his knees and uttered a prayer. Being asked the meaning of all this, he replied that he had extinguished the light lest the guilty person should prove to have been a favourite, the view of whom might have shaken his just resolution; but, on being relieved from this apprehension, he had returned thanks to Heaven.*

His love of Justice.

The people of Ghizni were thus well secured by Mahmoud against the injustice of their fellow-subjects; but their lot was different in regard to the deeds of extortion and iniquity which were too often committed by himself. Mention is made of a wealthy citizen of Nishapour, against whom he chose to make a charge of impiety and heresy. The accused person came to him and said, "O

His oppressions.

* This anecdote is given with considerable variations by the different authorities; the above version (which is that of D'Herbelot, Bibliothèque Orientale, art. Mahmoud) appears the most probable and consistent

king, I am neither idolater nor apostate, but I am possessed of wealth; take it, therefore, but do me not a double injustice, by robbing me of my money and of my good name." The rapacious ruler, it is said, unblushingly closed with the proposal, and after having stripped the man of his property, gave him a certificate testifying the soundness of his faith.

Religious zeal.

Religious zeal was not only avowed by Mahmoud, but under a certain shape supplied the main impulse to all his actions. Yet its exercise, as already observed, was productive of earthly gains so immense as to involve its purity in some suspicion. Still a religious profession is not always insincere, because it is somewhat alloyed in the mind of him who admits a mixture of worldly motives. That the Moslem faith, as the exclusive path to salvation, ought to be propagated by the sword, is one of its fundamental dogmas; and by a monarch whose ambition and avarice this tenet so greatly favoured, we cannot wonder that it should have been zealously embraced. Yet one incident, related as having occurred at the end of his mortal career, shows that the vanities of earth still held full possession of his heart. Two days before his death, he caused all his jewels, pearls, and golden ornaments, collected from so many different regions, to be spread out before him, that he might satiate his eyes by a display of riches, from which he was about to be separated for ever. We can more easily sympathize with his taking a last review of his troops, including the long array of his elephants, and with the deep emotion which this spectacle excited in the breast of the dying warrior.

Patronage of letters.

Mahmoud, as soon as the rays of wealth and prosperity began to illumine his throne, stood forth as the distinguished patron of letters and poetry; and Ghizni, under him, became the most literary and classical city of the East. It shone indeed at first by a borrowed light from Bagdad, which, even amid the complete overthrow of its political greatness, still retained an intellectual empire over all the nations speaking Arabic and studying the

CHAP. VI. — A.D. 1030.

Koran. Yet the splendour of Mahmoud's court, and the great events of his reign, called forth poetical talents more brilliant than had adorned even the celebrated courts of Haroun and Almamon. Ferdusi, who, in the Shah Nameh, celebrated the exploits of his patron, ranks as the second poet in Asia. The materials for the literary history of Ghizni are indeed exceedingly scanty; yet enough transpires to warrant the suspicion, that this great author, though attracted by the pomp and patronage of a court, shared the evils which appear inseparable from high endowments, and only passed a life of splendid misery. It is related, that having completed his great work, he sought the due reward, which he estimated at 60,000 *dinars;* but the king, taking advantage of a verbal resemblance, paid only the same number of *dirhems*, not exceeding a tenth of the sum demanded. This was a miserable pun upon which to deprive the greatest genius of the age of the hard-earned fruits of his labour. The indignant poet quitted the court where he had been so unworthily treated, and, retiring to a istance, sent forth various satirical effusions against his former patron, of which D'Herbelot gives the following specimen:—"The magnificent court of Ghizni is a sea, but a sea without bottom and without shore; I have fished in it long, but have not found any pearl." Mahmoud, it is said, was mortified, and endeavoured by flattering offers to induce him to return, but could never prevail with the offended bard.

Asiatic poets.

Treatment of Ferdusi.

The presiding star in the literary circles of Ghizni was Oonsuri, equally celebrated as a philosopher and a poet. Mahmoud placed him at the head of the university which he had founded, and gave him such a complete jurisdiction over a body of four hundred learned men, that no work was to be submitted to the sovereign, which had not been stamped with his approbation. We have not as yet in the West the means of duly estimating the actual merit of this personage; but on considering that with posterity his name stands in such deep eclipse behind that of Ferdusi, above whom he was so

Oonsuri the poet.

highly honoured in life, a doubt must arise, whether his reputation was not partly earned by the arts of a courtier, and the absence of the troublesome pride incident to elevated genius. One channel to favour seems to have consisted in the permission which was allowed him to share the convivial hours of the sovereign. The Orientals relate an occasion when, to sooth his master's grief for having, the night before, when overcome with wine, cut off the long tresses of his beloved, Oonsuri composed some extemporary verses, which conveyed such delight, that in return the mouth of the fortunate minstrel was three times filled with jewels.

Men of science.

Among the men of science resident at Ghizni, the most eminent was Abu Rihan, sent by Almamon from Bagdad, where he was venerated almost as the rival of Avicenna. But, besides metaphysics and dialectics, he studied and appears to have drawn his chief lustre from attainments in the magical art. Of this, D'Herbelot relates a remarkable instance. One day Mahmoud sent for him, and ordered him to deposit with a third person a statement of the precise manner in which the monarch would quit the hall where he was then sitting. The paper being lodged, the king, instead of going out by one of the numerous doors, caused a breach to be made in the wall, by which he effected his exit;—but how was he amazed, when, on the paper being examined, there was found in it a minute specification of the precise spot through which he penetrated. Hereupon the prince with horror denounced this learned man as a sorcerer, and commanded him to be instantly thrown out of the window. The barbarous sentence was presently executed; but care had been taken to prepare beneath a soft and silken cushion, into which the body of the sage sunk without sustaining any injury. Abu Rihan was then called before the monarch, and required to say, whether by his boasted art he had been able to foresee these events, and the treatment through which he had that day passed. The learned man immediately desired his tablets to be sent for, in which were found regularly

Magic.

CHAP. VI.
A. D. 1031.

predicted the whole of these singular transactions. This incident does not, it must be owned, inspire a very lofty idea, either of the wisdom or the wit of the imperial court of the Ghiznevide.

Mahmoud's successor.

Mahmoud, after a short interval, was succeeded by Musaood, who nearly equalled him in bravery and enterprise, but who had to struggle against a series of adverse fortune. There poured forth from the interior regions of Asia one of those great tides of conquest and migration, which have so often changed the face of that continent. It consisted of the Turks or Toorks, under the dynasty called, from Seljuk its founder, Seljukian, which overran Khorasan. Under the successors of the chief just named, the Turkish empire rose to such a height of power as to eclipse that of all the other Asiatic kingdoms. Togrul, who subverted the imperial throne of Bagdad, and shook that of Constantinople,—Alp Arslan, who wrote on his tomb at Meru, "Ye who have seen the glory of Alp Arslan exalted to the heavens, come and see it buried under the dust;"—these were warriors with whom even the most gallant of the lineage of Mahmoud sought in vain to contend. These last saw wrested from them the fine plains of Khorasan and Iran, even that of Balkh, and their dominions confined within the mountain-barrier of Caucasus. On the eastern side they still held Lahore, and made some vigorous attempts, but only with partial and temporary success, to extend their sway over the Indian territory.

Rise of the Turkish empire.

House of Ghizni.

The house of Ghizni, during two centuries, continued still, though thus reduced by Turkish invasion, to maintain the boundaries above described. Family alliances were even formed between Ibrahim the First and Malek Shah, son of Alp Arslan. The downfal of this dynasty arose from an internal cause. Ghori or Ghoor forms a rude district, situated on the loftiest branch of Caucasus, or Hindoo Coosh, where it borders on Tibet and Turkestan. Its princes, commanding a race of hardy mountaineers, gradually made themselves nearly independent of the Ghiznian government, and even obtained possessions in Tartary and Khorasan. This excited so strongly the jealousy of Byram, who about the year 1115 had ascended the throne, that having drawn into his power Mohammed, prince of Ghori, he put him to death; a step which he had ample cause to repent. Sief-ul-Dien, brother to the latter, soon mustered a large array of his followers, eager to avenge the loss of their chief. Byram, unable to oppose him, evacuated his capital; but having re-assembled his forces, he soon afterwards recovered Ghizni, and took his enemy prisoner, whom he subjected to the most dreadful insult and cruelty. Mounted on a bullock he was led through Ghizni, amid the derision of the mob; then tortured and beheaded, and his vizier impaled alive. This barbarity on the part of a ruler otherwise mild and respectable, set the seal to the fate of his house. Allah, brother to the sufferer, soon summoned round him all the warriors of the tribe of Ghori to chastise the author of their wrongs. Byram marched to meet him; and the superior numbers of his troops enabled them to maintain a vigorous struggle against the rude courage of the mountaineers. But at length he yielded, and fled with his scattered army towards Hindostan, where he soon after died of grief. The victor, in 1152, marched upon Ghizni, and according to the too common practice of eastern conquerors, sought to surpass the cruelty which he came to punish. That magnificent city was given up to a general pillage, and to the sword of the enraged Ghorians. In seven days it was no more; and its palaces, so profusely embellished with the spoils of conquered India, were rased to the ground. A few tombs, spared by eastern piety, stood alone amid this appalling solitude. It revived indeed, and became for a short time the capital of the Ghorian chiefs; but it again sunk, and now only a few scattered ruins, with the spacious tomb of Mahmoud, at which a few priests perpetually read the Koran, are all that remain of this once proud seat of the conqueror of Asia.

Division in the government.

Cruelties of eastern conquerors.

The Ghiznevide dynasty continued for some time to retain their diminished authority; but it was finally ex-

CHAP. VI. A. D. 1174.

tinguished by Mohammed Ghori, the successor of Allah-ul-Dien. He pursued into Lahore the last of this mighty race, whose name was Chusero; but the unfortunate prince made a resistance so desperate in that strong retreat, that the invader was twice obliged to retire. At last, by a feigned alliance, he induced his unwary victim to come out to meet him,—then, by a circuitous march, cut him off from Lahore, surrounded his little camp, and obliged him to surrender. He at first showed a disposition to mercy, and only confined him in a strong castle; but at length, in the year 1186, alleging the predictions of some astrologer, secured his safety by putting all the family to death.

Last of the race of Mohammed.

Mohammed Ghori.

Mohammed Ghori or Ghoor obtained the government of Ghizni in 1174, and held it in his brother's right and his own thirty-two years, with a valour and fortune similar to those of his great ancestors whom he resembled in name. Commencing his career with the occupation of the frontier territory of Lahore, he made it his principal object to extend his dominion over India. Collecting all his forces he advanced against Ajmere, which at first submitted; but the King of Delhi, having formed an alliance with several neighbouring princes, hastened to its relief with two hundred thousand infantry, and three thousand elephants. Mohammed, trusting to the courage of his mountain-tribes, rushed fearlessly to the attack; but the view of this immense host wheeling round to enclose them, and the mighty array of its elephants, seems to have struck with panic these undisciplined warriors. Many of the chiefs with their followers fled, leaving the king surrounded by the enemy, whose superiority in numbers was now greatly increased. The Moslem on horseback encountered hand to hand the King of Delhi, seated on his war-elephant. The Ghorian prince, after a desperate struggle, was pierced in the arm, fell to the ground, and was with difficulty carried off by a trusty band of his adherents. The rout was complete, and the pursuit was continued forty miles.

His total rout.

The emperor spent a year in repairing the effects of

CHAP. VI — A. D. 1174.

this dreadful disaster, and organizing the means of a new invasion. He at first degraded the omrahs who had fled, subjecting them to the humiliation of marching round the city with bags of barley suspended from their necks, and of feeding out of them; but when proceeding on his next expedition, it was represented to him that he thereby deprived himself of the services of many of his choicest warriors; upon which he allowed them to resume their stations, and obtain an opportunity of redeeming their fame.

Renewed invasion of India.

Mohammed, having mustered all his forces, marched into India, where he met troops still more numerous than those who had vanquished him in the preceding year; all of whom had now bound themselves by the water of the Ganges to conquer or die. The Indian princes advanced with boundless confidence; sending at the same time a friendly remonstrance, that if Mohammed was weary of his own life, he should at least pity the men whom he was leading to so cruel a destiny. Retreat was still open to him; but if urged on by his evil genius, "we have sworn," said they, "by our gods to advance upon you with our rank-breaking elephants, war-treading horses, and blood-thirsty soldiers, early in the morning, to crush your unfortunate army." The wary commander returned an answer seemingly inspired by alarm; stating, that he carried on the war only in obedience to his brother, without whose orders he could not retreat, but would gladly arrange the terms of a truce till he should receive further instructions. The Indians, lulled by this submissive tone, gave themselves up to security, and spent the following night in merriment. Mohammed, watching the moment when they were completely off their guard, made an attack during the darkness, defeating and putting to flight several large bodies; yet so immense was the circuit of their camp, that there were rallied next morning numbers which seemed more than enough to crush the whole host of the invaders. The Mussulman then adopted the old Scythian warfare; with his squadrons of cavalry he

Policy of the leader.

CHAP. VI.
A. D. 1174.

alternately attacked and retreated, till towards evening, seeing the enemy completely exhausted, he charged them at the head of his chosen band of mailed horsemen, who bore down all opposition, and drove the whole of their army into a tumultuary flight. The King of Delhi fell, and immense spoil came into the hands of the conqueror. Having advanced to the capital, the victor was prevailed upon by a high ransom to spare it, but left a strong force under his lieutenant, Cuttub, to maintain his authority in that quarter. This officer soon after assembled a large body of followers, subverted the throne of Delhi, and reigned there as viceroy. Thus a Moslem dominion was for the first time established in the heart of India, and in one of its greatest cities.

Defeat of the King of Delhi.

After a lapse of a short period, Mohammed made another expedition into Hindostan. Being joined by Cuttub, he totally defeated the Prince of Kanouge, then marched against Benares, broke the idols of its thousand shrines, and loaded four thousand camels with the wealth of that sacred city. Following a career similar to that of the Ghiznevide, he made nine expeditions into India, and accumulated treasures which almost rivalled those of his great predecessor. But this splendid light of conquest was in one moment extinguished; for on his way from Lahore to Ghizni, he pitched his tent for the night on the banks of the Indus or one of its tributaries; where a band of the mountain-tribe of Gwickwars, many of whose relations had perished in war with Mohammed, had vowed, at whatever cost, to purchase revenge. The season being extremely hot, the *canats* or screens enclosing the imperial tents had been thrown open for the admission of air. Twenty conspirators, availing themselves of this circumstance, stole in unperceived, stabbed the sentry on guard, and, having drawn off the attention of the others, penetrated to the chamber of the king, who was lying asleep with two slaves fanning him. All their daggers were instantly plunged in his breast, and he sunk under their hands, pierced by twenty-two wounds.

Expedition into Hindostan.

Assassination of Mohammed.

Subdivision of the kingdom.

Thus perished this great conqueror, whose dominion was almost as extensive as that of Mahmoud of Ghizni. Like him, according to Ferishta, he was not devoid of virtues, yet has left behind a darker reputation, redeemed by fewer traits of refinement and humanity. With him the dynasty of Ghori rose and fell, for he left no descendants possessed of energy sufficient to support the weight of his ill-balanced empire. His lieutenants, Ildecuz in the mountain-territory, and Cuttub in India, soon erected for themselves independent sovereignties.

CHAPTER VII.

The Patan or Afghan Dynasty.

Cuttub-ul-Dien founds this Dynasty—Altumsh—Sultana Rizia—Mahmoud II.—His ascetic Severity—Balin—Brilliant Patronage of the Arts and Sciences—Kei Kobad and Kera—Allah I.—His brave and fierce Reign—Conquest of Southern India—Adventures of the Princesses Cumladè and Dewildè—Anarchy—Several short Reigns—Mohammed III.—His Cruelty—Ferose III.—Short Reigns and general Disorder—Timur—His Character—Invasion of India—Capture of Delhi, and dreadful Massacre—His Return—Succession of Emperors—Conquest by Baber—Close of the Patan Dynasty.

CHAP. VII. — A.D. 1206. The Afghan dynasty.

CUTTUB-UL-DIEN, the founder of the first Mohammedan, or what was called the Patan race of emperors, who ruled in India, was of the humblest birth; it was even made the reproach of his dynasty that it originated with a slave. Brought as a captive from Turkestan, he had been purchased by a citizen of Nishapour, who, finding his talents good, instructed him in various arts and sciences. Upon the death of his master, he was sold with the rest of the property, and came into the possession of Mohammed. His abilities and address soon raised him to the rank of principal page; whence he was promoted to a military command, and soon rose to the first station in the army. The high confidence reposed in him by the emperor, pointed him out as the fittest person to remain as viceroy of the conquered territories in India, when he himself retired to his native mountains. Cuttub remained faithful to his superior; yet, from his distant position, he reigned almost uncontrolled during that monarch's life, whom he survived four years, and

FORT GWALIOR

Page 221.

whose successor publicly owned him as king. He is celebrated as brave, just, and humane; and his liberality was so unbounded as to make it become proverbial in India to say of any one,—"He is as generous as Cuttub-ul-Dien." He waged war with the neighbouring potentates generally with success, though in a campaign against the Rajpoots he sustained a signal defeat. Sinking, however, towards the close of his reign, into indolence and luxury, he allowed his rival Ildecuz to seize upon Ghizni and several of the frontier territories. He died in the year 1210.

Generous character of its founder.

Altumsh his successor.

Altumsh, though a Tartar of noble birth, had, like Cuttub, been sold as a slave, and purchased by that prince. Having raised himself by his valour to be captain-general and son-in-law to the emperor, he mounted the throne, having overcome Aram, the rightful heir. He redressed all the evils caused by the weaknesses of his aged predecessor. He defeated Ildecuz, and took him prisoner; he extended the empire on every side; making Bengal and Bahar first tributary and then subject provinces, over which his sons were placed as viceroys. He reduced, after a long siege, Gwalior, considered the principal bulwark of Hindoo power. Seated on a lofty hill with perpendicular sides, defended by extensive works, and supplied with abundance of water, it was viewed as nearly impregnable. He distinguished himself also by the conquest of Malwa, the capture of Ougein, and the demolition of the revered statue of Vicramaditya. He is celebrated, on the whole, as a good and wise prince.

Zingis attacks India

About this time a mighty tempest swept along the borders of India, happily without touching her rich provinces. Zingis, after ravaging Asia from the Pacific to the Caspian, and reducing numberless kingdoms under his dominion, attacked the Prince of the Afghans, whom he drove before him, and compelled to take refuge beyond the Indus. Altumsh refused to shelter him, and hence the arms of Zingis were turned aside from the wealthy regions which stretch towards the south. Per

CHAP. VII. A.D. 1236.

haps his horsemen, accustomed only to scour the plains of Tartary and Persia, felt themselves unable to act with vigour in the rugged steeps of the Caucasus.

After the death of Altumsh, which took place in 1236, there followed a succession of princes, most of whom occupied, during a very short period, a disputed throne, but without any material alteration of boundaries or relations in regard to the neighbouring states. A few, however, were so remarkable as to deserve notice.

Queen Rizia Begum.

Rizia Begum stood perhaps alone among Mohammedans as a reigning queen. In her earliest youth she displayed such talents for administration that Altumsh, her father, when departing on his expedition against Gwalior, left her sole regent, regarding her as better fitted than any of his sons to sustain the weight of government; and Ferose, one of the princes, having been afterwards deposed for incapacity, the chiefs unanimously vested the empire in this accomplished lady. She assumed the imperial robes, took her seat on the musnud, administered the laws strictly and impartially, and suppressed with vigour all attempts to take advantage of the supposed weakness of a female reign. Yet Rizia stooped at length to the frailty of her sex; she became doatingly attached to an Abyssinian slave named Jammal, whose sudden elevation to the highest dignities was ill brooked by the great lords and omrahs of the empire. Their discontent was soon matured into insurrection, which, though it was at first successfully resisted, became truly formidable when it was headed by Byram, her brother, who had a more natural right to the throne. The fair ruler of India was finally defeated, imprisoned, and, by a consequence too common in that part of the world, afterwards put to death.

Her courage and weakness.

Mahmoud II.

Mahmoud II., a younger son of Altumsh, had been oppressed by the jealousy of his sister and brother, and kept in long confinement. In his adversity he acquired virtues which afterwards eminently fitted him to adorn a throne. Disdaining the subsistence allowed by his ungenerous relatives, he earned his own livelihood by writing or rather copying books. Released from prison by a more humane prince, and intrusted with a small government, he obtained such a reputation for justice and wisdom that his accession to the throne was hailed with universal satisfaction. Nor was this high expectation in any degree disappointed. According to Ferishta, he was the patron of learning, the protector of the people, and the friend of the poor. Without embroiling himself in unnecessary war, he defended his territories with vigour against numerous and formidable enemies. Yet these elevated virtues were somewhat alloyed by a pedantic and fantastic ostentation of simplicity. Seated on the most splendid throne of the East, he practised the austerity of a hermit. Applying all his revenues to the exigencies of the state, he continued to earn by the pen his own support, which was limited to a supply of the humblest necessaries. He not only rejected the vain and culpable privilege of a numerous seraglio and confined himself to one wife, but he compelled that lady to discharge the most menial functions. Even when her majesty complained that she burned her fingers in the process of cooking, and asked for a maiden to aid her in that humble task, he rejected the request. This was very extravagant; yet there appears a fine and amiable feeling in the following anecdote. He had shown part of his daily task of copying the Koran to an omrah whom he much respected, and who pointed out an erroneous word. The emperor immediately erased it; but as soon as the chief departed, he restored the characters; and being asked the reason, answered, that the word was right; but that he did not wish to give pain to a worthy man by telling him he was mistaken.

Liberal character.

Affectation of simplicity.

Amiability.

The good government of Mahmoud had been in a great measure due to the happy choice of his prime minister, Balin or Baleen, who made himself universally popular; so that when the emperor died without posterity, the vizier, not being much attached to a family who had treated his master so ill, stepped into his place almost without a struggle It is scarcely possible, however, for

His successor Baleen

CHAP. VII. A.D. 1260.

a usurper to ascend a throne without being drawn into crime. Balin was one of forty Turkish chiefs who had associated to divide the empire among them on the monarch's decease. Mutual jealousy had already dissolved this bond; but the minister, notwithstanding, determined to consult his own security by making the whole of them perish either by poison or by the sword. This crime having quieted his fears, he did not again dip his hands in blood, but began a career which, for justice, mildness, and popularity, has scarcely an equal even among the many illustrious sovereigns who have ruled Hindostan. Balin was another of the *slave-emperors*. Having been captured by the Moguls, he was carried to Bagdad, and sold to a merchant of Bassora, who, learning that he was a relation of Altumsh, brought him to Delhi, and disposed of him with great advantage to that ruler. His talents soon raised him to a military command; and having openly attached himself to the cause of Byram, he was one of the most active instruments in the fall of the Empress Rizia. On succeeding to Mahmoud he made an entire change in the outward aspect of the court, restoring all those gay appendages of which it had been so closely shorn by his predecessor. He appeared in public with a blaze of pomp unwonted even in the East, which, however, he professed to exhibit solely in order to conciliate the respect of his people. He found ample scope for the exercise and perhaps the ostentation of kindness and generosity in the vast number of princes, some of them the greatest in Asia, who had been dethroned and forced to flee before the warlike hordes of Zingis and his successors. Upwards of fifteen of these fallen sovereigns, including two sons of the caliph, were accommodated with spacious apartments, and with every thing which could make them forget the miseries of their lot; and on occasions of state they were ranged round his throne in the order of their respective dignities. They brought with them a multitude of bards and ingenious men, who had constituted the ornament of their courts; to all of whom the emperor extended a patronage

Crimes of a usurper. Total change at the court. His hospitality.

Patronage of learning.

the most liberal and humane perhaps that has ever been bestowed by any monarch. Learned men, poets, and artists, were invited from the remotest extremities of Asia; and every effort was made, though without success, to induce Sadi, the pride of Persia, to quit the delights of Shiraz. The king's two sons, Shehid and Kera, vied with him in rendering the court of India the most refined and polite in the world. The former held at his palace a nightly assembly of divines, philosophers, and poets, at the head of whom was the bard Chusero; while Kera, the younger prince, in another apartment, convened musicians, players, story-tellers, and such as were possessed of the lighter talents. Amid these elegant pursuits, Balin did not aim at the glory of a conqueror; he even rejected opportunities that were presented for extending his dominions, though he vigorously defended his people against every aggression. He defeated with great slaughter the Rajpoots of Mewar, who by their predatory inroads had rendered a great extent of country almost uninhabitable; and though he could not altogether subdue these hardy sons of the desert, he cut down an extensive forest in which they were accustomed to find shelter, and by a line of forts so secured the district, that it was soon brought under full cultivation.

Successor of Balin.

On the death of Balin, in 1286, his eldest and most accomplished son, Shehid, being dead, and Kera absent in Bengal, Kei Kobad, son to the latter, was raised to the throne, which could not safely be left vacant even for a short interval. This prince was considered a youth of great promise, being imbued with the elegant tastes of his family; but on mounting the throne he soon allowed these qualities to degenerate into license and voluptuousness. He abandoned the reins of government to Nizam, an unworthy favourite, who oppressed the people, and put to death all who endeavoured to oppose his tyranny. Meantime Kera, who had remained at first content with the government of Bengal, distressed by the accounts of his son's conduct, and not unwilling

CHAP. VII.

A. D. 1290.

perhaps to take into his own hand the reins of empire, assembled a large army and marched into Bahar. The emperor met him with his whole force on the banks of

Invasion of Kera.

the Gogra; but Kera, moved by parental tenderness, sent a message, earnestly entreating that before affairs should come to extremities, he might obtain a conference with his child. An interview was accordingly arranged; but the latter, swollen with pride, seated himself on the imperial throne in the highest pomp, while the father, in approaching, was obliged at three different stages to do obeisance to him by kissing the ground, the mace-bearers exclaiming,—"The noble Kera to the king of

Noble conduct of Kera.

the world sends health." The aged sovereign, seeing himself exposed to this indignity, burst into tears. Suddenly at this spectacle the soul of the young monarch was moved; he sprung from his throne, threw himself at his parent's feet, and sought forgiveness. Kera raised him up, and the father and son mingled tears and embraces. An intimate communication was opened, and continued for twenty days, during which they agreed each to rest satisfied with his actual possessions; but the former most earnestly entreated his son to change his conduct, to distrust Nizam, to renounce his dissolute habits, and apply himself to the good government of his empire. Kei Kobad made the fairest promises, and set out for Delhi with the resolution of performing them.

Effeminacy of Kei Kobad.

For some short period he persevered; but the vizier, having assembled from every quarter the most seductive sirens, particularly one described as of almost supernatural beauty, caused the emperor soon to relapse into his former pleasures. His health was ruined, and he became an object of contempt to his people, till at length he was murdered, together with his infant son, by Ferose, an Afghan chief, who mounted the throne in his stead. This usurper, though he had in the usual manner stepped through blood to power, was afterwards rather blamed for too great lenity in its exercise.

Allah

Allah, who murdered and succeeded his uncle Ferose in the year 1295, was perhaps of all the sovereigns of

Hindostan the most energetic and terrible. The people sympathized deeply in the fate of the late monarch, whose head he caused to be fixed on a pole, and carried through camp and city. To pave the way to the throne by the death of its possessor had become indeed an established practice, of which Ferose himself had set the example. But there was something peculiarly barbarous in the manner in which the new emperor perpetrated this murder, and subsequently that of all the imperial family. He not only, as Ferishta observes, began in cruelty, but waded through blood to the end. He abandoned himself at the same time to the most unbridled voluptuousness, and courted the favour of the omrahs by leaving them also at full liberty to indulge their licentious propensities. Yet the fame of Allah as a warrior stood in the foremost rank. Before mounting the throne, he had begun his military career by marching with a corps of 8000 men against Deoghire or Dowlatabad, capital of the great kingdom of Aurungabad. Causing it to be believed that this force was only the vanguard of the main army, he intimidated the city into a surrender; put to flight a vast body of troops assembled for its defence; and returned laden with a treasure which had been accumulating for ages. He afterwards sent his vizier, Kafoor, to conquer the Carnatic and other southern kingdoms,—an undertaking which proved completely successful, and produced a plunder that has been estimated, doubtless extravagantly high, at £100,000,000 sterling.

Cruelty of the new sovereign.

Invasion of the Mongols.

Allah found a more legitimate occasion of triumph in repelling the invasion of the Mongols (whom the historians of India call Moguls), successors to Zingis, who had formed a kingdom in Mavar-ul-Nahar. Their first army was met in Lahore, and completely defeated by Elich, the emperor's brother. Two years after, they poured in a force of two hundred thousand men, which they loudly boasted would effect the conquest of all India. Every thing gave way before them as far as Delhi, which was crowded to excess with multitudes seeking refuge from

CHAP. VII. A.D. 1298.

Defeat of the Mongols.

this barbarous invader. Allah, having mustered his forces, marched out to battle. Ziffer, the greatest of his generals, at the head of the right wing and of the elephants, charged with such impetuosity, that the enemy were completely broken and pursued for many miles. Not being duly supported, however, he fell into an ambuscade, where he was surrounded and killed; yet the Moguls had suffered so severely that they did not resume the attack, but immediately retreated westward. It was suspected, as being not at all inconsistent with the character of Allah, that he was instrumental in this desertion of his own brave commander, and considered his fall almost as great an advantage as the defeat of the enemy.

Projects of the emperor.

The emperor, intoxicated with success, began to conceive the most extravagant projects. Two in particular were deeply and fondly cherished. He hoped to emulate at once the glory of Mohammed and Alexander, names which in the East stand above those of all other men. Although so ignorant that he could neither read nor write, he undertook to prepare for the human race a new religion, which was to unite the Moslem and the disciple of Brahma in one common worship. Next, he was to leave a viceroy to rule over India, and to set out himself, like a second Macedonian, to conquer the world. His flatterers applauded, and men of sense, overawed by his furious temper, withdrew and were silent. At length Alla-ul-Mulluck, the aged and venerable magistrate of Delhi, determined at all hazards that the truth should for once be heard by this formidable despot. Being summoned to the palace, he entered on a full discussion of these two insane projects; beginning with the theological scheme, whereby, as a Mohammedan, he had been struck with the deepest horror. He did not dwell on Allah's utter incapacity for the task, but urged the impossibility of commanding the minds of men on such a subject,—the alienation which this attempt would produce among the Moslems, on whom alone he could rely,—and the hopelessness of converting the Hindoos, who had resisted

Alla-ul-Mulluck.

so many successive invaders. As to the plan of conquest, he reminded him that his possession of India itself was by no means secure,—that many districts were still unsubdued,—and that even in his immediate dominions there were various elements of dissension;—nay, that the empire, in his absence, would probably pass from him either by revolt or invasion, while he would have a very doubtful chance of gaining another in its place. Allah, who did not want strong natural sense, meditated on this remonstrance; and instead, as was expected, of cutting off the head of his sage adviser, acknowledged the justice of his observations, and dismissed from his mind for ever these two chimerical designs. Although the emperor had thus shown a certain portion of wisdom, his mode of governing was still very loose and irregular; giving rise to repeated insurrections, to one of which he had very nearly fallen a sacrifice. This event so strongly affected his mind, that he determined upon completely reforming his method of rule. He suppressed the license of the grandees, and introduced so rigid an administration of justice, that the merchant, formerly exposed to every species of spoliation, now travelled in safety from Bengal to Cabul, and from Cape Comorin to Cashmere. He renounced the use of wine, emptied his cellars into the street, and compelled his omrahs to imitate his example; so that Delhi for several days streamed with that precious liquor. The collectors of the revenue, who had been amassing large fortunes, were reduced to a bare subsistence. Yet this improved system was accompanied with many relics of a blind and violent despotism. He employed spies to give information of the most secret incidents in the interior of families, and in the remotest provinces. The omrahs were not permitted to marry, or even to entertain a company of friends, without a written authority from him; and by fines and confiscations levied on various pretences he ruined a number of the overgrown nobles. He reduced the pay of the army; but that the soldiers might not suffer, he undertook to lower the prices of grain and other necessaries in the

Good sense of the emperor.

Singular reform.

System of spies.

CHAP. VII.

A. D. 1300.

same proportion; and for this purpose issued edicts, and adopted the most violent measures, which, though of course abortive, must have occasioned great inconvenience and oppression. To diminish the value of horses, he prohibited every one from keeping them beyond a certain time; and many poor dealers, accused of contravening this arbitrary statute, were whipped or put to death.

General character of his reign.

In spite of all this, the strict administration of justice, and the check put on the licentious domination of the omrahs, made his reign at this period be regarded as a blessing by the great body of the people. Allah even showed a desire for that higher species of glory which is derived from letters. He invited to his court the most eminent men; and the presence of Casi Molana, Corami, and Cuzi Biana, with other sages, was considered as rendering this one of the most brilliant eras of Mohammedan literature.

Late attention to literature.

The emperor himself, ashamed of his profound ignorance, applied with such zeal to acquire the first elements of knowledge, that he was soon able to read the Persian language. Still it was a very delicate affair for these sages to hold conversation with the monarch without making him sensible of his own extreme deficiency. Nicer still was the duty of expounding to him the Mohammedan law, to which his practice formed in many respects a complete contrast; yet this is said to have been done faithfully, though not without fear and trembling.

Love adventures.

The history of Allah contains some record of love-adventures, which may afford an idea how this branch of the imperial economy was conducted:—On taking Nahrwalla, the capital of Guzerat, he became possessed of the wives as well as of the treasure of its unfortunate prince.

Cumladè.

Among the former was Cumladè, universally esteemed the flower of India, and who, by her beauty, wit, and accomplishments, so charmed the conqueror, that, regardless of all other ties, he made her his queen. She does not seem to have felt her situation very irksome, since she afterwards expressed an earnest wish to be joined by her daughter, Dewildè, then thirteen years of age, and who had succeeded her mother in the reputation

CHAP. VII.

A. D. 1300.

of being the greatest beauty in the East. Allah readily undertook to satisfy her, and sent his general, Alip, with a strong army to bring the young princess to Delhi, without any reference to her own or her father's inclinations. These, it seems, happened to point in a different direction; for Dewildè was found already on her journey to be united to Singeldeo, prince of the Deccan. Alip, aware that he had to deal with one who accepted no excuse, pushed on with such speed, that he overtook and completely defeated the escort. They fled into the mountains, but were met by a party of the imperial troops. A combat ensued, the fair object of which, being herself in the field, had her horse pierced by an arrow; and she might have fallen, had not her women by their screams made known who she was, when the assailants paused, and received her with the utmost respect. The beautiful captive was immediately conveyed to her mother at Delhi, where Chizer, the emperor's son, became enamoured of her; their loves are said to have been happy, and to have inspired one of the most elegant effusions of the poet Chusero.

Her daughter Dewildè.

Another attempt which Allah made to gratify a similar passion had a less fortunate issue. Having defeated and taken captive the Rajah of Chittore, one of the greatest Rajpoot princes, he offered him liberty on the condition of adding to the imperial seraglio his daughter, reputed one of the most beautiful and accomplished princesses of the age. The rajah, overcome by his distress, gave a reluctant consent; but the young lady, regarding this proposal as full of the deepest dishonour, obtained leave to make trial of a plan which she had contrived for saving her father. She announced her readiness to accede to the marriage, and having procured a passport from the imperial court, fitted out a long train of close travelling-chairs, in the most splendid of which she herself was understood to take her seat. The procession advanced to Delhi, and on its arrival an earnest request was made on the part of the princess that she should without delay be allowed an interview with her

Rage of Chittore's daughter

CHAP. VII. A. D. 1316.

parent. A petition so natural was readily granted; and the whole train was admitted into his prison. The chairs being then opened, presented, not a fair retinue of female attendants, but, like the Trojan horse, a band of hardy warriors clad in full armour, who instantly cut in pieces the guards, snatched up the monarch, and having placed him on a swift horse, soon eluded pursuit.

Close of Allah's career.

Allah, towards the end of his life, abandoned himself again to dissolute habits, and is suspected to have been poisoned by Kafoor, his profligate favourite, who immediately put out the eyes of his sons Chizer and Shadi, and undertook to reign himself in the name of Omar, an infant. But he was soon assassinated; and in the year 1316 the crown was placed on the head of Mubarick I., one of the emperor's sons.

Mubarick I.

There seem to have existed hitherto in the Patan dynasty certain hereditary rules of good government, to which even bad men, after the first crimes that raised them to the throne, seldom failed to conform. Allah broke the series, and his wicked example was but too faithfully followed. Mubarick, during a reign of three years, disgraced himself by plunging into all those excesses of debauchery which have consigned to infamy the names of Nero and Heliogabalus. At length Chusero, an abandoned courtier, hired a band of ruffians, and having entered his sleeping-apartment, seized him by the hair, and engaged in a desperate struggle, the issue of which his extraordinary strength would have rendered doubtful, had not one of the conspirators cut off his head with a sabre. The murderer now attempted to reign, but India was not yet sunk so low as to endure his usurpation. An insurrection was raised, and the wretch, deserted by all his adherents, fled into a tomb, where he was put to death. Amid this confusion, Tuglick, a slave belonging to the warlike border-tribe of the Jits, seized the opportunity of ascending the throne. Like all the sovereigns derived from this low origin, he ruled well and wisely; and it was a misfortune to the empire when, at the end of four years, he was killed by the accidental fall of a pavilion.

His assassination.

Tuglick.

CHAP. VII.

A.D. 1323.

Mohammed III.

Tuglick was succeeded by his son Jonah, who assumed the title of Mohammed III.; but instead of following his father's example, his crimes surpassed those of his most guilty predecessors, and made him, during a reign of twenty-seven years, the execration of the East. Mubarick was a monster of debauchery,—Mohammed of cruelty. His actions exceeded in atrocity the greatest enormities of the worst of the Cæsars. On conceiving umbrage at any class of the inhabitants, he assembled his warriors as for a hunt, then told them that men, not animals, were to be the objects of chase. The devoted district was subjected to military execution; the people were massacred, their eyes were put out, or their heads were carried to Delhi and suspended in rows along the walls. Among his minor oppressions were those of grinding the cultivator with enormous taxes, and debasing the coin; and when by these proceedings he had driven the farmers in large bodies to abandon the fields, he became enraged, and set out on one of his bloody hunts. Notwithstanding, he professed himself a friend to religion and a patron of learned men; he was besides energetic, temperate, attentive to business, suppressed vigorously the rebellions which his cruelty excited, and continued during his life to tyrannize over India.

Horrible cruelties.

Oppressions.

Plans of conquest.

This prince seems in many respects to have followed the evil example of Allah. The conquest of the world, which the one only meditated and wisely renounced, the other actually attempted. He began by sending a hundred thousand men against China; but in advancing through the steeps and defiles of the Himmaleh, for which they seem to have been entirely unprepared, they suffered so severely that the greater part of them perished, and only a handful returned to Delhi. He had prepared also an immense force for the conquest of Khorasan and Mavar-ul-Nahar, comprehending the territories of Samarcand and Bokhara; but the alarm of insurrection at home deterred him from this wild expedition. Rebellion stalked round him on every side, and shook almost all his provinces; yet his energy, military skill,

CHAP. VII. A.D. 1351. and barbarity, enabled him to suppress it, and to maintain his reign of terror. Only the noble and distant kingdom of the Deccan, the conquest of Allah, finally

His ambition. defied all his efforts. Such was his eagerness for its preservation, that he at one time relinquished the grandeur of imperial Delhi, and removed his court and residence to Deoghire, the tributary capital, which he named Dowlatabad, or the Fortunate City. The pressure of circumstances, however, compelled him to resume his wonted seat of government, and he ultimately saw the Deccan formed into an independent monarchy. Hassen Caco, a Mogul chieftain, assumed the title of Allah I., and became the founder of a mighty dynasty. Mohammed, it appears, had at length resolved to adopt a milder system; but death interrupted him before he could realize his intentions, and delivered India from the dreadful scourge of his government in the year 1351.

Ferose III. This monarch was succeeded by his cousin, Ferose III., a prince happily of a very different temper. Under him the arts of peace flourished and the rights of humanity were respected. He is said to have built thirty reservoirs for irrigation, a hundred bridges, forty mosques, thirty colleges, with many other works of splendour and

His wise and vigorous rule utility. He has been accused of being unwarlike, yet he showed no want of vigour in suppressing the few insurrections which arose under his government. In a particular case he was even charged with an excess of severity. That he did not attempt to reconquer the Deccan, a great kingdom, now firmly established under a powerful sovereign, was probably a resolution as wise and beneficial for his people as it was for himself. India, during his reign of thirty-eight years, enjoyed a respite from her many calamities; industry reared its head; but after his removal the empire was involved in fresh disasters.

Tuglick II. The short reigns of Tuglick II., Abu Bicker, and Mohammed IV., exemplified the precarious nature of oriental power. Mahmoud III. was a minor; the crown was disputed by Nuserit, grandson to Ferose III., and almost all the provinces were setting up for independence, when, in the year 1397, India was assailed by an enemy whom her utmost strength, guided by her ablest monarchs, would scarcely have been able to resist.

Timur.

Timur (whom we shall not, with Colonel Briggs, name Teimoor) was certainly one of the most remarkable among the conquerors of Asia. If his career of invasion did not, like that of Zingis, include China and Muscovy, his successes in India, Persia, and the Turkish empire, which he almost totally subverted, brought him more conspicuously into the view of the western world. High panegyrics have been pronounced in the East on his justice and humanity; and these have been studiously repeated by the long line of princes who derived their lineage from his house. Timur, it is true, in the Book of Institutes written at least with his sanction, shows some correct ideas as to the duties of a sovereign, which, in a formal dissertation, he endeavours to prove that he himself had signally fulfilled. Yet he numbers among them extensive conquest, the spreading of Islamism by dint of arms, and the most rigid enforcement of his own despotic principles. He even applauds the maxim, that when a prince has commanded any thing, though he become sensible that it is wrong, he ought not the less to urge the mandate, lest his authority should be in any degree compromised. His partisans boast of his humanity to a submissive enemy; but this submission he required to be at once instant and entire,—such as could scarcely ever be expected from a country wantonly invaded. His mercy seldom availed to protect a people from the horrors of conquest; and his triumph usually appeared in indiscriminate massacre and huge pyramids of heads reared as proofs of victory. To go round the world exterminating nations with the words of humanity in his mouth, seems more odious than even the blind and barbarous ravages of Genseric and Attila. That Timur, in the countries subjected to his sway, might secure a regular administration of justice, and study to promote the public prosperity, may be believed, since this, in oriental

Character of his clemency

CHAP. VII. — A. D. 1397. history, is often combined with the most boundless and savage ambition. Yet the narrative of Clavijo the Spanish ambassador, who visited his court at Samarcand and describes its rude pomp, shows that his system of rule was thoroughly despotic. For example, he sent one day for the governor of the city, and, charging him with having abused his trust, caused him to be beheaded without a moment's delay; and two chiefs who had ventured to intercede for the sufferer shared the same fate. Having once ordered a broad street to be formed in twenty days, the workmen began with such furious haste, demolishing every house that stood in their way, that the owners had scarcely time to remove with their most precious effects. They humbly requested some small compensation; but he sternly replied that all Samarcand belonged to him. When his couriers halted at any stage, they immediately began to apply the whip in every direction till relays were furnished; and if they met a horse on the road which appeared to answer their purpose, they instantly seized it, striking off the owner's head if he offered any resistance.

Character of his rule.

Invasion of India.

Timur seems to have had no pretext for the invasion of India, except the desire of possessing it, and the hope of success afforded by its distracted condition. He set out from his capital in 1397, and advanced without difficulty along the immense plains of Bactria; after which he had to scale the tremendous barrier of the Indian Caucasus, whose steep and rugged passes were peculiarly unfit for the march of the Scythian horsemen. He scornfully disdained to use any means for conciliating the fierce and warlike natives; they accordingly opposed him at every step, and, though they could not arrest his progress, they inflicted upon him extensive losses. Yet it appears an exaggeration to say, that there were certain points where he could not advance without being lowered down from the cliffs by means of ropes. His cavalry, it is obvious, could not proceed in such a country, or be aided by any such expedients; and if there was a road for them, he might follow on foot. At length having crossed the Indus, he marched towards Moultan, already occupied by his nephew, Peer Mohammed, who had, however, been hard pressed by the Patan omrahs, especially the governor of Batneir; and by joining his forces to those of his relative, he became superior in the field. It was determined to begin with the capture of Batneir, a fortress considered almost impregnable, yet he went against it with only 10,000 of his chosen veterans. The troops within the walls, encouraged by the smallness of his numbers, marched out and gave battle; but they could not withstand the shock of the Mogul cavalry, who pursued them to the city, entered it along with them, and were soon masters of all except the citadel. He then ordered the execution of five hundred of those who had shown the greatest enmity to his nephew; a barbarous deed, which drove the Hindoos, who still held the fort, into a phrensy of desperation. They immediately set fire to the place, killed their wives and children, then rushed wildly forth to sell their lives as dearly as possible. Every individual perished, yet not before several thousands of the Moguls had fallen,—a loss by which their leader was so exasperated, that he gave orders for an indiscriminate massacre.

Capture of Batneir.

His barbarity.

The conqueror, collecting all his forces, now advanced upon Delhi, ravaging the country as he passed; and whatever good might have been displayed by him elsewhere, India knew him only in crime and terror. Finding himself encumbered with an enormous multitude of captives, and alarmed lest they should rise against him, he issued the horrid mandate for a general butchery; and a hundred thousand are said to have been forthwith put to death.

Advance on Delhi.

Mahmoud having shut himself up in Delhi with 40,000 foot and 10,000 horse, the invader became apprehensive that if his opponent should resolve to remain with this large force in a strongly-fortified position, the siege might be arduous, or at least ruinously protracted. To allure him into the field, he directed that only small parties should present themselves in front, with a studied dis-

Dreadful butchery.

CHAP. VII. A. D. 1400.

play of weakness and timidity, as if only waiting a serious attack to commence their retreat. The Mohammedan fell into the snare, marched out, and presented his whole army, with a numerous body of elephants, drawn up in battle array. The fortune of the field was then in the hands of the Tartar; his troops, rendered hardy and skilful by a life of warfare, were opposed only to an effeminate and tumultuary crowd, who were instantly broken and pursued to the gates of the city. The emperor fled into Guzerat, while his capital submitted and received a foreign garrison. Historians vary as to the extent of Timur's guilt in the fatal scene which ensued. The adherents of the Mogul dynasty assert, that while the victor was celebrating a great festival in his camp, he was surprised by the view of the flames ascending from the town. Ferishta, however, gives more credit, and seemingly with reason, to the report, that some of his troops having acted with violence towards the citizens, the latter killed several of their number, upon which the barbarian gave up this immense metropolis to an unrestrained pillage. The unhappy Hindoos, in a state of distraction, slew their females, then rushed out upon the enemy; but the efforts of this undisciplined crowd availed nothing against the warlike array of the Moguls; the streets soon streamed with blood; and, after a short contest, the natives were led captive by hundreds from the desolate walls.

Capture of Delhi.

Progress through India.

Timur, under what impulse does not appear, instead of advancing into the rich countries of Oude and Bengal, directed his march towards the Upper Ganges, and reached that river near Hurdwar. He then suddenly formed the resolution of retracing his steps, and proceeded along the lower borders of the Himmaleh range, maintaining severe combats with its brave inhabitants, and every where marking his path with blood. Having suppressed an insurrection at Lahore, he recrossed the Indus, and entered without delay upon the grand expedition in which he vanquished Bajazet and laid prostrate for a time the rising empire of the Ottomans.

After his departure, he exercised scarcely any authority over India. Money was indeed coined in his name, and its princes owned themselves nominally his vassals; but in other respects his inroad served only to aggravate the anarchy under which that hapless empire was doomed to groan. The governor of each province asserted a temporary independence; while Delhi, for some time abandoned, began to be repeopled, and passed from one hand to another. Mahmoud sometimes resigned himself to a private station, and then renewed his efforts to resume the rank of emperor; nor was it till 1413, when he died, and Chizer, viceroy of Moultan, seized the throne, and held it as the representative of Timur, that any amelioration was felt. This governor conducted affairs with vigour and wisdom, and the empire began to recover its wonted form and strength. There was no longer indeed any attempt to comprehend in it Bengal, Guzerat, or the Deccan; but it still comprised Delhi, Agra, with the other provinces of Hindostan Proper, and even held by a precarious tenure those of Moultan and Lahore.

Distracted state of India.

There are few remarkable features in the race of princes who now succeeded. Mubarick, after a mild and rather enlightened administration of thirteen years, was assassinated by his vizier. The weak reigns of Mohammed V. and Allah II. had nearly dissolved the empire, when it was seized and held for thirty-eight years by the firm hand of Bheloli. His son, Secunder I., supported his reputation; but Ibrahim II., who followed, though vigorous and brave, was unpopular. He was therefore very ill prepared for the great crisis which impended over the country.

Race of princes that succeeded him.

After the death of Timur and his accomplished son, Shah Rokh, his vast dominion fell to pieces. Not only were its distant provinces severed, but its original domain of Transoxiana was split into portions, for which the different branches of his family eagerly contended. The territory of Kokaun, or Ferghana, a fine valley nearly enclosed by mountains, and extending along the Upper Jaxartes, was inherited by a son of a great-grandson of Timur, aged only twelve, named Baber.

Fate of his dominion.

CHAP. VII.

This youth proved perhaps the most singular personage in oriental history. He was the knight-errant of Asia, and spent his whole life in losing or winning kingdoms. The adventures which the romance-writers of the Middle Ages ascribe to their heroes were realized in him. At one moment he was ruler of a great empire, in the next he had scarcely a hut to shelter him; now he was at the head of a numerous army, and now he was scarcely able to muster a hundred adherents. Once, when ejected from his native land, and seeing his followers reduced to two hundred and forty, he determined to attack Samarcand, the military capital of Asia, and defended by a strong army. He approached at midnight, scaled the walls, was joined by a number of friends, made the city resound with shouts of victory, and produced such an alarm, that Shubiani the sovereign fled, abandoning his metropolis and dominions to Baber, who held them for a considerable time. Driven afterwards from this and other possessions, and having no longer any district which owned his power, he resolved to carry war into Cabul. The state of anarchy in which that country was involved made the people eagerly welcome a chief of vigorous character and high reputation, who might suppress the rival claims by which it was distracted. On the same grounds he was invited to Candahar. A formidable insurrection was raised against him; but challenging successively five omrahs, he slew them in single combat, when the hostile army was moved with such admiration that they at once submitted.

Baber.

Singular adventures.

Attacks Cabul.

Expeditions into India.

Baber having established himself in Cabul, undertook several expeditions to the borders of Hindostan, and the countries on the Indus. A considerable time, however, elapsed ere, in his own figurative language, he finally "placed his footstep in the stirrup of resolution," and stood forth as a candidate for the imperial throne. He marched upon Delhi with only 13,000 horse, while Ibrahim came to meet him with a hundred thousand cavalry and a thousand elephants; but the bravery and experience of the hardy sons of the mountains more than compensated the inequality of numbers. The Moslems, ignorant of the military art, drew up their army in one extended line, which the active charge of the Moguls soon threw into confusion. The emperor, however, gallantly advancing in person with his chosen troops, attacked the enemy's centre, where the combat was almost confined to the two competitors for the sovereignty. But he fell in the midst of the fight; all his army fled; and Baber, in the year 1526, seated himself on the throne of Delhi.

Acquires the throne of Delhi.

This closed the dynasty, or rather the successive dynasties, of the Patan sovereigns. During the three hundred years that they occupied the throne of India, there was scarcely one family which swayed the sceptre for three generations. Not a few were slaves purchased from the regions of Afghanistan and Tartary, raised to high office by imperial favour, and to the empire by crime and treason. No country could be in a more humbled state than India during this long period; the slave of slaves, trampled upon by a foreign soldiery bigotedly hostile to all her creeds and institutions; and yet so mysteriously are human things ordered, that with the exception of a few partial shocks, and some short intervals of misrule, she was, throughout this era, well governed, prosperous, and happy.

Close of the Afghan dynasty.

CHAPTER VIII.

The Mogul Dynasty to Aurengzebe.

Baber—His Death and Character—Humaioon—His Exploits—Driven from the Empire—Misfortunes—Reign of Shere—Humaioon returns, and again mounts the Throne—Akbar succeeds—His daring Achievements—Mode of governing—Ayeen Akberry—Portuguese Missions from Goa—Reign of Jehangire—Visit of Hawkins—Embassy of Sir Thomas Roe—The Mogul Court—Rebellions against Jehangire—His Death—Reign of Shah Jehan—Rebellion of Lodi—Sons of Shah Jehan—Their Contests for the Sovereignty—Success of Aurengzebe—Dethrones his Father and becomes Emperor.

CHAP. VIII.

A. D. 1526.

Baber.

BABER was now seated on the throne of India; but it was not as yet either secure or firmly established. The Patan omrahs, holding sway each in his separate province, detested the Mogul rule as a foreign usurpation, while they had gained to their interest the leading Rajpoot princes, the bravest part of the Hindoo population. An army of 100,000 men was mustered in the west, headed by Mahmoud, brother to the late emperor. The young ruler, surrounded on all sides by open enemies or false allies, and having none on whom he could repose confidence except the small band whom he had brought down from the mountains, was in a truly critical position. His troops were struck with panic; some even of his boldest captains advised him to retreat into Cabul, or at least to the provinces on the Indus. But his lofty spirit indignantly repelled the idea of renouncing without a struggle so great an empire. He proclaimed that the voice of honour was loud in his ear, and with an enthusiasm which communicated itself to his adherents, exclaimed, " Since

His daring spirit.

death is inevitable, it is glorious to meet him with courage, face to face, rather than to shrink back, to gain a few years of a miserable and ignominious existence; since what can we inherit but fame beyond the limits of the grave;"—quoting to the same effect some verses from the Shah Nameh. Availing himself of the circumstance that a great proportion of the enemy professed the Hindoo faith, he appealed to the religious zeal of his troops, and made them swear on the Koran to conquer or die. There were some particulars in his own life which ill fitted him for acting the part of a Moslem champion; but he made a vow henceforth to renounce the use of wine, in which he had profusely indulged; and the golden goblets which had graced the imperial banquets were broken in pieces and given to the poor.

Influence of religious zeal.

Baber, having thus duly seasoned the minds of his troops, proceeded to the military arrangements, which he conducted with singular ability. The enemy had an immense superiority in brave though not highly-disciplined cavalry; while he had only bands of light horse, fitted rather for pursuit and plunder than for the duties of a regular field. His chief strength consisted in a body of musketeers and a train of artillery; forces hitherto little employed in the wars of India. The cannon, ranged in front, and chained together, presented a kind of wall to the enemy. Behind were the infantry, while squadrons of horsemen filled the intervals. Early in the morning the Patan army advanced, spread their wings, and enveloped the little phalanx opposed to them. But, by means of his fire-arms and guns, he repelled the attacks which they continued to make during a great part of the day. At length, when he saw them exhausted and dispirited by repeated repulses, he collected two brigades of chosen troops, and led them on to a grand charge, before which the whole adverse army gave way, and many of its most distinguished chiefs remained dead on the field of battle.

Great military skill.

Total rout of his adversaries.

Although this powerful confederacy against him was thus entirely broken, the descendant of Timur did not

CHAP. VIII. A.D. 1530

yet hold peaceful possession of the great throne which he had ascended. He was disturbed by insurrections both in India and in Cabul; and at length, after reigning as emperor only five years, he died in 1530.

Baber's character.

Baber may be ranked as the most accomplished prince that ever ruled over Hindostan, although not perhaps either the greatest or the best. His valour was brilliant; and several of his exploits are considered as surpassing even the most heroic of those achieved by his renowned ancestor. Yet his talents are observed to have been rather those of a daring partisan than of a skilful leader. He was almost as often defeated as victorious, and for a long period lost kingdoms as fast as he won them. But in the latter part of his reign his military policy seems to have assumed a more fixed character, and in the great battles on the plains of Hindostan he showed no want of the most consummate generalship. His bodily strength and dexterity both in sports and warlike exercises are described as almost preternatural. He was a master in the arts of poetry and music; and the Commentaries in which he has related the events of his own life, and of which Doctor Leyden and Mr Erskine have furnished an excellent translation, though they display not any profound habits of philosophical reflection, manifest much strong sense, combined with an active spirit of observation, as applied to the various scenes which passed before him. They exhibit also an interesting view of the manners of oriental courts and camps. The high moral qualities which have been ascribed to him appear somewhat more problematical. His disposition was amiable, generous, and open; and though his conduct in the field was stained by some examples of the barbarity incident to his nation, clemency and humanity were often signally displayed even towards his most inveterate enemies. His protection of mercantile caravans, on occasions when the laws of war would have authorized him to plunder them, and thus to supply his most urgent wants, marks an equitable and liberal disposition. Yet we nowhere see in him the pleasing picture of a monarch devoting

His generalship. His commentaries. His virtues.

CHAP. VIII. A. D. 1530.

himself in peace to the improvement of his country and the happiness of his people,—a spectacle so repeatedly exhibited even by the slave-sovereigns of the Patan dynasty. It is true the unsettled state of his fortunes left him little leisure for these tranquil and benignant cares; yet this also was owing in no small degree to his restless temper, which impelled him continually to new schemes of conquest and personal aggrandizement. Although, at one period of his life, he rigidly abstained from wine, he afterwards indulged to great excess, and even gives a disgusting account of the orgies celebrated with his jovial comrades; irregularities which appear to have shortened his life, though they never diverted his attention from affairs of state.

Baber's successor.

Baber bequeathed his troubled empire to his son Humaioon, an amiable and accomplished prince, possessed of refined though somewhat fantastic tastes. He was particularly devoted to the study of the heavenly bodies, which in that age and country was much tinctured with judicial astrology. He fitted up seven halls of reception, and dedicated one to each of the planets. Military commanders were received in the hall of Mars, judges and secretaries in that of Mercury, ambassadors, poets, and travellers in the hall of the Moon. From these recreations he was roused by the urgent cares of empire, to which he showed himself fully equal. He was soon involved in war with Bahadur, who had obtained the sovereignty of Guzerat. A mistaken religious zeal induced him to leave that prince unmolested while engaged in hostilities against the Pagan prince of Chittore; but he now advanced with so great a force, and conducted operations so ably, that the other was obliged to retreat into Guzerat, unable to meet his antagonist in the field. He next fled to Ahmedabad, having deposited his treasures in Chupanni, which was then considered an almost impregnable fortress. The young emperor, however, at the head of a chosen band, mounted the face of the perpendicular rock by fixing in it iron spikes, and carried the place by surprise,—an exploit still celebrated as equal to any achieved

Astrology.

Bahadur, Sovereign of Guzerat, defeated.

CHAP VIII. A. D. 1530. either by Timur or Baber. After this glorious termination of his first war, he might have expected a peaceful and prosperous reign; but it was speedily disturbed by his brothers, Camiran and Hindal, who were emboldened in their criminal designs by his excessive mildness and lenity. Having divisions of the army placed under their command, they successively laid claim to the supreme power. These dissensions encouraged Shere Khan, a Patan chief, still in possession of Bengal, to advance with a powerful host against Humaioon; who, unable from the distracted state of his affairs to muster a sufficient force, was worsted, and returned in a discomfited condition to Agra. The brothers, seeing that their disunion was about to produce the ruin of their house, rallied round the emperor, though not with the requisite cordiality. This last, having recruited his ranks, marched against Shere, but was again completely defeated, obliged to abandon his capital, and to seek refuge among the minor princes on the border. Few, however, remained faithful to the fallen monarch. After being obliged to flee from several courts, he sought protection in that of Maldeo, who had been the most urgent in his proffers of amity and alliance; but finding that this base chief had resolved to seize and deliver him to the enemy, he felt himself compelled to remove instantly with his few remaining adherents across the Western Desert to the banks of the Indus. In this march he experienced a pressure of calamity such as scarcely ever befell even the most unfortunate princes of the East. His horse having dropped down dead with fatigue and thirst, the lord of the world could not procure another, till a common trooper desired his own mother to quit that on which she rode, and give it to him. After suffering dreadful agonies from want of water, the party came to a well in which there was abundance; but they had only one bucket, and when it was drawn up, such crowds rushed forward, that, the rope breaking, it fell to the bottom, and several were precipitated after it. Meantime the rearguard was repeatedly obliged to turn and repulse the enemy, who

Insurrection.

Complete defeat of the emperor

Extreme sufferings.

pursued close behind. Many of them perished ere they reached Amercot, on the opposite boundary of the desert. In the depth of this calamity, it was announced to the emperor that his sultana had given birth to a son, the celebrated Akbar, afterwards the greatest prince of the East; but meantime he was obliged to pursue his flight, leaving his infant child to fall into the hands of a treacherous chief, by whom he was delivered over to Camiran, his brother and mortal enemy.

Hospitality of the Shah of Persia.

Humaioon sought refuge in Persia, and was received with the most magnificent hospitality by Shah Tamasp, who enabled him even to maintain the outward forms of imperial rank. Having agreed to embrace the Shiite creed or heresy, which in that country is held the only true faith, he was furnished with ten thousand men, to be employed in the recovery of his lost empire. He marched first into Cabul, where he was again encountered by fraternal rivalry, that province having been usurped by Camiran. He next advanced and laid siege to Candahar, which soon surrendered to him, when he proceeded with a superior force against Cabul. There his brother awaited his approach; and, on his arrival, exhibited on the walls his boy Akbar bound to a funeral-pile, intimating that he would forthwith put the child to death if the father should proceed to an attack upon the city. The latter, unmoved by this painful spectacle, expressed his determination to persevere, only adding the most dreadful threats if the horrid deed were perpetrated. The barbarian renounced his meditated crime, and, with his adherents, commenced a retreat. Humaioon entered the gates, embraced the young prince, and found himself again a king. He reigned nine years in that city, though constantly harassed by his relative, who, after reducing him repeatedly to great distress, was at last completely vanquished.

Recovers his kingdom.

Shere Khan.

Meantime Shere had become undisputed master of the empire, and extended its limits on every side. He swayed the sceptre wisely and well; at which the Mogul historians are astonished, considering the treason by

CHAP. VIII. which he gained it; but, as a Patan, he owed only a
A. D. 1547. very slight allegiance to the house of Baber. His arrangements for the accommodation of travellers, which, in the East, devolve generally upon the sovereign, were on a scale of which no former reign afforded an example.

His virtuous government.

Across the entire breadth of Hindostan, from the Ganges to the Indus, there was formed a high-road bordered with fruit-trees, with a well every two miles, and caravanseras at every stage, where the traveller was accommodated at the public expense. Justice was maintained inviolate; general security reigned; and his death, at the end of five years, was considered a national calamity.

His successor Selim.

His son, Selim, supplied his place nine years, though neither with equal wisdom nor ability; but when he died, leaving his heir a minor, the empire, during the short reigns of Mohammed and Ibrahim, was distracted by dissensions among the royal family, and by the revolt of numerous omrahs and viceroys. The friends of Humaioon then assured him, that his appearance with an army in any degree formidable would at once lay in the dust this ill-cemented dominion. Not being yet very firmly seated on the throne of Cabul, he felt considerable hesitation in answering this call; but at length he mustered 15,000 horse, and marched to the Indus, where Byram, his best general, joined him with a body of veterans from Candahar.

Encounter with Tartar Khan.

The army having crossed the river, first encountered Tartar Khan, governor of Lahore, whom Byram surprised and defeated. Meantime the Patan omrahs had placed on the throne Secunder, nephew to Shere, a prince qualified to lead them with vigour and talent. Having assembled 80,000 men, he proceeded to meet the invader; and the battle was fought with an obstinacy suitable to the great prize for which the parties contended. On the side of the Moguls, it was conducted with energy and prudence by Humaioon and Byram; but it was chiefly distinguished for the splendid heroism exhibited by the young Akbar, then scarcely thirteen, whose example inspired the troops with almost supernatural

Heroism of Akbar.

ardour. The Patan host was at length completely routed and dispersed, and Secunder fled into the mountains of the north, leaving all the fine plain of Hindostan open to the conqueror.

Humaioon gains his father's throne.

Humaioon advanced to Delhi, and seated himself on his father's throne, from which he had been thirteen years excluded. He mounted it, however, only that he might die in possession; for in less than a year after, descending the marble stairs of the palace, he fell, and was so severely bruised that he expired in a few days. He was a prince, brave, amiable, and learned, and his life was diversified with greater vicissitudes than that perhaps of any other eastern monarch. These are imputed in a great measure to his excessive lenity, especially towards brothers who ill deserved it; Ferishta even decides, that had he been a worse man, he would have been a greater ruler. No example, indeed, can afford a stronger apology for that cruelty which deforms the history of oriental kings. The principle of primogeniture, so firmly established in Europe, has there scarcely any hold on the feelings of the people; and any prince of the blood-royal, who can form a party, or become popular, may cherish the hope of expelling the reigning sovereign, and investing himself with the imperial purple.

Akbar's accession.

In 1556, Akbar began his reign of fifty-one years, during which he proved himself perhaps the greatest and wisest of all the monarchs who have swayed the sceptre of India. Seated, while yet a boy of thirteen, on the throne of so great an empire, he could not find his position very secure. The country teemed with rebellion, raised often by noblemen who had a better right than himself to the provinces for which they contended,—the Patan omrahs, the Rajpoot princes, and sometimes by his own discontented officers. These enemies he encountered with a display of talent and heroism somewhat better suited indeed to a knight-errant than to the commander of a great army. Marching to encounter the rebel chiefs of Bengal, he was impatient at finding himself separated from them by the Ganges, without any

CHAP. VIII. A. D. 1560.

means of transporting his army across that river. He suddenly conveyed to the other side a hundred chosen horse, and having collected a few adherents in the adjoining district, advanced directly to the attack. The enemy, considering themselves completely secured in their camp by the broad stream, had been indulging in mirth and festivity; so that the sound of the drums beating the imperial march struck them with amazement and panic, which, as usual in the undisciplined armies of the East, were soon followed by confusion. Akbar immediately rushed against the tents of the insurgent commander Zeman, who fell after a gallant resistance; and then the whole of his immense host, deprived of its head, fled in irretrievable rout before a handful of assailants.

Defeats the rebel chiefs of Bengal.

Rebellion of Mogul chiefs.

At another time, he received intelligence that some Mogul chiefs had raised a rebellion in Guzerat, and besieged Ahmedabad, the capital. He instantly despatched from Agra two thousand cavalry, whom he himself followed with a chosen troop, and marching at the rate of eighty miles daily, reached in little more than a week the scene of action. When the enemy's scouts, inquiring whose army it was, were informed that it was led by the king of kings, and brought the news to their camp, the rebels, struck with this event as almost miraculous, were with difficulty withheld from immediate flight. They were, however, compelled into the field; but, after a brisk action, were completely defeated, and their commander taken. Akbar, while his soldiers were engaged in the pursuit, remained with 200 men on the top of a hill, where he saw advancing against him a body of 5000 horse, whom the enemy had not been able to bring forward to the main battle. His officers urged the necessity of instant retreat; but, rejecting this ignoble counsel, he caused the imperial drums to beat, and led on his small detachment as if it had been the van of a great army. The others, thus deceived, fled, and were pursued for several miles. On the same day the emperor entered Ahmedabad, and the insurrection was finally

Their total defeat.

suppressed. On a different occasion, with not more than 150 horse, he attacked the rear of a large detachment, and gained some advantage, which struck the whole host with such astonishment that they dispersed in every direction. Having afterwards to contend with Daood, the suba of Bengal, he challenged him to single combat in so daring a manner, that the latter slunk off without venturing to face the emperor in the field.

CHAP. VIII.

A. D. 1565.

Estimate of Akbar's exploits.

These proceedings were much out of military rule, and unsuitable to the monarch of fifty millions of men, and the commander of a mighty army. Yet the Hindoos, and the Orientals in general, are wonderfully acted on by impressions of the marvellous, and are prone to exaggerate whatever has any tincture of that quality. The daring exploits of Akbar, therefore, invested him in their eyes with a mysterious and preternatural character, which withered the hearts of his enemies, and secured victory better than the most ably-conducted operations of a regular campaign. Thus he not only preserved the central provinces in complete tranquillity, but reduced Guzerat, Bengal, part of the Deccan, and nearly all that had ever been included under the Mohammedan dominion.

His literary labours.

One of his most valuable performances was the work called the Ayeen Akberry, which contains a complete survey of the empire, executed under his own direction and that of Abul Fazel, his able and enlightened minister. It comprises a full account of every thing connected with his dominions, government, and occupations, from the highest affairs of state down to the catching of partridges and the training and feeding of hawks; for even the games which served for the emperor's recreation afforded him, as he boasts, the opportunity of studying the temper of the officers whom he employed. The statistical details, describing the extent and productions of the different provinces, are of the greatest value. They seem to have been collected chiefly with a view to the regulation of the revenue, in which respect Akbar represents himself as having relieved the

Popular administration.

people from a great part of the taxes levied from them by his predecessors. Yet the portion which he himself exacted was by no means light, amounting to no less than a third of the whole produce of the land. He admits that under the ancient Hindoo administration the proportion was only a sixth, and in Iran or Persia only a tenth; but these governments, he maintains, imposed a number of other burdens, which pressed on the people with much greater severity. He, on the contrary, took off all the imposts except this one on the produce of land. Among those abolished, he enumerates a capitation-tax, poll-taxes on labourers and on fishermen, a tax on every kind of tree, on oxen, on the sale of cattle, with others either bearing hard on the poor, or obstructing the regular course of commerce. His system of finance, therefore, notwithstanding the large amount extorted by it, afforded probably a considerable relief to the great body of his subjects.

First Christian missionaries at the Mogul court.

During Akbar's reign, the first European mission of a religious nature arrived at the Mogul court. He appears not indeed to have attached himself to any particular faith, but to have felt an ardent curiosity respecting the different classes into which mankind were divided, and their respective forms of worship and belief. Having heard, therefore, of a new people from a distant region of the earth, professing a religion altogether different from any held in India, he expressed a desire to see and converse with them. A letter was sent to the Portuguese at Goa, requesting that certain missionaries would come with all the books of their law and gospel, assuring them of the most honourable reception. The name of the Mogul conveyed to European ears some impressions of terror; but the pious individuals selected for this duty determined that no such motives should induce them to decline an opening which might lead to important results. On the 3d December 1568, accordingly, three,—Aquaviva, Monserrate, and Enriques,—took their departure for Surat.

Having reached that capital, the missionaries, under

CHAP. VIII. A.D. 1568.

the escort of a body of horse, crossed first the Tuptee and then the Nerbudda; after which they passed Mandoo, which they concluded must have been one of the greatest cities in the world, as its ruins covered a space sixteen leagues in circumference. They next came to the large town of Ougein. On their way they had an opportunity of observing the superstitious practices of the Banians, who would neither kill nor witness the death of any living thing, and who, while they neglected the sick and infirm among their brethren, maintained highly-endowed hospitals for various species of birds and beasts. A Portuguese captain contrived to extort money by merely collecting a number of dogs, and threatening to kill them if a ransom were not paid. There were seen also in every town pyramids of various form and size, reared in memory of ladies who had burned themselves on the tombs of their husbands. The missionaries, from the peculiarity of their appearance and dress, were sometimes exposed to insult, and sometimes excited immoderate bursts of laughter; but the Mogul guard protected them from any serious annoyance. Bands of pilgrims were met coming from the ceremony of holy ablution in the Ganges, to obtain the full benefit of which they had been shaven all over. At length, on the 19th February, the Christians were received by a large body of troops mounted on horses, camels, and dromedaries, by whom they were honourably escorted to Futtypore, where the emperor then resided.

Extravagancies of the Banians.

Reception of the missionaries by Akbar.

Immediately upon their arrival they were admitted into the presence of Akbar, whom they describe as a man about fifty, of European complexion, and bearing on his countenance strong marks of intelligence. He gave them the most gracious reception; offering them every thing, even money, though he was greatly edified by their refusing it. When an image of the crucifixion was exhibited, he testified a respectful impartiality, by successively bowing, kneeling, and falling prostrate; conforming thus to the respective modes of Moslem, Christian, and Gentoo worship. He is described as having been dazzled, more

CHAP. VIII.

A. D. 1568.

than his character would lead us to expect, by a richly-ornamented image of the Virgin, which he declared to be indeed a worthy representation of the Queen of Heaven. Being presented with a Bible in four languages, he kissed it and placed it on his head. They then solicited the favour of a public controversy with the mollahs, or Mohammedan doctors. It was soon granted, and they are pleased to state that their arguments were completely triumphant; though they are compelled to admit that they made no impression on their blinded antagonists. The emperor, however, declared his satisfaction, and expressed himself so as to afford hope that he would ultimately prove a convert. But time passed on, and though he retained all his complaisance, he evaded, on various pretexts, taking any decisive step. At length one of the courtiers privately assured the missionaries that they were fed with vain hopes; that his majesty was merely gratified by having at his court persons of various characters and opinions, especially such as were odd and uncommon, without having the slightest idea of adopting their tenets. Indeed, from some circumstances mentioned by themselves, it may be suspected that he was not unwilling to find amusement at their expense. He informed them that a great Mohammedan doctor had undertaken to leap into a furnace with the Koran in his hand, and by sustaining this awful trial with impunity, to prove the superior excellence of his faith; he invited them to do the same with the Bible. The friars, who were not without some pretensions to supernatural power, were considerably embarrassed by this proposal. They urged, however, that after having so triumphantly supported the truth in successive conferences, which they were ready to repeat, it could not be justly expected that they should expose themselves to such an irrational and perilous test. Another disputation was held, which had the same issue as the foregoing; but Akbar returned to his proposal, undertaking that the mollah should leap in first, provided one of the friars would engage to follow; and hinting that he

Reception of the Bible.

Novel test of faith.

merely wished to see how the other would extricate himself from his daring pretensions; but, after deliberation, they wisely determined not to appeal to such a questionable criterion of religious faith. The emperor having been disappointed of this exhibition, and the attractions of novelty having worn off, he saw them more and more rarely; and his attention being finally distracted by insurrections which had broken out in Cabul and Bengal, he seemed wholly to forget his pious visiters; who, finding no longer any motive to protract their stay, returned to Goa in May 1583.

Return of the missionaries to Goa.

In 1591, he sent to request another mission, the members of which went through the same round as their predecessors, being well received, and finally neglected. Their stay was not of very long duration. Four years after he was again seized with a similar desire, and despatched a letter, with so many promises and kind expressions, that the government could not refuse to gratify him a third time. The court being then at Lahore, the Portuguese were obliged to proceed by Damaun to Cambay, and thence to cross the great Western Desert. Near the city just mentioned, they saw 20,000 persons setting out on a pilgrimage to the Ganges, and were considerably edified by their solemn and serious deportment. The wilderness was crossed in company with a large caravan, comprising 400 camels, a great body of horsemen, and multitudes on foot. After a dreary march of 220 leagues, the mission came to the banks of a fine stream, and on journeying ten leagues farther, reached Lahore, described as a delightful city. They were conducted to the imperial residence, situated on an island in the river, and were most graciously received. An image of the Virgin, studiously and splendidly adorned, and still more beautiful than that formerly presented, drew forth expressions of the deepest admiration. The hopes of the missionaries were raised still higher when they observed that Akbar showed so little partiality for the Mohammedan religion, that, when in want of money, he made no scruple to plunder the mosques. Yet they were dis-

Second missionary enterprise.

Pilgrims to the Ganges.

CHAP. VIII.

A. D. 1605.

couraged by observing the assiduous worship which he paid to the sun; they even accuse him of the folly of aspiring to a species of divinity in his own person. He presented himself every morning at a window, and saw the multitude fall prostrate before him; sick infants were also brought to receive his benediction; but perhaps they mistook for worship the profound testimonies of oriental homage. Finding no prospect of gaining their object, they took advantage of his departure for the seat of war in the Deccan, to accompany the army part of their way to Goa.

Akbar succeeded by his son.

Akbar died in 1605, after a reign of fifty-one years. He left only one son, named Selim, a prince of distinguished promise, who somewhat boastingly assumed the title of Jehangire, or Conqueror of the World. A powerful party intended to raise against him Chusero, his own son; but their intrigues were defeated, the prince was compelled to submit, and was forgiven. Soon after, however, having gained fresh adherents, he was encouraged to attempt the same object by force; though he still retained enough of good feeling to reject indignantly a plan for the assassination of the emperor, declaring that he would try the fortune of the field, but never ascend a throne stained with a father's blood. He had at first some success, laying waste the country between Delhi and Agra; but being overtaken by a superior army, retreated upon Lahore, near which he was totally routed, and made prisoner in attempting to pass the Indus. Chusero was led before his parent and confessed his guilt; but, with those sentiments of honour which seem to have been always strong in his mind, he refused to give any information which might lead to the detection of his accomplices. Being, however, placed in close confinement, he had the agony of being led out day after day to see his dearest friends and most devoted adherents put to death amid the most cruel tortures. He was released ten years after, though only to be assassinated by his brother, Shah Jehan.

Insurrection against Selim.

Jehangire began his reign with a crime, to which he

was impelled by an unhappy combination of circumstances. A young Tartar lady, born in the Desert, of poor though noble parents, was brought to Delhi, where she grew up, and was considered the most beautiful and accomplished woman in India. She received the title of Mher-ul-Nissa, or the Sun of Women, but was afterwards called Noor Jehan, and sometimes Noor Mahal. The emperor, before mounting the throne, saw and was dazzled with her charms; the passion was mutual, but she had been betrothed to Shere Afkun, a Turkoman of distinguished merit, and a tie was thus formed, which, according to Indian ideas, was indissoluble. Akbar honourably, though perhaps not wisely, insisted that his son's passion should not interfere to prevent the completion of the union. But the latter no sooner became the ruler of India, than he discovered the means of gratifying his guilty inclination. Shere Afkun, however, was so brave and so popular that he durst not openly put him to death, but found it necessary to have recourse to the meanest stratagems. He contrived to involve him in combats with an elephant and a tiger, under such circumstances as seemed to ensure his fate; but Shere, in both instances, extricated himself by exertions of almost preternatural strength. At length a nobleman, whose name was Kuttub, received the high office of Suba of Bengal on the base condition of ridding his master of this hated rival. Yet forty assassins employed for this purpose were beaten off, and it was necessary to make the attack with a little army. Even then Afkun performed prodigies of valour, slew Kuttub himself, his worthless enemy, as he sat on an elephant, together with several of his principal lords, and was overpowered only by clouds of darts. The fair but ambitious object of this execrable policy submitted meekly to her fate; but her royal lover, to whose temper crime so atrocious seems not to have been congenial, was struck with such horror, that during four years he refused to see her, and she lived neglected in a corner of the palace. At length she contrived to rekindle his passion, and became his favourite

Noor Mahal.

Assassination of Shere Afkun.

CHAP. VIII. queen. All her relations were raised to the highest

A. D. 1608. offices, her father becoming grand vizier. Happily he possessed every quality which could adorn that exalted rank; his elevation excited no envy, and though Jehangire gave himself up to ease and luxury, India is described as having been well governed.

English missions.

The reign of this prince was distinguished by the arrival of two English missions; from the narratives of which we may derive somewhat more precise ideas respecting his court, than from the vague and pompous language of the oriental historians.

Captain Hawkins.

In 1607, Captain William Hawkins was sent out by the Company, along with Captain Keeling, to endeavour to open a commercial intercourse with India, and especially with the dominions of the Mogul. Hawkins, who, separating from Keeling at Socotora, arrived at Surat on the 24th August 1608, immediately waited on the governor; but was informed that no permission could be granted to land his goods till a communication were held with Mocrib Khan, the viceroy, who resided at Cambay. A messenger was presently despatched thither; though, in consequence of the heavy rains and inundation of the rivers, an answer did not arrive for twenty days. At the end of this period permission was granted to land, and to buy and sell for the present voyage; but intimation was given at the same time that no factory could be established, nor permanent settlement made, without the sanction of the monarch, which might probably be obtained by proceeding to Agra, a journey of not less than two months.

Jealousies and rivalry.

As soon, however, as the goods began to be disposed of, the utmost uneasiness was observable among the native merchants, who, in their conferences with each other, anticipated the most alarming effects from this new rivalry. They were seconded by a Portuguese Jesuit, whose antipathy, both religious and political, led him to make the utmost efforts to ruin the English. One day, Hawkins received the disagreeable intelligence, that two of his boats, on their way between the ship and the shore, had been seized by the Portuguese; whose commander, on having a remonstrance addressed to him respecting this outrage, did not deign an answer, but spoke to the messenger in the most contemptuous terms of the British monarch, whom he described as a king of fishermen, and master only of an insignificant little island. Hawkins having afterwards met an officer of that nation, and represented to him the impropriety of this conduct, was told that those seas belonged to the King of Portugal, and none were entitled to trade in them without his license. The British captain requested him to convey to his superior a retort at once most indignant and scornful, accompanied with a challenge to single combat, which was not accepted. The boats, mean time, with their captured crews and cargoes, were sent to Goa; and the Englishman, instead of seeing any hope of redress from the Hindoo authorities, found reason to believe that the delays which he had endured were contrived solely to enable the enemy to collect their vessels, and accomplish their outrageous designs. They now laid wait for him, and attempted to break into his house; nor could he go about his affairs in the city without the danger of being murdered. Lastly, Mocrib himself arrived; but, instead of affording to him either relief or compensation, only amused himself with picking out from among his goods whatever appeared desirable, and taking them at his own price, which was always most inadequate and very ill paid.

Insults of the Portugese

Hawkins seeks an interview with the Mogul.

Under these accumulated grievances, Hawkins determined to follow the advice, early given to him, of visiting the Mogul himself at Agra; but Mocrib, the author of this suggestion, conscious of the just complaints which might now be urged against himself, had become anxious to prevent the journey. He furnished only a very slender escort, with the intention, it was suspected, of intercepting it on the road; but the other hired soldiers at his own expense, and applied to a captain of the Viceroy of the Deccan, who gave him a body of brave Afghan horsemen. His coachman, however, having got drunk

CHAP. VIII

A. D. 1609

on the road, confessed that he had entered into a covenant to assassinate him,—an engagement in which it was found that the interpreter had also concurred. The former being apprehended, Hawkins arrived at Burhanpoor, the residence of the viceroy, who courteously received and forwarded him to Agra, where he arrived on the 16th April 1609. As he was inquiring for lodgings, the emperor sent for him in such haste that he had scarcely time to dress. On repairing to the palace, he found Jehangire elevated on his "seat royal," and presented his letter, which, as well as the king's seal, the monarch for some time carefully examined. He then desired it to be read by an old Jesuit who happened to be present. That personage gave a very unfavourable report, saying "it was basely penned;" but the sovereign, finding his visiter could speak Turkish, had begun a conversation which pleased him highly. Hawkins was invited to visit the palace daily, and his majesty held long discourses with him, making inquiry respecting the different countries of Europe, and also the West Indies, the existence of which it seems he had been taught to doubt. He mentioned his conviction that the English had been ill-treated by Mocrib Khan, to whom the most positive orders were now sent to supply them with every thing necessary for their trade. Jehangire then earnestly requested the captain to remain in India till he himself could send an embassy to Europe, assuring him of an income of upwards of £3000 a-year, to be derived, according to their usage, from a command of four hundred horse, and a district of which he was to receive the revenues. Hawkins, considering with himself that he might thus benefit his masters, the Company, and also "feather his own nest," allowed himself to be persuaded. He was then urged, in addition to so many other donations, to accept a wife. After what had passed, he thought it unseasonable to refuse the offer, though it was much against his inclination; yet he hoped to escape by saying that his conscience would not allow him to marry any but a Christian, trusting that none

Visits the emperor.

Favourable reception.

Marriage and settlement in the country

such would be found in this quarter of the world. However, the emperor's search was so diligent that he produced a young Armenian maiden, with whom the captain could not refuse to join his fates; and to this union, though he afterwards found that it was not legal in England, he honourably adhered, and declares that he was thereby made extremely happy.

Influence of Hawkins.

Hawkins being now in the full stream of favour, and learning that another vessel, the Ascension, was coming to Surat, had no difficulty in obtaining an imperial commission, under the great seal with golden letters, authorizing his countrymen to trade. His satisfaction was complete when, in consequence of accumulated complaints from other quarters, his arch-enemy Mocrib was summoned to court, and punished with the confiscation of all his effects. These were so exceedingly numerous, that it afforded for two months a daily task to the emperor to examine them and select the best for his own use. The captain had the satisfaction of pointing out several articles which he himself had lodged as presents for his majesty, though they had never reached their destination.

Change of royal favour

The tide of royal kindness, which had now reached its height, from this moment began to ebb. Mocrib, after being stripped of his most valuable property, was restored again to favour, and allowed to resume his government, being simply exhorted to conduct himself with greater circumspection; but before his departure he took care to do the English every ill office in his power. All those who were about the emperor,—the omrahs, the officers of state, and more especially the Jesuits, united with him in their endeavours to undermine the influence enjoyed by strangers and infidels. It was represented to Jehangire, that by opening his trade to this strange people he would altogether disgust the Portuguese, a much more opulent and powerful nation, who would not only themselves desert his ports, but were able to prevent others from entering them. These arguments, enforced by a balass ruby of uncom-

CHAP. VII. A. D. 1611

mon size and brilliancy, so wrought upon the prince, that he exclaimed, "Let the English come no more!" and Mocrib departed with the instruction never again to allow them to touch his shores. Hawkins did not directly venture to face this tempest. He allowed his enemy to leave; and when the suspicions of the unfriendly cabal had been somewhat lulled, watched his opportunity, presented himself before the emperor with a splendid *toy*, as he terms it, and urging the great advantages which his kingdom might derive from the proposed commercial intercourse, obtained an order for the vizier to prepare a decree, in terms as ample as the former, in favour of the British. These tidings were immediately circulated throughout the hostile faction; an express was despatched to Mocrib, and such activity exerted, that after the decree had been sealed and was ready to be delivered, the sovereign was persuaded to withdraw it. The succeeding transactions continued to present the same woful picture of imbecility and vacillation. When the captain could find a friend at court, or seize a favourable moment, or present some valuable gift, he appeared again on the eve of having all his wishes accomplished; but the activity of his adversaries always produced a speedy reverse. During the whole of this time he suffered much annoyance from Abdul Hassan, the prime minister and his mortal enemy, who at court carefully excluded him from the space within the red rails, the scene of honour, and the spot where opportunities of conversing with the monarch usually occurred: And though he could not altogether withhold the grant of territory made for Hawkins' subsistence, he contrived to allot it in a district so disturbed by insurrection, that little or no revenue could be drawn from it. After two years and a half, therefore, of sickening and fruitless attendance, the English captain determined to take his leave. On the 2d November 1611, he departed, not only without obtaining any confirmation of commercial privileges, but even without a letter to his own king;—having some time before, with the deepest indignation,

Judicious policy of Hawkins.

Vacillation of the court.

Annoyances suffered by Hawkins.

heard from Abdul Hassan, that it was unsuitable to the greatness of the Mogul emperor to write to so petty a prince. CHAP. VIII. A. D. 1615.

English embassy to the emperor

A few years after, it was determined to make an attempt to place the British affairs in India on a more satisfactory footing, by sending out an embassy direct from the king, with ample presents and all such circumstances of pomp as might produce an impression on the proud oriental potentate. Sir Thomas Roe accordingly sailed from Gravesend on the 24th January 1615, with the Lion and Peppercorn, commanded by Captains Peyton and Boughton. After passing along the eastern coast of Africa, and touching at Socotora, he arrived in September at Surat, where he was landed in great pomp, with eighty men-at-arms. By asserting his privileges as ambassador of a powerful monarch, he escaped in a great measure the "barbarous search," as well as various exactions usually practised on merchants. On the 15th November he reached Burhanpoor, and had a splendid audience of Prince Purvez, second son to the sultan, who in this place represented the Mogul sovereignty, though the real power rested with Khan Channa, commander of the forces. The young viceroy is described as mounted on a species of stage, like the mock-kings at a theatre; and the ambassador expressing a wish to go up, was told that neither the Grand Turk nor the King of Persia could be so honoured. On his requesting a seat, he was told no man ever sate in that place. The prince, however, promised to admit Sir Thomas presently to a more private audience; but unluckily, among other gifts, his highness had received a case of bottles, of which he made such diligent use as to be soon wholly out of a condition to fulfil his engagement.

Sir Thomas Roe's arrival at Burhanpoor.

Proceeds to Ajmere.

As the Mogul sovereign was then resident at Ajmere, Roe proceeded thither through the country of the Rajpoots. On his way he admired the situation of Chittore, which he compares to a tomb of wonderful magnificence. Above a hundred temples, many lofty towers, and houses innumerable, were seen crowning the lofty rock on

CHAP. VIII. which it stood; but it was at this time entirely deserted.
A.D. 1616. On the 23d December, Sir Thomas arrived at Ajmere, but did not go to court till the 10th January 1616, when he waited on the emperor at the durbar, or place of public audience. He delivered the royal letter and presents, and met a reception so cordial, that he was assured no other ambassador, either Turk or Persian, had ever obtained the like. At the next interview he was allowed, and ever afterwards retained, a place higher than that of all the courtiers; and being permitted to state the grievances which the English trade suffered at Surat and Ahmedabad, was assured that these should be fully redressed. Many other conferences followed, and much familiar and even jocular conversation passed between the ambassador and the monarch. Sir Thomas for some time fondly hoped to obtain all his requests, but soon found himself opposed by the same hostile cabal that had caused so many reverses to Hawkins. Mocrib Khan, the rooted enemy of England, was at court, where he was supported by Asiph Khan, who had now succeeded as prime minister, and by Churrum, afterwards Shah Jehan, then the favourite son of Jehangire. It was surprising how he could at all maintain his ground against such powerful adversaries, who produced continual fluctuations in the mind of this inconstant prince; but the ambassador's address and perseverance at last enabled him to procure a firman, though not to the full extent which had been promised and expected. He even received a letter to the British sovereign, addressed, "Unto a king rightly descended from his ancestors, bred in military affairs, and clothed with honour and justice."

Favourable reception.

Mocrib Khan's evil influence.

Observations on the manners of the court.

During his stay, Sir Thomas had a good opportunity of observing the pomp and ceremonies of this court, the most splendid perhaps that ever dazzled the eyes of mankind, though scarcely possessing a corresponding share of polish and refinement. A remarkable degree of publicity, and even popularity, seems to have distinguished all its proceedings. The emperor spent as it were his whole life in public. In the morning he came to a window overlooking a wide plain, and exhibited himself to a numerous crowd there assembled. At noon he returned to the same place, where he was entertained with combats of wild beasts, particularly of elephants; and in the afternoon he seated himself in the durbar, the regular place of audience for all who presented themselves on business. At eight in the evening he once more appeared in an open court, called the Guzel Khan, where he spent the time chiefly in gay and easy conversation with his favourites. In the durbar, the royal throne was surrounded by two successive railings, the innermost of which enclosed a place for the ambassadors, officers of state, and persons of the first distinction. The outer space was filled with chiefs of secondary dignity; while a wide open area at a greater distance was assigned to the multitude; all of whom, however, enjoyed a full view of his majesty's person. To this routine the emperor was completely enslaved, and could not be excused for a single day, unless he were sick or drunk, which it was necessary to explain; but "two days no reason can excuse." All the state-proceedings and ordinances were equally public, being daily written down, and allowed to be perused for a trifling fee. Thus every event and resolution was immediately known to all the people; and even Sir Thomas' English feelings were scandalized by seeing the most secret councils of the prince, and his changeful purposes, "tossed and censured by every rascal."

CHAP. VIII

A. D. 1616

Royal pomp and forms.

Our traveller, on several occasions of gayety and festival, had other opportunities of beholding the pomp of the Mogul court. It consisted chiefly in the immense profusion of precious stones, which this sovereign made it his aim, by presents, purchase, or plunder, to collect from every quarter. The person of the emperor on high anniversaries was not only covered, but completely laden with diamonds, pearls, and rubies. Even the elephants, when they went in procession, besides having all their trappings richly gilded, had their heads adorned with valuable jewels. The ambassador was particularly dazzled,

Wealth of the court.

CHAP. VIII.

A.D. 1616.

after the monarch had taken the field, with the range of the royal tents surrounded by a wall half a mile in circuit. Those of the nobles exhibited the most elegant shapes and brilliant variety of colours. He declares it "one of the greatest rarities and magnificences" he ever saw, the whole vale resembling a beautiful city. But amid all this show we see few or no traces of any refined or intellectual tastes. On the sovereign's birth-day, his chief amusement was to take two boxes, one full of rubies, and the other of gold and silver almonds, and scatter them on the ground in presence of his omrahs; when these mighty lords of the greatest court in the world threw themselves on the floor and scrambled for them as children do for sugar-plums. On another occasion, much delight was afforded by the "royal weighing," at which time the emperor's person, arrayed in full pomp, was put into the scales, first against rupees, then against gold and jewels, next against rich cloths and spices, and, lastly, against corn, meal, and butter. Intoxication, carried to the utmost excess, completed the circle of court gayeties.

Royal encampment.

Frivolous pastimes.

Character of Jehangire.

The view given by both these travellers of the character of Jehangire scarcely accords with the high panegyrics pronounced by the oriental writers. His facility and kindness of temper appear combined with so much of weakness and vacillation as nearly to have unfitted him for conducting the concerns of so great an empire. Sir Thomas seems to describe him accurately, by saying:—"He is of so good a disposition, that he suffers all men to govern, which is worse than being ill." His justice, and more particularly his hatred of injustice, which Dow so highly extols, becomes somewhat equivocal, when we find it chiefly displayed in confiscating to his own use the goods of suspected individuals. After having pronounced Mocrib Khan guilty, and seized his most valuable possessions, there was a strange inconsistency in restoring him to his government and to full confidence, and being swayed by his advice on the most important occasions. It is difficult to know whether we should ascribe to superstition or policy the absurd caresses which he was seen to bestow on a miserable fakir or beggar, whom he conversed with for an hour, took in his arms and assisted to rise, and into whose lap he finally poured a hundred rupees.

Influence of his favourite.

The last years of this sovereign's life were spent in much misery; and it was still his fatal passion for Noor Jehan by which they were imbittered. This fair but haughty favourite governed him entirely, misled his easy temper, and alienated him from his best friends. The belief prevailed, apparently not without foundation, that she was studying to raise to the throne Shariar, her own son, to the prejudice of the elder branches of her husband's family; and this was at least the alleged motive of the formidable rebellion raised against the emperor by Shah Jehan, the ablest of his children, who had gained great reputation and influence by a successful war in the Deccan. That prince, by another crime, paved his way to the throne. Chusero, his elder brother, whose rebellion had chequered the opening of Jehangire's reign, was released from his long confinement, and placed under the shah's care; but one morning his favourite wife entered his tent and found him weltering in his blood, shed by an assassin. She filled the camp and city with her cries: Jehan repaired to the spot, and by the deep concern he expressed, escaped at first all suspicion; yet his father and the public became afterwards convinced that the guilt of this murder rested upon his head.

Shah Jehan's rebellion

Mohabet Khan.

The emperor, in the dangerous situation in which he was now placed, had, however, a faithful friend and servant, Mohabet Khan, who supported his crown with devoted zeal, and whose valour gained for him repeated victories over the rebellious Shah Jehan. Even when that prince repaired successively to Guzerat and Bengal, where he succeeded in raising several new armies, Mohabet still pursued him, and at last reduced his affairs to a desperate condition. When this commander, however, had returned to court, expecting the gratitude due for such signal services, he found a complete change in the senti-

CHAP. VIII. A. D. 1625.

ments of his sovereign. Noor Jehan, never ceasing to be the evil genius of Jehangire, joined with other enemies in making him believe that this virtuous guardian of his throne had entered into a conspiracy for his deposition. Mohabet, soon learning how affairs stood at court, determined not to sacrifice himself by obeying the order to repair thither, but withdrew to his castle at Rintimpour. At length, after repeated calls, he proceeded to the seat of government, accompanied, however, by 5000 brave Rajpoot cavalry, whom he deemed sufficient to secure his personal safety. He found the emperor encamped near Lahore; but on approaching the tents, met the most unworthy reception, being ordered to advance no farther till he had accounted for the revenues and the plunder which had come into his possession. Mohabet, though virtuous, was proud; hence his indignation was raised to the highest pitch, and he contrived, and immediately executed a truly bold scheme. The army, now on its march to Cabul, crossed next day the bridge over the Jelum, while the monarch, who dreaded nothing, lingered behind with a small party of courtiers. The general then pushed forward with his Rajpoots, caused one detachment to secure the bridge, while with another he dashed on to the tent of his master. Surrounded by five hundred of these troops, who had alighted in full armour, he entered with a countenance pale but determined. The omrahs at first made some show of resistance, but yielded as soon as they saw the amount of the force which assailed them. The chief, after some search, found Jehangire in the bathing-tent, when the latter immediately exclaimed, "What dost thou mean, Mohabet Khan!" The other replied, "Forced by the machinations of my enemies, who plot against my life, I throw myself under the protection of my sovereign." Being asked the object of the armed men behind him, he answered, "They want full security for me and my family, and without it they will not retire." Jehangire denied having entertained any design against his life, and endeavoured to sooth him; when the other

Daring of Mohabet.

Obtains possession of the emperor.

observed that this was his usual hour of hunting, and that a horse was in waiting. The emperor saw the necessity under which he was placed, and went, accompanied by a guard of valiant Rajpoots.

Rage of the queen

Meantime Noor Jehan, with her brother, Asiph Khan, the prime minister, had passed with the main body of the army to the opposite side of the river; and it is easy to imagine the consternation and rage of that proud princess on learning the disaster which had befallen her husband. After consultation, it was determined, at whatever peril, to attack Mohabet, and make a desperate effort for the release of their sovereign. The broad stream, however, was to be crossed in the face of the hostile Rajpoots; but the empress, to encourage her troops, rode into the current, exposing herself in the thickest of the conflict, and emptying four quivers of arrows with her own hand. Three of her elephant-drivers were killed; and her youthful daughter, who accompanied her, was wounded in the arm. The Rajpoots, however, attacked the several parties as they reached the shore, and successively defeated them. At length a large body, headed by the most gallant of the omrahs, crossed at a different point, and came upon the enemy's rear. They penetrated nearly to the emperor's tent, which was pierced with numerous arrows, and his person was only secured by being carefully covered with shields. But Mohabet finally restored the battle, and gained a complete victory. Noor Jehan fled to Lahore; whence, by letters from Jehangire, she was induced to repair to his camp. Under these circumstances, we know not how to justify the resolution formed by the conqueror of putting her to death. He even extorted the imperial warrant to that effect; when the artful princess, pretending to submit to her fate, solicited one interview with her lord,—a request which the general granted, on condition that it should take place in his own presence. She entered and stood before her husband in deep silence, "her beauty shining with additional lustre through her sorrow." He instantly burst into tears, and entreated so earnestly for the life of his beloved queen,

Her courage and daring.

Complete victory of Mohabet.

Tact of the queen.

CHAP. VIII

A. D. 1626.

that the victorious chief was overcome, and acceded to his wishes.

Magnanimity of Mohabet.

Mohabet now carried his sovereign into Cabul, treating him with the highest respect, maintaining the full pomp of his court, and allowing him to transact all the ordinary affairs of state. At length, having obtained the most ample promises of indemnity and future favour, he proved his disinterestedness by resigning his power, setting the monarch at full liberty, and retiring into a private station. But he had gone too far to recede with safety. The emperor, indeed, was capable of forgiving, and even of forgetting; but the deepest resentment rankled in

Vindictiveness of the queen.

the mind of his lady, who soon began to demand the life of the general, though the former had sufficient sense of justice to repel her proposal with indignation. She then proceeded to form plots for effecting her object by treachery. Jehangire, on learning these designs, gave information to the intended victim, at the same time owning his inability to afford him the protection to which he had so just a claim. It was evident, therefore, that no choice was left him but to flee; and the man who had so lately been the real master of this great empire became a solitary fugitive, after abandoning all his property. Noor Jehan immediately seized it, and in his absence obtained an entire sway over the mind of the weak sovereign; the other was declared a rebel; a price set upon his head; and a diligent search was ordered to be made for him through all the provinces.

Asiph and Mohabet.

Asiph, the reigning minister, disapproved of his sister's violence, and of the questionable measures into which she urged the government, but knew not how to resist. One evening after dark he was informed that a man in a mean dress besought an audience. With wonder and sympathy, he saw before him the chief who had so lately been the ruler of India. They withdrew into a secret cabinet; and Asiph having acknowledged the empress' violence and the miserable weakness of Jehangire, Mohabet urged, that the only chance for having the empire governed with a firm hand would be obtained by raising to the throne Shah Jehan, the same man of whom he himself had so long been the determined enemy. The other, after some consideration, concurred in his views, and a communication with the royal youth was immediately opened; but several circumstances suspended the execution of this project till it was rendered unnecessary by the illness of the emperor. An asthmatic complaint under which he laboured being severely aggravated by a residence in the cold climate of Cashmere, he expired on the 9th November 1627, leaving behind him a very doubtful reputation.

CHAP. VIII. A. D. 1627. Death of Jehangire.

Jehangire left only two sons, Shah Jehan and Shariar, to the latter of whom he had bequeathed his crown; but Mohabet and Asiph took immediate steps for the elevation of the former, and before that prince could arrive from the Deccan, his competitor was defeated, taken prisoner, and deprived of sight. The new emperor, on reaching the capital, immediately adopted the most dreadful expedients to secure himself against a rival. He caused not only his brother, but all his nephews who were alive, to be put to death; and there remained not a drop of the blood of Timur, except what flowed in his own and his children's veins. This horrible tragedy has been palliated as founded on oriental precedent; yet though in Eastern courts fraternal enmities have usually been fatal, Hindostan had afforded no instance of such a fearful proscription. Nor could Jehan fail to foresee that this guilty example was likely to be followed, if not against himself, as it actually was in some degree, at least against those in whose welfare he was most deeply interested.

Shah Jehan

Barbarous cruelties

He did not even escape the danger of an immediate claimant for the empire. Lodi, an omrah of distinguished spirit and valour, and who boasted a descent from the Patan emperors of India, had been employed as commander of the army in the Deccan. In this capacity he was opposed to Shah Jehan, and having, when the throne became vacant, attached himself to

Rivalry of Lodi.

CHAP. VIII. — A. D. 1627.

Reception at court.

Shariar, obstructed and even insulted the new sovereign on his way to Agra. The prince sent an army against him, but with liberal offers in case of submission. Lodi laid down his arms, and was appointed to the government of Malwa; whence, on a mandate from the imperial court, he repaired to the capital. At the first audience, however, he was received with such marked disrespect, as showed that some hostile purpose was meditated. Azmut his son even drew his sword; a tumult ensued, and the omrah hastened to his own house, which was capable of defence, where he shut himself up with three hundred followers. Thus enclosed, however, in the midst of enemies, his situation seemed desperate, and he was agitated with the most perplexing emotions. Suddenly a scream was heard from the apartment of the females,—he rushed in, and saw them weltering in their blood. In the prospect of captivity and dishonour, with that desperate fidelity not unfrequently displayed by Hindoo females, they had plunged the sword into their own breasts. At the sight his mind was worked up almost to phrensy. He sprang on horseback with his two sons, caused his men to follow him sounding trumpets, while he himself called aloud, "I will awaken the tyrant with the sound of my departure, but he shall tremble at my return." A hot pursuit was immediately commenced; yet he would have distanced his pursuers, had not the stream of the Chumbul, then flowing rapidly and swollen by heavy rains, arrested his progress. Overtaken by a greatly superior force he was obliged to plunge into the stream, and reached the opposite shore, but not without losing the greater number of his followers, among whom was Azmut his favourite son. He pushed onward, however, to the Deccan, where he openly raised the standard of rebellion, and, besides collecting his own adherents, engaged the kings of Golconda and Visiapour to enter into a league against the Mogul, by whose overwhelming power they had long been oppressed. Shah Jehan was so deeply alarmed that he hastened to the theatre of war; but not being disposed to take the field in person.

His bold flight.

Escape.

League organized against Shah Jehan.

yet afraid to intrust the sole command to any single chief, he sent detached corps under Eradut Khan and other generals to attack the combined forces at different points. Lodi being nominated generalissimo, conducted his operations with such valour and skill that he baffled all the efforts of the invader. Shah Jehan, greatly mortified, at length committed the entire conduct of the war to Asiph, who brought to it talents and a reputation of the first order. His very name struck the confederates with such terror that they immediately retreated. The insurgent chief, with only the troops personally attached to himself, determined to try the fortune of battle; but it proved adverse. The King of Golconda instantly began to treat with the emperor; and Lodi, well aware that the first article would be the delivery of his own person, lost no time in withdrawing from his territory. Shah Jehan endeavoured to shut against him all the passes leading into Hindostan; yet the fugitive chief evaded all his precautions, and with a chosen band, who remained faithful in every extremity, found his way into the high country of Malwa. The emperor immediately directed Abdallah, one of his officers, to pursue him with ten thousand horse. Lodi, weakened by the attacks which he encountered in his march, at length found this powerful body pressing close behind; while Mohammed Azâz, his eldest son, had fallen in endeavouring to cover his retreat. His troop was reduced to thirty, so closely hemmed in as to exclude all hope. Seeing a strong detachment of the enemy advance, he called together these faithful followers, and after expressing the warmest gratitude for their adherence to him amid so many calamities, begged as a last favour that they would no longer cling to a cause devoted to ruin, but each seek his own safety. They burst into tears, and declared their determination to share his fate to the last. He silently gave the signal to follow, and spurred his horse against the enemy. A ball pierced his breast, and his thirty gallant companions fell around him. Shah Jehan received the tidings with unbounded exultation, not tempered with

Asiph intrusted with the command.

Flight and pursuit of Lodi.

Fall of Lodi.

CHAP. VIII. A. D. 1630. the generous sympathy which was due to the valour and misfortunes of his fallen rival.

Firmness and justice of the emperor. The emperor, thus secured in the possession of the sceptre, added another to the list of princes who, after seizing it by crimes and violence, wielded it with firmness and justice. The sternness of his temper was now employed in overawing the haughty viceroys, and guarding the people against oppression. He derived, doubtless, much aid from the wise counsels of Asiph Khan and Mohabet, whom, notwithstanding some fits of jealousy, he continued to employ. Sometimes their intercession softened the extreme rigour of his justice, particularly in the case of the Rajah of Bundelcund, whom he had ordered for execution. When Mohabet pleaded for the life of the guilty chief, the monarch not only granted it, but restored him to his full dignity. Toleration. At one time, though wholly indifferent to the Mohammedan religion, he was so provoked by the manifold absurdities of the Hindoo worship, that he began to make it an object of persecution; but, seeing the eagerness with which the people clung to their proscribed ritual, he became sensible of his error, and resumed the system of toleration which his family had been accustomed to extend to both creeds.

His armed proceedings. Had there been a theatre open for foreign conquest, Shah Jehan would probably have been ambitious of that glory; but the empire was now so extensive, and all its enemies at so great a distance, that such projects must have been carried on under many disadvantages. He led armies, however, into the Deccan, and reduced its princes to a still humbler state of vassalage than before. He also sent expeditions against Candahar and Balkh, on the western and north-western frontiers; but the war was waged with difficulty in those remote and mountainous regions, while the vigorous rule of the Persian princes, Abbas and Sefi, rendered it impossible to make any permanent impression in that quarter. On the east, indeed, he added to the empire the rude province of Assam,—a precarious acquisition of no very great value.

To this prince India is indebted for the most splendid

THE TAJ MAHAL.

Page 267.

CHAP. III.

A. D. 1650.

and elegant monuments of architecture with which it is any where adorned. At New Delhi, which he made his residence, and called, from himself, Shah Jehanpoor, he erected a palace of red granite, considered by Bishop Heber one of the noblest he ever saw, and far superior to the Kermlin at Moscow. The gateway in particular is finely ornamented.* The Jumma Musjed, too, in the same city, is a magnificent mosque, not excelled by any other in India. But all his erections were surpassed by the mausoleum called the Taj Mahal, raised at Agra in honour of Noor Jehan, his favourite queen. It is built of white marble, inlaid with precious stones, and forms a quadrangle of 190 yards, with a lofty dome 70 feet in diameter rising from the centre. It stands on an elevated terrace, surrounded by a highly cultivated garden. The construction is said to have cost the immense sum of £750,000; and it is generally esteemed the finest edifice in the empire.

Love of architecture

This reign flowed on for more than twenty years in the most smooth and prosperous tenor. The emperor lost his valuable ministers Asiph and Mohabet; but this only induced him to apply more closely to public business, which he continued to administer to the entire satisfaction of the nation. His felicity seemed crowned by possessing four sons, whose accomplishments, and even virtues, fitted them to adorn the throne of the greatest of empires, and to be the idols of the people. As the most perfect cordiality reigned between them and him, he placed them in all conspicuous situations, which they filled both honourably and ably. But when they grew to manhood it was impossible to prevent mutual jealousies from arising. Each began to contemplate in the event of his parent's death a struggle for the vacant sovereignty; and each anticipated on that occurrence either a throne or a grave. Dara, the favourite of the aged monarch, was kept near his person, and for him the succession was destined. He was, perhaps, the most

Prosperous reign.

Family jealousies.

* See plate at the end of this chapter.

CHAP VIII. A. D. 1650. amiable of the family, shunning the licentious indulgences incident to a court, and employing his leisure in the cultivation of letters; but in action he was hasty and impetuous. Sujah, voluptuous, yet mild and also brave, held the government of Bengal. Morad, magnificent, proud, daring, delighting in war and danger, commanded in Guzerat. There was yet a fourth, of a character very different from that of any of his brothers, or from what is usually found in the bosom of royalty. Aurengzebe. Aurengzebe maintained a reserved deportment, rejecting pleasure, and devoting himself to business and public affairs with an intensity like that of one who was to raise himself from a low condition by his own exertions. Another circumstance gave a peculiar stamp to his pursuits and destiny. The princes of the house of Akbar had scarcely made even a profession of the Mohammedan faith, though it was zealously maintained by their armies and great lords. They seem to have viewed religion itself with a careless indifference, chiefly as a subject of philosophical speculation, and studiously avoided making it any ground of distinction among the various classes of their subjects. Devotion to Mohammedanism. He, on the contrary, had adopted the Arabian creed in all its rigour; conforming strictly to its observances, and professing himself more ambitious of the reputation of a saint and fakir than of a great monarch. He thereby made himself odious to the Indian population; but the Moslem chiefs, who wielded the military power, hailed the appearance of a sovereign that had renounced the scandal ous negligence of his ancestors, and identified himself with them upon this important subject. Having commanded also for a long time the troops in the Deccan, the main theatre of war, he found himself at the head of a better-disciplined army, and had acquired more military skill, than any other of the princes.

Illness of the emperor. This state of things, however painful and alarming, might have been of long duration, had not a sudden and severe illness seized the emperor. He continued insensible during several days, and no hopes were entertained

CHAP. VIII. A. D. 1650.

of his recovery. Dara, by his direction, immediately assumed the government, and administered it as if he were already on the throne. In particular, he showed a very jealous feeling towards his brothers, prohibiting all communication with them, seizing their papers, and sending into exile all the omrahs attached to their interest. Thus he precipitated, and in some measure justified, the hostile measures to which they were of themselves but too much disposed. Notwithstanding every precaution they obtained information of their father's illness, and were even led to suspect that he was already dead. They immediately entered upon a line of conduct, professedly prompted not by ambition but by regard for their personal safety. Sujah, in Bengal, first put his troops in motion; and soon after Morad, in Guzerat, communicated to Aurengzebe the recent events, inviting him to unite in counteracting the obvious designs of their relative;—in which views that ambitious prince readily concurred.

Dara assumes the government.

Meantime Shah Jehan, beyond all expectation, obtained a complete recovery, and Dara, in the most dutiful manner, resigned back into his father's hands the reins of empire. This intelligence was instantly conveyed to Sujah, and a hope expressed that the measures which he had taken, solely in anticipation of the emperor's death, would be discontinued. But he had gone too far; the flame of ambition was kindled in his breast; he affected disbelief of the statement, and even treated as forgeries the letters which the sovereign wrote to him with his own hand. Being met, however, on the banks of the Ganges by Solimân, the son of Dara, a youth of distinguished talents, he was totally defeated, and obliged to shut himself up in the fortress of Monghir, where he was closely invested. Meanwhile the expedition from the south assumed a more formidable character.

Recovery of Shah Jehan.

Insurrection of his sons.

Aurengzebe lost no time in obeying the invitation of his brother, and hastened to join him with all the forces he was able to collect. But, conscious that he viewed

CHAP. VIII. A.D. 1652. Morad also as a rival, and was likely to excite in his mind a similar feeling, he used every false and flattering expression which could inspire with confidence his naturally open and unsuspicious heart. He professed to consider him as alone fitted for the throne of Hindostan, to which he was called by the desire of the people; and as one to whose elevation it would be his pride to contribute, though his own wish was only to find some tranquil retirement, where he might devote the rest of his days to religious contemplation. Perhaps there was not another individual in Hindostan, knowing the parties, who could have been deceived by such language; but so great was the vanity and credulity of Morad, that Aurengzebe knew he might confidently use it. The two princes, with their armies, met on the banks of the Nerbudda, crossed that river, and totally defeated Jesswint Singh, the Rajpoot chief, who, in the service of the emperor, commanded a numerous body of cavalry.

Victory of Aurengzebe.

Dismay of the emperor.

Shah Jehan learned these events with the deepest dismay. He saw the formidable character of the rebellion, and dreaded that, whatever the issue might be, he himself could scarcely fail to be crushed. He therefore used all his power to support his destined heir; and even expressed an ardent wish to take the field along with him, though he was unfortunately persuaded to give up his intention. Orders were sent to Solimân to grant favourable terms to Sujah, and to hasten against the more dangerous enemy; and Dara was strongly advised to await his arrival with a large reinforcement. That prince accordingly placed his army, consisting of 100,000 horse, in a strong position along the banks of the Chumbul, which commanded the approach to Agra, and covered his camp with a powerful line of intrenchments. When the confederates advanced, and saw his force thus posted, they felt considerable embarrassment. Morad, with characteristic ardour, proposed to attempt forcing the lines; but this undertaking appeared too hazardous to the cautious prudence of Aurengzebe. Having obtained information of a pass through the mountains, by which the

Forces of Dara.

CHAP. VIII

A. D. 1652.

enemy's position might be turned, and leaving only the appearance of a camp to deceive his adversary, he effected his object, and marched upon Agra. The imperial lieutenant had then only the alternative of abandoning that capital or of giving battle, and his ardent spirit impelled him to prefer the latter. This engagement, which decided the fate of the Mogul empire, is related by historians in a manner very confused, and seemingly much darkened by oriental exaggeration. It is asserted that, after various changes of fortune on either side, the whole of both armies fled from the field, leaving only a thousand horse under Dara, and a hundred under Aurengzebe; and that when the latter had given up all hope, a retrograde movement by his brother's elephant, and the circumstance of that commander being induced to dismount, struck dismay into his troops, and caused his total defeat. The following may perhaps be considered as the real events which marked this important scene. The two principal divisions were commanded by Morad and Aurengzebe, and the former, opposed to Dara, was attacked with such impetuosity, that notwithstanding the most strenuous exertions his line was broken, he himself wounded, and his life in danger. His ally, meantime, after a very obstinate struggle, completely defeated and put to flight the force with which he had to contend; then, wheeling round, came to the aid of the other wing, restored the battle, and gained a complete victory.

Decisive battle.

Confused accounts of the engagement.

The confederate armies advanced upon Agra, where Morad being, most conveniently for Aurengzebe, confined with his wounds, the entire command devolved upon himself. His first care was to send an emissary to corrupt the troops of Solimân, in which he easily succeeded, or rather they corrupted themselves by following the usual Asiatic system of going over to the prosperous party. His next anxiety was to obtain possession of his father's person. This was a measure both delicate and difficult, for the fortified palace in which Shah Jehan resided was capable of withstanding a long

Defection of Solimân's troops.

CHAP. VIII. A. D. 1658. siege; which, pressed by a son against his parent, a monarch so popular and highly respected, would have placed him in a very odious position. It was most desirable, therefore, to effect his purpose by stratagem; but he had to deal with one versant in all the wiles of policy, and in all the forms of human deceit. Determining, however, to make the trial, he sent a messenger to the emperor, expressing deep regret at the situation in which he found himself, assuring him that he still retained all the affection of a son and the loyalty of a subject. Shah Jehan gave very small credit to these professions, yet he resolved to temporize, and sent his favourite daughter, Jehanara, to visit her brothers, and endeavour to ascertain how affairs really stood. She went first to Morad, who, knowing her to be entirely devoted to the interests of Dara, received her with very slender courtesy. The offended princess returned to her palanquin, and was hastening out of the camp when she met Aurengzebe, who saluted her with the utmost kindness and respect, complained of her having held so little communication with him, and prevailed upon her to enter his tent. He there professed the deepest remorse for the conduct into which he had been hurried, and his anxiety by any means to make reparation. He even expressed a willingness to espouse the cause of Dara, were it not that it already appeared quite desperate. Jehanara was thus induced to lay open all the resources of that prince, and to name the chiefs who remained still attached to him; disclosing to her brother many most important state-secrets, of which he afterwards fully availed himself. He then declared that he was entirely satisfied, promising to second all her views, and added, that in two days the emperor would see at his feet his repentant son.

The princess Jehanara.

Politic conduct of Aurengzebe.

Plan of the emperor.

Jehanara now hastened to her father with this joyful intelligence. But the monarch did not place full reliance on these professions; yet, believing that Aurengzebe really intended to pay him a visit, he determined to take advantage of the opportunity to secure his person. He was not aware that he was playing the game

CHAP. VIII.

A. D. 1658.

of treachery with one who possessed skill superior to his own. This other sent an humble message, representing that the guilty are always timid,—that being scarcely able to conceive how crimes such as his could be forgiven, he could in no way be reassured, unless his son Mohammed were allowed previously, with a small guard, to enter the palace. Shah Jehan was so bent on his object, and so convinced of the sincerity with which the proposal was made, that he hesitated not to agree to it. The youth entered, and being cordially received, stationed his party in a convenient situation. But his eager eye soon discovered a large body of troops occupying a very suspicious position. He went to the emperor and stated the apprehension to which this circumstance could not fail to give rise, observing, that unless these men were removed, he must immediately inform his father, who would then probably renounce his intended visit. The old man, still credulous, and determined to make every sacrifice rather than fail in his object, consented that the soldiers should quit the palace, thus rendering Mohammed and his party its real masters.

Superior sagacity of Aurengzebe.

Then indeed it was announced that Aurengzebe had mounted his horse and was approaching with his retinue. The monarch seated himself on his throne in the highest exultation, expecting to see the complete accomplishment of his schemes and hopes. He soon learned, however, that his son, instead of entering the presence, had proceeded to pay his devotions at the tomb of Akbar. Considering this as a decided slight to himself, he indignantly asked Mohammed, "What means Aurengzebe by this behaviour?" The other deliberately answered, "My father never intended to visit the emperor."—"Then why are you here?"—"To take charge of the citadel."

Proceedings of the conqueror.

Shah Jehan saw at once the abyss into which he had plunged himself, and burst into a torrent of fruitless invective and self-reproach, which induced his grandson to withdraw. On sober reflection he sent again for the youth, and, painting the miseries of his condition, urged the most pressing entreaties that the prince would

Shah Jehan's fruitless indignation

CHAP. VIII

A. D. 1658

restore to him his liberty, promising in reward even the empire of India, which his influence with the army and people would be sufficient to secure. Mohammed appeared to hesitate for a moment, but then, hastening out of the apartment, turned a deaf ear to every subsequent solicitation.

Ruin of Morad.

Aurengzebe had now only Morad to dispose of, and from that quarter he had not much to apprehend, though this prince, having recovered of his wounds, had repaired to Agra, and resumed the command of the army. His brother received him with the warmest congratulations, saluted him emperor, and declared all his wishes to be now fulfilled, since he had succeeded in raising so deserving a ruler to the throne of his ancestors. For himself he wished only to perform the pilgrimage to Mecca, on which he was intent as the commencement of a life to be entirely devoted to religion. The other, after some affected opposition, gave his consent, thinking himself too happy that his relative should thus voluntarily retire. This farce having been successfully acted, the ruin of Morad was secretly prepared; and the design soon became so obvious, that even his credulous spirit could no longer be beguiled. His friends assured him that the preparations for the visit to Mecca were sufficient to acquire the dominion of India; that by ample largesses Aurengzebe was gaining the affections of the soldiery; and, in short, that no time was to be lost in securing his own safety. Being at last undeceived, he determined to employ against his brother his own weapons of treachery.

Policy of Aurengzebe.

Unsuccessful attempt to assassinate him.

He invited him to a splendid banquet, where every thing was prepared for his death; but the penetrating eye of the guest discerning something suspicious, he pretended a sudden illness, and hastily withdrew, without exciting any suspicion of the motive. On the contrary, Morad soon after accepted his invitation to an entertainment, in which the finest musicians, and the most beautiful damsels that India could afford, were studiously assembled. The host, laying aside his austerity, invited to gayety and indulgence this voluptuous prince, who yielded to the seduction, and, after revelling in luxury, fell asleep in the tent. He then sent in some of his most unscrupulous partisans, who proceeded to bind their victim. The prince awoke, made violent efforts to extricate himself, calling for his sword, which had been taken away; when his brother, lifting a curtain, exclaimed,—"He has no choice but death or submission; despatch him if he resists." Morad, after venting loud reproaches, yielded to his fate, and was immediately conveyed a prisoner to Agra.

Fate of Morad.

Aurengzebe, having thus overcome every obstacle, considered it now time "to exalt the imperial umbrella over his head." He felt, however, considerable difficulty in taking a step so inconsistent with all his professions, and especially with that of his being entirely devoted to religious retirement and abstraction. It was contrived that his friends should come forward to urge upon him the important duty of sacrificing his ease and pious resolutions for the public good, and of submitting to this painful necessity. In due time he allowed himself to be persuaded, though he adhered so far to his former character as to suppress all the pomp with which the ceremony of coronation was usually attended. But the shouts of the people reached the ears of the captive monarch, who felt assured that something fatal to himself had been determined. He asked Jehanara to go and inquire; yet immediately recalled her, lest she should see the head of Dara exposed to public view. She, however, soon learned and communicated to him the real fact. The unfortunate sovereign rose, walked through the room in silence, then fixing his eyes on the figure of a crown suspended over his head, said,—"Take away that bauble;—yet stay, this would be owning the right of Aurengzebe." After standing long involved in thought, he said,—"The new emperor, Jehanara, has prematurely mounted the throne. He should have added the murder of a father to the other crimes which have raised him so nigh." It was now announced that Mohammed wished to be admitted, that he might state the reasons which

Aurengzebe assumes the throne.

The captive emperor

CHAP. VIII.

A. D. 1658.

Indignant remonstrance.

had induced the victor to mount the throne; but the degraded ruler indignantly replied,—" Fathers have been deposed by their sons; but it was reserved for Aurengzebe to insult the misfortunes of a parent. What motives but his ambition has the rebel for assuming the empire! To listen to his excuses would be to acknowledge the justice of his conduct."

Aurengzebe, smarting under remorse for the step to which his bold ambition had irresistibly impelled him, and having indeed very little to say in his own defence, did not press the unwelcome explanation. He had now reached the summit of his wishes, having deceived and vanquished one of the ablest monarchs of the East. He did not therefore push his triumph any farther, and maintained his father during the rest of his life, in strict confinement indeed, but honoured and respected.

CHAPTER IX.

Aurengzebe—Decline of the Mogul Dynasty.

Aurengzebe opposed by his Brothers, Dara and Sujah—Defeat of Sujah—Capture and Death of Dara—Defection of the Prince Mohammed, who is obliged to surrender—Death of Sujah—Aurengzebe's Treatment of Shah Jehan—His Administration—Defects of Mogul Government—Anecdotes furnished by Bernier—Danger of Persian War—Fakir Insurrection—Disturbance in Cabul—Conquest of the Deccan—Rise of the Mahratta Power—Exploits of Sevajee—His Death and Character—Sambajee's Reign and Death—Character of the Mahratta Armies—Bigotry of Aurengzebe—His Death and Character—Shah Allum—The Seiks—Their Progress checked—Character and Death of Shah Allum—Contests for the Empire—The Syeds—Nizam-ul-Mulk and Saadut Khan—Invasion by Nadir Shah—Sack of Delhi—Distracted State of the Empire—Invasion by the Afghans—Contest between them and the Mahrattas—Battle of Pannipút—The Mogul Dynasty reduced to entire Insignificance.

CHAP. IX

A.D. 1658.

Aurengzebe's position.

AURENGZEBE was seated on the throne of India; but his position could not be considered secure while his brothers Dara and Sujah lived, and were at the head of powerful armies. The former, from his brilliant qualities, and his designation to the empire by Shah Jehan, inspired the greatest apprehension; and against him the first efforts of the new sovereign were directed. Having withdrawn into Lahore, Dara had collected a host more numerous than that of his adversary, composed, however, chiefly of new levies, whom he was afraid to bring into the field against his brother's veteran forces. He therefore retired beyond the Indus; but retreat in these circumstances, and with such troops, was not less disas-

Dara retreats.

CHAP. IX.

A. D. 1658.

trous than actual defeat. His ranks gradually melted away, and he arrived at Tatta with only a small body of faithful adherents.

Advance of Sujah.

It would now have been the policy of Aurengzebe to pursue Dara without intermission till he had completed his destruction; but he was necessarily checked by the intelligence that his brother Sujah, with a large force, was advancing from Bengal. He found this rival very strongly posted near Allahabad; but, trusting to the valour and hardihood of his own troops, he resolved to attack him. Early in the day, however, the Rajpoot bands, who had accompanied him only through compulsion, fled from the field, and even began to assail his rear; so that the Mogul warriors, left alone, were soon very hard pressed. The elephant on which Aurengzebe rode received a severe shock, and fell on its knees; whereupon the emperor drew one foot out of the stirrup, preparing to alight,—but, as in an Indian battle the presence of the monarch on his war-elephant is the rallying point round which the army fights, Jumla, the vizier, called out, "You are descending from your throne." The prince felt the truth and importance of the remark, resumed his seat, and even ordered the feet of the animal to be chained to the spot. Thus, cased indeed in strong armour, he remained exposed to the darts and arrows of the enemy. His men, encouraged by the gallant example of their chief, rallied, and making the most desperate efforts, caused their opponents to give way. Sujah, finding his elephant disabled, committed the error which his rival had avoided, and mounted a horse. The view of the royal quadruped, moving into the rear without a rider, spread general dismay, which ended in a total rout; and the prince found present safety only by throwing himself into the strong fortress of Monghir.

Critical position of Aurengzebe.

Flight of Sujah.

Dara's reinforcement

Aurengzebe was again obliged to allow some respite to a vanquished adversary; for Dara, after reaching Tatta, recrossed the Indus, and proceeded through the great desert into the province of Guzerat. There he prevailed upon the governor, whose daughter had been married to Morad, to espouse his cause; and having raised a considerable army, he advanced into Rajpootana, and in the neighbourhood of Ajmere, its capital, intrenched himself in a position of extraordinary strength. The conqueror, on hastening thither, saw with dismay the commanding ground on which his brother had encamped. He endeavoured, by presenting his men in order of battle, and even by studied insults, to provoke the proud Dara to come forth and fight; but the prince had the prudence to decline these challenges. The emperor, however, always fertile in stratagem, devised a new scheme. Having in his camp the two chiefs who had been mainly instrumental in gaining over the army of the young Solimân, he caused them to write a letter to the father, assuring him that they had been induced only by imperious circumstances to forsake his cause, which they were anxious again to embrace; and that if he would leave open a certain gate at a particular hour, they, with all their followers, would enter and place themselves under his command. In vain did the oldest and most prudent counsellors warn Dara of the danger to which this step would expose him, and of the wiles of Aurengzebe. Rash, credulous, and inaccessible to advice, he allowed himself to be dazzled by the prospect of an accession to his force, which would have given him a complete superiority. The gate was opened at the appointed time; the chiefs rushed in, and were soon followed by the whole imperial army. Undeceived too late, he still attempted a gallant, though vain resistance, but being totally routed, was obliged to flee with a very small remnant of his troops. He bent his way to the capital of Guzerat, hoping there to find an asylum; but the governor refused him admittance. A band of Mahrattas, his sole remaining troops, seeing his fortunes lost, took the opportunity to plunder the camp, leaving nothing except what was concealed in the tents of the women. Dara was then compelled to undertake, without any preparation, a march across the desert, in a plight still more miserable than that in which the same

Strength of his position.

Duplicity of Aurengzebe

Total rout of Dara.

CHAP. IX. A. D. 1658.

disastrous journey had been performed by his ancestor Humaioon. Amid the horrors of fatigue and thirst, beneath a burning sun, a number of his faithful followers successively lay down and expired. At the head of a few survivors he reached Tatta, and might thence have pushed on into Persia, where he would probably have been well received; but at this crisis Nadira Bana, his favourite wife, was at the point of death, and he could not endure the thought of leaving this beloved object to die among strangers. He sought the hospitality of Jihon Khan, a neighbouring ruler; another rash or unfortunate act. This was a violent and bloody chief, who, after being twice condemned to death by Shah Jehan, had been pardoned at the prince's intercession. Dara had indeed the melancholy satisfaction of paying the last duties to his sultana; but, on attempting to depart, found himself surrounded by a body of troops, who delivered him to Khan Jehan, the imperial general, then in close pursuit of him. When at length he saw his fate inevitable, he assumed a demeanour of majestic fortitude, and maintained during the whole journey a calm dignity, soothing his grief by verses composed by himself on his own eventful history. He was led through Delhi miserably mounted and almost in rags. But Aurengzebe had miscalculated the effect of this exhibition; for the multitude, when they beheld their once noble and gallant ruler led to death under circumstances so fearfully changed, and beside him his son, a spirited and graceful boy, over whom so dark a destiny impended, were seized with the deepest sympathy, and melted into tears, mingled with curses against the tyrant. Jihon, the betrayer, was killed on his way home, while the capital seemed on the eve of insurrection. The emperor felt that he must hasten to close the tragedy. Assassins were accordingly introduced in the night, beneath whose blows his unfortunate brother fell after a desperate resistance; and, through the address of the monarch, the commotion in the city quickly subsided.

Seeks shelter from Jihon Khan.

Made captive.

His betrayer slain.

Aurengzebe had now only to dispose of Sujah, who,

under favour of this diversion, had rallied his broken forces. But as little apprehension was felt in that quarter, it was thought enough to detach against him Prince Mohammed and Jumla the vizier. This expedition, however, received a striking interest from a very unexpected and moving incident. The young warrior had been early betrothed to a daughter of Sujah, for whom he had conceived a strong attachment; and though in the late tumult of events he had forgotten the first impression, a letter which the princess, in concert with her father, now wrote to him, led to a revival of all his tenderness. He determined to quit the army, and espouse the cause of his uncle; nor does it seem improbable that he cherished some secret intention of imitating the example of Aurengzebe himself, by fighting his way to the empire. Being highly elated with the part he performed in the late revolution, and the offer made to him by his grandfather, he had often been heard to boast that it was he who placed the crown on his parent's head. He fondly flattered himself that the army would follow his example, and, when combined with that of Sujah, would compose a force so overwhelming as to defy all resistance. He embarked on the Ganges, as if upon a party of pleasure, and returned not. The soldiers, on discovering his intention, were at first greatly agitated; but the prudence and vigour of Jumla preserved their attachment to their master, and prevented any desertion. Sujah received his illustrious relative with the highest distinction; and, the nuptials having been celebrated with great pomp, he led out his men and offered battle. Mohammed placed himself in the foremost line, and when he saw the flower of the opposing cavalry bear down upon him, vainly imagined that they came to join his standard. But their fierce onset soon undeceived him. Both he and his kinsman behaved with the greatest valour; but the effeminate troops of Bengal could not withstand the veterans led by Jumla, who gained a complete victory. The situation of the prince was now deeply distressing, and the arts of his father rendered it

Expedition against Sujah.

Desertion of Prince Mohammed.

CHAP. IX. A.D. 1660.

desperate. Aurengzebe wrote a letter, addressed to him as if in answer to one from himself, treating of a plan for deserting the cause of his father-in-law. It was so arranged that this epistle should fall into the hands of Sujah, who thereupon conceived suspicions which the most solemn protestations could not remove. No violence was indeed offered to him; but he was informed that he and his wife must depart from Bengal. All India being now under the sway of the relentless emperor, the youth had no resource but to throw himself upon the mercy of one who never trusted those that had once deceived him. Mohammed was immediately arrested and sent to the strong fortress of Gwalior, where he pined away the remainder of his life, which terminated in seven years. Sujah having fled into Arracan, was betrayed by the rajah, and he with all his family perished. Solimân, the son of Dara, was taken prisoner among the Himmaleh mountains, whither he had fled for refuge; and thus Aurengzebe was left without a rival.

Deceit of Aurengzebe.

Captivity of Mohammed.

Close of Shah Jehan's life.

Shah Jehan survived for eight years the loss of empire; and it may be mentioned, to the credit of his ambitious son, and as some palliation of his crimes, that he treated his captive with all the respect and delicacy which were compatible with the condition of being dethroned and immured. He even tolerated the violent sallies of pride and indignation to which his unfortunate parent gave vent. Aurengzebe sent to solicit the daughter of Dara in marriage for his son Akbar, hoping by this connexion to strengthen his family interest with the nobles. But both Shah Jehan himself and his household received this proposal with the deepest resentment. The former returned for answer, that the insolence of the usurper was equal to his guilt; and the young princess herself kept a concealed dagger, declaring that she would rather die a hundred times than give her hand to the son of her father's murderer. All this was reported to the ruling sovereign, who quietly desisted from his solicitation. At another time he made a request for some of the imperial jewels, which were deemed

His indomitable pride.

necessary to adorn his throne. The Shah replied, that the hammers were ready to pound them into dust, if he should ever attempt to enforce such a demand. The other then exclaimed, "Let him keep his jewels, nay, let him command all those of Aurengzebe." The old monarch was so much affected by this moderation, that he sent a number of them, accompanied with a letter, in which he said,—"Take these, which I am destined to use no more.—Wear them with dignity, and by your own renown make some amends to your family for their misfortunes." The emperor burst into tears, which, on this occasion, appeared to be sincere. In short, by habitual respect and forbearance, and by occasionally asking advice, he succeeded, not indeed in reconciling the fallen sovereign to his fate, but in reviving a certain measure of friendly intercourse. On receiving intelligence that his father's end was approaching, he did not, it is true, venture into his presence, but sent his own son Shah Allum, who, however, arrived too late. The master of Hindostan then exhibited every mark of undissembled grief, and hastened to effect a reconciliation with his sister Jehanara, who had hitherto remained devotedly attached to her unfortunate parent.

Aurengzebe moderation.

Death of the Shah.

Aurengzebe continued for many years to occupy the throne of the Mogul dominion, which, under him, attained to its greatest extent and its highest glory. After he had added to it the kingdoms of the Deccan, it included nearly the whole peninsula of India, with the neighbouring regions of Cabul and Assam,—territories, the population and wealth of which probably exceeded those of the Roman empire during its most flourishing period. The revenues amounted to 32 millions sterling, which, though inferior to the immense income of one or two modern European states, was then probably unexampled. His internal administration seems to have been decidedly superior to that of his immediate predecessors. Amid the somewhat ostentatious display and matchless splendour of his court, his personal conduct remained pure and even austere; he neither allowed to himself, nor per-

Aurengzebe's reign.

Immense revenues.

CHAP. IX.

A. D. 1670.

mitted in his palace, any species of disorder or licentiousness. Early in the morning he was seated in the hall of justice, accessible to the meanest of his subjects, administering the law with the strictest impartiality, redressing their wrongs, and even relieving their sufferings by his bounty. India, therefore, under his long reign, apparently enjoyed all the happiness of which a country is susceptible in a state of subjection to the despotic power of a foreign prince. Indeed, were we to place implicit reliance in the Mohammedan historians, and in the English writers who copy their narratives, we should imagine the period from the accession of Akbar to the death of Aurengzebe to have been in the East an age of gold, an era of felicity almost unparalleled in the history of mankind. It cannot indeed be denied, that during all this time the central regions enjoyed a considerable measure of peace and prosperity; for the civil wars, though frequent and sometimes tragical, were usually decided in a single battle, and were not accompanied with extensive desolation. On looking narrowly into the subject, however, we shall find reason to suspect that the picture is too flattering, and that the empire throughout this period groaned under many of the evils incident to arbitrary rule. The very fact that at the time when Britain succeeded to this vast inheritance, the class of cultivators were all sunk into such abject poverty, that it was scarcely possible to discover by what tenure the land had been originally held, seems to invalidate the testimony of those historical eulogists.

Purity of his conduct.

Narratives of Mohammedan historians.

Evils incident to arbitrary rule.

Bernier's narrative.

It was during the reign of Aurengzebe that Bernier, an intelligent and reflecting traveller, spent some years in India, and applied himself with diligence to investigate the state of the Mogul government and empire. The description he gives is that of a country going to ruin, rather than of one flourishing under a just and impartial government. He observes, that supposing the sovereign inclined to enforce justice, he might perhaps succeed within his own immediate circle, in Delhi, Agra, and the close vicinity of these capitals; but in the provinces

Unprotected state of the provinces.

and remote districts the people had no adequate protection from the rapacity of the governors, who ruled with arbitrary power, and whom he characterizes as "men fit for ruining a world." This was confirmed by the mean garb, and the anxiety to assume the semblance of poverty, which prevailed even among those whom other circumstances proved to be possessed of exorbitant wealth. The people could appeal to no court of justice, no administrators of the law, no independent tribunals. The monarch himself could call to his service no men endowed with honourable principles, inspired with feelings of genuine loyalty, or identifying their glory with that of their prince. These functionaries were generally "men of nothing, slaves, ignorant and brutal, raised from the dust, and retaining always the quality and temper of beggars." The only object of those intrusted with any power was to amass wealth during the short and precarious tenure of their possession, regardless if afterwards the whole state should fall into ruin.

Evidence of disregard for justice.

Even as to the feelings of justice and regard to the rights of their subjects, which are said to have characterized this dynasty, Bernier mentions several particulars, which, agreeing in a remarkable manner with those reported by Hawkins and Roe, tend to cast great doubt upon the panegyrics of native writers. Anecdotes, even of a somewhat familiar description, may illustrate the tone of manners at this oriental court. A young man laid before Shah Jehan a complaint, that his mother, a banian, was possessed of immense wealth, amounting to two hundred thousand rupees, who yet, on account of alleged ill-conduct, withheld from him all participation. The emperor, tempted by hearing of so large a fortune, sent for the lady, and commanded her, in open assembly to give to her son fifty thousand rupees, and to pay to himself a hundred thousand; at the same time desiring her to withdraw. The woman, however, by loud clamour, again procured admittance, and coolly said:—"May it please your majesty, my son has certainly some claim to the goods of his father; but I would gladly know

Familiar anecdotes.

CHAP. IX.
A. D. 1680

what relation your majesty bears to the merchant, my deceased husband, that you make yourself his heir." This idea appeared to Shah Jehan so droll, that he desired her to depart, and no exaction should be made. Such an incident may prove an accessible temper, and a degree of good humour on the part of the sovereign, but gives a very low idea of the general character of that justice which oriental writers are pleased to ascribe to him.

Personal freedom enjoyed.

The other anecdote is of a still more odd description. There were in Delhi a class of females called Kencheny, who, though of somewhat doubtful reputation, were not altogether abandoned, and were allowed to contribute to the amusement of this very gay court. A French physician, named Bernard, then resident at Delhi, endeavoured to obtain a young damsel of this class as his mistress; but her mother, probably from motives of prudence, opposed the connexion. The medical man, however, having gone in the evening to wait upon the Emperor Jehangire, and being about to receive a present in return for a cure which he had effected in the seraglio, pointed to the Kencheny, who happened to be among the multitude paying her court to the prince, and besought, in place of any other gift, that she might be bestowed upon him. His majesty burst into a fit of laughter, and called out, "Lay her on his shoulders, and let him carry her away."—"So said, so done." The young lady was immediately given up to him, and Bernard departed laden with this unlawful booty.

Bernier's account of the Mogul armies.

Bernier was among the first to dispel the impression which prevailed in Europe of the mighty and unconquerable armies engaged in Mogul warfare. Even the numbers had been greatly exaggerated. The only efficient department was the cavalry, of which the portion immediately attached to the monarch's residence did not exceed 35,000 or 40,000, nor was it supposed that the whole under his command could much exceed 200,000. The infantry, including the artillery stationed at the capital, might amount to 15,000. The innumerable hosts of foot-soldiers, said to compose the mass of the army, consisted chiefly of servants, victuallers, foragers, and others, who followed in its train, conveying tents, and supplying provisions, cattle, and every thing wanted for the men and officers. This attendance was so numerous that, when the imperial troops marched, all Delhi and Agra might be described as proceeding along with them ; and, indeed, these cities could be considered as little more than standing encampments ; while the actual camps, on the other hand, with their streets of tents and regular markets, might be viewed as moving cities. Still lower was Bernier's estimate of the quality of these warriors. Often, it is true, they fought with great bravery ; but, being destitute of all discipline, they were frequently struck with panic, and then became altogether incapable of command. He was persuaded that a force of 20,000 or 25,000 men, led by a Condé or a Turenne, would easily trample all these barbarians under foot,—an anticipation amply verified by subsequent events in the annals of British India.

Cumbrous attendance on the army.

The foreign history of this reign was chiefly distinguished by the danger which threatened the new sovereign of being involved in war with Abbas, king of Persia, the most powerful and warlike prince in Asia. Dow, following the native historians, represents this rupture between these two mighty potentates to have arisen from the error of a secretary, who addressed a letter, "From the emperor of the world to the master of Persia." On receiving the epistle thus directed, Abbas, it is said, rejected all explanation and apology, and instantly prepared for war. Such a mistake seems not very probable, much less that a monarch so distinguished for talent and policy, and now of mature age, should have engaged in so formidable a contest on a ground so trivial. Possibly he might use it as a pretext ; and, seeing the throne of India filled by a prince not yet firmly seated, and rendered odious by the steps which had led to his elevation, might conceive the hope of making this important addition to his dominions. Many circumstances conspired to favour his

Threatened rupture with Persia.

CHAP. IX.

A. D. 1685.

expectations. Of the great omrahs at the court of Delhi a number were of Iranian extraction; many also, of Patan or Afghan origin, looked back with regret to the period when princes of their nation sat on the imperial throne. Aurengzebe had room to suspect that Abbas was seeking to open a communication with the Persian chiefs in his service, and was even attempting to seduce the vizier, who was of that descent. He felt himself in a very delicate situation; for this body was so numerous and powerful, that to drive them into open hostility might have rendered his position still more critical. The minister and the other nobles, however, strenuously denied the charge; and the whole affair was amicably adjusted. The emperor, notwithstanding, continued to suffer the utmost anxiety till he was relieved by the intelligence that Abbas, in consequence of a neglected illness, had expired in his camp on the frontier. Sefi, his grandson and successor, looking forward with uneasiness to the scenes of disorder which usually follow a vacancy in an eastern throne, had no inclination to embarrass himself farther by a foreign war, and readily concluded a treaty.

Secret plots of the Persian king.

His sudden death.

We must not omit to mention a ridiculous incident, by which Aurengzebe was exposed to great danger. An old female devotee, called Bistamia, in the Rajpoot territory of Marwar, having, by her bounty, collected around her a number of fakirs and other Hindoo sectaries, formed them at length into a sort of army, with which she defeated the rajah and some inferior officers. Having at length assembled a force amounting to twenty thousand, she marched upon the imperial city. Superstitious terror paved the way for her victories; for it was believed that she prepared a mess, composed of the most horrid ingredients, which rendered her followers on the day of battle invisible, and consequently irresistible. Having made their way victoriously almost to the gates of Agra, they looked on themselves as masters of the empire, and proclaimed their leader Queen of India. The emperor, seriously alarmed on finding even his own troops struck with awe, was convinced that it would be vain to contend

Ridiculous cause of danger.

Bistamia's victories.

Aurengzebe's policy.

against such a host with mere human weapons. Having, by his Moslem zeal, acquired a holy character in the eyes of his soldiers, he wrote sacred sentences on pieces of paper, and causing them to be stuck on the points of spears, which he placed in front of the battalions, he assured his men that they would protect them against the necromantic influences of their fanatical adversaries. Their fears being thus dispelled, the superiority of their arms soon enabled them completely to rout the fakir host, which was almost entirely cut to pieces.

Insurrection in Cabul.

The reign of this great monarch was again disturbed by an insurrection in Cabul, where he soon reduced the open country, though he wisely desisted from the attempt to deprive the inhabitants of their independence. But the grand object of his ambition was to effect the final subjugation of the Deccan kingdoms of Golconda and Bejapore, which, although their force had indeed been broken by repeated victories gained by his predecessors, and even by himself previous to his accession, still retained a considerable share of power.

Invasion of the Deccan.

Various occurrences and dissensions prevented this expedition from being carried into effect till the year 1686, the twenty-eighth of Aurengzebe, when the whole imperial force marched by three directions into the Deccan. Operations were begun by Shah Allum, the heir-apparent, who laid siege to Golconda. The king solicited peace on very humble terms, which the invader granted, that he might turn his whole force against Bejapore. This kingdom made a more obstinate resistance; but afterwards the troops being induced by treachery to desert, the city was closely invested, and at length compelled by famine to capitulate. Secunder Adil Shah, the last of a long line of powerful princes, became a captive in the hands of the emperor. The victor forthwith employed his arms to complete the conquest of Golconda; when his son Shah Allum, by remonstrating against this breach of faith, incurred his resentment, and was thrown into prison. That city, after a siege of seven months,

Capitulation of Bejapore.

Conquest of Golconda.

CHAP. IX.

A. D. 1686.

was taken by treachery; and the death of its king, Abou Houssein, after being treated with the utmost indignity, terminated another powerful race of monarchs.

Rise of the Mahratta power.

But an event which influenced the whole reign of Aurengzebe is still to be mentioned. This was the rise of the Mahratta power, which, from small beginnings, was one day to subvert the proud fabric of the Mogul empire, and even dispute with Britain the supremacy of Hindostan. The north-western part of peninsular India composes the territory of Maharashtra, which, according to Mr Grant Duff, includes a surface of 102,000 square miles, and a population of about six millions. It is traversed by branches of the Ghauts and Vyndhia mountains, and comprises a large portion of the provinces of Malwa, Candeish, Aurungabad, and Bejapore. The whole bears a very different aspect from the extensive plains of the Deccan and of Hindostan Proper. It is elevated, rugged, diversified with bleak table-lands, and broken by numerous streams and torrents. Being throughout unfit for the movements of heavy cavalry, in which the strength of the Mogul armies consisted, it could be reduced only to very imperfect subjection. All the hills and fastnesses were occupied by petty chieftains, who paid a mere outward homage to the imperial throne or the kingdom of Bejapore. Amid the constant wars, however, of the Mohammedan nations with one another, and the disputed successions of the great empire, opportunities were afforded to a leader of daring and comprehensive mind to erect them into an independent community. Such a person was Sevajee, the founder of the Mahratta dynasty.

Character of the country.

Lineage of Sevajee.

This hero, though he began with slender resources, was by no means of ignoble descent. His great-grandfather, Babjee Bhonslay, was a son of the Rana of Oodipoor, whose blood is considered the highest and purest in all Hindostan; but his mother was a woman of inferior caste, and the stain thus incurred induced him to quit his native country, and seek employment and distinction in other courts. Having risen to eminence in the service of a rajah in the territory of Candeish, he procured a zemindary near Poonah, then only a village, but which the prosperity of his family raised afterwards into a great capital. His son Malojee acquired celebrity under a Mahratta chief, whose daughter he obtained in marriage for his son Shahjee. This last having quarrelled with his father-in-law, entered the army of the King of Bejapore, and was employed in Tanjore and the Carnatic. While serving in this quarter, he left his son Sevajee at Poonah with his mother, under the tuition of Dadajee Konedeo, who seems to have bestowed very great pains in training the future warrior. He initiated him, not indeed in letters, which are despised by those mountaineers, but in military exercises, in national legends and poetry, and in a deep veneration for the Hindoo faith and observances. At the age of seventeen, the pupil was impelled by his daring spirit to a warlike enterprise; he collected a band of Mawulees, natives of the neighbouring glens, and commenced that ambiguous profession of a warrior and a robber, which is generally pursued by the half-civilized tribes of Asia. Heavy complaints were lodged with Dadajee on account of these exploits, against which he felt himself bound to make the most solemn remonstrances; but he is alleged, at the same time, to have secretly encouraged the youth to persevere in his pursuits, for which he conceived him eminently qualified; foreseeing, probably, in some degree, the greatness to which such an adventurous life would conduct him.

CHAP. IX.

A. D. 1625.

His son Malojee.

Collects a band of followers.

Sevajee accordingly followed his aspiring course; and obtaining possession of the almost inaccessible castle of Torna, gave the first alarm to the King of Bejapore, whom, however, he conciliated by the promise of an increased tribute. As he continued to seize or erect fort after fort, the king not only redoubled his remonstrances, but also appealed to Shahjee, the father of the marauder, whom he first threatened and then imprisoned, disregarding all his protestations that he neither knew nor approved of his son's proceedings. The youth was distress-

Sevajee acquires the Castle of Torna.

CHAP. IX. A. D. 1640.

ed at the disaster in which he had involved his parent; yet, very unwilling to effect his release by a change of system, he bethought himself of an application to Shah Jehan, whose vassal he professed himself, and by whose powerful intercession the deliverance of Shahjee was in fact obtained. When Aurengzebe came to make war against Bejapore, Sevajee continued to represent himself as an ally of the Mogul, and hence, as even his neutrality was of importance at so eventful a period, he was allowed to retain unmolested all his possessions. But, as soon as he saw these two great monarchies fully occupied in their sanguinary contest, he hesitated not to seize plunder and territory from either as opportunity offered. At length Aurengzebe suspended the contest, that he might prosecute those ambitious schemes which effected his elevation to the throne of Hindostan; during the progress of which he had of course no leisure to resent the conduct of the young freebooter. This rising chief, however, had to encounter the undivided hostility of the court of Bejapore, which had long considered him as a rebel, and now exerted its entire force to accomplish his destruction; and he boldly determined to face the storm with the combined power of arms and stratagem.

Sevajee's pliant policy.

Collision with the court of Bejapore.

The army of Bejapore, under the command of Afzool or Abdul Khan, a leader of distinction, advanced against this restless insurgent, in full confidence of speedily subduing him. Sevajee, finding it necessary to ply all his arts, gave intimation that he had resolved to submit, but dreaded to place himself in the power of an enemy so justly offended. He therefore prevailed upon his adversary to arrange a meeting, to which each party should come with one attendant only. In contemplation of this interview, he secretly filled the woods in front of his castle with armed men, put on a complete suit of chain-armour under his cotton robe, a steel cap on his head, and concealed in his clothes a dagger with other deadly weapons. He had soon the satisfaction to discover Afzool Khan approaching with an escort of 1500 men, whom he left at some distance, and repaired to the appointed spot

Sevajee's unprincipled stratagem.

Approach of Afzool Khan.

with a single follower. Sevajee meantime had performed the most solemn religious ceremonies, and besought his mother's blessing, like one going forth on some deed of glorious peril. He then proceeded to the place apparently unarmed, and looking frequently back as if afraid to advance. At length he stepped forward, embraced Afzool after the Indian fashion, and at the same moment struck him through the body. The Bejapore chief instantly drew his sword, and aimed a blow at the head of his treacherous assailant; but it was intercepted by the helmet beneath his turban; and the next stab laid the khan lifeless on the ground. The Mahratta troops, warned by the sounding of a horn, started from their ambuscade, and soon put to flight the surprised and terrified escort. Asiatic armies can only be rallied round the person of their commander, and on his fall lose all their courage. The enemy's soldiers having dispersed, Sevajee was left at full liberty to carry on his operations, and overrunning a great extent of country, he pushed his inroads to the very gates of the hostile capital. He took occasion in particular to possess himself of the Concan, called by the ancients the Pirate Coast, and became master of its key, the strong fortress of Panalla, which, by enabling him to equip a fleet, greatly augmented his means both of conquest and plunder. The King of Bejapore recruiting his forces, sent repeated expeditions against this rebel chief, which reduced him indeed to great extremities; but he always extricated himself, and at last concluded a peace that left in his possession an extensive range of mountain-territory, with an army of 50,000 foot and 7000 horse.

Treacherous assassination of the Bejapore chief

Acquires the fortress of Panalla.

Aurengzebe meantime, by civil war and treason, had attained the undisturbed possession of the Mogul throne; and he now resolved to make himself complete master of India. For this purpose it was necessary to put down the rising power of Sevajee, which was assuming so formidable an attitude. He despatched on this service a well-appointed army under Shaista Khan, an omrah high in his confidence. The new general carried on

Aurengzebe's plans of conquest.

CHAP. IX. A.D. 1660.

the campaign for some time with great success, reduced many forts, including Poonah, the original seat of the military adventurer, who in this extremity had recourse to one of his bold exploits. Having selected a small band of resolute soldiers, he obtained admittance, favoured, as was suspected, by the jealousy of a Mogul chief, into the residence of Shaista. The assailants with pick-axes forced their way into the cook-room, whence they rushed into the interior of the house with such fury that the omrah had scarcely time to leap out at a window; in effecting which he was wounded, and had one of his fingers cut off. His son was killed; and he himself was at once so intimidated by this disaster, and filled with such a degree of jealousy of his own officers, that he solicited his recall; after which the military operations against the Mahrattas for some time languished.

Bold exploit of Sevajee.

Recall of Shaista.

This interval was improved by their active chief for the accomplishment of one of his most adventurous undertakings,—the plundering of Surat, at that time the chief emporium of India, and perhaps the richest city in the world. Confident in its greatness and wealth, the citizens seem to have rested secure, having only surrounded it with a slight earthen wall, incapable of even retarding the intrepid bands of Sevajee. That leader, according to some authors, went in disguise three days through the town, marking the fittest objects for attack and plunder. He then formed two camps at once, before Bassein and Chaul, and seemed solely occupied in pressing the sieges of these important places, when suddenly he ordered the main body of his troops to withdraw from the former, leaving only small parties, who were instructed to keep up lights, noise, and every appearance of a large army. The Mahratta force thus presented itself quite unexpectedly, and entered Surat without resistance, the governor retiring into the fort, while the English and Dutch remained within their factories; so that the victorious army for three days ranged through this vast city, busying themselves in the appropriation of every valuable article on which they could lay their hands.

Plunder of Surat.

Mock sieges.

Sudden entrance of Surat.

CHAP. IX. A.D. 1664.

The booty in treasure, jewels, and other precious commodities, was valued at a million sterling.

Resolute effort of Aurengzebe.

Aurengzebe, more and more exasperated at being thus baffled by a petty chieftain, determined to make the most vigorous efforts to crush him; and with this view he sent a formidable army under the maraja, or Mirza Rajah, a gallant officer, who had been accustomed to make war in a mountainous country. The Mahratta was quite unable to face this new commander in the open field; and, castle after castle being reduced, he was soon driven to a more perilous extremity than ever. At length Poorundur, his main place of strength, in which he had lodged his family and treasure, was closely invested, without any hope of his being able to relieve it. He then gave up his cause as desperate; and on receiving the pledged faith of the maraja, that he should find at Delhi safety and an honourable reception, surrendered himself to the Mogul. He seems to have gone to court with the expectation of being treated as an omrah of the first class, and was therefore deeply mortified when he found himself received by the emperor with studied contempt, and consigned to quite a secondary rank. If we may believe some respectable historians, the daughter of Aurengzebe, seeing the young stranger from behind a curtain, became enamoured of him,—of which Sevajee being apprized, he made overtures for her hand, which were rejected by the monarch with the deepest indignation. More diligent inquirers regard this tender interlude as altogether apocryphal; but at all events, the discomfited chief saw himself a closely-watched and unhonoured captive, in the hands of one whose wiles were as deep as his own. All his invention, therefore, was on the rack to effect his escape. Having lulled the suspicions of his keepers by counterfeiting madness, he contrived to have himself and his son deposited in two large baskets that had been employed for carrying sweetmeats, and was conveyed to a spot outside the city. Here, mounting in disguise a miserable horse, he travelled onward without suspicion to Muttra, and thence to

Submission of Sevajee.

Contemptuous treatment of him.

CHAP. IX. A.D. 1670.

Effects his escape.

Benares and Juggernaut, taking this occasion to visit these holy seats of pilgrimage. From the latter he went round by Hydrabad, and at length found himself amid his native hills, with his devoted and gallant followers rallying around him.

Resumes his predatory career.

Sevajee at once resumed his predatory and victorious career, which placed him in a state of avowed warfare with the Mogul; but Aurengzebe, disgusted, perhaps, with the manner in which he had been overreached, and occupied with the arms of Persia and the insurrection of the Patans, did not for a long time direct his attention to this marauder, who pillaged merely a wild district of his dominions. The Mahratta prince accordingly extended his ravages almost undisturbed along the western coast; he again plundered Surat, and on a third occasion, though he did not enter, he levied a large contribution. In the sack of Rajapore, he robbed the English factory of 10,000 pagodas, which, however, were afterwards repaid. Singurh, a hill-fort, deemed next to impregnable, had been wrested from him by famine during his late disasters; but a thousand of his daring Mawulees, mounting at the highest point by a ladder of ropes, carried the place sword in hand. Immediately on his return he had assumed the titles of royalty, and caused coins to be struck bearing his name. He now determined to satisfy his pride and dazzle his followers by a formal coronation, modelled upon that of the Mogul, in which the weighing against gold, and other childish ceremonies, were not omitted. Gifts to an immense value, bestowed on Brahmins, gave lustre to this as well as to several other political festivals.

Second plunder of Surat.

Assumes the titles of royalty.

In the year after his coronation, Sevajee was seized with an illness which confined him eight months; but, upon recovering, he renewed his warlike operations on a more extended scale than ever. Golconda, almost at the opposite side of the peninsula, and considered far beyond his reach, saw itself suddenly surrounded by upwards of 12,000 Mahratta horse, who rushed to the assault so suddenly as to leave no time to put the city in any pos-

Assault of Golconda.

ture of defence. An immense ransom was paid to save it from plunder; and the assailant, having entered at the head of a large body of followers, held an audience on quite an equal footing with its great and potent sovereign. He even appears, without abating any part of his claim for ransom, to have formed an alliance for common defence against the Mogul. He penetrated next year across the territories of Bejapore into the Carnatic, which afforded an entirely new scene of conquest. He made himself master of Gingee, Vellore, and other strong places, in the name of the King of Golconda, but carefully garrisoned them with his own troops; then pushed his victories to the neighbourhood of Madras on the one side, and of Seringapatam on the other. After his return he alarmed and had nearly obtained possession of Bombay; but having to encounter Dilleer Khan, the imperial general, to whom Sambajee, his son, with the usual treachery of Indian princes, had deserted, he sustained a defeat, and was obliged to retreat to Rayree, his capital. Afterwards, being reconciled to the runaway, he set out, and making an immense circuit, seized near Burhanpoor a large convoy bringing treasure to the enemy's army. He returned rapidly and safely to his metropolis; but the extreme fatigue of this journey, joined to what he had endured in so many other expeditions, caused an inflammation in the lungs, which terminated his life on the 5th April 1680, at the age of fifty-three. On receiving the tidings, Aurengzebe is said to have shown extraordinary marks of exultation; having at the same time the magnanimity to bear witness to the great talents by which, while he himself had been employed in subverting all the ancient kingdoms of India, Sevajee had been able, in defiance of numerous and well-appointed armies, to erect a new one on a broad and firm basis.

Immense ransom. *Invasion of the Carnatic.* *Desertion of his son.* *His death.*

The character of Sevajee has been variously drawn; though the delineations appear to us, on the whole, somewhat too favourable. He certainly presented a complete example of a character not uncommon in the East or in barbarous countries, but seldom brought

Character of Sevajee.

CHAP. IX.
A. D. 1680.

into view in our happier forms of society; in which the monarch, general, partisan, bandit, and even the expert thief, are blended in nearly equal proportions, and each part is performed with equal success, according to the scene on which it is acted. In all these capacities Sevajee showed himself what we should call an excessively clever fellow; and the history of his tricks and surprises, repeated and exaggerated for the sake of amusement, has rendered his name highly popular among the Hindoos. Yet there seems nothing, either in his objects or in his mode of pursuing them, which can entitle him to be ranked as a great man, actuated by high or enlarged views of policy. In regard to his moral qualities, again, it seems difficult to ascribe any merit to the man who scrupled at nothing whatever by which he could compass his ambitious designs; for if he had the principles of faith or honour, it is obvious that they were never allowed to interfere with any important interest. Not to have been addicted to wanton cruelty is, indeed, in an eastern warrior, a subject of praise; yet blood was never spared by him if the shedding of it could serve a purpose. Perhaps, had he ever attained the peaceable possession of an extensive kingdom, he might have atoned for the evils which his predatory warfare inflicted, by a beneficent and protecting system; but for this he had scarcely an opportunity. At the same time his habits were simple and temperate; he mingled frankly and familiarly with his followers; and, without guard or precaution, felt himself among them always in perfect safety. He was strictly observant of the rites of the Hindoo religion, professing in its cause the most fervent zeal; nor would we hastily pronounce this attachment to have been purely political, though it proved one of the chief instruments of his aggrandizement. He proclaimed himself its champion against the bigoted enmity, degenerating at last into persecuting zeal, manifested by Aurengzebe.

His mercenary views. Unscrupulous policy. Simplicity of manners.

Sambajee's accession.

The Mahratta cause was placed in imminent peril by the premature decease of its founder. Sambajee, according to the usual fate of an Indian prince, opened his career by contending with a brother for the sovereignty. He was next invaded by a large Mogul force; but, showing himself not an unworthy descendant of his father, compelled it to retire with great loss. Aurengzebe, however, soon afterwards pushed all his armies into the Deccan, with the view of making a final conquest of the south of India. He commenced, as we have already related, with the entire reduction of the kingdoms of Bejapore and Golconda, which had so long braved his power. He then turned his whole array towards the Mahrattas, and began to practise against them their own arts. Having learned from one of his spies that Sambajee, in the pursuit of the irregular pleasures to which he was addicted, had set out almost unattended, he sent a detachment of soldiers who surprised and made him prisoner. The emperor, according to his usual ungenerous conduct, ordered the captive to be immediately put to death, and is alleged even to have feasted his eyes on the sufferings which that unfortunate prince bore with unshaken fortitude. The final downfal of the Mahratta cause was now fully anticipated; but Rama, a brother of the deceased, hastened to the Carnatic, and concentrated his troops round the almost impregnable fortress of Gingee, the reduction of which, interrupted by desultory warfare, occupied the imperial army several years. Meantime the people, throughout their native mountains, were mustering their irregular bands, with which they poured down, not only upon the newly-conquered countries of Golconda and Bejapore, but even upon the old territories of Candeish, Malwa, and Berar.

Military capacity.

Aurengzebe's invasion of the Deccan.

Sambajee's capture and death.

His brother Rama.

The Mahratta army, which was destined for more than a century to exercise great influence over the fortunes of India, was, like that of the Mogul, composed chiefly of cavalry, but very differently organized. The latter, cased in strong defensive armour, rode heavy and powerful steeds, while the chiefs, mounted on elephants, were enclosed in a species of fortification. Such squa-

Mahratta army.

CHAP. IX.

A.D. 1690.

drons, when acting on the vast plains of Hindostan Proper, or even on the wide and level table-lands of the Deccan, bore down all opposition. But Maharashtra is a region of hills neither so lofty nor so rugged as to obstruct altogether the movement of horse, yet not affording ground on which the enormous masses of heavy cavalry could make their impetuous charge. The inhabitants, therefore, raised a force suited to their country and to their own habits, composed of small, swift, active horses, with riders lightly dressed and equipped, fitted for march rather than for battle; to sweep over a wide extent of territory, and return without allowing an enemy to overtake them. They were intermixed with infantry, armed partly with matchlocks, partly with arrows; but the favourite national weapon is the spear, with a short sword and shield. An annual campaign was regularly opened at the termination of the north-west monsoon, and announced by the hoisting of the *ghoonda* or royal standard. In forming a camp, the flag of the prince or general is first displayed, whence the bazaar or range of shops extends in a parallel line from front to rear. Along these, on each side, the chiefs raise their ensigns, around which their followers, with their horses and cattle, crowd in masses. The army sets forth without any provision except what can be contained in two cotton bags or pouches thrown over the front of each rider's saddle. They march onward, trusting to supply all their wants on their route, either by forcible seizure, or by means of the numerous brinjarries, or merchants, who resort to a Hindoo encampment as a market for their commodities. Although plunder is indispensable, it is not pursued by lawless violence, nor does each individual trooper appropriate to himself what falls into his hands. It is extorted from the rich according to a regular system, and the produce is thrown into the public stock. A liberal pay is allowed to the soldier, not indeed always very regularly distributed, but he is indulged in great freedom while suing for its liquidation. In these excursions the troops not only

Character of the country. — Annual campaign. — Mode of provision. — Systematic plunder.

CHAP. IX

A.D. 1700.

load themselves with booty, but add much to their numbers; for men of an adventurous spirit, who have no tie to home, if they can only provide a horse are easily induced to join the ranks of this roving army. Thus the Mahratta force, without any decisive victory, swelled as it proceeded; and even amid successive defeats, while losing battle after battle and castle after castle, they continued to overspread the extensive provinces of Candeish, Malwa, and Berar, and to occupy a large portion of Central India.

Accession of adventures.

Latter years of Aurengzebe.

The latter years of Aurengzebe, though they were not marked by any serious reverse, and though his power continued on the whole unbroken, were yet rendered gloomy by the disappointment of several important enterprises, and by the many omens of decline which thickened around his empire. His bigotry, always increasing, impelled him at length to the most violent measures for extirpating the Hindoo religion. The superb temples of Muttra and Benares were rased to the ground, and mosques erected on their site. The pagoda of Ahmedabad, one of the most splendid of the national structures, was desecrated by killing a cow within its walls. These outrages, viewed by the superstitious people with the deepest horror, did not indeed excite them to direct rebellion; but still they spread throughout the empire a universal detestation of the Mogul yoke, and an eager disposition to rally round any standard whether erected by a chief or a government. To them may be ascribed in a great measure the rapid progress of the Mahratta state, and the successful resistance of the petty Rajpoot principalities. The days of Aurengzebe were also more and more imbittered by the disposition which his children showed to follow his example. Mohammed, his eldest son, had already died in prison,—the punishment of rebellion. During a dangerous illness, under which he suffered at an early period of his reign, Shah Allum, the second, had too clearly shown how intently his mind was fixed on the succession; and though he had done nothing absolutely

Bigoted zeal.

Influence on his popularity.

CHAP. IX.

A. D. 1707.

Rival jealousies of his sons.

undutiful, or which would have justified his disgrace, the intercourse between him and his father was ever after marked by suspicion and distrust. Akbar, another son, distinguished by the high rank of his mother, was guilty of open insurrection, and joined successively the hostile standards of the Mahrattas and the Rajpoots. Two others, Azim and Kaum Buksh, were near him in his last illness; and he foresaw too clearly that his death would be the signal for dreadful conflicts, to be terminated only by the blood of all his male descendants except one. Amid these troubles and gloomy presentiments the fatal term at length arrived; he expired in his camp on the 21st February 1707, in the ninety-fourth year of his age, and in the forty-ninth of his reign.

His death.

Estimate of his character.

Historians have found much difficulty in forming a correct estimate of the character of this extraordinary monarch. His crimes, written in deep and legible characters, cannot be concealed, while the general tenor of his life was marked by many virtues. In the administration of justice he was assiduous and impartial; he was liable neither to fits of passion nor caprice; his charities were almost unbounded, and he usually showed much concern for the welfare of his people. Surrounded by the most ample means of licentious indulgence, of which the example had been set by the greatest of his predecessors, the habits of his private life were pure and even austere. Our opinion of his character must be materially affected by the degree of credit which we attach to that religious profession which he maintained through life with so much apparent zeal. It is exposed to much suspicion, from the manifest exaggeration with which it was sometimes exhibited, and still more from its having been made an instrument of ambition, and even of crimes. Yet there seems reason to believe that, as in the case of Cromwell, whom in many respects he resembled, there may have been, beneath a good deal of interested and hypocritical pretension, a fund of sincerity. This conclusion seems

Purity of his private life.

strengthened by his persecution of the Hindoo religion, the imprudence of which, in a worldly point of view, was too manifest to have escaped a prince of his penetration, and, however blamable in itself, must, in the professor of a creed essentially intolerant, admit of some palliation. There seems reason to believe, that amid the greatest aberrations his moral feelings remained strong; that though the tempest of ambition, when it arose, swept all before it, the deeds to which it prompted him were afterwards a subject of painful remorse. The blood of his kindred which he had shed seems never to have been effaced from his mind; so that, seated on the greatest throne of the world, and possessed of every quality which could support and adorn it, Aurengzebe was miserable. Several letters have been preserved, written to his sons in the prospect of death, which are apparently genuine, and give a striking picture of the emotions felt at the approach of that awful hour when the earthly greatness which he had purchased at so dreadful a price was about to disappear. He says,—"Old age is arrived: weakness subdues me, and strength has forsaken all my limbs. I came a stranger into this world, and a stranger I depart. I know nothing of myself, what I am, and for what I am destined. The instant which passed in power hath left only sorrow behind it. I have not been the guardian and protector of the empire. My valuable time has been passed vainly. I had a patron in my own dwelling (conscience), but his glorious light was unseen by my dim sight.—I brought nothing into this world, and, except the infirmities of man, carry nothing out. I have a dread for my salvation, and with what torments I may be punished. Though I have strong reliance on the mercies and bounty of God, yet regarding my actions fear will not quit me; but when I am gone, reflection will not remain.—My back is bent with weakness, and my feet have lost the powers of motion. The breath which rose is gone, and left not even hope behind it. I have committed numerous crimes, and know not with what punishments I may be seized.—

Evidence of his sincerity.

His remorse.

Letters to his sons.

CHAP. IX. A. D. 1707.

The guardianship of a people is the trust by God committed to my sons.—I resign you, your mother, and son, to God as I myself am going. The agonies of death come upon me fast.—Odiporee, your mother, was a partner in my illness, and wishes to accompany me in death; but every thing has its appointed time.—I am going. Whatever good or evil I have done, it was for you.—No one has seen the departure of his own soul; but I see that mine is departing."

Shah Allum's temperate overtures.

On the death of Aurengzebe, the struggle for empire immediately commenced; yet it was neither so obstinate nor so bloody as had been anticipated. Shah Allum, the eldest son, and whose cause was embraced by the more powerful party, was of a temper peculiarly mild and amiable; he made the most liberal offers to his brothers, proposing to grant them the government of some of the finest provinces; but ambition and evil advisers urged them on to try the fortune of battle. They were vanquished; one of them was killed in the field, the other put an end to his own life; and Shah Allum, by painful steps, but without guilt, ascended the throne.

His peaceful policy.

The chief aim of this monarch seems to have been to restore peace to the empire, even at the cost of resigning some of the pretensions advanced by its rulers during the long period of progressive prosperity. He effected an accommodation with the Rajpoots, on terms which required from those haughty chiefs little more than the shadow of submission. The Mahrattas, during the latter part of the reign of Aurengzebe, had offered to cease their depredations on condition of receiving the *chout*, or fourth part of the revenue of the districts which were exposed to their inroads; but that proud sovereign, though unable to repel them, indignantly rejected the idea of listening to proposals made by the leaders of a predatory horde. Shah Allum, however, finding that the empire did not afford the means of subduing these plunderers, determined, wisely perhaps, to accede to their terms, and thereby to deliver several of

Amicable arrangements with the Mahrattas.

his finest provinces from so dreadful a scourge. On other occasions, when circumstances were more favourable, he showed himself not destitute either of enterprise or military skill. These qualities he had occasion to display against a new enemy, who about this time rose into political importance.

First appearance of the Seiks

The Sikhs or Seiks made their first appearance during the reign of Baber simply as a religious sect. Nannuk, the founder, is said to have been an amiable and intelligent man, of a mild and philosophic temper, who, seeing with pain the violent dissensions between the votaries of the Hindoo and Mohammedan creeds, formed a scheme by means of which he hoped to effect a reconciliation. Borrowing some of the leading ceremonies of each, he endeavoured to inculcate the grand principles of a superintending providence and a future retribution acknowledged by both. The numbers of the Seiks rapidly multiplied, being swelled by accessions from other sects; but they still conducted themselves as peaceable citizens, and, under the philosophic reigns of Akbar and his immediate successors, suffered not the slightest molestation. It was the persecuting bigotry of Aurengzebe which converted them into mortal enemies. He caused their chief or patriarch, Teeg Bahadur, to be seized, brought to the fort of Gwalior, and there put to death. This furious proceeding changed entirely the character of the people; and Gooroo Govind, son to the murdered prelate, devoted his whole life to the task of vengeance. He succeeded in inspiring all his followers with the same sentiments; and, having armed and mounted them, he changed peaceful fakirs into daring troopers and fierce marauders. Being obliged, however, with these newly-levied bands, to encounter Aurengzebe in the plenitude of his zeal and power, he was unable to make an effectual resistance. His troops were scattered; his two sons were taken and put to death; he himself became a hopeless exile; and, overpowered by so many calamities, died bereft of reason. But the spirit of the association did not sink; on the contrary,

Accessions to their numbers.

Influence of persecution.

Death of Gooroo Govind.

CHAP. IX. A. D. 1710.

under the pressure of wrong and suffering, it became more savage and resolute than ever. After lurking for many years amid the hills and fastnesses on the rude border of the Himmaleh, they were encouraged by the death of Aurengzebe again to approach the northern provinces. They were now led by Banda, a follower of the late chief, who assumed also the name of Gooroo Govind; and their devastations are represented to have been truly dreadful, inspired by an imbittered feeling of revenge, and an entire disregard of humanity. Banda had occupied Sirhind, when he learned that the emperor with his whole force was advancing against him; he then fell back upon Daber, a hill-fort situated among the steeps of Himmaleh, on an elevated summit which could be approached only by craggy rocks and ravines. According to the account of Eradut Khan, who appears to have been present, his majesty regarded the position as so strong that he wished to decline the attack, and proposed rather to remain inactive, and, by appearing afraid of the enemy, to allure them into the open field. The Khan Khanan or general, however, was animated with a more daring spirit; and having obtained permission to advance with a party to reconnoitre, he immediately began to attack and drive the enemy from the heights surrounding the fortress. This success roused the military ardour of the whole army, who instantly rushed forward in great numbers to join in the assault; and their imperial leader, with mingled anger and satisfaction, saw his troops, in defiance of his injunction, carrying all before them. They had driven the enemy into the central fort, which, relying chiefly on the strength of its approaches, was not calculated for any serious resistance; but darkness now fell, and the commander contented himself with closing all the avenues, and keeping strict watch through the night. In the morning, however, he was disappointed to find that, by a narrow path which had eluded his notice, the Seik chieftain had effected his escape, and was retreating into the wildest recesses of the Himmaleh. His progress, notwithstanding, was

Banda, their new leader.

Assault of Daber.

Escape of the Seiks.

checked for the present, though the sect retained their power unbroken, and were destined at a later period to act a conspicuous part on the theatre of India.

CHAP. IX. A. D. 1712.

Character of Shah Allum

Shah Allum, according to the account of Eradut Khan, who enjoyed his intimate confidence, appears to have been one of the most accomplished and amiable princes that ever swayed the sceptre of India. His liberality though censured by some as extreme, was always exerted towards the most deserving objects. He was strongly attached to the Moslem faith, and deeply versant in its theology, which he studied, however, in a liberal manner, making himself acquainted with the opinions of all sects, and even of freethinkers, to a degree that somewhat scandalized the more rigid doctors. Instead of the dark jealousy which had usually reigned between the members of the Mogul family, he had seventeen sons, grandsons, and nephews, constantly seated at his table, who showed no disposition to abuse this kind confidence. Though he did not possess the full energy suited to the trying circumstances of his government, his moderation and the general respect in which he was held might probably have averted the calamities which impended over this great empire; but unhappily, after a reign of five years, he was seized with a violent illness, and died in his camp at Lahore in the year 1712.

Amiable disposition.

His death.

Struggle for the empire.

He left four sons, who, notwithstanding their peaceful conduct during his life, immediately began to contend with one another for the empire. The cause of Moiz-ud-Dien, the eldest, was espoused by Zulfeccar Khan, one of the most powerful of the omrahs, who succeeded in defeating and putting to death the three others, and placing the crown on the head of this prince, who assumed the name of Jehander Shah. The new monarch, however, was found wholly incapable of supporting, even with an appearance of decency, the exalted rank to which he had been elevated. Neglecting altogether the business of the state, he abandoned himself to dissoluteness, and was even seen strolling in the vicinity of Delhi in the company of mean and abandoned females. In a

Accession of Jehander Shah.

CHAP. IX.

A. D. 1719.

His incapacity and death.

government of so little vigour, there were not wanting bold spirits to avail themselves of the opportunity which the weak character and bad administration of the emperor had created. Two brothers, Abdoolla and Hussein, who boasted the high rank of Syeds, or descendants of the Prophet, undertook to recommend a successor, in whose name they might rule Hindostan. They nominated Feroksere, the offspring of Azim Ooshaun, who was the favourite son of Shah Allum. An army was soon raised, and though Zulfeccar bravely defended the unworthy object whom he had placed on the throne, he was, after a short struggle, entirely overthrown, and both he and his master put to death.

Feroksere Shah.

The Syeds having thus elevated their candidate to power, considered him as their vassal, and proceeded to administer the empire at their pleasure. They discovered no want of vigour in the conduct of affairs. Banda, the Seik prince, having descended to the plains bordering on the Indus, was defeated, taken, and put to death with the most cruel tortures. The great omrahs, however, soon began to murmur at the supremacy of these chiefs. Even the emperor himself felt their yoke burdensome; and favourites were also found who exhorted him to submit no longer to this thraldom, but to assume real power in his own person. Thus his reign of seven years was spent in a continued series of intrigues, the issue of which was that the Syeds completely prevailed, put Feroksere to death, and looked around for another high-born pageant on whom to confer the semblance of sovereignty. They chose first a great-grandson of Aurengzebe by his rebellious son Akbar; but in five months he died of consumption. Next his brother Ruffeh-ul-Dowlah was named to succeed, but he survived his elevation only three months. The Syeds then placed on the throne Rooshun Akter, a grandson of Shah Allum, under the name of Mohammed Shah.

His troubles and death.

His successors.

Mohammed Shah.

This prince, like Feroksere, paid at first implicit deference to the two individuals who had raised him to the empire; but he also soon listened to other counsellors, who exhorted him to emancipate himself from their tyrannical sway. He was at length induced to join in a regular conspiracy formed for that purpose. A misunderstanding had arisen between the two brothers and Nizam-ul-Mulk, a powerful chieftain who held the government of Malwa, and refused to resign it at their mandate. It was arranged that the emperor and Hussein should set out together, and subdue this refractory commander. A plot for the assassination of the Syed was however matured; the three conspirators cast lots which of them should do the deed, and it fell upon one whose name was Hyder. Approaching the palanquin in which Hussein was seated, as if to present a petition, the murderer stabbed him so dexterously that he died in a few moments. He had only time to show his suspicion of the motive by calling out, "Kill the emperor!" and his nephew, at the head of a few resolute soldiers, made a desperate effort to fulfil this dying injunction; but precautions had been taken against the attempt. Mohammed then marched upon Delhi, where the remaining Syed, determining to make a stand, set up a new monarch and collected an army; but he was defeated and taken prisoner. The victor made his triumphal entry into the capital, as if he had just begun to reign.

Plot against Hussein.

Triumph of the Shah.

But he was no sooner in full possession of sovereign power than he displayed that incapacity which seemed to be now inherent in the Mogul race. He had two able and not unfaithful ministers, Nizam-ul-Mulk and Saadut Khan; but, disgusted with their grave and severe manners, he resigned himself to youthful advisers, who were easily found within the precincts of a court. Those two chiefs, irritated at finding themselves thus overlooked, withdrew, and endeavoured to establish a separate authority in other quarters; Nizam in the Deccan, where he has transmitted his name and title to a race of princes still nominally independent; and Saadut in Oude, where a branch of his family likewise continues to reign. In this crisis the Mahrattas, who had been continually extending the range of their incursions, began

His incapacity.

Rival kingdoms of Deccan and Saadut.

CHAP. IX.

A. D. 1730.

Ambitious schemes of the Mahrattas.

penly to contend for the empire. After overrunning he greater part of Malwa and Guzerat, they pushed forward to the very gates of Agra, and struck terror into the imperial capital. Saadut Khan, who alone seemed to retain any regard for the honour and safety of the state, marched down from Oude, and gave them so great an overthrow as would have completely broken their power, had he been permitted to follow it up; but the weak emperor desired operations to be suspended till his favourite minister should have collected troops, and marched forth to take the chief command. Saadut then retired in disgust; after which the enemy rallied, made a fresh incursion as far as Delhi, plundered the environs of that capital, and returned laden with booty to Malwa. But, as if this combination of imbecility with intestine war were not enough, an assault from abroad, of the most formidable character, burst upon the sinking fabric of the Mogul empire.

Incapacity of the emperor.

The Afghans invade Persia.

Persia, had been recently exposed to the most violent revolutions. The Afghans, a warlike race inhabiting the mountainous region which separates that country from India, took advantage of the weakness into which the once-powerful dynasty of the Sophis had sunk. They marched into its territory, defeated its troops, and laid close siege to Ispahan. Having reduced that capital, they put to death Hussein, the reigning sovereign, with all his family except one son, named Thamas. This young prince sought refuge among the pastoral tribes who occupy those elevated plains which extend over a great part of the Persian empire. These hardy and warlike shepherds, animated with loyal and patriotic feelings, warmly espoused the cause of this last branch of their royal house, and assembled round him in numbers, which became every day more formidable. Among these volunteers a young chief, named Nadir, but who on this occasion assumed the title of Thamas Kouli Khan, or the noble slave of Thamas, soon distinguished himself by such zeal and ability as raised him to be their leader. After having gained successive victories, he at

Siege of Ispahan

The chief Nadir.

length retook Ispahan, and drove the invaders completely out of the empire. In the course of so many successes, the troops contracted a stronger attachment to Nadir than to him for whom they had taken up arms; and this bold chief, finding himself within reach of the supreme power, placed the prince under restraint, allowing him the mere epithet and shadow of royalty. He afterwards put out his eyes, and seized the kingdom in his own person, under his original name of *Nadir* Shah.

Recovery of Ispahan.

The new monarch was not content to be master of Persia; but, confident in the bravery and affection of his followers, he resolved to carry his conquests into the neighbouring countries. He invaded the territory of the Afghans themselves, and having reduced Cabul and Candahar, at length approached the frontier of India. He professed to have no intention or wish to penetrate into that region,—for which historians in general give him credit; but we should hesitate in ascribing to the daring usurper so much moderation. At all events, sufficient grounds or pretences were not long wanting. A number of his countrymen who had fled from him found an asylum in Hindostan. An ambassador and his escort, whom he sent to demand that these fugitives should be delivered up, were murdered by the inhabitants of Jellalabad; and Mohammed, under the advice of his arrogant and imprudent courtiers, refused to grant satisfaction for this outrage. The Persian prince advanced, burning for revenge, and, probably not without some secret anticipation of ulterior objects, marched with such rapidity, by way of Peshawer and Lahore, that he was within four days' march of Delhi before the supine emperor was aware of his approach. The latter then hastily mustered his troops, and obtained the able assistance of Saadut Khan; but that officer, not duly aware of the high talent and valour opposed to him, committed the fatal error of quitting his intrenchments, and hazarding an engagement in the field with the veteran forces of Nadir. The effeminate pomp of an Indian host was quite unfit to contend with the rude valour of these pastoral

Nadir Shah.

Reprisals on the Afghans.

Folly of Mohammed.

Saadut Khan.

CHAP. IX.

A.D. 1738.

Total rout of Mohammed's army.

bands; hence the imperial army was totally routed, and their commander taken. A series of transactions now followed, which are not very distinctly related by historians. Saadut, it is said, negotiated a treaty, by which the other agreed to evacuate the empire on the payment of a subsidy of two crores of rupees (two millions sterling). The Persian seemed so entirely satisfied with this arrangement, that the emperor and Nizam-ul-Mulk hesitated not to visit him, and thus put themselves within the grasp of the invader. Then, however, as is reported, the captive general, disappointed at finding that the office of vizier which he claimed as the reward of this service, was to be conferred on the nizam, disclosed to the enemy the secret of the unbounded wealth contained in the palace and capital of India, and for which two crores of rupees were a most inadequate ransom. We should require fuller evidence before we could believe such treachery in one whose conduct had hitherto been so honourable; nor was it likely that the riches of Delhi were so little known as to be confined to the honour and fidelity of a single chief. May we not suppose, with greater probability, that the terms of the treaty were discussed by Nadir, and his friendly professions made, solely to induce the emperor and the nizam to commit the almost incredible imprudence of placing themselves in his power. Certain it is, that having thus obtained possession of their persons, he marched forward and made himself master of the metropolis.

Alleged treachery of Saadut.

Probable policy of Nadir.

Intended moderation.

Nadir seems to have entered it with the intention of acting moderately, and of protecting the inhabitants from outrage. For two days the strictest discipline was observed; but unfortunately, in the course of the second night, a rumour was spread of his death, when the Hindoos, emboldened to a vain resistance, killed a number of his troops. Their commander, whose fierce spirit had been with difficulty restrained, roused to the utmost fury by this outrage, issued orders for a general massacre in every house or lane where the body of a murdered Persian could be found. Till mid-day the streets of

Rash attack by the Hindoos.

Delhi streamed with blood; after which the conqueror suffered himself to be appeased,—and so complete a control did he exercise over his rude followers, that at his mandate the sword was immediately sheathed. The imperial repositories were now ransacked, and found to contain specie, rich robes, and, above all, jewels to an almost incredible value. The Mogul emperors, since the first accession of their dynasty, had been indefatigable in the collection of these objects from every quarter, by presents, purchase, or forfeiture; and the store had been continually augmented without suffering any alienation, or being exposed to foreign plunder. The invaders continued during thirty-five days to extract, by threats, torture, and every severity, the hidden treasures of that splendid capital. Historians hesitate not to estimate the spoil carried off by the Iranian monarch and his officers at thirty-two millions sterling, of which at least one-half was in diamonds and other jewels.

CHAP. IX.

A. D. 1739.

Immense spoils of Delhi

Nadir made no attempt to retain India, though it lay prostrate at his feet. He had probably the sagacity to perceive that so vast a country and Persia were incapable of being united into one kingdom. He contented himself with exacting the cession of Cabul, Candahar, and all the provinces west of the Indus; then, seating Mohammed anew on the Mogul throne, he gave him some salutary advices, and departed without leaving a soldier or retaining a fortified post in Hindostan. Yet the empire, already greatly sunk, lost by this discomfiture the little remnant of respect which it had hitherto commanded. In Rohilcund, a hilly district closely contiguous to the capital, some refugee chiefs of the Afghan race, with the brave inhabitants of the country itself, formed an independent state, which defied the imperial power. They were, it is true, obliged to give way before the united force of the vizier and the Nabob of Oude; but they held themselves in readiness to take advantage of those convulsions to which the successors of Akbar were constantly becoming more and more exposed.

Abandonment of India.

Restoration of Mohammed.

Independence assumed in Rohilcund.

The western nations had learned the route to Delhi

CHAP. IX. A. D. 1747.

and were not likely to forget it. Nadir, eight years after leaving India, was assassinated in his tent at Meshed, in Khorasan; whereupon the dominion which had been formed by him, and kept together by his prudence and vigour, fell quickly to pieces. Ahmed Abdalla, one of his officers, an Afghan by birth, being joined by a part of the army, hastened home, and forthwith proclaimed himself king of his native land, and, amid the distractions that followed the death of his master, succeeded without difficulty in making good his claim. Finding himself thus seated in the undisturbed possession of a strong country, with a brave population, which had often given conquerors to Hindostan, he could not resist the temptation of following the footsteps of Nadir. In 1747 he passed the Indus, plundered the city of Sirhind, and defeated the vizier, who fell in the engagement; but being disconcerted by some unexpected obstacles, and particularly by the explosion of a magazine, he did not then push his conquests any further.

Assassination of Nadir.

Ahmed Abdalla.

Accession of Ahmed Shah.

Soon after this expedition the emperor died, and was succeeded by his son, Ahmed Shah, during whose short reign, as if foreign enemies had not been sufficient, the court was perpetually distracted by intestine dissension. The sovereign and his vizier were now almost in regular opposition. Ahmed being oppressed by one of these officers, Suffder Jung, employed against him Ghazee-ud-Dien, grandson to Nizam-ul-Mulk, who had died at the age of 104. This young man, holding the rank of Ameer-ul-Omrah, made considerable efforts to retrieve the affairs of the empire. He compelled the vizier, who had even set up another monarch, to relinquish his station. He undertook an expedition against the Jits or Jauts, a wild tribe inhabiting the hilly tracts in the most western provinces, and who, amid the general anarchy, had shaken off the yoke. But, while thus employed, he excited the jealousy of his master the emperor, who, adopting the views of a new favourite, concerted with the enemy a plan for his destruction. Aided, however, by the Mahratta chief Holkar Mulhar, he

Distracted state of the kingdom.

completely baffled these designs, obtained possession of his master's person, put out his eyes, and raised to the throne a son of Jehander Shah, under the empty but imposing title of Aulumgire the Second.

CHAP. IX.

A. D. 1750.

Aulumgire Shah.

The empire was now in a most distracted condition; there was scarcely a power so insignificant as not to think itself sufficiently strong to trample on it. The Afghans had completely conquered the provinces of Moultan and Lahore; the Seiks, in the same quarter, daily augmented their numbers and strength; the Jauts and Rohillas continued their predatory inroads; while the Mahrattas extended their incursions, in the course of which they had even passed the Jumna, and obtained an important settlement in Rohilcund. Ghazee-ud-Dien precipitated the disaster by a rash attempt at conquest, to which his power was wholly inadequate. An Afghan lady having been intrusted by Ahmed Abdalla with the government of Lahore, the vizier, under pretence of negotiating a marriage with her daughter, seized her person, and brought her a prisoner to Delhi. At this outrage the indignation of the barbarian king knew no bounds. He hastened at the head of a vast army, and made an unresisted entrance into the capital, which was given up to a sack almost as dreadful as it had suffered from Nadir. A most extraordinary scene then ensued. The emperor besought the invader not to leave him without protection against his own vizier, who had raised him indeed to nominal power, but treated him as a mere pageant, while he himself exercised all the real authority. Ahmed accordingly made some arrangements for this purpose, placing Aulumgire under the guardianship of a Rohilla chief; but these measures, after his departure, proved wholly insufficient. Ghazee-ud-Dien (for so, to prevent confusion, we shall continue to call him, though he now chose to entitle himself Umad-ul-Mulk), having formed an alliance with the Mahrattas, easily obtained possession both of the capital and the sovereign. That unfortunate prince at first pretended a reconciliation, but, being soon after detected in a correspondence

Second sack of Delhi.

Ghazee-ud-Dien.

CHAP. IX. — A.D. 1757.

with the adverse party, was assassinated, and his body thrown into the Jumna. Yet Ghazee-ud-Dien himself, unable to withstand the numerous enemies who surrounded him, was at no distant period obliged to seek refuge in a castle belonging to the Jauts.

State of the Mogul empire.

Without attempting to thread further this labyrinth of treason, we may observe generally, that the Mogul throne had now almost ceased to retain any degree of weight or importance. The contest for the empire of India lay entirely between the Afghans and the Mahrattas; and the latter, taking advantage of the absence of their rivals, determined upon a grand attempt to secure complete possession of Hindostan. Bringing up from the Deccan an immense body of cavalry, and being aided by the Seiks, they overran not only the metropolitan provinces of Agra and Delhi, but also those of Moultan and Lahore, and drove the Afghans beyond the Indus. Ahmed Abdalla, however, was not of a character tamely to allow these fine countries to be wrested from his kingdom. He soon crossed the river with a formidable army, and was joined by many chiefs who were exasperated at the incursion of the Mahrattas. These plunderers at first retreated, and allowed him to occupy Delhi; but immediately intrenched themselves in a strong camp, which he did not venture to attack. Pressed, however, by want of provisions, they imprudently came out and gave battle, when they experienced a total defeat; their army of 80,000 men being almost entirely destroyed, and Duttah Sindia, their general, killed. Another body under Holkar was surprised near Secundra, and so completely worsted, that he himself fled naked with a handful of followers.

Combined claimants of Hindostan.

Ahmed Abdalla enters Delhi.

Defeats the Mahrattas.

New forces assembled.

The Mahrattas, though humbled by this disaster, were not discouraged; and they resolved to make the most extraordinary exertions for retrieving their fortunes. Before the close of the year, they had assembled a force of 140,000 men, commanded by Sewdasheo Rao, called the Bhow, nephew to their peishwa or supreme prince; and that chief, being joined by the vizier and the Jaut leaders, advanced upon Delhi. The deep stream of the Jumna, swelled by the rains, separated the armies; but, though it could not be forded, the daring spirit of Abdalla impelled him to plunge into its waters, and swim across with his whole army. This achievement, which was almost without example, struck dismay into the host of the Mahrattas. Though triple the number of their antagonists, they did not venture to face them in the open field, but shut themselves up in an intrenched camp at Panniput, on a spot where the fate of the empire has been repeatedly decided. Ahmed for some time merely hovered round them and cut off their supplies; at length he ventured on an attempt to carry their position, but was obliged to retire without any important success. Encouraged by this result, and distressed as formerly by the want of provisions, his active foe determined again to risk a battle in the open plain. Placing their artillery in front, they advanced with that impetuosity by which they were accustomed to carry all before them. The Afghan commander caused his troops to hold themselves in reserve till the enemy had nearly come up;—then gave the signal for a general charge. The light horse of the mountains were never able to resist, even for a short interval, the heavy cavalry of the more northern nations. On the first onset a complete rout took place; their host was so scattered in every direction that only a remnant reached the Deccan: while 22,000 prisoners, 50,000 horses, with an immense booty, fell into the hands of the conquerors.

Passage of the Jumna.

General engagement.

Total rout of the Mahrattas.

It was now easy for the victorious Abdalla to seat himself on the vacant throne of the Mogul; but he seems not to have felt any ambition for this high dignity. Perhaps he was sensible that, amid such a general agitation throughout Hindostan, and with so many nations in arms, such an acquisition was too distant from the centre of his dominions to be retained with advantage. Contenting himself with the provinces west of the Indus, he quitted in a few months the seat of government, leaving

Vacant throne of the Mogul.

CHAP. IX. A. D. 1760. Alee Gohur.

there Alee Gohur, eldest son of Aulumgire II., in possession of the empty but still venerated title of Great Mogul, to be the tool or the captive of the first daring warrior who should seize the capital. Having traced the decline of this mighty empire to so low an ebb, we shall now pause till we have marked the progress of that new power from a distant continent, which has seated herself on its ruins, and obtained a complete supremacy over all the states of India.

CHAPTER X.

British Conquest of the Carnatic.

First Territorial Acquisitions—War between France and England—Early Settlements of the French—Their Establishment at Pondicherry—Enterprises of Labourdonnais—He takes Madras—Superseded by Dupleix—Pondicherry besieged—Conclusion of Peace—English Expedition to Tanjore—Contests for the Sovereignties of Southern India—The French interpose—Gain a complete Victory—They are expelled by Nazir Jung—The English join him—His Death—Succession and Death of Mirzapha Jung—Salabat Jung—Exploits of Clive—Advantages over the French—Their Influence in the Deccan—Form a Confederacy against the English—Siege of Trichinopoly—Acquisitions of the French—Recall of Dupleix—Treaty concluded—The Colleries—War of 1756—Lally takes the Command—Reduces Fort St David—Siege of Madras—Raised—French defeated at Wandewash—Siege of Pondicherry—Its Surrender—Cruel Treatment of Lally in France.

CHAP. X.

A. D. 1689.

Early English voyages.

THE voyages of the English, related in a former part of this work,* were personal adventures, undertaken with a mingled view to discovery, commerce, and piracy, rather than to any fixed scheme of conquest or dominion. Their forts accordingly were erected as depositories for goods, or to supply commercial facilities, but not with any aim at territorial possession. It was not till 1689 that their views seem to have extended to the latter object. In the instructions issued to their agents during that year, they intimate that the increase of their revenue was henceforth to occupy as much attention as their merchandise; that they wished to be "a nation in India;"

* Chapter V.

CHAP. X.

A. D. 1715.

and they quote with unmerited applause the conduct of the Dutch, who, they assert, in the advices sent to their governors, wrote ten paragraphs concerning tribute for one relative to trade. The means of gratifying this disposition were as yet very limited; as certain small portions of territory around Bombay and Madras comprised the whole extent of their Indian sovereignty. They held themselves ready, however, to purchase every city or district which the native princes could, by any motive, be prevailed upon to alienate; and in this way they acquired Tegnapatam on the Coromandel coast, which they garrisoned, and gave it the name of Fort St David. Nine years after they made a more important acquisition. Azim Ooshaun, whom his father, Aurengzebe, had nominated Viceroy of Bengal, but who, contemplating a struggle for the succession to the empire and standing in need of treasure to forward his schemes, was induced, in 1698, to sell to the Company the zemindarships of the towns and districts of Chutanutty, Govindpore, and *Calcutta*,—the last destined soon to become the capital of British India. Here they began, though not without due circumspection, to erect Fort William, which, in 1707, was made the seat of a presidency.

Limited possessions of the English Company.

Possessions acquired by purchase.

The superior skill of Europeans in medicine, which had first enabled them to obtain a footing in Bengal, now afforded an opportunity of greatly extending their influence. In 1715, under the reign of the Emperor Feroksere, the residents sent two factors, with an Armenian merchant, on a commercial mission to Delhi. The principal object was defeated, in a manner similar to that of Roe and others, by the intrigues of the omrahs, and of Jaffier Khan, governor of Bengal. But his majesty happening to labour under a severe illness, which the ignorance of the native physicians rendered them unable to treat with success, was completely cured by a medical gentleman, named Hamilton, who accompanied the embassy. For this signal service he not only received large presents, but obtained the valuable grant of three villages in the vicinity of Madras, with liberty

European medical skill.

Cure of the emperor.

to purchase in Bengal thirty-seven additional townships; an arrangement which would have secured a territory extending ten miles upwards from Calcutta. The emperor conferred also the still more important privilege of introducing their goods and conveying them through the province without duty or search. But the acquisition of these districts was frustrated by the hostility of the nabob, who by private threats deterred the owners from consenting to the purchase. Still, the permission of free trade, though limited to foreign exports and imports, proved of the greatest importance, and soon rendered Calcutta a very flourishing settlement.

Important privileges conceded.

A considerable time now elapsed without any farther change in the territorial relations of the Company. They complain of the extravagance of their servants, which involved them in debt to the native shroffs and merchants; but this evil seems to have been in a good measure remedied. Having establishments supported at a moderate expense, which enabled them to carry on trade with security and advantage, they gradually extended their operations till the annual sales amounted to the considerable sum of about two millions sterling; whence they were enabled to pay a dividend of seven or eight per cent. on their capital. Perhaps it would have been fortunate had this state of things remained unaltered; but the war which broke out in 1744 between the French and British produced an entire change in the position of the Company, both in regard to its internal management, and relatively to the powers of Europe and of India. To understand this, we must look back for a moment to the first establishments formed by the French in the eastern world.

Gradual progress of the Company.

Influence of war with France.

That people, though they had suffered themselves to be far outstripped in the progress of maritime greatness by the English and Dutch, had yet at an early period displayed a spirit of enterprise. Even in 1503 an expedition had been fitted out by some merchants of Rouen; which, however, experienced a complete failure, in consequence probably of the imperfect nautical skill then

Early French enterprise.

CHAP. X.

A. D. 1664.

Establishment of a French settlement at Madagascar.

possessed by their mariners. Attempts, though on a small scale and generally unsuccessful, were made early in the next century; but it was not till 1642 that a considerable company was at length established. Unluckily that body directed their main attention to the formation of a settlement on Madagascar, a large and fruitful island, which it was easy to describe as affording ample scope for cultivation and commerce. But it yielded no commodity suited to the markets of Europe; its inhabitants, too, were numerous and ferocious, and soon became formidable to a power which attempted to take possession of their territory. The settlers were involved in a harassing warfare, and with difficulty maintained, at certain points on the coast, a few wooden tenements dignified with the title of forts, which involved them in expense without yielding any profit.

French East India Company.

The first real establishment of a French East India Company took place in 1664, under the auspices of Colbert, who, prompted by the aspiring genius of his master Louis XIV., devoted himself indefatigably to the promotion of agriculture, manufactures, and commerce. He proceeded upon the principles of that age, which was by no means enlightened in respect to the sound doctrines of political economy; and hence, exclusive grants, exorbitant privileges, and the removal of competition, were the expedients by which it was then attempted to make any branch of industry flourish. Such was Colbert's system, when he submitted to the king the plan of an East India Company, to carry on trade with a capital of 15,000,000 livres (£625,000), and supported by the most extravagant encouragements. They received an exclusive charter for fifty years; they were exempted from all taxes; and the government came under the singular obligation of reimbursing them for all the losses which they might sustain in the course of the first ten years,—a stipulation which actually subjected the state to the payment of a large sum. The funds supplied by individuals not being equal to the amount of the proposed capital, limited as it was, three millions

Colbert's system.

were advanced out of the treasury; while the nobles, and all the opulent classes connected with the court, were induced to follow the example.

Mismanagement of the Company.

The management of the Company was neither judicious nor fortunate. They began by endeavouring to turn Madagascar to some account, and sent thither a large colony, most of whom perished under the influence of climate, fatigue, and the hostility of the natives. The survivors were afterwards employed in occupying the islands of Cerne and Mascarenhas, which at a later period, under the names of Mauritius and Bourbon, rose to some degree of prosperity. After the failure of the attempt at Madagascar they sent vessels to India, and formed settlements on different points of its coast. In 1668 they established their principal factory at Surat, under the direction of Caron, one of their countrymen, who had spent most of his life in the service of Holland. The prospects at first appeared rather promising; but, being involved in dispute with the native powers, and finding the trade ultimately unprosperous, they thought fit to take their departure very suddenly, leaving their debts unpaid,—an omission which of course precluded their return. Attempts were afterwards made to secure a position at Trincomalee in Ceylon, and at St Thomas on the Coromandel coast; but both were defeated by the jealousy of the Dutch. Their affairs, therefore, would have become desperate, had not M. Martin, an officer possessed of talent and patriotism, collected the scattered adventurers and fixed them at Pondicherry; where, by judicious and conciliatory conduct, he gained the attachment of the inhabitants, opened an advantageous trade, and soon raised the settlement to a very prosperous condition.

Settlements in India.

Rivalry with the Dutch.

State at the period of collision with the English.

When the French and English first came into mutual collision, the former had no station of much consequence on the continent of India except that just named; but it was of very considerable importance, being well fortified, and having some extent of territory attached to it. They had smaller factories at Mahé and

CHAP. X.

A. D. 1746.

Carical, as well as at Chandernagore in Bengal. In 1744 hostilities broke out between the two nations, which were carried on in Europe with great animosity. The French Company appear to have been rather desirous that the war should not extend to the Indian Seas; but their naval officers, on the contrary, were fired by hopes of glory from an attack on the English settlements in that quarter, before they could be placed in a posture of defence. Labourdonnais, a person of great talent and most indefatigable activity, who had raised himself through all the ranks of the navy, was now governor of Mauritius and Bourbon; and these islands, by his exertions, almost without assistance from home, had become very flourishing. Happening to be in France when the war was in preparation, he made proposals, both to the Company and the ministry, for an attack upon the enemy's establishments. The former were altogether averse to his scheme; but the government unknown to them sanctioned it, and even engaged to furnish two ships, which however were afterwards withheld. The adventurer returned to his command with the most resolute determination to prosecute his design, though possessed of very slender resources. With this view he detained the vessels which happened to touch there, and employed them in the expedition; he brought the sailors, many of whom had never fired a gun, into regular training; and he supplied by various inventions the defective means of equipment. In June 1746, he arrived at Pondicherry, after a slight action with an English naval force on the coast. Here, too, he had to overcome certain obstacles raised by Dupleix, before he was permitted to sail with his squadron to attack Madras.

Project for attacking the English settlements.

Obtains the sanction of government.

Governor Labourdonnais' zeal.

Expedition against Madras.

This city was not only the capital of the English possessions, but one of the chief settlements at that time formed by the Europeans in India. It comprised within its district a population of not less than 250,000, of whom, however, only 300 were from this quarter of the globe, including 200 soldiers. These lived in Fort St George, surrounded merely by a slender wall, with four ill-constructed bastions and batteries; and hence, it is obvious, they had very small means of defence, and did not, in the use of them, display any heroism. After sustaining a bombardment of five days, in which two or three houses were demolished, and four or five men killed, they capitulated on the 10th September 1746. They obtained, indeed, the singular condition, that Labourdonnais, after having regularly occupied the place and taken possession of the Company's magazines and warehouses, should, within a stipulated period, and on payment of a fixed ransom, restore Madras to the English. That officer, having made this important acquisition without the loss of a single man, returned to Pondicherry.

Capitulation of Madras.

But there he did not meet with such a reception as he merited. Dupleix, an aspiring and ambitious man, who could not brook any rival in power, thwarted all his schemes, and exposed him to repeated mortifications, till at length he gave up the contest, and sailed for France. There, too, on the representations of his superior officer, he was treated in a manner altogether unworthy of his long and faithful services, being thrown into the Bastile, whence he was not liberated till the end of three years, soon after which he died.

Rival jealousies of the French.

Dupleix, who was thus left in the supreme command of affairs in India, was a very extraordinary character. From his father, who had been a farmer-general and a director of the East India Company, he inherited an immense fortune, which he was taught to employ in the pursuits of commerce. Being sent out originally as first member of the council at Pondicherry, and afterwards as superintendent at Chandernagore, he at once, by his public measures, rendered this last settlement extremely prosperous, and by an extensive trade largely augmented his private wealth. His talents and success recommended him to the important station of Governor of Pondicherry. Although, from feelings of jealousy, he had quarrelled with Labourdonnais, and succeeded in removing him, yet his mind was enthusiastically and intensely devoted to the same system of policy. Neither

Dupleix the French governor.

Talents and success.

CHAP. X.

A. D. 1746.

Vast schemes of conquest.

Cæsar nor Alexander ever formed more magnificent schemes of conquest than this mercantile ruler of French India. His first object was to follow up the advantage gained over the English, and thoroughly to root out that rival nation from the coast of Coromandel. Labourdonnais had, as already mentioned, stipulated on certain conditions to restore Madras, after a temporary occupation of it; and as a man of honour he was resolved to make good his engagement,—a design wholly foreign to the grasping ambition of Dupleix. Unable otherwise to accomplish his object, he made such arrangements as to delay the period of surrender till the departure of that officer, and then contrived to draw forth from the citizens of Pondicherry a remonstrance against giving up a place the possession of which was so important to their security. In pretended compliance with this request, Madras was not only retained, but exposed to a species of plunder, while the governor and principal inhabitants were carried prisoners to the French settlement.

Breach of faith with the English.

Expedition against Fort St. David.

This step was forthwith followed by an expedition on his part for the reduction of Fort St David, while his confidence was greatly heightened by an event which forms a memorable era in the annals of Indian warfare. The Nabob of Arcot, having espoused the English cause, had sent his son with 10,000 men, to endeavour to retake Madras on their behalf. The French had only 1200 soldiers to defend the city, with which force they hesitated not to attack the numerous army of the nabob; when, by their superior discipline and the expert management of their artillery, they gained a complete and decisive victory. The superiority of even a handful of Europeans over the tumultuary bands which compose an Asiatic host had long ago been proved by the Portuguese; but the example of their success was nearly forgotten; and both French and British had been accustomed to view the Mogul as a powerful and mighty monarch, whom it was vain with their slender means to think of resisting. The spell was again broken; and the settlers of either nation learned a lesson which they

Success of French arms.

failed not soon to reduce to practice with the most extensive and terrible effect.

CHAP. X.

A.D. 1748.

Disparity of French and English forces.

The present object of Dupleix was simply the reduction of Fort St David, against which he led a force of 1700 men, mostly European; while the English had only 200 of their own troops, with a body of undisciplined natives. As the French, however, were advancing in full confidence, the nabob's army surprised them by a sudden attack, and obliged them to retreat with some loss. A detachment was afterwards sent by sea to attempt the surprise of Cuddalore, a town immediately contiguous to Fort St David, but a heavy gale springing up obliged them to return. He then employed all his address to gain over the nabob; being particularly careful to impress on that prince a lofty idea of his own power, trusting to the maxim regularly acted upon by Indian grandees of studying only immediate advantage, and espousing always the side which they believe to be the strongest. His highness being informed of the arrival of a great additional force, was led to credit the pretensions of the French; and, deserting our countrymen, of whom he had been the sworn and active ally, concluded a treaty with their enemies, which was cemented by a visit from his son, who was received with all that ostentatious pomp in which eastern rulers delight.

Negotiations of Dupleix with the English allies.

Attack on St. David resumed and abandoned.

Dupleix now vigorously resumed his enterprise. He crossed the river, and took up a strong position in front of Fort St David, when a fleet under Admiral Griffin with a considerable reinforcement of troops, was seen to enter the road. The French again retreated, and the English received some further recruits. At length, in January 1748, Major Laurence, an experienced officer, assumed the command; after which the two nations remained for some time so equally matched that neither ventured upon any serious movement. The governor o Pondicherry indeed undertook a midnight attack upon Cuddalore; but his approach being discovered, his men were repulsed with considerable loss.

The face of Indian affairs was soon entirely changed

CHAP. X.

A.D. 1748.

by the arrival of an English expedition of nine ships of war, having on board 1400 men, who, with those already in the country, formed the largest European army ever seen in that part of India. The British were then completely in a condition to undertake offensive operations; and they determined to strike a blow at the main strength of the enemy by besieging Pondicherry. As the French had no force which could oppose them in the field, the siege was undertaken with the fairest prospect of success. It was not, however, carried on with due promptitude and vigour. A long delay was incurred in reducing a small fort two miles distant from the city; and when the trenches were at length opened before the place itself, they were not found to be sufficiently near for the artillery to fire with effect; and before this error was amended, the rainy season had set in, sickness spread among the troops, and it was deemed necessary to desist from the attempt. The French felt extraordinary exultation at this repulse, which they boasted of as a splendid victory; but, before they could derive any advantage from it, tidings arrived that peace had been concluded in Europe, of which one of the conditions was the relinquishment of Madras. Hence the two nations were placed exactly in the same position as before the war.

Large accession of English forces.

Siege of Pondicherry.

Restoration of Madras.

Influence of peace in Europe.

But this treaty, instead of restoring tranquillity to India, served only to give a wider range to warlike operations in that quarter of the world; for the two parties, having each a large disposable force, began to look round for some object on which it might be advantageously employed. The events of the preceding war had disclosed the weakness of the native governments, and left room to hope for the establishment of a wide dominion over this rich and beautiful region.

First war with the native government.

The English made the first movement. A prince of Tanjore named Sahujee, who had been dethroned by a brother, craved their aid to reinstate him, and offered in return the fortress and district of Devicottah, advantageously situated on the banks of the Coleroon. In 1749, they undertook an expedition against that stronghold;

but, disappointed by want of concert between the fleet and the army, and receiving no aid from the natives, they returned without having even attempted its reduction. Mortified by this failure, they proceeded a second time against the place, the ships now conveying the soldiers to the mouth of the river, whence they ascended in boats to the town. After considerable difficulties, and a severe contest, in which Lieutenant Clive, afterwards so eminent in Indian history, distinguished himself by daring valour, they obtained possession of the fort. Its capture was immediately followed up with a treaty, by which its occupation was secured to the English, who, in return, abandoned the cause of the prince for whom they had taken arms. They stipulated even to keep him in confinement, and thereby render him incapable of troubling his rival, provided he received a pension of £400 a-year. This arrangement, it need not be remarked, was far from being honourable to our countrymen, who seem, however, to have been altogether deceived in their expectations of co-operation from the people of Tanjore.

Lieutenant Clive.

Dishonourable arrangements.

The French, meantime, were playing a much higher game, and openly aspiring to a direct ascendency in Southern India. We despair of conducting our readers in a satisfactory manner through the dark maze of Carnatic intrigue, or the barbarous names and uninteresting characters who were employed in it. It may be premised, that whenever an Indian prince dies, no respect is paid to the principle of primogeniture, or to any fixed law of succession. His sons, grandsons, nephews, or even more distant relations, advance claims to the sovereignty, which they forthwith endeavour to support by an appeal to arms. The dissensions of the Deccan arose upon the death of Nizam-ul-Mulk, who may be remembered as acting a part in Mogul history, and of Sadatullah, nabob of the Carnatic. Both these offices, originally subordinate appointments under the Emperor of Delhi, had, in the decline of that dynasty, become gradually independent. For these, instead of Nazir

French schemes.

Indian law of succession.

CHAP. X. A.D. 1749. Jung and Anwar-ud-Dien, the rightful or at least actual possessors, there appeared Mirzapha Jung and Chunda Saheb, who aspired, the former to be Subahdar of the Deccan, the latter to be Nabob of the Carnatic. Having united their interests, they had assembled an army of 40,000 men, and eagerly courted the aid of Dupleix.

Scheme of Dupleix for obtaining the mastery of Southern India.

This ambitious governor conceived that, by filling the two great thrones of the south of India, to which exploit he judged his forces adequate, he should become the undisputed master of that extensive country; and therefore he sent D'Auteuil with 2300 men, of whom 400 were Europeans, to join the allied troops. The combined armies then marched to attack Anwar-ud-Dien, the reigning nabob, who, with 20,000 followers, was encamped at Amboor, a strong post guarding one of the principal passes into the Carnatic. He had thrown across the ravine an intrenchment defended by cannon, served by a small band of Europeans; when D'Auteuil, ambitious to display the valour of his countrymen and their high discipline, offered with only his few French soldiers to storm the lines. The Indian chiefs closed with the proposal; though the undertaking proved somewhat more formidable than had been anticipated. The artillery of the enemy, being strong and well-directed, repulsed two successive attacks; but the assailants, animated by the consciousness that they were fighting in the view of three armies, rushed on a third time, and carried the fortifications. They then pushed forward against the main body, where the nabob, mounted on an elephant, with his standard displayed, and surrounded by his chosen cavalry, was loudly encouraging the troops. But almost immediately a ball fired by a Caffre soldier went through his heart, and he dropt to the ground dead. A total rout instantly ensued; the camp, a very ample booty, sixty elephants, with all the artillery and stores, fell into the hands of the victors. The princes forthwith resolved to march upon Arcot, which surrendered without resistance.

Fortification of Amboor carried.

Fall of Anwar-ud-Dien.

Mohammed Ali, son to the fallen nabob, and heir of

PAGODA OF TANJORE.

The town of Tanjore, bordering on the delta of the Coleroon and the Cavery, was wealthy and splendid, adorned with a pagoda which eclipses in magnitude all other structures in the south of India.—Page 333.

CHAP. X.

A.D. 1749.

his throne, fled to Trichinopoly, a very strong city, the possession of which gave him still a hold upon the Carnatic. Dupleix pressed in the most urgent manner upon the confederate generals that they should not lose a moment, but hasten to the attack of the fortress, which was probably in a very imperfect state of defence. The Indian princes, however, chose rather to begin by marching into Arcot and Pondicherry, where they made a display of their pomp as subahdar and nabob; and when they at last took the field, it was to proceed, not, as he had recommended, against Trichinopoly, but against the more remote and unimportant city of Tanjore. This decision, however, proceeded from a secret motive; their treasury being completely exhausted, they felt the necessity of securing a supply by extorting from the rajah some heavy arrears of tribute. The town, bordering on the delta of the Coleroon and the Cavery, was wealthy and splendid, adorned with a pagoda which eclipses in magnitude all other structures in the south of India. From the opulent ruler of this state they demanded the payments due to the Mogul, and claimed by them as his representatives. Had they even prosecuted this demand with vigour and promptitude, they might probably have brought it to a speedy issue; but they suffered themselves to be amused by the rajah, who sometimes negotiated, and at other times fought, till at length they succeeded in bursting open one of his gates, whereby he was intimidated into an agreement to pay about £900,000. He reluctantly consented to advance the first instalment; but by sending first a quantity of gold and silver plate, then a lot of old coins, and lastly a quantity of jewels, he contrived to spin out the time till tidings arrived of the appearance of a new actor on the scene, who was destined entirely to change the aspect of affairs.

Mohammed Ali.

Attack of Tanjore.

Policy of the rajah.

Ghazee-ud-Dien, the eldest son of the nizam, had attached himself to the Mogul court, at which we have seen him act a conspicuous part. Nazir Jung, the second son, had therefore succeeded to the subahdary, of

Nazir Jung.

CHAP. X. A.D. 1749.

which he took upon him the full dignity and titles. He was summoned, however, on a peculiar emergency, to join the imperial standard, and had already reached the Nerbudda when he learned the successful usurpations of Mirzapha Jung and Chunda Saheb. He then retraced his steps; and, under the assumed authority of the imperial court, assembled all its adherents and his own to join in the suppression of this daring rebellion: he enlisted also 30,000 Mahrattas to act as light cavalry. Although he moved with the slow and encumbered pomp of an eastern army, he at length arrived on the Carnatic frontier with a force which Orme supposes not to have fallen short of 300,000 men. It then behoved the allies to put themselves on their defence, and Dupleix backed them with all his resources. Having learned their pecuniary difficulties, he gave them a loan of £50,000, while he increased the French contingent to 2000 men. The English meantime, though they had viewed with jealousy and alarm the late progress of their rivals, were very slow to embark in actual warfare. They had supported the cause of Mohammed Ali only by sending very small detachments to Trichinopoly and Tanjore; but when Nazir Jung arrived with so great an army, invested with the full authority of the Mogul, Major Laurence no longer hesitated to march and join him with a corps of 600 men. This reinforcement was not necessary to secure that prince's triumph. The French troops were brave, but under bad management; a mutiny arose among the officers, thirteen of whom in one day resigned their commands. At this untoward event D'Auteuil, losing all presence of mind, determined immediately to march with his division to Pondicherry. The cause of the confederates was then altogether desperate. Chunda Saheb sought safety in the French settlement, while Mirzapha Jung surrendered at discretion, and was immediately thrown into irons.

Approach of relief to Tanjore. *Defensive movements of the allies.* *English reinforcements of Mohammed Ali.* *Failure of the schemes of the allies.*

Courage of Dupleix.

Dupleix, notwithstanding this complete fall from the proud position which he had so lately reached, did not

CHAP. X.

A. D. 1749.

lose courage. He attempted a negotiation with Nazir; and though the mission sent for this purpose failed, it was learned that, as the prince was of a weak and voluptuous character, some warlike chiefs of Afghan extraction, who held the principal commands in his army, had entered into a conspiracy to dethrone him.

Native conspiracy against Nazir.

The French governor formed a connexion with these malecontents, and likewise endeavoured to give effect to their intrigues by a military movement. D'Auteuil again took the field, surprised during the night a quarter of the Mogul camp, while the troops were buried in slumber and the fumes of opium, and committed great havock. Another detachment sent by sea reduced Masulipatam, long the chief emporium of this part of India, and began to fortify it.

French alliance with the conspirators.

Meantime Major Laurence, disgusted with repeated irregularities in the conduct of his Indian allies, who refused to be at all guided by his advice, withdrew the English troops from the service of the subahdar, affording thereby full scope for the operations of the French commandant. That officer having sent a body of men, who defeated the nabob and obliged him to flee to Arcot, despatched a force into the interior to attack Gingee, the most powerful stronghold in all the Carnatic. In a midnight assault they stormed successively the three fortified mountains which constituted the strength of that important place, and carried it with the loss of only twenty men.

English abandon their allies.

Gingee taken.

Nazir Jung, roused by this loss from his voluptuous supineness, at length took the field with an army which, notwithstanding some reductions, still exceeded 100,000 men,—a movement desired by the conspirators as extremely favourable to the execution of their scheme. Time, however, passed on without any decisive event; and the subahdar, tired of a dull contest, which kept him from his favourite enjoyments, made such advantageous overtures that Dupleix entered into a negotiation. The latter, notwithstanding, imitating the wiles of Indian policy, still kept his communications open with the rebellious omrahs; and it has been said that the treaty

Nazir Jung takes the field.

CHAP. X.

A. D. 1750.

with Nazir Jung was actually signed, though not communicated to Latouche who had succeeded to the command of the French troops, when that officer was summoned by the Afghan insurgents to co-operate in the execution of their seditious design. Latouche accordingly advanced, and at four next morning attacked that part of the camp where the subahdar commanded in person. The conflict was sharp, the Indian cavalry fighting with great bravery; but the discipline of the French, and the rapidity with which their cannon was served, enabled them gradually to penetrate into the heart of the hostile encampment. Nazir Jung, not destitute of personal valour, indignantly saw his troops giving way before a handful of Europeans; and being told that a large corps, under the direction of the confederate chiefs and their adherents, were not joining in the action, he rode up and began to reproach them bitterly for their cowardice. Cudapah, the leader whom he first addressed, made an insulting reply, and then discharged a carabine, by which two balls were lodged in the heart of Nazir, who fell dead on the spot. For an Indian army to pass from one prince to his assassin and enemy is only the work of a moment. Mirzapha Jung was taken out of irons, led forth, and universally acknowledged Soubah of the Deccan, a region superior in magnitude to any European kingdom.

Proceedings of Latouche, the French commander.

Assassination of Nazir.

Mirzapha Jung installed in his throne.

This revolution had the effect of completely establishing the influence of the French in Southern India. Mirzapha, reposing entire confidence in Dupleix, visited him at Pondicherry, and was there installed with the greatest pomp in the throne of the Deccan. This officer, in return, was created governor under the Mogul, and collector of the revenue in all the countries south of the Kistna, a territory little inferior in extent to France; considerable districts round each of the three towns of Pondicherry, Carical, and Masulipatam, were also ceded in perpetuity. But the victorious parties found themselves in that anxious and difficult position which inevitably arises from the alliance of those who own no

Influence acquired by the French.

CHAP. X.

A.D. 1751.

law human or divine. The Patan chiefs made most enormous demands,—to which, according to the maxims of oriental treason, they seemed entitled. Yet the fulfilment of these, and of others which would have followed, must have reduced Mirzapha Jung nearly to a cipher. Dupleix strongly represented to them the necessity of accepting much lower terms; and probably, from feeling themselves to be in his power, they appeared at the moment cordially to acquiesce. When, however, Mirzapha left Pondicherry, and advanced into the interior of the Deccan, he learned that the defiles in his front were occupied by those very traitors assembled in arms to dispute his passage. The prince, ambitious to display his valour, marched and began the attack before his European allies came up, in consequence of which he suffered some loss. Afterwards, with their aid, he had the prospect of a complete victory, when he engaged in single combat with the Nabob of Canoul, by whom he was pierced through the head with a javelin, and instantly expired. Bussy, the French minister, was at first in the deepest consternation, imagining the influence of his countrymen in Indian affairs would now be terminated, when he recollected that three brothers of the deceased monarch were prisoners in the camp. Obtaining the concurrence of the principal native leaders, he raised to the throne Salabat Jung, the eldest, in preference to the infant son of the fallen soubah. The new sovereign, feeling himself indebted to these foreigners for his elevation, espoused their interests with an ardour equal to that of his predecessor.

Demands of the Patan chiefs.

Defection from Mirzapha.

He is slain in single combat.

Salabat Jung's accession.

The English for some time contemplated with singular apathy this extensive aggrandizement of their rivals. Major Laurence, who seems to have been no politician, having formerly, by his desertion of Nazir Jung, lost all influence in the Indian councils, now, in the most critical period of French ascendency, left the East and returned home on private business. At length the subjects of Louis began to assume a deportment so lofty as convinced the British of their danger, should this ambi-

Apathy of the English.

CHAP. X. A.D. 1751.

tious enemy continue masters of the south of India. They despatched, therefore, a body of troops under Captain Cope to defend Trichinopoly, the only strong position which their ally, Mohammed Ali, still retained in the Carnatic; but this officer lost a great part of his men in an unfortunate attempt upon Madura. Captain Gingen was then sent from Fort St David with a larger detachment; but neither did they gain any earnest of that glory which their countrymen were afterwards to earn in Indian warfare. Having encountered the enemy near the fort of Volconda, they were instantly seized with a panic, and while the natives stood their ground, they fled; thus rendering themselves an object of derision even to their undisciplined allies. They fought better on two subsequent occasions; but at length, without attempting to master their antagonists in the field, they hastened to throw themselves into Trichinopoly.

Unsuccessful measures.

Disgraceful conduct of the British.

Fresh reinforcements.

The English afterwards sent another detachment, which raised the European part of the garrison to 600 men; but as Chunda Saheb, then nabob of Arcot, and his auxiliaries, were besieging it with a force greatly superior, there was much reason to fear, that without some effort this last barrier against French dominion must ultimately fall. A new character, however, at this crisis began to act a brilliant part on the scene. Mr Clive, the son of a gentleman of small property in Shropshire, had gone out in a civil capacity; but his violent and turbulent conduct had displeased his superiors, and made him be considered as an intractable youth. On the breaking out of the war he obtained leave to enter the army as an ensign, and soon showed himself better qualified for this active profession; where, indeed, he distinguished himself so much as to be employed in several confidential situations. He proposed to make a diversion in favour of Trichinopoly, by an attack on Arcot, the nabob's capital. Having obtained 500 men, of whom only 200 were Europeans, and partly made up by volunteers from the civil service, he proceeded on this daring expedition. He approached

Appearance of Clive.

His military genius.

Arcot; and the garrison of the fort, merely on witnessing the intrepidity with which his people advanced amid a tempest of thunder and rain, were seized with a panic, and evacuated the city. He did not allow them to recover from their consternation, but pursued and obliged them to retreat from one point to another. CHAP. X. A. D. 1752.

The object of this enterprise was forthwith realized, as a large body of the besiegers of Trichinopoly were drawn away to attempt the delivery of Arcot. Troops were brought to the amount of 4000, reinforced by 2000 from Vellore. According to his bold policy, Clive endeavoured to intimidate them by an attack on the city, in which these forces were stationed,—an imprudent step; for the most undisciplined hordes, fighting under the cover which streets and buildings afford, are a match for the bravest warriors. The natives from the houses poured down a destructive fire, and obliged the English commander to retreat with a loss which he could very ill spare. He had then a hard task, to defend with 300 men fortifications a mile in circuit, consisting only of a feeble wall, and a ditch fordable in many places. He had thus full scope for the splendid military talents with which he was endowed. Lieutenant Innis, sent with a reinforcement from Madras, was intercepted and obliged to return; but Morari Rao, now at the head of a body of 6000 Mahrattas, who had deserted the nabob's cause when it appeared desperate, was animated by the valour of his ally, and promised his support. At length, on the morning of the 14th of November, the great Mussulman festival, and a day deemed peculiarly auspicious for warlike achievements, the enemy made a general assault. They rushed on with a species of madness, and when one detachment was driven back, another instantly followed. Clive was obliged to stand to the guns himself, and assist in firing them. But the assailants were at length repulsed, and finally raised the siege; and the young soldier, being thus left master of the field, scoured the country in different directions, took possession of several important posts, and then returned to Madras.

Bold policy of Clive.

Difficulties of his task.

Complete repulse of his assailants.

CHAP. X.

A.D. 1753.

Arrival of British reinforcements.

Meantime the force defending Trichinopoly was receiving continual accessions. Major Laurence, having arrived from Britain with a large reinforcement, set out himself for that city with 400 Europeans and 1100 sepoys. Mohammed Ali allured into his service Morari Rao, and by liberal promises even induced the Regent of Mysore to come to his assistance; and these together formed a corps of 20,000 men. By such additions the English and their friends became decidedly superior to their opponents, whom they determined without hesitation to attack in the open field. The French and their confederates no sooner discovered this intention than they retreated and took up a position in the fortified pagoda of Seringham, strongly situated in an island formed by the branches of the Coleroon and the Cavery. Here, however, they were closely pressed by the combined armies; while the adherents of Chunda Saheb, considering his cause as desperate, deserted in large bands. That unfortunate prince at length delivered himself up to the King of Tanjore, under a promise of protection, which was basely violated, and he was immediately put to death. The French troops also capitulated, and were conveyed prisoners of war to Fort St David and Trichinopoly.

Total defeat of the French and their allies.

Satisfaction of the British.

The highest satisfaction was now felt by the British, who considered themselves complete masters of the Carnatic. But at Pondicherry this loss spread the deepest consternation, relieved only by the secret joy of those who viewed with disgust the haughty conduct of Dupleix, and exulted in the failure of his ambitious schemes. Yet at this very time he was acting a splendid part on a greater scale. His agent, Bussy, having, in the manner above related, placed Salabat Jung on the throne of the Deccan, after assisting to inflict punishment on the murderer of his predecessor, marched along with the prince to Golconda and Aurungabad, where he assumed the government with every circumstance of oriental pomp. His pretensions, however, were not sanctioned by the Mogul court, who conferred the sove-

Politic system pursued by Dupleix.

reignty on Ghazee-ud-Dien, the legitimate claimant, as eldest son to Nizam-ul-Mulk. At the same time the country was harassed by the attacks of a numerous Mahratta force; so that Salabat Jung could hope to maintain his power only by French aid, and therefore made Bussy the chief director of his councils.

CHAP. X.
A.D. 1753.

Efforts to restore French ascendancy

Dupleix, not content with these advantages, was indefatigable in his efforts to restore the French ascendency in the Carnatic; and the continual fluctuation in the plans and alliances of Indian potentates afforded him the means sooner than could have been expected. With such persons, when in distress and applying for aid, it is the invariable practice to promise whatever is asked; but when their deliverance is effected to perform as little as possible. After the complete triumph of the British arms and those of Mohammed Ali, Major Laurence was astounded by the intelligence that this prince had stipulated, as the price of the assistance which he obtained from the Mysorean chief, the surrender to him of Trichinopoly and its territory; and the fulfilment of this engagement was now imperiously demanded. On being interrogated, he at once admitted the promise, which he imputed to the necessity of circumstances, but strenuously abjured the slightest intention of adhering to it. He affected even to believe it impossible that his ally could have seriously expected the execution of so unreasonable a contract; and he undertook to induce him to rest satisfied with the present cession of Madura, and the illusory hope of obtaining Trichinopoly at some future period. After much negotiation, and seeing that he could gain nothing more, the other feigned to appear contented. Yet Major Laurence, clearly perceiving the regent's secret resentment, advised the Company either honourably to deliver up the city, or resolutely to seize his person and that of Morari Rao, and thereby prevent the hostile machinations which might easily be foreseen. The Directors followed neither of these counsels; and the disappointed chief continued to meditate on plans of vengeance. The commanders of several

Rash agreement of Mohammed Ali.

Mode of fulfilling its conditions.

Temporizing policy of the Company

CHAP X.
—
A. D. 1754.

districts were encouraged, by the knowledge of his present disposition, to make head against Mohammed Ali,—among whom was the Governor of Gingee, the strongest of all the fortresses; and the English, in attempting to reduce it, were repulsed by the French. Dupleix sent a large body of troops, which entered the territory of Fort St David, and at the same time captured a detachment of Swiss proceeding thither by sea from Madras. Laurence then marching out, encountered him at Bahoor, about two miles from the city; and his men charging furiously with the bayonet, broke the centre of the enemy, who instantly throwing down their arms, fled in such confusion that, had not the native cavalry occupied themselves in securing the plunder, the rout would have been complete. This advantage was followed up by Captain Clive with the reduction, under considerable difficulties, of the forts of Covelong and Chingleput; after which the state of his health obliging him to return home, deprived the army of his important services.

Partial successes of the French.

Advantages gained by the British.

Native treaty with the French.

The Mysorean general, after beginning to negotiate with the French, had been induced to pause by the intelligence of the victory gained by the English; but, learning that it had not been followed by any decisive results, he concluded the treaty in conjunction with Morari Rao, who had also been much dissatisfied with his share of the booty. Dupleix likewise drew over Mortiz Ali, the governor of Vellore, by holding out to him the hope of being himself raised to the dignity of nabob; and then the French troops, in conjunction with the native forces, laid close siege to Trichinopoly. Major Laurence was stunned by the unexpected intelligence that, through the negligence of the commander, this important place did not contain provisions for more than fifteen days. He was therefore obliged to hasten instantly with his whole army to its relief. The men suffered considerably by a rapid march in the midst of the hot season; but they succeeded without opposition in entering the city. The major was then able to open a communication with the southern districts for a supply

French lay siege to Trichinopoly.

of necessaries, and obtained some assistance from the Rajah of Tanjore, whose alliance, however, like that of all Indian princes, wavered with every variation of fortune. It became impossible in this scarcity to supply the inhabitants of so great a city as Trichinopoly, who, to the number of 400,000, were compelled to quit the place, and seek temporary shelter elsewhere; and the immense circuit of its walls was occupied only by the 2000 men composing the garrison. The provisioning of this important fortress now became the principal object of contest, the entire strength of both sides being drawn around it; and the French, with an immensely superior force, placed themselves in such positions as enabled them to intercept completely the entrance of convoys from the south. The brave Laurence twice attacked, and, though with very inferior numbers, drove them from their posts, and opened the way for his supplies. On no former occasion, indeed, had the valour of the English troops, and their superiority to those of the enemy, been more signally displayed. The garrison, however, had nearly, by their own supineness, forfeited the benefit of all these exertions. One morning at three o'clock, the guard having fallen fast asleep, the French advanced to the assault, applied their scaling-ladders, made themselves masters of a battery, and were advancing into the city, when several of the soldiers happening to fall into a deep pit, their cries alarmed their companions, some of whom fired their muskets. The assailants thus conceiving themselves to be discovered, made a general discharge, beat their drums, and advanced with shouts of *Vive le Roi*. Happily a considerable body of British was quartered near the spot, who were immediately led on by Lieutenant Harrison to such an advantageous position, and directed with so much judgment, that the foremost of the storming-party were soon cut down, the ladders carried off or broken, and all of the enemy who had entered, to the number of 360, were made prisoners. Thus the enterprise, at first so promising, caused to them a loss greater than any sustained by their arms during the course

British defence of Trichinopoly

Bravery of the English.

Neglect of sufficient guard.

Timely rescue.

CHAP. X.

A.D. 1754.

Surprise of an English detachment.

of this memorable siege. Soon afterwards, however, an English detachment, being sent out to escort a convoy of provisions, was attacked by a corps of 18,000 natives and 400 Europeans. An inexperienced officer, who had the command, drew up his men in small parties at wide intervals. Suddenly Morari Rao and Innis Khan, with 12,000 Mysorean horse, advanced with loud shouts at full gallop and charged this ill-constructed line. Our countrymen had scarcely time to fire one volley, when they found their ranks broken by the enemy's cavalry. Deserted by the sepoys, they were left, only 180 in number, without any hope of escape; upon which they determined to sell their lives as dearly as possible. The whole were either killed or taken, including a company of grenadiers, who had acted a prominent part in all the late victories.

Protracted siege of Trichinopoly.

Amid these gallant exploits, the siege of Trichinopoly was protracted a year and a half, during which neither the French nor their numerous allies obtained any decisive advantage. Mr Mill considers the object as very unworthy of such strenuous efforts; yet it ought to be remembered, that the Company were deciding on that spot the destiny of the Carnatic, and perhaps the very existence of their establishment in India. To have yielded in such circumstances might have realized the views of Dupleix, whose boast it had been, that he would reduce Madras to a fishing-village.

Salabat Jung's court.

Important events were meantime taking place at the court of the Deccan, where we left Bussy with his followers dictating or directing every movement. This influence indeed he seemed entitled to expect, both from the generosity and prudence of Salabat Jung, who had been raised by the French to his present lofty station, and by them alone was maintained in it against the Mahrattas, and Ghazee-ud-Dien, whom the Mogul had authorized to expel him. The latter, however, as he was approaching with a prodigious army, died suddenly, not without suspicion, perhaps unjust, of having been poisoned by the adherents of his rival. Salabat being

CHAP. X.

A.D. 1755

thus relieved from apprehension, the great men around him, viewing with much indignation the thraldom of their master to a handful of strangers, urged him to adopt measures for extricating himself from this humiliating situation; and at their suggestion he took certain steps, which were favoured by a temporary absence of Bussy. The pay of the troops was withheld, and on plausible pretexts they were broken into detachments and sent into different quarters. The foreigner, however, on his return, immediately reassembled them; and his own force, aided by the alarm of a Mahratta invasion, enabled him completely to dictate terms to the subahdar. He procured the dismissal of the hostile ministers; and, taking advantage of the accumulated arrears of pay, demanded and obtained, as a security against future deficiencies, the cession of an extensive range of country on the coast of Coromandel and Orissa, including the Northern Circars. This, in addition to former acquisitions, gave to the French a territory 600 miles in extent, reaching from Medapilly to the pagoda of Juggernaut, and yielding a revenue of £855,000.

Jealousy of French supremacy

Influence of Bussy.

The heads of the two European presidencies, being urged by instructions from home to endeavour to bring their differences to a termination, opened a negotiation for peace. They began with the farce of examining the titles by which each held their respective possessions from the native powers, and particularly the Mogul; but the English alleging, seemingly with some reason, that the documents produced by the French were forged, proposed to reject this mode of decision altogether, and proceed at once to the only effectual plan of treating, that, namely, which had a reference to the actual strength of each party. Upon this ground some mutual propositions were made, but were found too inconsistent to afford any hope of agreement.

Negotiations for peace.

Meantime this Indian contest had given rise to warm discussions between the two governments in Europe. France had never favoured the system of encroachment followed by her viceroy; and this aversion was greatly

Views of the Indian war in Europe.

CHAP. X.
A.D. 1755.

strengthened by the warm remonstrances of the English cabinet, who began to fit out a somewhat formidable expedition for the East. After some discussion, it was agreed that commissioners from each state should be sent, with full powers to adjust the differences, rather upon equitable principles satisfactory to both parties, than from any consideration of their comparative strength and acquisitions. When Godheu, the French envoy, arrived at Pondicherry to supersede Dupleix, considerable anxiety was felt as to the manner in which the tidings would be received by that haughty ruler. He had assumed the most lofty bearing, invested himself with the dress and ensigns of a Mogul viceroy, and had often obliged the officers whom he admitted to audience to fall down on their knees before him. His whole soul, too, was understood to be absorbed in the magnificent project of making his country supreme in India. But he was too sound a politician not to perceive that all resistance was now vain; and yielding with a good grace, he was well treated and sent home with honour and respect. The Company indeed gave him a cold reception, and refused to repay nearly £400,000 which he had expended out of his private fortune and credit in extending their dominion. All the historians inveigh bitterly against this treatment; yet it is impossible not to remark, that the ambitious and warlike policy of this governor, in furtherance of which he lavished immense treasures, was in direct opposition to the system which the merchants, wisely we think, were anxious to pursue. They thought themselves not at all obliged to him for spending such sums in the attempt to make them masters of vast provinces against their will; and, therefore, they did not hold their association bound to replace advances which, although made on their account, were made not only without but even contrary to their instructions. The government, when appealed to, sanctioned the conduct of the Company, though at the same time they gave to Dupleix a strange and iniquitous compensation, by granting letters of protection against any prosecution which might be raised by his creditors.

Commissioners appointed.

Assumption and politic submission of Dupleix.

His reception by the French Company.

Defence of their conduct.

The French commissioner, and Mr Saunders, the English governor, immediately proceeded to arrange a treaty, with a view at once to the protection of the native states against encroachment, and the equitable adjustment of the points in dispute between the two European powers. It was stipulated by the very first article, that all the cessions obtained from the Moors (as the Indian princes were then called) should be restored by both parties, with the exception only of certain maritime stations, to be retained for the security of trade; and these were to be so selected, that the two nations should in each particular district of the coast be nearly on a footing of equality. The terms of this arrangement were in general very favourable to the British. The portions of territory which they were obliged to renounce were comparatively small, and their ally, Mohammed Ali, was left undisputed ruler of the Carnatic; while the French resigned the immense possessions which they had acquired in Orissa and the Northern Circars.

Adjustment of rival claims in India.

Favourable arrangement for the British.

But this compact, which was expected to have adjusted all differences between the two countries, scarcely produced a suspension of hostilities. The English, having secured Mohammed Ali, their candidate, as nabob of the Carnatic, considered themselves bound, and perhaps felt inclined, to support him against the numerous enemies by whom he was still surrounded. The Regent of Mysore declared himself determined not to recede from his pretensions to Trichinopoly, which rendered it necessary to maintain troops for the defence of that fortress. The enemy, however, were considered so little formidable, that Captain Kilpatrick, who commanded in the place, learning that the regent was forming a plan for its attack, sent a message, that if he chose to come, he himself would throw open the gates and meet him. The Company also agreed to send another corps to establish the rajah's authority and collect the revenue in the provinces of Madura and Tinnevelly. This promised to be an easy and profitable task, in which some share of the proceeds would probably fall into their own hands; but

Trifling influence of this compact.

Claims of the Regent of Mysore.

CHAP. X.

A. D. 1755.

The Colleries.

they were very much disappointed in both respects. These countries are occupied by an almost savage race, called the Colleries, who, in their habits of robbery and predatory warfare, can scarcely be surpassed. They have their abode in the heart of dense and inaccessible forests, whence they issue to plunder the cattle of the surrounding districts, and boast of their dexterity in performing these thefts, as if they were the most heroic exploits. Their chief ambition is to enrich their family and tribe, for which they brave death with the utmost intrepidity.

Rude ideas of virtue.

Two brothers who had stolen a vast number of horses were apprehended and brought before Major Laurence, who ordered them to be hanged. One of them offered, if leave were given him, to go and bring back, within two days, the stolen animals, while his brother should remain as a hostage. His request was granted; but the time having elapsed, the prisoner was sent for and examined, when he very composedly expressed his astonishment that they should have been so silly as to imagine his brother would think of restoring so many valuable prizes, which were sufficient to make the fortune of the whole family. It was a clever trick: as for himself, having often hazarded his life for objects comparatively trifling, he was quite ready to die in so honourable a cause. Laurence was so amused with the fellow's impudence, that on Clive's intercession he dismissed him. The Col-

Native fortresses.

leries occupied a range of hills, the passes or intervals of which were fortified with walls of large loose stones, and with a broad deep ditch, in front of which was planted a hedge of bamboo-canes, so thick that it could not be penetrated but by fire or the axe. The natives defended these fastnesses with the utmost obstinacy: and, though they did not face the English in the open field, were continually on the watch to cut off their detachments. One small body being found asleep, were all speared in a few minutes; and the whole army, as it once marched in a careless manner through a defile near Madura, had its rear suddenly assailed, and suffered great loss. Thus, after a hard campaign, the troops did not collect revenue enough to defray the expense of the expedition, and had afterwards to struggle through several years of tedious and fruitless warfare.

French resume operations.

The French, when they saw their enemies thus actively employed, felt disposed to imitate their example. Finding them entirely occupied with the war in Madura, they made a hasty march upon Trichinopoly, which was then nearly defenceless; but it was saved by a very rapid movement on the part of Captain Calliaud. A predatory warfare was for some time waged between the two nations, when events ensued that gave a new and more important character to the contest.

War between Britain and France.

On the breaking out of the memorable war in 1756 between Britain and France, the latter determined to make the most vigorous efforts to acquire an ascendency in India. The ministry fitted out an extensive armament, the command of which they intrusted to Count Lally, an officer of Irish extraction, who, among many brilliant displays of personal valour, had, at the battle of Fontenoy, taken several English officers with his own hand. Cherishing the strongest attachment to his late master, the unfortunate and misguided James II., he felt also the most deadly antipathy to the people who had expelled him, and looked, as his highest pride, to his being the chief instrument for subverting their eastern dominion. He sailed from Brest on the 4th May 1757, but had so tedious a voyage, accompanied with severe sickness among his crew, that he did not land at Pondicherry till the 25th April 1758.

Count Lally

So eager was he to accomplish his great object, that though he did not reach the shore till five in the afternoon, before night closed he had troops on their march to besiege Fort St David, which was still considered the strongest and most important of the English settlements. By this indiscreet haste, in which no regard was paid to the convenience, opinion, or prejudices of his followers, he created a spirit of animosity and even of resistance, which much impeded his future movements. He even arrived at the place without due information as to the

Rash proceedings.

CHAP. X. A.D. 1759.

strength or position of the works. However, he pushed the siege with extraordinary vigour; while the garrison made an injudicious defence, throwing away their shot on insignificant objects, till at length, when they were hard pressed, their ammunition proved extremely deficient. The enemy having, on the 1st of June, advanced their trenches to the foot of the glacis, and opened such a fire that the artillerymen could scarcely stand to their guns, it was judged necessary to surrender; the troops became prisoners of war; and this fortress, the capital of our eastern settlements, was rased to the ground.

Capture of Fort St. David.

Lally's exultation.

Lally returned to Pondicherry in the highest exultation, fully determined to lose no time in following up his design of driving the English from the whole of India. With this view he took a step which involved him in deep reproach. Bussy, amid the violent revolutions at the court of the Deccan, and the most deadly jealousy among its leading men, had succeeded in completely maintaining the French influence. He had acquired the full command of the Circars, where he reduced Vizagapatam, an important factory belonging to the British. Now, however, he was ordered by Lally to quit this court, that he might be able to unite all his forces, first in reducing Madras, and then in attacking our newly-formed settlements in Bengal. Bussy remonstrated strongly against renouncing his brilliant prospects for such uncertain advantages; but the other, imperious and self-willed, would listen to nothing, and insisted upon an instant and implicit compliance with his own views.

Unwise dismissal of Bussy.

Expedition against the Rajah of Tanjore.

Notwithstanding the reinforcement obtained by so great a sacrifice, the new leader, from the want of funds, was scarcely in a condition to attempt any enterprise of importance. In hopes of relieving this distress he resolved upon an expedition against the Rajah of Tanjore, to extort the fulfilment of an old engagement to pay five millions of rupees. This enterprise, however, was conducted in a manner rash and revolting to the natives; and even after penetrating to the town, and commencing the siege, he was obliged by the scarcity of provisions and ammunition to withdraw. He soon obtained possession of Arcot and certain other places in the Carnatic, from whence he drew some supplies; and being then joined by Bussy, he deemed it expedient to commence the siege of Madras, which he carried on upwards of two months, though under great difficulties. The garrison, meanwhile, consisting of 1758 Europeans and 2420 natives, commanded by Governor Pigot and the veteran Laurence, made the most gallant defence. The blockade was terminated by the appearance, on the 16th February, of a squadron of English ships, having on board six hundred fresh troops. As soon as this fleet hove in sight, the French army, without waiting their commander's orders, began to retreat with the utmost precipitation, and he had not time to execute his cruel purpose of burning the Black Town.

Siege of Madras.

Precipitate retreat.

It is admitted by Lally himself, that, owing to their deep hatred of him, his return in this discomfited state to Pondicherry was viewed as a subject of triumph by the principal officers, and even by the greater part of the inhabitants. Every thing now presented to his eyes a disastrous aspect. When the English took the field, and began to reconquer the Carnatic, the French, in attempting to check their career, were defeated at Wandewash, and obliged to retreat upon their presidency. It was evident that their dominion in India was fast approaching to a close; and their general has acknowledged, that if, after their late success, our countrymen had marched direct upon their chief city, they might have become masters of it in a few days. But they spent the next three months in reducing the different strong places in the Carnatic, including Carical, the only other seaport which remained to their adversary. Having obtained repeated reinforcements, which the enemy looked for in vain, they were enabled to close in around Pondicherry, and make preparations for its actual siege. Lally, in this desperate state of his affairs, obtained by high promises an auxiliary force from Hyder, now master of Mysore; but his troops, after remaining about a month, became

Reception of Lally at Pondicherry.

Slow proceedings of the British.

Desperate state of the French leader.

CHAP. X.

A.D. 1761.

Deserted by his allies.

discouraged by witnessing the manifest weakness of their allies; and, being impelled by urgent matters at home, they broke up without giving notice, and departed for their own country.

Spirited attack on the British camp.

Lally made a spirited attempt to retrieve his affairs by a midnight attack on the British camp, and succeeded in carrying several posts of some importance; but the gallantry of our soldiers, and the tardy arrival of one of his divisions, caused his final repulse. By the end of September 1760, Pondicherry was so closely blockaded both by sea and land, that only a very scanty supply of provisions could be introduced; and two large ships that were lying in port were surprised in the night and carried off. On the 27th November, the commander, who had long urged the necessity of the measure, insisted on carrying into effect the expulsion of the black inhabitants. To the number of 1400 they were thrust out of the gates, but were refused a passage by the besiegers, who foresaw that the garrison would thereby be enabled to hold out a somewhat longer period. The unhappy creatures wandered about the glacis, picking up plants and roots of grass, and imploring either an entrance into the city or leave to pass through the army. Both parties stood firm for a week, at the end of which time Colonel Coote's humanity induced him to allow this wretched band to retire into the country. They were in the most exhausted state, and had nowhere to look for refuge; yet they were extremely grateful even for this chance of preservation.

Blockade of Pondicherry.

Cruel policy of the Europeans.

Opening of the trenches.

It was not till the 12th January 1761, that the trenches were regularly opened,—an operation which was effected with ease and rapidity, as the enemy scarcely offered any resistance. Their spirit seems to have been completely gone, and they had provisions left for only two days. On the 14th two deputations arrived,—one from Lally, and the other from the governor and council. The former merely stated, that certain alleged violations by the English of the faith of treaties prevented him from entering into any regular capitulation, but that,

CHAP. X.

A. D. 1761.

pressed by the necessity of circumstances, he yielded the place, and surrendered himself and his garrison prisoners of war. The governor and council asked some terms for the inhabitants; but, as matters stood, every thing rested with the discretion of the conquerors, who, however, promised to act with consideration and humanity. Colonel Coote entered the city, and three days afterwards the defeated general set sail for Europe.

Surrender of Pondicherry.

On his arrival in France, a tragical scene ensued. The nation were by this time worked up to a great degree of discontent by the severe disasters which, throughout the war, when the British resources were directed by the genius of Pitt, had befallen their arms in every quarter of the globe. The loss of India raised their indignation to the highest pitch; and they loudly demanded a victim. Lally, with his usual violence, presented a formal accusation against Bussy and three others connected with him in the administration, as having, out of enmity to himself, ruined the French affairs. The impeachment appears to have been ill founded, and the parties accused retaliated by charging him with having caused that unfortunate issue by a series of acts, which, as they alleged, inferred more than incapacity. The voice of individuals returning from India, who had been alienated by his hasty temper, was generally hostile to him. On their testimony, the attorney-general thought himself justified in founding a charge of high treason; which appears to have been altogether groundless. Many of his proceedings, it is true, were rash and imprudent, and his outrageous manner, provoking the enmity both of his own people and the natives, was very injurious to the interests of the Company and the government. But to constitute high treason there must have been an intention to betray these interests; instead of which his faults appear to have rather proceeded from a blind and headlong zeal. Being arraigned of this high crime, he was removed from the Bastile to an humbler prison, and, according to the ungenerous practice of France, was denied the aid of counsel. The parliament of Paris, a

Indignation of the French.

Mutual recrimination

Lally accused of high treason.

CHAP. X.

A.D. 1761.

Unjust condemnation and execution of Lally.

too numerous though highly respectable body, were so far wrought upon as to pronounce sentence of death; against which Seguier and Pellot, two of their most distinguished members, protested; and Voltaire hesitates not to call it a judicial murder. The unfortunate Lally, when it was announced to him, lifted his hands to heaven, exclaiming—"Is this the reward of forty-five years' service!" and endeavoured to stab himself with a pair of compasses. He was prevented, and conveyed next day in a common cart to the *Place de Grève*, where he underwent the unjust sentence of the law.

CHAPTER XI.

British Conquest of Bengal.

Difficulties of the early Settlements—Reign of Aliverdi Khan—Succeeded by Surajah Dowlah—His Jealousy of the English—Captures Cossimbuzar—Advances upon Calcutta—Plans of Defence—Proceedings of the Enemy—Garrison deserted by the Ships and the Governor—Surrender—Confinement in the Black Hole—Dreadful Sufferings—Conduct of the Nabob—Armament from Madras under Clive and Watson—Their Landing and first Encounter with the Enemy—Calcutta surrenders—Surajah Dowlah attempts to retake it—Treaty—Capture of Chandernagore—Plan of dethroning the Nabob—Intrigues—Treachery of Meer Jaffier—Advance of Clive—Battle of Plassey—Elevation of Meer Jaffier—Capture and Death of Surajah Dowlah—Invasion by the Shazada—Defeat of the Mogul and the Nabob of Oude—Bad Conduct of the new Nabob—Succeeded by Meer Cossim—His Disputes with the Company—Rupture—Patna taken and retaken—Victory gained by Major Adams—Massacre of English Prisoners—Meer Cossim's Flight into Oude—Repeated Defeats of Sujah Dowlah—The Mogul joins the English—Death of Meer Jaffier—Clive returns to India—Restores Sujah Dowlah—Obtains for the Company the Dewannee of Bengal, Bahar, and Orissa.

CHAP. XI

Difficulties of early British settlements.

The British establishments in Bengal had, during a long period, held only a secondary place to those formed on the coast of Coromandel; but the time was now arrived when they were to become the theatre of the most interesting events, and finally the centre and chief seat of our Indian dominion. The manner in which the factory at Calcutta was first founded has been already mentioned,* and it continued to extend its importance, notwithstanding the opposition it experienced during the vice-

* Page 320.

CHAP. XI. — A.D. 1754.

Progress of Calcutta.

royalty of Jaffier Khan. Its situation became greatly improved when the office of nabob was occupied by Sujah; but on the death of that prince, his son Suffraze, a weak and imprudent ruler, was dethroned, and his place usurped by Aliverdi, a chief either of Patan or Afghan extraction, and possessed of great military talents.

Wise administration of Aliverdi.

Notwithstanding the irregular elevation of the latter, he administered the government, not only in an able, but a mild and beneficent manner. This he did under difficult circumstances; for the Mahrattas, invited it is said either by the Mogul court or the subahdar, found their way in vast bodies into Bengal; and, though often repulsed, repeatedly renewed their inroads. The prudence and valour of Aliverdi preserved his dominions from conquest, but not from ruinous depredation. He secured the attachment of his Hindoo subjects by protecting their property, as well as by employing them in all the civil departments of government; and he was therefore not likely to oppress industrious strangers settled in his dominions.

Dealings with the English.

The English had only to complain, that amid the various exigencies of his situation, he made repeated demands upon their generosity in return for the countenance granted to their trade; yet his entire exactions, during an administration of twelve years, did not exceed £100,000. He felt no objection, when there was an alarm of invasion, even to their enclosing Calcutta with a moat, meant to extend seven miles in circuit; though, as soon as the danger passed by, they discontinued the work, which was afterwards known by the name of the Mahratta ditch.

Jealousy of French and English settlers.

Considerable uneasiness, indeed, is supposed to have been felt by him with reference to the ascendency of the English and French in the Carnatic, who were said to create and depose governors at their pleasure. Finally, the downfal of Angria, of whose naval strength he had been led to form an exaggerated idea, made him begin to look on them as somewhat too formidable neighbours.

When Aliverdi died, he was succeeded by his grand-

CHAP. XI. A. D. 1755.

Secession of Surajah Dowlah.

son Surajah Dowlah, a dissolute and tyrannical prince, who adopted these jealousies to a much greater extent. He was also irritated by the protection afforded, seemingly without design, to a young man by the English whom he viewed as a pretender to the office of nabob. Lastly, his very exaggerated conceptions of the wealth to be found within their factory, made him seek with avidity any pretext on which he might be justified in plundering that establishment. The ostensible cause of complaint arose from a report that they were making certain additions to the works around Fort William. Mr Drake, the governor, on being called upon to account for this proceeding, defended it by a reference to the hostile relations of his countrymen with the French on the coast of Coromandel, and the danger lest the war should spread thence into Bengal. This ill-judged explanation inflamed at once the pride and the fear of the nabob; who considered it an insult to suppose that he, in his own dominions, was unable to protect them, while he felt alarmed at the idea of the war being transferred to his country. He immediately began his march from Rajemahl towards Calcutta, stopping at Cossimbuzar, where the Company had a factory very slightly fortified, without ditch or palisade, and of which the curtains formed the outer wall of a range of apartments. Under these circumstances, he summoned first Mr Watts, the governor, and then the two other members of council, to repair to his camp, a step which these gentlemen judged it vain to decline; and though Mr Holwell in one place seems to blame them for not having attempted a few days' defence, yet the danger of a general massacre was in that case so great, and the probable benefit so small, that we do not perceive any good ground for censure. They were then required to sign a paper, promising compliance with all the nabob's demands; when, instead of being allowed to return to the presidency, they were detained as prisoners, while his troops plundered their warehouses.

Unwise proceedings of the English governor

Capture and plunder of Cossimbuzar

Conciliatory proceedings.

The council at Calcutta, sensible of their weakness, had hitherto made every possible effort to conciliate the

CHAP. XI

A.D. 1756.

Imprudent delay.

nabob; and as his chief ground of complaint respected the new intrenchments which they were adding to Fort William, they suspended these works, and thus lost twenty precious days, during which they might have placed themselves in a good posture of defence. As soon, however, as they learned the capture of the factory at Cossimbuzar, they gave up all hopes of accommodation, and thought only of increasing their means of resistance, which were very slender. The garrison did not muster above 514 men, of whom only 174 were Europeans, and of these not ten had ever seen service beyond the parade; and even this duty had been enforced so negligently that many, according to Mr Holwell, did not know the right from the wrong end of their muskets. The fort, though of some extent, was defended by a wall only four feet thick, which in many parts, as at Cossimbuzar, enclosed chambers whence windows opened, and whose terraced roofs formed the top of the rampart. All around were erected warehouses, clusters of buildings, and even little streets; some commanding the castle, others affording cover for the operations of an assailant. Under these circumstances the officers determined to draw their defensive line around the whole range of buildings, and endeavour to prevent the enemy from penetrating into them. This plan seems justly censured by Orme, since they had no force to defend so extensive a circuit pervaded by so many avenues. They ought to have demolished the houses close to the fort; or, if time did not allow this operation, have removed at least the roofs and upper floors, while a few buildings, that were defensible and overlooked the works, should have been occupied by strong bodies of troops, and a ditch and palisade then drawn round the whole. By such means they might, in our author's opinion, have kept their ground till the annual fleet arrived, which would at least have secured their retreat. In this extremity, they importuned the French and Dutch to make common cause against the Indian tyrant; but they only received from the former the insulting offer of shelter in Chandernagore.

Slender garrison of Fort William.

Unskilful plan for its defence.

Vain appeal to the French and Dutch.

Assault of Fort William

Meantime the nabob marched upon Calcutta with such furious haste, that a number of his men perished from strokes of the sun, or other accidents occasioned by excessive heat; and having left Cossimbuzar on the 9th June 1756, he arrived on the 16th in view of Fort William. He was arrested for some time by the Mahratta ditch, not being aware that it extended round only part of the circuit; but having overcome this obstacle, he commenced, on the morning of the 18th, a general attack on the outposts, defended by three batteries, which were for some time vigorously served. The Indians, however, having kept up a brisk fire from under the bushes, and also penetrated through avenues which had not been secured, all the three batteries in the course of the day were abandoned, and the whole garrison sought refuge within the fragile walls of the fort. From this time the most sanguine lost almost every hope of a successful resistance; and yet no measures were taken for withdrawing the troops. At night, indeed, the women and children were conveyed on board a vessel, and two members of the council, who superintended the embarkation, thought it prudent not to return. At two in the following morning the leaders met, to deliberate whether they should immediately effect their escape, or delay it till next night. After much discussion, they broke up without any decision; which amounted practically to the adoption of the latter alternative. The attack being warmly renewed at daybreak, the enemy continually gained ground. While affairs were assuming every hour a more alarming aspect, the ship, on board of which were the women and children, was seen to weigh anchor and stand down the river, while the other vessels most culpably followed the example. The situation of the garrison became then truly critical. Drake, the governor, who had all along been very inefficient as a commander, was seized with a panic, threw himself into the last remaining boat, and left his troops to their fate. Struck with astonishment and indignation, they chose Mr Holwell to fill his place; but all their concern now was in

Hopeless state of the garrison.

Shameful desertion of the governor

CHAP. XI.

A.D. 1756.

Mr. Holwell chosen governor

what manner to effect their deliverance. One vessel which was ordered to approach, being still within reach, ran on a sandbank, and was deserted by the crew. The most earnest and repeated signals were then made to the ships that had gone down to Govindpore; but it is very mortifying to state, that not one of them, to save so many brave men, chose to encounter the danger, which was by no means formidable, of approaching the walls of the fort. Mr Holwell then saw no alternative but to open a negotiation for surrender, and in the morning a letter was thrown over the ramparts, which was answered in the afternoon by a flag of truce. Meantime the troops, taking advantage of the confusion, had obtained access to the liquor, and were so intoxicated as to be incapable of action. The enemy, discovering how matters stood, stepped into the fort, and took possession of it without resistance.

Negotiations for surrender

Proceedings of Meer Jaffier.

The Indian army, upon their first entrance into Fort William, did not commit any outrage; but when the nabob entered, accompanied by his general Meer Jaffier, he sent for Mr Holwell, and burst into violent reproaches at his having attempted to defend the place against the ruler of Bengal. He expressed also the most extreme dissatisfaction at finding in the treasury only the small sum of 50,000 rupees; yet, after three interviews, he dismissed him with assurances, on the word of a soldier, that no harm should be done to him. The Englishman then returned to his people, and found them surrounded by a strong guard, who led them into a veranda, or arched gallery, constructed to shelter the garrison from the sun and rain, but which excluded the chambers behind it from light and air. Some quarters of the fort being on fire, they were involved in so thick a smoke as inspired them with the apprehension that a design was formed to suffocate them; but their keepers were merely looking out for a proper place of confinement. They pitched upon a chamber employed as the common dungeon of the fortress, called the *black hole;* it consisted of a space eighteen feet square, with only two small windows barred

Treatment of the prisoners.

Black hole of Calcutta.

with iron, opening into the close veranda, and scarcely admitting a breath of air. Into this narrow receptacle the whole of the officers and troops, 146 in number, were compelled to enter; and on their venturing to remonstrate, the commander ordered every one who should hesitate to be instantly cut down. Thus were they forcibly thrust into this fearful dungeon, into which the whole number could with difficulty be squeezed; and the door was then fast barred from without. Their first impression, on finding themselves thus immured, was the utter impossibility of surviving one night, and the necessity of extricating themselves at whatever cost. The jemautdars, or Indian guards, were walking before the window, and Mr Holwell seeing one who bore on his face a more than usual expression of humanity, adjured him to procure for them a room in which they could breathe, assuring him next morning of a reward of 1000 rupees. The man went away—but returned, saying it was impossible. Thinking the offer had been too low, the prisoners tendered 2000 rupees. The man again went,—and returned, saying that the nabob was asleep, and no one durst awake him;—the lives of 146 men being nothing in comparison to disturbing for a moment the slumbers of a tyrant. Mr Holwell has described in detail the horrors of that fatal night, which are scarcely paralleled in the annals of human misery. Every moment added to their distress. All attempts to obtain relief by a change of posture, from the painful pressure to which it gave rise, only aggravated their sufferings. The air soon became pestilential, producing at every moment a feeling of suffocation; and while the perspiration flowed in streams, they were tormented with the most burning thirst. Unfortunately, as the stations near the windows were decidedly the best, the most dreadful struggles were made to reach them. Many of the prisoners being foreign soldiers, and now released from all subordination, made the most frightful efforts, and the sufferers, as they grew weaker, were in some instances squeezed or actually trampled to death. Loud

Dreadful position of the British.

Sufferings of the prisoners.

CHAP. XI. A.D. 1756. cries being raised of "water!" the humane jemautdar pushed through the bars several skins filled with that liquid; but this produced only an increase of calamity, owing to the very violent endeavours made to obtain it. The soldiers without found a savage sport in witnessing these contests, and even brought lights to the windows in order to view them to greater advantage. About eleven, the prisoners began to die fast; six of Mr Holwell's intimate friends sank at his feet, and were trodden upon by the survivors. Of those still alive, a great proportion were raving or delirious; some uttered incoherent prayers, others the most frightful blasphemies. They endeavoured by furious invectives to induce the guards to fire into the prison and end their miseries, but without effect. When day dawned, the few who had not expired were most of them either raving or insensible. In this last state was the governor himself, when about six o'clock Surajah awoke and inquired for him. On learning the events of the night, he merely sent to ascertain if the English chief yet lived, and being informed that there were appearances as if he might recover, gave orders to open the fatal door. At that time, of the 146 who had been enclosed, there breathed only twenty-three. Mr Holwell, being revived by the fresh air, was immediately supported into the presence of the nabob, who, on his beginning the dismal tale, ordered for him a seat and a draught of water, but showed no other mark of sympathy. He forthwith commenced a strict interrogatory about the supposed treasure, discrediting extremely the assertion that there was none; but not being able to learn any thing on this subject, he sent that gentleman, with three others, prisoners to Muxadavad. In this voyage they suffered severely, their bodies being covered with boils, that had broken out in consequence of their confinement; though these eruptions were considered beneficial. The other survivors were liberated; while the dead bodies were, without any ceremony, thrown into a ditch.

State of the survivors.

Interview of Mr. Holwell with the nabob.

Mr Holwell seems to be of opinion that the nabob had

CHAP. XI. A.D. 1756.

no actual intention of causing the dreadful catastrophe, but that some inferior officers had seized this opportunity of gratifying their revenge. The utter insensibility displayed by him, however, seems to fix thoroughly upon that prince the guilt of this frightful transaction. We cannot concur with Mr Mill in throwing the blame upon the English themselves for having used this apartment as a prison. A room eighteen feet square might afford ample space for two or three soldiers, the greatest number probably they were ever accustomed to confine in it. The fatal effects evidently arose from the crowd thus thrust into an apartment wholly unfit to contain them.

Probable cause of the treatment of the garrison.

All was lost in Bengal before the presidency at Madras were apprized that any thing was in danger; and the melancholy tidings, too, arrived at a moment when the most brilliant prospects had just opened in the Deccan. Salabat Jung, after having long shown the most extreme impatience under the thraldom in which he was held by the French, resolved at length upon an effort to extricate himself. Bussy was ordered to depart; and the subahdar, to secure his person against the resentment of that people, as well as the other evils from which their presence had protected him, requested from the English a subsidiary force, by sending which they would have supplanted their rivals as the arbiters of Southern India. The opportunity was tempting; but the crisis in Bengal was so urgent as made it indispensable to forego the advantage, though by their refusal they should compel the subahdar to solicit the return of Bussy, and throw himself again into the arms of the French.

Effects of the news at Madras.

Influence on the policy of that Presidency

All the force, naval and military, which could possibly be spared, was now despatched to Calcutta, under the command, the former of Admiral Watson, and the latter of Colonel Clive. This armament, destined to establish the British empire in India, consisted only of 900 Europeans and 1500 sepoys; and two of the ships, having on board 700 troops and many stores, were separated in a storm. The remainder arrived in the

Armament despatched to Calcutta

CHAP. XI. A. D. 1756.

middle of December at Fulta, a town at some distance below Calcutta, where the remnant of the English had taken refuge. Letters for the nabob were then transmitted to Monickchund, governor of that city; conceived, however, in so fierce and threatening a tone, that he declared he could not venture to transmit them. The British commanders then resolved to commence hostilities without delay. Admiral Watson moved up the vessels to the vicinity of Moidapore, purposing on the following day to attack the fort of Budge-Budge, about ten miles below the town. Clive, however, determined to advance direct upon the capital itself; and being unable to procure boats, he disembarked and proceeded by land. As evening approached, the troops, being extremely fatigued, were allowed to ground their arms and consign themselves to slumber. They were not aware that a large force of the enemy was encamped within two miles, who, having much better means of information, advanced during the night and commenced a very unexpected attack. They gained at first a considerable advantage, and even captured two field-pieces. The English commander, however, on being roused from sleep, refused to retreat, and soon with characteristic energy rallied his men. The enemy, notwithstanding their superior numbers and partial success, proved altogether unable to cope with disciplined troops, and were in the end entirely defeated and dispersed.

Hostilities commenced.

Proceedings of Clive.

This issue, displaying so completely the superiority of a European military force, struck Monickchund with such a panic that he precipitately quitted Calcutta, leaving only a garrison of 500 to make a show of resistance; and almost as soon as Admiral Watson opened his batteries, the surrender took place. The merchandise belonging to the factory was found entire. Some jealousy arose between the colonel and admiral, the latter wishing to appoint another governor of the city, and even to exclude the Company's troops; while the former strenuously and successfully vindicated his claim to that office. Collisions continued between these two

Surrender of Calcutta.

Jealousy between the admiral and Clive.

commanders, though as both were zealous for the public service and at bottom esteemed each other, the Company's interests were not materially impeded. Captain Coote was sent up against Hoogley, which after a slight resistance was taken, and plunder obtained to the extent of £15,000.

A native army marches on Calcutta.

The nabob, on receiving intelligence of the arrival and success of the English, immediately assembled his army and began to march upon Calcutta. Clive, not yet fully aware of the weakness of Indian potentates, was by no means forward to rush into a contest with the ruler of twenty millions of people. He considered it also of great importance to return as soon as possible to Madras, where the affairs of the Company were in so critical a state as to require his presence, and he hoped that Surajah might be induced to accede to moderate proposals. Watson, on the contrary, insisted that he would never become inclined to peace "till he had been well thrashed." But the other so far prevailed, that a mission was sent to him, who were honourably received, and had terms proposed that were considered admissible. He did not, however, discontinue his march, and by various evasions avoided bringing the treaty to a conclusion. In the end of January 1757, having arrived with his whole force, he commenced intrenching himself in the neighbourhood of Calcutta; and then all parties began to be persuaded that his only object in negotiating had been to gain time. Two gentlemen, meanwhile, were sent to request that he would withdraw; but he received them with haughtiness and refused compliance. Being warned by a friendly Indian to be on their guard against treachery, they departed abruptly, and reached headquarters in safety.

Temporizing policy of the nabob.

Clive attacks the Indian army.

Clive now determined to attack the Indian army. With the addition of 600 seamen he possessed a force of 2150, with which on the morning of the 5th of February he advanced against the nabob. The action was fought on both sides with obstinacy and determination, but in a confused and straggling manner; for so thick a mist enveloped the two armies that they could scarcely descry each other. The English, exposed to repeated and furious charges from the enemy's cavalry, as well as from a strong battery of artillery, suffered a severe loss, amounting to 220 men. They finally repulsed, however, every attack; and Surajah, mortified that his powerful host could make no impression on this small band, became not indisposed to terms of accommodation. As the inclination was mutual, the articles were adjusted by reciprocal concession. The prince permitted the English to fortify Calcutta, to carry on trade, and enjoy the same privileges as before the war; while they dropped their high though most just claims for redress and vengeance. Even an alliance offensive and defensive was concluded, and the ambitious potentate then led his troops into the interior.

Articles of peace.

Renewed war between France and England.

A delicate and important question now arose; intelligence having arrived of war being declared between France and England. The subjects of the former, who had a strongly fortified position at Chandernagore, agreed that neutrality should be observed within the province; admitting, at the same time, that they could not pledge themselves for its permanence without the sanction of the government at Pondicherry. Clive felt inclined to accept the offer, foreseeing that an attack on this post would offend the nabob and involve the British too deeply in the affairs of Bengal. On the other hand, it was considered that the security offered by the French was very precarious, and that when united with the native ruler, whose good will was exceedingly doubtful, and reinforced, as they might easily be, from their presidency, they could soon assemble a force which the English would be unable to resist. It was urged, therefore, that our countrymen ought to avail themselves of their present superiority to crush them,—an opinion which, supported by Watson as well as by urgent representations from Madras, finally prevailed. An attempt was made to gain the prince's consent; but he at once imposed a strict prohibition. Admiral Watson, however, wrote a letter earnestly de-

Delicate position of the British in India.

manding this sanction, with somewhat formidable threats in case of refusal. This drew forth a reply of vague consent, saying, "Whatever you think right, that do;" and to Mr Watts, the English resident at his court, he intimated that he would not intermeddle. As soon, however, as he learned that the expedition was in motion, he retracted, and wrote in the most peremptory style commanding them to stop. This was treated as an indignity and totally disregarded. Clive pushed on, commenced the siege on the 14th May 1757, and immediately drove in the outposts. A brave resistance was made; but the admiral soon came up with the fleet, opened a heavy cannonade, and carried on operations with such skill and vigour as to compel in a short time unconditional surrender. The garrison, consisting of 500 European and 700 native troops, became prisoners of war, and a vast quantity of stores was captured.

Vascillation of the nabob.

Siege and capture of Chandernagore.

Complete success had crowned this undertaking; yet Clive soon felt the critical situation in which his very triumph had placed him. The nabob was raving in a furious, though childish manner, menacing destruction to Mr Watts; and he was emboldened by the retreat of Ahmed Abdallah, the Patan chief, who had threatened an invasion of Bengal. He was now sure of support from the French, of whom a small body was still left, while reinforcements were expected, and said even to be on the march by way of Cuttack. As the English insisted that the whole of that nation should be banished from his dominions, he professed to have already done so, but complained that their demands were endless. Continuing in the same state of puerile irritation, he one day offered to Meer Jaffier, his prime minister, ten lacks of rupees if he would march and destroy the British, but next morning repented. This lamentable exhibition of weakness, with the vicinity of the Company's establishment, led to events which gave an entirely new turn to Indian affairs.

Critical situation of Clive.

Imbecile proceedings of the nabob

An oriental court, especially in so disorganized a state as those of India then were, in which no regular law of

CHAP. XI.

A.D. 1757.

succession was recognised, usually presents numerous elements of treason. Among the nabob's principal chiefs, several who were disgusted with his violent and capricious behaviour were at the same time ambitious of filling his place, and Mr Watts, who still continued resident, afforded a channel through whom applications could be made. The first overture came from one named Khuda Yar Khan Lattee, who proposed with the aid of the British to dethrone his master, assuring them that they would be aided by the Seits, a family of native merchants and bankers possessed of immense wealth. This transaction acquired a greatly augmented importance when it was announced that Meer Jaffier, the premier, was ready to engage in it on condition of being raised to supreme power in the room of the other. Clive, on receiving this intimation, considered the revolution as already effected. His eyes seem to have been at once opened to the demerits of Surajah, whom he describes as a villain who could not be trusted, but must be overset,—"he or we must fall,"—at the same time, to prevent any suspicion, he wrote him a soothing letter. Nothing remained but to arrange the terms, with which view the colonel hastened to the presidency, and laid the project before the Select Committee. They gave their cordial concurrence, and Admiral Watson agreed to afford his co-operation.

Dissensions at the nabob's court.

Policy of Clive.

Extravagant demands of the British.

It was determined to demand the cession of all the French factories and effects, and the entire exclusion of that nation from Bengal; the grant of a considerable territory around Calcutta, with a pecuniary compensation for losses sustained, amounting to 10,000,000 of rupees for the Company, 5,000,000 to the British inhabitants, and 2,700,000 to the natives and Armenians. For the army 2,500,000 were demanded, and a like sum for the navy. One of the members of the committee chancing to ask why they should not claim something for themselves, his proposal obtained a unanimous concurrence, and 1,200,000 rupees were fixed, to be distributed among each, corresponding to their respective ranks. The most boundless and extravagant ideas prevailed in general respecting the wealth of Indian princes; wild reports had represented that of the nabob as amounting to forty-five millions sterling; and it was supposed certainly not to fall short of four millions and a half; though, as Mr Orme observes, the consideration that Aliverdi Khan had been employed during his whole reign in repelling a series of formidable invasions, might have proved even this last estimate to be very unreasonable. When these demands, amounting to nearly three millions sterling, were laid before Meer Jaffier, his minister Roydoolub declared it utterly impossible for the Bengal treasury to defray them; but as the English refused to make any abatement, and conciliated the official by high expectations, he at last adopted the Indian plan of promising every thing, leaving the performance to be regulated by circumstances. It may be mentioned as a characteristic feature in this negotiation, that Omichund, a native who had been let into the secret, threatened to make a disclosure unless his silence were purchased at an immense price. To defeat this manœuvre, Clive caused two treaties to be drawn up, one real, which contained no stipulation whatever in favour of that person, the other prepared solely for the purpose of being shown to him, and comprising an agreement to pay him not less than two millions of rupees. The colonel having signed the latter, presented it to Admiral Watson, who honourably refused his signature. On being asked, however, whether he would allow another to write it for him, he gave a sort of half consent, saying, "he left them to do as they pleased." His handwriting was then counterfeited, and, by showing this treaty to Omichund, his silence was secured; but the discovery of the deceit afterwards drove him into a state of derangement, terminating in confirmed idiotism. Mr Mill brands this as an act of the most consummate baseness; while Sir John Malcolm contends, that in a case of glaring and avowed treachery, like that of this Hindoo, a similar act, employed solely to counterwork the other, became justifiable. His arguments certainly have considerable force; yet we cannot,

False ideas of native wealth.

Omichund outwitted.

Opinions entertained of Clive's proceedings.

CHAP. XI.

A.D. 1757.

on the whole, reconcile the transaction to our ideas of English honour.

Clive musters his troops.

Clive having mustered his troops at Chandernagore, began his march on the 13th June 1757, with 3100 men, of whom only 750 were British; and with this force undertook to effect the subversion of a mighty kingdom. As he approached the encampment of the nabob at Plassey, near Cossimbuzar, unpleasant notices were received as to the conduct of Meer Jaffier, who having held frequent conferences with his master, had apparently accommodated all differences, and bound himself by the most solemn oaths to make common cause with him. He privately, indeed, transmitted assurances that these were only feints to lull the prince's suspicions; but, from his evidently keeping up the same appearances to both parties, there remained doubts as to which he really intended to betray. For this reason, when the British commander arrived opposite the island of Cossimbuzar, at some distance above which lay encamped the native army of 35,000 foot, 15,000 horse, and a strong train of artillery, he paused. On the 21st he called a council of war, —a measure which, it has been observed, almost invariably issues in a determination not to give battle. He opened the debate by expressing his own conviction against attacking the enemy under present circumstances. The other speakers concurred, with the exception of Major Coote, who argued that the troops, now full of courage and confidence, would feel their spirits entirely damped by the proposed delay; that the enemy would soon obtain fresh reinforcements, more particularly a large detachment of French now in the interior; in short, that there was no alternative, but either to attack now, or, renouncing all their ambitious projects, march back and shut themselves up within the walls of Calcutta. The opposite opinion was carried by a majority, with whom Clive himself voted; but on dismissing the council, he took a solitary walk in an adjoining grove, and after an hour's meditation became convinced, that Coote's advice was the soundest, and determined to

Suspicious conduct of Meer Jaffier.

Council of war.

Change of opinion by Clive.

follow it. Accordingly, next day he crossed the river, and marched fifteen miles towards the enemy, who at dawn on the following morning were seen encamped at the distance of a mile.

Battle of Plassey.

The battle of Plassey, which virtually transferred to Britain the sceptre of India, was by no means fought witb a vigour corresponding to the great interests at stake. The enemy commenced the attack on the 23d of June at six in the morning, while the English, covered by a grove and a high bank, remained almost the whole day on the defensive, keeping up a straggling cannonade. At one time, indeed, several brisk movements were made by the adverse cavalry, which were repulsed by the steady fire of the field-pieces; but so languidly did the contest proceed, that Colonel Clive is reported to have fallen asleep in the midst of it, which Mr Orme accounts for by the great fatigue he had undergone. The nabob, however, as cowardly as cruel, remained in his tent, and was much discouraged to learn that his antagonists had not fled, and still more that Meer Murdeen, the best and most faithful of his generals, had fallen. The chief interest was felt respecting the course to be followed by Meer Jaffier, which remained for a long time mysterious; and his corps, even when it began to make a movement towards the left, not being recognised by our countrymen, was treated as hostile. Soon, however, it was seen decidedly to separate from the rest of the army, and Clive then determined to make an immediate and brisk assault upon their camp. It was attended with complete and instant success; for scarcely had the onset begun, when the enemy fled, abandoning their tents, baggage, and artillery. The pursuit was continued six miles; several officers of distinction were slain, and forty pieces of cannon taken. The loss on the British side was only twenty-two killed and fifty wounded. The nabob, seized with panic, gave up all for lost, mounted a camel and fled, escorted by 2000 of his chosen cavalry.

Desertion by Meer Jaffier to the English.

Total defeat of the nabob.

Interview with Meer Jaffier.

Next day an interview was appointed at Daudpore between the English commander and Meer Jaffier. The

CHAP. XI. A.D. 1757.

latter approached with evident symptoms of fear, dreading resentment on account of his cold and doubtful co-operation. On his entrance, the guard in sign of respect presented arms, when, interpreting this as a menacing attitude, he started back in alarm. Clive however advanced, and saluted him Nabob of Bengal, Bahar, and Orissa; after which entire cordiality prevailed during the conference, and measures were concerted for the pursuit of Surajah Dowlah. That prince had arrived at Daudpore about midnight after the battle; and several of his principal officers being already there, he assembled them in council. Rejecting the advice urged by some of them, that he should surrender to the English, he concurred with those who recommended that he should give donations to the troops, and place himself next day at their head. But when he returned to the seraglio, and learned the near approach of Meer Jaffier, his timid disposition gained the ascendency. He disguised himself in an humble garb, and, with his favourite eunuch and concubine, carrying a casket of his most precious jewels, placed himself in a barge and endeavoured to push up the river to Patna, where, from the fidelity of the governor, he expected to be in safety. He arrived at Rajemahl, where the boatmen, overcome by fatigue, insisted on resting for the night, and the ex-nabob sought concealment in a deserted garden. In the morning, however, a man of low rank, whose ears in a fit of rage he had formerly caused to be cut off, discovered him, and made the report to a brother of Jaffier, who gave notice to the soldiers engaged in the pursuit. They hastened to seize their prey, and conveyed him down the river to Muxadavad, treating him on the passage with every species of indignity. The unhappy prince was dragged like a felon into the palace which he had so lately occupied in all the pomp of eastern royalty. Jaffier showed himself somewhat affected at this spectacle, not indeed without reason, having owed every thing to Aliverdi Khan, grandfather to Surajah, of whom also he had no serious ground of complaint. He desired the captive prince to retire,

His reception by Clive.

Flight and capture of the nabob.

His reception by Jaffier.

and assembled his counsellors to deliberate on his fate. Some recommended clemency; others, among whom was his son Meeran, aged about seventeen, urged the cruel but safe expedient of putting him to instant death. The new nabob still hesitated, when the youth entreated him to go to bed and leave to him the care of the royal captive. He consented, not without an obvious presentiment of what would follow. Meeran lost no time in sending a band of assassins to the apartment of the prisoner, who met his end with weak and pusillanimous lamentations; and the view of his remains, placed on an elephant and carried through the streets, induced the servile crowd to yield implicit submission to his successor. Surajah Dowlah perhaps deserved his fate; yet the circumstances attending it, and the persons by whom it was inflicted, rendered it an act of the basest treachery.

His assassination by Meeran.

Meanwhile the English made all due haste to commence the important investigation into the contents of the Bengal treasury; and the result, as Meer Jaffier's minister had intimated, created the most bitter disappointment. To pay the stipulated amount of 22,000,000 rupees, there was found in the exchequer only 15,000,000, and it could not be entirely emptied. It was necessary, therefore, to be content with the immediate receipt of one-half, and to accept the promise of paying the rest in three annual instalments. Even of this half, our countrymen were obliged to take a third in jewels and other precious effects; yet there was paid down in cash £800,000,—the largest sum of prize-money, it is presumed, which they or any other European nation ever received in India. The chiefs also were graciously pleased to accept in return for their services presents of very large amount,—a mode of remuneration accordant, it is said, with Indian ideas, though one cannot view it as particularly honourable. Clive acknowledged to have received £160,000, while to each member of council there fell £24,000. As Watson did not come in regularly for a share, one was made for him by deducting a tenth from that of the others,—an arrangement with which several of the officers were extremely dissatisfied.

State of the Bengal treasury.

Large prize-money

Share of the spoils.

CHAP. XI.

A. D. 1757.

New difficulties of the Bengal government.

Soon after, the government of Bengal was involved in peculiar difficulties. The distracted state of the province excited the hopes of the native princes, who expected that it would fall an easy prey; and the eldest son of the Mogul, called the shazada, having obtained from his father the investiture as Subahdar of Bengal, Bahar, and Orissa, proceeded to establish his claim by arms. The force which he could command was exceedingly small; but he was supported by two distinguished officers, now established nearly as independent rulers. One was the Nabob of Oude, a fine province north of the Ganges, once the seat of a powerful empire. The other was the Subahdar of Allahabad, a fertile region along the same river, the capital of which, situated at the junction of the Ganges and the Jumna, is one of the largest and most venerated cities of the empire. Akbar made it a favourite residence, and erected at the angle of the currents the *Chalees Satoon*, a spacious fortress, which, having its gateways ornamented with domes and cupolas, exhibits one of the most striking specimens of Indian architecture. The British have since added new defences, and chosen it as their chief military depot for the upper provinces. The interests of his country, and the treaty with Meer Jaffier, alike impelled Clive to aid that ruler in repelling the invasion. This conduct is branded by Mr Mill as "undisguised rebellion;" but when we consider that the power of the Mogul over all distant provinces had for a long time been quite nominal, and that prince merely a tool in the hands of others, who regarded his authority almost as little as Jaffier did, we are brought to view the subject somewhat differently. The English, having united their forces at Moorshedabad to those of the nabob, marched upon Patna, which was with difficulty defended by Ramnarain, one of his adherents. A very serious contest would now have ensued, had not the native chiefs, instead of forwarding the views of their master, begun to quarrel among themselves. The Nabob of Oude seized Allahabad, and the subahdar, having proceeded to its defence, was inveigled into the

Native confederacy.

Opinions of Clive's proceedings.

Dissensions among the native chiefs

THE CHALEES SATOON AT ALLAHABAD.

Page 374.

power of his enemy. The shazada was left without support in any quarter, and, as Mr Mill observes, "the descendant of so many illustrious sovereigns, and the undoubted heir of a throne once among the loftiest on the globe, was so bereft of friends and resources, that he was induced to write a letter to Clive, requesting a sum of money for his subsistence, and offering in requital to withdraw from the province." It was granted, on the condition of his presently evacuating the district; and the British commander was thus enabled, with remarkable ease, to bring this important affair to a happy termination. Jaffier was so eager to testify his gratitude, that, notwithstanding his necessities, he bestowed upon him, in name of jaghire, the rent due by the Company for the territory round Calcutta. About this time the colonel sent a force against the Circars, which obtained at least their nominal submission; and having repulsed an attack made by the Dutch, he resigned the government in February 1760, and sailed for Europe.

Dependent position of the shazada.

Meantime the interior was by no means tranquil. The young prince, who, on his father being put to death by the Mahrattas, succeeded to the almost empty title of Great Mogul, renewed his pretensions upon Bengal, and was again seconded by the Nabob of Oude, on whom he had conferred the still imposing rank of vizier. Their combined forces had advanced upon Patna, and gained a considerable advantage over the garrison, before Colonel Caillaud, now commanding the English army as well as the native troops under Meeran, Jaffier's son, could arrive to their aid. He made the attack on the 22d February, 1760; and though the Indian auxiliaries were rendered nearly useless by a very injudicious position, the British and sepoys alone poured in so effective a fire as drove the enemy off the field, and obliged them to retire to Bahar. Meeran, however, who had received a slight wound, re-entered Patna, and resigned himself to ease and pleasure. The defeated army then conceived the bold design of marching across the country by the shortest route to Moorshedabad, and surprising the nabob in his

State of the interior

Partial success of the British.

CHAP. XI. A. D. 1760.

Bold design for surprising the nabob.

capital. It is believed, had this enterprise been as promptly executed as it was ably planned, that the object might have been accomplished; but the chiefs indulged in the usual dilatory habits of an oriental army, and Caillaud had time, by rapidly conveying troops down the river, to reinforce his ally, and deter the enemy from the meditated attack. Returning hastily by the same route, they reached Patna before the English, and, aided by M. Law with a French force, reduced that city to great extremity. Captain Knox, however, marching above two hundred miles under a burning sun in thirteen days, relieved it, and obliged the enemy to fall back.

State of affairs in Bengal.

Affairs in Bengal meantime were by no means in a satisfactory state. Jaffier proved an indolent, voluptuous, and tyrannical ruler. Instead of being able to pay up the instalments due to his allies, he could not find funds for his own extravagant expenses; and he endeavoured to fill his coffers by plundering the native chiefs, three of whom at one time rose in rebellion. The revenues of three districts indeed were assigned for the liquidation of the British debt, while the monopoly of saltpetre and other exorbitant commercial privileges were granted; but it soon became sufficiently evident that he had forgotten all his obligations to the English, and yielded only from fear or the impossibility of otherwise maintaining his power. On a full survey of these circumstances, the heads of the council formed the determination of supplanting Meer Jaffier, or at least of placing the real power in the hands of another. After much deliberation, it was resolved that his successor should be his own son-in-law, Meer Cossim, who alone appeared to possess the energy necessary to retrieve the sinking affairs of the country. Mr Vansittart repaired to Moorshedabad, and endeavoured to prevail upon the nabob to consent to an arrangement, by which he should retain the pomp and state of royalty, while the government would be administered by Cossim; but Jaffier, though he felt it impossible to resist, proudly refused the mere shadow of authority, and

Misgovernment of Meer Jaffier.

His dignified resignation.

preferred to pass the remainder of his days in Calcutta as a private individual. CHAP. XI A. D. 1760.

Meer Cossim applied himself with talent and vigour to the task of governing. By judicious arrangements, and by extracting money from the native chiefs, he succeeded in paying up the arrears due to our countrymen. But urgent circumstances soon called the allied powers to the frontier; for the emperor, still aided in some degree by the sovereign of Oude, contrived to make several harassing incursions into the nabob's territory. Major Carnac marched to its defence, and having soon brought the Mogul army to action, completely defeated it. The most remarkable event was the capture of M. Law, who, with a handful of French troops, had hitherto been the chief support of the native armies against the English. Deserted by his men, he bestrode one of the guns, and in that attitude awaited the approach of death. The Hindoos, strangers to any refined laws of war, were much surprised to see the British officers approach, courteously invite him to their camp, and treat him as an honoured and respected guest. The major, after the battle, sent overtures of accommodation, accompanied even with an offer to wait upon the emperor in his camp; and though these proposals were at first rejected, the prince, on mature reflection, not only received the victorious commander, but proceeded with him to Patna. He was there met by Meer Cossim, and a treaty was concluded, by which the latter was invested Subahdar of Bengal, Bahar, and Orissa; and in return for this he stipulated to pay the annual sum of twenty-four lacks of rupees, or three millions sterling. Some reason was even given to expect that our countrymen might aid in restoring the prince to the imperial power; but the embarrassed state of the finances, and other circumstances now to be related, prevented any steps from being taken in fulfilment of that object.

Meer Cossim

Capture of M. Law.

Treaty agreed to.

The first measures of Meer Cossim's government were prudent and vigorous; and, had he been left to the exercise of independent power, he might have become a

First measures of Meer Cossim's government.

CHAP. XI. A. D. 1760.

very good ruler. But he stood in a relation to his patrons which a high-spirited prince could scarcely continue to brook. After having twice deposed and set up a nabob, they not only felt themselves, but were viewed by others, as the real masters of Bengal; and their most subordinate officers conceived that they were entitled to the obedience of the highest native authorities. This bad feeling was fomented by a party in the council hostile to the governor, who not only soon became the majority, but, having been originally adverse to the elevation of Meer Cossim, delighted to thwart him in every possible manner. This body, mindful of the circumstances which attended Jaffier's elevation, made the modest demand of twenty lacks of rupees as personal presents. Cossim positively denied the promise and refused payment. His conduct was highly approved by the Company, while that of the council was strongly condemned,—a circumstance, it may be feared, which still farther imbittered their feelings against the nabob. Ellis was at the head of the ruling party; and being stationed with a detachment at Patna, obtained permission to act there as he pleased, and he behaved in the most domineering manner towards the prince. The complaints of this ruler assumed a serious shape, in consequence of the privileges with regard to trade which the English claimed in virtue of a former grant from the Mogul. They were thereby exempted from those heavy transit duties which, according to the impolitic system prevalent in India, were imposed on all goods passing up and down the river, and from city to city. This immunity, which gave to them an immense advantage over the natives, was farther abused by affording the sanction of their name to agents, by whom the regular merchants were entirely driven off the field. In consequence of the heavy complaints lodged by the nabob upon this subject, Mr Vansittart, at Monghir, concluded an agreement, according to which the same duties were to be paid by the Company's servants and by the country traders. This judicious arrangement, after the Indian prince had somewhat hastily

Effects of mutual jealousy.

Serious and well-founded complaints.

begun to act upon it, was annulled by the majority of the council, and affairs were again thrown into their former confusion. The nabob then determined to end the controversy by abolishing at once all those inland duties,—a measure salutary in itself, but of which the English unreasonably and loudly complained, because it left no distinction between them and his own subjects.

Mutual preparations for war.

As the tide of discontent swelled, both parties began to assume a warlike attitude. His highness busied himself in raising money, levying troops, and disciplining them in the European manner. Learning that some boats with military stores were proceeding up the Ganges to Patna, he ordered them to be detained; but soon after, feeling this to be a questionable step, he allowed them to proceed. No sooner, however, had Mr Ellis received news of the first detention, than he resolved, agreeably to conditional instructions from the council, to attack that city, which, being ill-provided for defence, was quickly carried.

Declaration of war against Cossim.

Cossim, on receiving intelligence of this violent measure, became exceedingly furious, and thenceforth breathed nothing but war. He was, however, soon gratified, by learning that the victors, having resigned themselves to security and plunder, had been surprised by the late governor, driven from their conquest, and, in attempting to escape up the river, had been all taken prisoners. The factory at Cossimbuzar, with its garrison, was also captured.

Renewed negotiations with Meer Jaffier.

The English now again raised to power Meer Jaffier, whom the blind desire of governing induced to forget all his wrongs. At the same time Major Adams, who commanded the troops, was ordered to open the campaign with the utmost possible vigour; and he found Meer Cossim better prepared for resistance than any Indian sovereign who had yet been encountered. The British had first to defeat a strong advanced guard in front of Moorshedabad, and afterwards to storm the lines constructed for the defence of the city; when continuing to press forward, they discovered the subahdar with his whole force drawn up in the plain of Geriah. The troops presented

CHAP. XI.

A.D. 1760.

Character of the subahdar's army.

the aspect of a European army; being brigaded, clothed, and accoutred in the English style, and supported by a fine train of artillery. Their number did not exceed 20,000 horse and 8000 foot; but to oppose this force Major Adams had only 3000 men. He led them on, however, to the attack, which the enemy withstood four hours with great intrepidity; at one period they had even surrounded and broken a part of his line, and captured two pieces of cannon. But at length, the steady and disciplined valour of the assailants carried every thing before it; and the native warriors fled, abandoning all their artillery and provisions. Their prince, notwithstanding, retired to an intrenched camp on the Oodwa, so strongly enclosed between the river, the mountains, and a swamp, that its reduction detained the army nearly a whole month. In the end it was surprised and carried; after which he never again attempted to face his adversaries in the open field. Adams immediately marched and laid siege to Monghir, which the subahdar had made his capital, and carefully fortified. After nine days of regular operations the place capitulated, which threw the Indian chief into a dreadful paroxysm of rage. He sent notice, that the moment the English force should advance upon Patna, he would avenge himself by putting to death the whole garrison who had been taken in that city. The commanding officer, much distressed by this menace, addressed a letter to the prisoners, entreating them to suggest some expedient by which their release might be effected. Ellis and Hay, however, with a truly Roman spirit, answered, that there was no hope of escape,—that they were resigned to their fate,—and entreated that the march of the army should not be suspended on their account for a single moment. Vansittart wrote to Meer Cossim, at once deprecating his intended cruelty and threatening the most signal vengeance; but as soon as the troops began to move, the tyrant fulfilled to the utmost his bloody purpose. The whole garrison of Patna, consisting of 50 gentlemen and 100 soldiers, were put to death, with the single exception of Mr Fullerton,

Success of the British.

Barbarous cruelty of Cossim.

who was spared on account of his medical skill. The nabob killed also the two Seits, the most opulent and distinguished native inhabitants of Bengal, solely for their known attachment to the English. By these barbarities he forfeited the interest which his spirited conduct and hard treatment would otherwise have excited.

CHAP. XI.

A.D. 1760.

Investment of Patna.

The nabob's only hope henceforth rested on Patna, which was soon afterwards invested. He reinforced the garrison with 10,000 men, and supported the defence by strong bodies of irregular cavalry. The resistance was vigorous; the garrison took one of the English batteries, and blew up their magazine; yet in eight days a breach was effected, and the place was taken by storm. Cossim then gave up all for lost, and fled into the country of Oude to implore the aid and protection of the subahdur, Sujah Dowlah. That prince had then a still more illustrious refugee, in the individual who by legitimate descent bore the mighty name of the Great Mogul. At this court the fugitive viceroy was well received, and Sujah, probably with a view to his own aggrandizement, undertook to support his cause; after which these three distinguished personages marched with their united force to attack the British army, which happened then to be very ill prepared to sustain so formidable an encounter. The troops, composed in a great measure of foreigners and sepoys, complained that, after such a series of brilliant victories, they were left not only without reward, but suffering severely from the climate and scarcity of provisions. Their discontents broke forth into open mutiny, and numbers even separated from the main body. Major Carnac, who in these circumstances assumed the command, did not feel himself in a condition to undertake offensive operations, but waited the attack in his camp near Patna. The soldiers, when engaged in battle, forgot their mutinous propensities, and behaved with the utmost steadiness. After a protracted conflict, they completely repulsed the enemy though from extreme fatigue they were unfit for any lengthened pursuit. Sujah

Flight of Cossim

Discontented state of the British forces.

CHAP. XI.

A.D 1764.

Dowlah was obliged to retreat into Oude, whither the English commander did not attempt to follow him.

Major Monro.

In May 1764 the command devolved upon Major Hector Monro, an enterprising officer, who determined to follow up the advantages gained by his predecessors. It appeared indispensable, however, to begin by completely checking the spirit of insubordination, and to employ for this purpose measures of imposing rigour. A battalion of sepoys having left the camp soon after he had joined, was pursued and brought back; when, selecting twenty-four of the ringleaders, he ordered them to be blown from the mouth of a cannon,—a fate which they met with much intrepidity. No disposition to mutiny being thenceforth manifested, Monro marched against Sujah, whom he found strongly intrenched at Buxar on the river Soane. The difficulty of attacking the enemy in this position was obviated by their advancing against the British at eight in the morning of the 23d October; when, after a combat of three hours, they were defeated. They made their retreat, however, without being pursued to any great distance, but losing an immense quantity of stores, and 130 pieces of artillery. The emperor had already made overtures to Major Carnac, which that officer did not think himself authorized to accept; these he now renewed, complaining that Dowlah treated him with indignity, and detained him as a mere state-prisoner. Major Monro gave a favourable answer, and only delayed the final acceptance of his proposals till they should receive the sanction of the presidency, which was readily granted. Even before it arrived, the Mogul had come over with the corps personally attached to him, and begun to march under the banner of his allies.

Treatment of the mutineers.

Overtures for peace.

New native alliance against the English.

The nabob, having retreated into the interior of his dominions, obtained the aid of a body of Mahrattas under Mulhar Rao, and of Ghazee-ud-Dien, who, as we have seen, were once the most powerful adherents of the Mogul throne. With these auxiliaries he hoped to make a stand against the victorious English. Sir Robert

Siege of Allahabad.

Fletcher, however, who held the temporary command, laid siege to Allahabad, which surrendered as soon as a breach had been effected. Carnac, now raised to the rank of general, succeeded him, and immediately advanced to attack the army of the vizier, which, with scarcely an effort, was completely dispersed; whereupon that prince was obliged to abandon all his dominions.

Splendid British campaign.

The British had now certainly made one of the most splendid campaigns that occur in the annals of any nation. They had gained five victories against much superior forces; they had reduced every strong place which attempted to oppose them; they had vanquished the Mogul emperor and all his principal feudatories; and, in short, had made themselves the virtual masters of the great central plain of India. Various opinions, however, prevailed as to the best mode of improving these important advantages.

Death of Meer Jaffier.

Meer Jaffier had died, partly it should seem, of vexation at not having been able to meet the enormous pecuniary demands of the English rulers. The council, after some hesitation, filled his place with his son, Nujeem-ul-Dowlah, a youth of twenty, whom they reduced, however, to a much more dependent situation than his predecessors. They took upon themselves the whole defence of the province, and consequently kept in their hands the entire military force; assuming, at the same time, an extensive control over the internal administration of affairs.

Anxiety of the directors at home.

Meantime the directors at home, amid the triumphs which had crowned their arms, were agitated by many anxieties. It was not from any impulse imparted by them that the career of conquest had been pursued. They do not appear indeed to have desired any farther possessions than were necessary for the security of their trade. Without absolutely censuring the council for their proceedings relative to Meer Jaffier and Cossim, they expressed some apprehension lest their character for good faith and moderation should be thereby injured. Three revolutions had occurred in the course of as many years,

CHAP. XI.

A.D. 1765.

by which their very existence in India had been exposed to hazard. In particular, they complained of the enormous and incessant expenses in which these transactions involved them, and which they had not been able to defray without reducing their dividend 25 per cent. They had also found extreme difficulty in answering the demand for men, which indeed would have been impossible, had not government supplied them with some regular troops; it was not even very easy to charter vessels for their conveyance. They soon discovered the reckless profusion and even gross corruption which prevailed among their Indian servants. A statesman of comprehensive views and vigorous character seemed wanting to place their affairs in the East on a stable and tranquil footing, as well as to introduce order and regularity into the various branches of so extended an administration. With this view, their attention was directed to the same person who had been the real founder of their dominions; and Lord Clive, about three years after his return, was proposed a second time for the supreme command of the British provinces in India. He refused to accept unless invested with the most ample powers, and placed entirely beyond the control of the council. This was strongly objected to, yet finally sanctioned by the small majority of thirteen to eleven.

Cost and precarious position of their Indian possessions.

Want of a vigorous and able governor.

Appointment of Lord Clive.

His arrival at Calcutta.

His lordship arrived at Calcutta early in the year 1765;—but we shall reserve till another occasion our notice of his internal regulations, and proceed at present to record those measures by which he achieved the farther extension of the Company's territory. Sujah Dowlah, though defeated in successive battles, and driven even beyond his frontier, still possessed energy and great resources. Having collected his scattered troops, and obtained a reinforcement from the Mahrattas, he formed an army with which he again ventured to face General Carnac. At Calpy however he was completely routed, and compelled to flee precipitately with great loss across the Jumna. Considering his cause as altogether desperate, he repaired to the camp of the English, and threw him-

Defeat of Sujah Dowlah.

CHAP. XI. A. D. 1765.

self entirely upon their mercy. He had been strongly urged, and high offers were even made to induce this prince to bring with him Meer Cossim; but with a sense of honour not usual in an eastern potentate, he determined not to betray a person who had sought and received his protection. He allowed him, and a German, Sumroo, his associate in the work of blood, to seek shelter in the countries bordering on the Indus. Thus Carnac had at once in his camp two princes holding the highest rank in India, and the direct representatives of an empire lately the most splendid and powerful in the world

Favourable reception of Sujah by Lord Clive.

Lord Clive, on receiving this intelligence, immediately repaired to the British encampment at Allahabad, where these two illustrious personages awaited his decision upon their fate. It had been determined, in consequence of the obstinate hostility displayed by Sujah, to deprive him of all his territories and bestow them on the emperor. But his lordship, on forming a personal acquaintance, conceived so favourable an opinion of him, and judged him likely to be so much more effective as an ally and formidable as an enemy than the young Mogul, that he resolved to restore him to his dominions, by whose inhabitants he was greatly beloved. To the emperor, the districts of Corah and Allahabad were assigned; and he agreed, that is, was compelled, to grant to the Company the dewannee or collection of the revenue, including in fact the entire sovereignty, of the fine provinces of Bengal, Bahar, and Orissa; in return for which he was to receive annually twenty-six lacks of rupees, which, after all, was greater than he had ever enjoyed. Soon after, Nujeem-ul-Dowlah, the nominal subahdar of these provinces, was obliged to retire on a pension of forty-two lacks. Clive then boasted, that the revenues of the ceded territory would amount to more than 250 lacks of rupees, which, after the deductions now stated and the liberal allowance of 60 for the expenses of government, would leave 122 of clear gain to the Company. These financial anticipations were very imper-

Determination to restore him.

Clive's financial anticipations.

CHAP. XI. A.D. 1765.

fectly realized; but it was difficult for England not to be dazzled with a succession of such splendid victories, by which her possessions, that ten years before had included only an almost defenceless fort at the mouth of the Ganges, now extended over all the finest portion of that vast region. The most valuable part of the great central plain of India, westward as far as the Jumna, was either in the immediate possession or under the entire control of the British nation.

CHAPTER XII.

War with Mysore

Formation of the Kingdom of Mysore—Influence of the Ministers Deoraj and Nunjeraj—Hyder—His Parentage—His early Destitution—Begins to distinguish himself—Mode in which he forms a Body of Adherents—Commands at Dindigul—His Power augmented—Violence of Nunjeraj, who is reduced to Distress—Hyder relieves and then supplants him—His own Danger—Extricates himself, and becomes complete Master of Mysore—Conquest of Bednore—Invasion by the Mahrattas—Conquest of Calicut—The English join a Confederacy against him—The Mahrattas make Peace—Nizam joins Hyder against the English—They invade the Carnatic—Threaten Madras—Battle of Trinomalee—Nizam quits the Alliance—Invasion of Mysore—Successes of Hyder—He overruns the Carnatic—Again threatens Madras—Conclusion of Peace—Another great Inroad of the Mahrattas—Hyder concludes a Treaty with them, and makes farther Conquests—His Resentment against the English—Weak Conduct of the Madras Government—Hyder invades and desolates the Carnatic—Fate of Colonel Baillie's Detachment—Sir Eyre Coote sent from Calcutta—He gains several Advantages—Loss of Colonel Brathwaite's Detachment—Negotiations—Operations on the Western Coast—Death of Hyder—Tippoo succeeds—Dissensions in the Madras Government—Death of Sir Eyre Coote—Peace between England and France—Bednore surrenders to General Mathews—Retaken by the Sultan—Siege o Mangalore—Peace with Tippoo.

In the general breaking up of the Mogul empire and its great viceroyalties, India was reduced almost to a state

CHAP. XII
A. D 1740.

CHAP. XII. — A.D. 1740.

of anarchy. Any bold adventurer, who could summon round him the warlike and predatory bands with which that region abounded, might aspire to rule over extensive districts, several of which were entitled to rank as kingdoms. Among such communities a conspicuous place was held by Mysore, the territory of which forms one of the most remarkable of those elevated table-lands that diversify the southern provinces. It stretches more than half-way from sea to sea, closely approaching the Malabar coast on the one side, and on the other reaching to the border of the Carnatic. A circuit of lofty hills, forming a barrier round the country, raise its general surface to the height of almost 3000 feet; a happy circumstance, which secures for it a climate unusually temperate and salubrious. The soil is generally well suited for producing the most valuable grains and fruits, and by a rude but careful cultivation is rendered extremely fertile. This kingdom, under the direction of a daring soldier, rose to such power as to threaten the very existence of the British dominion in the East.

Kingdom of Mysore.

Government of Mysore.

Mysore, down to a recent period, had not been entirely subjected to the Mohammedan sway; it was still ruled by native princes, who paid homage, and sometimes tribute, first to the kings of the Deccan, and after their fall to the Mogul. In the decline of the latter sovereignty both these were withheld, unless when the imperial lieutenant could assemble a force sufficiently strong to wrest payment from the local sovereign. This independence, however, was of little avail to the original rajahs, who, sinking, according to the custom of oriental princes, into voluptuous indolence, allowed the government to pass almost entirely into the hands of their ministers. When the war in the Carnatic first led the English into hostility with Mysore, two brothers, Deoraj and Nunjeraj, of whom the latter possessed the more vigorous character, had risen to the head of affairs. At this time, however, there was coming into notice a young adventurer, destined to effect a complete revolution in that country, and in all Southern India.

Its state at the period of the war in the Carnatic.

Colonel Wilks, from native authorities, has given an account of the origin of *Hyder* with a degree of minuteness which it is unnecessary for us to follow. His family appears to have sprung from the northern territory of the Punjaub; they were of low station, and so poor, as in some instances to subsist upon alms. Futtee Mohammed, the father, reared by a charitable hand, entered the army of a Mysorean chief, and having served with distinction was raised to the rank of a *Naik*, an officer of peons or foot-soldiers. A lady of some quality, whose husband had been robbed and murdered by banditti, being reduced to the utmost want, was prevailed upon to give her two daughters successively in marriage to this adventurer. By the youngest he had two sons, named Shabaz and Hyder; but, when they had attained only the respective ages of nine and seven, their father and the prince his master were killed in battle. The mother and her boys then fell into the power of a rapacious chief, who not only seized all the property he could find, but employed the most cruel torture to make them yield up their hidden possessions. The widow of Futtee Mohammed, having "lost every thing but her children and her honour," found refuge with her brother Ibrahim, by whose bounty the family were supported. Hyder, accordingly, had his fortune entirely to make; and for some time he gave but slender promise of reaching any high advancement. He did not even learn to read or write; and, on arriving at manhood, spent his whole time either in voluptuous riot or in the pleasures of the chase. Thus he reached the age of twenty-seven before he would submit to the restraints even of military service. His elder brother, meantime, had been more meritoriously employed in the army of Nunjeraj, where he distinguished himself, and was raised to a subordinate command; and he was at length induced to join him while employed in the siege of a fortress called Deonhully, which occupied nine months. The wild youth, having once embarked in this active career, soon displayed daring valour, presence of mind, and all the qualities which constitute an eminent warrior. He received the charge

CHAP. XII — A.D. 1749.

Hyder.

His origin.

Hyder Ali.

Tardy developement of his qualities.

His first display of warlike faculties.

CHAP. XII. A. D. 1759.

of a small corps, with a commission to increase its numbers by all the means in his power.

Expedition to Trichinopoly.

At this time Nunjeraj, having formed an alliance with the French, undertook the expedition to Trichinopoly, of which some account has been already given; and Hyder accompanied him, making diligent use of the opportunities which this campaign afforded, both to distinguish and advance himself. He soon assembled round him a numerous body of those freebooters with which India swarmed, who asked no pay, but trusted solely to the plunder that they might collect under the auspices of an active chieftain. Instead of his giving to them, they gave to him; being required to contribute one-half of all the booty which they might succeed in capturing. They were doubtless very much disposed to evade this partition; but their leader, though unable to write the numerals, could boast of an extraordinary expertness in the operations of mental arithmetic; and he was assisted by Kunde Row, a Braminical accountant of remarkable skill. They established a system which the operative maurauders found it vain to attempt eluding; and the practices of a common London thief may be considered just and honourable, compared with those by which Hyder rose to the rank of an Indian monarch. Not only the great and regular objects of pillage, such as convoys of grain, horses, or herds of cattle, but clothes, turbans, earrings, the most trifling ornaments taken from the persons of females, and even of children, were alike welcome. Nor did his friends enjoy any exemption, provided the theft could be executed with secrecy; and by these means, before he left Trichinopoly, he had collected 1500 horse, 5000 infantry, with elephants, camels, and all the other appendages of a chief of high rank. Having distinguished himself also by his military services, he continued in great favour, and was appointed Foujedar of Dindigul, an important place recently acquired in the country of the Polygars. Here he enlarged his forces and increased his wealth, not only by the plunder of the surrounding territories, but by the most scandalous impositions practised on his own

Hyder raises a band of freebooters.

Dishonourable source of Hyder's rise to power.

Appointed Foujedar of Dindigul.

sovereign, as well as on the commissioners sent to inquire into his conduct. He managed to bring his troops to what was called a *circular* muster, in which ten thousand men counted as 18,000; thereby obtaining pay for a fictitious number, and also at a rate much above his actual expenditure. Having an allowance for every wounded soldier, he imposed on the inspector by presenting many who were perfectly sound, but had their hands and feet tied with bandages dipt in turmeric. By these gross frauds he completely deluded Nunjeraj, who thought it wonderful that so great a force could be maintained, and the war successfully carried on at an expense so moderate.

CHAP. XII

A. D. 1761.

Shameless imposture.

Hyder had now collected so much strength both of arms and treasure, and had acquired so high a reputation, that he began to aim at the throne of Mysore. His views were greatly favoured by the violent dissensions which prevailed at court. The young rajah, whom Nunjeraj kept as a convenient tool, determined to make an effort to extricate himself from this thraldom, and had already secured the support of a large body of adherents: but having made a premature display of his designs, the palace which he had fortified was attacked and easily carried. The minister, after this victory, though he treated his sovereign with a semblance of respect, caused his supporters to be either thrown into chains, or, having their noses and ears cut off, to be thrust out into the street. Deoraj, indignant at this cruelty on the part of his brother, abandoned his interests, and went to reside in a different quarter of the country.

Ambitious projects.

Cruel policy.

Nunjeraj himself was soon exposed to an exigency to which a Hindoo prince is almost always liable. His troops began to clamour for a large amount of arrears, and, obtaining no satisfaction, proceeded to the expedient of seating themselves in *dherna* at his gate. According to this institution, which in India is held sacred, he could neither taste food nor drink while the claimants remained in that position; and the soldiers, occupying the entrance of the palace, took care that this rule should

Singular expedient of Nunjeraj's troops.

CHAP. XII.

A. D. 1761.

Politic interposition of Hyder.

be strictly observed. In this extremity Hyder gladly took occasion to interpose his services. He repaired to Seringapatam, and by seizing all public property within his reach, as well as judiciously collecting the sums due to government, obtained as much money as satisfied the immediate claims of the military. He had also effected an accommodation between the two brothers, which Deoraj, however, did not long survive; and thus by appearing as a disinterested friend to all parties, he became extremely popular. Having raised a large force of his own, and attached to his views the army of Nunjeraj by his exertions for their relief, he soon felt himself to be the real master. His influence was greatly increased by the occurrence of a formidable invasion on the part of the Mahrattas, when, being appointed to the chief command, he brought the contest to an issue, not triumphant indeed, but much more favourable than had been anticipated.

Matured scheme for the ruin of Nunjeraj.

He now determined to make his way to the supreme power on the ruin of that chief through whose kindness he had risen to his present elevation. Kunde Row, who had all along been his agent and partisan, opened through the medium of a dowager princess, a woman of talent, a negotiation with the rajah, who, with the view of being enabled to resume the real authority in his own kingdom, agreed to concur in the removal of Nunjeraj. Circumstances favoured their designs. A fresh arrear of pay having accumulated, the troops again established themselves in *dherna* before his gate; when Hyder, instead of studying as before to appease their discontent and relieve his patron's distress, sought only to foment the one and aggravate the other. Nay, with a semblance of grief and reluctance, he concurred with them in stooping to the position of *dherna*.

Accomplishment of Hyder's purpose.

Nunjeraj, thus pressed, at length agreed to retire with a liberal allowance of treasure and troops, and leave the field open to his rival; upon which the rajah, having assumed the government, intrusted the whole administration, civil and military, to Hyder and Kunde Row. It was not likely that the deposed minister should remain long satisfied with his altered condition. Retiring to the city of Mysore, only nine miles distant from the capital, he recruited his forces with the utmost diligence. A demand was hereupon made, that he should discharge his troops, remove to a greater distance, and be content with a fixed allowance for his private expenses. He indignantly wrote in answer to Hyder:—"I have made you what you are, and now you refuse me a place in which to hide my head. Do what you please; or what you can. I move not from Mysore." The other immediately proceeded to besiege the city, which, after an obstinate resistance, surrendered; and Nunjeraj was obliged to accept the hard conditions imposed by the victor.

Final humiliation of Nunjeraj.

Hyder seemed now at the height of power; yet he was soon after involved in the most serious peril he had ever encountered. The rajah and the dowager were not long in discovering, what indeed they could scarcely fail to foresee, that by this change of affairs they had merely substituted one sovereign minister for another, and were as destitute as ever of any real power. They gained over Kunde Row, who then watched in conjunction with them the opportunity of striking a blow against the man of whom he had been so long the devoted adherent; and it occurred sooner than might have been expected with one so conversant in all the intricacies of treason. Hyder, suspecting nothing, had dispersed his forces in different directions, and lay encamped with a handful of troops under the walls of Seringapatam. Suddenly, with amazement and consternation, he saw its batteries begin to play upon him; he called for Kunde Row, his resource in every difficulty, but that person was seen on the ramparts directing the operations of the artillery Perceiving the snare into which he had fallen, he summoned all his presence of mind in this desperate extremity. Having placed his men under the best shelter that could be obtained, he transmitted the most humble overtures and supplications to his former servant, now his successful rival; but could obtain no other terms than to be allowed to steal off in the night with a few

New perils of Hyder.

Desertion of Kunde Row.

Humiliation and flight of Hyder.

CHAP. XII. A.D. 1763.

soldiers, leaving behind him nearly all his treasures, the accumulated fruit of so much crime and extortion, and even his family, among whom was his son Tippoo, then nine years old. These last, however, were received into Seringapatam, and treated with kindness.

Renewed efforts of Hyder.

The expelled chief sought refuge first at Anicul and then at Bangalore, places under his immediate command, and of which the governors proved faithful even in this extremity. He soon collected his forces, called in his detachments, and endeavoured, by the reputation of his name, to attract fresh adventurers to his standard. Thus in a few months he took the field against Kunde Row; but that able politician, having still a superior army, brought on a general action, in which Hyder was defeated. His affairs being thus rendered nearly desperate, he had recourse for relief to a very singular quarter. With two hundred horse he hastened during the night to the residence of Nunjeraj, presented himself in a suppliant posture, confessed his guilt and ingratitude, and intreated his former patron to resume his place, and treat him again as a servant. All historians express astonishment that the fallen minister should have been won over by protestations so manifestly insincere; but we are to consider, that by closing with this proposal he obtained perhaps the only chance of regaining his former power and dignity.

His defeat.

His successful stratagems.

Upon this successful stratagem Hyder founded another still deeper. He affixed the seal of Nunjeraj to a number of letters, seeming to contain a treasonable correspondence, addressed to the principal officers in Kunde Row's army. They were sent by an emissary, who appeared to exercise the strictest vigilance lest they should fall into the hands of that chief, yet took effectual means that they should be intercepted. This leader, with all his experience and profound policy, was completely deceived; and seeing himself, as he imagined, betrayed by his own followers, he abruptly quitted the camp and hastened to Seringapatam. The army was thus thrown into a state of complete disorganization, when Hyder, attacking them unexpectedly, put them

CHAP. XII. A. D. 1763.

to a total rout, capturing guns, stores, baggage, and all the infantry, who were then incorporated with his own troops; the cavalry alone by an early flight effected their escape. Kunde Row discovered the deceit, and soon began to rally his men, when his antagonist had recourse to another artifice. He lay several days in apparent inaction, as if not intending to follow up his victory; then suddenly, by a rapid night-march, came on his opponents at unawares, and gained a signal advantage. After reducing many of the surrounding places, he advanced against the remaining force of 5000 or 6000 cavalry intrenched under the guns of Seringapatam. By entering into a feigned treaty, he lulled anew the suspicions of his adversaries, who suffered themselves to be again completely surprised, with nearly the entire loss of their horses and baggage. All Hyder's enemies were now at his mercy; still he wished that the terms which he meant to exact should appear as if offered and pressed upon him by the vanquished rajah. He sent a message, merely soliciting that the defeated general should be delivered up, and the large balance due to himself from the state be liquidated; adding that his highness might then either continue him in his service, or allow him to seek his fortune elsewhere. He privately transmitted, however, an intimation as to what he would be pleased to accept; and accordingly, under the impulse of necessity, the rajah was at length compelled to entreat the victor to relieve him from the toil of governing Mysore, and for that purpose to draw all its revenues, except three lacks for his own use and one for Nunjeraj; to which conditions the victor, with well-feigned reluctance, submitted. The sovereign and the ladies of the palace joined in earnest entreaty for mercy to Kunde Row; the other replied, that he would treat him like a paroquet, by which they understood a favourite or pet; but he literally fulfilled his insidious promise, by enclosing the unhappy man for life in an iron cage, and sending him a daily portion of rice and milk. It is needless to add, that the lack of rupees was all that Nunjeraj obtained

Total defeat of Kunde Row.

Politic dealings with the Rajah.

Barbarous revenge on Kunde Row.

CHAP. XII. A. D. 1765.

of the promises lavished upon him by the conqueror at the period of negotiation.

Extended conquests of Hyder

Hyder, having thus become the real sovereign of Mysore, applied himself to extend his sway in every direction. He made himself master of Sera, Chittledroog, and other districts properly included in that country; but whose rajahs and polygars, during the late troublous period, had rendered themselves in a great measure independent. His richest prize, however, was afforded by the conquest of Bednore, a territory situated on the loftiest crest of the Ghauts, 5000 feet above the level of the sea, where the profuse rains nourish magnificent forests and copious harvests. Its sequestered position had hitherto preserved it from invasion, and its rulers had applied themselves most diligently to that chief object of ambition in India, the accumulation of treasure. On the approach of the Mysorean army, the timid inhabitants of the capital, after setting fire to the palace, fled into the adjoining woods, leaving a splendid city eight miles in circumference entirely open to plunder. Wilkes estimates the booty, we suspect with much exaggeration, at twelve millions sterling; though Hyder himself, it is said, always owned that its capture was the principal instrument of his future greatness.

Conquest of Bednore.

Immense booty.

Successful rivalry of Madoo Rao.

But this successful career soon met with an interruption. Madoo Rao, one of the most renowned generals among the Mahrattas, entered Mysore with an immense host of cavalry. They covered the face of the country, and so completely cut off all communication, that even the vigilant Hyder was surprised by the appearance of their main body, when he imagined them to be still at a distance. He was defeated, and after several unsuccessful attempts, during a campaign of some length, to retrieve his affairs, was compelled to purchase peace by extensive cessions, and the payment of thirty-two lacks of rupees. That tumultuary horde then retired, and left him at liberty to pursue his farther acquisitions. He directed his arms against Calicut, still ruled by a personage entitled the zamorin, and esteemed the prin-

CHAP. XII

A. D. 1766.

Submission of Calicut.

cipal maritime city on that coast. Its troops opposed him with the same desultory but harassing warfare by which they had baffled the attack of Albuquerque. The rude soldier, however, forced his way through these obstacles and approached the capital, when the zamorin, despairing of being able to prolong the resistance, came out with his ministers and endeavoured to negotiate a treaty. He was favourably received, and on his offering ransom to the amount of £190,000 sterling, the invader agreed to abstain from farther aggression. But this did not prevent him from attacking and carrying Calicut by surprise; and, as the money was produced very slowly, he sought to hasten payment by placing the sovereign and his nobles under close restraint, and even by applying torture to the latter. The prince, dreading that he would be exposed to a similar indignity, shut and barricaded the doors of the house in which he was confined, set fire to it, and before the flames could be extinguished, he had perished. Several of his attendants are said to have thrown themselves into the burning mansion, and suffered the same fate. A conquest achieved by such deeds of violence soon excited a fierce rebellion, which was suppressed only by severe executions, and by the transportation of a great number of the people to a remote quarter of Mysore.

Cruelty of the conqueror.

Confederacy formed against Hyder.

These rapid successes, and the additional resources derived from them, alarmed the great powers of Southern India. Nizam Ali, subahdar of the Deccan, and Madoo Rao, the Mahratta commander, united in a confederacy to crush the assailant; and the English agreed to place an auxiliary force at the disposal of the former, with the vague commission "to settle the affairs of his government in every thing that is right and proper." It was distinctly understood, that they were to co-operate in the invasion of Mysore; and Colonel Smith proceeded to Hydrabad to arrange measures for that purpose. This seems to have been a very doubtful policy, when the Mahrattas alone were fully equal to contend with Hyder; so that the two parties might have been advan-

CHAP. XII.

A. D. 1767.

tageously left to weaken each other by mutual warfare; whereas the aggrandizement of the one by the downfal of the other tended directly to overthrow the balance of power.

Want of combination among the allies.

The three allied armies began to move early in 1767, but in a straggling and ill-combined manner. A month before the two others were ready, Rao had covered with clouds of cavalry the high plains of Mysore; and his force alone was more than Hyder dared to encounter in the field. This last endeavoured to pursue a desultory mode of defence, causing the grain to be buried, the wells to be poisoned, the forage to be consumed, and the cattle to be driven away. Every expedient proved unavailing to stop the progress of these rapid and skilful marauders: their horses fed on the roots of grass; by thrusting iron rods into the earth they discovered from the sound, the resistance, and even from the smell, the places where corn was deposited; while the cattle, to whatever spot they might be removed, were traced out and seized. The Mysorean leader, finding them already in the heart of his dominions, where he had no means of arresting their progress, determined at any price to detach them from the confederacy. Apajee Ram, a Bramin, was sent, and opened a negotiation in a style much differing from European diplomacy. He was received in full durbar by the Mahratta general, who declared his determination not to treat with an opponent who held his legitimate prince in such unworthy captivity; and a murmur of approbation ran through the assembly. The envoy humbly confessed the charge, but took leave to add, that his master, whenever an opposite example was set by his betters, would immediately follow it. Every one now recollected that Madoo Rao held the descendant of Sevajee in exactly the same thraldom as the rajah of Mysore was kept by Hyder; the approving sound was changed into suppressed laughter; the Mahratta chief hung down his head; and a serious negotiation was immediately commenced. He consented, on the payment of thirty-five lacks of rupees, to quit the country and

Expedients of Hyder.

His successful diplomacy.

withdraw entirely from the grand alliance. He had gained his end; and when Colonel Tod was sent to urge him to fulfil his engagements, the whole court laughed in that officer's face.

Proceedings of the English.

Colonel Smith, meantime, supported only by the poor, ill-paid, and undisciplined troops of the nizam, had entered Mysore. He soon began to suspect that this would prove a very futile expedition; and in fact it was about to assume a character much more disastrous than he anticipated. His Indian ally had taken umbrage on various grounds at the English presidency. They had procured from the Mogul, now a merely nominal potentate, the grant of the valuable territory of the Northern Circars. Mohammed Ali, their confederate, whom they had raised to be Nabob of the Carnatic, had meantime advanced pretensions to the dominions and rank of the nizam, which the latter suspected the British of secretly favouring. Hyder therefore employed Maphuz Khan, brother to that chief, who, actuated by the fraternal jealousies usually prevalent in India, had come over to the Mysorean interest, to open a secret correspondence with the subahdar. This last was easily persuaded, that he should most successfully realize his views of aggrandizement by entering into a league with Hyder against Mohammed and that foreign power, of which he was rendering himself the instrument; and accordingly these two parties, who were so lately vowing each other's destruction, united in an offensive treaty against our countrymen. Colonel Smith, both from his own observation and from notices given by his faithful ally, soon obtained a clear perception of this change in the position of affairs. It bore rather a serious aspect, considering the distance to which he had advanced into the enemy's territory; but on his remonstrances the nizam concurred in the propriety of his retreat, only desiring that a corps of three battalions should remain with him,—a request which was very unaccountably complied with. Yet the Indian prince, on this occasion, displayed honourable feelings very unusual with persons of the same class.

Faithlessness of their allies.

Dangerous position of the English.

CHAP. XII.

A.D. 1767.

Before commencing hostilities he allowed the whole detachment to depart, except five companies, and afterwards these also, without the least molestation.

Overwhelming alliance against the English.

Colonel Smith, seeing himself now threatened by the united attack of these two great powers, with an army of 43,000 horse and 28,000 foot, while he himself had only 6000 foot and 1000 horse, limited his efforts to fortifying the passes of the Ghauts by which they might be expected to descend into the Carnatic; but, from ignorance of the local positions, he left undefended those very openings which were the most favourable for their purpose. Through these they very easily penetrated, and, threatening the rear of his column, obliged him instantly to fall back.

The fruitless victory of Colonel Smith.

The confederates attacked him near Changama, but were completely repulsed; though, in consequence of their horsemen having plundered the slender store of rice belonging to his army, this victory was converted almost into a defeat, and he was obliged to retreat day and night till he reached Trinomalee. The war now assumed a most alarming aspect. The British officer indeed had his force raised to ten thousand, for the most part regular infantry, which gave him a superiority in the field; but his cavalry were few and inefficient, while the enemy covered all the country with the finest light-horse in the world, which cut off all his supplies, and left him no command over any spot beyond that on which he was actually encamped.

First appearance of Tippoo.

At the same time Tippoo, son to Hyder, afterwards so deadly an enemy to the English name, then only a boy of seventeen, made a rapid excursion with 5000 horse to the vicinity of Madras, and had nearly surprised several of the European residents in their country-houses. The Indian princes expected to see their adversary reduced to extremity by the want of provisions; but this was averted by the discovery of some hidden stores, which, according to national custom, had been buried in the earth. The nizam, imprudent and impatient, insisted that they should no longer wait the slow operation of famine, but bring on a general action. They made the attack at Trinomalee, confident in their superior numbers and vast masses of cavalry; but Smith, by an able movement round a mountain, and by the skill with which his artillery was served, completely baffled the efforts of this great though irregular host. The pursuit was marked by a singular occurrence. The Indian chief, according to his absurd practice, had ranged in the rear a long line of elephants, on which his favourite ladies, seated in pomp, surveyed the battle. When the field was seen to be lost, orders were sent that this cavalcade should retreat at full speed; but a female voice, issuing from a splendid vehicle borne by one of these animals, exclaimed, "This elephant has not been instructed so to turn, he follows the standard of the empire!" The consequence was, that before the flag passed several of these huge quadrupeds had fallen, and the balls were already flying among the fair fugitives.

Successful manœuvres of Colonel Smith.

Singular native cavalcade.

The nizam, on witnessing these disasters and the disappointment of all his hopes of aggrandizement at the expense of the English, began to waver in the alliance. Another check sustained near Amboor, and the invasion of his territory by a detachment from Bengal, confirmed him in the resolution to withdraw himself from Hyder. and agree to a separate treaty, which was concluded on the 23d February 1768. Under the pressure of such circumstances he obtained tolerable terms; but was obliged to confirm the grant of the Circars made by the Mogul. There were to be paid to him, however, five lacks annually; not in name of tribute for this district, but as a friendly subsidy. Even from this there was to be deducted, for the expenses of the war, 25 millions, at the rate of three every year. Nor was any opposition to be made to the appropriation by the British of a considerable extent of Hyder's dominions.

Wavering of the Nizam.

His defection from Hyder's alliance.

The presidency of Madras felt now the highest exultation, and sent immediate orders to Colonel Smith to enter Mysore, and strike a blow at the centre of Hyder's power. That officer represented the impossibility of subsisting his army in the elevated and barren territory

Rash proceedings of the English Presidency.

CHAP. XII.

A. D. 1768.

around Bangalore, which upon this plan must have been the first object of attack. He rather proposed, in the first instance, to occupy the fertile country extending along the foot of the Ghauts, and make it the basis of future movements. The council adopted the very questionable policy of combining these two plans; directing Smith to march upon Bangalore, while Colonel Wood with a separate detachment should conduct operations in the district adjoining the mountains. With this scheme they coupled the very injudicious measure of sending two commissioners to direct and assist, but more properly to obstruct the proceedings of the commander, while they engaged Mohammed Ali, the most unfit of all persons, to collect the revenue of the conquered territory. This plan was meantime favoured by the advance of some British troops from Bombay, who had reduced Mangalore, Onore, and other important places on the western coast. Colonel Wood was thus enabled to overrun all the territory against which his arms were directed, capturing every post of consequence, while Smith arrived in the vicinity of Bangalore, and made preparations to besiege that important key of the kingdom.

Injudicious measures of the Presidency.

Temporary discomfiture of Hyder

Thus in a few months Hyder had lost one-half of his dominions, and saw the centre of his power menaced. Having, however, in the first instance, directed his whole force against the western districts, he succeeded in completely retrieving affairs there, and driving the English out of all the places which they had occupied. He then returned to the eastward to make head against the Madras army, which, though it had subdued an extensive tract of country, held it by a very precarious tenure. His numerical force was indeed much diminished by the defection of the nizam; but the remaining troops, being entirely under his own guidance, proved nearly as effective.

Judicious views of Colonel Smith.

The presidency incessantly urged Smith to besiege Bangalore, as the only step by which the war could be brought to a crisis; but he replied that it was impossible to do so without previously defeating Hyder's army; and though that chief continually hovered round

CHAP. XII. — A. D. 1768.

and harassed the English, he skilfully shunned a general action. Sensible, however, of the great superiority of his opponents, he showed a willingness to submit to very considerable sacrifices. He even offered to relinquish the frontier district of Baramahl, and to pay ten lacks of rupees for the expenses of the war; but the leading persons at the presidency, still buoyed up with hopes of conquest, made such enormous demands, both of money and territory, as confirmed his resolution to persevere in arms.

Extravagant hopes of the Presidency.

The council, on pretence of consulting Smith, recalled him to Madras, leaving the command with Colonel Wood, who had gained reputation by his rapid subjection of the lower districts. This officer, however, proved himself wholly unable to contend with Hyder. Being surprised at Baugloor, he was obliged to retreat with confusion and loss, and must have suffered greatly but for the prompt arrival of Major Fitzgerald with a reinforcement. He was forthwith sent a prisoner to Madras, and the charge devolved on the officer just named.

Recall of Smith, and incompetency of Colonel Wood.

The British force had now been considerably weakened by remaining so long in the open field, insufficiently supplied with food, and exposed to the unfavourable influences of the climate. The Indian chief, who had gained continual accessions of strength, determined on a bold movement, not in front of the English, but by one of his circuitous marches among the hills. First his general, and then himself, aided by their thorough knowledge of the passes of the Ghauts, descended suddenly into the level country of Coimbetoor and Baramahl, with the conquest of which our countrymen had been so highly elated. He found the Company's troops scattered in numerous small bodies, and occupying indefensible positions, which fell one after another, almost without resistance, while several were betrayed by the native commandants; so that in six weeks he had re-annexed to his territory all these boasted acquisitions. On this occasion a detachment under Captain Nixon being surrounded by the whole force of the enemy, was, after a gallant resistance, almost entirely destroyed. Hyder

Complete success of Hyder

CHAP. XII.

A. D. 1768.

then marched upon Eroad, which was under the command of Captain Orton, whom he invited to come to his tent under promise of safety. This officer, with a rashness which Wilks can only account for by supposing that he had previously dined, went and placed himself in the power of his enemy. The rajah, it is said, always piqued himself upon not breaking faith without some plausible ground; but there happened to be in the English army a captain named Robinson, who was formerly a prisoner and released on his parole, which he had not scrupled to violate. On this pretext he not only detained Orton, but induced him, by force or threats, to sign an order to Robinson to surrender the important fortress of Eroad,—a mandate which this last thought it his duty to obey. The same pretext was used for breaking the capitulations with the troops in the garrison of Caveriporam, and sending them to Seringapatam, where they were immured in dungeons, and treated with the utmost severity.

Folly of Capt. Orton.

Successful overreaching of the English.

Triumphant progress of Hyder

Hyder, in his triumphant progress, now began to menace the rear of his adversaries; and the English, awakening from their dreams of conquest, saw the depôts and posts on which their military operations rested in danger of falling into the hands of the enemy. Their pride was so far lowered, that they despatched Captain Brooke to attempt a negotiation with the sovereign of Mysore. The latter received him extremely well, and seems to have explained his views with a candour not usual in the tortuous proceedings of oriental policy. He declared that it was, and had always been, his earnest wish to be on good terms with the British, an object defeated solely by themselves and their worthless ally, Mohammed Ali. He confessed that this desire was prompted by an enlarged view of his own interest, especially as being liable to a periodical visitation from the Mahrattas, whose usual time was now fast approaching. He frankly owned to Brooke, that as he was quite unable to resist both them and the English, he might find it advisable in such an extremity to form a union

Mission of Capt. Brooke.

Frank response of Hyder.

with them against his European enemies,—an arrangement in which he would find little difficulty. He desired him, therefore, to assure the council that no time must be lost in making him either friend or foe. The presidency accordingly sent Mr Andrews, an individual greatly in their confidence, to the Indian camp; but still their terms were too high. Hostilities were resumed, and Smith being restored to the command, checked the progress of the marauder, who, however, engaged at last in a most daring enterprise. With a body of 6000 chosen cavalry, and 200 picked infantry, he made a rapid sweep of 130 miles in less than four days, and appeared to the astonished council within five miles of Madras, who, then thoroughly awakened from their dreams of ambition, were seized with the deepest feelings of despondence. The British army could easily have returned in time to secure the fort; and they had only to fear the plunder of the country-seats, and perhaps of the native town, though this last danger is considered as doubtful; but they agreed at once to the demands which he made, that Colonel Smith should be ordered to suspend his march, and that M. Dupré, nominated as the future governor, should come out to settle the basis of a peace. In the present temper of the belligerents, the negotiation was neither long nor difficult; a treaty was concluded in April 1769, on the condition of placing the possessions of both parties, with scarcely an exception, on the same footing as before the war. Hyder solicited an alliance offensive and defensive; the English granted only the last, which, however, was found to involve them in all the responsibility that, by refusing the first, they had sought to escape.

Colonel Smith restored to the command. Daring enterprise of Hyder. Hasty concessions of the council.

Having thus terminated with advantage and glory this great contest with the British, he felt himself better prepared to encounter a still more formidable enemy. The Mahrattas, under Madoo Rao, entered his dominions with a force supposed to be at least double that of his army, and led by able commanders. He endeavoured a second time to check them by laying waste his territory;

Hyder's war with the Mahrattas.

CHAP. XII. — A. D. 1769.

but the invaders, as before, surmounted every obstacle, and, forming a regular plan of conquest, reduced successively all his strong places, and committed the most monstrous cruelties. At one fortress, which had made an obstinate resistance, the barbarian leader ordered the noses and ears of the garrison to be cut off; and sending for the governor, asked if he was not conscious of deserving to be thus mutilated and disgraced? The other replied:—"The mutilation will be mine, the disgrace yours;" an answer, the truth of which so forcibly struck the Mahratta, that he dismissed him uninjured.

Cruelty of the conqueror.

Madoo Rao being obliged, by severe indisposition, to yield the command to Trimbuck Mama, Hyder determined to make a stand, and intrenched his army in a very strong position covered by a range of rugged mountains. The new general did not attempt directly to force this camp, but pointed against it day after day such a harassing cannonade, that the Mysorean chief at length determined to fall back upon his capital. He began his march early in the night, hoping before morning to be beyond reach of the enemy; but the rash discharge of a gun by one of the officers betrayed the secret, and the numerous squadrons of Mahratta horse were soon in full pursuit. A most extraordinary scene then ensued. The critical condition of the army had not prevented Hyder from indulging in habits of evening inebriety, to which he had become addicted, and which now rendered him wholly unfit for directing the movement of the troops. Having in this state met his son Tippoo, he assailed him with the bitterest reproaches; then seizing a thick cane, applied it to his back with such vehemence, that the marks remained visible for upwards of a week. The prince, burning with indignation, went to the head of his division, dashed to the ground his turban, sword, and splendid robe, exclaiming:—"My father may fight his own battle, for I swear by Allah and his prophet that I draw no sword to-day." The army, thus left to itself, soon became a crowd of scattered fugitives, and their bold leader, while the Mahrattas were busied in plunder,

Temporary command of Trimbuck Mama.

Retreat of Hyder.

His habits of inebriety.

Total rout of his army

mounted a fleet horse, and almost alone reached Seringapatam. Tippoo, having assumed an humble garb, begged his way undiscovered through the midst of the enemy, and arrived the same night in the capital.

Inability of the Mahrattas to follow up their success.

Trimbuck Mama immediately marched upon that city, and seemed on the very point of putting a period at once to the career of the great usurper. The Mahrattas, however, possessed no skill adequate to the siege of so strong a fortress. They kept up during a month a daily cannonade, which produced no effect, while the resources of Hyder were constantly recruited. He now proceeded to operate with success on their rear, and, after a tedious and desultory warfare of a year and a half, prevailed on them to accept the terms which he offered; namely, the cession of a great part of his northern dominions, and the immediate payment of fifteen lacks of rupees, and fifteen more *hereafter*,—a term of which he fully understood the value.

Evasion of their treaty by the English.

The English during this war did not fulfil their engagement to aid the Mysorean ruler in the defence of his dominions. After it was concluded, the Company wrote to their principal officers, strongly condemning their interference in the wars of the Carnatic, the formation of any alliances which might involve them in hostilities, and particularly the supplying arms and ships to Hyder, or any other native power. To enforce these views, Sir John Lindsay was sent out as a sort of minister plenipotentiary, to act as a check upon the council. He, however, soon went much beyond his commission, for he formed a close intimacy with the nabob Mohammed Ali, whom he joined in urging that the presidency should embrace the cause of the invaders. They successfully resisted so gross a violation of their treaty; but these opposite impulses rendered the whole conduct of the British weak and vacillating. The Court, on being made acquainted with the doings of Sir John, superseded him, and appointed in his place Admiral Harland, commander of the fleet, to whom such instructions were given as were expected to prevent a similar collision. But he, neglecting

Division in their councils.

CHAP. XII. A.D. 1772.

their advice, proceeded in the very same manner, opening treaties of his own accord, and urging to warlike operations. The Court at length gave up this ill-judged attempt to check the council by a separate and co-ordinate power. The anxiety of the Company to follow a neutral and pacific system, and the total absence of any wish for a farther acquisition of territory, was, however, strongly impressed upon them.

Views of the East India Company.

Hyder's invasion of Malabar.

Hyder, as soon as he had extricated himself from this invasion, employed the most active exertions to regain his lost territory; turning his attention first to the Malabar coast, the communication with which could only be maintained through the intervening district of Coorg. He suddenly invaded that country, which he found almost wholly unprepared, and made a singular display of barbarian cruelty. He proclaimed a reward of five rupees for every head presented to him, and sat in state to receive and pay for these bloody trophies; but after seven hundred heads had been brought in, there appeared two with such peculiarly fine and handsome features, that he was moved with unwonted pity, and ordered the carnage to cease. Coorg was subdued; and the once powerful state of Calicut, distracted by internal commotions, scarcely made any resistance. His next aim was to recover the extensive territories wrested from him by the Mahrattas; and in this he was much favoured by the distractions in which that powerful confederacy was soon involved. Madoo Rao, their warlike chief, died in 1772, and after a short interval was succeeded by Ragonaut Rao, better known under the name of Ragoba, whose authority, however, was by no means fully acknowledged. The Mysorean prince, therefore, fearlessly entered and overran a large portion of the ceded country. Ragoba, indeed, hastened to its defence, but being recalled by a violent insurrection, which ended in the overthrow of his power, he concluded a treaty allowing Hyder to occupy all the provinces south of the Kistna. Another army sent afterwards under Hurry Punt, the leader of the party which ex-

Barbarian cruelty.

Death of Madoo Rao.

pelled Ragoba, penetrated into Mysore; but the rajah, having gained over a detachment of the Mahratta troops, baffled all his attempts, and obliged him to desist. CHAP. XII. A.D 1772

Immediately after the treaty with Ragoba, the indefatigable Hyder began operations against a number of independent chiefs, some of whom possessed fortresses on the borders, and others within the limits of his territory. Among the most remarkable of these was Gooty, the castle of Morari Rao, a fierce Mahratta freebooter, who had long acted a conspicuous part on the theatre of India. This stronghold consisted of numerous works, occupying the summit of several rocky hills. After the lower stations had been reduced, the upper made so obstinate a defence that a treaty was agreed on, granting peace on the payment of a large amount of treasure. A young man sent as a hostage, being well entertained in Hyder's camp, was induced to betray the secret cause of submission, namely, that there was only a supply of water for three days in the fort. He took no notice at the moment; but soon afterwards contriving to find a defect in the articles, he renewed the siege, and Morari Rao in the end was compelled to surrender at discretion. The most obstinate resistance was experienced from the Polygar of Chittledroog, who ruled over a warlike and fanatic tribe, called Beder. They had reared in the most elevated part of their citadel a shrine to Cali or Doorga, the Indian goddess of destruction, and they firmly believed that, so long as it was duly served, the place would never fall. Every Monday morning solemn devotions were performed to the goddess; then a loud blast with the bugle was blown, upon which the garrison rushed forth in a desperate sally, with the object chiefly of procuring human heads to be ranged in pyramidal rows before the dread temple of the destroying deity. Although, contrary to every military rule, they thus gave to the enemy full warning of the period of attack, it was made with such fury, and at such various points, that the goddess was scarcely ever defrauded of her bloody offerings; and when the place fell, two thou-

Siege of Gooty.

Breach of faith of Hyder.

The Beder.

CHAP. XII. — A. D. 1769.

sand heads were found piled in front of her portal. Hyder was obliged by Mahratta invasion to abandon the siege, which, however, he afterwards renewed; but it was only through treason that the governor was obliged to own that the mighty spell of Cali was broken, and to admit an enemy within the impregnable bulwarks of Chittledroog.

Hyder's dissatisfaction with the English.

Deep discontent against the English was now rankling in the mind of Hyder. He had, as formerly mentioned, earnestly courted their alliance; for his own purposes doubtless, but on the fair and honourable principle that the parties should mutually support each other against the overwhelming power of the Mahrattas. Their conduct, however, in the late war, when they saw his very existence so long endangered without making a single effort to relieve him, seems to have thoroughly disgusted him. He gave up every hope of profiting by their alliance, and even centred all his prospects of aggrandizement in their destruction. The Mahrattas again, whose councils had undergone a complete change, instead of threatening further invasion, sent proposals to Hyder for an alliance against the British; and a treaty preparatory to that object was accordingly concluded. By a singular fatality, the views of the government at Madras had been altered in the opposite direction, having become sensible of the advantages which might be derived from a union with the chief of Mysore. They even made overtures for a close alliance, with promises of co-operation in case of attack from any foreign enemy. His irritation, however, seems to have been only heightened, by having that aid which was denied at his utmost need thus pressed upon him at a moment when he could maintain his own ground. At this crisis the war, consequent upon the American contest, broke out between France and England, and was extended to India. The subjects of Louis, with their usual diplomatic activity, immediately opened a communication with Hyder, whom they found most favourably disposed towards them; and he engaged accordingly in that confederacy

League against the English.

French negociations with Hyder.

to which his house so long adhered, and with results so fatal to their own interests.

CHAP. XII. — A.D. 1769.

Comprehensive plans of the English.

As soon as hostilities commenced, the English government formed a comprehensive plan for the reduction of all the French possessions in India without any exception. Pondicherry soon fell; to which conquest no opposition was made by Hyder, who even pretended to congratulate them on their success. When, however, they announced their intention of reducing Mahé, on the Malabar coast, he decidedly objected; urging, that the territory around it having been conquered by him, was now included in his dominions. The British not considering this argument of sufficient weight to deter them from attacking a French fort, sent a body of troops who speedily reduced the place, although the ambitious warrior gave all the aid he could at the moment supply, in order to defend it. It has been supposed, that his resentment at this step was one cause of the rooted enmity which he ever after displayed against England; but the real motives of his conduct probably lay deeper, and were connected with a more extended view of his peculiar interests.

Reduction of Mahe.

Short-sightedness of the Madras Government.

The government at Madras, while they adopted a more judicious policy in regard to the chief of Mysore, unfortunately shut their eyes to the possibility of its failure, and could not be convinced that they were in any danger from his hostility. Yet he made no secret of his feelings, and seems even to have amused himself by trying how far he could proceed without rousing them from their security. They sent to him Swartz, the Danish missionary, a highly respectable and amiable man, whom he received with kindness; and on his return intrusted him with a letter, recounting a long list of wrongs sustained from the English, adding the ominous words—"I have not yet taken revenge: it is no matter." Mr Gray was afterwards despatched to him, but seemingly very ill provided for an Indian mission, having no presents except a saddle and a gun, both of bad workmanship, which were disdainfully refused.

Ominous message of Hyder.

CHAP. XII. A.D. 1780

Unsuccessful mission of Mr. Gray.

He was lodged, or rather imprisoned, in a miserable shed near the capital, and annoyed with the impertinence of one of the court-menials. He obtained only formal audiences; while Mohammed Osmân, a confidential officer, brought to him messages by no means of an encouraging tenor. Hyder asked, "Of what avail were treaties? Of the treaty of 1769 the English had broken every article; his affairs had been reduced to the brink of ruin by their refusal to aid him against the Mahrattas: after such an example, it was unnecessary to enumerate minor grievances." As it was likewise evident that an expedition on a great scale was preparing in Mysore, Mohammed Ali represented to the government in the strongest manner the impending danger, and the necessity of taking the most vigorous steps to prevent it. But his system of policy was no longer in favour with the council; every thing hostile to the rajah was disregarded as coming from one who had long misled them on this subject. The government were therefore completely unprepared for the tremendous blow with which they were about to be struck.

Obstinate blindness of the English.

Sudden attack of Hyder.

Early in June 1780, after prayers had been offered in the mosques, and the solemn ceremony called *jebbum* performed by the Hindoos, for the success of the proposed expedition, Hyder quitted Seringapatam, and found mustered on the frontier perhaps the finest army that had ever taken the field in Southern India. It consisted of 28,000 cavalry, 15,000 regular infantry, and 40,000 troops of the class called peons, many of whom, however, were veterans,—in all 83,000, besides 2000 rocketmen, 5000 pioneers, and about 400 Europeans. In the middle of July he marched through the pass of Changama, and began a career of devastation in the Carnatic, which he covered with the most dreadful suffering. A few days after, while the ruling party in the council would scarcely admit the existence of danger, black columns of smoke, mingled with flame, were seen approaching within a few miles of Madras. Colonel Wilks, however, controverts the idea generally received that the whole country was

Madras menaced.

reduced to ashes. This would have been contrary to Hyder's object in pursuing a plan of conquest; he merely drew round the capital a wide circle of desolation, calculating that a tedious blockade would be necessary to reduce so strong a city.

Insufficient means of resistance.

As soon as the first alarm of the government had subsided, they began to consider the means of resistance, which, with an empty treasury, disunited councils, and the impossibility of placing any confidence in Mohammed Ali, appeared extremely deficient. The first object was to secure different strong places now held by the troops of the nabob, who, it was not doubted, would surrender them to the enemy on the first attack. Several fell; but two were saved by the exertions of very young British officers. Lieutenant Flint, with a corps of 100 men, having proceeded to Wandewash, was refused admittance by the killedar or governor, who had already arranged the terms on which the fortress was to be given up. Flint, however, having with four of his men procured access, seized the commandant, and, aided by the well-disposed part of the garrison, made himself master of the stronghold.

Courageous proceedings of an English officer.

The next object was to unite into one army the different detachments spread over the country; the most numerous and best equipped being under Colonel Baillie, who had advanced far into the interior with a view to offensive operations. This corps amounted to 2800, the main body not exceeding 5200. Lord Macleod, who had recently arrived in India and held the actual command, strongly, and apparently with reason, recommended that the point of junction should be fixed in front of Madras, not in the heart of a province entirely occupied by the enemy. Sir Hector Monro, the commander-in-chief, however, undertook to unite the armies at Conjeveram, fifty miles distant from the capital; but Baillie, in order to reach that place, was obliged to take an inland route, in which he was exposed to the hazard of being attacked by the whole force of the invader. He was detained ten days by the swelling of the river Cortelaur,

Lord Macleod's plan for united operations.

CHAP. XII. A.D. 1780.

and, after effecting his passage, was assailed by a large detachment under Tippoo, which he repulsed, but not without sustaining some loss. Hyder then, under cover of a feigned movement against Sir Hector, interposed his whole army between the two English divisions. They were then only fourteen miles distant, within hearing of each other's cannon, and, could they have acted in concert, would have easily defeated the irregular host opposed to them. Baillie wrote, urging Sir Hector to join him; but this commander, conceiving that he would thereby lose Conjeveram with its small supply of provisions and stores, chose rather to send to his support Colonel Fletcher, at the head of 1000 soldiers,—a most hazardous movement across a country already covered by the enemy's detachments. Yet Fletcher, with great skill and activity, and by deceiving his own deceitful guides, succeeded, amid every danger, in joining the corps that he was ordered to assist, which he raised to upwards of 3700 men. Hyder burst into the most furious invectives against his officers for not having prevented this union; and the French, conceiving it preparatory to a combined attack by these two divisions, exhorted the chief, by a speedy retreat, to shun a general action. The rajah had formed a juster estimate of those with whom he was to contend. Colonel Baillie first attempted a night-march, by which a great extent of ground might have been gained, and where, in case of a battle, superior discipline would have given him the advantage; but meeting with some obstacles, he determined, contrary to Fletcher's advice, to delay till morning. Departing at dawn, he soon found himself opposed by the entire strength of the Mysore army. The English troops were at first harassed only by flying detachments; but when they came into a narrow and exposed part of the road, upwards of fifty pieces of cannon began to play upon them with the most terrible effect. The several narratives vary somewhat as to the farther issues of this dreadful day. According to official and other statements, our countrymen repulsed repeated

Divided position of the English forces.

Skilful manœuvre of Colonel Fletcher.

Rash delay of Colonel Baillie.

charges with prodigies of valour. Their bravery indeed is nowhere denied; but private accounts assert that Baillie, quite unaccustomed to a separate command, and fleeing in an agitated manner from post to post, took no fixed position, and did not avail himself of his real advantages. The grenadiers called out to be led on, and not exposed without the means of resistance to the destructive fire of the enemy. Suddenly two tumbrils exploded, spreading dismay, and threatening a failure of ammunition. The Mysorean cavalry, headed by a desperado named Scindia, made a furious onset, by which the whole sepoy force was broken, and mingled with the enemy in inextricable confusion. The handful of British troops still kept their ground; but as no hope could be entertained of their being able to withstand the whole army of Hyder, Baillie advanced into the front, waved his handkerchief, and concluded that he had obtained the promise of quarter. But when the enemy rushed in, either disregarding their pledge, or indignant at a straggling fire which was still kept up by the sepoys, they treated the troops with the utmost cruelty, stabbing those already wounded, and even women and children. The only humanity exercised was through the exertions of the French officers Lally and Pimorin. The greater part of the corps perished on the field; all the rest, including 200 Europeans, were taken prisoners.

Incapacity of Baillie for command.

His total defeat.

Such was this miserable catastrophe, on which Colonel Wilks hesitates not to pronounce, that if either of the commanders had followed the dictates of ordinary experience, both corps would have been saved; and if the two chiefs had acted well, the discomfiture would have been on the side of the enemy. Sir Hector approached within two miles of the fatal spot; but observing the firing cease, and no return made to his signals, he withdrew; and, on learning the fate of the detachment, fell back to Chingleput, where he was joined by a smaller party under Colonel Cosby, who had conducted his retreat with ability and success. The prisoners were conveyed to Seringapatam, where they were used with the greatest

Opinion of this catastrophe.

CHAP. XII.

A.D. 1780.

Cruel treatment of the prisoners.

inhumanity. All those not wounded were put in irons, and lodged in a kind of open shed, with sleeping-places at the corners, supplied simply with mats. Only sixpence a-day was allowed for food, and no medicine was provided under the severe maladies caused by this mode of life, and to which many fell victims.

Reduction of Arcot.

The first advantage that the ruler of Mysore drew from this victory was the reduction of Arcot, which, after a respectable defence, surrendered on the 3d November 1780. He held also in close siege Wandewash, Vellore, Chingleput, and other important bulwarks of the Carnatic.

Sir Eyre Coote appointed to the command.

The intelligence of this signal disaster being conveyed to the chief seat of government at Calcutta, Mr Hastings immediately took the most active steps to repair it. Sir Eyre Coote, a veteran officer enjoying the highest military reputation of any in India, was appointed to the chief command, and sent from Bengal with 560 European troops, while a corps of sepoys prepared to march along the coast as soon as the rainy season should terminate. At the same time the governor of Madras was suspended, and his place in course supplied by the senior member of council, who had always opposed his inactive policy; but the funds for the prosecution of the war were placed in the hands of the new commander-in-chief.

Small available force.

General Coote, on arriving at the presidency, and preparing to take the field, found at his disposal not more than 7000 men, of whom 1700 only were Europeans. Yet with this force, so far from fearing, he anxiously desired to encounter in the field the numerous, brave, and well-commanded troops of the enemy. What he dreaded was the harassing warfare carried on by Hyder in a country which he had already converted almost into a desert. The English army, when it left Madras, was like a ship departing on a long voyage, or a caravan preparing to cross the deserts of Arabia. Every thing by which life could be supported must be carried along with it; and the soldiers, continuing to depend on the capital alone for supply, were in danger of absolute famine. As they moved in a close body through this desolated region, never occupying more than the ground which they actually covered, clouds of the enemy's cavalry hovered round them; who, finding that they did not choose to waste their ammunition on individual objects, even rode up to the line, and held an occasional parley, uttering from time to time a fierce defiance or an invitation to single combat. Dallas, an officer of great personal prowess, successfully encountered several of the Indian chiefs, and his name was called out by the most daring of the champions. In this mode of fighting, however, the natives in general had the advantage.

Single combats.

Harassing as such a warfare was, and though the Mysorean chief continued to refuse battle, he was obliged to raise the siege of every place upon which the English directed their march. In this manner the important fortresses of Wandewash and Permacoil were relieved, and a stop was thereby put to the career of the enemy. The British commander, however, in following the rapid movements of this indefatigable adversary, found his troops so exhausted, and reduced to such destitution, as left no prospect of relief except in a general action, which he scarcely hoped to accomplish. But Hyder at length, encouraged by the appearance of a French fleet on the coast, and by a repulse sustained by our countrymen in attacking the pagoda of Chillumbrum, intrenched his army in a strong post near Cuddalore, where he at once maintained his communication with the sea, and cut off the supplies of his opponent. This station was extremely formidable; but Sir Eyre Coote skilfully leading his men through a passage formed by the enemy for a different purpose, drew them up in the face of several powerful batteries as well as of a vast body of cavalry, and finally carried all before him. The rajah, seated on a portable stool upon an eminence in the rear of the army, was struck with amazement at the success of the attack, and burst into the most furious passion; refusing for some time to move from the spot, till a trusty old servant almost by force drew the slippers on his legs, and

The career of the enemy arrested.

Skilful leadership of Coote.

CHAP. XII. A. D. 1780.

placed him on a swift horse, which bore him out of the reach of danger.

Great want of supplies by the English commander.

This victory enabled the English commander to relieve Wandewash a second time, which was again closely pressed by Tippoo; but it did not supply his urgent want of money, provisions, and equipments. After sundry marches and countermarches, Hyder once more took the field, and waited battle in a position chosen by himself, being no other than the fortunate spot, as he deemed it, near the village of Polilloor, where he had gained the triumph over the corps of Colonel Baillie. Here General Coote led his troops to an action which proved more bloody than decisive; for though he placed them in various positions, he found them every where severely annoyed by a cross-fire from the enemy. Mr Mill's authorities even assert, that his movements were paralyzed by a dispute with Sir Hector Monro, and that had the Mysorean captain made a vigorous charge he would have completely carried the day. But he at length yielded the ground on which the battle was fought, and the English reached it over the dead bodies of their yet unburied countrymen, who had fallen in the former action. The natives, according to some accounts, boasted of this encounter as a complete victory; but Colonel Wilks says they represented it merely as a drawn battle, which was not very far from the truth.

Disputed victory.

Rapid movements of General Coote.

Neither the fame nor strength of the British army was much improved by this engagement. The commander, however, having learned that the important fortress of Vellore was besieged and reduced to extremity, determined upon a vigorous attempt to relieve it; and having understood that Hyder was posted at Sholinghur, resolved upon another effort to bring him to action. On the morning of the 27th September, he pushed forward with such vigour as very nearly to surprise the Indians before their ranks could be fully formed. They rallied indeed, and made several brisk charges, but were finally obliged to betake themselves to flight with the loss of 5000 men, while only a hundred fell on the side of the assailants. General Coote was thus enabled, though not without difficulty, to march upon Vellore, the siege of which was abandoned on his approach.

Fall of the Dutch settlements.

The war continued with various fortune. Intelligence having been received of hostilities between the English and Dutch, Lord Macartney, now president at Madras, formed the design of reducing Negapatam, the capital of their settlements; and, upon finding Sir Eyre Coote opposed to the measure, he completed, without drawing any from the main army, a detachment of 4000 men, placed under the command of Sir Hector Monro. The enterprise was conducted with the greatest vigour, and five successive lines of redoubts were carried by the besiegers with such energy and intrepidity, that the garrison, though consisting of about 8000, capitulated in fourteen days. All the other Dutch settlements on the same coast fell along with it; and even their important station of Trincomalee, on the island of Ceylon, was carried by storm.

Temporary success of the English in Tanjore.

Meantime Colonel Brathwaite, at the head of 2000 men, was recovering for the English their ascendency in Tanjore; though his corps, when the whole country was occupied by the Mysorean cavalry, seems to have been too small to remain with safety detached from the main army. Hyder not only cut off from the British all sources of accurate information, but studied to deceive them: all the spies who pretended to give them intelligence were in his pay; and Brathwaite remained encamped on the banks of the Coleroon, without a suspicion that the flower of the enemy's forces were hemming him in on every side. Even when assured of the fact by one of the natives, he was so misled by opposite intimations as to think the assertion unworthy of credit, till he found himself enclosed by an army of more than ten times his number. All accounts agree that the resistance of this devoted little corps was truly gallant, and that, during the protracted contest, they repulsed repeated and desperate attacks. But at length an onset by the French troops broke the sepoys; the whole were thrown into confusion, and finally either killed or obliged

Spy system of Hyder.

Total defeat of Colonel Brathwaite.

CHAP. XII. A.D. 1781.

to surrender. The French officers displayed their usual humanity, and even Tippoo, who commanded, did not on this occasion treat the prisoners with his accustomed barbarity.

Fears of Hyder.

Notwithstanding this triumph Hyder felt deep anxiety as to his future prospects. He learned that, through the indefatigable exertions made by Mr Hastings from Bengal, the Mahratta government had withdrawn from his alliance, and had even bound themselves to guarantee the British territory as it stood at the period of their last treaty. At the same time a detachment, which he had sent to besiege Tellicherry on the Malabar coast, met with a very unexpected resistance; they were not only unable to make any impression, but, on a strong reinforcement being received from Bombay, were beaten and compelled to surrender. So much depressed was he by these unfavourable circumstances, that he had even formed the design of evacuating the Carnatic, when tidings arrived of a strong body of French troops having arrived on the coast; and accordingly, on the 10th March, they landed to the amount of 3000. These auxiliaries and their allies, regarding themselves now decidedly superior in the field, immediately laid siege to Cuddalore, which, having been imperfectly provided with the means of defence, surrendered almost without resistance. They then proceeded to attack the important position of Wandewash; but General Coote having presented himself, and offered battle for its relief, the combined army, with all its boasted strength, declined that issue and retreated towards Pondicherry. The British general followed, and defeated them with considerable loss near Arnee. At the same time he threw supplies into Vellore, and undertook an expedition against Cuddalore, which failed only through the want of naval co-operation. Thus, even after obtaining a powerful reinforcement from France, Hyder remained still unable to face the English army in the open field.

Arrival of French allies

Superiority of General Coote.

In the meanwhile, the latter were employing vigorous efforts to make an impression on the side of Malabar.

After the triumphant repulse of the enemy from Tellicherry, Major Abingdon reduced Calicut; and Colonel Humberstone, an able and intelligent officer, landed with additional strength from Bombay, which rendered the British completely masters of the field. The nayrs, hailing him as a deliverer, immediately joined their forces to his, and the combined troops proceeded into the interior. The enemy having imprudently waited their approach in a disadvantageous position, with a river in their rear, were totally defeated, and a great number drowned in the flight. Yet, on advancing into the country, the conqueror found himself so encumbered by the difficulties of the march, and harassed by parties acting in his rear, that he was obliged to commence his retreat. This movement it was soon necessary to make very rapid, as Tippoo and Lally had hastened with a large army to retrieve the Mysorean interests on this coast. The English fell back to Paniani, where Colonel Macleod, who arrived to take the command, intrenched himself so strongly, that Tippoo was repulsed with a severe loss. This prince, however, was preparing with a superior force to renew the attack, when he was recalled by an event of the most momentous character, to which he very naturally considered every other as secondary.

Successes of the English.

Counter operations of Tippoo.

Hyder's health had for some time been in a state of rapid decline, and symptoms now appeared of that severe imposthume called the rajhora, or royal boil, said to be peculiar to the country and even to the higher ranks. When decidedly formed, it baffles the skill of the native physicians, and invariably proves fatal. He expired on the 7th December 1782, at an age not precisely ascertained, but believed to have exceeded eighty. Of the numerous race of Indian adventurers he was perhaps the most remarkable. Destitute of the first elements of education, unable to write or read, he made his way to the throne of a mighty kingdom, which he governed with brilliant talent and profound political wisdom, though without the least tincture of honour, principle,

Death of Hyder.

CHAP. XII. — A. D. 1782.

or humanity. His death formed a crisis the most alarming for the power which he had reared. An Indian army is held together by no sentiment of patriotism, public duty, or professional character, but simply by fealty to their chief, and to him personally. When he disappears, his soldiers are converted from an organized body to a scattered crowd of individuals, who either disperse entirely or are formed into bands, each following the leader who attaches them to him by his exploits, or can bribe them by his wealth. This danger was great as it respected the family of Hyder, whose active mind was the soul of every movement in the court and army. His sagacity, however, enabled him to choose instruments who, in the hour of trial, proved faithful to himself and his house.

Designs of Hyder's ministers.

The affairs of his treasury were administered by the joint instrumentality of Poornea and Kishen Rao, two Bramins of opposite sects, speaking different languages, and serving as checks upon each other. These two persons, as soon as they saw Hyder's last hour approaching, formed in concert the extraordinary design of concealing it from the army and the world. The state of his health had for some time prevented him from receiving any but his most confidential servants; to them the two treasurers, with awful injunctions of secrecy, communicated the fact; while to all the others they gave regular reports of the progress of the malady, which they still represented as favourable. Only Mohammed Ameen, cousin-german to the monarch, with another chief, contrived the plan of raising to power his second son, a youth of defective intellect, as a pageant in whose name they themselves might govern. But their plot was discovered; and they were apprehended and sent off under a strong guard, as if by the personal orders of the sovereign. The instant that the rajah expired, his faithful ministers despatched notice to his eldest son, which reached him in four days. Tippoo instantly suspended his operations against the English, and accomplished a march with extreme rapidity across the peninsula. As

Discovery of their plot.

he approached, and learned that every thing was tranquil, he slackened his speed, and on the 2d January, 1783, made a private entry into the camp, where, after the usual distribution of pay and donatives, he was soon recognised as commander of the army and as sovereign of Mysore. He had now at his disposal troops estimated at 88,000 men, and a treasure amounting to three millions sterling, besides a great store of jewels and other precious effects.

Accession of Tippoo.

Notwithstanding this studied concealment, the government at Madras received early notice of the death of Hyder. They immediately transmitted the intelligence to their commander-in-chief, urging him to make a rapid movement to take advantage of that disorganization which usually follows such a crisis in an Indian government. But unfortunately the most violent insubordination and dissension reigned among the different members of the council themselves. The dictatorial power, independent of the civil government, intrusted to Sir Eyre Coote, was perhaps necessary under the circumstances of that period, and had been attended with signal advantage in the conduct of the war; but it formed a precedent to which future commanders were too much inclined to appeal. General Stuart, who had succeeded Sir Eyre, claimed equal authority; while Lord Macartney required the entire subordination of the military to the civil administration. The former, to vindicate his supposed right, seems to have acted in studious opposition to the instructions issued by the presidency. He first expressed doubts of the death of Hyder; then said that he would move at the proper time; next declared that his army was in no condition to march; and, in short, did not undertake any thing till thirteen days after Tippoo was fully established in the sovereignty.

Proceedings of the Madras government.

Dissensions in the council.

This state of dissension between the civil and military authorities, each seeking rather to inculpate the other than to promote public objects, could not but be highly injurious to the service. The supreme government seem to have laid the chief blame upon that of Madras. They

Injurious delays.

CHAP. XII. A. D. 1783.

say, "You favour us with a collected mass of complaint and invective against this government; against the Nabob of Arcot and his ministers; against the commander-in-chief of all the forces in India; against the commander-in-chief of his majesty's fleet; against your own provincial commander-in-chief; and again, against this government." It was observed, that the efforts of the presidency, when they had the entire management of the war and the most liberal supplies, had been altogether unavailing for the delivery of the Carnatic. Sir Eyre Coote was accordingly sent to resume the command, with nearly the same unlimited powers as before, to which Lord Macartney very decidedly objected. But the gallant general, overcome by the hardships of the voyage, suffered a renewal of some former disease, and expired on the 26th April 1783, two days after reaching Madras, and about four months after the decease of the great Indian prince whose career he had checked.

Death of Sir Eyre Coote.

Policy of the new sultan.

The war in the Carnatic had now assumed an aspect favourable beyond expectation. Tippoo, from causes which we shall presently notice, considering the west of India as having become the principal theatre of hostilities, withdrew his troops from the former, in order that he might act in the latter with more effect. In consequence of his departure it was determined to attack Cuddalore, where the French had now concentrated their main strength. As this place was receiving continual reinforcements, it was desirable to proceed speedily to its investment; but the Madras government lodged heavy complaints of the tardy progress made by General Stuart, who performed only a daily march of three miles, and thus required forty days, instead of the usual period of twelve, to reach his destination. He was censured also for immediately calling Colonel Fullerton from Tanjore, an expedient which was understood to be reserved for a case of urgent necessity. The fact, however, appears to have been, that with every reinforcement which could be obtained, the task was beyond his strength. Bussy, the French commander, had under him a numerous and

Complaints against General Stuart.

brave army, with a considerable body of native troops. In an attack, which took place on the 13th June, the English gained indeed the contested position, but with the loss of upwards of a thousand men. The garrison was afterwards repulsed with considerable loss in a midnight sally;* yet Suffrein, the French admiral, having made himself master of the sea, and landed no fewer than 2400 men, the enemy acquired a decided superiority, and prepared for an enterprise which threatened the most disastrous consequences to the British. Stuart, irritated and disgusted, and considering himself abandoned by the government at Madras, had recklessly determined to expose his followers to whatever hazard the course of things might present. At this critical moment, however, tidings arrived that peace was concluded between the two nations. Bussy soon after suspended offensive operations, and even sent orders to his countrymen to withdraw from the service of Tippoo, offering likewise his mediation between the two belligerent parties; but, though some advances were made, they were not productive of any immediate result.

Overwhelming French force.

Tidings of peace.

We shall now turn our attention to the proceedings on the western coast, which were rapidly rising in importance. After Tippoo had retired so hastily to make good his claim to the crown, the English became again decidedly superior; having obtained a very considerable reinforcement under General Mathews, who assumed the command. That officer received from the presidency of Bombay positive orders to commence operations, and push forward without delay, by the most direct road, against the important city of Bednore. Instructions thus peremptory, issued by a civil government placed at so great a distance, were manifestly inexpedient. Mathews wrote, remonstrating in the strongest manner against the danger of the course thus prescribed, and the disadvantage of depriving him of discretionary power;

Proceedings on the western coast.

* Bernadotte, the present King of Sweden, was taken prisoner in this action, and treated by General Wangenheim with a humanity which he afterwards cordially acknowledged.

CHAP. XII. A. D. 1783.

and yet, though there must be always some measure of discretion implied in such circumstances, he proceeded precipitately to carry his orders into effect. He landed his troops at the point of the coast nearest to Bednore, and began to scale the steepest part of the Ghauts, regardless of several detachments of the enemy which were hovering on his flank and rear. He experienced a degree of success which there was little room to anticipate; every thing gave way before him, and Bednore itself surrendered without a blow. He is supposed to have found in that city a treasure exceeding £800,000, and was accused of appropriating to himself a considerable portion of it; but, from the events which followed, this charge could never be fully investigated. It would appear from Colonel Wilks, that treason, unknown to the general, had afforded the means of his triumph. Sheik Ayâz, the governor, had been raised to a high command by Hyder, who was accustomed to reproach Tippoo with the superior qualities of this slave as contrasted with his own. Hence the prince conceived the most deadly hatred against the favourite, who, soon after the late monarch's decease, intercepted a letter from the new sultan ordering him to be put to death. Under this impulse, he hastened to the citadel, and effected its delivery to the English. He did not, however, join in active warfare against his cruel master, but contented himself on his approach with retiring to the coast.

Temporary success of General Mathews.

Source of unexpected triumph.

Counter movement of Tippoo.

Tippoo was greatly annoyed on learning the fall of this important place, and the near advance of the enemy towards his capital. Mathews was soon informed that successive corps were throwing themselves on his rear, and surrounding him with a force against which he would be unable to cope. He had by this time obtained permission from the Bombay government to act according to his own discretion; but he was now so elated by his easy victory, that he placed blind confidence in fortune, and even, according to certain statements, believed himself aided by some supernatural power. Thus, reposing in full security, he allowed his communi-

Rash security of the English general.

cations with the sea to be intercepted, while his troops were surrounded by Tippoo's whole force, aided by the science of Cossigny, a French engineer. The garrison were driven into the citadel, and, after a brave defence, were reduced to the necessity of capitulating, though on favourable terms, receiving a promise that they should be safely conducted to the coast. When the Indian prince obtained admission into Bednore, he proceeded to the treasury; but, to his rage and dismay, found it empty. Orders were then given to search the persons of the English officers, on which unhappily was found a large sum both in money and jewels, considered always in that country as public property. Upon this discovery he considered himself absolved from all that he had stipulated; the prisoners were thrown into irons, and committed to the most rigorous durance in the different fortresses of Mysore.

Compelled to capitulate.

The sultan immediately marching down to the low district, invested Mangalore, which, though a fortress of very secondary strength, was defended in the most gallant manner by Colonel Campbell. Having stood a siege of fifty-six days, it was reduced almost to a heap of ruins, when tidings arrived of the peace concluded between France and England. The French officers, Cossigny, Lally, and Boudenot, then withdrew with their troops from the army of Tippoo,—a measure viewed with great indignation by that prince, who considered them as united to him in a personal alliance during the war. Indeed it was not without difficulty that they escaped the effects of his resentment. Having made some vain attempts to prosecute the siege alone, he at length agreed to an armistice, which was to extend over the whole coast of Malabar. One condition was, that a certain supply of provisions, sufficient to keep up the present stock, should be allowed to enter Mangalore every month. But, although this stipulation was nominally observed, its spirit was completely violated, the food provided being so deficient in quantity, and of such very bad quality, that the health of the garrison rapidly sank; while General

Defence of Mangalore.

News of peace between France and England.

Armistice agreed to.

CHAP. XII. A.D. 1783.

M'Leod, with an exceedingly ill-timed scrupulosity, declined taking any effective means for introducing proper supplies. The consequence was, that Campbell, after sustaining a siege of nearly nine months, was obliged to surrender, and was so overpowered by the fatigues of the service, that he soon afterwards died.

Advantage gained in the south.

Meantime in the south, under the able direction of Mr Sullivan the civil resident, and through the military talents of Colonels Lang and Fullerton, very important advantages were gained. First Caroor and Dindigul, and afterwards Palgaut and Coimbetoor, were reduced. The last of these officers was even preparing to ascend the Ghauts and march upon Seringapatam, when he was ordered to stop, and directed to restore all his recent conquests. Tippoo had applied for two English commissioners to proceed to his camp and treat for peace; and, with a courtesy which Colonel Wilks considers blamable, the Madras government had acceded to his request. These envoys, however, on discovering his proceedings with regard to Mangalore, sent orders to Fullerton to suspend the process of restoration. But at length a treaty was concluded, founded on the basis that each party should retain his former possessions, and that the sultan should release such of his prisoners as had survived the cruelties with which they had been treated.

CHAPTER XIII.

Conquest of Mysore.

Power of Tippoo—His Persecution of the Christians, and of the People of Coorg—Confederacy against him—His Successes—Conclusion of Peace—Cruel Treatment of the Natives in Calicut—Attack on Travancore—Repulse—Final Success—Arrival and Views of Marquis Cornwallis—He resolves to make War upon Tippoo—Treaty with the Nizam—General Medows opens the Campaign—Reduction of Dindigul and Palgaut—Successful Manœuvres of Tippoo—He lays waste the Carnatic—Cornwallis assumes the Command—Advances upon Bangalore—Reduces that Fortress—Nizam's Contingent—Advance upon Seringapatam—Engagement, Distress and Retreat of the English—General Abercromby's Advance and Retreat—Junction with the Mahrattas—Reduction of several Hill-forts—Second March on Seringapatam—Defeat of Tippoo—Overtures from him—Terms accepted—The young Princes received as Hostages—Difficulties—Final Conclusion—General Results of the War—Pacific Policy of Sir John Shore—Arrival of Marquis Wellesley—His System—Tippoo's Negotiation with the French—British Influence established at the Court of the Nizam—Negotiations with the Sultan—Army advances against him—He attacks the Troops from Bombay—British march on Seringapatam—Action at Malavilly—Despondence of Tippoo—Siege commenced—Its Operations—Tippoo attempts to negotiate—His Alarm—Storming of Seringapatam—Death of the Sultan—His Character—Anecdotes—Disposal of the Kingdom of Mysore.

CHAP. XIII. A.D. 1783.

Power of Tippoo.

TIPPOO, after having concluded this treaty, became the most prominent personage in the political world of India. Equal perhaps to his father in talents and ambition, sometimes even displaying a superior military genius, he was yet, as already observed, a very different character.

CHAP. XIII.

A.D. 1784.

Character of Tippoo.

The former always proceeded in a direct course to realize his schemes of interest or ambition, from which no other object could turn him aside; but the latter was agitated by various passions and caprices, which disqualified him from pursuing a decided line of policy. Instead, too, of manifesting the indifference of Hyder on the subject of religion, he was inspired with a furious zeal in the cause of Islamism, which prompted to the most odious and tyrannical measures. The issue was, that he was buried under the ruins of the empire he inherited, and which his predecessor, by so many arts and crimes, had raised out of nothing.

Persecution of the Christians.

His first religious persecution was directed against the Christians on the coast of Canara, who had been converted by the Portuguese. In this case, indeed, he seems to have had a somewhat plausible pretext. In his narrative he asserts, probably not without truth, that the Europeans had originally employed violent means to compel the natives to adopt the new creed. Having therefore collected 60,000, by his own statement, but, according to Wilks, only 30,000, he forcibly inflicted on them the rite of circumcision; then hurried them to the capital, and distributed them in the different garrisons; a barbarous treatment, by which it is said that many perished. By a strange inconsistency, he represented it as the highest honour to be thus urged to the profession of the Moslem faith, yet made it the punishment of rebellion and contumacy. The rude mountainous territory of Coorg had always formed a reluctant appendage to the kingdom of Mysore. The people had taken advantage of the war with the English to reassert their independence; holding their conquerors in equal abhorrence on account of their religion, and their disregard for the rights of landed property. As they now presented the aspect of a formidable resistance, Tippoo was obliged to march against them with his whole force, when they retreated into the depth of their forests, which appeared almost inaccessible. Having, however, divided his whole army into detachments, which formed a complete circle

Cruel and inconsistent proceedings.

round the unhappy fugitives, and closing in upon them as huntsmen do in pursuit of game, he at length penetrated into their most secret haunts, and carried off 70,000 victims to undergo the abhorred penalties of circumcision and captivity. Elated by these cruel triumphs, the sultan hesitated not to assume the title of *padsha*, which our historians have not very accurately translated king. It was hitherto appropriated exclusively to the Great Mogul, whose supremacy had till that period been acknowledged in Mysore; but no sooner did the conqueror invest himself with this high distinction, than public prayers were offered for him instead of Shah Allum.

The sultan assumes the title of *padsha*.

Confederacy against the sultan.

The increasing influence and lofty pretensions of this potentate raised against him, in 1786, a confederacy the most powerful that had for a long time been formed in Southern India. The Mahrattas had repeatedly shaken to its foundation the throne of Hyder; and, though now much disunited, they were still the greatest among the native powers. They held possession of the person as well as the capital of the Mogul, and had no rivals for empire except in the Afghan sovereigns. With the nizam, who ranked second in strength and dignity, they formed an alliance, which had for its object the subversion of the new kingdom in the south, and the division between them of all its possessions. So confident were the Mahrattas of a triumphant issue, that they did not even call in their own contingents, and declined courting the aid of the English, lest they should be obliged to share with them the expected spoil. The confederates advanced towards the Toombuddra, the chief barrier between their dominions and those of Tippoo; they besieged and took the strong fortress of Badamee; and their cavalry spread themselves over the country. The sultan did not attempt directly to oppose this invading force; but by a circuitous movement came rapidly upon Adonic, the principal fortress of the nizam south of the river just named, and considered by this ruler so strong, that he had formed in it a sort of royal esta-

Confidence of the Mahrattas.

Investment of the fortress of Adonic.

CHAP. XIII
A. D. 1786.

blishment, which included the harems of his brother and nephew. The son of Hyder pushed the siege with his characteristic impetuosity; but having prematurely attempted to storm a breach, found it so bravely defended by its commander, that he sustained a complete repulse. The confederate armies were thus enabled to come to its relief, and obliged him to retire. But it was now the season of the year at which the Toombuddra undergoes its periodical inundation, when it became necessary for the allies to have the whole of their armies, their materials, and supplies, either on the one side or on the other of that river. To transport so many men and so much baggage to the southern bank, in the face of an active enemy, appeared too hazardous; they therefore recrossed to the northern side, leaving Tippoo's dominions secure during the period of the monsoon. They were even reduced to the necessity of abandoning Adonie, after hastily withdrawing its distinguished inmates; and the victor on entering found numerous apartments still fitted up with all the splendour of a royal palace.

Impetuous attack and repulse of Tippoo.

Abandonment of Adonie.

The sultan had now just ground to boast of his success; yet he aimed at extending it still farther. He caused a great quantity of timber to be felled in the forests of Bednore, and floated down the swollen stream, where it was converted into rafts and basket-boats for conveying his forces across. All his officers dissuaded him from the daring scheme of carrying beyond this river offensive operations against such powerful armies. He rejected every argument, and in the course of a week had actually transported the whole of his troops to the other side. The confederates, who could not be made to believe in any such attempt, had neglected all precautions against it; and their indecisive movements soon showed how completely they were taken by surprise. After repeated marches and countermarches, Tippoo, with his whole force in four divisions, made a midnight attack upon their camp. Through a want of co-operation between these detachments, the undertaking did not completely succeed; yet the enemy were thereby compelled

Daring scheme of Tippoo.

Partial success.

to quit their position, and when they afterwards attempted to regain it, were repulsed with considerable loss The general issue of the day was such as induced them to retreat, abandoning to the conqueror the important city and district of Savanoor. Soon after, overtures were made for a treaty, which was concluded on the condition that the sultan should acknowledge the tribute stipulated by Hyder; amounting still, after some liberal deductions, to forty-five lacks of rupees, thirty of which were actually paid. He restored also Adonie and the other towns taken during the war, and was in return recognised as sovereign of nearly all India south of the river Toombuddra.

Mutual treaty concluded.

By this successful contest against such a powerful confederacy, Tippoo had earned perhaps the greatest military name in Hindostan; having displayed even prudence and moderation in the terms on which he concluded peace. He now considered himself the undisputed ruler of the south, and at liberty to propagate the Mohammedan faith by violence of every description. His first movement was to descend the Ghauts, into the territory of Calicut or Malabar Proper, which, by a hard-won conquest, Hyder had annexed to the dominion of Mysore. Here he found a race inspired with such deadly enmity to his favourite creed, that if a Mussulman touched the outer wall of a house, they thought it necessary to reduce the whole to ashes. Their religious profession, indeed, derived little honour from their moral conduct, since custom among the nayrs, or natives of high rank, sanctioned a mode of living so extremely dissolute, that Tippoo did not exaggerate when he told them, that "they were all born in adultery, and were more shameless in their connexions than the beasts of the field." But notwithstanding these habits, they possessed the utmost bravery, and were prepared to make the most determined resistance to the resolution entertained by the sultan of compelling them to undergo circumcision and eat beef. Even when vanquished they submitted to both conditions with extreme reluctance,

Strong position acquired by Tippoo.

Descent on Mysore.

CHAP. XIII.

A.D. 1788.

and many sought refuge in the heart of forests, or in the surrounding mountains, till at length the whole were either circumcised or driven from their fields and homes. The victor then commenced a war against the religious edifices. He publicly boasted that he had rased to the ground eight thousand temples, with their roofs of gold, silver, and copper, after digging up the treasures buried at the feet of the idols; but there is reason to believe, that in this instance he greatly exaggerated his own enormities. At length he became so elated with these exploits, that he appears to have considered himself as really endued with supernatural powers, and little if at all inferior to Mohammed himself. Being strongly advised by his counsellors not to attempt passing the Ghauts during the height of the rainy season, he replied, that "he would order the clouds to cease discharging their waters until he should have passed." But he had soon to encounter a mortal foe, against whom neither his earthly nor his celestial powers were found to avail.

Religious war.

Extravagant elation of the conqueror.

Kingdom of Travancore.

The little kingdom of Travancore, forming the western part of the most southerly extremity of India, amid the revolutions which shook the greater states in its vicinity, had hitherto succeeded in maintaining independence and neutrality. It was protected not only by a lofty chain of mountains, extending as far as Cape Comorin, but by the more imperfect defence of a wall and ditch covering its whole frontier. Tippoo, however, had fixed his eyes with intense eagerness on the conquest of a territory which lay as it were enclosed within his recent acquisitions, and would complete their circuit. He fabricated several grounds of dissatisfaction. The territory of Cochin, which had now been reduced under complete vassalage to Mysore, happened so to intersect that of Travancore, that the wall formed for the defence of the one surrounded some portions of the other; and Tippoo could complain that his passage to a certain part of his dominions was obstructed by this barrier. The Rajah of Travancore again, with the view of securing his frontier,

Grounds of rupture.

had purchased from the Dutch the forts of Cranganor and Ayacotta, which the latter had long ago conquered from the Portuguese. This measure was deeply resented by Tippoo, who remarked that these forts stood within his territories, and alleged, though seemingly without reason, that the Dutch had owned his superiority, and paid a rent for the land. Lastly, the refugee nayrs, fleeing from his persecution, had found a friendly reception in Travancore. On these, or any other grounds, the sultan would not have been slow to execute his purpose, had it not been checked by a defensive alliance formed during the last war between the rajah and the English. It was therefore necessary to afford explanations to the government at Madras, who appear to have felt the strongest disposition to preserve pacific relations with Mysore. They professed themselves ready to listen to all reasonable grounds of complaint, and proposed sending two commissioners who might examine and adjust the several matters in dispute. This did not harmonize with the design of Tippoo, who hastened with his whole force to attack the weak barrier of the Travancore lines. The extent of such a fortification necessarily rendered it inefficient; and accordingly, on the 29th December 1789, while a numerous body, comprising apparently the whole army, by a feigned attack on the principal gate, occupied the attention of the inhabitants, the sultan himself with upwards of 14,000 men, the flower of his troops, had effected his entrance at an unguarded point on the right flank. He then pushed along the interior of the rampart to reach the nearest gate and open it to his soldiers. For some time his progress was almost unresisted; the inhabitants retreated from one tower to another; though, as reinforcements arrived, they began to make a more vigorous stand. They maintained their defence particularly in a large square building that served the joint purpose of a magazine and barrack; and here Tippoo, seeing his first division considerably diminished by successive contests, ordered it to be strengthened by a fresh corps. This operation being ill understood, was im-

Defensive alliance with the English.

Attack on the Travancore lines.

Fresh troops ordered to advance.

CHAP. XIII.
A. D. 1790.

perfectly executed; and, as the troops were advancing in some disorder, a party of twenty Travancoreans, from under a close cover, opened a brisk fire on their flank. The commanding-officer fell, upon which the whole body was thrown into irretrievable confusion. The mass of fugitives drove before them a detachment which was advancing to their support, and who again impelled those behind. Many of the men thrown down were trampled to death; and the ditch was filled with heaps of bodies. The sultan himself was borne along by the torrent, and some servants with difficulty conveyed him over the ditch, after he had twice fallen, and suffered such contusions as occasioned a lameness from which he never entirely recovered. His palanquin, the bearers of which had been killed in the crowd, was left behind; and his seals, rings, and other ornaments, fell into the hands of the enemy. He hastened forward, partly on foot and partly in a small carriage, and arrived at his camp in the most miserable plight, after losing 2000 of his men. So precarious is the fortune with which war, and especially barbarous war, is often attended!

Their disorder and defeat.

Flight of Tippoo.

Rage of the sultan at his repulse.

It may be easier to conceive than describe the rage and humiliation of Tippoo at seeing his fine army thus completely repulsed by a despised foe; and he made a vow that he would not leave the encampment till he had retrieved and avenged the disaster. All his detachments were called in, his heavy cannon was brought down from Seringapatam and Bangalore; and though more than three months were employed in these preparations, he succeeded completely in lulling the suspicions of the British, and in persuading them that he was still desirous of maintaining amicable relations. At length, his arrangements being completed, about the beginning of April 1790, he opened regular batteries against this contemptible wall, and soon made a breach nearly three quarters of a mile in extent. The troops of Travancore, thus exposed in the open field, fled with little resistance, and he soon saw the whole country lying defenceless before him. Immediately after he laid siege to

Deception of the British.

CHAP. XIII. A. D. 1790

Cranganor, near which, on the neighbouring island of Vipeen, the English had a small force stationed to assist the rajah. These were reinforced by three battalions under Colonel Hartley, who, on finding that he could not undertake offensive operations, withdrew the native garrison from the place, and took up a defensive position, in which the enemy did not attempt to molest him. The Mysorean commander now overran a great part of the conquered territory, committing his usual devastations, and carrying great numbers of the inhabitants into captivity. Many, however, retired to their southern fastnesses, where they could with difficulty be pursued; and the season becoming unfavourable, Tippoo, who was also alarmed by the movements of our countrymen, returned to Seringapatam, after having levelled to the ground the wall which had proved so unexpectedly formidable.

Siege of Cranganor

Reformed system of Indian policy

The Marquis Cornwallis had arrived in 1786 as governor-general, with a view to effect a complete reform in the system of Indian policy; and to avoid by every possible means war with the native powers was one of his leading instructions. He began, accordingly, by proclaiming, in a manner that has been censured as too full and undisguised, the resolution to engage in no hostilities not strictly defensive. Yet his views very early underwent a change; and he then considered it necessary, or at least highly expedient, to enter upon an extended warfare with the view of humbling completely the power of Mysore. It seems difficult to discover any good ground for altering his determination so entirely. Tippoo had no doubt shown himself very formidable; yet there was no reason to apprehend, while the whole of Central India was united by the alliance between the nizam and the Mahrattas, that the balance of power would be actually endangered; on the contrary, it was likely to be in greater peril from the downfal of one of these parties and the immoderate aggrandizement of the others. The new governor-general, in adopting this policy, was greatly influenced, we suspect, by the restless

Change of the Marquis Cornwallis' views.

CHAP. XIII.

A. D. 1790.

and violent disposition of the sultan, and by an abhorrence of the cruel persecutions which he continued to inflict upon the inhabitants of the Malabar coast.

The cession of Guntoor demanded.

The views of the marquis were soon developed by a treaty formed with the nizam. He had been instructed to take the earliest opportunity of demanding from this prince the cession of Guntoor, one of the Northern Circars, considered necessary for completing the circuit of that important territory. This claim was founded on the agreement of 1768, originally concluded with a view to offensive war against Hyder, and to a partition of his dominions. The pretension was somewhat exorbitant, considering that the treaty had been repeatedly broken; that war had since been waged between the two parties; and that peace was twice contracted with Mysore without any regard to its stipulations. A military force, however, was despatched to support the claim, which the nizam showed a very remarkable and unexpected facility in granting. Hatred and fear of Tippoo had at this time overcome all other considerations, and he readily agreed to execute the conditions of the treaty relative to Guntoor, provided all the others, including extensive cessions promised to him from the expected spoil of his enemy, were also inserted. The governor-general could not grant this to the full extent, but he acceded to the proposal in case future circumstances should admit of its fulfilment. At the same time, agreeably to treaty, a subsidiary force was to be sent to the nizam, and securities were introduced that it should not be employed against certain other powers. No such saving clause being added in reference to the sultan, the negotiation with respect to him bore altogether a hostile character.

Unexpected and prompt compliance.

News of Tippoo's proceedings.

While actuated by these dispositions, Lord Cornwallis was probably gratified upon hearing that Tippoo, by his attack on the Travancore wall, had afforded a regular ground on which to declare war. He made a most indignant reply to the presidency at Madras, who, expressing their opinion that this prince still desired peace, were themselves entering into treaty, and making no preparation for hostilities. In fact, the Travancore affair, though it called for attention, does not seem to have pressed so closely on any British interest that an attempt might not have been made to adjust it by pacific arrangements. The marquis, however, announced, that it ought to have been considered, and must still be viewed, as at once placing the two powers in a state of enmity. He had determined to repair to Madras and take the command in person, but relinquished this intention on learning the arrival of General Medows, in whose vigour and capacity he placed the utmost confidence. At the same time he hastened to conclude an alliance with the nizam and the Mahratta government, who each engaged to employ their whole force against the sultan; in return for which, upon the success of the war, all their claims upon the territory of Mysore were to be granted in their fullest extent. The former pressed earnestly for a guarantee that, while his troops were absent on the projected expedition, his country should not be pillaged by his warlike allies; but, though it was impossible to deny the reality of the danger, it would have been exceedingly ungracious, in a public document, to have supposed that great power capable of such a dereliction of duty and decency. The governor-general, however, gave private assurances of protection, with which he prevailed upon the Indian prince to be satisfied.

Arrival of General Meadows.

Alliance with the Mahratta government.

Tippoo seems not to have been prepared for the prompt movement of the English. In June 1790, they commenced the campaign on the boldest system of offensive warfare; their aim being nothing less than by the most direct route to ascend the Ghauts from the south, and advance upon Seringapatam. This march had already been projected and considered practicable by Colonel Fullerton at the termination of the last war. As compared with the northern road through the frontier-district of the Baramahl, it had the disadvantage of being more remote from Madras, and consequently from all military supplies and stores; but it led through a country more abundant in forage and provisions, and avoided

Prompt movements of the English.

CHAP. XIII.

A.D. 1790.

the obstacle presented by the powerful fortress of Bangalore. It was necessary, however, to begin by reducing the strong places possessed by the sultan in the low country; and General Medows, fixing his head-quarters at Coimbetoor, employed in this service Colonel Stuart, who had acquired much experience in Southern India.

Reduction of the fortresses of the low country.

The most important of these fortresses, and that which was considered the main bulwark of Mysore in this quarter, was Palgaut, about thirty miles west of Coimbetoor. Stuart immediately marched against it, but had on his way to encounter an unexpected obstacle. At this season the monsoon, which deluges the coast of Malabar, conveys only cooling and refreshing showers to the interior and eastern districts; but, in advancing westward, he met its full force, which rendered the country wholly unfit for military operations. After giving a formal summons to Palgaut, he returned, and was then despatched to Dindigul, more than 100 miles distant in the south-east. Having formed a very inadequate idea of the strength of this place, he had carried only a small stock of ammunition, which was found nearly exhausted after effecting only a very imperfect breach. No alternative was left but an attempt to storm it, in which he was repulsed; the enemy, however, were so struck by the spirit with which the assault was conducted, and so ignorant of the deficiency under which he laboured, that they sent proposals of surrender, on terms which he was too wise not to accept.

Siege and surrender of Dindigul.

By the time he returned from Dindigul, the season admitted of his again proceeding against Palgaut. Here he had been equally misinformed, though to quite a different effect, having been led to expect a very formidable resistance. He accordingly employed great efforts in sending forward a considerable train of artillery; but on the morning of the 21st September, two batteries having been opened, the guns of the fort were speedily silenced, and before night a breach was effected in the curtain. The garrison soon made offers of submission, asking scarcely any conditions except that they should

Surrender of Palgaut.

be protected from the fury of the nayrs in the British service, who were ready to vent on all that belonged to Tippoo their deepest resentment for his barbarous persecution.

While Colonel Stuart was thus employed, considerable progress was made by the army towards the high land of Mysore. A chain of posts along the rivers Cavery and Bahvany, namely, Caroor, Eroad, Sattimungul, had been successively reduced; and the last of these, commanding the important pass of Gujelhutty, which opened the way into the heart of the country, was occupied by Colonel Floyd with a force of 2000 men. By this arrangement the different corps were very ill connected together; for General Medows at Coimbetoor was sixty miles distant from the division of Floyd, and thirty from that of Stuart. The second of these officers pointed out the danger of his situation, and the intelligence he had received that the enemy was collecting a great force to attack him; but the commander paid no attention to this warning, and ordered the detachment to continue in its present position. The Mysore cavalry, under Seyed Saheb, had indeed, in their attack, been very easily repulsed, and even compelled to retire behind the Ghauts; still, this failure of the advanced guard under a pusillanimous chief afforded no ground to judge of what might be expected when the whole force under the sultan himself should be brought into action. Early in September his horsemen were seen in large bodies descending the Ghauts; and as, when crossing the Bahvany at different points, they endeavoured to surround the handful of English and sepoys, the latter soon felt themselves in a very critical situation. They nevertheless made a gallant defence, and the enemy, having entangled their columns in the thick enclosures which surrounded the British position, were charged very effectually with the bayonet, and several squadrons entirely cut off. The Mysoreans, however, still advanced with increasing numbers, and opened a battery, which did great execution among the native soldiers; yet these mercenaries stood their ground with

Reduction of posts in Mysore.

Rash policy of Colonel Stuart.

Critical position of his detachments.

CHAP. XIII. A. D. 1790.

great bravery, saying,—"We have eaten the Company's salt; our lives are at their disposal." They accordingly maintained their position, and Tippoo thought proper to withdraw during the night to the distance of several miles: but the casualties had been so very severe, and the post proved so untenable, that Colonel Floyd considered it necessary in the morning to commence his retreat, leaving on the field three dismounted guns. The sultan, at the same time, having mustered his forces, began the pursuit with about fifteen thousand men, and after midday overtook the English as they retired in single column. The latter, repeatedly obliged to halt and form in order of battle, repulsed several charges; yet, as soon as they resumed their march, the Indians hovered round them on all sides. They were compelled to abandon three additional guns, and their situation was becoming more and more critical, when some cavalry being seen on the road from Coimbetoor, the cry arose that General Medows was coming to their aid. This report, being favoured by the commander, was echoed with such confidence through the ranks, that though Tippoo had good information as to the real fact, he was deceived, and withdrew his cavalry. Colonel Floyd was thus enabled to prosecute his retreat towards the main army, which had already marched to meet him, but by a wrong road; so that the two divisions found much difficulty, and suffered many hardships, before they could rejoin each other.

Retreat of Colonel Floyd.

Fortunate diversion in his favour.

Derangement of the English plans.

The English, in the course of these untoward events, had lost above 400 in killed and wounded; their plans for the campaign had been deranged; the stores and magazines formed on the proposed line of march lay open to the enemy, and were therefore to be removed with all speed. General Medows, notwithstanding, resumed offensive operations, and had nearly come in contact with the army of the sultan; but this ruler, by a series of manœuvres, eluded both him and Colonel Maxwell, then stationed in Baramahl, and by a rapid march descended into the Coromandel territory. After menacing Trichinopoly, he turned northwards, and swept the Carnatic with nearly as little opposition as was experienced by his father during his first triumphant campaign. At Thiagar, indeed, he was repulsed by his old friend Captain Flint, whom he had learned to know at Wandewash; but scarcely any other place made even a show of resistance. He began by burning and destroying every thing in his way; but soon considered that it would be more profitable to levy contributions, and thereby to replenish his somewhat exhausted treasury. On approaching Pondicherry, he endeavoured to open a negotiation with the French, which was rendered fruitless by the pacific disposition of Louis the Sixteenth.

Lord Cornwallis resumes the command.

General Medows in the field displayed courage and talent; but he had not shown himself equal to the intricate operations of an Indian campaign. Lord Cornwallis, therefore, determined to resume his original design of directing in person the course of the war; and having arrived at Madras, on the 29th January 1791, he took the command. He brought considerable reinforcements; and having ordered Medows to join him, resolved without hesitation to carry hostilities into the centre of Tippoo's dominions. In weighing the advantages of the two lines of operation, the north and the south, by which he could penetrate into the interior of Mysore, he preferred the former. Probably the failure of the late campaign a good deal influenced his choice; he reflected also on the distance to which his military movements would in the other case be withdrawn from their point of support at Madras, and therefore decided upon braving all the difficulties presented by the fortress of Bangalore, and the bleak region in which it is situated.

Motives of his policy.

March of the governor-general.

On the 5th February the governor-general began his march, and on the 11th passed through Vellore towards Amboor, as if he had meant to ascend the mountains by some one of the passes directly opposite to Madras. Tippoo, meantime, was lingering near Pondicherry, in hopes of concluding his French negotiation, and being thereby reinforced by six thousand troops. He trusted, too, that with his light cavalry he might reach the passes

CHAP. XIII. A.D. 1791.

towards which the English were advancing, in time to place himself in their front. Cornwallis, however, suddenly wheeled to the right, and by a circuitous march of four days attained the pass of Mooglee, where he found neither fear nor preparation on the part of the enemy. In a similar period he entered without resistance the high plain of Mysore, and was now in the heart of the sultan's country. This able movement, with which the commander-in-chief opened his career, struck his antagonist with consternation, and inspired the most favourable anticipations as to the manner in which the campaign would be conducted.

Able movement of the general.

Siege of Bangalore.

Tippoo, taken completely by surprise, hastened to the defence of his dominions; but he acted on no distinct or effective plan. He lost much valuable time in superintending personally the removal of his harem from Bangalore; and, notwithstanding several attempts to harass the British, scarcely opposed an obstacle to their taking ground before that stronghold, which they did on the 5th March. The siege was immediately begun with the utmost vigour, yet under peculiar disadvantages. The fortress was too extensive to be invested; operations were therefore carried on solely by breach and battery; the garrison received all the reinforcements and supplies of which they stood in need; while the sultan, with the whole of his brave and active army, well skilled in desultory warfare, hovered round, making continual efforts to support the besieged, and to annoy their assailants. Yet the only serious disaster which the latter experienced was occasioned by the too forward valour of Colonel Floyd, when despatched with the cavalry to cover a *reconnoissance.* Being about to retire, he saw the enemy's rear in a position exposed to an advantageous attack, and could not resist the temptation. He pushed on, and though soon entangled in broken and irregular ground, drove successive detachments before him, when suddenly a musket-ball entered his cheek, passed through both jaws, and he fell down apparently dead. The second in command being in the extreme left, there was no one to

Disaster of Colonel Floyd.

CHAP. XIII.

A.D. 1791.

give orders or encourage the troops at this critical moment. They began a retreat, which, as the different corps of the enemy rallied, and a cross-fire was opened from the fort, was soon changed into a confused flight. The overthrow might have been very serious, had not Colonel Gowdie come up with a body of infantry, and checked the advance of the pursuers. The loss of the British in men was only 71, but the destruction of nearly 300 horses was very severely felt.

Taking of the town of Bangalore.

Another enterprise, which proved somewhat hazardous, was the carrying of the town, or pettah as it was called, of Bangalore, a place of very considerable extent and importance. It was surrounded with an indifferent wall, but the ditch was good, and the gate was covered by a very close thicket of Indian thorns. The attack was made, too, without any due knowledge of the ground; and the soldiers, both in advancing and in endeavouring to force an entrance, were exposed to a destructive fire from turrets lined with musketry. Colonel Moorhouse, one of the most accomplished characters in the service, received four wounds, which proved fatal. At length, when the gate was almost torn in pieces, Lieutenant Ayre, a man of diminutive stature, forced his way through it, and Medows, who preserved an inspiring gayety in the midst of battle, called out, "Well done! now, whiskers, try if you can follow and support the little gentleman." On this animating call, the troops dashed into the town; though its great extent rendered the occupation difficult. Tippoo likewise threw in a strong corps, which renewed the contest, opening a heavy fire with small arms; but, when the English betook themselves to the bayonet, they drove the enemy with irresistible fury through the streets and lanes, and soon compelled them to evacuate the pettah. Our loss, however, amounted to 131.

Bravery of the English officers.

Breach effected in the fortress.

Notwithstanding every obstacle, the besiegers by the 21st had effected a breach, and though it was not in a condition for being stormed, yet, on considering the active movements made by the sultan, it was determined to

CHAP. XIII.
A.D. 1791.

make the attempt that very night. It was bright moonlight,—eleven was the hour named,—and a whisper along the ranks was the signal appointed for advancing in profound silence. The ladders were planted, and a few men had reached the rampart before the alarm extended through the garrison. The killedar or governor hastened to the spot, and fought with the utmost bravery, but he fell; and the assailants, charging with the bayonet, soon established themselves on the top of the walls. They spread to the right and left; columns descended into the body of the place; and in an hour they were masters of Bangalore. Tippoo had received the intelligence, and was marching with his whole force to save the place, when crowds of fugitives announced to him the disastrous event; and he remained the whole night sunk in silence and stupor. It is asserted that he was aware of the intended attack, and had made preparations to meet it; but the occurrences which actually took place do not seem very consistent with this statement.

Fortress of Bangalore taken.

After this triumph, Lord Cornwallis was still in extreme distress for provisions, and especially forage. Before making his grand movement upon the capital, he proceeded northward, in hopes of obtaining supplies, and of being joined by 10,000 horse which the nizam had promised. After a long march, the expected contingent made its appearance; but a woful disappointment was felt at the very aspect of such grotesque auxiliaries. According to Wilks, "it is probable that no national or private collection of ancient armour in Europe contains any weapon or article of personal equipment which might not be traced in this motley crowd,—the Parthian bow and arrow, the iron club of Scythia, sabres of every age and nation, lances of every length and description, and matchlocks of every form, metallic helmets of every pattern." These singular accoutrements were combined with "the total absence of every symptom of order or obedience, excepting groups collected round their respective flags; every individual an independent warrior, self-impelled, affecting to be the champion whose single arm

Distress of the English forces.

Strange auxiliaries.

was to achieve victory." This corps, it was evident, could never be of any use in regular operations; but hopes were at first cherished that they might relieve the English from some of the harassing duty belonging to light troops. It was soon found, however, that they did nothing but plunder the natives and consume the stores of the camp, already almost entirely exhausted.

Resolute plans of the general.

Lord Cornwallis, though he had been so completely disappointed in his allies, and though all his departments, especially those of conveyance, were in the most imperfect state, was yet anxiously desirous to bring the war to a termination, which could be effected only by advancing upon Seringapatam. For this end all possible resources were called into action; the officers were invited and agreed with alacrity to contribute their private means, and to hire from the natives accommodations, which the latter would not willingly have placed under the control of a public department. Cannon-balls were carried even by women and children; and thus, almost without any regular equipment, the army was enabled to march upon the capital. This movement struck Tippoo with alarm; he had even made arrangements for conveying his harem and treasure to Chittledroog; but his mother represented to him the fatal impression of despondency which such a step would make upon his troops and subjects. He yielded to her judgment, and determined to hazard all in the defence of his chief city. His mingled apprehension and rage were oddly displayed, in effacing from the walls of the town numerous caricatures with which he had caused them to be embellished, representing the English in the most ridiculous attitudes, and also in the secret murder of a number of his prisoners.

Alarm of Tippoo.

Change of the sultan's tactics.

The sultan had hitherto confined himself to a desultory warfare, endeavouring to cut off the British by detachments, in the manner which, during the last contest, had been so successful. But in his campaign with Lord Cornwallis, he had been unable to achieve any exploit of this description; and now the danger of his

CHAP. XIII.

A. D. 1781.

capital, and it is said the reproaches of his wives, urged him to hazard a general battle rather than allow it to be formally invested. He drew up his men with great judgment on a range of heights in front of the Cavery, which here separated his army from the island on which Seringapatam stood. The governor-general, by a night-movement, placed himself on the enemy's left flank; but Tippoo, with great promptitude, had anticipated the object of his opponent by occupying a succession of steep hills in front of his position, from the possession of which he derived a great advantage. The battle was of long continuance, and maintained with great obstinacy. The English, unable to employ their own artillery with any effect, suffered considerably from that of the enemy, and were also seriously annoyed by numerous flights of rockets furnished from the arsenal. Yet, on coming to close combat, they carried, by successive charges, one point after another, till the whole of the sultan's army was obliged to seek shelter under the fortifications of the city.

General battle.

Unfruitful victory of the British.

Lord Cornwallis, at the expense of 500 men in killed and wounded, had gained the honour of the day; but he was in such a situation that only a decisive victory, and scarcely even that, could have enabled him to achieve his object. Tippoo had practised, with the utmost diligence, his old system of laying waste the country around the English. They had marched through a desert, and in vain, by sending scouts in every direction, endeavoured to find a human being who could afford either aid or information; and the army was now suffering most deeply from famine, disease, and all those evils which, in a campaign, are often more fatal than the sword. Their means of conveyance were so deficient that the men were compelled, in view of the enemy, to drag the baggage, and even the heavy cannon, as if they had been beasts of burden. In short, after several marches and countermarches, the British commander felt himself under the painful necessity of immediately retreating, with the sacrifice of all the battering-train and heavy equipments with which he was to have besieged Seringapatam. He was obliged also to stop the progress of another expedition which was advancing to his support.

War in Malabar.

Although Madras was the main centre of the English operations, yet the war had extended to the coast of Malabar. There Colonel Hartley held the command, with a force numerically small, but aided by the zealous co-operation of the natives, who had been thoroughly alienated by the violence of the sultan. This enmity towards him rendered it impossible for his troops to carry on that desultory warfare in which they excelled; they were therefore obliged to fight a regular battle, and were completely defeated. Soon after, in December 1790, General R. Abercromby landed with a large force, reduced Cananor, and easily made himself master of every other place held by the enemy in Malabar. He met with another auxiliary, who opened for him a passage into the midst of Tippoo's dominions. An account has been given of the injurious treatment suffered by the people of Coorg from the ruler of Mysore. Their youthful rajah, after a long captivity, had lately contrived to effect his return. The greater part of his subjects were groaning in exile; but in the depth of the woody recesses there was still a band of freemen, who rallied round him with enthusiastic ardour. By a series of exploits, that might have adorned a tale of romance, the young prince recalled his people from the distant quarters to which they had been driven,—organized them into a regular military body, drove the oppressors from post after post, and finally became undisputed ruler of Coorg, expelling the Mohammedan settlers who had been forcibly introduced. A common interest soon united him in strict alliance with General Abercromby, who thus obtained a route by which he could transport his army, without opposition, into the elevated plain. The conveyance of the heavy cannon, however, was a most laborious task, as it was often necessary to drag them by ropes and pulleys up the tremendous steeps, which form on this side the declivity of the Ghauts.

Rajah of Coorg.

Alliance with General Abercromby.

CHAP. XIII. A. D. 1791.

At length the general had overcome every difficulty, and was in full march to join Lord Cornwallis, when he received orders to retreat, which, in this case too, could be effected only by the sacrifice of all the heavy artillery.

Arrival of Mahratta auxiliaries.

As his lordship was retiring, in a most shattered condition, upon Bangalore, the strength of the men failing for want of food, and the sick being with the utmost difficulty dragged along, his troops were alarmed by the appearance on their left of a large body of cavalry, apparently the vanguard of a numerous army; but as they were preparing for resistance, one of the horsemen rode up and called out that he was a Mahratta. This proved in fact to be no other than the first division of those potent allies, under the command of Purseram Bhow and Hurry Punt. These chiefs had taken the field in good time, and this unfortunate delay had been occasioned by the siege of Darwar, a very strong place considerably to the northward, which Tippoo had carefully fortified and garrisoned with his best soldiers. Purseram, seconded by a small detachment of English, broke ground before it in September 1791; but our officers were almost distracted to see the manner in which this important siege was conducted. The Mahrattas, in working a battery, never pointed their cannon so as to make a breach in a particular spot, but aimed at random all round the wall. After loading a gun they sat down, smoked, and conversed for half an hour; then fired, reloaded, and resumed their conversation. Two hours at mid-day, by mutual consent, were set apart for meals and recreation. Our engineers calculated that seven years would be spent before a breach could be effected; and Colonel Frederick, an officer of high spirit, and animated with the most eager anxiety for the success of this important service, was seized with such chagrin that he fell sick and died. However, at the end of six months the garrison, finding their provisions become scarce, and discouraged by the fall of Bangalore, proposed terms of capitulation, which were granted, though ill observed. The great Mahratta army then moved leisurely forward

Siege of Darwar.

Mahratta gunners.

Capitulation of Darwar.

into Mysore, where, in the manner before mentioned, they met with their European allies. Had Cornwallis been aware that this large force was advancing to his aid, he would probably have made every exertion to maintain his ground before Seringapatam; but the activity of the enemy's light troops completely intercepted the intelligence.

Seasonable supplies.

As soon as these auxiliaries arrived, the scarcity in the cantonments of the English, which previously amounted almost to famine, ceased, so far as they were willing to pay the enormous prices that were extorted from their necessities. Every article abounded in that predatory host: it exhibited "the spoils of the East, and the industry of the West,—from a web of English broadcloth to a Birmingham penknife; from the shawls of Cashmere to the second-hand garment of the Hindoo; from diamonds of the first water to the silver earring of a poor plundered village-maiden;" while "the tables of the money-changers, overspread with the coins of every country of the East, gave evidence of an extent of mercantile activity utterly inconceivable in any camp, excepting that of systematic plunderers by wholesale and retail." These allies, moreover, introduced the commander to a most useful class of men, the brinjarries or grain-merchants, who, travelling in large armed bodies with their wives and children, made it their business to supply all the militant powers of Hindostan. They distributed their corn with the strictest impartiality to all who could pay for it; and the general, now amply supplied with funds, was no longer exposed to want, and easily obtained a preference over Tippoo, whose pecuniary resources were beginning to fail.

Miscellaneous spoils.

Brinjarries or grain merchants.

Change of tactics.

Although the army was thus relieved from the immediate pressure of distress, Lord Cornwallis did not conceive it possible to advance again upon the capital till the arrival of a more favourable season, and till a fresh battering-train and other extensive supplies should be forwarded from Madras. In the mean time the troops were employed in the reduction of some of the tremen-

CHAP. XIII.

A.D. 1791.

dous *droogs*, or precipitous rocks, which rise like so many fortresses in this as well as in other of the elevated plains of India. Among these Nundidroog, almost inaccessible by nature, had been fortified with every care to render it impregnable, and was placed under the command of one of Tippoo's ablest officers; yet Major Gowdie, after some successful experiments upon minor forts, undertook its reduction. The only one of its faces at all capable of approach, had been strengthened near the top by a double wall; while the labour of establishing works on its steep and craggy sides, and conveying cannon to the batteries, was excessive. In twenty-one days two breaches were effected, and one morning, by clear moonlight, the assault was made by General Medows in person. The defence was vigorous; huge masses of granite were rolled down, with tremendous crash, from steep to steep; the assailants nevertheless overcame every obstacle, and forcing the interior gate, effected an entrance. During the whole siege they had only 120 killed and wounded, of whom thirty fell in the assault, chiefly by the stones precipitated from the summit.

Reduction of the droogs or rock fortresses.

Nundidroog taken.

Savendroog attempted and taken by storm.

The *droogs* being now viewed as no longer impregnable, Colonel Stuart undertook Savendroog, which bore a still more formidable character, and had been considered by the commander as a place not to be attempted. Yet after seven days' approaches and five of open batteries, it was carried by storm without the loss of a single life. Ootradroog, struck with dismay by these successes, fell with little effort; and a *coup-de-main* had meantime been attempted against Kistnagherry, the capital and bulwark of the Baramahl. This attempt failed; Colonel Maxwell being only able to burn the town, that it might not serve as a cover to predatory inroads. The sultan, in the interval, had sent an expedition to the south, which succeeded, by a series of manœuvres, in carrying Coimbetoor with its English garrison; and, violating the capitulation, by which they were to be allowed to join in safety their countrymen at Palgaut, he caused them to be marched prisoners to Seringapatam.

Ootradroog surrendered.

Lord Cornwallis completes his preparations

After some abortive attempts at negotiation, Lord Cornwallis, having completed his preparations and brought his army into a state of full equipment, determined no longer to delay his march upon the capital. He was now joined by the troops of the nizam, under his son Secunder Jah, which had been hitherto detained by the siege of Goorumconda. His followers consisted of a tumultuary host, closely resembling the corps already described, and giving little hope of an effective co-operation. Purseram Bhow, who at the head of his numerous Mahrattas might have performed with great advantage the services assigned to light cavalry, had concluded that it would be more profitable to himself to turn aside and plunder the rich country of Bednore; and to this personal interest he hesitated not to sacrifice all the grand objects of the confederacy. Captain Little, who, with a body of about a thousand men, had been attached to the host of the Bhow, was obliged to second him in all these irregular pursuits; the most arduous services devolving upon himself and his followers. At one time he was urged to attack a large detachment of Tippoo's army, stationed in an almost impenetrable jungle, covered by a deep ravine. With less than 750 bayonets he undertook the service, and, after a severe and even doubtful contest, dislodged the enemy with great loss,—an exploit considered one of the most brilliant by which this war was distinguished.

Gallant service of Captain Little.

Available forces.

By these circumstances Lord Cornwallis was reduced to depend on the force under his own immediate command, amounting to 22,000 men, including forty-two battering-guns and forty-four field-pieces; and on that of General Abercromby, consisting of 8400 men, which he ordered immediately to approach Seringapatam. He began his march on the 1st February 1792, and by proceeding in three lines instead of one, with his ordnance and heavy baggage in the centre, his infantry and light troops on the flanks, he avoided much of the annoyance hitherto experienced from the attacks of an active enemy.

CHAP. XIII. A. D. 1792.

Meeting of Cornwallis and Tippoo.

On the 5th of the month, the English army having reached a range of heights, discovered the Mysorean metropolis, in front of which Tippoo, with his whole force, amounting to between 40,000 and 50,000 infantry and 5000 cavalry, appeared strongly intrenched. In Colonel Wilks' opinion, the sultan would have practised with greater advantage his original system of desultory warfare, by throwing into the city a strong garrison under a faithful commander, while he himself, with his light cavalry, might have endeavoured to intercept the supplies and communications of the enemy. It is probable, however, that he fully trusted to the strength of his present position, and also hoped, by maintaining it, that he might weary out and finally exhaust his antagonist, in the same manner as Hyder in 1767 had baffled the formidable invasion of the Mahrattas. His encampment was exceedingly strong, covered on one side by a thick bamboo-hedge and by a small river and canal, while the main body of his army was secured in front by a fortified hill and a chain of redoubts, and its rear by the works of the town and island, which, at the same time, afforded a secure retreat. This position was such as, in the opinion of many, and particularly of all the native officers, precluded every idea of attack. Lord Cornwallis, however, considered, that while his movements were delayed, this intrenchment would be continually strengthened by new works, and that his own situation, in the midst of a hostile country and of allies so little to be trusted, would become always more precarious. He determined, therefore, to make an immediate and general attack; though it appeared necessary, as in the storming of a fortress, to carry on his operations under cover of night, when the batteries by which the camp was defended could not be directed with any degree of precision.

Strength of Tippoo's position.

Its immediate assault resolved upon.

Arrangements for the assault.

The troops to be employed in this hazardous service were divided into three columns, under General Medows, Colonels Stuart and Maxwell; the commander with the reserve following close behind; and the whole, under a bright moon, began to move at eight in the evening. The operations of this memorable night have been very minutely narrated, yet they are somewhat enveloped in the obscurity of the scene in which they were acted; and we should despair, without minute topographical details, of conveying to our readers a distinct comprehension of them. The officers experienced to a considerable extent the casualties and dangers of a nocturnal attack; the divisions of Colonels Stuart and Maxwell being once on the point of charging each other with the bayonet. Lord Cornwallis having entered the boundary-hedge, and searching in vain for General Medows, was attacked by a greatly superior force, against which he with difficulty maintained his ground. The general issue of the contest, however, was, that the English, when regularly brought to bear upon the enemy, carried all before them. The most critical moment was when the two divisions above mentioned, after having found a ford, undertook to force their way across the river. Being aided by an able movement of Colonel Knox, they succeeded more easily than was expected, though it was so deep that all their cartridges were spoiled by the water, and they were accordingly compelled to place their sole reliance on the bayonet. Tippoo, during the early part of the engagement, occupied a strong redoubt on the river, where he took his evening meal; but, on seeing the English divisions advance to the ford, he felt alarm as to his communication with the city, and hastened to cross it before them. He almost touched the head of the column, and had several of his attendants killed before he could reach a detached work in an angle of the fort, where he again took a station. But morning soon dawned, and discovered the British army fully established on the island, and facing the fortress without any interposing barrier. The sultan lost, it is said, no less than 23,000 men, chiefly in consequence of the multitudes who dispersed amid the confusion, and returned to their homes. A body of ten thousand, with their wives and children, rushed along the Mysore

CHAP. XIII. A.D. 1792.

Nocturnal attack

Passage of the river.

Immense loss of the sultan.

CHAP. XIII.

A.D. 1792.

bridge to reach the western territory. The loss on the side of our countrymen amounted only to five hundred in killed and wounded.

Vigorous efforts of Tippoo to recover his position.

Tippoo, on discovering the extent of his disaster, made the most vigorous efforts to retrieve it. By the advice of Poornea his treasurer, he announced that two lacks of rupees would be distributed among the troops, as the most effectual mode of alluring back the numerous fugitives. He urged his soldiers to recover if possible the positions in which the British were not fully established; and several of their attacks, being supported by the artillery of the fort, were very formidable, though they were all finally baffled.

His perilous position.

It was no longer possible for the sultan to conceal from himself that his crown and kingdom were in the most extreme peril, and indeed that a peace dictated by his enemies could alone save them. The English force under Cornwallis had singly defeated his army and besieged his capital; and that force was now about to be increased by the corps under General Abercromby, by another from the south, which had ascended the pass of Gujelhutty, and even by the Mahrattas under Purseram Bhow, who had at length been shamed or frightened out of his predatory course. There was nothing, therefore, it has been justly observed, but the general uncertainty of human things, which could leave a doubt as to his approaching downfal. He accordingly determined to seek peace on almost any conditions. Two English officers, Lieutenants Chalmers and Nash, who had been taken at Coimbetoor, and made prisoners contrary to the terms of capitulation, were still detained at Seringapatam. They were sent for, and the first was asked if he was not an officer of rank, and a near relation of Lord Cornwallis. Notwithstanding his reply in the negative, he was released, and desired to convey to that commander the sultan's earnest wish for peace, and the proposal to send an envoy to treat for it. His lordship's answer, though it expressed deep dissatisfaction at the treatment of the captives, contained an acceptance of

Tippoo sues for peace.

this overture. An officer of distinction, Gholaum Ali, arrived in the camp, and several days were busily spent in negotiation, to which the allies, though they had been so entirely useless, were admitted on equal terms. The following was at length fixed as the ultimatum to be delivered to Tippoo:—The surrender of half his dominions, taken from districts contiguous to the territory of the confederates; the payment of three crores and thirty lacks of rupees (about £4,000,000 sterling); and the delivery of two of his sons as hostages. Hard as these conditions were, they were powerfully enforced by events which had occurred in the course of the negotiation. On the night of the 18th February, while the attention of the enemy was attracted to the south side of the fort by the operations of a flying corps under Major Dalrymple and Captain Robertson, the trenches were opened on the north side with such silence and caution, that though the fort was kept blazing with blue lights for the purpose of observation, morning had arrived before the sultan discovered that this operation, so fatal to him, had commenced. A nullah or ravine had been converted into a wide and extensive parallel, where the assailants were placed so fully under cover, as to render ineffectual every attempt to interrupt their operations. This parallel was carried on and improved till the 21st, when it was completed; and in the night the line was marked out for a second. It was finished on the 23d, and the ground was fixed for the heavy batteries about 500 yards from the fort, in so advantageous a position, as to leave no doubt of a practicable breach being speedily effected.

Terms of peace.

Trenches opened before Seringapatam.

As the crisis of his fate thus rapidly approached, Tippoo felt the necessity of coming to a prompt decision upon the proposals submitted by the British commander. He called his principal officers to meet in the great mosque, and laying before them the Koran, adjured them by that sacred book to give faithful advice in this dread emergency. He stated the terms demanded by the enemy, adding,—"You have heard the conditions

Critical position of the sultan.

CHAP. XIII.

A. D. 1792.

of peace, and you have now to hear and answer my question, *Shall it be peace or war?*" A reference made in such words, could leave no doubt as to the course which he felt himself under the necessity of following, and that he merely sought the sanction of his chiefs. They unanimously agreed that, under present circumstances, there remained no alternative. The scene is said to have been peculiarly affecting, and Colonel Wilks met with few that had been present who could even allude to it without tears in their eyes.

Council with his officers.

Accepts of Lord Cornwallis' conditions.

That very night Tippoo sent off, signed and sealed, the conditions transmitted to him by Lord Cornwallis. Early in the morning orders were sent to the English troops to cease from their labour in the trenches, and to forbear farther hostilities. The injunction was received with a deep feeling of disappointment. Their enthusiasm had been raised to the highest pitch; they cherished the most sanguine hopes that they should triumphantly scale the proud walls of Seringapatam, and with their own hands rescue their countrymen immured in its dungeons. The commander-in-chief, however, issued very judicious general orders, in which he exhorted them to display moderation in their present success, and to avoid any insult to their humbled adversary.

Tippoo's hostages.

An interesting scene occurred in the fulfilment of that article of the treaty which related to the delivery of the two royal youths as hostages. We confess ourselves unable fully to perceive the object of a stipulation, conformable indeed to Indian ideas, but contrary to the more improved feelings of modern Europe. Supposing the treaty violated in the most flagrant manner, what use could have been made of the boys, or what injury done to them? However, such being the course adopted, Lord Cornwallis softened it by every species of kindness and indulgence; and in consequence of the deep distress which was understood to prevail in the palace, a day's delay was granted. Tents having been sent from the fort, and erected for their accommodation, the general offered to wait upon them; but their father wrote that it was his particular wish they should be brought to his lordship's tent, and delivered into his own hands. They set out at one in the afternoon of the 26th, the walls being crowded with spectators, among whom was the sultan himself. They rode on elephants richly caparisoned, dressed in white muslin robes, having round their necks several rows of large pearls, intermingled with valuable jewels. The marquis received them at the door, and taking their hands in his, led them into his tent. The chief vakeel then said,—"These children were this morning the sons of the sultan, my master; their situation is now changed, and they must look up to your lordship as their father." Their reception was in fact truly paternal; they were soon relieved from all apprehension; and though the one was only eight and the other ten years of age, yet, having been trained with infinite care in every thing relating to external behaviour, they astonished all present by the dignity and ease of their deportment, and by that union of politeness and reserve which characterizes oriental courts.

Their delivery to Lord Cornwallis.

After the hostages had been delivered, and a crore of rupees paid, a serious difficulty arose. The treaty stipulated the surrender of one-half of Tippoo's dominions, where they bordered on those of the allies; but there was no specification of the actual territories to be ceded,—a point so essential, that it ought, one would imagine, to have preceded the execution of any of the articles. The ceded districts were to be rated according to the revenues which they yielded. His majesty presented statements by which the produce of those contiguous to the possessions of the allies were grossly exaggerated, and the others underrated; while the nizam and Purseram Bhow were not slow to err on the opposite side, and hence the discrepancy became enormous. Meantime reports were spread of suspicious conduct on the part of the sultan, and in particular that, contrary to treaty, he was actively strengthening the fortifications of Seringapatam. When remonstrated with on this subject, he replied that, if they thought proper, he would throw down a bastion

Unforeseen difficulties.

Grounds of suspicion.

CHAP. XIII. A. D. 1792.

and let the English see into the fort,—an answer so wild and extravagant, that it tended little to dispel apprehension.

Statement of the sultan's revenues.

At length his vakeels produced documents which were supposed to be authentic, and whence it appeared that the entire revenue of their master's dominions did not exceed £2,960,000. Each of the allies then picked out what best suited him; the Mahrattas extended their frontier to the Toombuddra; and the nizam carried his beyond the Pennar. The English took their share in detached portions; on the east the frontier-territory of Baramahl; in the south Dindigul; on the west a great extent of the disputed coast of Malabar, including Tellicherry and Calicut. No objection was made till it was observed that this last section included Coorg, long the subject of much deadly contest. On seeing this condition, the sultan burst into a paroxysm of rage that approached to absolute phrensy. "To which of their territories," said he, "is Coorg adjacent? Why do they not ask at once for Seringapatam? They know that I would sooner have died in the breach than have consented to such a cession, and durst not bring it forward till they had treacherously obtained my children and my treasure." Some English authors endeavour to prove that the demand ought not to have been unexpected; and yet it cannot be denied that, while all the other cessions consisted of frontier-territories, leaving untouched the mountain-barrier which encloses Mysore Proper, this included a portion of its very summit, and opened a ready access to the capital. But the truth is, that as long as Tippoo was eagerly intent on pouring his vengeance on its brave people, Lord Cornwallis could not abandon to his fury faithful allies, and a race unjustly oppressed. Upon this refusal all was again in movement,—the princes were separated from their native attendants, and arrangements entered into for despatching them to the Carnatic under an English escort,—preparations were made for renewing the siege,—the army was full of new hope and animation,—Purseram

His indignation at the demand for Coorg.

Threatened renewal of hostilities.

Bhow began once more to plunder. In less than two days, however, the sultan again felt the weight of the necessity which pressed upon him, and sent notice that the demand was acceded to. A considerable delay still intervened; but, on the 18th March 1792, the definitive treaty was transmitted to the young princes, that by their hands it might be delivered. At ten in the morning of the 19th they waited on Lord Cornwallis, and the eldest presented to him all the three copies of the treaty; but as the vakeels of the two allied chiefs, who did not choose to appear in person, soon after entered, his lordship returned their copies, which the boy delivered to them in a manly though evidently less cordial manner; and on hearing something muttered by the Mahratta envoy, asked what he grumbled at, hastily adding, "they might well be silent, as certainly their masters had no reason to be displeased."

The demand acceded to.

General Dirom calculates, that after deducting the Company's share of the sum exacted from Tippoo, the extraordinary expenses of this war would scarcely amount to two millions sterling. Every department had been conducted with the strictest economy. Instead of the large grants that had accrued to individuals from the conquest of Bengal, the prize-money in three campaigns amounted only to £93,584, which, after Cornwallis and Medows had given up their shares, and the Company had added a large gratuity, only allowed to a colonel £1161, 12s., and to a private soldier £14, 11s. 9d. The losses sustained by the sultan during the period of hostility are estimated by the same author at 49,340 men, 67 forts, and 801 guns.

Cost of the war.

This celebrated treaty has been the subject of much controversy; nor do the views which influenced Lord Cornwallis seem ever to have been fully understood. It appears to have effected either too little or too much. The cessions extorted were such as to preclude all hope of future friendship; for they inevitably created in the mind of a proud, ambitious, and restless prince, a feeling of deadly enmity, as well as an incessant desire to retrieve

Opinions on the treaty.

CHAP. XIII. A.D. 1794.

his lost greatness; while they left him a degree of power which might easily become formidable in the hands of such an enemy.

Fulfilment of treaty, and return of the hostages.

Notwithstanding these unpromising circumstances, six years elapsed without any violation of the treaty; and all its conditions being fulfilled, the two young hostages were sent back to their father in 1794. Tippoo saw no prospect of making war with advantage; and Sir John Shore, who succeeded as governor-general, followed a strictly pacific system, which he was even accused of carrying to excess. His policy was particularly questioned in the case of the nizam, when the Mahrattas, his late allies, carried into effect their long-cherished design of invading and plundering his territories. The engagements entered into with this ruler previous to the commencement of the Mysore war, though somewhat vague, were such as reasonably led him, in that event, to look for British protection. The new governor, however, considered himself as strictly precluded by his instructions from engaging in any contest that was not purely defensive. The nizam, in the exigency to which he was thus reduced, had recourse to a Frenchman named Raymond, who possessed no ordinary share of enterprise and martial skill. He succeeded also in alluring into the service of his employer a great number of French officers, and with their aid organized a large body of troops, who were superior to any native force, with the exception of the sepoys trained in the British army. Tippoo, meantime, was busily employed in attempting to improve his military system, though, from want of means and practical information, he met with very imperfect success.

Mahratta aggressions.

The nizam seeks French aid.

Wellesley appointed governor-general.

Such was the state of affairs, when in May 1798 the Earl of Mornington, afterwards Marquis Wellesley, went out as governor-general. This nobleman, whose splendid career was destined to eclipse that of Clive, was sent with the most solemn injunctions to follow a course directly opposite to that which, throughout the whole of his administration, he did actually pursue. He was instructed not to engage, if possible, in hostilities with any native power; and yet he waged deadly war with every one of them. He was desired not to add by conquest a single acre to the Company's territory, and he subdued for them all India from the Himmaleh to Cape Comorin. Yet his adherents contend that he acted steadily and uniformly in the spirit of his instructions; and that, in deviating so widely from the wishes of his employers, he was carried along by a current of circumstances which existed prior to any step taken by him in the government of that country.

CHAP. XIII. A.D. 1797.

His instructions and proceedings.

He had no sooner assumed the exercise of authority, than his attention was roused by a most remarkable proceeding on the part of the sovereign of Mysore. That prince, like his father Hyder, had been long connected in close alliance with the French, as the power by whose aid he hoped to subvert the dominion of the English. This connexion was in a great measure broken by the expulsion of those allies from India upon the breaking out of the revolutionary war; but Tippoo had listened with the utmost eagerness to the accounts of their success against Britain and the continental nations, and had been led to hope for their assistance in the re-establishment of his own greatness. While he was in this disposition, Ripaud, the captain of a French privateer, arrived at Mangalore, in the beginning of the year 1797, to solicit the means of repairing his shattered vessel. There he met with Gholaum Ali, whom the sultan had formerly employed on an embassy to France; and, finding a field open for the display of a little vain-glory, he represented himself as second in command at the Mauritius, and stated that he had come to give notice of a large force being ready at that island to co-operate with them in driving from India their common enemy. He was immediately forwarded to Seringapatam, where the monarch, contrary to the advice of his most prudent counsellors, who assured him that this stranger was an impostor, received him into his entire confidence. After a number of little arrangements and transactions, he

New schemes of Tippoo.

Fresh hopes of French alliance.

Ripaud's reception by Tippoo.

CHAP. XIII

A. D. 1798.

sent two ambassadors along with Ripaud to the Isle of France, to adjust the terms of a treaty offensive and defensive. This mission arrived at the Mauritius, where they were altogether unexpected; but when Malartic, the governor, learned their purpose, animated by that desire to promote national interests which generally characterizes his countrymen, he determined to give them a cordial reception. They landed under a salute of artillery, were conducted to the government-house, and received there in state. Malartic expressed the utmost readiness to accede to the proposals of their master, which were no less than that he should send an army of 25,000 or 30,000 men to assist in conquering the English, the nizam, and the Mahrattas, and to divide all India between them. The arrangement was fully completed, with the important exception that, to compose the powerful force by which these mighty projects were to be accomplished, there did not exist a single soldier. All that could be done was to transmit the plan, accompanied with strong recommendations, to the Executive Directory; and, in the mean time, to invite as many as possible of the Frenchmen and natives resident on the island to enrol as volunteers. With the most palpable imprudence, the governor issued a proclamation, announcing the arrival of the ambassadors and the object they had in view, and calling upon all the citizens who had any martial spirit to enlist under the banners of the Mysorean sovereign, who made the most liberal offers of pay and allowances. They thus succeeded in levying exactly ninety-nine persons,—a motley group,—Europeans, creoles, citizens, soldiers, sailors; and with this troop, for want of more and better, the ambassadors were fain to depart. They landed at Mangalore on the 26th April 1798; when the sultan, though galled at the utter disappointment of his expectations, and the rash exposure made at the Mauritius, had still the means of averting the danger. He might have disowned the envoys, and refused their mock auxiliaries, while, by secret explanations he might at the same time have contrived to keep

Mission to the Mauritius.

Projected invasion of India.

Extravagant proceedings of the governor of Mauritius.

Insignificant results.

CHAP. XIII

A. D. 1798.

open the communication with France. But he seems to have been in a state of blind and violent excitation. The embassy, with their slender accompaniment, were welcomed to the capital, where they founded a Jacobin club, planted the tree of liberty surmounted with the cap of equality, and on the public parade hailed the bigoted Mohammedan as "Citizen Tippoo." In these republican forms he cordially concurred, although wholly ignorant of their true meaning; imagining them to be the badges of a mystic association, whose members were to devote themselves to his aggrandizement.

Citizen Tippoo.

These proceedings were fully communicated to the governor-general, who immediately transmitted to the Court of Directors his decided opinion, that they were equivalent to "a public, unqualified, and unambiguous declaration of war," and that "an immediate attack upon Tippoo Sultan appeared to be demanded by the soundest maxims both of justice and policy." These conclusions have been generally assented to by British officers and politicians; yet Mr Mill, with his usual anxiety to escape national partialities, has not hesitated to assert, that the above incidents afforded no ground for attacking, or reason for dreading, the sovereign of Mysore, beyond what previously existed. No doubt, it is said, could be entertained, ever since the last peace, of his deep hostility against the English, and his disposition to embrace any opportunity of regaining his lost territories. There was, we admit, the most reasonable presumption of the existence, in his mind, of such sentiments. Well-founded, however, as this suspicion was, the governor had no right to proceed upon it without some overt act; it being something very different from the positive conclusion of a compact aiming directly at the destruction of the British power in India. It is argued, moreover, that the treaty, having been entered into without any means of fulfilling it, might safely have been regarded as nugatory, and altogether neglected. This reasoning cannot be held conclusive, unless there were some certainty that the sultan could not obtain the means of carrying into

Steps taken by the governor-general.

Opinions on his policy.

CHAP. XIII. A.D. 1798.

Hostility of the French.

effect those hostile schemes in which he had so eagerly engaged. But it is well known that he could depend upon the co-operation of the greatest military power in the world, animated, too, with the most rancorous feeling towards Britain, and peculiarly desirous to strike a blow against her in this very quarter. The only security lay in the dominion of the seas, which England had fully established; though experience has shown that no fleet, however triumphant, can hermetically seal the ports of a great country, or even prevent a squadron from finding its way to the most distant regions. This had just been made evident, as Bonaparte, in the face of the British navy, had recently landed in Egypt a force sufficient to conquer it; an expedition, too, which was generally believed to be undertaken with an ultimate view to India. The perils of a French invasion of that country were then, perhaps, generally overrated; now, after the event, they are probably too much despised; for it seems highly probable that the republican government, had they not been involved in a series of continental wars, would have attempted to transport a large army into the East,—and it is by no means certain that they would not have succeeded.

Dangers to be apprehended from Tippoo.

The dangers to be apprehended from Tippoo were moreover greatly increased by the actual position of the neighbouring states. The only two by which his power could be balanced were the Mahrattas and the nizam. The former confederacy, notwithstanding its great extent, was now in so distracted a state that the peishwa, its nominal head, could scarcely maintain his authority against the turbulent chiefs who were struggling for supremacy. The dominions of the other were also ill organized, and his troops quite undisciplined. His chief military strength lay in the corps trained after the European manner by Raymond, which in a few years had been raised from 1500 to 10,000, and arrangements were now making to increase it to 14,000. These troops, however, were so far from affording a ground of confidence to the English that they were felt

Disorganized state of his native rivals.

as sure and deadly enemies. It had long been a fixed policy of the French government thus to employ their officers among the native powers, in the view of exalting their own influence and depressing that of their rivals. Little doubt was entertained that, if Tippoo once raised a hostile standard, this and similar corps would soon flock round it, and make a formidable addition to his forces. That prince, moreover, was carrying on active intrigues with the courts both of Poonah and Hydrabad, the fidelity of which to the British alliance was by no means assured. He had sent also an embassy to the Afghan potentate Zemaun Shah, the most powerful of those who then held sway over the destinies of India, and an invasion from whom was considered very probable. Thus, it was clear, a very trifling change of political relations might lead to the formation of an overwhelming confederacy against the English provinces.

French policy.

Intrigues of Tippoo.

Under these circumstances, the Marquis Wellesley considered it of great importance to commence immediate operations with a view to the attainment of certain concessions which he was sensible would never be voluntarily made. These included the giving up by Tippoo of all his territory on the coast of Malabar, and his complete exclusion from the sea,—the banishment of all Frenchmen from his dominions,—the admission of a permanent resident at his court, and the reduction of his resources by making him pay the expense of the contest. The governor-general hoped, by a *coup-de-main*, to have suddenly carried these objects before the Indian prince could make preparations or procure alliances. Great, however, was his mortification to learn that the Coromandel army, so far from being adequate to such an achievement, was quite insufficient to the defence of the Carnatic. This arose chiefly from the want of cattle and other means of transport, which rendered it wholly unable to keep pace with the rapid movements of the sultan, who, had he then invaded the British territories, might have ravaged them unresisted from one end to the other. The earliest period when it

Plans of Wellesley.

Inefficient state of his forces.

CHAP. XIII.

A. D. 1798.

was supposed this deficiency could be supplied was three months; while Lieutenant-colonel Close, a high authority, thought it would require six. On the 8th September, Lord Clive, then governor of Madras, considering that the season of action was only from January to May, did not think the campaign could be opened till the beginning of the year 1800; yet such activity did the marquis infuse into the conduct of affairs, that in October 1798 an adequate force was assembled, and early next January preparations were in so advanced a state as to afford the prospect of its being speedily able to move. Meantime an important preliminary operation had been effected.

Activity of the governor.

Negotiations at Hydrabad.

Immediate attention was required to the strong corps formed under French officers at the capital of Hydrabad, and upon this point the governor-general determined to adopt the most decisive measures. Captain Kirkpatrick, resident at that court, was instructed to lay before the nizam the plan of an alliance, offensive and defensive, by which he was to be guaranteed against the attack of all his enemies. In support of this pledge, four English battalions, with a body of artillery, in addition to the two already stationed there, were to be sent to his capital; but he was informed that the regiments commanded by the French must be immediately dissolved, and themselves dismissed. The movement of a large body of troops to the frontier intimated that these propositions were not meant to be optional. The nizam was involved in much doubt and perplexity. He is said to have been disgusted by the insolent and domineering conduct of the foreign officers; but he dreaded to see his country made the theatre of a contest between the rival nations; still more, perhaps, he foresaw that, by the proposed arrangement, he would become completely the vassal of England. At length, on the 1st September 1798, he signed the treaty, which was ratified at Calcutta on the 18th, and carried into effect with such expedition, that on the 10th October the new subsidiary force arrived at Hydrabad. His highness again relapsed into all his doubt and irresolution, and endeavoured to evade or delay every

Measures to enforce them.

Treaty signed.

decisive step, till Colonel Roberts, the commander, cutting short all discussion, marched up to the French cantonments, and on the 22d formed a circle round them. The troops, at once dreading a conflict with the English, and discontented on account of their arrears of pay, rose in mutiny against their chiefs; when, on being assured of the money due to them, and of future service under other leaders, they laid down their arms. Thus, in a few hours, without a blow being struck, was dissolved a corps of fourteen thousand men, having an arsenal filled with military stores, and a handsome train of artillery.

Decisive proceedings of the British.

Wellesley, having by these means secured the co-operation of the Hydrabad forces, and, at the same time, by indefatigable exertions rendered his military establishment efficient, determined to bring affairs to an immediate crisis. His correspondence with Tippoo had continued friendly till the 8th November 1798, when he wrote a letter, in which, after discussing some general topics, he observed, that it was impossible the sultan could suppose him ignorant or indifferent as to the intercourse maintained by him with the French, the inveterate foes of Britain. He and his allies, he added, had on that account been obliged to adopt certain measures of precaution and self-defence. Anxious, however, to suggest a plan which might promote the mutual security and welfare of all parties, he proposed to depute Major Doveton, an officer well known to the sultan (having been employed in 1794 in conveying back to him the young princes detained as hostages), "who," said he, "will explain to you more fully and particularly the sole means which appear to myself and to the allies of the Company to be effectual for the salutary purpose of removing all existing distrust and suspicion." On the 10th December the governor-general forwarded another communication, announcing that he was on the point of setting out for Madras, where he hoped to receive his reply.

Direct communication with Tippoo.

Major Doveton proposed as negotiator

Tippoo, apparently before receiving the first despatch, had written, on the 20th November, an expostulation, in rather amicable terms, upon the military preparations

CHAP. XIII. A. D. 1798.

of the English, and a profession of his own pacific disposition; but the letter of 8th November was followed by a long and suspicious silence. The demands of the governor-general would, at this time, have been very moderate, confined to the dismissal of French emissaries, and the exchange of a part of the coast of Malabar for a territory of equal value in the interior. But the sultan, who foresaw that some demands were to be made upon him, could not bring down his mind to the necessity of submission. He still placed a vague confidence in destiny, in the aid of foreigners, and in alliances which he hoped to form with the northern powers of India. At length, on the 18th December, probably after receiving the despatch of the 10th, though he did not acknowledge it, he wrote a long explanatory paper. He represented the French affair as only the casual arrival of a party of strangers in search of employment, which he had granted to a few; and he expressed extreme surprise that there should be any idea of the interruption of mutual amity. Referring to the proposed mission of Major Doveton, he observed that "the treaties and engagements entered into were so firmly established and confirmed, as ever to remain fixed and durable, and be an example to the rulers of the age. I cannot imagine that means more effectual than these can be adopted for promoting the security of states, or the welfare and advantage of all parties." It seems impossible to regard Lord Wellesley's interpretation as strained, when he considered this note as implying an absolute rejection of the embassy, and a determination against any concession beyond those made by former treaties.

Hesitation of Tippoo.

His explanations.

Reply of Wellesley.

In reply to it, accordingly, his lordship, having arrived at Madras, wrote, on the 9th January 1799, a long memorial, fully explaining all his grounds of complaint. He gave a narrative of the transactions at the Isle of France, enclosing a copy of Malartic's proclamation, and finally inferred, that "his Highness' ambassadors had concluded an offensive alliance with the French against the Company and its allies; that they had demanded military succours and levied troops with a view to its prosecution; that his Highness had sanctioned the conduct of his ambassadors, and had received into his army the troops which they had levied; that having made military preparations of his own, he was evidently ready, had the succours obtained been sufficient, to have commenced an unprovoked attack on the Company's possessions, and had broken the treaties of peace and friendship subsisting between him and the allies." Deeply regretting that the offered mission of Major Doveton had not been accepted, he still urged it as a means of conciliation, but earnestly requested that not above one day should elapse previous to its acceptance. On the 16th he sent another letter, enclosing one to the sultan from the Grand Seignior, transmitted through Mr Spencer Smith, and also that monarch's declaration of war against the French. At this stage of the proceedings attempts were made to work upon the Mohammedan zeal of Tippoo, and to induce him to resent the attack made by that people upon the head of his religion; at the same time the reception of Doveton was again pressed. After a long silence, there arrived at Madras on the 13th February 1799, without date, the following short and singular epistle:—

Major Doveton's mission again proposed.

Attempt to influence his religious zeal

Tippoo's reply.

"I have been much gratified by the agreeable receipt of your lordship's two friendly letters, the first brought by a camel-man the last by hircarrahs, and understood their contents. The letter of the prince, in station like Jumsheid, with angels as his guards, with troops numerous as the stars; the sun illumining the world of the heaven of empire and dominion; the luminary giving splendour to the universe of the firmament of glory and power; the sultan of the sea and the land, the King of Room (the Grand Seignior), be his empire and his power perpetual! addressed to me, which reached you through the British envoy, and which you transmitted, has arrived.—Being frequently disposed to make excursions and hunt, I am accordingly proceeding upon a hunting-excursion. You will be pleased to despatch Major Dove-

CHAP. XIII. A.D. 1799.

ton, about whose coming your friendly pen has repeatedly written, slightly attended. Always continue to gratify me by friendly letters notifying your welfare."

Its meaning.

This strange reply might certainly have created a doubt whether it was not designed as an evasion, or even an insult; though Colonel Wilks afterwards learned from the Mysorean chiefs, that it was meant for a real consent, though somewhat forced and ungracious. The letter of the 9th January had fully opened Tippoo's eyes to his alarming situation. He was thrown into a state of suspense and violent agitation, venting imprecations against all who had been concerned in the mission to the Isle of France, and exclaiming, "the fractured mast of Ripaud's worthless vessel will cause the subversion of an empire." He made, however, a reluctant movement to the eastward, with the view of meeting Major Doveton;

Wellesley's policy.

but Wellesley now considered the time as passed when such an arrangement could be advantageously admitted. The monsoon, which begins in June, would put a stop to military operations, so that to enter at present upon a negotiation would enable his enemy to gain a whole year, in the course of which he might hope to procure allies and reinforcements from various quarters. On receiving, therefore, no answer by the 3d of February, the governor-general had ordered the armies to advance; and on the arrival of the sultan's letter, he wrote to him on the 22d February, announcing that the mission of Doveton could no longer be attended with the expected advantages; that his long silence had rendered it necessary to command the approach of the troops; but that

Tippoo invited to send an embassy.

General Harris was empowered to receive any embassy, and to enter into any explanations by which a treaty might be arranged, on such conditions as should appear to the allies indispensably necessary to the establishment of a secure and permanent peace. Tippoo, however, even before receiving this notice, either suspecting that his consent had not produced the intended effect, or moved by his own inconsistent disposition, had determined to try the fortune of arms.

The army appointed to invade the kingdom of Mysore consisted of 4381 European and 10,695 native infantry; 884 European and 1751 native cavalry, with 608 gunners; forming in all 18,319 fighting-men, with 104 pieces of cannon, and 2483 lascars and pioneers. To these were added 10,157 infantry and 6000 horse belonging to the nizam, and which, under British command, now formed an effective body of troops. In the mean time General Stuart, a veteran in Indian warfare, was advancing with 6420 men from Malabar to join and co-operate with the main army.

CHAP. XIII.

A.D. 1799.

British forces.

General Harris was furnished with the plans of two treaties, to be selected according to circumstances. The first, which was to be produced in the event of the army merely arriving before Seringapatam, required the cession to Britain of the coast of Malabar, and an equal extent of territory to each of the two allies; the reception of a resident ambassador; the expulsion of all natives of European countries at war with Great Britain, and the payment of 150 lacks of rupees. In case, however, the events of the campaign should not open the prospect of a successful termination this season, these terms might be modified according to circumstances; but every effort should be made to inspire the sultan with fear, from which alone any concession could be hoped. If again the trenches were actually opened before the capital, with the prospect of its speedy reduction, the second treaty was to be produced, in which peace was to be granted only upon the cession of half his dominions.

Conditions on which a treaty was to be agreed to.

Tippoo, anxious to strike a blow at the commencement of the campaign, had the penetration to discern the advantage which he derived from the detached state of the invading armies proceeding from Malabar and Coromandel. He might thus attack the former, when it had just ascended the Ghauts, and taken a defensive position amid the hills and forests which enclose the territory of Coorg. Accordingly, by a rapid movement to the westward, he arrived, on the 5th March 1799, very unexpectedly in their neighbourhood; and the Eng-

Rapid movement of Tippoo.

lish, who conceived that the main force of the enemy was still on the opposite side of India, were somewhat disconcerted. General Stuart had stationed a corps under Colonel Montresor eight miles in advance, on the hill of Sedaseer, to observe any signal which might be made by the eastern army. Much surprise was felt when a number of tents appeared on the ground in front, which gradually swelled to several hundreds, and composed a formidable encampment. Among others, belonging apparently to chiefs of distinction, there was a very large one covered with green, which was concluded to be that of the sultan himself; and yet so contrary was this to all previous intelligence, that Stuart merely reinforced the party on the hill with a single battalion, and waited to act according to circumstances. At daybreak, General Hartley, from a height, discovered an appearance of activity among the opposite troops. It does not appear very clear why the commander did not immediately concentrate his forces, by either marching forward himself, or ordering the advance under Montresor to fall back.

Surprise of General Stuart.

Secrecy and expedition of Tippoo's attack.

In fact, the Indian army penetrated through the jungle with such secrecy and expedition, that between nine and ten in the morning they had completely surrounded that officer's brigade, attacking it at once in front and rear. It maintained most gallantly an arduous conflict till after two o'clock, when General Stuart came up, and after a brisk charge obliged the enemy to retreat in all directions through the thicket. The advanced corps being immediately withdrawn, Tippoo had a pretence for claiming a victory; but the casualties on our side, which amounted only to 29 killed, 98 wounded, and 16 missing, sufficiently showed that he had failed in his object of striking a decisive blow. Even by his own statement, his loss included several chiefs of rank; and this was the last action in which he displayed any military genius. He effected a complete surprise, and the destruction of the English corps was averted only by its own extraordinary valour and the inferiority of his troops in a pitched battle.

Failure of his purpose.

The sultan hastened back to oppose the main army

advancing against him from Coromandel. It might now have appeared evident that his only resource was, by recurring to the ancient military policy of his house, to throw a strong garrison into Seringapatam, to keep the field with large bodies of cavalry, and by continual movements to intercept the enemy's communications, cut off his supplies, and surprise his detachments. He might thus either have defended his throne, or have remained powerful after its fall. His plan, however, appears to have been to contend with the English according to their own method, in regular warfare and by pitched battles. To this system he had been partial ever since Lord Cornwallis' first retreat after the engagement fought near his capital. But even there Tippoo was beaten; and the subsequent retreat had been occasioned solely by the want of supplies and equipments, produced by the desultory warfare previously waged. During the peace, he made great exertions to assimilate his force to a European army, and his success had been such as to render him an overmatch for any of the native powers; but the cavalry, the instrument by which all the triumphs of his family over the English were achieved, had been comparatively neglected.

False policy of Tippoo.

The British were now advancing into the heart of his dominions; and the comprehensive mind of Marquis Wellesley instantly saw it to be his true policy not to detain himself with any secondary object, but to strike at once at Seringapatam, the reduction of which would be followed by the entire downfal of the sultan. All our writers agree in stating, that no army could be in a higher state of equipment than the one which now took the field under General Harris; yet the march, though he did not encounter any serious resistance, was very slow. He passed the frontier only on the 5th, and made the first united movement on the 10th March 1799, the time that had been fixed as the latest at which he ought to have arrived at the capital. Certain authors speak as if in this tardy progress there were some mystery which could never be developed; but the delay seems suffi-

Advance of the British.

Slow progress.

CHAP. XIII. — A. D. 1799.

Cause of delay.

ciently explained by an allusion to the ample supplies which he carried with him. He conveyed, by means of sixty thousand ill-trained oxen and careless drivers, several months' provisions for his whole army, and a battering-train to reduce a fortress, the fall of which was expected to bring with it that of the whole kingdom.

Battle of Malavilly.

When he had reached Malavilly, about thirty miles from the capital, the sultan's encampment was observed from the heights, and General Floyd, with the advance, having approached within a mile of that village, discovered their whole force posted on the elevated ground behind it. An attack being immediately determined on, it was led by Colonel Wellesley, supported by Floyd's cavalry, and directed against the enemy's right. A column of their troops advanced in perfect order and with great gallantry; but the English infantry, reserving their fire, received that of their antagonists at the distance of sixty yards, rushed upon them and broke their ranks, when a resolute charge by the horse drove them off the field. The whole of the Indian line then gave way, and a general retreat ensued, which Harris, who was greatly inferior in cavalry and light troops, did not attempt to molest. The loss was not very serious on either side; but an additional proof was given how unable even the flower of the Eastern armies was to contend in pitched battle with the British.

Tippoo's plans circumvented.

Tippoo made another attempt to carry into effect his plan of desultory warfare. He had removed or destroyed all the forage, and almost every blade of grass on the highway between his enemy's position and the capital; and he hovered round, ready to fall upon their rear, as they marched along this desolated route. But he was completely disappointed by the movement of General Harris, who after leaving Malavilly turned to the left, crossed the Cavery at the fords of Sosilla, and proceeded to Seringapatam along the southern bank of that river, a resolution which, being wholly unexpected, no pre-

His dismay.

cautions had been taken to defeat. On seeing their last scheme thus baffled, the sultan and his principal officers were struck with deep dismay and despondence. Having assembled them in council, he said :—"We have arrived at our last stage; what is your determination?" "To die along with you," was the universal reply. A unanimous resolution was formed to try again the fortune of the field, with the alternative only of victory or death. All present were deeply affected; one of the chiefs, before taking leave, threw himself prostrate and clasped the feet of his master, the usual sign in India of the most solemn farewell. The latter could not refrain from tears; his example quickly spread through the whole assembly; and they parted as men who had met for the last time in this world. But the final crisis was not yet arrived. Tippoo had expected that the English commander would proceed to the *eastern* extremity of the island of Seringapatam, cross the branch of the Cavery that enclosed it, and establish himself on the ground formerly occupied by Lord Cornwallis. But General Harris chose to make a circuit, which would bring his army opposite to the western point of the island and fortress; thus avoiding the wasted tract prepared for him, and, at the same time, opening a more ready communication with the Bombay army under Stuart, and the fertile districts in the south. Besides, in that quarter he had every reason to expect a more favourable opportunity for attack. This expedient also enabled him to avoid the ground on which the sultan had purposed to give battle; and that chief, thwarted in all his measures, threw himself into the town, with the resolution of defending it to the last extremity.

CHAP. XIII.

A.D. 1799.

Despondency of his chiefs.

Thwarted in his measures.

On the 5th April, the British took their station opposite the western front of the fortress, at the distance of about two miles. The position was strong; their right resting on elevated ground, their left upon the river Cavery; and several *topes*, or groves of trees, afforded ample materials for the construction of the works. The enemy still occupied a defensive line behind an aqueduct, on which Colonels Wellesley and Shawe made a night-attack and were repulsed; but, be-

British position.

CHAP. XIII. — A. D. 1799.

ing reinforced, they carried it in open day. Meanwhile Floyd was detached to meet and escort General Stuart and the Bombay army. On the evening of the 13th, their signal-guns were heard; and they arrived late on the 14th, having been beset on their way by the whole body of the Mysorean cavalry, yet without sustaining any serious loss. General Floyd then marched to the southward in search of provisions; for an unexpected and alarming discovery had been made, that there was grain in the camp for only eighteen days' consumption. This extraordinary failure, into which Colonel Wilks mysteriously says, that after the lapse of nearly twenty years it was not yet time to inquire, did not, however, as supplies were obtained from various quarters, prove an impediment to the progress of the siege.

Arrival of the Bombay army.

Plan of attack on Seringapatam.

Meantime deep deliberation had been held as to the point whence the town might be most advantageously attacked. There was a south-western angle, by assailing which the besiegers could have obtained a lodgement on the island, and been thereby secured from the expected swelling of the Cavery, while at the extreme west, the walls, extending along the very brink of that river, could be reached only by crossing its channel. The fortifications at the first point, however, appeared both strong and complicated; while the most western angle projected beyond the main body of the fortress, and was not duly flanked or protected by the other defences. Besides, while regularly attacked from the south, it could be enfiladed from the northern bank of the Cavery. The river, too, evidently appeared fordable, as both men and cattle were seen passing without difficulty; and it was confidently expected that before the monsoon had augmented its waters, the campaign would be over. In pursuance of these views, General Stuart crossed the stream, and notwithstanding a vigorous resistance, and one very brisk sally by the garrison, succeeded in gaining a position in which he could effectually co-operate with the main attack.

Letter from Tippoo

On the 9th April, Tippoo wrote a letter to General

Harris, in which he merely asked why the English had entered his country, and made war upon him contrary to subsisting treaties, which he had never violated. The general in return briefly referred him to the communications of Marquis Wellesley, which had put an end to the correspondence. Wilks, who usually lets us into the interior of the Mysore councils, leaves us here in the dark as to the views by which the Indian chief was actuated. Meantime the trenches had been opened, and the works proceeded regularly and rapidly. On the 20th and 26th, two strongly-intrenched posts, which guarded the approaches to the wall, were carried by attacks under the direction, the one of Colonel Sherbrooke and the other of Colonel Wellesley. Before the second of these actions, the sultan, seeing his defences successively fall, and the siege quickly advancing to its termination, resolved again to solicit peace, though sensible it must be purchased with extensive sacrifices. He wrote, referring to the despatches of the governor-general, and proposing a conference of ambassadors. General Harris, in reply, after taking a view of recent events, announced, as the positive ultimatum, the cession of half his dominions, the payment of two crores of rupees, one immediately, and another in six months; finally, the delivery of four of his sons and four of his principal chiefs as hostages. These conditions were to be accepted in twenty-four hours, and the hostages and specie delivered on the following day; otherwise he reserved the right of extending these demands, till they should include even the provisional occupation of Seringapatam.

Trenches opened.

Tippoo proposes to negotiate.

Terms offered.

These terms, certainly not favourable, roused in the proud mind of Tippoo a violent burst of indignation. He raved against the arrogance and tyranny of the English, and declared his determination to abide the worst decrees of fate, and rather to die with arms in his hands, than drag a wretched life as a dependant upon infidels, thereby swelling the list of their pensioned rajahs and nabobs; he resolved, in short, not to give a reply. But six days afterwards, when the parallel had been com-

Indignation of Tippoo.

CHAP. XIII. A.D. 1799.

pleted, and nothing remained except the erection of the breaching-batteries, he again brought down his mind to the attempt to gain either delay or mitigation in the conditions of the treaty. A communication was received from him on the 28th, acknowledging the letter of General Harris as a friendly one, but adding, that as the points in question were weighty and not to be concluded without the intervention of ambassadors, he proposed to send two vakeels, or confidential messengers, to treat upon the subject. The general, however, was fully determined not to admit any such overture. In his reply he claimed credit for not making an advance on the terms already proposed, when by non-compliance they had been virtually declined. They were still offered; but no ambassadors could be admitted, unless accompanied by the hostages and the treasure; and the time during which they would be received was to terminate next day at three o'clock. On perusing this answer, the energies of his mind seemed entirely to fail. Yielding to despair and grief rather than rage, he sunk into a state of stupor, alternating with paroxysms of extravagant and groundless exultation. He no longer took any steady view of his danger, or rationally followed out the means by which it might still have been averted.

Renewed proposals of treaty.

Decisive reply.

Arrangements for effecting a breach.

At sunset, on the 28th, the place was marked out for the breaching-batteries; and, as they were only four hundred yards from the wall, no doubt was entertained of their speedily effecting their object. Two, of five and six guns respectively, were erected, seventy yards distant from each other; but as only one could be completed by the morning of the 30th, its shot was directed, not against the spot intended to be breached, which it was not desirable the enemy should yet know, but against the adjoining bastion, whose fire might have taken the assailants in flank. Enfilading batteries were also constructed, which were expected to render it impossible for the enemy to remain on the walls during the assault. On the 2d May, the two principal batteries were completed, and opened their full fire upon the part of the wall called the curtain. In the course of that day the works sustained extensive damage, and in twenty-four hours the breach became nearly practicable: in which view fascines, scaling-ladders, and other implements of storm, were brought into the trenches. During the previous night Lieutenant Lalor had crossed the river, which he found easily fordable, with a smooth rocky bottom, the retaining-wall of the fortress being only seven feet high, and presenting no obstacle whatever to the passage of troops. On the night of the third there was a practicable breach of a hundred feet wide, and one o'clock on the following day was fixed as the hour of assault.

Breach effected.

The sultan, meantime, as the term of his life and empire approached, instead of employing the usual means of deliverance from this extreme peril, occupied himself only in superstitious and delusive modes of prying into futurity. He had recourse, in his despair, even to the hated and persecuted Bramins, whom he desired to practise, though at immense cost, their wild and mystic incantations. All the astrologers, whether from hostile feelings to his highness, or from seeing that their credit could not be otherwise supported, announced the most imminent danger; prescribing, however, some absurd ceremonies and oblations by which it might possibly be averted. Under their directions he went through a solemn ablution, offered a pompous sacrifice, and steadily contemplated his face reflected in a jar of oil. Somewhat reassured by these sage precautions, and persuading himself that no attempt would be made during that day, he had sat down to his forenoon meal, when tidings arrived that the enemy were scaling the ramparts. He ran to meet them.

Superstitious resorts of Tippoo.

Responses of the astrologers.

The morning of the fourth day of May 1799 had been busily spent by the English in completing the breach and making preparations for the assault. The storming-party was composed of upwards of 4000 men, divided into two columns, who were instructed, after entering the breach, to file to the right and left along the top of the rampart. The command was intrusted to

Arrangements for storming the breach.

CHAP. XIII. A.D. 1799.

Sir David Baird.

Sir David Baird, who had been nearly four years immured as a captive in the gloomy dungeons of that fortress which he was now about to enter as a conqueror. The troops, in silent and awful expectation, awaited the decisive moment. A few minutes before one o'clock, Baird sent orders to the several regiments, desiring every man to be ready at an instant's notice. When the crisis came, he mounted the parapet, and stood in full view of both armies, in an heroic attitude, heightened by his noble and commanding figure. He then said, "Come, my brave fellows, follow me, and prove yourselves worthy the name of British soldiers." Both columns sprung forward like lightning; and seven minutes had not elapsed, when, in the face of a dreadful cannonade, the foremost assailants had crossed the river, leaped over the ditch, mounted the breach, and planted their colours on its summit. They were met by a gallant band of Mysoreans, from whose attack they suffered severely; but the breach was soon crowded with our soldiers, who overcame every obstacle, and established themselves on the rampart. Then, according to the orders received, they pushed on to the right and left along the top of the wall. The right detachment being supported by a powerful enfilading fire from the batteries, drove before them the enemy, who scarcely making any resistance fled out of the fort in great numbers,—and many, letting themselves drop from the wall by their turbans, were dashed against the rocky bottom and killed. The English thus cleared the whole of the southern rampart, and arrived at the eastern, where their advanced guard came in view of the palace.

British colours planted on the battlements.

Brave defence of the left walls.

The left column, meantime, encountered much more serious obstacles. On reaching the top of the wall they discovered, to their surprise, a deep ditch separating it from an inner rampart, where the enemy, in great force, kept up a destructive fire. The garrison at this point, too, animated by the arrival of the sultan in person, gallantly defended successive traverses, formed across the path of the assailants. The situation of the latter now became critical; all the commissioned officers who led the attack were either killed or wounded; and Lieutenant Farquhar, having assumed the command, immediately fell, and was succeeded by Brigade-major Lambton. Meantime, Captain Goodall, with a detachment from the right, had forced his way over the ditch, seized the inner rampart, and commenced upon the enemy a flanking-fire similar to that with which they had so severely annoyed his countrymen. The Mysoreans were accordingly driven to a spot where they beheld in their rear the other column which had advanced in the opposite direction. Seeing themselves thus completely hemmed in, they fled tumultuously, escaping by every possible outlet from the fortress, which was thus left completely in the hands of the besiegers.

Critical position of the assailants.

Rout of the Mysoreans.

General Baird, meantime, after the triumphant success of the right column, had allowed his troops an interval of rest, when certain officers brought notice that they had discovered the palace, and seen in a species of durbar or court a number of persons assembled, several of whom appeared to be of high consideration. The commander immediately directed Major Allan, who seems to have been well qualified for this delicate task, to summon them to an immediate surrender, in order to avert the calamities that would be inevitable were the royal residence to be taken by storm. This officer, on going towards the palace, saw several persons on a sort of balcony, to whom he announced his message. They manifested the greatest consternation, and soon brought the killedar or governor, who appeared much embarrassed, and endeavoured to gain time; but the major insisted upon entering with two other officers, by a broken part of the wall. He found a terrace, on which there was a numerous assemblage of armed men, before whom he laid his conditions, and laboured to tranquillize their minds, not only by presenting a white flag, but by placing his sword in their hands. They appeared alarmed and irresolute, positively declaring that Tippoo was not in the house, though his family and two of his sons were; but, on

State of the palace.

Major Allan summonses it to surrender.

His delicate mission.

CHAP. XIII. — A.D. 1799.

the major's urging the necessity of speedy decision, they withdrew as if for consultation. Persons were observed moving hastily backward and forward through the halls, in a manner that caused some anxiety; but Major Allan, fearing to excite suspicion or betray any symptom of doubt, declined the advice of his companions to take back his sword. At length, on his urgent solicitation, he was admitted to see the princes, whom he found seated on a carpet, surrounded by numerous attendants. "The recollection," says the major, "of Moiz-ad-Dien, whom on a former occasion I had seen delivered up, with his brother, hostages to Marquis Cornwallis,—the sad reverse of their fortunes,—their fear, which, notwithstanding their struggles to conceal, was but too evident,—excited the strongest emotions of compassion in my mind. I took Moiz-ad-Dien by the hand, and endeavoured by every mode in my power to remove his fears." This prince concurred with the others in giving assurance that the *padsha* was not in the palace,—and, on the urgent representation of the English officers, he agreed, with strong reluctance, that the gate should be thrown open. General Baird had already approached with a considerable force, and instantly sent back the major with Colonel Close to bring out the princes. After expressing much alarm and many objections, they allowed themselves to be conducted into the presence of the British commander. The general was greatly irritated, from having just heard that thirteen prisoners had been murdered during the siege; and his feelings were probably heightened by the recollection of his own sufferings in the same place; but, when he saw these unfortunate youths led out as captives, every harsher sentiment yielded to that of pity, and he gave them the most solemn assurances that they had nothing to fear. They were escorted to the camp with arms presented, and all the honours due to their rank.

Admitted to see the princes.

The gate thrown open.

Moderation of General Baird.

Search for the Sultan.

Sir David's object being now to obtain possession of the person of the sultan, he proceeded with a body of troops to make the most diligent search in every corner of the palace. He forbore, indeed, to enter the zenana, but strictly guarded every passage by which any one could leave it. No trace of the individual he sought could any where be found; till at length, by severe threats, a confession was extorted from the killedar, that his royal master was lying wounded, as he supposed, in a gateway, to which he offered to conduct the conqueror. The latter immediately accompanied him to the spot, where he beheld a mournful spectacle: it was here that the fiercest combat had raged; the wounded and dead were lying piled in heaps over each other; while the darkness which had just fallen rendered the scene still more dismal. It was indispensable, however, immediately to ascertain the fact; torches were brought, and the bodies successively removed till they discovered the sultan's horse, then his palanquin, and beneath it a wounded man, who was soon recognised as a confidential servant, and who pointed out the spot where his sovereign had fallen. The body was found, and forthwith identified by the killedar and the other attendants. The features were in no degree distorted, but presented an aspect of stern composure; the eyes were open, and the appearance of life was so strong, that Colonel Wellesley and Major Allan could not, for some time, believe him actually dead. It appears that, after having issued armed from the palace, with a band of trusty followers, he saw the English advancing along the rampart, and his men fleeing. He rallied them by the utmost efforts of his voice and example, shooting several of the enemy with his own hand; and he thus called forth that resistance which had proved so formidable. At length, when the determined valour of the British troops prevailed against all opposition, he was left at one time almost alone, and obliged to accompany the fugitives; but, with a few resolute adherents, he maintained the combat, till, being exposed to a fire from different quarters, he received two musket-balls in the side. His horse was killed under him; and, becoming faint with loss of blood, he was unable to make his way through the crowd. He was over-

Finding the body of Tippoo.

His gallant exertions.

CHAP. XIII. A. D. 1799.

taken by a party of the conquerors, when one of his attendants besought him, as the only means of saving his life, to make himself known; but he peremptorily forbade the disclosure. An English soldier then made an attempt to detach his sword-belt, when the sultan, with all his remaining strength, made a cut at him, and wounded him on the knee. The man presently fired, the ball entered the temple, and the wound proved speedily mortal. The body was carried to the palace, and was afterwards interred, with royal honours, in the splendid sepulchre of the Lâll Baug, erected by Hyder.

His death-wound.

Thus terminated a dynasty, which, though short, and limited in respect of territorial dominion, was undoubtedly the most vigorous and best organized of any that had sprung out of the wreck of the Mogul empire. It arose, indeed, from the distracted state of India, and rested almost entirely on the personal character of its two rulers, the qualities of whose minds, striking though dissimilar, we have had repeated occasion to describe. It may be farther noticed, however, that, while Hyder entered on his career unable to read or write, and remained always a stranger to these primary elements of human knowledge, Tippoo, amid the most active cares of government, retained the habits and character of a man of letters. He read and wrote almost incessantly, carried on an extensive correspondence, and became the historian of his own exploits. Yet the adoption of hasty and superficial theories, in preference to the practical good sense which had guided his predecessor, led him often into crude and rash innovations, which were followed by disastrous consequences. The absolute indifference with which the subject of religion was viewed by Hyder, though marking a degraded state of moral feeling, induced him in his administration to adopt the wise measure of general toleration. His son's mind, on the contrary, was occupied and almost engrossed by his Mussulman zeal, which became the chief source of his crimes and follies. He fancied himself a sort of militant apostle, who was to spread his faith over the world.

Termination of the dynasty.

Acquirements of Tippoo.

His Mussulman zeal.

Combining this design with his projects of ambition, he waged sacred wars on every side; against the Nazarene English, against the Bramin Mahrattas, and against the Pagan and licentious nayrs. Ultimately, as we have seen, he sunk into the most childish superstition, calling not only upon the Mohammedans, but the persecuted Hindoos, to practise their arts of divination. After the capture of Seringapatam, when his repositories were searched, along with treaties, state-papers, and political correspondence, there was found a record of his dreams and their interpretation, of which Colonel Beatson has preserved some curious specimens. At one time, when he was threatened with an invasion of the Mahrattas, he dreamed that a young man came up and accosted him, who in the course of conversation proved to be a female. Hence he sagely inferred that his enemy, who at first had a manly and formidable appearance, would in battle prove no better than women. On another occasion, when he was about to make war with the native Christians, he was favoured with the vision of a cow and a calf, the former resembling a tiger in aspect and fierceness; it had a slight motion in its fore-legs, but no hind-legs. He resolved to kill this cow, but awoke before he could accomplish his purpose. Hence, however, he thought himself entitled to infer, that he would kill the Christians as he had proposed to kill the cow; that the slight movement of the fore-legs indicated faint attempts at resistance, while the absence of the hinder-legs proved that they would have no alliances to support them. These lucubrations form a strange contrast to his display of talent on other occasions; nor can it be wondered that public measures resting upon such conclusions should not always have proved very prosperous.

CHAP. XIII. A.D. 1799.

His ambitious projects and superstition.

His dremas.

This prince, owing to his long wars with the English, his cruel treatment of the captives, and the imbittered enmity which he manifested, was regarded by them almost as a monster in human shape. Yet when their armies penetrated into the interior of his kingdom, they found it flourishing, highly cultivated, and seemingly

Opinions entertained of him.

CHAP. XIII. A. D. 1799.

Attachment of his people.

well governed. His people always showed a strong attachment to him, and the inhabitants of the ceded districts were ever ready to embrace his cause. But to the conquered nations he was at all times a cruel master, and rendered himself the object of their inextinguishable hatred; a cause to which his downfal may, in a great measure, be attributed. It has been said, with the general approbation of British authors, that "Hyder was born to create an empire, Tippoo to lose one;" yet it may be observed, that he maintained a complete ascendency over all the native states, some of which had matched, and even overmatched, his father. He fell beneath the English power, employed on a scale, and wielded with an ability, of which, in the course of Indian history, there had been no example.

Mysore at the disposal of the British.

Mysore, having been thus completely conquered, was placed, as to its future arrangements, entirely at the disposal of the British government. The Mahrattas had taken no share in the expedition, and the nizam knew that he must content himself with whatever the victors might choose to give. The governor-general took for the Company, in full sovereignty, the coast of Canara, the district of Coimbetoor, the passes of the Ghauts, and Seringapatam itself, the capital and main channel of intercourse. He thus secured the whole sea-coast, and an easy communication across the peninsula. To the nizam was assigned a large tract of territory adjoining to his dominions. Another portion was reserved for the purpose of being offered to the Mahrattas, on conditions which, however, as will be hereafter seen, they did not choose to accept. There remained yet an extensive district in the interior of Mysore, which Marquis Wellesley judged most expedient not to partition, but to form it into a native kingdom under the protection and control of Britain. The question then arose, as to the prince in whom the supreme dignity was to be vested. The governor-general would not have been disinclined to bestow it on one of the family of Tippoo; but he justly considered, that the recollection of the

Its dismemberment.

Partial reconstruction

recent greatness of their house must have rendered them always hostile to the power by whom its downfal had been achieved. It appeared, therefore, more advisable, after making a liberal provision for these princes, to draw forth from their deep humiliation the ancient race of rajahs, to whom the people were still fondly attached. The representative of this house, a minor of five years old, and his mother, were found in great poverty and neglect; from which, amid the applauses of their countrymen, they were raised to the splendour and to some share of the power of Asiatic royalty.

Heir of the ancient rajahs.

CHAPTER XIV.

Mahratta War, and Conquest of Central Hindostan.

Great Power of the Mahrattas—Shao succeeds as Rajah—Able Administration of Ballajee Wishwanath—Bajee Rao succeeds—Rise of Holkar and Scindia—Great Power of the Peishwa—Reduction of the Pirate Angria—Madoo Rao becomes Peishwa—His able Government—Ragoba—He is expelled by the Ministers—Forms an Alliance with the Government of Bombay—Keating's Expedition—Proceedings at Bombay disallowed—Treaty—War renewed—March against Poonah—Shameful Capitulation—Campaign of General Goddard—Exploits of Popham and Camac—Mahrattas allied with Britain—Increased Power of Mahadajee Scindia—His Death—Death of Madoo Rao—Various Intrigues—Jealousies of Britain—Dissensions of Scindia and Holkar—Defeat of Scindia and the Peishwa—Subsidiary Alliance with Britain—Opening of the Campaign—General Wellesley enters Poonah—Negotiations with Scindia and the Rajah of Berar—Hostilities commenced—Battle of Assaye—Of Argaom—Siege of Gawilghur—Treaty with the Rajah of Berar—Force of the Enemy in Central Hindostan—Battle of Coel—Capture of Alighur—Reduction of Delhi—The Mogul Emperor—Final Defeat of the Enemy—Treaty with Scindia—Rupture with Holkar—Retreat of Colonel Monson—Siege of Delhi—Defeats sustained by Holkar—Siege of Bhurtpore—Repulse of the English—Treaty—Hostile Conduct of Scindia—New System of Policy in Britain—Marquis Cornwallis comes out as Governor-General—Dies, and is succeeded by Sir George Barlow—Treaties with Scindia and Holkar—Lord Minto's Administration.

CHAP. XIV.

A.D. 1680.

Mahratta kingdom.

In prosecuting, without interruption, the train of British conquest in Southern India, we have lost sight of the Mahrattas, except in reference to their relations with the government of Mysore. The reader, however, will recollect the steps by which that people raised themselves on the decline of the Mogul empire, and became the most powerful instrument in its overthrow. They would even have occupied its place, had they not encountered the more regular and formidable armies of the Afghans, from whom they sustained two such mighty defeats as would have annihilated any force which did not possess in itself a strong principle of vitality. But they soon recruited their strength out of the warlike and roving population of their mountain-districts; and as the Afghans did not attempt a permanent establishment in the Indian peninsula, the Mahrattas acquired again a decided preponderance among the native states. Only Mysore, in the height of its greatness, for a short time disputed their supremacy; but when that throne was first shaken, and then subverted, the foreign power by which this triumph had been achieved became the only rival to them; and the question soon arose, which of the two was to rule Hindostan. Before coming to the decisive struggle, however, some internal movements of this government, and some previous transactions with the English presidencies, seem to demand our notice.

Checked by the Afghans.

Sevajee had exercised a power nearly absolute over his rude followers, and the reverence cherished for his name enabled him to transmit the Mahratta sceptre to his posterity. But the princes born to his throne did not possess the active and daring hardihood necessary for treading in the steps of such a progenitor. Indulging in ease and voluptuousness, they gradually intrusted the arduous concerns of government and war to their ministers and generals. Then followed a consequence almost inevitable in oriental dynasties: the minister, or still more the general, in whose hands the actual administration was lodged, and who had the disposal of all favours and offices, soon became the real depositary of power, whom the sovereign would have sought in vain to displace, being in fact his master and that of the kingdom. Yet a certain veneration attached to the original race, and the recollections connected with the his-

Power of Sevajee.

Influence of luxury on his successors.

CHAP. XIV. tory of its founder would have made it unsafe actually

A.D. 1708. to depose the legitimate rajah. It was much easier as well as safer to maintain him in ease and luxury, as a splendid pageant, while all the real authority was exercised in his name by the individual who presided in the council or army.

Shao, the grandson of Sevajee.

This consummation, which always took place in the course of two or three generations, was, in the case now before us, precipitated by a remarkable accident. At the capture of Rayree, in 1690, by the troops of Aurengzebe, the grandson of Sevajee and his mother, having fallen into the hands of the conquerors, were carried to the Mogul country, where Begum Sahib, the emperor's daughter, took an interest in the young captive, and obtained permission to educate him under her own eye. His majesty, when visiting the princess, contracted a great fondness for the youth, whom, instead of his proper name of Sevajee, he used to address by that of Shao, which alluded, in an ironical manner, to the thievish vocation of his ancestors. He married him successively to the daughters of two considerable chiefs of his own nation, and celebrated his nuptials by rich presents, among which was the sword of his father, taken in his capital, and distinguished in the East under the name of Bhowanee.

Shao's return to the Mahrattas.

After the death of Aurengzebe, Shao remained with that emperor's son, Azim, who, wishing to excite divisions in the Mahratta nation, then carrying on a furious predatory warfare against the Moguls, sent home the young prince. During his absence the regency had been held by his cousin, Rajah Rama, and afterwards by the widow of that officer, Tara Bye, who felt exceedingly inclined to continue in the exercise of her high functions; but the people retained such an attachment to the direct line of Sevajee, that she was obliged to give way, and Shao, in March 1708, was seated on the throne of his ancestors. During a long reign he displayed some ability, and did not absolutely sink from his place as a sovereign; yet the debilitating influence of oriental

Recovers the throne.

habits was heightened in his case by his education in the Mogul seraglio. He soon discovered a lively taste for pleasure, and a disposition to devolve on others the burdensome cares of government; but fortunately for himself, or at least for the greatness of the state, he placed his chief confidence in Ballajee Wishwanath. This future head of the Mahratta confederacy occupied originally an inferior situation in the revenue; and at his first rise had so little of the adventurous character of his tribe, that he could not sit upon horseback without a man on each side to support him. His consummate talents and address, however, soon raised him to high consideration with Shao, whose object was rather to re-establish order, and cement his power by a conciliatory system, than to lead his countrymen in their predatory campaigns. By a very able negotiation, this minister extricated his master from a quarrel with Angria, and induced that powerful chief to own his supremacy. Shao was so highly pleased with him on this occasion, that he raised him to the dignity of *peishwa*, usually translated general; but which, embracing as it did all the branches of administration, seems to have had more analogy to the office of vizier in the Ottoman empire. Ballajee soon engrossed the whole power, and ruled successfully, but rather as a legislator than a warrior. He contrived, by ties of common interest, to unite together the somewhat discordant elements of which the Mahratta confederacy was composed, and to fit them for those united efforts that afterwards rendered them so formidable. He introduced order into the finances, encouraged agriculture, and brought all the branches of the administration into a regular system.

Love of pleasure.

Ballajee Wishwanath.

His diplomatic skill.

After a brief government of six years, which, however, was found sufficiently long to effect these important objects, Ballajee died in October 1720, leaving two sons, the eldest of whom, Bajee Rao or Row, had been trained under his own eye both to business and arms, and had proved himself in the former equal, in the latter superior, to his parent and preceptor. He urged his

Bajee Rao succeeds his father.

CHAP. XIV. master to much bolder schemes of ambition than had occupied the views of Wishwanath; drawing his attention to the Mogul empire, in which all the Indian ideas of greatness were centred, reduced now to such a state of weakness and disunion, that it must present an easy prey to the first bold assailant. Shao, though not personally a soldier, was dazzled by these prospects of dominion, and gave his entire sanction to the designs of his minister. The peishwa, however, disturbed by domestic rivalry, and involved in a contest with the nizam, or Subahdar of the Deccan, could not for some years follow out his scheme of aggrandizement: And when at length he assembled his forces, and began his march to the main seat of Mogul power, he was seized with a sudden illness, and died on the banks of the Nerbudda in 1740, after holding office nineteen years. Under him two chiefs, Holkar and Scindia, who, with their posterity, were destined to dispute the sovereignty of Hindostan, rose from very low stations into considerable importance. The former, who sprang from the class of Sudra or labourers, had, by his military talents and spirit, collected a small party of horse, with which he attached himself to the army of the peishwa. Scindia, though claiming descent from a family of the high-born tribe of Rajpoots, belonged to a decayed and illegitimate branch, which had sunk so low that he began his career by carrying the general's slippers; yet, by the diligence and dexterity with which he executed this menial function, he attracted the notice of that commander, and laid the foundation of his own greatness. These two chiefs, having distinguished themselves by several daring exploits, rose gradually, till at length they were intrusted with separate commands; and favoured by the general propensity of the Hindoos to obey only their immediate superiors, they subsequently acquired an independent political power.

A. D. 1740.

Bold schemes of empire.

Death of Bajee Rao.

Holkar.

Scindia.

Hereditary peishwa.

The office of peishwa was now nearly established as hereditary, and the eldest son of Bajee Rao, who prefixed to his father's name that of Balajee, after some

CHAP. XIV.

A.D. 1749.

opposition from Raghojee Bhonslay, another aspirant, succeeded to that high station. The disputes with this last chieftain, however, and other occurrences, suspended the design of subverting the imperial throne. The ordinary exaction of chout, or a fourth of the tribute, was stipulated to be paid by the Mogul, while Raghojee made the most desolating inroads into Bengal. In 1749 Shao died, when the dignity of rajah, which had been in some degree maintained by his personal character as well as his descent from Sevajee, sank into total insignificance. Ballajee even intended to suppress it altogether, especially as there was some doubt as to the legitimacy of the young prince nominated to the succession; but after some consideration he determined to preserve, though with reduced state and expense, this shadow of royalty. His measures were strenuously opposed by Suckwar Bye, the favourite wife of the late rajah; but that lady, among other manœuvres, had rashly announced an intention to devote herself to the flames on the death of her husband. The peishwa contrived, even while apparently dissuading her from fulfilling this design, to bring it before her family and the public in such a manner as made it impossible for her, according to Indian ideas, to avoid this dreadful sacrifice. Having gained over Raghojee Bhonslay, and transferred the seat of government from Satara to Poonah, the peishwa became the sole and undisputed head of the Mahratta confederation. For several years he was involved in foreign connexions, the wars and politics of the Deccan and Carnatic, and the reduction of the piratical power of Angria. The last of these objects gave rise to certain achievements of a memorable description, in which the English bore the most conspicuous part.

Death of the rajah.

Suckwar Bye.

The coast of the Concan, between Bombay and Goa, which belongs to the Mahratta territory, has always been the seat of tribes who exercised in piratical expeditions those predatory habits which elsewhere impelled them to inroads by land. In the middle of the seventeenth century, during the first rise of the Mahrattas,

Concan coast.

CHAP. XIV
A. D. 1755

Conajee Angria's ambitious schemes.

and while they were carrying on a maritime war with the Mogul, one of their officers, Conajee Angria, conceived the design of founding an independent kingdom. He was greatly aided in his project by the barrier of precipitous rocks, which on this coast rise out of the sea, like the hill-forts from the Indian plain. On the two insulated cliffs of Gheria and Severndroog reigned this chief and his successors of the same name, where they became more and more formidable, till at length they felt themselves able to cope with the greatest European powers, and even aspired to the dominion of the adjacent seas. They made many valuable captures from different nations, who, through dread of their ravages, could not proceed along the shore without a convoy. In February 1754, a Dutch squadron of three ships, carrying 50, 36, and 18 guns respectively, was attacked, and the whole either burned or taken. The British then considered themselves called upon to take vigorous steps for putting down this growing and dangerous power; and the Mahrattas willingly afforded their co-operation. In March 1755, Commodore James sailed with a squadron against Severndroog, where Angria's ships were stationed; but these last, on the approach of the enemy, slipped their cables and ran out to sea. They were of light construction, and the crews, by fastening to flagstaves their robes, quilts, and even turbans, caught every breath of wind, and completely outsailed the English. The commodore then steered for the place itself, which was found to consist of several forts on the island and opposite coast, the works of which were either cut out of the solid rock, or strongly framed of blocks ten or twelve feet square. By throwing in bombs, however, which blew up a large magazine, and caused a general conflagration in the principal stronghold, he spread such an alarm, that the inhabitants and garrison successively evacuated the different posts. Rear-Admiral Watson having arrived with a much larger fleet, proceeded to the attack of Gheria, the capital, which Colonel Clive undertook to blockade on the land side. On the 11th

Opposed by the British.

Expedition against Angria.

Attack of Gheria.

February 1756, the several ships took their positions, and next day opened so tremendous a fire that the batteries were soon silenced. On the 13th the enemy delivered up the town, solely, as it appeared, through terror at this overwhelming discharge of artillery; for the fortifications were of such strength, that no weight of metal could ever have effected a breach. The treasure, vessels, guns, and every thing constituting the strength of this piratical state, fell into the hands of the victorious squadron.

Capture of the town.

The influence of the Mahratta confederation continued constantly to increase. Scindia and Holkar, on the invitation of the Nabob of Oude, had crossed the Jumna, and invaded the Rohilla territory, which they soon overran, but were obliged to retire on the approach of the Afghan monarch. But it was not till 1760 and 1761 that several grand expeditions were undertaken, which promised at first to make them masters of the Mogul throne, and extend their dominion over the whole of India. Having, however, provoked the resentment of Ahmed Abdalla, they experienced those signal overthrows, particularly in the battle of Panniput, which we have already noticed in tracing the fall of that empire. The tidings of that fatal day filled all Maharashtra with mourning; and the disaster pressed with peculiar weight on Ballajee Rao, who, having suffered for some time under declining health, now sunk under a load of grief, and died in June 1761.

Power of the Mahratta confederation.

Death of Ballajee Rao.

As the office of peishwa had become quite hereditary, Madoo Rao, son of the deceased minister, was immediately elevated to that distinguished rank, under the regency of his uncle, Ragonaut Rao. This chief, afterwards well known to the English under the familiar name of Ragoba, had already acquired considerable military reputation. Four years, however, had not elapsed, when his young nephew showed a power and decision of character, which fitted him for executing in person the duties of his exalted station. In 1764 and 1765 he undertook his celebrated expedition against Hyder, the triumphant issue of which displayed at once his own

Madoo Rao.

CHAP. XIV

A.D. 1772.

His great energy

abilities, and the almost inexhaustible resources of his military system. He carried on also, chiefly through the agency of his general Trimbuck Mama, the other enterprise against the same ruler, which is mentioned in the history of Mysore. Finally, towards the close of his reign, the peishwa again undertook to establish his supremacy in the very centre of the imperial dominions. A great army under Scindia overran Rohilcund, and Shah Allum, who inherited the mighty name of Great Mogul, having exchanged the protection of the English for the aid of the Mahrattas, enabled the latter people to seize all that was left of the power which had so long been held supreme over India.

Improvements in the administration

The young ruler made considerable improvements in the different branches of the state, especially in the collection of the revenue and the administration of justice. He could not extirpate the corruption so deeply rooted in all Indian governments; but he studiously afforded protection to agriculture, which, allowing for the inferior fertility of the country, was then more flourishing in Maharashtra than in any other part of Hindostan. The revenue drawn from the people is estimated by Mr Grant Duff at ten millions sterling, though little more than seven is understood to have entered the treasury.

His army.

The army consisted of 50,000 good cavalry, while the contingents of Scindia, Holkar, and other feudatory chiefs, raised it to about 100,000. They were followed to the field by crowds of irregular infantry, who were little better than camp-followers, and by bands of Pindaree horse, fit only for plunder, but very eminently skilled in that vocation.

Narrain Rao.

Madoo Rao died in 1772 without issue, and was succeeded by his next brother, Narrain Rao, a youth not more than seventeen. He was placed in a difficult situation; for the office of peishwa, after having crushed beneath it that of rajah, was itself beginning to lose its influence. His uncle, Ragoba, was not likely to view without jealousy the elevation of so young a rival; while a body of experienced ministers, trained under successive peishwas to a thorough acquaintance with the affairs of state, were beginning to contend for the supreme direction. In these circumstances, a temporary and apparent calm was followed by a dreadful commotion. On the morning of the 30th August 1773, Narrain Rao, having observed some unusual agitation among the troops, desired one of the ministers to be on the alert; but the warning was neglected. The unfortunate prince had gone in the afternoon to repose in a private chamber, when a band of soldiers burst by an obscure entrance into the palace. They at first pretended that they came to demand arrears of pay, about which they had for some time been clamouring; but it soon appeared that they were impelled by a much darker purpose. Narrain, roused from slumber, ran into his uncle's apartments, and threw himself into his arms, entreating that he would save him. The latter at first appeared to interpose in favour of his relative; but Somer Sing, the ringleader, said,—"I have not gone thus far to ensure my own destruction; let him go, or you shall die with him." He then extricated himself from the grasp of the youth, whom, as well as a faithful servant that had also clung round his neck, the conspirators instantly despatched with their swords.

His fate.

All eyes were turned to Ragoba, as the person by whom this crime must have been suggested. For some time no proof could be obtained, till Ram Sastree, one of the most respectable and upright of the ministers, having collected various evidences, brought the charge so home to him, that he at length confessed he had signed the order to seize the person of his nephew, but denied having in any degree sanctioned his death. A numerous body of Indian politicians still believe that such was the truth, and that a more criminal hand made an alteration in the writing, of which traces were asserted to be visible. In these cases, however, the strong feelings of the public always adopt the darker belief; yet Ragoba mounted without opposition the throne to which he had thus cleared the way, and soon after departed on an expedi-

Ragoba.

His criminality.

CHAP. XIV. — A.D. 1773.

Expedition against Hyder.

tion against Hyder, who was in the field attempting to regain some of the territory lost in the former war. But during his absence on this occasion, the ministers, partly sharing the indignation of the public,—partly seeing the opportunity of drawing into their own hands the supreme authority,—entered into a combination for raising to the office of peishwa the unborn son of Gunga Bye, widow of the late peishwa, who had been left in a state of pregnancy. The lady was conveyed to the fortress of Poorundur, accompanied, it is alleged, by a number of Bramins' wives in the same condition, that in the event of the issue proving a female, a male child might be immediately substituted. Ragoba, meantime, had been completely successful in his warlike enterprise; but learning the dangers to which he was exposed at home, hastily concluded a peace, and having endeavoured, by extensive concessions, to conciliate the nizam, hastened back towards Poonah. The ministers sent against him Trimbuck Mama, the most martial of their body, who confidently expected to raise his military fame still higher by the defeat of the peishwa; but he was fatally disappointed. That ruler, though with an inferior army, charged in person at the head of a select corps of ten thousand men, and in twenty minutes completely routed the army of Trimbuck, who fell mortally wounded into the hands of his adversary. Had the conqueror proceeded direct upon Poonah, where, on the arrival of the tidings, the utmost confusion and consternation prevailed, he might probably have resumed, almost without opposition, his wonted power and dignity. But, on the contrary, he marched northward towards the Nerbudda, in hopes of being joined by Holkar and Scindia, who had encamped in that quarter. By this step he lost a favourable opportunity; the government of Poonah recovered from its panic, and collected a force of 50,000 men, while by intrigues and high offers they had induced the nizam to break his treaty with their enemy, and to co-operate in their designs. To crown their good fortune, Gunga Bye produced a son, declared, indeed, by the opposite

Plan for supplanting him.

His success.

Impolitic course of procedure.

party to be supposititious, but now believed to have been the genuine offspring of Narrain Rao. At the age of forty days, the infant was formally inaugurated in the office of peishwa.

Deserted by his army

Ragoba's own army were so disgusted with the course he had followed, that they deserted in great numbers, and, after passing the Nerbudda, he found himself at the head of only 7000 cavalry. At Indore, notwithstanding, he met Scindia and Holkar, from whom he received a cordial reception and liberal promises, and was empowered to recruit his thinned ranks from their territory. He then advanced to the banks of the Tuptee, with the view of completing the negotiation into which he had entered with the English government at Bombay.

Views of the Company.

It was at this period a very favourite object with the Company to secure their possession of that settlement, by adding to it the port of Bassein, with Salsette and several smaller islands in its vicinity. Permission had been given to maintain an envoy at the court of Poonah, who was instructed to watch every opportunity of obtaining these much-desired cessions; and the Bombay government, on receiving the application from Ragoba for aid to restore him to supreme power, determined to employ it as the means of accomplishing their own purposes. It was contrary, indeed, to the orders and policy of the Directors to interfere in the internal disputes of the native powers; and the support of a usurper and assassin was no very creditable mode of realizing their objects. But these considerations were overlooked; and indeed on this last point their defenders assert that they were very imperfectly informed, and really believed the peishwa innocent of the murder, and the infant illegitimate. Even that prince, however, started when he heard the enormous conditions which his new allies attached to their assistance, particularly the cession of Bassein and Salsette. But seeing that Scindia and Holkar, on whom he placed much dependence, had been gained over by his enemies, he felt the necessity of submitting to every demand of the English, who, in the mean time, had taken

Neglected of their established policy

CHAP. XIV. — A. D. 1777.

the liberty of possessing themselves of Salsette and its dependencies. In respect to their requisition, indeed, of a large sum of money, he was obliged to profess, what his circumstances rendered exceedingly probable, an absolute inability to furnish it, but deposited jewels to the value of six lacks of rupees, and stipulated the cession of an extent of territory, from which the sum demanded might afterwards be drawn.

British forces landed at Cambay.

With a view to the fulfilment of this treaty, Colonel Keating landed at Cambay with a force which was raised to 2500 men. Having begun his march, he was joined by an army, or rather mob, under Ragoba, amounting to about 20,000, bearing a very martial appearance, though quite incapable of acting with effect in combination with regular troops. The Indian chief was inclined to delay offensive operations; but the English urged the propriety of advancing upon Poonah, as the only course by which the war could be brought to a decisive issue. They proceeded accordingly as far as Arass, where they were attacked by a large Mahratta force composed chiefly of cavalry. The enemy made several desperate charges, and the battle continued long with various and even doubtful fortune, though at length it ended in the complete repulse of the enemy. Keating's loss was, however, so severe, amounting in his small detachment to 222, including eleven officers, that he suspended his intention of advancing at present upon the capital, and awaited at Dubhoy the termination of the rainy season and the arrival of further reimforcements. This partial success, meanwhile, produced an impression favourable to the British and their ally. Several of the late adherents of the ministry espoused their cause,—even the nizam began to waver. The next campaign was therefore expected to open under very promising auspices, when circumstances occurred which gave an entirely new turn to affairs.

Defeat of the Mahratta force.

The Company, who had hitherto left the three provinces of Bengal, Madras, and Bombay, separate and independent, were now induced, by the inconveniences which had arisen from this arrangement, to establish one central authority. They vested in the governor-general and council of Calcutta a controlling power over the two other presidencies. The latter, however, were not as yet much inclined to acquiesce; and that of Bombay in particular had, in the late transactions, made very little reference to their new superiors. The supreme council, on being apprized of their proceedings, strongly condemned them, as unjust in themselves, and contrary to the policy inculcated by the Company, of avoiding all interference in the internal concerns of Indian states. This step is generally blamed by English politicians, though, as it appears to us, without any good reason; but there does seem room to question the propriety of superseding entirely the Bombay government, and sending Colonel Upton direct from Bengal to conclude a fresh treaty. This had certainly the effect of placing the inferior presidency in a disadvantageous position, and of exposing it to the contempt of the native powers. It has also been observed, that the Hindoo courts interpret every conciliatory step as a sign of weakness, and immediately rise in their demands. Nana Furnavese, a Bramin minister, who had attained an entire ascendency at Poonah, assumed a lofty tone; and indeed, as the English continued to demand the cession of Bassein and Salsette, he complained, not without some cause, that, after having frankly admitted the unwarrantable ground on which their claim to these places rested, they should still wish to retain possession of them. In short, the negotiation took so unfavourable a turn, that Colonel Upton announced to the councils both of Calcutta and Bombay, that in all probability it would be immediately broken off. Suddenly, however, the Mahratta minister, seeing that the British authorities were really determined to renew the war, and consequently had in no degree been actuated by fear, yielded almost every point in dispute. A treaty was concluded in Poorundur, by which they obtained all the places demanded; while a month was fixed as the period within which the army of Ragoba

Governor-general and council.

Conflicting policy.

Concessions to the British.

Treaty of Poorundur.

CHAP. XIV. — A.D. 1778.

was to be reduced, and their protection entirely withdrawn from him.

New elements of confusion.

Affairs seemed amicably settled, when the wheel of events brought round another remarkable change. The Court of Directors at home, on being apprized of the arrangement made by the government of Bombay with that chief, were more swayed by its immediate advantages than by their general principles, and sent out a cordial approbation of the measure. Their despatch to this effect arrived immediately after the conclusion of the treaty of Poorundur. It was impossible at once to annul so solemn a transaction; but the council at Bombay exulted in an extraordinary degree over the superior presidency, which had so harshly censured their conduct, and became accordingly disposed to find pretexts for placing themselves again in a hostile attitude towards the administration at Poonah. They by no means withdrew entirely their protection from Ragoba; they even derived encouragement from intrigues carried on to re-establish his influence, which, however, were baffled by the profound political skill of Furnavese. The latter received with great favour a Frenchman named St Lubin, who appears to have held out to him the expectation of a strong military force from Europe. It was concluded, on the whole, that Nana had shown a hostile disposition; and Mr Hornby, the governor of Bombay, entered on the minutes a general review of Mahratta affairs, in which he concluded that they were fast verging to a crisis that would compel the English either to take some active and decisive part, or to relinquish for ever the hopes of improving their own condition in the west of India. Mr Hastings, too, though he had concurred in the censure on the Bombay government, now began to think that better terms might have been gained by the treaty of Poorundur. He granted authority to them "to assist in tranquillizing the dissensions of the Mahratta state;" to promote which object he sent Colonel Leslie with a strong detachment to march across the centre of India from Bengal to the western coast.

Proceedings of the Bombay council.

Presumed necessity for action.

Hasty proceedings.

The authorities at Bombay were not only highly elated by the sanction thus given to their schemes, but even adopted the rash resolution of accomplishing them with their own resources, lest the glory should be shared by the troops under Leslie. In vain did Mr Draper represent to them the importance of delay till their forces should be concentrated. Mr Carnac, who had now the lead in the council, not only carried his point of immediately opening the campaign, but was himself placed at the head of a committee to aid in the direction of military operations. The command, in consequence of the claims of seniority, devolved on Colonel Egerton, whose health was extremely infirm, and who had acquired all his experience, as a soldier, in Germany, so that an Indian war presented a scene altogether new to him. However, a force of 3900 men, of whom only 600 were British, landed at Panwell, and advanced to attack the capital of the Mahratta empire. The march of an army in that country, encumbered with baggage, bullocks, and beasts of burden, is always slow; but the tardiness of this movement was altogether unprecedented. In eleven days they had not proceeded above eight miles. A week more brought them, on the 9th January 1779, to the village of Tullygaom, where they found in front a mass of about 50,000 men, who began to skirmish in their usual desultory manner. They did not, however, venture on a serious attack; but though nothing had occurred which might not have been foreseen with the utmost certainty, Mr Carnac and Colonel Cockburn, who, in consequence of Egerton's sickness, had succeeded to the command, formed the fatal determination, from which nothing could dissuade them, of immediate retreat. Such a step, in the face of a Mahratta host, with clouds of cavalry, was more perilous than the boldest advance. The English troops had scarcely begun to fall back, when their rearguard was assailed by the whole force of the enemy. Fortunately it was commanded by Captain Hartley, a young officer of high and rising reputation, who gallantly withstood several most furious charges; and they were finally un-

Tardy operations.

Rash determination to retreat.

Gallant conduct of Captain Hartley.

CHAP. XIV. able to make a serious impression on any part of the line.
A. D. 1779. The loss, however, was very severe, amounting to upwards of three hundred, among whom were fifteen European officers.

Disgraceful convention of Worgaom. After this action, the military authorities decided that even retreat was no longer practicable, and consequently that there remained no resource but negotiation. This, in such circumstances, was equivalent to offering the enemy a *carte blanche* as to the terms on which the invaders should be allowed to return to Bombay. In vain did Hartley remonstrate against that humiliating step, and point out a course by which the retreat might have been effected; in vain did Carnac advance objections, which, however, he forbore to press; nothing could shake the pusillanimous determination of the commanders. They were even prepared to give up Ragoba, had not that chief made a private agreement to surrender himself to Scindia. The British themselves, by treating with the latter, obtained somewhat more favourable terms: still the convention of Worgaom, if not the most disastrous, was much the most disgraceful event which had marked the annals of our army in India. All the points in dispute were yielded; all the recent acquisitions were to be restored; and orders were sent that the troops now marching from Bengal should proceed no farther.

Indignation excited by it. Both at Bombay and at home the utmost indignation was felt at this convention. Mr Carnac, Colonels Egerton and Cockburn, were all three dismissed from the service. Their conduct in the present instance certainly appears quite indefensible, and it is not a little remarkable, that it formed a decided contrast to their characters as displayed on former occasions. Cockburn, in particular, had distinguished himself by exploits of the most daring valour, and was considered one of the best officers in the service; but the qualities which had fitted him for a secondary part, proved insufficient to guide his judgment in this higher and more arduous station. Treaty annulled. The treaty was immediately annulled, as having been concluded without sufficient authority, and the arrival of Colonel Leslie with his detachment was alone waited for in order to commence offensive operations. This officer, however, had not made the despatch which was expected. His march being harassed by some of the Rajpoot chiefs, he absurdly allowed himself to be drawn into several petty contests, and in the course of five months had not proceeded above 120 miles. Mr Hastings was obliged to supersede him, and send in his place Colonel Goddard, who, by passing over three hundred miles in twenty days, reached Surat, having avoided the snares formed by the enemy to interrupt his progress.

Tardy progress of Colonel Leslie.

Colonel Goddard.

This commander, who, though acting on a conciliatory system toward the Bombay government, was invested with a jurisdiction nearly independent, began with an attempt to negotiate. This being found impracticable, on account of the lofty tone assumed by the cabinet of Poonah upon its recent success, hostilities were immediately commenced; and the English appeared no longer as auxiliaries to Ragoba, but as principals. On the first of January 1780, Goddard, now a general, crossed the Tuptee, and before the end of the month reduced Dubhoy, and carried by storm Ahmedabad, the great but decayed capital of Guzerat. Then, however, he received notice that Scindia and Holkar, with upwards of twenty thousand horse, had passed the Nerbudda, and were advancing against him. The former chief opened a negotiation with the British, for whom he professed a warm attachment. But, as it was soon perceived that he sought only to gain time, Goddard determined if possible to bring him to a general action; and attacking his camp by night, he succeeded in surprising some of his outposts. The day, however, dawned in time to enable the main body to mount their horses and present themselves in order of battle: they even made a movement as if to charge, but being received with a brisk fire, they galloped off and were soon out of sight. The English commander, who imagined he had gained a decisive victory, soon learned with surprise that they had taken a fresh position quite entire, at a little distance. He again endeavoured to

Unsuccessful attempt at negotiation.

Storming of Ahmedabad.

Desultory engagements with the Indian army.

CHAP. XIV.

A. D. 1780.

bring them to action; but on his near approach they merely discharged a flight of rockets, and disappeared as before. Wearied with these fruitless and harassing operations, he at length removed his army, and placed it, during the rains, in cantonments on the Nerbudda.

Siege of Bassein.

In the course of the dry season, which commenced in October, the general employed himself in the siege of Bassein, while Colonel Hartley covered his operations, spreading his force over a great part of the Concan, whence he drew both supplies and revenue. This campaign was very successful; Bassein surrendered on the 11th December, while Hartley, taking a judicious position, completely repulsed the whole combined force of the Mahrattas, which attempted to overwhelm him.

Proposals for negotiating.

Thus the English affairs were beginning to assume a prosperous aspect, when Goddard was apprized of an intention on the part of government to open an immediate negotiation. He was directed, therefore, to hold himself in readiness to cease hostilities as soon as intelligence should be received from Poonah of a corresponding disposition. This resolution was connected with certain events of the war in the south of India related in a former chapter.

British affairs in southern India.

Hyder, having formed an alliance with the nizam and the Mahrattas, had made a terrible irruption into the Carnatic, and was threatening the very existence of the British establishment at Madras. Under these circumstances, it was determined to make sacrifices to a great extent, in order to detach the court of Poonah from this formidable confederacy. The treaty, however, proceeded slowly, especially after tidings had arrived of the catastrophe that had befallen Colonel Baillie's detachment.

Unsuccessful manœuvring of General Goddard.

In these discouraging circumstances General Goddard conceived that an advance with his army beyond the Ghauts, and the placing it in such a position as to menace the Mahratta capital, might produce a favourable effect. Accordingly, with about 6000 men he succeeded in penetrating the barrier of hills. Nana Furnavese, however, still refused to separate from his ally; and the general was so harassed by attacks on his rear, by having his convoys intercepted, and by seeing the country laid waste around him, that he felt at length the necessity of retreating to Bombay. In this march he was assailed by the enemy with so much fury, that although he reached the coast without dishonour, he sustained a loss more severe than had been incurred in the campaign which terminated in the convention of Worgaom.

Severe losses of the British.

Mr Hastings, meantime, attempted to influence the war by military movements from Bengal, directed towards the very heart of India. Captain Popham, with 2400 men, crossed the Jumna, and attacked the fort of Lahar; but finding it much stronger than was expected, and labouring under the want of battering-cannon, he could effect only a very imperfect breach. He determined, however, to storm it; and, though both the officers who led the assault fell, the troops followed with such intrepidity that the place was carried with the loss of 125 men. But the most brilliant exploit was that against Gwalior, a stronghold repeatedly mentioned as being considered in Hindostan Proper the most formidable bulwark of the empire, though it could not rank with the impregnable hill-forts of the south and west. After two months of observation and contrivance, on the 3d August 1780 a party was employed to make a night-assault. They mounted the scarped rock by a regular escalade, then ran up the steep face of the hill, and by ladders of rope ascended the inner wall, thirty feet high, when they found themselves within the place; and though some of the men gave the alarm by firing prematurely, they nevertheless stood their ground. The garrison were panic-struck; and the sun had scarcely risen when the British, with almost no resistance, became masters of this celebrated fortress.

Plan of operations by Mr. Hastings.

Storming of the fort of Lahar.

Taking of Gwalior.

In pursuance of the same system, Mr Hastings sent Colonel Camac to carry the war into the territories of Scindia. He penetrated without difficulty into Malwa; but the Mahratta chief then hastened to oppose the invasion, and by the rapid manœuvres of his numerous cavalry, soon reduced the British to great distress; keep-

War in the territories of Scindia.

CHAP. XIV — A. D. 1781.

ing up an incessant cannonade during the long period of seven days. The colonel, however, by remaining for some time inactive, lulled the suspicions of the enemy, then suddenly burst by night into his camp, and defeated him with great loss. This success, although he was not able to follow it up, raised considerably the reputation of the English, who also succeeded, by a large sum of money, in detaching Moodajee Bhonslay, rajah of Berar, from the other Mahratta leaders. Thus, after various transactions, a separate convention was first concluded with Scindia on the 13th October 1781; and finally, on the 7th May following, a general peace was signed at Salbye, on terms as favourable as the chequered events of the war could give room to expect. The limits of the respective territories were fixed nearly on the same footing as by the treaty of Poorundur; and a monthly pension of 25,000 rupees was assigned to Ragoba. Thus closed the first Mahratta war, by which our countrymen, it must be confessed, had earned very little either of glory or advantage.

Successful manœuvre of Colonel Camac.

Close of the first Mahratta war.

Friendly alliance with the Mahrattas.

From this time the relations of that people with our government were for many years those of amity and alliance; a union which was produced by a common dread of the exorbitant power and pretensions of the house of Mysore. We have seen them joined with the British in successive leagues, and affording a tumultuary aid in the contests which brought to an end the power of Tippoo. The history of the confederation, however, was remarkably distinguished by the rise of Scindia to a pre-eminence which made him decidedly superior to all its other leaders. His territory being contiguous to the southern states and to the fragments of the Mogul empire, he added to it successively these different possessions. On the east he subdued Bundelcund; on the west he rendered tributary the warlike princes of Rajpootana; and at length, amid the dissensions of the imperial court, Shah Allum, who still retained the name, revered even in its downfal, of Mogul emperor, placed himself under his protection. In this manner that chief became master

Superiority acquired by Scindia.

of Agra, Delhi, and the surrounding territories; while he exercised all that now remained of imperial power. He was so elated by these successes, that he ventured upon a demand of chout or tribute from the government of Bengal; a claim which Mr Macpherson, then governor, repelled with the highest indignation, and insisted upon its formal renunciation.

CHAP. XIV

A. D. 1781.

Demands tribute from the British.

Scindia's elevated position was in other respects precarious and difficult. Labouring under an extreme deficiency of funds, he was obliged to levy exorbitant contributions from the Rajpoot chiefs. That proud race rose in insurrection, and were joined by Mohammed Beg and Gholaum Kawdir, to whom, as well as to the emperor himself, the domination of the Mahratta ruler had become odious. In an invasion of Rajpootana, he was completely defeated, and though the feudal bands of that country, as usual after a victory, dispersed and went to their homes, he was no longer able to resist the power even of the Moslem princes. He was again worsted, and reduced to the greatest extremity, when he entreated, though with little success, that Nana Furnavese would forget all grounds of quarrel and jealousy, and aid him in the general cause of the Mahratta confederation. He was extricated by the savage violence of Gholaum Kawdir himself, who, having obtained possession of Delhi and of the emperor's person, treated him, his family, and adherents, with the most wanton barbarity. With his own hand he used the point of a dagger to put out that prince's eyes; and committed other cruelties which rendered him the object of general horror and disgust. At length his own associate, Ismael Beg (who had succeeded to Mohammed), went over to Scindia, who also at length obtained a reinforcement from Poonah. By this means he was enabled to enter Delhi,* and pursue Kawdir, who was taken and put to death; and having thus regained almost the entire plenitude of his dominion, the Mahratta chief sought to strengthen his military power by means not resorted to by any of his predecessors. He enlisted into his army the various warlike races in the north of India,

Precarious position of Scindia.

His defeat by the rajpoot chiefs.

Savage cruelties of Gholaum Kawdir.

His capture and death.

CHAP. XIV — A. D. 1794.

—the valiant Rajpoot horsemen, the Goseins, a religious sect, whose tenets did not prevent them from taking arms, and even Mohammedan soldiers who had been thrown out of the Mogul service. But the force on which he chiefly relied was a corps of regular infantry, organized and disciplined in the European manner by a French adventurer named De Boigne. This body, at first consisting only of two battalions, had been rapidly augmented, till it amounted to three brigades, each comprising 5600 infantry, 500 cavalry, and forty pieces of cannon. He had besides a separate train of artillery, and was supported by a mass of irregular foot. A considerable territory was assigned for the support of this corps; which included officers of all nations, among whom was a considerable proportion of English.

Scindia recovers his position.

Ambitious projects of Scindia.

Having thus rendered himself the most powerful among the Mahratta princes, Scindia's next object was to acquire a preponderance at the court of Poonah. He proceeded thither with the professed purpose of conferring on the peishwa the dignity of Vakeel-i-Mootluq, or supreme deputy, which he had caused the Mogul to bestow; a most unwelcome visit, which Nana Furnavese sought in vain to decline. He arrived at length, and was received with every mark of outward respect. The peishwa, amid great state, was invested with this new title, which was considered an addition to the splendour even of his rank; while the gallant warrior, being appointed his perpetual deputy, with the right of nominating a successor, acquired all the real power attached to the function. Besides dazzling the eye of the youthful prince by the pomp of this ceremony, he gained his favour by inviting him to field-sports and other amusements, from which he had been in a considerable degree withheld by the austere maxims of the aged Bramin, his minister. In short, Scindia seemed about to supplant Furnavese as the arbiter of the Mahratta state, when he was seized with a violent illness, which terminated his life on the 12th February 1794.

Reception at the court of Poonah.

His sudden death.

Mahadajee Scindia, who had been the chief instrument

in raising his house to be the first in Hindostan, was a person of very great activity and address, long experience, and of so much principle as to be supposed incapable of committing any very enormous crime,—a praise which cannot often be bestowed on the great men of India. His death at the present moment, when a danger of the greatest magnitude impended over the state, may probably be considered as the main cause of the ultimate decline of the Mahratta power. Dying without issue, he adopted as his successor, not the nearest heir, but Dowlut Rao, his nephew, the son of his youngest brother; a youth not more than fifteen years of age, who, though possessed of talents and enterprise, was without that knowledge which would have been necessary to guide him through the difficult circumstances in which he was soon placed.

Character of Scindia.

His successor Dowlut Rao.

Nana Furnavese, on the death of his rival, seemed again replaced in the supreme direction of affairs; but the very eagerness with which he clung to power soon involved him in a deeper calamity. While he kept Madoo Rao, the peishwa, in very strict tutelage, he held also in close confinement Bajee Rao, the son of Ragoba, who, on approaching manhood, displayed high accomplishments and engaging manners, which rendered him an object of general interest. This was particularly felt by his cousin Madoo Rao. An epistolary communication was opened, and a romantic friendship formed by these two young men, who stood in a position of such deadly rivalry. In their correspondence they were wont to anticipate the moment when, delivered from their present thraldom, they might form a personal intimacy, and emulate the great actions of their ancestors. This innocent exchange of sentiment, being discovered by Nana, excited his most violent rage. He increased the rigour of Bajee's confinement, and, at the same time, loaded Madoo with the severest reproaches. The high-spirited youth, in a paroxysm of grief and indignation, threw himself from a terrace in the palace, and died in two days. This was a most disastrous event to Furna-

Nana Furnavese.

Romantic friendship between Madoo and Bajee Rao.

Death of Madoo Rao.

CHAP. XIV.

A. D. 1794.

vese; for Bajee, whom he had done so much to make his enemy, was, in fact, the legitimate heir. The minister attempted at first to parry this fatal circumstance, and proposed that the widow of the deceased prince, though she had not reached the age of womanhood, should adopt a son, whom he might establish as peishwa, and in his name conduct the government. He found this measure, however, to be quite repugnant to public feeling; and learning that Scindia had declared in favour of the imprisoned youth, endeavoured to make the best of his situation by employing his influence in raising the latter to the vacant dignity. Bajee Rao, on this intention being announced to him, was so much surprised, that he obliged the messenger to take hold of a cow's tail, and swear by the holy waters of the Godavery that no stratagem was intended. He then repaired to Poonah, and was placed on the musnud. The reconciliation, however, could not be durable. The court from this time became a complete chaos of political intrigue, between the peishwa, who endeavoured to exercise his own authority, and Nana, Scindia, Purseram Bhow, and other chiefs, who sought to administer it in his name. These individuals appear in the confused scene one day united in close alliance, the next plotting one another's destruction. We shall not now follow the thread of these intricate transactions, nor encumber our pages with the uncouth names of humbler individuals who, amid the general confusion, contrived to thrust themselves into notice. Some attempts were even made to employ as an instrument the long-imprisoned rajah, whose title was still dear to the Mahratta people. Nana Furnavese, after passing through various fortunes, and being reduced to the greatest distress, was restored to some share of his former power, but died soon afterwards, leaving the reputation of one of the ablest and most skilful politicians that India had ever produced; and there remained no individual possessed of those comprehensive and statesman-like views, which were soon much wanted to direct the affairs of the confederation.

Dilemma of Furnavese.

Bajee Rao appointed peishwa.

Fate of Nana Furnavese.

CHAP. XIV

A. D. 1794.

Situation of the court of Poonah.

Even before the death of Furnavese, the court of Poonah had been placed for some time in a critical situation. It was united in a triple alliance with Britain and the nizam, against the power and pretensions of the house of Mysore, and had repeatedly co-operated, though in an irregular and unsatisfactory manner, with th English in their wars with that dynasty. Lord Cornwallis, though he had much reason to complain of the conduct of their army, so far from expressing any anger, granted to them a third, or equal share with the Com pany and the nizam, of the ceded lands: and Marqui Wellesley afterwards, when he entered upon the las and decisive contest with Tippoo, called upon the Mahratta government to fulfil the stipulations of this alliance. By that time, however, they had begun to cherish a deep and not ill-grounded jealousy respecting the rapid progress of the British power; and although they chose to temporize, their wishes were now completely in favour of Mysore. Nana strongly shared this feeling; nevertheless he decidedly objected to any measure which might commit the state in a war with so formidable a nation But Scindia and the peishwa, those young and ardent spirits, embraced with enthusiasm the cause of the sultan; a fact which was proved by a correspondence found at Seringapatam, breathing unequivocal hostility, and leaving no doubt, that had fortune favoured the son of Hyder, he would at once have been joined by these chiefs. They were arrested, however, by the intelligence of the fall of that capital, the death of its ruler, and the downfal of his formidable dynasty. Then, indeed, every effort was made to excuse their inactivity as allies, and to explain away every symptom of a hostile intention.

Jealousy of the British power.

Proposed alliance with Tippoo.

Though the failure on the part of the Mahrattas had been undeniable, Marquis Wellesley declined showing any resentment; he even set apart for them a portion of the sequestered territory. But he determined to avail himself of his present commanding position to establish if possible an effective control over this great and turbulent state. He tendered to them a share in the spoils

Politic proceedings of Wellesley.

CHAP. XIV.

A. D. 1802.

Proposed treaty with the Mahrattas.

of Mysore, coupled with the condition, that the peishwa, on terms similar to those of a treaty just arranged with the nizam, should receive a British subsidiary force, and cede a portion of territory, the clear revenue of which might be sufficient for their maintenance. But this proposal, after some months of delay and evasion, was decidedly rejected. It evidently appeared that his highness would never agree to any such measure, unless under the pressure of an irresistible necessity; and the governor-general, entertaining sanguine hopes that such a crisis might erelong occur, carefully watched his opportunity. He calculated, that the distractions in the Mahratta confederacy, as they must increase, could scarcely fail of compelling that prince to have recourse to British aid; for, though the nominal head of the other chieftains, and himself a man of spirit and ambition, he saw his power every day more and more controlled by the pretensions of those military adventurers. Scindia began to act as the real sovereign of Maharashtra, commanding a force superior to that of his master, whom he evidently intended to treat as a mere state pageant. Holkar, too, having assembled round him a vast predatory army, was not unwilling to measure his strength with any rival, however mighty. Yet these turbulent elements continued for some time to ferment without producing an actual explosion; and hence, more than three years elapsed from the conquest of Mysore, before the expected crisis arrived. Marquis Wellesley was even preparing to return to Europe in January 1803, when the unexpected intelligence induced him to remain. The convulsion which he had long waited for, occurred on a greater scale, and in a form more favourable to his views, than he had ever anticipated.

Divisions among the native allied powers.

The expected crisis.

Jeswunt Rao.

The rival houses of Scindia and Holkar, after recently emerging from the lowest obscurity, had for some time ranked nearly equal; but after the former had once risen to greatness, his family acquired a very decided preponderance. The power of the Holkars, however, revived under an illegitimate branch, Jeswunt Rao, who by boldness, enterprise, and a peculiar talent for predatory warfare, soon raised himself, notwithstanding the stain on his birth, to be the head of his house, and the leader of all who fought under its banners. Dissensions soon arose between him and Scindia, whose territory he did not spare in the course of his ravages. After various movements, the two armies engaged near Indore, Holkar's capital, when that chief was completely routed, with the loss of ninety-eight pieces of cannon; and his power was supposed to be so completely crushed, that the other very imprudently neglected any farther pursuit. No force is so easily or so rapidly recruited as that of the Mahrattas. The vanquished leader, having undertaken some inroads into the surrounding territories, soon rallied round him all the bold youths who delighted in plunder and adventure: large bands even from the ranks of his adversary, tired of an inactive life, flocked to his camp. In short, he soon found himself in a condition to march upon Poonah. Scindia and the peishwa united their forces to oppose him; and there ensued in the vicinity of that city one of the most obstinate battles recorded in the annals of Indian warfare. Holkar fought with the utmost desperation, and led his men to successive charges with such fury, that the enemy were completely broken, and fled in every direction. Colonel Close, the British resident, while the engagement lasted, hoisted his flag, which was respected by both parties; and next day he was asked to visit the victorious general. He found him in his tent, ankle-deep in mud, wounded both with a spear and a sabre. He received the colonel with the utmost politeness, professed a cordial attachment to the English, and expressed a wish that they would assist in adjusting his differences with Scindia and the peishwa.

Total rout of Holkar.

Aggressive movement by the vanquished leader.

His complete success.

Solicits British intermediation.

The latter prince, however, had already entered into engagements with the British. On the first approach of the crisis which had now overwhelmed him, he began to make overtures for a subsidiary force, though on the narrowest possible conditions. It was not even to enter the country, but to be posted on the frontier, ready to

Negotiations of the peishwa.

CHAP. XIV.

A. D. 1802.

advance when circumstances might call for its services. His object evidently was, not to incur the odium and danger of introducing these powerful foreigners into his dominions, but by the mere dread of their approach to overawe the contending chiefs, and restore his own supremacy.

Accommodating policy of Wellesley.

The marquis was not, however, unwilling to close the arrangement, even under this jealous restriction; but the treaty for the maintenance of the corps was attended with great difficulties. An ample extent of territory was indeed offered, but being situated in Hindostan Proper, where the peishwa had a mere nominal authority, it was really occupied by Scindia and Holkar, from whom it must be wrested by force of arms. The assignment was required of a tract of country over which the English could hold command; even money would be accepted, notwithstanding the uncertainties of obtaining payment. Thus the negotiation

The peishwa adopts the British alliance.

was spun out till the very day before the battle, when the prince, foreseeing that whoever prevailed he would be reduced to a state of vassalage, signed the compact. After Holkar's signal victory, he determined to throw himself entirely into the arms of the British. This intention he intimated from Singurh, to which he had fled, and was then invited to repair to the coast, where the arrangements could be conducted with security. Having repaired to Severndroog, he embarked for Bassein, where he was met by Colonel Close; and at that place, on the

Treaty of Severndroog.

31st December 1802, was signed the celebrated treaty by which the alliance was settled on a more extended basis. The Company not only engaged to furnish 6000 men, for the support of whom was assigned a territory yielding twenty-six lacks of rupees; they engaged, moreover, to bring forward all the force they could command, and which might be necessary to re-establish the peishwa in his full rights as head of the Mahratta confederacy.

Great Mahratta war.

In entering on the greatest war which England ever waged in India, and which was destined completely to establish her supremacy over that region, it is impossible to refrain from some inquiry respecting the necessity and the wisdom of this eventful measure. Mr Mill, in a very masterly discussion upon this subject, argues, that the war arose out of the treaty of Bassein, which was manifestly the spontaneous act of the governor-general; and that the Mahratta chiefs, engrossed by their own contests for power, had no immediate intention or wish to involve themselves in hostility with the British government. The object of each was to obtain possession of the peishwa's person, and to exercise in his name a general control over the whole state. But an arrangement which altogether withdrew that ruler from the control of all of them, and transferred to a foreign power the whole weight of his name and resources, besides humbling their national pride, presented a common obstacle to the ambitious views of each chief, and was therefore to all an object of equal resentment. He goes on to maintain that the Company might have safely looked on, and seen the different leaders waste themselves in internal conflicts, while courted by each they might have secured advantages to themselves, and held the balance between them. This part of the question, however, depends upon circumstances that are extremely complicated; and the arguments urged on the other side appear to be at least equally plausible.

Its necessity and source.

British supremacy the subject of general apprehension.

Probable result of the conflict.

It has never been denied, that a power which sees its neighbours engaged in war may be justified in interfering, either from generosity to defend the oppressed, or from policy, lest any one state, by conquering the others, should attain a dangerous ascendency. But the conflicts of the Mahratta chiefs now bore much less the character of internal disturbance, than of regular war between independent princes. The common national tie served little more than to inspire the design and hope of a general dominion,—the object which, it is clear, had kindled the ambition of the several aspirants. There was therefore, perhaps, a strong probability that erelong some one of these leaders would gain the supremacy, and wield the entire resources of the Mahratta power. It seems impossible to deny that in such a case an able warrior

General view of the question

CHAP. XIV — A. D. 1802.

might have become very formidable to Britain, both by the great extent of territory which he would have commanded, and by the success which might have been expected from disciplining his troops after the European manner. He would also have enjoyed the prospect of being aided by the French, while the English would have had to dread the doubtful faith of the nizam and other native princes whom they held in vassalage.

Anticipations of the Marquis Wellesley.

The Marquis Wellesley, from his confidential correspondence recently published, evidently cherished sanguine hopes that the mere influence of this treaty, without any actual appeal to arms, would have re-established tranquillity and a due balance of power in the Mahratta state. Scindia, it was hoped, after so overwhelming a blow, would have been happy to co-operate with him and the peishwa, under the offered pledge of regaining all he had lost, and having its preservation guaranteed to him. Holkar's resources were considered too unsolid and ephemeral to make any stand against these three united powers. The only doubt respected Raghojee Bhonslay, who had become Rajah of Berar, and whose ancestor, as formerly mentioned, had even laid claim to the rank of peishwa. He had, however, been observed to attach himself so very decidedly to the successful party, that there appeared little chance of his espousing a cause so desperate as that of Holkar. In fact, had these chiefs been guided by sound views of policy, they would have at least temporized till Scindia had recruited his shattered forces, and till his rival, who had retired beyond the Godavery, and seemed disinclined to take any decisive step, could be induced to join the confederacy.

Raghojee Bhonslay.

Adverse influence of Scindia and Raghojee.

These hopes, though resting on plausible grounds, were not fulfilled. Scindia and Raghojee felt such a hatred and dread of British power, as not only suspended the strongest feelings of enmity between themselves, but impelled them to make precipitate efforts against a treaty which appeared to render the Company supreme over Maharashtra. Yet the former, who, after his defeat, had retired to Burhanpoor, where he had reas

CHAP. XIV.

A. D. 1802.

sembled a considerable force, did not at first declare himself. Being invited to accede to the treaty of Bassein and to share its advantages, he expressed an intention to comply, only wishing previously to correspond with and obtain some explanations from the peishwa. Afterwards he declined acceding, but declared he would do nothing to obstruct its execution. Alarm was naturally excited by his continuing posted at Burhanpoor, which could apparently have no other object but that of regaining his ascendency at Poonah; wherefore Collins, stationed as resident in his camp, again pressed upon him the acceptance of the treaty, though intimating that his refusal would not be considered as a ground of offence. In that case, however, it was expected he would prove the absence of any hostile intention, by immediately recrossing the Nerbudda, to the north of which his own dominions lay. He made friendly professions, but urged that his present position was necessary to watch and keep in check the movements of Holkar. The marquis afterwards intimated to the resident, that if this should appear to be the case, he would accept any other unequivocal proof of pacific dispositions; and he continued long to cherish the hope, that this warrior would not venture any opposition without the concurrence of Holkar and the Rajah of Berar. He wrote both to him and the rajah, assuring them of being left secure and unmolested in the possession of their dominions; at the same time, in allusion to certain unfavourable reports, he warned them, that all attempts on the part of any state or power to obstruct the execution of the treaty of Bassein, would place them in a state of hostility with Britain. The rajah replied, disclaiming any hostile views; though a letter was at the same time communicated, which he had written to a chief, Azim-ul-Omrah, expressing his desire to meet Scindia, and concert measures with him for opposing the fulfilment of the said treaty. Although this intention was denied, and amicable professions continued, yet the movements both of Scindia's army and that of Berar entirely corresponded to it. The governor-general there-

Caution of Scindia.

Disguise of his motives.

Overtures of the Marquis.

CHAP. XIV.

A. D. 1803.

Preparatory measures of the governor-general.

fore determined to place all his armies in such positions as might enable them to act with the utmost vigour, the moment it should be determined to strike the blow. General Wellesley from Mysore, Colonel Stevenson from the nizam's capital of Hydrabad, and some regiments under Colonel Murray from Bombay, had been ordered to advance upon Poonah, and after re-establishing the peishwa, to be ready if necessary to act against the turbulent Mahratta chiefs. Lord Lake, stationed with a large force at Cawnpore, on the Bengal frontier, had instructions, immediately on learning the commencement of hostilities, to advance.

Plan for combined operations.

His objects were to conquer Scindia's territories in Hindostan Proper, capture the Mogul capitals of Delhi and Agra, obtain possession of the emperor's person, and open a friendly communication with the Rajpoot chiefs. At the same time, detachments were to be sent against Cuttack, belonging to the Rajah of Berar, and from Bombay against Baroach and the neighbouring coast of Guzerat. The success of these last expeditions would render the Company masters of the whole circuit of the Indian coast, and cut off all connexion between their European and native enemies.

Major-general Wellesley enters the Mahratta territory.

On the 9th of March 1803, Major-general Wellesley marched from his position at Hurryhur, and on the 12th entered the Mahratta territory. Colonel Stevenson, at the same time, broke up from Hydrabad with the subsidiary force of about 8000 men, and 16,000 troops furnished by the nizam. On the 15th April the two divisions united at Aklooss, about 70 miles south-east of Poonah.

Retirement of Holkar.

Holkar, on hearing of the approach of the English, determined not to involve himself in hostile proceedings, but early in April retreated to Chandore, a place 130 miles to the northward of Poonah,—leaving Amrut Rao, whom he had invested with the dignity of peishwa, with only a small detachment in that capital. Sir Arthur then judged it unnecessary to lead his whole army to a place where it could not without much difficulty procure subsistence; but being informed by Colonel Close that there was reason to apprehend Amrut Rao would set fire to the capital, where part of the family of the peishwa still resided, he formed a select corps of cavalry, and advanced with such speed, that in thirty-two hours, on the 20th April, he reached Poonah, which Amrut had hastily quitted without attempting any violence. The English power being thus established in the Mahratta metropolis, the sovereign was escorted from Bombay by the detachment under Colonel Murray, and resumed his seat on the musnud amid the congratulations of the British and native armies.

Rapid march of Sir Arthur Wellesley.

General Wellesley now paused till he could ascertain the disposition of the other Mahratta chiefs. Though great difficulty was found in procuring supplies and the means of transport, no aid was derived from the peishwa, who was either unable, or, as was strongly suspected, disinclined to command the exertions of his subjects for this object. However, by his own activity and the assistance forwarded from Bombay, the English leader was at length enabled to put his troops in marching condition.

Difficulty of procuring supplies.

As the conduct of the native rulers became daily more suspicious, the governor-general, to avoid the delays of communicating with Calcutta, invested his brother on the 26th June, not only with the supreme military command in the Mahratta territories, but with the decision of the question of peace or war. In the first capacity, indeed, he was still inferior to Lord Lake and General Stuart; but the former was on an entirely different line of operations, and the latter, it was understood, would not interfere. Sir Arthur hereupon instructed Colonel Collins urgently to demand from Scindia an explanation of his present menacing attitude, and to solicit his retirement into the interior of his own dominions. That chief gave the most positive assurances of a pacific disposition, and even of an intention to acquiesce in the treaty of Bassein; but as, in conjunction with the Rajah of Berar, he still maintained his menacing posture, and was understood to be issuing orders to his officers to hold themselves in readiness to act on the shortest notice, it

General Wellesley invested with supreme military command.

Suspicious position maintained by Scindia and his allies.

CHAP. XIV.

A. D. 1803.

Ambiguous message of Scindia.

was judged farther necessary to require that he and the rajah should withdraw their troops to their ordinary stations in the centre of their respective territories, while a corresponding movement should be made on the part of the British army. To this demand, Scindia replied, that he expected in a few days to have an interview with the Rajah of Berar, when the resident would be informed "whether it should be peace or war." This ambiguous expression, so strongly indicative of the latter alternative, induced the general to advance to Walkee, a strong post near Ahmednugger, whence he could with advantage commence military operations.

Protracted manœuvres.

On the 3d June, the rajah arrived, and had a meeting with Scindia, though the principal conference did not take place till the 8th; and when the resident, on the 12th, demanded to know the result, he was met only by delays and subterfuges. The two princes acknowledged themselves to be in some respects dissatisfied with the treaty of Bassein, but declared that their troops were in their own territory, without any hostile intention. They admitted, however, that they were intending to march towards the nizam's dominions; and from this and other circumstances, the general formed the decided opinion that they were determined upon war, and were only desirous of waiting till their preparations should be completed, and the negotiation which they had opened with Holkar brought to a conclusion. Every delay, in fact, was in their favour. Colonel Collins was therefore instructed to demand, in a peremptory manner, that the Rajah of Berar should immediately retire to his capital of Nagpoor, and Scindia beyond the Nerbudda, provided the state of the rivers permitted; if not, at least to Burhanpoor. These remonstrances, seconded by a letter from General Wellesley, procured for the colonel an audience on the 25th July; though he obtained nothing beyond shifts and excuses till the 31st, when he threatened an immediate departure. He was then invited to the rajah's tent, and a proposal was made that the allies should retire to Burhanpoor, fifty-eight miles in their rear, pro-

Manifest determination for war.

Remonstrances and delays.

vided the English commander would withdraw his troops to their usual stations at Madras and Bombay. This arrangement, which would have left the Mahratta territory entirely at the disposal of the confederates, was at once rejected; and they at length offered to march back to their respective capitals, provided the British army should commence a retrograde movement on the very same day. This proposition was judged worthy of being transmitted to the general. The letter, however, purporting to convey it, on being delivered, was found to contain no such offer, but merely the first and rejected proposition. The resident, then concluding that the sole object of the allies was to gain time, at once quitted the camp, and the war immediately commenced.

Unreasonable proposals of the confederates.

War resolved on.

Sir A. Wellesley was at the head of 7000 infantry, 1900 cavalry, with 5400 native horse, independently of the corps of Colonel Stevenson, which covered the nizam's frontier. He now with characteristic promptitude marched upon Ahmednugger, and on the 8th August 1803 summoned that fortress, which was considered one of the bulwarks of the Deccan. On the first day the town was stormed, and on the 10th a battery was opened against the fort, which on the 12th was evacuated by the garrison. He then proceeded to the city of Aurungabad. Meantime, however, the confederates with their numerous cavalry had passed Colonel Stevenson, and appeared resolved to cross the Godavery and make a rapid march against Hydrabad, the capital of the nizam. The British general, however, by a judicious movement, obliged them to return northwards; but as the flying warfare, which they seemed inclined to pursue would have been exceedingly harassing, he resolved to bring them, almost on any terms, to close combat. With this view, the two English corps marched separately, though at a short distance, along the two roads by which the enemy was expected to pass.

Prompt measures of General Wellesley

Capture of Ahmednugger.

Plans of the confederates overturned.

The general had arranged that Stevenson and himself should unite on the 24th September, and in concert attack the enemy; but as it was reported that their cavalry had

CHAP. XIV. A. D. 1803.

Unexpected meeting with the enemy.

begun to move, he pushed forward to reconnoitre, or to prevent their manœuvre. His information, which in that hostile country was extremely imperfect, led him to suppose that they were posted at Bokerdun, twelve or fourteen miles distant; but after marching six miles, he discovered their whole force, consisting of 38,000 cavalry, above 18,000 infantry, and about 100 pieces of artillery, drawn up on the plain of Assaye. He could not now retreat without being pursued under a great disadvantage by their immensely superior body of horse, and without greatly dispiriting his followers. He determined, therefore, notwithstanding the vast disparity in the number of his troops, to lead them directly on to the attack. Far from being struck with any apprehension, they exultingly exclaimed, "They cannot escape us!" As they advanced, however, the enemy's artillery, the best organized part of their army, opened a most destructive fire, which greatly thinned their ranks. The general, being informed by one of the officers in command that his guns could not be got forward, owing to the number of men and bullocks that were disabled, said, "Well, tell him to get on without them." The British infantry continued to move forward in the face of this tremendous fire with a steady pace, and bore down all opposition. The Mahratta cavalry, meanwhile, on seeing the opposite ranks so much reduced, made a desperate attempt to break them; when they were encountered by a most gallant charge of the English horse, which soon compelled them to join their foot in a rapid retreat. The victory seemed complete, when it was for a moment rendered doubtful owing to a very unexpected incident. By a stratagem not unexampled in the East, a considerable number of Indians had thrown themselves on the ground, and been passed as dead by the advancing troops; they now started up, seized some of the captured guns, and commenced a brisk fire from behind, under favour of which a few of the fleeing squadrons rallied. Sir Arthur Wellesley, however, with his usual presence of mind, detached several corps, by whom this alarming resurrection was soon put down;

General engagement.

Battle of Assaye

Retreat of the enemy.

Daring stratagem of the Indians.

CHAP. XIV.

A. D. 1803.

and the whole Indian host was forthwith involved in one promiscuous flight, leaving on the field twelve hundred dead, with ninety-eight pieces of artillery. The loss of the conquerors was very severe, amounting to 409 killed and 1622 wounded. Much of this was occasioned by the mistake of an officer who led his corps direct against the formidable battery at the village of Assaye, instead of attacking another quarter, which being carried would have caused that post to fall of itself. Scindia's infantry fought better than Tippoo's, and his ordnance was so superior that it could be used by the British, while that taken in Mysore was found quite worthless.

Severe loss of the British.

Such was the battle of Assaye, which established the fame of the greatest commander of the age, and fixed the dominion of Britain over prostrate India. Yet his conduct on this occasion has been the subject of considerable controversy, and many consider that he led on his troops too daringly to an unequal combat. The panegyrists of the general, on the other hand, argue, that he availed himself of this apparent disadvantage as the only footing upon which the enemy could be induced to engage in regular battle. But this plea is refuted by one of his interesting letters to Sir Thomas Munro, where he disclaims any intention of acting separately from Colonel Stevenson, and admits himself to have been taken considerably by surprise, when he discovered the whole Indian army assembled on the extensive plain. He judged, however, that under existing circumstances, he could not retreat without disastrous consequences. Sir Thomas, rather a severe military critic, observes, "If there was any thing wrong, it was in giving battle; but in the conduct of the action every thing was right. General Wellesley gave every part of his army its full share; left no part of it unemployed; but supported, sometimes with cavalry, sometimes with infantry, every point that was pressed at the very moment that it was most necessary." In regard to the result also, it has been said, that the enemy suffered so little of actual loss

Opinions on the conduct of General Wellesley.

Observations of Sir Thomas Munro.

CHAP. XIV — A. D. 1803.

Effect of the battle.

as to render the battle very indecisive. But besides the capture of their formidable artillery, and the extensive dispersion which in undisciplined armies always follows defeat, it appears probable that this triumph, achieved by such a disparity of numbers, produced a moral effect greater than would have arisen from a much more decisive victory gained under ordinary circumstances. There is something extremely sensitive in the Indian mind, that is acted upon with extraordinary force by whatever is strange or unexpected. Such displays of valour they never fail to exaggerate, attaching to them a mysterious efficacy which partakes deeply of the supernatural. It was on the field of Assaye that the spirit of India was vanquished; and Hindostan, after that fatal day, was viewed by its people as having passed into the hands of invincible conquerors.

Overtures of Scindia.

After this victory Scindia proceeded to make separate overtures; but as they were presented at first through private and unaccredited channels, which he might afterwards disown, no proceeding could be founded upon them. The commander-in-chief directed Colonel Stevenson to reduce the great city of Burhanpoor and the adjoining fort of Asseerghur, which bore the reputation of being almost impregnable. The town yielded without opposition, and the fort after a surprisingly short resistance. The Mahratta chief then sued for peace in earnest, and the terms of an armistice were arranged for all his territories south of the Nerbudda. The British general next led his army against Berar, and found the rajah with his troops on the Plains of Argaom, where, contrary to the convention, he was still supported by a strong body of Scindia's cavalry. He attacked them without the slightest hesitation, and, after a contest less obstinate than at Assaye, gained a complete victory, taking 36 pieces of artillery, and losing only 46 killed and 308 wounded. Siege was then laid to Gawilghur, one of those hill-forts which are esteemed the bulwarks of India. It made a more vigorous defence than any of the other strongholds, and severe labour was required to

Capture of Burhanpoor and Asseerghur.

Victory of Argaom.

plant the cannon on its steep sides; but in a very few days a breach was effected, and the outer wall was carried by storm. There remained still an inner rampart, which for some time defeated the efforts of the assailants, till Captain Campbell (now Lieutenant-general Sir Colin), with a detachment of light troops, carried it by escalade, and opened the gate to the rest of the army.

Capture of Gawilghur.

Sir Arthur could now have advanced upon the rajah's capital, and completed the extinction of his power; but a vakeel had already arrived in his camp to solicit a conference preparatory to negotiation. This envoy endeavoured to prove that his master had never entertained any hostile intention; and after some unprofitable discussion on this question, asked the terms on which peace might now be obtained. The British commander demanded the cession of the maritime district of Cuttack, which was desirable for completing the Company's dominion over the eastern coast; also the surrender of a territory on the river Wurda, the authority over which had hitherto been inconveniently shared between the rajah and the nizam. Some further demands were made, but withdrawn; and the arrangements, being hastened by the fall of Gawilghur, were completed on the 16th, and the treaty signed at Deoghaun on the 17th December 1803.

The treaty of Deoghaun.

Meantime, the central regions of Hindostan were the theatre of events equally memorable. Scindia's force there consisted almost exclusively of the large corps formed on the European model by De Boigne, who, having returned to France, had, as we have already stated, been succeeded by Perron. These troops were considered very formidable, consisting of 16,000 or 17,000 regular infantry, from 15,000 to 20,000 cavalry, a large body of irregulars, and a well-appointed train of artillery. General Lake, having been informed of the failure of the negotiation with their master, moved from Cawnpoor on the 7th August 1803; on the 28th he passed the frontier, and next day found the whole of Perron's horse in a strong position near Coel, a town on the Doab. He presently led his

Formidable force in central Hindostan.

Advance of General Lake.

CHAP. XIV. A. D. 1803.

troops to the attack; when the native army, deemed so efficient and well equipped, after a short random fire retreated with such rapidity that the English could not overtake them. The next object was the fort of Alighur, the main depot of the enemy. It was a very strong place, surrounded with a good glacis, and a broad and deep ditch always filled with water. It would have been unassailable had the entrance been confined to a drawbridge; but a terrace had been imprudently formed for that purpose, over which Lake concluded his troops might force a passage. Colonel Monson, who led the storming-party, soon penetrated across the mound and over the breastwork; but the wall was so strongly guarded by spearmen, that he could not attempt escalade. A twelve-pounder was brought forward to burst open the gate; but before it could be pointed the soldiers remained exposed to a most galling fire, which severely wounded and disabled their leader himself. Major M'Leod succeeded to the command; and, after the first gate had been forced open, pushed his way through a long and intricate passage and two successive gateways to a fourth, against which, however, the gun was employed without effect. The situation of the assailants would now have been serious, had not the major succeeded in forcing the wicket, and thus opening an entrance to his countrymen, who soon became masters of the place.

Sudden retreat of the enemy.

Capture of the fort of Alighur.

Desertion of Scindia's cause by Perron.

It being understood that Perron was discontented with the service of Scindia, Lord Lake was authorized to make large offers on condition of his coming over to the English, and bringing his troops with him. In fact, a letter was received from him on the 7th September, requesting to be allowed to repair with his family, servants, and property, in safety to Lucknow, but without expressing any disposition to detach his army from their allegiance. His request was readily granted; and he afterwards stated his desertion to have been occasioned by the appointment of another officer to supersede him in the command.

After the capture of Alighur. Lake marched directly

upon Delhi, the imperial capital, and the residence of him who still enjoyed the rank and title of Great Mogul. He had advanced within view of its walls, when he discovered the army, organized under French command, drawn up in a strong position to defend its approaches. Though he had only 4500 men against 19,000, yet he determined to give battle without delay; but as the enemy could not without difficulty and severe loss have been dislodged from their present ground, he used a feigned retreat as a stratagem to draw them from it. This delicate manœuvre was executed by the British troops with the most perfect order; and the enemy, imagining the flight real, quitted their intrenchments, and eagerly pursued. But no sooner were they fully drawn forth on the plain than Lord Lake faced about, and in a single charge drove them from the field, with the loss of three thousand in killed and wounded, as well as their whole train of artillery.

CHAP. XIV.

A. D. 1803.

March on Delhi.

Successful stratagem of General Lake.

The British general now entered Delhi without resistance. He immediately requested and obtained an audience of the sovereign, with whom a secret communication had previously been opened. He beheld this unfortunate descendant of a long line of illustrious princes "seated under a small tattered canopy, the remnant of his former state, his person emaciated by indigence and infirmities, and his countenance disfigured with the loss of his eyes, and marked with extreme old age and a settled melancholy." He is described as deeply sensible to the kindness of Lake, on whom he bestowed several titles, such as "the sword of the state, the hero of the land, the lord of the age, and the victorious in war." All his adherents, and especially the inhabitants of Delhi, expressed delight on this occasion, and the journalists, in the language of oriental hyperbole, proclaimed that the emperor, through excess of joy, had recovered his sight. Mr Mill derides these rather pompous descriptions of the "delivering" of Shah Allum, as he was in fact merely transferred as a state-prisoner from one custody to another; yet, besides having suf-

His reception at Delhi.

His welcome by the people.

CHAP. XIV.

A. D. 1803.

Influence acquired by means of the Mogul.

fered the most barbarous usage from some of the native chiefs, he had endured from all of them very great neglect. The French officers seem to have been inclined to treat him with respect; but the funds obtained from Scindia for his support were exceedingly scanty. The English did not indeed restore any shadow of his former power; still they maintained him in comfort, and with some semblance of the pomp by which the Mogul throne had been anciently surrounded. In return, they obtained for all their measures the sanction of a name still venerated throughout the empire; in fact, they were thus virtually seated on the throne of India.

Capture of the town and fort of Agra.

The conquerors now marched upon Agra, the rival capital, which still possessed the advantage of being defended by a strong fort, occupied by a large body of troops. Anarchy however prevailed in the garrison, and the officers, being chiefly of English extraction, had become objects of suspicion, and were thrown into confinement. At the same time seven battalions of Scindia's army, having been denied admittance, lest they should claim a share of the riches it contained, still kept their post in the town and principal mosque. It was considered necessary to begin by dislodging them, which was effected, though not without an obstinate resistance; and the soldiers, to the amount of 2500, immediately transferred their services to the victors. The Mahratta leaders meanwhile resolved to propose a treaty of surrender; but as the time for its ratification approached they suddenly recommenced firing. The trenches were forthwith opened, and a breach being effected on the 17th October 1803, the enemy capitulated the same evening, stipulating only for the safety of their persons and private property. The treasure found here, amounting to no less than £280,000, was divided among the troops as prize-money.

Immense spoils.

Forces still in the field.

There remained still in the field a corps composed of troops detached from the Deccan, reinforced by fugitives from the different armies. General Lake hastened in pursuit of this force; and, considering it only as a collection of runaways deserted by their officers, little apprehended that he was about to encounter the most obstinate resistance he had sustained during the whole campaign. This body, consisting of 9000 foot, 5000 horse, and a numerous train of artillery, were rapidly retreating, when, on the 1st November, he overtook them with his cavalry alone, and determined, by an immediate attack, to prevent their escape. The enemy, however, having their motions concealed by a cloud of dust, speedily threw themselves into an advantageous position, which they strengthened by cutting the embankment of a reservoir in their front. The dragoons were led on, and had gained some advantages, when they suffered so severely by the fire from a number of well-served guns, that it was judged necessary to withdraw them, and wait till the infantry should come up. That force accordingly advanced; but the 76th regiment and a few companies of sepoys, having arrived earlier than the others, were exposed to so destructive a fire, that the general deemed it his wisest as well as safest plan, to lead singly to the charge "this handful of heroes." They accordingly carried all before them, though with severe loss; and when the Mahratta cavalry attempted to break their thinned ranks, the British horse triumphantly repelled the charge. The remainder of the foot soon appeared, and, after a desperate stand, the enemy, for the most part, were either destroyed or made prisoners. In short, by this brilliant success, the entire army, formed and disciplined under Scindia by British officers, and considered the finest possessed by any native power, was completely annihilated.

Their unexpected strength and vigour.

Bold movement of General Lake.

Total annihilation of Scindia's army.

Besides these achievements, the expeditions detached under Colonel Woodington into Guzerat, under Colonel Harcourt into Cuttack, and under Colonel Powell into Bundelcund, were all conducted with the most favourable results; though we have already hinted our doubts whether these troops might not have been more advantageously employed in strengthening the armies in the principal seat of war, and rendering the success there more prompt and decisive.

Achievements of detached bodies.

CHAP XIV.
A. D. 1803.

Scindia's submission.

Scindia, thus vanquished at every point, deserted by the Rajah of Berar, and seeing his finest levies destroyed, felt the necessity of relinquishing those expedients by which, till now, he had hoped to avert the necessity of a humiliating peace. On the 30th December 1803, a treaty was signed in General Wellesley's camp, by which he ceded the Doab, or territory between the Ganges and the Jumna, with considerable provinces beyond the latter river; surrendering thereby to the British

Terms of treaty.

dominion Delhi and Agra, the two capitals of the Great Mogul, and with them the person of the nominal emperor. He sacrificed also Baroach, with the rest of his maritime territory in Guzerat; while on the south he yielded Ahmednugger to the peishwa, and some extensive districts to the nizam. But he regained the other places conquered from him in the course of the war. Finally, pressing offers were made to him of a treaty on the same terms as that concluded with the peishwa, by which he should admit into his territory a subsidiary force that would relieve him to a great extent from the cares of government; but this courtesy was for the present positively declined.

Equivocal proceedings of Holkar

Meantime Holkar, while witnessing the downfal of the other members of the Mahratta confederacy, had maintained a very uncertain and equivocal position. At first he gave them ground to suppose that he would join their league; but on the actual commencement of hostilities he remained inactive, and seemed to watch the opportunity when the other powers should have exhausted themselves by mutual conflict, to throw himself in and secure a preponderance. He was struck with consternation at the victorious career of the English, who proceeded with such rapid steps, that before he could come to any decision they had completely realized their object.

Excites the alarm of Scindia.

He seems then to have shown some disposition to take advantage of the reduced state of Scindia, and to strengthen himself at his expense. That prince at least was so much alarmed, that he accepted the offer made by the Company of a subsidiary force of 6000 men, to be stationed, however, only on his frontier, while their maintenance was to be defrayed out of the districts already ceded. Holkar, seeing himself thus completely hemmed in, and all his schemes of conquest about to be checked by the British, seems to have hastily determined to plunge into a contest with them. He threatened the territory of their ally the Rajah of Jyenagur; he made extravagant and even insulting demands; and in a letter to Sir A. Wellesley, he said, "Countries of many hundred coss shall be overrun and plundered; Lord Lake shall not have leisure to breathe for a moment; and calamities will fall on lacks of human beings in continual war by the attacks of my army, which overwhelms like the waves of the sea." At the same time he earnestly invited Scindia, and the other princes who remained still independent, to unite against the English as a common enemy.

Hasty proceedings of Holkar.

The governor-general, in coming to the resolution of opening the campaign against Holkar, considered it necessary not merely to reduce and limit, but altogether to extirpate a power whose existence seemed incompatible with the repose and security of all the other states. To display, however, the disinterested views of the Company, it was determined not to retain any part of the conquered territory, but to distribute it among those chiefs who adhered even formally to her alliance. Scindia was to receive the largest share, provided he gave cordial aid in overthrowing the pretensions of his rival.

Liberal plan of conquest by the governor-general.

Holkar, however, was by no means a contemptible adversary. His cavalry, swelled by the wreck of the other defeated armies, and by numerous adventurers, amounted to 60,000, to which were added 15,000 well-disciplined infantry and 192 pieces of artillery. General Wellesley was unable to advance in consequence of a famine which prevailed in the Deccan; and Lake, after reducing the fort of Rampoora, left Colonel Monson, with five battalions and 3000 horsemen, to watch the enemy's movements. The prudence of this arrangement may be questioned. Holkar, who was a second Hyder for de-

Formidable power of Holkar.

Questionable arrangements of General Lake.

CHAP. XIV.

A.D. 1804.

Disastrous retreat of Colonel Monson.

sultory warfare, succeeded in bringing his whole force to act against this single detachment; yet it has been supposed, that, had Monson promptly led his men to the charge, he might have encountered with success the large undisciplined host opposed to him. But he resolved upon retreat, a movement always disastrous before Mahratta forces, which of all others are the most rapid and vindictive pursuers. Every thing, besides, combined to render his march unfortunate; the swelling of the rivers, the inundated and swampy plains, the scarcity of provisions, the desertion or hostility of the native troops, among whom was a strong party belonging to Scindia. These last, in the hour of distress, turned their arms against the British, whom they had undertaken to assist. The detachment, indeed, did not forfeit their honour, having triumphantly repulsed every attack; but they lost all their artillery and baggage; many of the sick, the exhausted, and the wounded were left behind, and cut to pieces; and when, on the 31st August 1804, they reached Agra, most of the regiments were in a state of total disorganization.

Rapid proceedings of General Lake.

Holkar advanced upon Muttra and took possession of it; but General Lake now proceeded with the utmost expedition from Cawnpoor, and having assembled his forces at Secundra, marched against the Mahratta army, which at once relinquished its position. The Indian chief, however, contrived, by alternately advancing and retreating with his cavalry, to occupy the attention of the British commander, while his infantry, by a rapid movement, succeeded in reaching Delhi on the 8th October, which they immediately invested. The city, ten miles in circumference, with a ruinous wall, was guarded only by a small body of sepoys. Lieutenant-colonels Ochterlony and Burn, however, led on these troops with such spirit and judgment, that all the enemy's attacks were repulsed, and after seven days of persevering efforts they were obliged to raise the siege.

Investment of Delhi by Holkar.

Lake, on receiving intelligence of the danger of Delhi, hastened to that capital, which he reached on the 17th October. Learning there that Holkar with his cavalry had begun a course of devastation along the Doab, he set out in pursuit of him. He sent at the same time his infantry, under General Fraser, to attack that of the enemy now stationed at Deeg, a strong fort belonging to the Rajah of Bhurtpore, who, on seeing the scale of fortune turn against the English, had embraced the opposite interest. Fraser found them on the 13th, skilfully intrenched under the stronghold just named, their front covered by a morass, and their left by a fortified village. The battle which followed was a repetition of the usual scene; the English rushing on in the face of a destructive cannonade, and suffering severely till they came to close quarters, then charging with the bayonet, and carrying all before them. Here there were successive lines of guns, which it was necessary to capture by repeated assaults. The general, a very gallant officer, received a wound that obliged him to quit the field, and afterwards proved mortal; the victory was completed by Colonel Monson. This action, like that of Assaye, was distinguished by a stratagem on the part of the Indian cavalry. Wheeling round and recovering several of the first line of guns, they turned them on the English rear; but they were soon chased off the field by twenty-eight men of the 76th, headed by Captain Norford, who, however, lost his life in the performance of this memorable exploit. At length the enemy were driven to the walls of the fort, with the loss of the greater part of their artillery, among which Monson recognised a portion of that lost during his late unfortunate retreat.

Pursuit of Holkar by General Lake.

Battle of Deeg.

Stratagem of the Indian cavalry.

Meantime the gallant Lake was in hot pursuit of the Mahratta chief, following him at the rate of twenty-three miles a-day; and at length, by marching fifty-three miles in twenty-four hours, he came up with him, on the 17th November, encamped under the walls of Furruckabad. The Indian horse, which never could stand a charge in the field, were routed, 3000 cut to pieces, and the rest saved only by the rapidity of their flight. Holkar then proceeded towards Deeg to join the remains of his in-

Rout of Holkar's horse.

CHAP XIV. A. D. 1804.

fantry: and the British general arriving at that fortress on the 1st December, determined immediately to undertake the siege. Ten days, however, elapsed before the battering-train could be brought from Agra, and thirteen days more before a breach could be effected in a detached work which commanded the approach. It was then carried by storm on the night of the 23d, and the enemy were so struck by the daring intrepidity of the assailants, that, in the course of the two following days, they evacuated both the town and fort, and retreated towards Bhurtpore.

Storming of Furrack-abad.

Holkar's reverse of fortune.

Holkar was now about to sustain a complete reverse of fortune. While the strength of his army was broken by recent defeats, his dominions, whence he might have drawn recruits and resources, had fallen into the enemy's possession. Colonel Wallace from the Deccan had reduced Chandore and the other strongholds in that quarter while Colonel Murray from Guzerat, having overrun nearly the whole of Malwa, and entered Indore the capital, was already preparing to intercept his retreat. The only point of resistance was Bhurtpore, the rajah of which still adhered to his alliance; and the reduction of that city was therefore considered necessary to complete the triumph over this turbulent chieftain. At first sight, the place did not present a very formidable aspect to an army before which many of the mightiest bulwarks of India had fallen. It was encircled by none of those rugged steeps which guarded the approach to Gwalior and Asseerghur. The only works were a lofty mud-wall and a broad ditch not easily fordable; and the very extent of its walls, which embraced a circumference of six or eight miles, increased the difficulty of protecting them. But the rajah applied himself to its defence with the utmost skill and resolution: the kingdom of the Mahrattas, he observed, was in their saddle; his was within his ramparts. Hitherto, in general, the reduction even of the strongest forts had proceeded in a sure and regular course; the trenches were opened, a storming-party was selected, who forced their way with

Bhurtpore.

Skilful measures of the rajah.

greater or smaller loss, and were masters of the place. But the defenders of Bhurtpore not only fought with the most daring valour, but called into action means of defence and annoyance which our people had never elsewhere encountered, and for which they were wholly unprepared. They rendered the breach impracticable, by raising behind it stockades and other bulwarks; they made the ditch unfordable, by damming up the waters; and during the assault, logs of wood, pots filled with combustibles, and burning cotton-bales steeped in oil, were thrown down upon the soldiers. In short, the British were repulsed in four successive attempts, sustaining in killed and wounded a loss of 3203,—greater than had occurred in any two battles during this obstinately disputed campaign. Even their glory was somewhat tarnished. The 76th, hitherto the bravest among the brave and the foremost in every triumph, along with the 75th, refused on one occasion to follow their officers, after the 12th Bengal sepoys had planted the colours on the top of the rampart. Being bitterly reproached by General Lake for having thus caused the failure of the assault, they were overpowered with shame, and entreated to be led to a last attack, in which they displayed a desperate but useless valour.

Obstinate defence of Bhurtpore.

Repulse and severe loss of the British.

It was now necessary to intermit the operations of the siege in order to repair the losses sustained, and to bring forward more adequate means of attack. The rajah, however, apprehensive of the final issue, and seeing that certain ruin must accompany the fall of his capital, made very advantageous overtures, including the payment of twenty lacks of rupees as the price of peace; while, on the other hand, the situation of affairs was such as induced the English general, on the 10th April, to embrace the conditions, and even to promise, in case of a steady adherence to treaty, the restoration of the fortress of Deeg.

Advantageous overtures of the rajah.

Holkar, during the siege, had made several exertions to interrupt or retard it by movements with his cavalry. He partly succeeded; but a large body of his men

Exertions of Holkar during the siege.

CHAP. XIV

A. D. 1804.

His desperate condition.

under Ameer Khan was entirely defeated, and some smaller detachments suffered so severely, that at length they fled at the mere sight of their antagonists. This chief, therefore, after being deserted by the Rajah of Bhurtpore, was reduced almost to the condition of a fugitive; and his situation seemed altogether desperate, when relief came from an unexpected quarter.

Unexpected relief.

Scindia, who had been strongly affected on witnessing the commencement of the war by Holkar, and the brilliant successes with which he had opened the campaign, evidently cherished the idea of seizing this opportunity to retrieve his own fortunes; but the indecisive character of Indian councils caused him to advance towards his object only by tardy and circuitous steps. He began by raising his demands upon the British; he marched his troops towards their frontier, and when remonstrated with, delayed upon various pretexts to withdraw them. At length, when Holkar, after the peace made by the Bhurtpore rajah, was retreating in a shattered and reduced condition, he received him into his camp; having already committed the almost unprecedented outrage of plundering the abode and seizing the person of the British resident.

Scindia's breach of faith.

Change of British policy in India.

Lord Lake, as the rainy season now approached, could not immediately follow the two hostile chiefs into the heart of their territories. Their power, however, was so completely broken that he entertained no doubt of soon reducing them to submission: but at this crisis the whole system of our policy respecting India underwent an important change.

Public opinion.

The vast scheme of conquest and subsidiary alliance, by which Marquis Wellesley had studied to place this great eastern empire under British control, had excited in the mother country a very deep sensation. The public were, to a certain degree, dazzled with its splendid success; yet a numerous body of politicians exclaimed that this course was contrary to all true principles of policy,—that it formed an interminable system of war, —that the Company, in seating themselves upon the throne of the Mogul, and endeavouring to effect the conquest of all Hindostan, had entirely relinquished the basis on which they had uniformly professed to act. The contest with Holkar, breaking out with so formidable an aspect after all the others had closed, gave rise to painful feelings as to the endless duration of Indian hostility. The Directors, strongly influenced by public opinion, and struck by the enormous expenditure in which the campaign had already involved them, determined to change entirely the system on which their affairs were conducted. Accordingly, in place of the Marquis Wellesley, who, with or without reason, had acquired the reputation of a war-governor, they substituted the Marquis Cornwallis. This nobleman had not, indeed, while in power, pursued a course materially different; yet his character was generally esteemed moderate and conciliatory, and he was understood to disapprove of the extent to which conquest had now been carried. His instructions were to proceed on principles every way opposite to those of his predecessor,—to conclude peace almost at any price,—to form a defensive line beyond which English interference was not to extend; and to allow the native powers to treat and to fight with each other as if situated at the extremity of the globe.

Marquis Cornwallis appointed governor.

The courts of directors and proprietors voted thanks to the Marquis Wellesley for his zeal, vigour, activity, and ability, to which they attributed in a great measure the brilliant successes which had crowned the British arms. They qualified the vote, however, by stating, that it was "without entering at present into the origin and policy of that war." This reservation was deeply felt by the marquis, who intimated that, while the votes of thanks to the commanders had been communicated in general orders to the army, and in an extraordinary gazette, he considered it his duty to forego the gratification of publishing his own. These expressions would, he thought, convey a universal impression of doubt and uncertainty respecting all the recent arrangements and the permanency of all treaties with the native powers.

Qualified acknowledgment of Wellesley's services.

CHAP. XIV. A.D. 1804. He pressed the question home upon the courts, by observing, "the general fame of your equity and magnanimity precludes any supposition, that in condemning the justice of our cause, you would retain the fruits of our success."

Questionable safety of abandoning his policy. Admitting that the policy of Marquis Wellesley was not quite so pacific as his friends contended, it was very doubtful how far it could now with safety, or even with justice, be thus abruptly relinquished. A great power can seldom be justified in withdrawing from all concern in the contests of its neighbours, from endeavouring to protect the weak against the strong, and thereby preventing any one of them from acquiring a decided preponderance. It was perhaps chimerical to suppose that the principal native chiefs would cultivate habits of sincere peace, or entertain a solid attachment for the British government. Character of the native chiefs. They were for the most part usurpers, who had started up amid the ruins of one great empire; each seeking to aggrandize himself at the expense of the rest, and viewing undivided dominion as a prize at which he might aim. They had all, however, through the interposition of the Company, seen their aspiring views checked or baffled, their armies vanquished, and some of the brightest jewels plucked from their diadems. There could be little doubt, therefore, that when left to themselves there would be a struggle for the mastery; and that either by him who should succeed in this object, or by a league of all united, an effort would be made to overthrow the ascendency of England, and to regain the possessions which she had wrested from them. According to the advocates of the Wellesley policy, the system pursued by that nobleman was so far advanced towards maturity that only one effort, of easy and assured success, was necessary to place all India in a state of tranquillity, and to keep down those discordant elements which would otherwise lay waste the country itself. By stopping short at this point, great part of the empire was involved in calamity and disorder, and the foundation laid for another expensive and even perilous struggle.

Danger involved in a change of policy.

Lord Wellesley, owing to the state of his health, had announced the necessity of returning to Europe as soon as the contest with Scindia and the Rajah of Berar should have been brought to a termination. On learning, however, the rupture with Holkar, he intimated his willingness to remain, and bring it also to a close: but the views of the government at home were different. On the 30th July 1805, Marquis Cornwallis arrived at Calcutta; where, learning that the war was still going on, he determined to proceed immediately into the upper provinces, and make personal inquiry into the state of affairs. In his zeal for the public service, however, and to fulfil the anxious wish of his countrymen, he had undertaken this duty at a period when his age and infirmities rendered him very unequal to its performance. Under the fatigue of the voyage his illness daily increased, till on reaching the village of Gazypoor on the Ganges, he was obliged to land, and after lingering some time died on the 5th of October. Having been unable to reach his destination, while his mind as well as body were impaired by indisposition, he had been little able to receive or consider any fresh information. His place was supplied by Sir George Barlow, the senior member of the supreme council, who had reached that station through various gradations of service, which he had filled with distinction; but his previous habits had not accustomed him to take comprehensive and statesmanlike views of public interests. Regarding with the deepest respect the views of his predecessor, and considering them as supported by the government at home, he refused to listen to any arguments, or admit any of the modifications suggested by Lord Lake.

Arrival of the Marquis Cornwallis.

His death.

Sir George Barlow.

That commander, although he disapproved of the new system, finding it was firmly established by the supreme power, judiciously sought to carry it into effect on the most advantageous footing. He managed, with great address, to draw the first overtures from Scindia; and as it had been determined to yield all the points in dispute, no difficulty was found in the conclusion of a treaty

Judicious proceedings of Lord Lake

CHAP. XIV.
A. D. 1805.

Concessions to Scindia.

on the 23d November 1805. The Mahratta leader obtained the highly-important fortress of Gwalior, which he made his residence and capital; the Chumbul was fixed as the boundary between his possessions and those of the British, who agreed to dissolve their alliance with the Rajpoot princes and others whom he claimed as tributaries. This last measure was in accordance with the new political system; yet in the case of the Rajahs of Boondee and Jyepore, who on the ground of this connexion had performed important services, it was considered scarcely compatible with national faith.

Advantages acquired by Holkar.

Holkar, after being deserted by his ally, retreated with the wrecks of his army into the western provinces to seek refuge among the Seiks. They refused to receive him; and, being closely pursued by Lord Lake, he must have been reduced to extremities had he not been saved by the new policy which the military commanders were compelled to observe. No sooner did he ask for peace, than it was granted on terms so advantageous, as allowed him to regain almost all that he had lost during the war.

Consideration of defensive alliances.

Amid this general dissolution of defensive alliances, those formed on the great scale with the nizam and the peishwa necessarily came under consideration. The connexion with the latter, founded on the treaty of Bassein, and out of which the late war had arisen, was described by the Company as one which they were desirous to relinquish. Yet even Sir George Barlow, when he came to consider the proposed measures, could not but view them as fraught with extreme peril. To dissolve the alliance with these potentates, and to withdraw the troops by which they were at present overawed, would have been to relieve the greater part of the powers of India from British control, while they were still animated by the most hostile feelings towards her; it would, in fact, have been to lay the foundation of a future confederacy for her downfal. The peishwa, likewise, notwithstanding his general aversion to the English, had motives, connected with the internal state of his dominions, which

Extreme peril involved in their dissolution.

made him desirous, for the present at least, to claim on that ground the fulfilment of the treaty of Bassein.

Lord Minto appointed governor.

Sir George Barlow was succeeded in 1807 by Lord Minto, a prudent and intelligent nobleman, who endeavoured in his general system to maintain the pacific policy recommended by the Company, without shrinking from vigorous and even hostile demonstrations, when the conduct of the native powers appeared to render these necessary. The great states during his administration retained their position nearly unaltered; but animosities continued to ferment, which were destined to burst into a violent tempest, and to involve India afresh in a sanguinary war.

CHAPTER XV.

Pindaree War—Conquest of the Mahrattas, &c.

Progress of the Pindarees—Their Character—Ameer Khan—Arrangements with the Peishwa—Trimbuckjee—He murders the Guzerat Minister—Is delivered up to the English—Escapes—Concessions required from the Peishwa—Marquis of Hastings arrives in India—Rupture with Nepaul—Death of General Gillespie—Successes of Ochterlony—Negotiations—Renewal of the War—Final Treaty—Alliance formed with Berar—Irruptions of the Pindarees—Opening of the Campaign against them—Treaties with Scindia and Ameer Khan—The Cholera attacks the Grand Army—Rise and Diffusion of that Malady in India—Alarming Accounts from Poonah—Operations against the Pindarees—The Adherents of Holkar join them—Battle of Mehidpoor—Treaty—Final Catastrophe of the Pindaree Chiefs—Movements of the Peishwa—He attacks the English—His Repulse and continued Flight—Repeated Defeats—Surrender—Intrigues at Nagpore—The Rajah attacks the English—Issue of the Contest—His Escape—Contest with Bhurtpore—Disturbances in Bengal and the Circars—Campaign against Coorg—Troubles at Gwalior—Jondpore—Jeypore—Lord Bentinck succeeded by Lord Auckland—Contest with Goomsoor—Succession of Oude—Charges against the Rajah—His Deposition—Discussions on the Subject—Local Disturbances in India.

CHAP. XV
A. D. 1807.
The Pindarees.

IN the aspect which India at this period exhibited, the most remarkable feature consisted in the marauding habits of the people by whom so large a portion of it was occupied. A new power which rose without any basis to rest upon, without country or territory to claim for its own, and without any regular place in the political system, was chiefly supported by the roving tribes named Pindarees, who carried to an extreme all the predatory usages characteristic of Mahrattas. The latter, indeed, regarded plunder as an essential part of their policy; still they had a country and a home to which they were fondly attached; and they had regular occupations which they followed in the intervals, unconnected with their more violent pursuits. Their chiefs aimed not merely to enrich themselves by booty, but also to attain political power. The Pindarees, on the contrary, were nothing more than robbers, elevated by their number into armies; and their boast was, not that they were able to encounter disciplined troops, but that they could elude them. If overtaken or surprised, the point of honour was, who should flee the most swiftly. No barrier arrested them; they penetrated the closest chain of military posts, finding a way even between the divisions of an army drawn up to oppose them; they desolated the countries in the rear; after which, making an immense circuit, they returned home by a different route. Their aim was, not to possess a district, but to sweep away all that was in it. Obliged to pass with a celerity almost preternatural, and to employ expeditious modes of extracting treasure, they inflicted the most merciless tortures to compel the owners to yield up their concealed hoards. Redhot irons were applied to the soles of the feet; oil was thrown on the clothes, and inflamed; the head was tied into a bag filled with hot ashes and dust. The proudest exploit of a Pindaree was to steal a horse; and this operation was conducted with a dexterity which might put to shame the most skilful of their fraternity in Europe. They could carry one off from amid a crowded camp: stretched on their bellies they crept to the spot, and lay concealed till a favourable moment, when they cut the cords, mounted, and galloped off among the bushes with a rapidity that defied pursuit. When an enemy was distant, they divided into small parties, moving in a circular direction, so as to sweep the whole country. Their numbers were continually augmented by disbanded soldiers, and by persons of idle and desperate character. The leaders annually raised their standard on the northern bank of the Nerbudda at the termination of the rains, that they might be ready, as soon as the rivers should become fordable, to commence a general movement.

Comparison of the Mahrattas and Pindarees.

Barbarous cruelties of the Pindarees.

Dexterous thefts.

Predatory system.

CHAP. XV.

A.D. 1809.

Mohammedan predatory bands.

The Patan and other Mohammedan troops, who, in the wreck of all the thrones occupied by their countrymen, had no longer a sovereign in whose service to fight, afforded another source whence predatory squadrons were formed and recruited. Most of them rallied round Ameer Khan, a bold and enterprising chief, who in the late war had fought under the banner of Holkar. He still retained his allegiance to that house, and attempted to direct its councils; but his main object was, with his chosen band of about 12,000 horse and 200 pieces of artillery, to overawe and extort contributions from the Rajpoot and other petty states in this part of India. Though equally destitute of fixed possessions, and as much devoted to plunder as the Pindarees, he acted more systematically, and aimed at the attainment of political influence; yet, in Sir John Malcolm's opinion, the Mohammedans, from their tendency to sink into indolence and luxury, are less to be dreaded than the Hindoos, who, though they yield for the moment, pursue their object, on the whole, with unwearied perseverance.

Ameer Khan.

Expedition against Berar.

Though Ameer Khan formed a power distinct from the Pindarees, he easily attracted large bodies of them to any enterprise that promised to gratify their appetite for plunder. Such was the expedition which, in 1809, he undertook against Berar, then governed by an effeminate unwarlike sovereign; and he would have succeeded in subverting that monarchy, had not Lord Minto wisely departed from his strictly defensive system. A strong detachment under Colonel Close was despatched into the territory of Nagpore, which, it was notified to Ameer, was under British protection. That adventurer made a blustering and indignant reply, but was soon, by a variety of circumstances, compelled to retreat into Malwa; and the governor-general, on farther consideration, gave up the design which he had once entertained, of finally crushing him.

Tactics of Lord Minto.

Tardy arrangements with the peishwa.

The arrangements with the peishwa, meantime, proceeded also in a very unsatisfactory manner. That prince began, indeed, by courting the English, and even solicit-

CHAP. XV. A. D. 1809.

ing the continuance of their subsidiary force in his territory; but his object was to regain the control which he had almost entirely lost over his own dominions. Besides the provinces possessed by Scindia and other independent princes, numerous districts, especially in the south, had been parcelled out into *jaghires*, which, like the European fiefs in the Middle Ages, were held on the mere tenure of homage and military service. To make the resemblance more complete, the jaghiredars, during the recent period of public confusion, had secured for themselves a condition of almost complete independence. The Company felt considerable difficulty when importuned for aid against these chiefs, with many of whom, during the late exigencies, they had formed an alliance; notwithstanding, they agreed to enforce over them the authority of the peishwa, not as an absolute sovereign, but as their liege lord. As these proud dependants, however, were little inclined to own even this imperfect obligation, they imposed on their head the frequent necessity of calling upon his allies to support his claims, and of declaring their possessions forfeited. Thus, in a few years, principally through the aid or fear of our countrymen, he had reduced most of these retainers, and enriched his treasury by extensive confiscation. Having completely recovered his power and provided the necessary funds, he resolved at once to shake off also the British yoke, and to re-establish his influence over the great feudatories of the Mahratta state. For this purpose he availed himself of the services of Trimbuckjee Dainglia, a bold, able, but very dissolute minister, raised from the lowest ranks, and entirely devoted to his master's purposes. The British resident from the first viewed with umbrage the elevation of this personage, and was soon brought into direct collision with him. The peishwa, among his other plans of aggrandizement, had revived certain ancient claims on the *guickwar* or sovereign of Guzerat, with whom also the Company had formed a subsidiary alliance. As the negotiations on this subject became extremely intricate, it was agreed that Gungadhur Sastree,

Jaghires.

Difficulty of dealing with them.

Bold position recovered by Scindia.

Trimbuckjee Dainglia.

CHAP. XV — A. D. 1809.

Gungadhur sastree.

the prime minister of that state, should repair to the court of Poonah, and endeavour to place them on an intelligible basis; having, however, previously obtained a safe conduct from the English. From being supposed favourable to our interests, as well as from some personal causes, he incurred the enmity of Trimbuckjee and the peishwa; and to gratify their revenge, they prevailed upon him to accompany them to Punderpoor, where a religious festival of peculiar solemnity was to be celebrated. After their arrival Gungadhur, though indisposed, was induced to repair to the temple with a few unarmed attendants. On the way certain persons were heard asking in a whispering tone which was the sastree; to this it was answered that it was he who wore the necklace; but the question, it was imagined, was prompted by mere curiosity. The minister, having performed his devotions, was returning with a diminished escort, when several men, with long twisted cloths used for the purpose, called aloud to clear the way: and the sastree being thus left alone, they rushed upon him with drawn swords, and quickly pierced him with numerous wounds. Every thing conspired to render it manifest that Trimbuckjee was the author of this daring crime; for the assassins, who had left him in the temple, were seen running back with naked weapons. On the most trivial pretexts, however, he declined to submit to any formal investigation. In short, the inquiries of Mr Elphinstone, the resident, left no room to doubt that he was the direct instigator of the murder, and had obtained the full consent of Bajee Rao to its perpetration.

His assassination.

Decisive measures of the British minister.

The British minister, on this emergency, determined to adopt the most decisive measures, and, with the view of giving effect to the negotiation, ordered the auxiliary force to approach nearer to Poonah. The peishwa, evidently apprehensive of being personally charged with the deed, evaded, on various grounds, all communication on the subject. At length, two persons in his confidence waited on the resident, apparently with a view to sound his intentions. Mr Elphinstone allowed them to understand that there was no design of fixing the crime upon the peishwa; indeed, when he made any allusion to the rumour of Bajee's guilt, it was with the air of entire disbelief, and only to show the necessity of his disproving it by bringing the real offender to justice. It was demanded that Trimbuckjee, who was openly charged with the murder, should, with his two principal accomplices, be placed in close confinement to await a full investigation. The prince studiously employed every expedient to save his favourite; sometimes endeavouring to justify him, and at other times declaring it beyond his power to effect his arrest. The suspicion thus afforded of a determination to screen the offender, induced the resident, with the concurrence of the governor-general, to demand that he should be delivered into British custody. This proposal was of course still more revolting to the peishwa, who began to augment his troops; and it was understood that he was on the point of making common cause with his minister,—to flee with him from the capital, and endeavour to raise the Mahrattas against the Company. Mr Elphinstone then considered it indispensable to order the subsidiary force to march upon Poonah; but Bajee Rao, when he saw the sword about to be drawn, lost courage, and Trimbuckjee was delivered into the hands of the English. This they esteemed an important triumph, having long foreseen that they must ultimately come to a rupture with this person, who had shown a disposition the most evidently hostile; yet to have driven him from power, merely because he supported his master's interests and opposed a foreign influence, would have been extremely odious in the eyes of the nation. But the crime with which he stood charged, being aggravated in the view of the natives by every possible circumstance, as having been committed on a Bramin of high sanctity, and within the precincts of one of their holiest shrines, threw a great degree of popularity on the vigorous steps taken by the resident for its punishment.

Efforts of Bajee Rao to screen his minister.

Trimbuckjee delivered up to the English.

Popular hatred of his crime.

Our countrymen conducted their prisoner to the strong fortress of Tannah in the island of Salsette, and watched

CHAP. XV. — A.D. 1816.

Jealous guard of their prisoner.

him so narrowly that they did not admit a single native into the guard. But this excessive precaution was perhaps the very circumstance which defeated their object. The vicinity was filled with the minister's adherents; and a groom in the service of one of the British officers, in passing near the terrace where the accused was allowed to walk, chanted gaily what was supposed to be a Hindoo song, but which really communicated a plan contrived for his escape. Through a small gap in the wall of the edifice, he reached a stable; and not being missed for a few minutes, succeeded in crossing the narrow channel which separates Salsette from the continent. He immediately hastened to the southern districts, where he began to levy troops, and raise the whole country against the English.

His escape.

Double dealing of Bajee Rao.

The peishwa disavowed all knowledge of the course taken by Trimbuckjee after his escape, as well as of the place of his retreat; and as no proof could be obtained of the falsehood of this declaration, the good understanding between the two states was not at first interrupted. Bajee's conduct, however, became more and more unsatisfactory. Troops were indeed sent, ostensibly to put down the insurrection; but they reported that they could not find an enemy; and, in fact, they held a friendly communication with the very individual whose plans they professed to oppose. The British resident farther learned that the prince was in active correspondence with the insurgents; that he had held an interview with Trimbuckjee at a village seventeen miles from Poonah; and had even forwarded to him liberal supplies of money; being at the same time employed in military preparations, with the intention, as was suspected, of co-operating with him. Secret negotiations were also carried on with Scindia, Holkar, and other Mahratta chiefs, for the purpose of uniting the whole confederation for the overthrow of British power. All remonstrances relative to these proceedings having been met by a positive denial, as well as by a refusal to adopt any of the measures demanded as proofs of an amicable disposition, it was

His correspondence with the insurgents.

Native confederation against the British.

CHAP. XV.

A. D. 1817.

thought inconsistent with sound policy to allow this combination to reach maturity. Mr Elphinstone ordered the subsidiary force to advance upon Poonah, and gave notice to the peishwa, that hostilities would commence within twenty-four hours, unless three of his strongest fortresses, Singurh, Rayree, and Poorundur, should be provisionally placed in the hands of the English, and assurance given that within a month Trimbuckjee would be again delivered up. Bajee Rao delayed some time to give any answer; but at length, with that infirmity of purpose which usually appeared in the hour of danger, he agreed unconditionally to all these terms. The fortresses were surrendered, and a price set on the head of the minister. Still the resident gave warning, that these concessions could not be considered as final; and that the peishwa, having forfeited the confidence of the Company, could not expect the treaty of Bassein to be renewed, unless under modifications, the extent of which must depend upon the next despatch from the governor-general. Accordingly it was soon after announced, that amicable relations could only be restored on the following terms:—That the subsidiary force should be augmented by 5000 horse and 3000 infantry, for the maintenance of which, territories yielding a revenue of 34 lacks of rupees must be ceded; that in this cession the strong city of Ahmednugger should be included; tha his highness should renounce the character of head oı the Mahratta confederacy, and cease to hold direct communication with any of the native powers. These severe conditions the peishwa sought by every effort to mitigate or elude; but as the resident remained inflexible, a treaty to this effect was signed on the 13th June 1817.

Decisive measures of the English minister.

Bajee Rao's unconditional surrender.

Severe conditions imposed.

In carrying on the narrative of the transactions at Poonah, we have been led beyond the commencement of the administration of the Marquis of Hastings, who arrived in the end of the year 1813. The Company, in appointing to this high station so eminent a military character, seemed to intimate a conviction that the pacific or merely defensive policy on which they had for some time acted

Marquis of Hastings appointed governor.

CHAP. XV.

A.D. 1813.

Change of policy.

could not be much longer maintained. Lord Hastings in fact soon indicated a disposition to resume the more active scheme of government so ably pursued by the Marquis Wellesley. He appeared resolved to suppress the growing power of the predatory associations; to renew the alliances with the Rajpoot and other minor chiefs; and generally to establish the control of the English over the Indian states. But his attention was for a time drawn off by movements in a new and somewhat unexpected quarter.

Fierce tribes of the Himmaleh.

The extensive region which slopes downward from the summit of the Himmaleh to the plain of Hindostan has always been occupied by fierce and warlike tribes. Being, as described in a former chapter, broken into a number of narrow valleys separated by steep and lofty ridges, it had been parcelled out among various independent chiefs, never before united in such a way as to prove dangerous to the central kingdoms. Lately, however, the Gorkhas, a rude but brave race of men, led by a warlike commander, had conquered the valleys of Nepaul, the finest which intersect that magnificent range of mountains. Thither they transferred the seat of their government, and having by a skilful policy conciliated the neighbouring princes, had made this acquisition a step to farther conquest. They accordingly proceeded to subdue different tracts, till their territory extended above 800 miles in length, and comprehended nearly the whole Alpine region of Northern India. They then cast a longing eye towards the wide plain that spreads beneath, covered with all the riches of tropical cultivation, and capable of affording an ample revenue. Being generally superior to the native troops, both in courage and discipline, they might perhaps in favourable circumstances have founded an empire equal to that of Aurengzebe. They had, however, to encounter, not the fallen fragments of Mogul greatness, nor the loose squadrons of Mahratta horse, but the disciplined strength of that new power which had become paramount in Hindostan. The British, by the numerous victories gained in the late war,

The Gorkhas.

New kingdom established in Northern India.

Plans of conquest.

CHAP. XV.

A.D. 1814.

had extended their boundaries along nearly the whole line of this mountain-domain. The Gorkhas, on seeing their career thus checked, hesitated for some time whether they should commit themselves against so formidable an adversary. Meanwhile they appropriated certain small portions of territory, to which, by the vague tenures prevalent in that country, they could found some ancient claim. Repeated complaints being made, they at length agreed that deputies from either side should meet in order to examine and decide the pretensions to the land in dispute. The commissioners assembled; but those of Nepaul, it is alleged, showed a singular insensibility to the clearest proof of the total absence of right on their part to the favoured spots of which they had taken possession; and even where they were obliged to yield, the supreme authority evaded or retracted its sanction. At length the governor-general, considering the claim to a particular district most clearly established, sent a detachment, which provisionally occupied it, till these endless discussions should terminate. The Nepaulese did not at first oppose this movement; but as soon as the troops had retired during the unhealthy season, leaving only a small party to guard the frontier, they advanced in force and drove them out, killing and wounding several of their number. After this there was no longer room to hesitate as to the immediate necessity of warlike operations.

Apprehensions of British power.

Evasive policy.

Interference of the governor-general.

Ameer Sing, the able and enterprising commander of the Nepaulese, on grounds which it seems impossible fully to understand or justify, had taken post on the western extremity of their conquests. Lord Hastings, who, in 1814, sent into the field a force of 30,000 men, availing himself of the position assumed by the enemy, formed the plan of enclosing his army, and cutting it off from the central territories. Generals Ochterlony and Gillespie, at the head of their respective divisions, marched, the one to attack Ameer in front, the other to occupy the passes by which he might effect his retreat. The latter speedily penetrated into the Deyra Dhoon, one of the finest valleys which diversify the Himmaleh, and

Ameer Sing's proceedings.

British forces take the field.

CHAP. XV.

A. D. 1814.

the main channel of communication between the eastern and western districts. Somewhat unexpectedly he found this passage commanded by the fortress of Kalunga, or Nalapanee, rendered formidable, not by artificial bulwarks, but by its situation on the top of a hill, where it could only be approached through a thick and entangled jungle. That gallant officer, however, perceiving that it formed the key of the territory, hesitated not to commence an attack. He divided his army into four detachments, which, advancing from different points, were to meet at the summit, and engage in a common assault.

Fortress of Kalunga.

Such a plan is at first view imposing; yet it appears founded on false principles, and in practice is likely to prove extremely perilous. The chances are many that the different corps will not all reach their destination at the same moment; and if one arrive before the others, it will have to encounter the united resistance of the enemy's force. Such was the case now; one division making their way through every difficulty, arrived in front of Kalunga before they could be supported by the rest of the army. The general then came up, and seeing his troops thus exposed to the whole fire of the besieged, led them at once to the assault, hoping, with this corps alone, to carry the place. They accordingly dislodged the outposts, and arrived under the very walls; but were twice driven back by showers of grape-shot, arrows, and destructive missiles peculiar to Indian warfare. Gillespie, nevertheless, determining to carry the fort or die, placed himself at the head of the storming-party, and cheered them on, waving his hat, and pointing with his sword to the gate. At this moment a ball pierced his heart,—he fell; and all hopes of success were at once abandoned. The arrival of another division served merely to cover the retreat of the former. Colonel Mawbey, however, who succeeded to the command, felt deeply the importance that this first and great military operation should not be finally abortive; but he was obliged to delay his meditated attack till a battering-train was procured from Delhi. Three days

Perilous plan of attack.

Death of General Gillespie.

afterwards a breach was effected, and an assault commenced, under the command of Major Ingleby; but the resolute defence, and formidable fire of the garrison. again baffled every effort. The batteries, notwithstanding, continued to play till the walls, which were by no means lofty, were reduced almost to a heap of ruins; and the natives then evacuated the place which they had so gallantly defended. General Martindale, who now took the command, advanced to attack the enemy stationed at the strong fort of Jytuk; but here again the British troops, through their too impetuous valour, were thrown into confusion, and obliged to fall back with considerable loss. At the same time, the army which was attempting to penetrate direct into Nepaul through the district of Sarun had two of its detachments surrounded and cut off; on which account operations on that side were completely paralyzed.

Evacuation of the fortress.

British repulses.

These events produced an alarming sensation at Calcutta, while they were received with the highest exultation in all the native courts, which were watching for an opportunity to effect the downfal of British power in India. Movements were made by Scindia and other princes, which seemed to call for an increase of the corps of observation stationed in their territories. Yet the Marquis of Hastings, judiciously considering that to obtain some decisive success over the Nepaulese and compel them to sue for peace was the only mode by which the evil could be remedied, augmented and concentrated his force already stationed on the theatre of war. General Ochterlony, hitherto checked by the losses of the division that was to act in combination with him, began vigorous operations on the offensive. He had already compelled Ameer Sing to retire from the heights of Ramghur to those of Malown, which were also exceedingly strong. He had likewise reduced Ramghur, Bellaspore, and the other fastnesses that commanded this mountain-region. At the same time the province of Kemaoon being left unprotected, a detachment was sent under Colonel Nicolls, who besieged, and, on the 25th April 1815, took Almora,

Alarm at Calcutta

Judicious proceedings of the governor-general

Operations of General Ochterlony

CHAP. XV. A.D. 1816.

its capital. Ameer, now closely confined to his fortified post at Malown, was obliged to capitulate, though on honourable terms, being allowed to join the main army with the troops under his charge.

Submission of Nepaul.

The government of Nepaul were so deeply discouraged by these reverses, that notwithstanding the opposition of several chiefs, and particularly of Ameer Sing, who proposed even to seek support from the Emperor of China, they determined to open a negotiation. The terms demanded by Lord Hastings were high,—including the cession of all the provinces conquered in the west, and also of the Teraee or Tarryani, the border of jungle which extends along the base of the mountains. This last

Obstacles to the proposed treaty.

article formed the chief obstacle to the treaty, not so much on account of the actual value of the territory, as because most of the principal chiefs at court had in it assignments of land from which they derived their income The marquis, considering the point to be of little consequence, had made up his mind, and given directions that it should not stand in the way of an adjustment. The

Negotiations broken off.

Nepaulese ambassadors had, in fact, agreed to the terms and signed them, but when transmitted for ratification, the court was induced, on the grounds just stated, to refuse its consent. In such circumstances, there appeared no longer room for the intended concession; and no alternative was left but the renewal of war. This was attended with considerable inconvenience, since, in confident expectation of peace, the preparations had not only been relaxed, but even part of the military stores sold off; however, extraordinary exertions were made, and the army, in January 1816, was again ready to take the field.

War renewed.

The enemy had intrenched themselves in the strong pass of Chereea-ghatee, which formed the entrance into their mountain-territory; but General Ochterlony, by a skilful though laborious march, turned this position, and penetrated to Muckwanpoor, in the vicinity of which they had erected several forts and stockades. Two successive defeats convinced them of the folly of their attempt to contend with British troops; they made overtures for a fresh negotiation, in which all the points in dispute were yielded; and in March a definitive treaty was concluded. The governor-general was then with a good grace able to grant, as a matter of favour, most of the districts for the possession of which they had been so extremely solicitous.

Negotiations resumed

The contest with Nepaul having been brought to a successful termination, the Marquis of Hastings turned his views to that new system of policy, which he was desirous to establish with regard to the central powers of India. It consisted partly in the renewal and extension of subsidiary alliances with the native princes, partly in the extirpation of the predatory states which had arisen in the heart of the empire. In the former view, overtures from Bhopal, when threatened by Scindia and the Rajah of Berar, were at first well received; but, amid the distractions occasioned by the Nepaul contest, it became necessary that they should be courteously evaded. A negotiation was opened with the Rajpoot prince of Jyepore, who had made heavy complaints of having in 1806 been deserted by the English, and exposed to the depredations of the Holkar family and other plundering tribes. The treaty for some time proceeded with promptitude; but, the very knowledge that he was about to be supported by the British having overawed his enemies and averted the present danger, the deep-rooted jealousy always cherished by the native sovereigns respecting the admission of foreign troops soon revived. A powerful party exclaimed against the ministers by whom the treaty was conducted, as betrayers of their country; and they thought it expedient, by advancing conditions that were inadmissible, to prevent its final conclusion.

New system of policy.

Difficulty of negotiating with native powers.

This disappointment was compensated by a more fortunate occurrence in another quarter. Raghojee Bhonslay, rajah of Berar, died, leaving a son, Pursajee, so infirm both in mind and body as to be incapable of maintaining even the semblance of royalty. In these circumstances, Appa Saheb, his cousin and also presumptive heir, assumed the authority of regent, to which he seemed

Death of Raghojee Bhonslay.

CHAP. XV
A.D. 1816.

to possess a legitimate claim. Another chief, however, Dhurmajee Bhonsla, having formed a powerful party, rendered it doubtful whether Appa would be able to maintain himself without foreign aid. The latter, therefore, made overtures to the British for a subsidiary alliance, coupled with the condition of supporting him in the administration. This, in the present temper of the councils of Calcutta, was most readily granted. The stipulated force was to consist of six battalions of infantry and one regiment of cavalry, partly attached to the regent's person; for the maintenance of which the annual amount of 7½ lacks of rupees was to be received in money-payments, instead of the invidious mode of territorial cession. This treaty, according to Mr Prinsep, was viewed at the presidency with the highest exultation, as an arrangement by which the state of Berar was finally detached from the Mahratta league, and fixed in our interests; and not as what it really was, a mere expedient for the attainment of personal objects, and to be thrown aside as soon as these were accomplished.

Disputed succession.

British alliance solicited.

Its illusory character.

Facilities for new operations.

The occupation of Berar afforded great facilities for operations against the predatory powers, whose main rallying-point was in Malwa, the hilly province to the northward of the Nerbudda. The governor-general, however, had not yet obtained permission to root them out of that strong country, and was obliged to content himself with drawing a cordon along the southern bank of the river, by which he hoped to prevent them from again penetrating into the Deccan. Unfortunately for themselves, Cheetoo and other chiefs had at this time acqured a considerable increase of strength. They had been left several years nearly unmolested; and had even received secret assurances of support from the principal Mahratta chieftains, who were meditating a fresh attempt, with the aid of the Pindarees, to subvert the ascendency of Britain. They were, however, considerably alarmed by the appearance of the force stationed on the Nerbudda; but seeing it remain inactive, while they themselves had mustered 23,000 cavalry, they conceived

Proceedings of native chiefs.

it possible to penetrate at some point the extended line along which the English were posted. Accordingly, with 10,000 horsemen, they crossed on the extreme right with such rapidity, that our infantry were unable either to arrest or overtake them. They then separated into two *lubhurs* or plundering bands, one of which proceeded due south into the country of the nizam, and reached the banks of the Godavery. The other marched eastward, and entered the Company's territory of Ganjam, where in the course of twelve days during the preceding year they had killed and wounded nearly 700 persons, and carried off or destroyed property to the value of £100,000. A third party crossed at Burhanpoor, and overran the dominions of the peishwa to some distance beyond Poonah.

Marauding incursion of the Pindarees.

The Pindarees had thus eluded the regular force appointed to check their inroad; yet though they were still liable to be attacked by several detached corps that were scouring the country in different directions, they never stationed sentries, nor took any similar precaution against an evil to which they were always exposed. While the large body who had reached the Godavery were deliberating on their future course, Major M'Dowal, with a party of light troops, came upon them so unexpectedly, that they had received a discharge of fire-arms before almost a man of them was mounted; and they were obliged to flee, abandoning nearly all their horses and plunder. One bold chieftain, with 260 troopers, crossed the Peninsula, swept along the western shore, and, ascending the Tuptee, reached his home with less indeed than half his original number, but all of them carrying in their saddles a rich booty. Major Lushington again, learning that the other band had passed Poonah, made a march of fifty miles, came upon them while busied in cooking, and gave them so complete a defeat that only a few escaped. In Ganjam, too, they met with several surprises, in one of which Lieutenant Borthwick beat up their camp with only fifty men. They abandoned their attempt to penetrate into the territory of Cuttack; and

Irregular mode of warfare.

The main body surprised by Major MacDowal.

Other bands surprised.

CHAP. XV.

A.D. 1817.

learning that a plan was formed to intercept their return, they endeavoured to effect their object by a circuitous route through Bundelcund, in the course of which Colonel Adams and other officers inflicted upon them very severe losses.

Apprehensions suggested by this campaign.

Although this campaign had been in some measure successful and even triumphant, it afforded reason to apprehend that India could never be secure from the inroad of these marauders, so long as they should have a place of safe retreat. Upwards of 30,000 troops had been employed against them, a number adequate to a regular war on the greatest scale, and involving an immense expenditure; yet they had penetrated through a strong line of defence, while their subsequent failure was occasioned only by an undue security, which they would probably learn to correct. The permission granted by the government at home to prosecute the war against them was far from being unlimited; but the marquis trusted that the events which had occurred during this campaign, and the success which he hoped would still attend his measures, would procure for him the sanction of the Company.

Efficient measures of the governor-general.

About the middle of the year 1817, the governor-general put in motion the most numerous and efficient host that had ever perhaps taken the field in India. Its entire amount is estimated at about 81,000 infantry and 10,000 cavalry; of which 57,000 advanced from the Deccan and Guzerat, and 34,000 from Bengal through Hindostan Proper. To the corps from the Deccan were attached 13,000 irregular cavalry, and to that from Bengal 10,000 of the same force, many of them good troops. The main body of the Bengal army, under the immediate command of the Marquis of Hastings, assembled at Secundra, and proceeded to cross the Jumna near Calpy. Another corps was instructed to pass that river at Agra; while two smaller sections were to act on the flanks, and to connect this with the other armies. The Deccan force was to advance in two divisions under Generals Hislop and Sir John Malcolm; Colonel Adams led the regiments from Berar, while Generals Doveton and Smith took post in the rear, ready either to support the main body, or to suppress any commotion that might arise at Poonah or Nagpore. General Keir meantime led the army of Guzerat into Malwa. All these divisions formed a complete circle around the Pindaree positions, closing in upon them as to a common centre. This system of tactics, which in contending with disciplined forces is accompanied with the danger that the enemy, availing himself of his central position, may successively attack and beat the different corps advancing against him, was attended with no such hazard when directed against troops who never encountered an adversary in pitched battle,—whose sole aim was escape, and to whom flight was victory. It was by such a movement only that they could be enclosed and finally crushed.

Judicious system of tactics.

There was one circumstance attending this campaign which could not be regarded without some degree of alarm, namely, that it led our army into the territories of princes who viewed with the most rancorous jealousy the height to which the British power had now attained. All of them, seeing in its success the downfal of their own ambitious hopes, and even of their independence, anxiously watched the favourable moment for striking a blow. Even the courts of Nagpore and Hydrabad, notwithstanding the treaties by which they professed to be bound, could not by any means be relied upon. Besides, the Pindaree war was to be carried on in the dominions of Scindia and Holkar, the most deadly foes to the British name. Of the former Sir John Malcolm justly observes, that he never could be expected to forget the loss of empire sustained through Britain:—"All his habits, his prejudices, his wishes, are against us; we have nothing in our favour but his fears. His faith and his promises cannot be relied on for a moment." It appears indeed that Cheetoo, the principal leader of the Pindarees, had made urgent applications that he would allow to him a place where his family might be secured from danger; adding, "that thereby my heart may be set at ease,

Dangers attending this campaign.

Natural apprehensions of Scindia.

CHAP. XV.
A. D. 1817.

and I may face the English with confidence. Then for once, by the blessing of God and the fortune of the exalted, the tumult shall be spread to the environs of Calcutta, the whole country shall be consigned to ashes, and to such distress shall they be reduced, that the accounts will not fail to reach you; but at present this must be delayed for want of a place of refuge." To this Scindia's ministers replied, that they could not take such a step without an immediate rupture with the British government; but that Cheetoo might depend on their utmost aid in secret. In these circumstances Lord Hastings considered it indispensable, before leaving Scindia's dominions behind him, to extort his consent to such a treaty as might withdraw from him the means of a hostile interposition in the approaching conflict. Colonel Close, the resident at Gwalior, was instructed to demand that he should place his troops entirely at the disposal of the governor-general; that he should furnish a contingent of 5000 horse, and supply funds out of which they might be supported; finally, that he should provisionally deliver up the forts of Hindia and Asseerghur, on which, to save his honour, his flag would continue to fly. There was even to be a private understanding, that while the contest lasted he should not quit his capital. Scindia manifested the most violent opposition, first to the English entering his dominions at all, and then to the terms attached to that movement; nor was it till Lord Hastings from one quarter, and General Donkin from another, were each within a day's march of his frontier that the treaty was reluctantly signed.

Plans of Cheetoo.

Secret assurances of aid.

Terms of British treaty with Scindia.

Terms with Ameer Khan.

A negotiation was next opened with Ameer Khan, and, as he was a principal member of the confederation, it was made a primary article that he should disband the whole of his turbulent corps. This demand was severe, for he must thereby lose every thing on which his importance and power had been founded; but in return he was offered the guarantee of the territories held by him under grants from Holkar, and of which his tenure was otherwise very precarious. Having submitted to the terms, the treaty was signed by his agent at Delhi, on condition that a month should be allowed previously to ratification; but the stipulated period had elapsed, and a British army was surrounding him on every side, before he would affix his name to it. His troops being then disbanded, he seemed thenceforth to place his hopes of aggrandizement solely in the English alliance, and cordially exerted himself in promoting its objects.

CHAP. XV

A. D. 1817.

Embarrassments of the Pindaree chiefs.

The Pindaree chiefs could not view this immense force, especially when it began to close in around them, without the deepest alarm. While the rainy season still suspended operations, they held frequent conferences on the state of their affairs. Their only hope, they were convinced, was to quit their present haunts and seek a temporary home in some remote quarter of India. But it was difficult to find a secure place in which to deposite their property and their families; for even amid their wandering life they were still susceptible of the strongest domestic attachments. This embarrassment and the violent dissensions which had long reigned between their two principal heads, Kurreem and Cheetoo, caused them to break up without having formed any definite plan. The invading armies began to move as soon as the rains had abated, and while the swelling of the rivers might yet impede the rapid movements of their adversaries.

Unexpected obstacles.

The opening of the campaign, meantime, was retarded by two very unexpected circumstances:—The first was the appearance in the main army of that terrible epidemic, usually denominated the *cholera spasmodica*, which, after creating desolation and dismay in the greater part of India, spread through Persia into Russia, and thence all over Europe, occasioning a very considerable loss of life in the British empire, and then reaching even to the American continent. In its first progress, it struck the world as a new and unheard-of visitation; but further researches have established, that the same disease has from time to time appeared in the East. Ancient writings, in the languages of Southern India, describe it very distinctly under the names of Sitanga or Vishúchi. Ex-

Cholera Spasmodica.

CHAP. XV.
A. D. 1817.

History of the disease.

tensive ravages are represented to have been committed by it in Bengal in 1762; in a division of troops which in 1781 were marching through the district of Ganjam; and in 1783, during the annual festival at Hurdwar. In 1787, a malady, the symptoms of which clearly establish its identity, prevailed at Vellore and Arcot on the coast of Coromandel. It had not however, during a long period, assumed any formidable aspect, and in the comprehensive tables published by the medical board at Madras, the column for cholera spasmodica in 1815 and the two following years exhibits nearly a continued blank.

Its first appearance

This disorder first showed itself, in August 1817, in the zillah of Jessore, about sixty miles north-east of Calcutta, in the marshy districts which form the Delta of the Ganges. The whole of the tract extending along the lower course of that river is intersected by numberless branches of its stream, whence are derived canals and tanks that diffuse the benefit of irrigation almost to every field. These artificial channels, however, are often in bad repair and filled with stagnant water, while even the river itself at certain seasons has not current sufficient to preserve its salubrious qualities. Added to this, the extreme violence of the heat in summer, and of the rains in winter, renders the whole of this part of Bengal liable to fevers and other climatic disorders. When any of these atmospheric phenomena occur in an extraordinary degree, and especially when, by injuring the cultivated fields, they render the grain scarce and bad, epidemics of the most malignant description are frequently generated. The years 1815 and 1816 were distinguished by very striking peculiarities of season and weather. In May of the latter year, the heat became most intense, the thermometer rose to 98 degrees in the shade, and various persons, both European and native, fell down dead in the streets. A deficiency in the periodical rains was also apprehended till the beginning of September, when there poured down a complete deluge, causing a more extensive inundation than was recollected by the oldest inhabitant. This was followed by attacks of low

Peculiarities of the climate.

typhus fever, and of malignant sore throat,—a disorder formerly unknown in that region, but believed on this occasion to be contagious.

Excessive rains.

The year 1817 was from the first uncommonly moist, and the annual rains began on the 25th May, about three weeks before the usual period. They fell to a depth greater by one-third than in ordinary years; so that, before the middle of August, nearly the whole district composing the Delta of the Ganges was one sheet of water. It was during the distempered state of the air thus produced, that the malignant cholera broke forth on a scale hitherto quite unprecedented. The disease, either in its common or violent form, appeared nearly at the same time in different parts of Bengal. But it was in Jessore, situated in the tract called the Sunderbunds, covered with thick jungle and surrounded by stagnant waters, that it assumed its most alarming aspect. At Calcutta, during the month of August, many cases of common cholera had occurred; but at the beginning of September it appeared in that city under its most malignant type; though whether it was imported from Jessore, or rose spontaneously under similar circumstances, is a question not yet decided. It spared Europeans for a few days, but began to attack them on the 5th, though without committing the same dreadful ravages as in the native town; yet the register of one of the life insurance societies exhibited a proportion of deaths four times as great as in several preceding years. The malady was diffused almost simultaneously through the different cities of Bengal, rapidly ascended the Ganges, and spread even to the west of the Jumna; sparing, however, the comparatively elevated territories of Oude and Rohilcund.

Occurrence of cholera in Calcutta.

Its appearance in the army.

In the beginning of November, in consequence, as is supposed by some, of the arrival of a detachment from the lower province, this disease in its most virulent form broke out in the army under the immediate command of the Marquis of Hastings. Troops on a march are observed to be peculiarly liable to its attack, which is imputed to the extreme heat of the tents, doubtless com-

CHAP. XV.
A. D. 1817

bined with the great exposure to the atmosphere. The cholera appeared while they were slowly marching through the low and unhealthy district of Bundelcund, which labours under a singular deficiency of good water. For about ten days it converted the camp into a large hospital. All the public establishments being engrossed by the care of the troops, the numerous camp-followers could not be accommodated except in the tents of their masters, who formed also their only attendants. The route over which the army moved was strewed with the dead and dying; the bazars were deserted; even those persons whose health was good suffered under severe depression of spirits; so that during the whole period the efficiency of this fine body of men was completely destroyed. The usual bustle and hum of a crowded camp was changed into an awful silence, broken only by the groans of the sick and lamentations over the dead. In the European patient death usually followed from six to twelve hours after the attack, while the sepoy was carried off in about half that interval. The malady raged with its utmost fury from the 15th to the 23d November, when it ceased almost at once; so that the army having reached a more salubrious camp, at Erich on the Betwa, became rapidly convalescent, and by the commencement of December were prepared to enter on the duties of the campaign.

Dreadful prevalence in the camp.

Mortality in the army

The loss sustained during this most gloomy crisis was very greatly exaggerated. It has been represented even by good authorities as amounting to three, five, or even eight thousand,* out of the whole division of ten thousand men. More precise statements by Mr Prinsep and Mr Kennedy, derived from personal and official knowledge, prove this inaccuracy to have arisen from the not taking into account the vast crowd of camp-followers, who, in an Indian army, always greatly outnumber the soldiers. When the proper distinction is made, it appears that the deaths among the troops amount-

* Bisset Hawkins' History of Cholera, p. 169.

ed only to 764; while the loss among the camp-followers was about 8000, which did not however exceed a tenth of their entire number.

Progress of the malady.

We cannot here follow in detail the progress of this severe malady, which made its way in every direction. After having spared in its first progress the provinces of Oude and Rohilcund, it reached them in April and May 1818, and in the following months penetrated to Catmandoo, Almora, and other very elevated positions on the chain of Himmaleh.

Its general diffusion

The march of armies into the centre of India, and the despatches sent through every province of that country, were supposed to diffuse more and more widely its fatal influence. The natives, instead of using any rational means of cure or prevention, sought to avert it only by pompous and crowded visits to the temples, which increased the danger of communicating the disease; or by sanguinary proceedings against certain persons who were suspected of producing it by witchcraft. In the course of the year 1818 it spread through every part of India. The report of the medical board at Madras contains an interesting map, showing its track through the Deccan and the south by an irregular course, sometimes along the high roads, sometimes in cross directions; but, in the end, leaving scarcely any point of importance untouched. It reached Nagpore on the 15th May,—Bombay by way of Poonah on the 14th August,—Hydrabad on 25th July,—Madras on 8th October,—and finally the extreme stations of Trivanderam and Palamcotta in January 1819. Throughout these provinces it manifested itself in various degrees of intensity. In general, however, this dreadful disease seemed to be marked, rather by its fatal effects than by the great number who were actually attacked. The entire amount of cases occurring in the army of Fort St George during 1818, the most severe year, was 1087 out of 10,652 Europeans, and 3314 out of 58,764 natives. Of the former 232, and of the latter 664 died.* In the

Irrational proceedings of the natives.

Its fatality.

---

* Report of Madras Medical Board, p. 28

CHAP. XV
—
A. D. 1817.

island of Bombay, which contains a population of about 210,000, the ascertained cases were 15,945, of which 14,651 were medically treated, and the deaths among these were only 938, or $6\frac{4}{10}$ per cent.,—perhaps the smallest proportion of mortality that has any where been observed.* Instances, however, are given of single corps, particularly on a march, suffering much more severely. The 2d battalion of the 20th regiment of native infantry was proceeding to Hydrabad, when of about 1150 men 200 were attacked, and 73 died. The 1st battalion of the 1st regiment, on its road from Nagpore to Hydrabad, out of 1010 men had 167 attacked, of whom 64 died. His majesty's 54th regiment, on their way from Madras to Bangalore, had 159 out of 632 attacked, and 54 died.

Unexpected attack by Bajee Rao.

Another unexpected crisis arrested Sir Thomas Hislop with the army of the Deccan, just as he had arrived on the frontier of Malwa. Intelligence then reached him that Bajee Rao had taken up arms and attacked the British residency in his capital; upon which Sir Thomas judged it necessary to fall back, that he might support the reserve corps, and aid in the suppression of this insurrection. General Keir, who had advanced from Guzerat, was induced by the same information to retreat. But Lord Hastings justly considered that the fortune of the campaign must ultimately depend upon the prompt success of the operations in Central India, and conceiving Smith's force, with another under Pritzler, quite sufficient at present to overawe the peishwa, ordered these commanders to return without delay to the scene of action.

Proceedings of the Pindarees.

The Pindarees, as soon as they saw themselves completely enclosed by the advancing corps of the British, made no attempt at resistance, and studied only how to escape. One party succeeded in penetrating into the rear of our army in Bundelcund, where they began to commit serious ravages, and were not dispersed without some difficulty. Cheetoo, with nearly 8000 men, effected a march westward into the territory of Mewar, where he

* Bombay Report, App. pp. 13, 14.

CHAP. XV

A. D. 1817.

was assured of support from several quarters, and had the strong mountain-fort of Kumulner as a refuge for his family. The escape of the Pindaree chiefs, when so great a force surrounded them, Colonel Blacker explains by a reference to the defective means of conveyance possessed by the British; to their having, in the dread of encountering a Mahratta army, encumbered themselves with ordnance; and, above all, to the agility of the native horses, which can pass over the most rugged roads and uneven ground with great speed. Kurreem, with one of his associates, attempted to push his way to Gwalior, where he hoped to find support from Scindia. All the passes in this direction, however, were most strictly guarded; and a strong corps was appointed to watch the motions of that ruler, whose secret enmity to the British was so fully understood. The first that came up with this body of Pindarees was General Marshall, who easily drove them before him. They escaped without much loss, but were obliged to change their direction and march for the territory of Jyepore, where they hoped to be joined by some of the disbanded troops of Ameer Khan. On their way thither they were surprised by General Donkin, who gave them a complete overthrow, capturing the wife of Kurreem, with all his state-elephants and kettle-drums. His army, therefore, no longer attempted to preserve any appearance of regularity, but broke into detachments, and sought for safety by fleeing in various directions. The greater number endeavoured to reach the corps of Cheetoo; and, accordingly, the final destruction of that warrior appeared all that was now necessary to finish the Pindaree contest, when there started up another head of the hydra which the English were labouring to vanquish.

Causes of their escape.

Complete overthrow of a large body of them.

House of Holkar.

The councils of the house of Holkar had been involved for some time in the utmost confusion. Jeswunt Rao, who had raised that family to power, after the unfortunate issue of the war with the British, became deranged, and died in a few years. His heir, Mulhar Rao, was a mere boy, and the administration during his minority

CHAP. XV. A. D. 1817. was agitated by the most violent dissensions. The chief parties were, on one side Toolsee Bhye, widow to the late Holkar, who had been invested with the office of regent; and on the other the Patan chiefs, who were strongly attached to the predatory system. The lady, with the direct view of maintaining her influence, made secret overtures to the English for receiving a subsidiary force. This measure was firmly opposed by the leaders just named, whose sentiments were shared by the military in general; and the weight of their opinions was so strongly felt by the regent, that she did not venture to proceed with the negotiation. The chiefs, however, being suspicious that something of that nature was still in progress, were fired with such indignation, that they seized her person, carried her down to the river, and put her to death. War was then only delayed till the completion of the necessary preparations. Troops, especially infantry, were collected with the utmost diligence, and their movements assumed so formidable an aspect, that Sir John Malcolm judged it advisable to fall back upon the corps of General Hislop, who, as already mentioned, had begun a retrograde movement, but was again advancing towards Poonah. These commanders having effected a junction, proceeded together, and found the native army strongly posted at Mehidpoor, with a steep bank in front, at the foot of which flowed the river Soopra, passable only by a single ford. Although this position might have been turned by a circuitous march, Hislop considered such an advantage more than counterbalanced by the impression which would be produced by pushing on promptly and directly to the attack. This mode of proceeding, it has been often observed, is better suited than more scientific manœuvres to the genius of English troops. A scene then ensued, similar to that which usually took place in Mahratta battles; the British regiments rushing forward with the most daring intrepidity in the face of a numerous artillery, by which they severely suffered, and at length, when they came to a close charge, carrying all before them. They lost 174 killed

Toolsee Bhye's secret overtures to the British.

Her death.

Junction of British forces.

Decisive attack on the native army.

and 604 wounded; there being among the former three, and among the latter thirty-five European officers. The Mahrattas, though they left 3000 on the field, retreated with a great part of their army entire: but they abandoned all the artillery; their courage and confidence were gone; and though their numbers were not greatly diminished, they were no longer a regular force. The chiefs therefore at once accepted the offered terms; namely, that young Holkar should be placed under the protection of the Company, who were to maintain an auxiliary force, and to have a contingent of 3000 men at their disposal; and that certain districts of moderate extent should be ceded, not for the purpose of being possessed by the conquerors, but distributed as rewards to those allies who had remained faithful during the present contest.

British terms accepted.

After losing the support of the Holkar family, the Pindarees found an unexpected asylum with Jeswunt Rao, one of Scindia's generals, who occupied several strong camps in the neighbourhood of Rampoora. After several fruitless remonstrances, General Brown attacked this chieftain, reduced his intrenchments, and obliged him to flee with only a handful of followers.

Jeswunt Rao

The hopes of the marauders were now reduced to the lowest ebb. Flight, they knew not whither, became their only resource. They had obtained Kumulner and other fortresses in the Rajpoot territory; but these being quickly invested, were, after a short resistance, all given up. Major Clarke having overtaken the party under Kurreem during the night, and finding them plunged as usual in profound security, delayed the attack till morning, that they might derive no advantage from the darkness. He divided his corps into two bodies, with one of which he made the charge, while the other occupied the only road by which the enemy could retreat. They sustained, accordingly, a complete overthrow, and were dispersed in every direction, leaving several of their chiefs dead on the field. After suffering some farther disasters, their whole body was reduced to a state truly

Desperate state of the Pindarees.

Total overthrow of a party under Kurreem.

CHAP. XV.
A.D. 1818.

miserable. Cheetoo and his adherents sometimes slept with their horses saddled, and the bridles in their hands, that they might be ready for instant flight. At length an intimation was circulated, that, in case of unconditional surrender, their lives would be spared, and the means of an honourable subsistence secured for the chiefs in some remote district. One after another submitted upon these terms; and at length Kurreem, after wandering for some time on foot through the jungles, gave himself up, on the 15th February 1818, to Sir John Malcolm. Cheetoo opened a negotiation; but, on learning the small allowance which was to be granted to one whom he thought entitled to a jaghire in his native country and a place in the British service, he hastily took his departure. He afterwards encountered a variety of distresses, which ended in a manner equally dismal and appalling, being devoured by a tiger while lurking in the forests of Asseerghur. His fate excited sympathy among our officers, who admired the spirit and intrepidity with which he had on all occasions braved the deepest reverses of fortune.

Terms offered and accepted.

Fate of Cheetoo.

Occurrences at the court of Poonah.

While the performances on the main theatre of Indian warfare were thus brought to a successful close, two separate dramas of a subordinate though eventful character were acted on other stages, of which the most remarkable occurred at the court of Poonah. The peishwa, ever since the last treaty which he was compelled to sign, had eagerly sought deliverance from a yoke which now pressed heavily upon him; and the employment of the British forces in the Pindaree campaign offered a tempting opportunity to reassert his independence. A little consideration indeed would have shown him that this contest could not engage his enemy beyond a very short period; after which they would find it easy to crush such resistance as he or any other of the Mahratta states could create. But the peishwa, like many other Indian princes, though possessed of talent and address, and skilled in pursuing the ordinary objects of eastern policy, was incapable of taking a comprehensive view of his actual situation. He was encouraged by the hatred of the English which he saw prevalent among his own chiefs, and by the general disposition of all the other leaders to unite in a confederacy against that people.

Secret designs of the peishwa.

For a considerable time he threw an impenetrable veil over his hostile designs. On intimation being given of an intention to go to war with the Pindarees, he professed his cordial concurrence in the object, and his desire to co-operate by all the means in his power. So great indeed was his address, that Sir John Malcolm, an intelligent and veteran politician, after living at his court several days, was completely deceived, and communicated his opinion, that nothing hostile was to be apprehended from the peishwa. But Mr Elphinstone, the official resident, entertained from the first an opposite opinion, which was soon fully confirmed. He saw that the utmost activity was employed in collecting troops, under the pretext of aiding in the projected war, though for a purpose directly opposite. At the same time, the jaghiredars, who had been studiously depressed and humbled, were courted and conciliated; while Bapoo Gokla, an officer of distinguished ability, who had hitherto been kept in a species of disgrace, was invested with the supreme direction of affairs. A numerous camp was formed close to the British cantonments, around which the Mahratta horsemen were seen riding in menacing attitudes. The brigade commanded by Colonel Burr, the amount of which had been fixed with a very undue confidence in the friendly disposition of the prince, did not exceed three sepoy battalions, with a European regiment not yet arrived from Bombay. As the hostile intentions of the court became more and more manifest, it was judged advisable to withdraw the troops into a strong defensive position formed near the city by an angle of the river Moola; but Mr Elphinstone, anxious to avoid the imputation of being the aggressor, resolved not to quit the residency till he should be driven away by force. Threatening notes began to be exchanged; and on the 5th November 1817, so sudden an attack was made that

Suspicions excited.

Measures taken against hostile proceedings.

Attack on the resident.

CHAP. XV.

A. D. 1817.

the resident and his suite had scarcely time to mount their horses, when his mansion was plundered, and all the property, including his books and papers, was either carried off or destroyed.

Understanding with General Smith.

General Smith, though placed in the rear of the grand army, had agreed, if a single day should pass without his hearing from Poonah, that he would conclude the communications were interrupted, and hasten thither with his whole brigade. A week, however, must necessarily elapse before his arrival, and to keep the sepoys in the mean time cooped up in a narrow space, harassed by the enemy's artillery and light horse, would, it was feared, damp their courage, and promote that tendency to desertion which had already been strongly manifested. Hence the officers determined to march out with their small corps and attack their foes, who, to the amount of 26,000, were already stationed in front. This movement was executed promptly, and with such vigour, that though the enemy's horsemen made some desperate charges, and reached several times the flanks of the English brigade, the latter finally remained masters of the field. They had not indeed done much damage to their adversaries; but the intrepidity of their attack, and the amount of their success against numbers so vastly superior, changed decidedly the moral position of the two armies. When General Smith, therefore, on the 13th November, after fighting his way through the peishwa's cavalry, arrived at Poonah, and prepared to attack the Mahratta camp, that prince at once commenced a retreat. He continued it upwards of six months without intermission, ranging over the wide extent of the Deccan; at one time approaching Mysore, at another proceeding nearly to the Nerbudda, always distancing his pursuers by the skill and rapidity of his march, and even passing between corps advancing from opposite quarters. At one time he made himself sure of cutting off a division of 800 men destined to reinforce Colonel Burr; but Captain Staunton the commander, taking post in a village, repulsed with desperate valour, though with severe loss, all his

Vigorous measures of the British officers.

Retreat of Bajee Rao.

Gallant repulse by Captain Staunton.

attacks, and he was at length obliged to desist. This was considered the bravest exploit performed in the whole course of the war. The peishwa finding himself now a hopeless fugitive, and learning the triumphs of his enemy in other quarters, made overtures for a treaty; hoping to be allowed to retain, though in a reduced condition, his rank as a sovereign. But the governor-general, on considering his long course of hostility, and the treacherous attack made at so critical a moment, had determined to erase his name from the list of Indian princes, and that there should be no longer a peishwa. Britain was to exercise the sovereign sway in all the territories which had belonged to him; though, in order to sooth in some degree the irritated feelings of the Mahratta people, the Rajah of Satara, the descendant of Sevajee, still deeply venerated even after his long depression, was to be restored to some share of his former dignity. To follow up this purpose, General Smith laid siege to Satara, which surrendered after a short resistance. The interval afforded a brief respite to the peishwa, and lulled his vigilance; so that when this officer had pushed on by forced marches, at the head of a division of light horse, he arrived unobserved within hearing of the Mahratta kettle-drums. Concealed for some time by the brow of a hill, he appeared on its summit to the astonishment of the Indian leaders. The fallen prince forthwith left the field with his attendants; but Gokla determined to hazard a battle rather than sacrifice nearly the whole of his baggage. He made the attack with the greatest vigour, and had succeeded in throwing part of the cavalry into some confusion, when he fell mortally wounded. His death was regretted even by the English, since his enmity to their nation, and zeal for the independence of his own, had been tempered with honour and humanity. The whole army immediately fled, and the British obtained possession of the person of the Rajah of Satara, who had before been a prisoner in the hands of his rival.

Overtures for peace.

Plan for extended British sovereignty

Total rout of the Mahrattas

Bajee Rao still continued his retreat, of which he as-

CHAP. XV.

A. D. 1817

Retreat of Bajee Rao.

sumed the sole charge; and gave out every morning the direction in which the troops were to move, having concealed it till that moment from his most confidential officers. After much and long wandering, he moved northward to the borders of Berar and Malwa, where he partially recruited his strength by collecting the remains of the beaten armies. But he soon found himself hemmed in still more closely; and in pursuing his march, in the absence of proper information, he met Colonel Adams at the head of a considerable force, and could not avoid a battle. He was defeated, with the loss of most of his infantry and all his artillery, saving only his horse and light troops. He then made an effort to reach the capital of Scindia, hoping for aid, or at least protection, from this most powerful of the Mahratta chieftains; but all the passes were strictly guarded. His distress became greater every day; his followers deserted in vast numbers; and the English drew their nets round him so skilfully that he could not hope long to escape. He then opened a correspondence with Sir John Malcolm. After some discussion, it was agreed that he should surrender, and that, on being secured in a pension of eight lacks of rupees (about £100,000), he should renounce the dignity of peishwa, with all his claims as a sovereign; spending the rest of his days in some holy city at a distance from the seat of his former dominion. The sum was regarded by the Marquis of Hastings as too large; though, considering it as the final adjustment with a prince who ranked in authority and power above all others at that time in India, it does not appear very extravagant. The apprehension that his revenue would be employed by him as an instrument for regaining his political influence has not been realized. He immediately resigned himself to voluptuous indulgences, to which, it is said, he had been always addicted, and sought to drown in them every recollection of his former schemes and greatness.

Defeat by Colonel Adams.

Terms of surrender.

While the territory of Poonah was agitated by these violent commotions, a scene almost exactly similar was

Proceedings at Nagpore

Appa Saheb.

passing at Nagpore. Appa Saheb had invited the British troops with the sole view of maintaining his own situation as regent; and so long as he judged them necessary for that object he remained faithful. At length he got rid by assassination of the young prince, and placed himself on the *guddee*, as the seat was called to which the dignity of rajah was attached. He then considered himself independent of foreign aid, and began to regard it with the dislike so generally felt by all persons in his condition. He was thus led to enter into that confederacy against the British power which was formed among the Mahratta chiefs in consequence of the Pindaree war; and was observed also to carry on an active correspondence with the peishwa while the latter was maturing his plans of aggression. The first treaty which that prince was compelled to sign greatly abated the courage of his ally, which was revived, however, by the intelligence of his having again taken up arms and attacked the English subsidiary force. The subsequent retreat of Bajee Rao threw him into much hesitation and uncertainty, though at length it resulted in the hazardous determination to follow his example. On the 24th November 1817, Mr Jenkins, the British resident, was invited to see his highness invested with a dress of honour; having assumed the juree putka or golden streamer, an emblem of high command, both of which had been transmitted by the peishwa. Our countryman declined attendance, not without expressing indignation at the rajah's acceptance of these honours at such a moment; and indeed it seems to have been an imprudent and premature insult, by which the Company's servants were warned of approaching danger.

Imprudent haste.

Critical position of the British residency.

The subsidiary force then stationed at Nagpore was very small. It consisted only of two battalions of native infantry, with detachments of cavalry and artillery; and the whole, being much reduced by sickness, did not amount to 1400 men. The rajah's army, on the contrary comprised 10,000 cavalry and 10,000 infantry, includ ing 3000 or 4000 very brave Arab troops. The residency

CHAP. XV.
A. D. 1817.

was situated outside the town, and separated from it by a ridge rising at each extremity into low hills, which were hastily occupied as defensive posts. At sunset the piquets were fired upon by the Arab infantry, and soon after a general discharge of artillery was opened upon all the positions, particularly those on the smaller eminence. This was continued till two in the morning with considerable effect, the first officer in command on that station being killed, and the second wounded. The English, during the remainder of the night, made the best preparations in their power against the more serious attack which was anticipated in the morning; and, accordingly, at daybreak the charge was renewed with increased fury. At ten a tumbril burst on the lower hill, which threw the troops into some confusion; the Arabs rushed on with loud cries, the sepoys were seized with panic and fled, abandoning the guns and the wounded, who were immediately put to the sword. The enemy then began a heavy fire on the larger hill, when several officers fell, and among them Mr Sotheby, the resident's assistant, a young man of distinguished merit, while he was endeavouring to rally and restore the courage of his men. The dismay of the troops, the cries of the women and children, the vast numbers and increasing confidence of the enemy, seemed to portend the most fatal result. Yet, even then, resources were found in British firmness and courage. Captain Fitzgerald, who had withdrawn the cavalry within the residency-grounds, seeing the critical state of the infantry, and the fire already extending to his station, felt that affairs could be retrieved only by one of those bold attacks which a native army can scarcely ever resist. He accordingly led his few horsemen to the charge, drove every thing before him, took two guns and turned them against the enemy. The troops on the other hill, animated by this example, resumed courage, and, raising loud shouts, opened a brisk fire on the assailants. A party dashed across to the smaller elevation, from which the rajah's followers were driven in their turn, and about noon were repulsed at every point. Yet the British had

Attack on the residency.

Desperate position of the British.

Gallant charge of the cavalry

lost a fourth of their number, and their ammunition was drawing to a close, so that had Appa persevered, he must have finally succeeded in cutting off the detachment,—an event which would have produced the strongest sensation over all India. But he remained inactive, while reinforcements poured in to his antagonists from every quarter. On the 12th December, for example, Doveton arrived with the strong reserve under his command, and it then became impossible for Saheb to hope for success; he had already obtained an armistice, and now inquired as to the terms on which a final accommodation might be effected. Mr Jenkins replied that nothing would be accepted short of entire submission,—the disbanding of his troops, the delivering up of all his forts and artillery, and his own presence as a hostage at the British residency. It was, however, intimated, that, on his complying fully with these requisitions, he would be restored to nearly his former condition, being required only to maintain a subsidiary force, and submit to a certain degree of control. When the troops, however, marched into Nagpore to take possession of the ordnance, they were saluted with a hot fire, and suffered some loss before they could seize the guns and compel the Arabs, who took the chief part in this resistance, to retire within the fort. As they refused to surrender, a siege was immediately commenced, and a practicable breach appeared to have been made in the gate; but when the assault was given, it was found to be so secured by interior walls, that the English were obliged to retreat with considerable damage. Preparations were then made to invest the place on a more regular plan; but the garrison, satisfied with the display of valour which they had already made, capitulated on condition of being allowed to march out with their baggage and private property.

Arrival of reinforcements.

Terms dictated to Saheb.

Capitulation of Nagpore.

As none of these transactions could be brought home to Appa Saheb, he was not made responsible for them; wherefore on the surrender of Nagpore he was liberated, and received notice of the terms on which he might retain his seat on the guddee. These consisted in his

Liberation of Saheb.

CHAP. XV

A.D. 1817

being placed entirely on the same footing with the nizam; having his military force subjected to the control of the Company, and even his ministers appointed by them. The rajah only so far expressed his dissatisfaction as to offer to retire altogether on a liberal pension,—a proposition which was not considered admissible. He therefore began forthwith to intrigue, with the view of shaking off this hated dependence. Troops were levied, the governors of fortresses and the mountain-chiefs were instructed to muster their forces, and give every possible annoyance to the enemy; finally, a secret correspondence was discovered with Bajee Rao, who being invited to join his army to the standard of the peishwa, had actually taken steps for that purpose. Mr Jenkins hereupon deemed it indispensable to call upon Appa to resume his place within the residency; and this not being complied with, a party was sent who effected his arrest, fortunately without having recourse to violence. It is less difficult, however, to seize Indian princes than to keep them: the rajah being mildly treated, and access procured to him by several of his adherents, a plan was arranged for his escape in the disguise of a sepoy. He went off at two in the morning, and the discovery was not made till daylight; so that, relays of horses having been provided, all pursuit was vain. But as the Pindaree war was now terminated, and Bajee Rao reduced to the last extremity, he was unable to do more than excite desultory hostilities in the mountainous districts. The English were thus able, on their own terms, to seat on the guddee Bajee Rao, a grandson of Raghojee Bonslay, while the administration was placed entirely under their own control.

Intrigues of the rajah.

His arrest and escape.

Retirement of the Marquis of Hastings.

In the beginning of 1822, the Marquis of Hastings was induced by certain family circumstances to intimate his wish to retire from the high situation which he had filled for nine years. The Court of Directors passed a unanimous vote of thanks for the unremitting zeal and ability with which he had discharged its functions; and this was subsequently confirmed by the Court of Proprietors. In the subsequent October, Lord Amherst was nominated his successor, and arrived at Calcutta on the 1st August 1823. The principal event of his administration was the war with the Birman empire, which, after some vicissitudes, was completely successful, and the Company acquired a considerable addition of territory on the eastern coast of the Bay of Bengal. As this contest, however, was carried on entirely beyond the limits of India Proper, it does not belong to the subject of the present work.

CHAP. XV.

A. D. 1825.

Lord Amherst appointed governor general

But in 1825 an important event occurred in the interior of India. After the death of the Rajah of Bhurtpore in that year, his legitimate heir, Bulwunt Singh, being dethroned by Doorjun Sâl, his cousin, applied for aid to Sir David Ochterlony, then resident at Delhi. That officer embraced the prince's cause; but his conduct in doing so was disavowed by the governor-general, who, at this crisis, showed a disposition to proceed upon the old principle of non-interference. Farther information, however, induced him to change this intention, and Lord Combermere was ordered to march upon the city and expel the usurper. This able commander accordingly, with 25,000 men and an ample train of artillery, proceeded to attack that celebrated stronghold. The siege was begun on the 23d December; but it was soon found that cannon-shot could not penetrate mud-walls sixty feet thick, and that it would be necessary to employ mining operations. By means of these a breach was effected on the 17th January 1826; the assault was given next morning, and after a gallant defence of two hours, in which many veterans who had triumphantly fought in the former siege took an active part, the place was carried; Doorjun was made prisoner; and there remained no longer in Hindostan a fortress that had successfully defied the British arms. While this conflict lasted, a general ferment was observable among the surrounding principalities; and Bishop Heber doubts not, that had the attack failed, the whole country westward of the Jumna would have risen in arms, at least so far as to resume the predatory system of warfare. This triumph, however.

Bulwunt Singh, Rajah of Bhurtpore

Siege and capture of Bhurtpore.

Important influence of success.

CHAP. XV. — A. D. 1827.

checked the disposition to revolt, and completely confirmed the supremacy of Britain.

Opinion of Lord Amherst's policy.

Lord Amherst's conduct both in the Birman and Bhurtpore contests, was the subject of severe criticism at home, especially by the liberal party, who had by that time acquired great influence. They particularly complained of his having continued the severe restrictions on the press introduced by Mr Adam, during his temporary possession of power in the interval after Lord Hastings' departure. Influenced by these and other motives, the Company, in 1826, determined to recall his lordship, who left India in the following year. Having ultimately afforded much greater latitude to public discussion, and being in his general conduct very amiable, he had acquired considerable popularity. He was created viscount and earl, and the Courts of Directors and Proprietors passed votes of thanks to him by large majorities, though not without some warm discussion.

His recall.

Lord William Bentinck appointed governor-general.

In July 1827, Lord William Bentinck was sworn in as the new governor-general. His election was peculiarly acceptable to Mr Canning, then premier, but who died before his departure. His lordship was understood to go out with the intention of introducing a liberal and economical system, which was now considered desirable. He arrived on the 2d July 1828, and soon after set out on a tour to the upper provinces, in order to survey the state of affairs, and endeavour to cement the relations of amity with the neighbouring independent princes. A visit was paid to Scindia's family at Gwalior, and some time was spent at Ajmere, where the Rajpoot chiefs were invited either to visit him, or to send ambassadors. Extensive military reductions were made, particularly on the field allowance called batta, which excited a great deal of discontent among the officers, many of whom were of good family, and had gone out in the hope of living in splendour, and acquiring fortunes. No general conflict took place during Lord Bentinck's administration, but some partial disturbances agitated the ruder borders of our Indian possessions.

Peaceful policy pursued by him.

The Chooars

In 1832 and the following year, considerable annoyance was sustained from a tribe named Chooars, inhabiting the jungly tracts on the eastern limits of Bengal. An extensive contraband trade in salt, favoured by this situation, gave them the habit of acting in large bodies, which they soon improved into an extensive and organized system of plunder. Individuals of high distinction were strongly suspected of exciting and supporting them; though this could not be legally proved. The ostensible leader was Gunga-narain, chief of a small village in a hill-pass, whose house was only a clay edifice, surrounded by sheds covered with grass. The depredations were at length committed on so great a scale, and with such impunity, that it became necessary to enter into an avowed war against them. Four regiments and a large body of irregulars were at one time employed, yet found much difficulty in putting down these marauders. Gunga-narain, who never appeared at the head of more than 400 men, was repeatedly defeated; the Chooar fortresses were successively taken and destroyed; yet the pillagers still lurked under the thick cover of their entangled forests. At length their daring captain was killed in a casual encounter with another tribe, after which his followers mostly dispersed, and did not again muster in any formidable numbers.

Gunga-narain.

Attack and defeat of the marauders.

The Fittoorydars.

About the same time, the hill-country behind the Circars became the scene of some serious disturbances; for in those rugged tracts, bands of robbers had begun to assemble and plunder the lower districts. Gradually they were organized into two great bodies called Fittoorydars, assuming the aspect of an insurrection, which was understood to be fomented by some great zemindary families. The first detachment sent to attack their principal stronghold was repulsed with the loss of about fifteen men killed and wounded. Reinforcements having been brought up, the insurgents evacuated the fort; and they were then hunted from place to place, being dispersed chiefly by surprises, to which their incautious system rendered them always liable. At length several of their leaders being

CHAP XV.

A. D. 1834.

taken and executed, the district was restored to a state of tranquillity.

The Coorg rajah.

In 1834 a more serious contest arose in the west of India. The Coorg rajah, as we had formerly occasion to mention, was an attached ally of the British, and had given material aid in the conquest of Mysore; but the sceptre had now descended to his son, a violent and tyrannical youth, who had exercised such excessive cruelties in his own family, that his sister and her husband were obliged to flee to the English for protection. The rajah demanded, in the most peremptory manner, that they should be given up, and on this being refused, addressed letters of an insulting tenor to the Madras presidency and the governor-general. One of the Company's servants being sent to treat with him, was put under confinement, and his release refused. He was accused at the same time of having assumed an attitude of hostility against us, and of receiving and encouraging our avowed enemies; on which grounds a proclamation was issued on the 1st April 1834 from Calcutta, deposing him from the office of rajah, and announcing that a force was about to enter and take possession of his territory.

Insulting letters to the governor-general.

Peculiar difficulties of the country.

This country, as to its capacity of coping with the British power, might, from the small amount of its population, have been considered as utterly contemptible. The extreme difficulty of the ground, however, composed altogether of lofty mountains, covered with the thickest and most entangled jungle, defended by a race of determined valour, gave to it a somewhat serious character. A force of 6000 men was placed under Brigadier Lindesay, in whom was vested the supreme command of the expedition; and marching from Mysore with the main body, he entered Coorg on the 1st April. The troops were harassed by the difficulties of the road, which were much increased by large trees cut down and laid across it, so that they could scarcely accomplish above five miles in fourteen hours. The enemy, however, did not venture to encounter him, and all the stockades were found deserted.

Tardy march through the country.

On the 6th the army entered without resistance Mudakerry, the capital, on which the British flag was displayed. The campaign thus seemed to have been easily and triumphantly terminated; and yet it acquired a somewhat disastrous character, from the operations of three other detachments which entered the territory at different points. Owning that we may not have full means of judging, we yet cannot help calling in question the policy of sending so many separate and unconnected bodies into the heart of so difficult a country. There was every ground to presume that the reduction of the capital would carry with it that of the whole district, as it actually did; and even had it been otherwise, these subordinate posts could scarcely have failed soon to follow the fate of the leading one.

The capital entered.

Questionable conduct of the forces.

Colonel Foulis, marching from Cananor, on the western coast, approached, on the 2d April, the entrance of the Hugul Ghaut, the principal opening from this side. The enemy had fortified it with three successive stockades, as well as with breastworks and felled trees at every hundred yards. Their posts were driven in, and on the 3d, at six in the morning, the attack began. The first stockade was carried with trifling loss; but from that time till four in the afternoon, a series of very hard conflicts was maintained in carrying the successive barriers, which the enemy defended with vigour, carrying on at the same time a continued skirmishing from the wood. The last stockade was only captured by attacking it in reverse as well as in flank. Next day, as the colonel continued to advance, a flag of truce appeared bearing a proposal from the rajah for a suspension of arms. He replied, that if the Coorg troops did not fire, his would also abstain from doing so; but that nothing should prevent him from passing through the ghaut. He accordingly effected this march without opposition, and on the afternoon arrived at Hugul. His service was now completed, with the loss of twelve killed and thirty-six wounded; but among the former was Lieutenant Erskine, a very promising young officer.

The Hugul Ghaut.

Proposed suspension of arms.

At the same time, Colonel Waugh, from the north,

CHAP. XV. — A.D. 1834.

Unsuccessful attack on Buck.

advanced upon a fortified position named Buck, seated on the brow of a steep ascent, and accessible only by a narrow defile through a dense jungle. The assailing party was divided into two, who were each to make a detour and take the stockade in flank; but being misled, it is said by native guides, they both met in front of that barrier. With characteristic valour they rushed forward to the attack; but the place was so strong and so vigorously defended, that all their efforts were vain, and their ranks were thinned by a most destructive fire. Upon encountering this resistance, the commander directed Lieutenant-colonel Mill to send part of his force to support the storming-party; and immediately that officer, inspired by a too ardent valour, led them on himself, and was followed by the whole detachment. An impetuous assault was then commenced against the stockade; but being in a great measure built of stone, it baffled every attempt, while a most murderous fire issued from it against our countrymen. Mill was shot dead on the spot, and several, while vainly attempting to rescue his body, fell around him. Major Bird then determined to withdraw the party, and, with little additional loss, brought it under cover. In this most unfortunate affair about forty-eight were killed, including three officers, and 118 wounded.

Retirement of Lieutenant-colonel Jackson.

Another column, under Lieutenant-colonel Jackson, advanced from Mangalore upon a position named Bullary Pett; and this officer, learning that there was a strong stockade five miles in front of him, sent Captain Noble with a detachment to reconnoitre it. The latter made his way through a narrow and winding path, till he arrived in front of the barrier; and having completed his reconnaissance, he began his return, when a running fire was instantly commenced from among the bushes. His party continued exposed during the whole of their retreat to this assault from an invisible foe, whom they could neither elude nor repel; and the casualties amounted to thirty killed and thirty-six wounded. Colonel Jackson, after considering this loss, and the reported strength of the position, thought it impossible to attempt carrying the stockade without further reinforcements, and fell back upon Coombla. This transaction was at first made a subject of official inquiry, but was ultimately decided to have arisen from inevitable circumstances, without any reproach on the commander.

Surrender of the rajah

The war, as formerly observed, was already decided by the primary movement of the main body upon the capital, where the rajah, in no degree emulating the courage of many of his subjects, did not even attempt resistance. On the 11th April he entered Mudakerry in pomp, with about 2000 attendants, mostly unarmed, and fifty palanquins containing his female establishment. He then surrendered himself, in the hope probably of being reinstated on certain conditions. But the British had already formed their determination; his territory was annexed to their dominion; and the rajah, receiving only an allowance fitted to support a suitable household, was removed to Bangalore. Prize-money to the amount of thirteen lacks of rupees was distributed among the army.

Gwalior.

Gwalior being the most powerful of the independent states now remaining, its interior movements were regarded as of considerable importance. Dowlut Rao Scindia having died, left the regency in the hands of his widow, the Baiza Bye; and that lady, to ensure a male successor to the throne, as none had been left by her husband, adopted a youth under the name of Jhundkoo Rao, and the title of Maharaja.

Ambitious projects of Jhundkoo Rao

This young man, on coming of age, aspired to the actual possession of the supreme power, which the Bye was by no means inclined to grant; while he, without any regard to his obligations to that lady, determined to use every means of enforcing his claim. When the governor-general visited the capital, he solicited his aid to place himself upon the musnud. Lord William, however, intimated, that Gwalior being an independent state, the British government could by no means interfere; then reminding him of what he owed to his patroness, advised him to pay the utmost deference to her, and await the time when she might be willing to place the government in his hands. But he

CHAP. XV.
A. D. 1833.

was by no means disposed to follow this advice, and in July 1833 made an attempt to seize the reins of power. This being frustrated, he repaired to the mansion of our resident, who, unwilling to interfere, had left it fast locked. The young prince sat the whole day in the court of this official dwelling without food, and under a burning sun; but having at last obtained an audience, and being refused all support, he made his submission to the Bye. Meantime, however, a large body of the military, impatient of a female government, discontented with Baiza, and perhaps desirous of change, applied a ladder to the maharaja's apartment, brought him out, and proclaimed him their sovereign. The lady took refuge with some troops who still adhered to her; but they were unequal to contend with the opposite party, who were more numerous, and possessed all the artillery. An agreement was made, under the mediation of the resident, that Jhundkoo Rao should be placed on the musnud, and acknowledged by Britain; while the regent should retire unmolested to Dholapoor. There she still attempted to make a stand; but being closely invested and reduced to great distress, she at length surrendered, was allowed a revenue of ten lacks of rupees, and took up her residence near Futtyghur. The Company in this case proceeded on the principle of non-interference, and of acknowledging the sovereign *de facto*, whoever he might be. Yet this conduct was criticised by some, who considered the change unfavourable to our interests, from a female ruler of pacific habits, to a military government with a violent and ambitious young man at its head. In fact, some serious disturbances followed, both in the durbar and army, in which British interests and wishes were not much regarded; however, Jhundkoo displayed a degree of vigour which enabled him at last to establish an uncontrolled authority.

His submission.

Settlement of the government.

Maun Sing Rajah of Joudpore.

An affair of a more serious aspect soon after arose with Maun Sing, rajah of Joudpore, who had been restored to power by the governor-general on the footing of a subsidiary and dependent ruler. He was considered, however, to have by no means duly fulfilled the conditions of his tenure; and having absented himself from the congress of Rajpoot princes, who assembled at Ajmere in 1832 to meet Lord William Bentinck, he could not be viewed as showing a friendly or respectful disposition. Besides, he had allowed the tribute to fall more than two years in arrear; he had given shelter to bands of marauders, and had refused, when called upon, to assist in putting down others. When remonstrances were made against these proceedings, his answers indicated no desire to comply or act according to his professed obligations; and it was therefore determined to march against him a force which might either compel unqualified submission, or dethrone him. For this purpose 10,000 men were ordered to assemble at Nusserabad on the 20th October 1834; but he had no sooner learned that matters were coming to so serious a crisis, than he sent a deputation of thirty persons, with a numerous attendance, to Ajmere, to treat with the residents there, Major Alves and Captain Trevelyan. The envoys made lavish professions of their master's attachment to Britain, and regret at having given offence. When informed, however, that no declarations would be esteemed of any value, unless followed up by certain specific actions, namely, the immediate delivery of the refugees, and payment of a large sum of money, they made many apologies, and showed an extreme anxiety to avoid compliance. But on inquiring what alternative awaited the rajah, and being informed that he would be forthwith dethroned, they showed the utmost consternation, and solicited a delay of at least two days. At the end of that time, after some farther attempts to parry the blow, they finally yielded an unqualified submission; and the storm which threatened the peace of Western India was thus averted.

Symptoms of enmity to the British

Active proceedings against him

His submission.

A part of the force prepared for this expedition was immediately after employed against the Shekhawuttees, a rude tribe occupying the almost desert territory westward of Rajpootana. A number of these petty chiefs has been accustomed to subsist by plundering the neigh-

The Shekhawuttees.

CHAP. XV. A. D. 1834.

bouring districts, and when these were held by native powers this was regarded as a matter of course. Having now, however, come into contact with the Company's territory, they continued towards it the same system of indiscriminate marauding; and yet when the British force under General Stevenson marched into the country, no attempt had been made for an organized resistance. The forts of the freebooters were rased to the ground, the district of Sambhur was retained as security for the expenses, and a detachment left to overawe the rude natives.

Their defeat.

Jeypore.

The Rajpoot state of Jeypore was soon after the scene of a tragical and distressing event. The rajah, a thoughtless and voluptuous youth, had left the whole administration in the hands of Jotaram, originally a banker, an able man, but believed to bear that unprincipled character too common among Indian statesmen. The prince died suddenly, leaving an infant as the heir; and as the inspection of his body was refused to the public, a strong suspicion arose that the minister, finding his master about to shake off his influence, had secretly murdered him. Amid the ferment thus occasioned, the British residency interposed, and procured the removal of Jotaram, and the transference of the government to a regency,—measures which appeared entirely accordant with public feeling. Soon, however, a jealousy was entertained that public affairs were placed entirely under the dictation of a few foreigners, and a feeling of enmity arose, which broke forth fatally on the following occasion:—On the 4th June 1835, Major Alves, the resident, with Mr Blake, Cornet Macnaghten, and Lieutenant Ludlow, had an interview with the Myesaheb or dowager-princess. After taking leave, as the first-mentioned gentleman was mounting his elephant, a man rushed out of the crowd with a drawn sword, and inflicted three wounds, one in the forehead; but these being immediately dressed, he was placed in a palanquin, and conveyed home in safety. The assassin having been seized, Mr Blake undertook to conduct him to the place of con-

Jotaram, the chief minister

Suspicions on the death of the rajah.

Attack on the British residency.

finement; but as he proceeded, the cry was raised, "The Feringees have shed blood in the palace!" A crowd instantly assembled, who are said to have been joined by many of the police; stones were thrown, and attempts made to stop him by maiming his elephant. He reached the city gate, which was found shut, whereupon he turned back, and sought shelter in a mundur or temple, which was then fastened on the inside; but the multitude burst in, and he fell pierced by numerous wounds. He is said to have been a very promising officer, and generally popular among the natives. Macnaghten, by galloping in another direction through the crowd, though assailed by stones and other missiles, reached the residency in safety. The government disowned all knowledge of this outrage, though five individuals, whose guilt was clearly proved, were condemned and executed. Suspicion, however, soon fell upon Jotaram, the late minister, and, after long preparation, he and several grandees connected with him were brought to trial before a native jury. Being found guilty of instigating and abetting the crime, sentence of death was pronounced upon them; but it was commuted to exile and imprisonment.

Assassination of Mr Blake.

Trial of Jotaram for the crime.

A strong sensation was caused in March 1835 by the assassination of Mr Fraser, commissioner and agent of the governor-general at Delhi. As he was riding out late one evening, a man rode up as if to speak to him, rapidly discharged three balls through his body, and galloped off. After some time, through the evidence of an accomplice, the crime was brought home, not only to Kurreem, the actual murderer, but to a native chieftain, the Nawab of Ferozepore, by whom he had been employed. Both were condemned and underwent the extreme sentence of the law. The execution of the former was attended by a vast concourse of natives, who, though kept in awe by an armed force, displayed a decided sympathy in his favour. It is somewhat unpleasant to learn that he was then in a manner canonized by them; that his grave was visited by great numbers, who sang songs

Assassination of the British agent at Delhi.

Execution of the assassins.

CHAP. XV.

A.D. 1835.

and strewed flowers over it. The rajah was executed without the gates, which were shut, and any large attendance of the people was thereby prevented.

Resignation of Lord William Bentinck.

In the course of the year 1834, Lord William Bentinck was obliged, from the state of his health, to make known to the government at home the necessity of resigning his high office, and in March 1835 he embarked for England. His departure was the subject of very general regret; for his administration had been marked by economy, a pacific spirit, and one of mildness and indulgence towards the natives. His system was considered by a party, especially among the military, as having been carried somewhat too far; but it was conformable to his instructions, and prompted undoubtedly by the best motives. His efforts to improve internal intercourse by the establishment of steam-vessels between the different Indian ports, and the formation of extensive lines of road through the interior, commanded universal applause. He favoured also the diffusion of education and knowledge among the Hindoos, and his views were seconded by the amiable and benevolent exertions of Lady Bentinck. A statue of his lordship was erected by subscription. His place as governor-general was supplied in the interim by Sir Charles Metcalfe; and on receiving intelligence of Lord William's resignation, the Court of Directors unanimously nominated Lord Heytesbury, a choice which was cordially sanctioned by Sir Robert Peel and the Duke of Wellington, then ministers. The proceedings in Parliament, however, soon led to their resignation, and the accession to power of the Whig party, who deeming it important to have a governor-general whose views accorded with their own, annulled the appointment. The Directors, though they expressed some dissatisfaction at this change, finally concurred in the nomination of Lord Auckland, who was entirely acceptable to ministers. On the 4th March 1836 his lordship landed at Calcutta, and assumed the reins of government.

His policy.

Nomination of Lord Heytesbury.

superseded by Lord Auckland.

About this time another mountain-struggle occurred

The Khoonds.

in a territory named Goomsoor, inhabited by a peculiar race named Khoonds, who had remained nearly independent. Their rajah having shown a refractory spirit, a considerable force was despatched against him; and the troops, on reaching the summit of the alpine chain, were surprised to see an extensive and fertile tract of country covered with fine villages in romantic situations. Little serious resistance was encountered; Goomsoor and the principal forts soon fell; the rajah, and afterwards his son, submitted; yet a number of detached chieftains, exercising a sort of feudal power over vassals devotedly attached to them, kept up for a time a desultory resistance. In one skirmish two British officers were killed. The prolongation, too, of the war in a country filled with jungle and marshy districts caused severe sickness among the troops, and two campaigns elapsed before this bold tribe could be brought under full subjection.

Difficulty of their subjection.

The throne of Oude.

A considerable sensation was excited in 1837 by the succession to the throne of Oude, the most important dependency of the Bengal government; an event the prospect of which had for some years attracted attention, as the king's infirmities indicated that the throne would soon become vacant. That weak prince had acknowledged as his sons two youths, Kywan Jah and Moonah Jaun; but the general belief was, that he had acted under the influence of certain females, and that they were not his children. He himself finally made a declaration to that effect, and, after a good deal of consideration, the British authorities determined to set them aside, and to support Nusseer-ood-Dowlah, his majesty's eldest surviving uncle, who, according to the peculiar tenor of Mohammedan law, was considered the legal heir. But the Padsha Begum, or queen-mother, a bold and ambitious princess, had, in the mean time, adopted Moonah Jaun, and was determined to espouse his cause.

Disputed succession

Death of the king.

On the night of the 7th July 1837, Colonel Low, the resident, received a message that the king was taken suddenly ill, and believed to be dying. This officer,

CHAP. XV.
A. D. 1837.

having ordered his troops to be in readiness, obeyed the summons, when he found that his majesty had just expired. Having in this crisis obtained from Nusseer-ood-Dowlah an engagement to sign such a treaty as the governor-general should dictate, he led him to the royal residence, where preparations were made for his immediate installation. Suddenly, however, a great noise was heard, and it soon appeared that the Padsha with an armed force of about 2000 men, was approaching the palace, which, as our soldiers were not yet come up, was very slightly guarded. In spite of a warm remonstrance, the natives burst open the gates, filled the edifice with shouts and clamour, seized both the prince and the Company's servants, in presence of whom Moonah Jaun was placed on the throne, the Begum being seated in a palanquin beneath him. The insurgents after some violent proceedings towards the resident, allowed him to retire, when, upon finding his men assembled, he sent repeated messages to the Begum, calling upon her to surrender. As she returned evasive answers, a battery was opened, and in a short time she and her minions were made prisoners. The old prince, whom, though he had endured many insults, they found safe, was immediately seated on the throne, and his accession announced by a royal salute to the inhabitants of the capital.

Preparations for installing Nusseer-ood-Dowlah.

Insurrection on behalf of Moonah Jaun.

All these proceedings were approved by the governor-general; but of the promise extorted from the king relative to a new treaty, it appears that no advantage has been taken.

Principles of Indian succession.

Claims were advanced by two nephews, sons of a deceased elder brother, who urged that, as their father, if alive, would have succeeded, they ought to inherit in his stead. This question, however, had early attracted the attention of the Indian government, who, after much consideration and reference to high authorities, as well as precedents (among which was that of the present King of Delhi), had concluded that, according to the principles of the Soonee sect, a son cannot succeed to rights or property to which his father was heir, if he died before coming into actual possession. In this case, the inheritance goes to a brother. A curious contest also arose between the two princes which was the elder; though, as both were excluded, there was no need to discuss this question. One of them spent a considerable time in England, but without being able to obtain any attention either from Parliament or the Company.

The Rajah of Satara.

Another political change, somewhat similar, excited a great interest in India. The Rajah of Satara, lineal descendant of Sevajee, the warlike founder of the Mahratta dynasty, had, as formerly mentioned, been drawn from the prison into which the peishwa and the other chiefs had thrown him, and invested, not indeed with the wide dominions of his house, but with a certain extent of valuable territory. He held it, however, under the avowed stipulation of paying the greatest deference to the advice of the English resident, and holding no intercourse with foreign states through any other channel. For several years he gave the highest satisfaction, showing the most cordial attachment to the British government, and exerting himself with diligence, unfortunately not usual among Indian princes, to promote the prosperity of his subjects. At length he began to show strong symptoms of an intriguing spirit; and about 1836, the charges against him assumed a definite form, being resolved into three heads:—1. That he had been guilty of an attempt to seduce certain native officers from their allegiance to the Company. 2. That he had carried on a treasonable correspondence with Appa Sahib, then a refugee at Joudpore. 3. That he had maintained a similar intercourse with the Portuguese governor of Goa. After long investigation, Sir Robert Grant, governor of Bombay, became thoroughly convinced of his guilt; and Lord Auckland, after a good deal of hesitation, acquiesced in the same judgment.

Manifestations of unfriendly policy.

Concurrent belief in his treason.

Sir Robert died, and was succeeded in 1839 by Sir James Carnac, who went out, it is said, with a strong prepossession in the prince's favour. He soon, however, became convinced that there was ground for the

CHAP. XV.

A.D. 1839.

An amnesty proposed.

charges against him, but obtained the approbation of Lord Auckland to an amnesty, by which past offences were to be buried in oblivion, on securities being given to adhere strictly in future to the treaty by which he had been placed on the throne. He was also required to dismiss his favourite minister, and not allow him, without our permission, to reside in his dominions Sir James on a visit to him, presented these proposals, but they met with a peremptory and indignant rejection. His friends admit that he was "proud, overbearing, strong in the assertion of his rights, impetuous, in short a regular Hotspur." It is added, on the other side, that the idea had been instilled into him, that the Company would not proceed to extremities, and great confidence was placed in extensive agencies maintained in England, Bombay, and Poonah, at an annual expense of above £35,000. The governor, in four successive interviews, sought in vain to change his resolution, and in departing on the 28th August, left instructions with the resident to forward any communications he might receive.

His deposition.

The rajah remaining inflexible, a proclamation deposing him was issued on the 5th September, and on the 7th December he was removed to Benares, to be entered on the list of pensioned princes. The vacant seat was bestowed on his brother, who was placed on the gadi on the 18th November 1839. Among his first proceedings was the abolition of suttee, which was followed by other measures decidedly calculated for the public good.

Proceedings in his favour at home.

A portion, meantime, of the East India proprietors, actuated by honourable motives, considered these measures oppressive, and even injurious to the British character. A special court being called on 12th February 1840, upon the requisition of nine of their number, Sir Charles Forbes moved, that they should recommend to the Directors and the Board of Control to withhold their sanction to the measure till after a full and fair investigation of the charges. This motion was opposed, until the subject should be considered by the Directors, and the proper documents laid before the proprietors; which be-

An investigation sought.

Discussion of the subject.

ing done on the 6th May, and a sufficient time afforded for consideration, the court again met on 14th July 1841, when a very long and animated debate ensued. Generals Robertson and Lodwick, who had been residents at the prince's court, took a very decided part in his favour. They urged, that none of the charges were confirmed by any thing in his own handwriting, or had been brought personally home to him; alleging that his agents and officers, especially the Bramins, cherished in many cases hostile feelings towards his person; that his brother, hoping for the succession, had an obvious interest in proving him guilty; that the very idea of defying British power by the aid of the Governor of Goa and the imprisoned Rajah of Nagpore, was ridiculous, and could never have been entertained by a prince who was admitted to possess ability; and at all events, that he was entitled, like every accused person, to a fair and open trial. In these views they were supported by others. It was answered, that the inquiry had been most impartial; that due allowance had been made for the defects in the evidence, much of which had been given by persons who had no interest in proving the rajah's guilt; that even his advocates, Robertson and Lodwick, had addressed severe warnings to him on his intriguing disposition, and the consequences which might follow; that there had certainly been some correspondence with Goa and the Nagpore rajah, which alone was a breach of the treaty placing him on the throne; and that though possessing ability, he was not a politician, and might easily form chimerical expectations from distant quarters. The public trial of a prince in his own dominions, it was admitted, was liable to many objections; but the charges had been stated to him, and no satisfactory explanation given. Finally, the terms on which continuance in power had been offered were extremely lenient, making no material difference from his position when first raised to it. The motion was finally negatived by 31 to 13, and several attempts made to revive it were unsuccessful.

Defence of the government.

Approval of their proceedings.

At Hydrabad, a somewhat serious conspiracy was

CHAP. XV. — A.D. 1839.

Conspiracy at Hydrabad.

formed among thirty or forty leading men, headed by the nizam's brother, a proud and daring chief; but, being discovered, it was baffled, and the prince conveyed to the fort of Golconda. During the investigation which followed, the Nabob of Kurnool, a place situated about 120 miles farther south, was found implicated. A force being immediately marched to reduce the town, it was entered without opposition; and the nabob, who had been carried away by his own troops, was pursued and captured after a sharp conflict. Within the fortress, however, were found a number of well-constructed furnaces, in which cannon and shot had been cast on a large scale, and in forms fitted not for defence only, but for active proceedings in the field. These preparations had been secretly carried on for a considerable time.

Capture of the nabob.

Submission of the Rajah of Joudpore.

The Rajah of Joudpore, after yielding in 1834 to all the demands of the governor-general, had constantly evaded their fulfilment, and now showed himself more than ever refractory. Six regiments, with some cavalry and artillery, were sent against him, on whose approach he abandoned the stronghold, which was entered without resistance, only one British officer being wounded. Thus, the troubles which had arisen in so many quarters were crushed, and our ascendency more fully than ever established throughout Hindostan.

Proceedings on the frontier:

While these movements were taking place in the interior, a most extensive and serious contest was waging on the western frontier. Although Afghanistan, its theatre, is not strictly part of India, the two regions have always been very closely connected, and sometimes united; and the events in question deeply affect the interests of our Eastern empire. The succeeding chapter is, accordingly, devoted to the history of the memorable transactions in Afghan, which seemed for a time to threaten the overthrow of British empire in India.

CHAPTER XVI.

The Afghan War.

Revolutions of Cabul—Dost Mohammed—Expedition of Shah Sujah—Intrigues of Russia and Persia—Siege of Herat—Treaty to restore Shah Sujah—March of the Army—Submission of the Ameers—Arrival at Candahar—Capture of Ghizni—Flight of Dost Mohammed—Death of Runjeet Sing—Troubles in Afghanistan—Invasion by Dost Mohammed—His Defeat and Surrender—Disturbances in various Quarters—March of General Sale—Great Insurrection at Cabul—Various Conflicts—Treacherous Negotiations—Disastrous Retreat—Fall of Ghizni—Transactions at Candahar—Gallant Exploits of General Sale—General Pollock passes the Kyber Defile—Repulse of General England—Death of Shah Sujah—Lord Ellenborough Governor-general—His Policy—Transactions at Jellalabad—Victories of General Pollock—He arrives at Cabul—General England's Return—General Nott's March on Ghizni and Cabul—Return of the Prisoners—Capture of Istalif—Proceedings at Cabul—Return of General Pollock—Conclusion.

CHAP. XVI

A. D. 1761.

Kingdom of Cabul.

THE kingdom of Cabul, under Ahmed Abdalla, had, towards the end of the last century, become one of the most powerful in Asia; and after his victory over the Mahrattas in the battle of Panniput, in 1761, the Mogul throne seemed completely within his grasp. He had the moderation or prudence, however, to content himself with the rich provinces on the Indus, and the fine valley of Cashmere. Having added Balkh, Herat, and Sinde, he formed a powerful monarchy, estimated to contain above fourteen millions of inhabitants; and this dominion Mr Elphinstone, on his mission to Peshawer in 1808, found still entire in the hands of his successor Shah Sujah ul Mulk. But it was then on the eve of a great revolution; and in a few months afterwards, that prince was driven out by his brother Mahmoud, whose

CHAP. XVI. A. D. 1831.

Mahmoud.

successes, however, were mostly achieved by his vizier Futeh Khan, of the Baurikzehee tribe. That minister, having incurred the jealousy of his master, was deposed and his eyes put out,—a cruel deed, which roused the vengeance of his numerous offspring. The usurper was driven from all his territories except Herat; and, after some vicissitudes, Cabul, Ghizni, Candahar, and Peshawer, were partitioned among members of the Baurikzehee house, the first two falling to Dost Mohammed, the most powerful of their number. Amid these distractions, Runjeet Sing, having acquired absolute authority over the warlike race of the Seiks, made himself master of the provinces eastward of the Indus, to which he added Cashmere. Balkh was seized by the sovereign of Bokhara; the chiefs of Sinde threw off their dependence; while the fine territory of Herat was occupied by Kamran, son to Mahmoud, the only branch of the house of Ahmed Abdalla to whom any thing now remained. In this manner, a monarchy, lately so great, was parcelled out into a number of disjointed fragments.

Partition of his kingdom.

Shah Sujah.

Shah Sujah, after his expulsion, resided at Loodiana, being allowed by the British government 4000 rupees monthly. He kept a longing eye upon his lost kingdom, and was encouraged by various chiefs of Afghanistan and Khorasan to attempt its recovery. With this view he made proposals, in 1831, to Runjeet Sing; and, after some difficulties, concluded a treaty with him on the 12th March 1833. The British agreed to give an advance of four months' allowance, but declined taking any further concern in the enterprise. Hence the exiled prince could not begin his march till the season was somewhat advanced. He passed first through the territories of the Rajah of Bahawulpore, from whom he received only an old gun and 1000 rupees; and then, with the consent of the chiefs of Sinde, he crossed the Indus, and established himself at Shikarpore. Those leaders, however, turned a deaf ear to his applications for money; and the shah, who had assembled a considerable force, determined to take that affair upon himself, demanding from the city

British share in his plans.

Summary proceedings at Shikapore.

a contribution of three lacs, and seizing all the crops in the surrounding districts. The Sindians thereupon levied a force, and marched to attack him; but being completely defeated, they agreed to the payment demanded, and even to send an auxiliary force. The conqueror, thus supplied, advanced, in February 1834, upon Candahar, and was joined on the road by numerous adherents. He defeated a force which attempted to oppose his progress, entered the city, and laid close siege to the citadel. The Baurikzehee brothers retreated upon Cabul, and, as disunion was understood to prevail between them, the complete and speedy success of the undertaking was anticipated. But Dost Mohammed, by indefatigable exertion, assembled an army, and marched upon Candahar, the chiefs of which sallied forth from the citadel, and an engagement ensued, in which the army of Shah Sujah was totally defeated and dispersed. He himself at the head of only 200 men fled in the direction of Herat, but afterwards regained India, though mortified by the total failure of this attempt to recover his crown. The "Lion of the Punjaub," however, succeeded on his part in capturing Peshawer, and annexing it to his dominions.

Enforced supplies.

Siege of Candahar

Its relief on the defeat of Shah Sujah.

Dost Mohammed, elated by his victory, and indignant, not without reason, at the conduct of Runjeet Sing, who certainly had acted without any provocation, became eagerly desirous, not only of recovering the lost territory, but of entirely overthrowing this ambitious potentate. Sensible that his own power was inadequate to the undertaking, he hoped to accomplish it by a general confederacy among the powers of Central Asia; and the one from whom he could look for the most effective aid was the sovereign of Persia.

Dost Mohammed.

The empire just named has been involved in a continued series of revolutions. The last century in particular was marked, first by the conquest of the Afghans, then by their expulsion on the part of Nadir, and the splendour to which he raised the monarchy; after his death, a long anarchy ensued, out of which she was raised by

Persian revolutions

CHAP. XVI. A.D. 1834.

Aga Mohammed, great grandfather to the reigning prince. Under him and his son, Futeh Ali Shah, she was supported in a respectable position, but having to contend against the advancing power of Russia, with whose numerous and disciplined troops hers could not cope, she was stripped of some of her finest provinces between the Caspian and the Black Sea. In this situation the government applied for assistance to England, which, jealous of the progress of the czar, supplied ome pecuniary aid and experienced officers to discipline the shah's troops. Nothing more was meant, however, than to maintain him in a purely defensive position, and with this view he was dissuaded from all schemes of war and conquest.

European interference with Persia.

Change in the councils of Persia.

An alliance thus founded on mutual interest, seemed to promise permanency; but a change gradually came over the councils of Persia. Although her improved discipline could not enable her to contend with Russia, it gave to her arms a decided superiority over the rude tribes of Khorasan and Afghanistan. The former country, long held by brave and turbulent chiefs, was, after a desperate struggle, reduced to submission. The adjacent province of Herat was next aimed at, and after its conquest, there appeared no difficulty, in the present distracted state of Afghanistan, to extend the Persian sway to the Indus. To these schemes the old king, Futeh Ali, unwillingly assented, chiefly on the impulse of his son, Abbas Meerza, whose younger brother he had made governor of Khorasan. In 1834 he died; and as Meerza had previously deceased, his son Mohammed now succeeded. This young and aspiring sovereign, who had actually led an expedition against Herat, embraced with ardour the new and ambitious system of policy. To carry it on successfully, the acquiescence of Russia was indispensable, while her aid might prove of the greatest advantage. England, on the contrary, had always opposed schemes of conquest, and would doubtless view with peculiar jealousy those carried in the direction of her own frontier. It might scarcely have been expected

Plans of conquest.

Accession of Mohammed to the Persian throne.

that Russia would favour the aggrandizement of an old enemy, from whom she had wrested so many valuable provinces, which there was doubtless an eager desire to recover. Yet there was in her cabinet a powerful party who urged the adoption of these views. They considered that attempts at distant conquest would only increase the dependence of Persia on so powerful a neighbour; and they had probably other views to be forwarded by such profound diplomacy.

Views of Russia.

The question, whether Russia contemplates the conquest of British India has been much canvassed, and in most cases with imperfect local knowledge. Her route is presumed to lie across the vast, almost desert regions of Turkestan, and then through the tremendous passes and eternal snows of the Indian Caucasus, by which it is argued that the complex apparatus of a modern army could never be conveyed. This was indeed the course followed by Alexander and Timur; but the former was obliged to pursue Darius into Bactria, while the latter came from Central Asia. There is, however, another route leading through Persia and Afghanistan, and along the southern verge of the great chain, which is beset with no peculiar difficulties; and this has been usually followed by the conquerors of Hindostan, the Ghisnevide, the Patans, Baber, and Nadir. At the same time, though Russia could send by this track 40,000 men, we imagine her too politic seriously to think of such a step. By employing, however, or even promising a much smaller force, she might acquire a preponderating influence in Western Asia, and might hope to overawe Britain by exciting alarm for her Indian possessions.

Her object in reference to British India.

Rout to India.

By communications from Mr Ellis, our envoy in 1835, it appears that both powers were strongly actuated by these views. The Persian court openly avowed its claim not only upon Herat but upon Candahar and Cabul; and great preparations were making for an expedition against the former city, the immediate prosecution of which was eagerly urged by Count Simonich, the Rus-

Claims avowed by Persia.

CHAP. XVI. A.D. 1836.

Supported by the Russian ambassador

sian ambassador. In April 1836, a deputy arrived from the chiefs of Candahar proposing an alliance offensive and defensive, even offering themselves as feudatories, and holding out the hope that through their aid the shah might follow the steps of Nadir to Delhi. He was received with great favour, and the alliance agreed to, though the Persian minister, in his communications with Ellis, represented such language as that of a madman.

Expedition against Herat.

Mr M'Neill, who succeeded that gentleman, reported, in September 1836, that the shah had actually marched against Herat. At Astrabad, the dearth of provisions and the insubordination of the troops reduced him to great distress; yet the Russian minister continued to urge even a winter campaign.

British remonstrance to the Russian cabinet.

Lord Durham being hereupon instructed to represent these particulars to the Russian cabinet, Count Nesselrode answered, that if Simonich had really acted in the manner alleged, it had been in direct opposition to his orders. Letters were afterwards shown from the ambassador, asserting that he had used all his influence to dissuade the shah from the expedition; yet Mr M'Neill declared, that his information was confirmed by all the Persians with whom he conversed, the prime minister not excepted. Preparations were avowedly making for a fresh expedition, when

Tribute offered by Herat.

an envoy arrived from Kamran, offering not only the redress of all positive complaints, but an annual tribute, and the aid when required of a military force. Our agent strenuously urged the acceptance of these terms, intimating that otherwise the intentions of Persia would evidently be conquest, which would give decided umbrage to the British government. The prime minister replied, that Herat was a province of their empire,—that the object required was submission, which would include all the other conditions, while the bare use of the term shah by its chief was expressive of disobedience. The entire conquest of Herat was thus openly contemplated, and without any regard to the remonstrances of our ambassador, Mohammed began his march. When he was near Meshed, a messenger employed by the British representative was seized, stripped, and carried to the camp, where he continued to be treated with indignity, even after the remonstrances of Colonel Stoddart. Mr M'Neill had no doubt the object was to show contempt for the English, and remove the unfavourable impression derived from their opposition. The Persian ruler meantime reached, and in ten days reduced, the frontier fortress of Ghorian, which had been considered very strong. Elated with this success, he proceeded to besiege the capital, where Kamran, having concentrated his forces, had begun a vigorous defence; yet the general opinion in Western Asia was, that he could not long resist the formidable force now brought against him.

Indignity offered to a messenger of the British minister

The British government in India, on receiving this intelligence, instructed our minister to use his utmost exertions to mediate a peace between Persia and Herat. He accordingly set out for the latter place, and, after many difficulties, succeeded in persuading the shah, who began to suffer from want of provisions, to enter into a negotiation, which seemed even in a fair train, when Count Simonich arrived at head-quarters. Then the views of Mohammed were entirely changed, and the treaty was suspended; for the Russian not only supplied money, but aided with his advice the operations of the siege. As, however, it advanced slowly, the shah, ten days after, sent for Mr M'Neill, and offered to close with Kamran's proposal, provided the ambassador would pledge the guarantee of Britain. The latter felt this somewhat beyond his powers, yet, on considering the very great importance of the object, he at last gave his consent; upon which the other altered his tone, advanced new demands, and resumed the siege.

Instructions to the British minister.

Counter movements of Russia.

The cause of this change was soon understood to be the arrival of a messenger from Kohundil Khan, ruler of Candahar, expressing the most friendly sentiments, and a disposition to co-operate against Herat. It was known in fact, that about four months previously Captain Vicovich, a Russian officer, had proceeded to that city through Persia, having been received on his way with distinction, and supplied with money. The result of this

Fresh allies of Persia.

CHAP. XVI.
A. D. 1838.

mission forthwith appeared in a treaty, by which the shah agreed to cede the town to the chiefs of Candahar and to defend them against attack from any quarter; in return for which he was to receive allegiance, peesh-cush (tribute), and military aid. This treaty was sanctioned in the name of Russia by Count Simonich; upon which Mr M'Neill, defeated in all his views and scarcely treated with common decency, quitted the camp on the 7th June 1838.

Renewed interference of Russia.

Uncertain views of Dost Mohammed.

Meantime, uncertainty reigned as to the views of Dost Mohammed at Cabul. Lord Auckland sent thither Captain Burnes to negotiate for the free commerce of the Indus, and if opportunity occurred, to endeavour to restore peace between him and Runjeet Sing. The former prince received the envoy well, and soon introduced political subjects, endeavouring to gain the support of Britain. He was assured, by a letter from the governor-general, that she would readily interpose her good offices to negotiate a peace with the Sheik chief, who had accepted her mediation, and he might thus be secured in all his actual possessions, though he must not expect any more; for even this was only on condition of his renouncing all political connexion with the powers to the westward. These terms were by no means equal to his expectations, so that Vicovich and a Persian envoy having arrived with great boasts and promises, he was induced to prefer their alliance. Captain Burnes was then allowed to depart, bearing with him a very ambiguous letter to Lord Auckland.

Offers of British intermediation.

Critical state of our Indian affairs.

This situation of affairs was considered by the governor-general as calling for the most serious consideration. The ultimate fall of Herat appeared still inevitable, all means of relief being apparently cut off by the Candahar treaty. The whole of Western Asia would then be united in one vast confederacy, under the influence of Russia, which would thereby be able to disturb at will the repose of India, where there were doubtless many princes eager to shake off all dependence on Britain. Under these circumstances, the system of non-intervention, hitherto pursued, was thought no longer practicable nor even safe. Shah Sujah had a legitimate claim to the throne of Cabul; and he had in his favour a strong party, which Major Wade reported to be decidedly superior to that by which the Baurikzehees were maintained in authority. He had formed an intimate alliance with Runject Sing, then engaged in hostilities with the ruler of Cabul. It appeared that Britain, by a union with these two powers, could easily replace the exiled monarch on his throne, and thus render the strong country of Afghanistan friendly, and a sure bulwark against all attacks from the westward. In pursuance of these views, a treaty between the three parties was signed at Lahore, on the 26th June 1838; and a considerable force was marched from the Bengal provinces upon the Indus, where it was to be joined by all the disposable troops of the Bombay presidency.

System of non-intervention abandoned

Treaty of Lahore.

Shah Mohammed continued to prosecute the siege, and on the 23d June made a general assault, planned by Count Simonich, who complained however that his directions had not been attended to. The Persians attacked with much bravery, but were repulsed with great slaughter, the Afghans pursuing them sabre in hand across the ditch. Yet as the blockade was continued, and the difficulty arising from want of provisions appeared to be in a great measure removed, on the 10th July Mr M'Neill sent Colonel Stoddart with a notice that its farther prosecution would be considered an act of decided hostility towards England. The message was doubtless rendered weighty by the prince's knowledge of the triple alliance, and the approaching march of British troops into Afghanistan. On the 14th August he announced his unreserved assent; but it was not till the 9th September, that he took his departure, and without attempting to negotiate the treaty with Kamran on the terms formerly stipulated.

Prosecution of the siege of Herat.

Decisive message of the English minister.

In October 1838, Lord Palmerston presented a remonstrance to the Russian government, reminding them of their professed desire to maintain Persia in a pacific state, and asking whether their policy was to be judged of by the declarations of their cabinet, or by the acts of their

Remonstrance with Russia.

CHAP. XVI. — A.D. 1839.

Evasive replies of the Russian minister.

ministers! Count Nesselrode, in two successive papers, reiterated the same pacific professions, particularly disclaiming any designs upon India, as impracticable and inconsistent with any sound and reasonable policy. Yet, by a singular course of reasoning, he defended the conduct of those officers, not excepting Simonich's active share in the siege of Herat, representing it as merely aiding a friendly power in distress, while the Candahar treaty had been a purely defensive one. It was, however, announced that both officers had been recalled, and the place of ambassador filled by General Duhamel, "so well known for the moderation of his character, that his nomination alone may be held as the surest proof of the line of conduct which he is instructed to follow." The emperor had also refused to ratify the treaty of Candahar, however harmless, as being "beyond the limits which he had fixed to his policy," and took no part in the civil wars of the Afghan chiefs. As this was written on the 5th March 1839, when the British expedition was fully known, it amounted to an engagement not to oppose that measure. Lord Palmerston, therefore, while declining to give any assent to the reasonings contained in these despatches, expressed entire satisfaction with the result.

Recall of the Russian officers.

Movement of the British force.

The British force was in motion by the end of 1838; and for various reasons, chiefly political, it marched not through the Seik territory, but by way of Sinde and Beloochistan. The troops from Bombay, under Sir John Keane, embarked on the 21st November for the Indus, on the banks of which they were to be joined by Sir Henry Fane, the commander-in-chief, with the force from Bengal. On the 3d December, the former disembarked at the branch of the river named Hujamree, and by difficult marches arrived on the 28th at Tatta, the ancient Patala, which, though much decayed, still presented some vestiges of its former grandeur. Here negotiations were opened with the Ameers, resident at Hydrabad, to whom on the 13th January, two officers were sent with an ultimatum, which included the free navigation of the Indus, the admission of a British force to

Plan for combined action.

Negotiations opened.

be stationed at Tatta and other points, together with the payment of 170,000 rupees, in part of arrears due to Shah Sujah. The mission returned on the 25th, reporting the entire rejection of these terms, describing the city as filled with large bands of warlike Beloochees, and stating that active measures had been taken to strengthen the fortifications. They advised, therefore, to defer the attack till after the arrival of the Bengal force. Sir John, however, on the 3d February, took post on the opposite side of the river; while Admiral Maitland, with the Wellesley seventy-four, moved upon Curachee, a large seaport west of the Indus, and communicating with it by a navigable channel. The governor at first showed a bold face; but as soon as a breach had been made the garrison fled, and the place was occupied without resistance. On receiving this intelligence, and seeing the British army, most of the Beloochees broke up from Hydrabad, and the ameers at once agreed to the terms demanded.

Terms rejected.

Occupation of Curachee.

Sir John now marched up the banks of the Indus, and on the 21st February reached Sehwun, where he met Sir Henry Fane with the Bengal army. These last had crossed at Bukkur, having, by a great exertion of skill and activity, thrown a bridge of boats over the river, here 490 yards broad. A long conference was held between the two officers; but the latter was obliged by severe illness to return to Britain, so that the chief command devolved on General Keane, and the second on Sir Willoughby Cotton. Mr Macnaghten, who acted as envoy, having urged an immediate advance, progress was resumed on the 22d; the whole force, according to Major Hough, being 19,350 men, with 6000 of the shah's contingent. Having reached Larkhanu on the 5th March, and halted there nine days for refreshment, they quitted the Indus, and struck into the interior. They had then to perform a march of 500 miles to Candahar, through a most difficult country, being partly the same in which Alexander, on his return from India, so severely suffered. Great part was quite a desert, and the heat so excessive, that Major Dennie reports two officers and fifty or sixty

Sir Henry Fane effects a junction with Sir John Keane.

Advance of the whole British force.

CHAP. XVI. — A. D. 1839. Bolan pass.

men in his division to have died from the action of its deadly simoom. The Bolan pass, through a range of mountains stretching from north to south, and at its head, according to Major Hough, 5793 feet above the sea level, is in its nakedness and desolation almost unparalleled. The Afghan princes certainly showed a great want of foresight in not bringing forward their main force, defending the strongest positions, and attacking the invader at every assailable point. Even without such opposition, the army was not a little annoyed by desultory attacks from the Beloochees and the Kakurs, tribes inured to plunder, who not only carried away camels, provisions, and other property, but murdered all whom they found straggling, or could entice by false promises to quit the main body. The distress became extreme from the want of water, the enemy having filled up the wells and diverted the mountain-streams. A pestilential air filled the close valleys, and a noisome stench arose from the numerous bodies of camels, and even men, that lay strewed on the ground. But through all these obstacles, they, on the 4th May, arrived without any serious loss, though in a very exhausted state, at the ancient city of Candahar. The chiefs, who at first came out to meet them, were seized with panic, quarrelled among themselves, and left the place, which was entered without even a show of resistance. It could not, it is true, have stood twenty-four hours against a British army. On the 8th, Shah Sujah was crowned with every circumstance of pomp and external honour; but accounts vary as to the cordiality displayed by the native inhabitants. Mr Fane mentions that few men of consequence made their appearance on the occasion.

Attacks of marauders.

Arrival at Candahar.

Fortress of Ghizni.

The army remained six weeks at Candahar, and received from its fruitful plain tolerable supplies of provisions. They then marched through the valley of the Turnuk upon Ghizni, the celebrated capital of Mahmoud, and still esteemed by the Asiatics an impregnable fortress. The British, indeed, when they arrived on the 21st July, found it considerably stronger than their information had led them to expect, and which had even induced them to leave behind their small battering train. The town is situated on high ground, the walls were lofty and in good repair, surrounded by a wet ditch, reported to be unfordable. This position was considered very unfavourable either for mining or escalade; and yet rapidity of operation was of the utmost importance. Captain Thomson, the principal engineer, after a careful survey of the whole circuit, reported that the Cabul gate could be approached, and suggested the novel expedient of conveying thither a heavy train of gunpowder, and blowing it up. General Keane having approved the plan, a party, consisting of three officers and twenty-one men, advanced, carrying 900 pounds of gunpowder in twelve sand-bags. On the 23d, at early dawn, they made their way unperceived to the spot, deposited the train, and, setting it on fire, hastily retired. It presently burst with a tremendous explosion, by which the gate was shattered entirely to pieces; the storming party, directed by Colonel Sale, and headed by Colonel Dennie, rushed in; the garrison, struck with astonishment and dismay, made a brisk but irregular resistance; and in a short time the whole works were in our possession. A number had kept up a fire at particular points, and from houses, exulting even in death if they had slain an infidel; whence our loss amounted to 17 killed and 165 wounded.

Novel engineering expedient.

Capture of Ghizni.

Dost Mohammed, trusting that the siege of Ghizni would have occupied the invaders a considerable time, had an army prepared to operate, according to opportunity, against the besiegers; but on receiving intelligence of what had taken place, he endeavoured through one of his brothers to open a negotiation. Being informed that the only terms which would be accepted were resignation of the crown and residence within the Company's territories, he refused compliance; but, deserted by his best troops, he did not attempt to defend even the strong passes leading to Cabul; his artillery was captured on the road; and the British entering his capital without resistance, he retreated by Bameean over the mountains into

Confusion of Dost Mohammed.

British enter Cabul.

CHAP. XVI.

A.D. 1839.

Turkestan. Haji, a native chief who had deserted his cause, was employed to pursue him with 2000 men and an escort of 100 English troops under Major Outram; but he performed the task carelessly and even treacherously, so that the fugitive prince without difficulty escaped. The whole country then submitted, excepting a few grandees who held strong positions in the Ghilzie territory, whom Outram obliged successively to yield.

Escape of Dost Mohammed.

Death of Runjeet Sing

In the end of 1839, an event took place which threatened a serious commotion. Runjeet Sing died, leaving a kingdom formed by himself, and supposed to be kept together almost solely by his talents and energy. Kurruk Sing, his eldest son, was understood to be well disposed, but devoid of such vigour and determination as were necessary to control the turbulent elements over which he must preside. Runjeet's abilities were in some degree inherited by Shere Sing, another son, whom, through certain feelings of jealousy, he had refused to acknowledge. Yet, as that prince grew up, and displayed eminent military qualities, he was received into favour, and even invested with the government of Cashmere, where he is said to have ruled tyrannically. Kurruk, being undoubtedly the legitimate heir, and on that ground supported by Britain, was at once placed on the musnud. He ventured, however, to transfer his confidence from Dhian Sing, the active minister of his father, to another chief named Cheyt Sing. Yet Dhian's influence being still paramount, he brought about the death of the new favourite; and placing Kurruk under restriction, lodged all the power in the hands of his son, Now Nehal, said to be a prince of spirit and talent. On the 5th October 1840, the deposed prince died, after a lingering illness, not without strong suspicion of poison; and at the funeral ceremony Nehal was killed by the falling of a beam, which was also believed to have proceeded from preconcerted design. Both these guilty deeds were ascribed to Dhian, who immediately after sent for Shere, and placed him on the musnud; but one of the widows of Nehal declaring herself pregnant, her cause was espoused

Shere Sing.

Influence of Dhian Sing.

by the mother of that prince, a person of determined character, and Shere, finding her influence at Lahore too strong for him, resigned his pretensions and left the city. His only object, however, was to muster his adherents, who held a species of feudal sway over different districts of this turbulent domain. He soon obtained ample assurances of support, and though commencing his return to the capital at the head of only 500 followers, he approached it with fair prospects of success. Dhian having joined him with a numerous band, completed his triumph; and the queen, though she still made some attempts to resist, was soon obliged to yield, on the promise of safety and honourable treatment.

Triumph of Shere Sing.

Passive policy of the British.

During this strange series of events, the British government kept a strong cordon of troops on the frontier, and carefully watched every movement; but there appeared no ground for interference, which could not indeed have been attempted without taking actual possession of the country. Agitations and alarms continued to be felt; but the dread of British hostility restrained Shere Sing for a time, while objects of more immediate interest engaged the attention of the British government.

Unfriendly conduct of Mehrab

On the west of the Indus, even after the conquest of Afghanistan, another serious contest was waged. Mehrab, khan of Kelat, whose dominions lay on the left flank of the British in their advance, had shown a very unfriendly spirit, and actively directed against them his predatory bands. It was judged necessary to chastise this conduct, and General Willshire, in November 1839, marched against his capital. He rejected all overtures, and the army arrived on the 12th before Kelat, which was found defended by three heights, each covered with infantry, and guarded by a parapet wall. As nothing decisive could be effected till these troops were driven from that position, the general ordered three columns to advance, who found when they reached the eminences, that the enemy had been dislodged by the fire of the artillery. Hopes were entertained of reaching a gate

British army before Kelat.

CHAP. XVI.

A. D. 1839.

before it was closed upon the fugitives. This could not be effected; but, by some well-directed discharges of heavy shot, one was nearly demolished, and the pursuers rushed in. The garrison, after making a gallant and determined resistance, retired into the citadel; but its gate being reached before it could be fully secured inside, was burst open. Mehrab and several of his chiefs fell fighting sword in hand, before the final surrender. The contest was more severe than that at Ghizni, the loss amounting to 31 killed and 107 wounded.

Surrender of the citadel of Kerat.

Shah Niwaz undertakes its defence.

The fort was now placed under Shah Niwaz, another Beloochee prince, who, with a party of thirty men, under Lieutenant Loveday, undertook its defence. Nusseer, however, heir to Mehrab, having assembled a considerable band, threw himself between that place and Quetta, the British head-quarters; and the force there being too much reduced to dislodge him, he cut off several small detachments. He then directed his march upon Kelat, which he closely invested. The defence was spirited; but extensive treachery being discovered within the walls, Shah Niwaz judged it necessary to submit. Loveday, who was thus made prisoner, was very harshly treated, and at last barbarously murdered. Nusseer then advanced upon Dadur, an important British post, which he took, and plundered its magazines; but Major Boscawen came up next day and obliged him to retreat. Larger reinforcements arriving soon after, General Nott took the command, and marched upon Kelat, which he reached on the 3d November, but found it abandoned by the enemy. At length, on the 1st December, Colonel Marshall from Kotra succeeded in surprising the enemy's camp, and routed and dispersed his force.

Successes of Nusseer.

Total rout of the enemy.

The Murrees.

Another troublesome contest soon afterwards arose. The Murrees, a brave tribe of Beloochistan, owned some allegiance to the Khan of Kelat, but were, it is said, not at all disposed to take part with him against Britain. By way of security, however, Captain Brown, with a detachment, occupied Kahun, their principal hill-fort. No resistance was made at the time;

but their feeling of patriotic independence being soon roused, they assembled in large bodies, cut off several detachments, and closely invested the place. Brown was thus placed in a critical situation, and Major Clibborn, who was sent with a party to relieve him, found the pass of Nufoosk very strongly guarded. He endeavoured to force it; but this being the hot and dry season, his troops were overpowered by thirst and fatigue; and though he gained considerable advantages, and a number of hostile chiefs fell, he could not clear the ravine. A party sent for water were entirely destroyed; he lost in all 150 men, and through the defection of the camel-drivers, was obliged to abandon stores, artillery, and baggage. After this disaster, there seemed no hope left for the detachment at Kahun. Brown, however, by dexterously deceiving the enemy as to the extent of his resources, succeeded in obtaining a treaty, which allowed him to return unmolested. It was honourably fulfilled, and no farther disturbance has been experienced from that quarter.

Critical position of Captain Brown.

The interior of Afghanistan, meantime, remained in a state of somewhat precarious tranquillity. Sir John Keane returned with a portion of the army into India, not through Sinde, but by the route of the Punjaub, crossing the Indus at Attock. It was found necessary, however, to leave still a considerable force under Sir Willoughby Cotton; for although all regular resistance had ceased, there were clear symptoms of the unpopularity of the new government, and especially of its foreign supporters. The conduct of the shah, too, as well as of his sons, is represented as neither prudent nor conciliatory. Officers and men found straggling were murdered; several of the mountain-chiefs openly resisted, and were not reduced without some difficulty. The most serious affair was at Peshoot, where Colonel Orchard's attempt to blow up the gate as at Ghizni failed through the bad quality of the powder, and he was finally beaten off with the loss of sixty-nine killed and wounded. The fort, however, with the adjacent one of Khatke, was then evacuated.

Uncertain state of Afghanistan.

Imprudent conduct of the Shah.

CHAP. XVI.

A. D. 1840.

Insurrection of the Ghilzies

In May a general insurrectionary movement took place among the Ghilzies, a tribe occupying the high mountain-territory between Candahar and Cabul; who, accustomed to a wild independence, brooked ill the stricter rule under which they were now held. Captain Anderson, marching against them with 1200 men, was attacked by more than double that number, who fought with such bravery as to render the contest for some time doubtful; however, they were at length repulsed with great loss. Colonel Wallace also took by surprise the fort of a leading chief; and the two corps having joined, composed a force which the insurgents could not face. The brother of Mohammed Khan, the leader of these revolted chieftains, then came into camp, and effected an accommodation.

Dost Mohammed's proceedings.

Dost Mohammed, after his retreat beyond the mountains, being favourably received by the chiefs of Khoolloom and Koondooz, had proceeded to Bokhara, hoping to obtain aid from that most powerful of the states in Central Asia. The khan, however, alarmed by the Russian march upon Khiva, and unwilling to offend Britain, not only refused his request, but placed him under confinement. In August 1840, he made his escape, and, being still favoured by the border princes, found no difficulty in raising among the Usbeck tribes and his own former subjects a very considerable force. The Wallee of Khoolloom even took the field along with him, and they advanced through the mountain-defiles upon Cabul. That capital, only about fifty miles from this great barrier, became seriously exposed. Dost Mohammed marched upon the strong frontier town of Syghan, then held by an Afghan corps organized under the eye of the British, and commanded by Captain Hopkins. On the approach of the enemy, they fell back on Bameean in a mutinous and disorderly state, several companies having deserted. Colonel Dennie, who with about 2000 men was then sent to encounter the invader, anticipated him in crossing the Irak pass, disarmed Hopkins' corps, and advanced from Bameean. He learned, on the 18th Sep-

Raises a considerable force

Faithless conduct of the Afghan allies.

tember 1840, that the enemy were advancing in great force from Syghan; and, being desirous to draw them on, suspended his movements. Being informed, however, that a party, supposed to be their advanced guard, had attacked a fortified post which claimed his protection, he pushed on with about a third of his troops. On arriving, he was surprised by seeing the whole of the Dost's army in front, estimated by him at 10,000; but finding his men full of ardour, and dreading the effect of halting or retreating, he promptly decided on an immediate attack. The enemy, who at first made a somewhat vigorous stand, seeing the steady advance of the British, lost courage after a few volleys, and fled in confusion into the pass, through which they were pursued by the cavalry four or five miles. Mohammed and the Wallee of Khoolloom fled with only 200 followers.

Bold and successful attack of Colonel Dennie.

Meantime, one of the sons of Dost Mohammed had occupied the strong defile of Ghorebund in Kohistan. General Sale was sent against him, and on the 29th found him stationed in a village covered by a garden-wall, and defended by a chain of forts. A column of attack was formed, and pressed forward with such energy, that, on its advancing within fifty paces of the wall, the enemy abandoned all their positions, and fled with precipitation into ground where the cavalry could not follow. The loss of the assailants did not exceed six wounded. The general, then learning that several rebel chieftains had sought refuge in a fort at Julga, sixteen miles to the north-east, succeeded on the morning of the 3d October in completely investing it; but from the state of the road, the artillery could not be brought into action till four in the afternoon. By three next day, a breach had been effected, and considered practicable; upon which Captain Tronson, with a detachment, undertook to storm it. They reached the crest of the breach, but were encountered by a close fire from the houses, which, after a desperate struggle, obliged them to retire under cover of a neighbouring ravine. The only use, however, which the enemy made of this advantage was to effect a safe retreat out of the fort, to the great regret

Ghorebund.

Assault of the fort of Julga.

CHAP. XVI.

A.D. 1840.

of the British commander, who took immediate possession of it. The loss amounted to thirty-four killed and wounded. About the same time, Colonel Wheeler, stationed at Kudjah, stormed the castle of a chief in the Wuzzeree valley, who had shown decided proofs of a hostile spirit.

Occupation of Syghan.

Meanwhile, Brigadier Dennie, after his victory at Bameean, advanced and occupied Syghan, but did not think it prudent to pursue the fugitive leaders in their retreat over the mountains. The Wallee, however, following the Asiatic rule of adhering always to the fortunate side, made overtures, and requested an officer to be sent to arrange the basis of a compromise. A conference accordingly ensued between him and Dr Lord, and a treaty was concluded on terms securing to him a considerable accession of territory, which was carried to the very summit of the Caucasus, called here Dundan Shikun. He declined to give up Dost Mohammed, but promised to afford no aid or protection, and even to advise him to surrender.

Proceedings of Dost Mohammed.

That prince, thus left to himself, hoped still to effect something by advancing into Kohistan. He was preceded by his son with a considerable force, and himself arrived about the middle of October. General Sale, to oppose his progress, hastened to Purwan, where he learned that the Afghan chief, with about 4000 men, was in the vicinity, and preparing to march upon the Ghorebund pass. He made arrangements to attack them; and, on the suggestion of Dr Lord, sent forward the 2d native cavalry to skirt the eminence on which they were posted, with the view of cutting off their retreat. When they had advanced about a mile, Dost Mohammed rushed down upon them with 200 horse. This corps, which had hitherto maintained a distinguished character, were seized with a sudden panic; they first faltered, and then gave way at all points. The officers were left alone to meet the charge of the enemy; their bravery was unavailing; Dr Lord, Lieutenants Broadfoot and Crispin, were killed, Captains Fraser and Ponsonby severely wounded. Sale, however, pushed forward his infantry, who successively dislodged the enemy from all the strong positions,

Disgraceful conduct of the native cavalry.

and drove them to a distance, though without being able to keep up a long pursuit.

Dost Mohammed reduced to extremities

The ex-ruler of Cabul notwithstanding the partial success now gained, soon found himself reduced to great extremity. His troops, discouraged by so much ill fortune, were no longer disposed to follow his standard; a victorious army was pressing upon him, and he had no retreat but into the territory of allies by whom he had been deserted. We are indeed informed by Colonel Dennie that he claimed refuge from the Wallee, who, however, refused to receive him; and in this extremity he determined to throw himself upon the clemency of his foe. Setting out with only one companion, he rode undiscovered through the camp, and arrived at Cabul, where he surrendered to the British authorities. By his orders his son, who still remained in arms, gave himself up also. He was thence conveyed into Hindostan, and his residence finally fixed at Loodiana, with a pension of £30,000 a-year.

Delivers himself up.

Auktur Khan.

For some time afterwards only partial outbreaks occurred. Auktur Khan, a chief on the extreme western frontier, had worsted the shah's general and assembled a considerable force; but Captain Farrington hastened up, defeated him, and captured his fort. Another movement took place in the Nizian valley, near Jellalabad, studded with eighty-four strongholds, which Brigadier Shelton reduced one after another, yet with the loss of fifty-two killed and wounded.

State of Sinde.

Sinde was still unsettled, Nusseer declining to place himself in the power of the British, and hovering about the hills. A rude tribe named Kujuks refused to pay the shah's tribute, under the plea of inability, which does not seem to have been duly considered. Colonel Wilson marched against them, but was repulsed, himself and some other officers being wounded, and Lieutenant Creed, who led the storming party, killed. Affairs continued thus unsettled till September, when it having been made known to Nusseer that the governor-general had determined to replace him in his khanate, he came to Quetta, and matters were amicably arranged. By this prudent step Sinde was restored to tranquillity.

CHAP. XVI.
A. D. 1840.

Meantime, in Western Afghanistan, the insurrection was becoming more formidable. Auktur Khan was again in arms, and fanatical moollahs were proclaiming a religious war against the British. Colonel Wymer defeated a large force near Kelat-i-Ghilzie, but had not strength sufficient to pursue the fugitives to any distance. On the 17th August, Captains Woodburn and Griffin encountered about 5000 men under Akram and Auktur Khan, whom they totally defeated, though with the loss of nearly 130 killed and wounded. In October, a force of Ghilzie insurgents occupied in great force the valley between Cabul and Jellalabad. As they held the strong pass of Koord Cabul, which interrupted the communications, General Sale was sent from the capital, with the 13th and 35th regiments, to clear the pass. He found the enemy stationed behind a breastwork, which they quitted on the approach of the assailants, but kept up a well-directed fire from the rocky heights on each side. Sale was wounded, and obliged to quit the field; but the troops under Brigadier Dennie drove the enemy from all the cliffs except the very highest, whither, as the object was only to clear the pass, it was thought needless to follow them. The Afghans, then retreating to Tezeen, occupied the surrounding heights, but were driven successively from all whence they could cause any annoyance. The chiefs sent proposals of negotiation, making friendly professions, and promising no longer to annoy the march of the column; but their sincerity was rendered more than doubtful by the continued molestation which the troops experienced. After passing Jugduluk, they entered a long winding pass, overhung by terrific eminences, every one of which was held by men showing the most obstinate determination to dispute their progress. An advance could only be effected by the arduous operation of scaling the heights, while from above a heavy fire was still maintained. A single company, however, having dashed through the defile, found its main outlet unguarded. The whole then passed, but their rearguard continued to be harassed till their arrival at Gundamuk. Respecting this long march, the commander generally

Affairs in western Afghanistan. *Pass of Koord Cabul.* *Friendly professions of the chiefs.* *Harassing conflicts.*

observes, "each succeeding morning brought its affair with a bold and active enemy, eminently skilful in the species of warfare to which their attempts have been confined, and armed with jezails, which have enabled them to annoy us at a range at which they could only be reached by our artillery." This march had doubtless a fatal influence, inasmuch as it showed to the natives the mode of warfare by which they could inflict upon us the most extensive injury.

General Sale compelled to leave Gundamuk.

General Sale remained at Gundamuk; but the armed natives, termed by him Ooloose, crowded round him in increasing numbers, while many of them in his own service showed symptoms of disaffection, or went over to the enemy. In these circumstances, he found it impossible to maintain himself in a mere cantonment, and had no choice but to push on to Jellalabad. He broke up on the 11th November, when the inhabitants rushed in, and blew up the magazine in such haste, that a number of themselves were killed. During that day, our troops were harassed only by predatory attacks; but on the 12th, a body of 2000 or 3000 pressed behind, and were joined by the whole population of the country. Colonel Dennie, commanding the rear-guard, for some time considered it sufficient to beat them off, but on coming to a level tract, contrived to allure them on, then suddenly attacked, and put them to flight with great slaughter. After this the army, with little molestation, reached Jellalabad.

Station at Jellalabad.

This place was found by no means defensible, surrounded merely by a weak wall, with a narrow rampart and insufficient parapet; while on the north angle, trees and old buildings afforded excellent cover for the enemy within pistol-shot. They soon assembled in great force on all sides, and particularly on this, whence they succeeded in burning a cantonment erected at a heavy expense in 1840, and kept up a harassing fire of musketry. It being deemed necessary to dislodge them from this position, a considerable body of horse and foot was placed under Colonel Monteath. That officer, after reducing three posts which might have harassed his advance,

Attack on the enemy.

CHAP. XVI. A.D. 1841. pushed forward against the great mass of the enemy who occupied the heights in front. On his approach, the whole suddenly gave way, and fled to a considerable distance, suffering severely from a cavalry charge by Captain Oldfield. The divisions on the other sides of the city being then attacked, made off with equal rapidity and in great consternation; there was soon scarcely an armed Afghan to be seen in the vicinity of Jellalabad. Advantage was taken of the interval to repair and strengthen the defences, so as to render them secure against any Asiatic force, unaided by siege artillery; also to collect grain from the adjacent villages. To guard both against famine and internal insurrection, it was judged necessary to remove all the inhabitants except the shopkeepers.

Defences of Jellalabad.

Eventful scenes in Cabul.

Meantime, Cabul became the theatre of scenes most deeply eventful, and which have indeed no parallel in the whole of our Indian history. The expedition into that country had, as we have seen, been undertaken, not with a view to its conquest, but under the belief that the exiled monarch, once replaced on the throne, had a party strong enough to maintain him in power. It now appeared, however, that he was solely supported by the arms of the British, who thus became the real masters of the country. The Afghans were perhaps the bravest and proudest people in Asia; from the time of Mahmoud of Ghizni down to that of Ahmed Shah, they had made several victorious expeditions into India; they had founded its two greatest dynasties, the Patan, which reigned more than three hundred years, and that which, though called Mogul, was established by Baber with native troops. They now saw themselves a conquered people, compelled to acknowledge the superiority of a distant nation, of strange language, religion, and manners. That in such a situation they should have felt at once indignant and vindictive, can excite no wonder; nor could we have avoided in some degree sympathizing with them, had they sought deliverance by legitimate means; but assassination and breach of faith cannot be palliated even by a good cause.

Character of the Afghans.

Cause of their indignation.

Notwithstanding the explosion at Koord Cabul, the

country was generally in a state of seeming tranquillity; though there were not wanting circumstances calculated to inspire apprehension. Strong discontent had arisen among the Ghilzie leaders, owing to a reduction of their stipends, ordered by Lord Auckland from motives of economy. Alarms were also spread among the principal chiefs, that they were to be seized and carried prisoners to London. Major Pottinger, who acted as envoy in Kohistan, reported the state of that rude territory to be such, that unless reinforcements were sent, a serious insurrection might be apprehended. British officers, when met singly, were insulted, and attempts made in some cases to assassinate them. These, however, were looked upon as only the ebullitions of private discontent, not as the symptoms of a universal antipathy.

Discontent among the Ghilzie leaders.

Sir Alexander Burnes, though intimately acquainted with the country and people, was so far deceived by a feeling of security that he did not hesitate to take up his residence at a house in the town, detached from the English quarters. On the 2d November 1841, it was attacked by about 300 Afghans; yet his confidence was such, that he refused to leave it, and attempted to appease the assailants by haranguing them from a high gallery. They soon, however, forced an entrance, overpowered all resistance, and mercilessly slew himself, his brother, Captain Johnson the paymaster, and Lieutenant Broadfoot, a promising young officer. General Elphinstone, on receiving this report, and seeing flames issuing from that part of the city, ordered Brigadier Shelton to march and occupy the Bala Hissar, or citadel-palace, where the shah resided. Captain Lawrence, who was sent to announce this intention, was attacked by a large band, and with difficulty escaped. Lieutenant Sturt, coming with another message, received three wounds, though none of them dangerous. The shah immediately ordered his guard, with some other troops, to attempt the restoration of tranquillity; but they were repulsed with great slaughter.

Misplaced confidence of Sir Alexander Burnes.

His assassination.

The standard of insurrection was thus openly raised; and the English, from the emergency being so wholly

Open insurrection.

CHAP. XVI. A.D. 1841.

Unprepared state of the British.

unforeseen, were little prepared for the events which now pressed upon them. Their force was divided into two parts, one in the Bala Hissar, the other in a cantonment about two miles distant, separated by the Cabul river and by a broad canal. The situation was low, commanded by adjacent hills and buildings; while the numerous camp-followers rendered the extent too great for the number of troops appointed to defend it. An error still more serious had been committed in making a weak fort at some distance the depository of all the commissariat stores.

Deficiencies of the commander-in-chief.

General Elphinstone, the commander-in-chief, is described as an amiable and intelligent officer; but age and declining health had induced him to obtain leave for his immediate return. He appears to have been peculiarly deficient in decision and promptitude, the qualities now most urgently required. Having under him about 5500 troops, it can scarcely be doubted that a brisk attack on the city would have been so successful as to have crushed the immediate rising.

False tactics.

A dilatory and defensive system was adopted: orders were sent to General Sale to rejoin him, and to General Nott to send two regiments from Candahar. A farther reinforcement was despatched to the Bala Hissar; but Major Swayne, in attempting to lead two more companies thither, was obliged by the heavy fire of the enemy to fall back.

Danger of the commissariat fort.

The most urgent object of attention was the commissariat fort, separated from the cantonment by the Shah Bagh or royal garden, which afforded large cover to the enemy. Captain Swayne, on the 4th, attempted to penetrate thither with two companies of the 44th, but was exposed to so severe a fire from a fort in possession of the enemy, that he himself and another officer were killed, and the troops driven back with great loss. A party of the 5th light cavalry were equally unfortunate. Captain Boyd of the commissariat, however, represented so forcibly the extreme importance of this post, that a stronger

Its abandonment.

detachment was prepared, but delayed till next morning; when Ensign Warren, who held the fort, came in with the garrison, stating that the enemy, by forming a mine and setting fire to the gate, had rendered it untenable. This failure in an object so essential, and seemingly so easy, produced a fatal effect on the spirit of both parties. The enemy became greatly emboldened, and were joined by many who had been hitherto our friends; while the British troops were deeply mortified, and ceased to display that courage which usually so much distinguishes them.

CHAP. XVI. A.D. 1841.

Dispiriting effects of its loss.

To retrieve this disaster, Major Swayne was sent on the 5th to attack a fort which commanded the one lost; and some success was at first gained; but not being duly followed up, the detachment was recalled. On the 6th, a stronger and more regular corps was employed, when the artillery having succeeded in making a practicable breach, the place was carried by storm. An attempt was also made, but without success, to occupy the Shah Bagh; when the enemy brought up large bodies of cavalry, hoping to intercept our retreat; but they did not ultimately make the attempt. Hence the general result of this day was somewhat favourable.

Brigadier Shelton takes the command.

On the 9th, the health of General Elphinstone was so much affected, that Brigadier Shelton was desired to take the command; and with him rested henceforth the chief direction of military operations. But the hope that he would revive the drooping energies of the troops was not realized; he having early formed the opinion that they could not hold their ground at Cabul, and advised, therefore, an immediate retreat to Jellalabad. Sir William Macnaghten, on the contrary, conceived the army bound to maintain their position, for which their power, if vigorously exerted, seemed to him quite sufficient. This opinion prevailed to the extent of making them remain; but the brigadier, retaining his own judgment, was disposed to preserve an attitude purely defensive, and was urged only by the strong remonstrances of the envoy to any active measures. Either a vigorous attack or an immediate retreat would probably have saved the army; but amid conflicting counsels, a middle course was adopted, which could produce only the very worst results.

Want of decisive measures.

CHAP. XVI.

A.D. 1841.

Storming of Rika-bashee.

On the 10th, the Afghans, with large bodies of cavalry, occupied the surrounding hills, and took possession of several forts. One of these, called Rika-bashee, somewhat commanded the cantonment, and interrupted the supply of provisions, which became now extremely scarce; the envoy, therefore, by urgent representations, obtained from the commander-in-chief an order that Shelton should attack it next day. The storming party then burst open what appeared to be the gate, but which proved a mere wicket admitting only two or three at once. The first who entered suffered severely; but when a few had forced their way, the garrison were struck with panic, and evacuated the post. Meantime, a body of cavalry had charged the British, who, deserted by their usual courage, precipitately fled. Shelton, however, who was always conspicuous for valour in the field, twice rallied them, and at last carried the fort, which the enemy had reoccupied. Unhappily, during their temporary possession, they had killed almost all the little party who first entered; only Lieutenant Bird and a sepoy maintained their ground in a stable, till relieved by their countrymen. Our object was indeed gained, four other stations being evacuated, and a supply of grain procured; yet 200 men were lost in killed or wounded. On the 13th, the enemy, occupying in force the adjacent heights, fired with some effect into the cantonment; when the envoy, by earnest entreaty, prevailed on the general to send a body of troops against them. They made an obstinate resistance, and at first repulsed the assailants, but by some skilful movements of the artillery and cavalry, were finally driven from the position. Our soldiers, however, under existing circumstances, could never hold any ground which they had gained, but were obliged to return to the cantonment, while the enemy, having rallied, pressed closely behind them.

Flight of British soldiers.

Renewed attacks.

Major Pottinger.

On the 15th, Major Pottinger arrived from Charekur, in the mountain-territory of Kohistan, north of Cabul, which he had defended at the head of 800 Gorkhas. He and some other officers occupied a small adjacent fort, when they were invited to a conference, and Captain Rattray, being inveigled to a little distance, was suddenly shot dead, while the major with difficulty escaped. A vast number of insurgents then assembled, who were at first repulsed with great slaughter; but their force increasing, and the post being untenable, the troops withdrew to Charekur. Here they maintained themselves twenty-five days, amid continual assaults from an overwhelming body, and the most severe sufferings from want of water. No resource then appeared but to cut their way to Cabul, amid incessant hardships and attacks. All the troops either perished or were dispersed, and only the Major and Lieutenant Haughton, passing during the night through the city, succeeded in reaching the cantonment.

Retreat and total destruction of the force.

A proposition was now started, and even urged by the envoy, that the force should quit the cantonment for the Bala Hissar, where the whole would be united in a much more defensible position. The military authorities, however, decided that this plan, including an extensive conveyance of stores, could not be accomplished without ruinous loss. The measure of retreat was then agitated, and would now really seem to have been the wisest course; but the envoy still urged a delay of eight or ten days, in the hope of some favourable occurrence. On the 22d, Mohammed Akbar, second son of Dost Mohammed, arrived at Cabul, and was invested with the command of the hostile army, to whose movements he gave an augmented energy. He had already distinguished himself by his military talents, having been employed by his father in defending the frontier against the Seiks.

Fatal delay.

Arrival of Mohammed Akbar.

The village of Beymaroo, lying to the north of the cantonment, on the road leading to Kohistan, was now the only quarter through which, at high prices, supplies of provisions were procured; and the enemy, by marching out in great force every morning, and occupying it during the day, much narrowed this resource. It appeared indispensable to take possession of the place; and on the 22d Major Swayne moved thither with a

Unsuccessful attack on Beymaroo.

CHAP. XVI. A.D. 1841.

strong detachment, but found it so well garrisoned, and the entrance so blocked up, that he considered it impossible to force a passage. He kept up a fire some hours, while his troops suffered severely, but without any result.

Storming of Beymaroo.

On the 23d, Shelton determined to employ a large corps in storming Beymaroo, as well as in maintaining the adjacent heights against any force the insurgents might send out. He marched at two in the morning, occupied the brow of the height, and threw the enemy into considerable confusion, but with doubtful prudence delayed the attack till daylight. Major Swayne then effected an entrance; but, as it proved, only through a small wicket, admitting merely a few, who could not long secure their post against a heavy fire. The natives then poured out from the city large bodies, estimated at 10,000 men, and covered all the surrounding heights. The British troops were led against them, and maintained a long contest with various fortune, suffering most severely from the jezails, whose range the musket could by no means equal. Yet the other party, having sustained several checks, and being discouraged by the fall of Abdoolah Khan, one of their greatest chiefs, began a retreat towards the city, abandoning a gun which they had captured. The cavalry were then called upon to pursue them; but that body, having been for a long time kept in an injudicious position, exposed to the enemy's fire, shrunk back, and would not obey the summons. This the Afghans no sooner perceived, than they renewed the assault with augmented courage and energy. The square of British infantry was broken; panic spread through the troops; all attempts to rally them were vain; and finally the whole rushed in confused and tumultuary flight to the cantonment. The spirited efforts of one or two corps prevented the enemy from entering along with them.

Partial success.

Failure of the cavalry.

Panic and flight of the British.

Severe loss of the army.

On this fatal day, the loss both of men and officers was immense; and the spirit of the army was completely broken. The proposal of removing to the Bala Hissar was renewed, but again rejected. On the 24th, a letter was received from Osman Khan, a chief believed friendly, boasting, seemingly with truth, that he had spared our troops in the preceding day's pursuit; and declaring himself earnestly desirous of terminating the war, on condition of our quietly evacuating the country, leaving it to be governed by a king and laws of its own. The general, on a reference from Sir William, strongly advised negotiation. Accordingly, on the 27th, an interview took place at the eastern gate with several Afghan leaders; but their demands were enormous, amounting to the unconditional surrender of the British force, with only a hope that their lives might be spared. These terms were indignantly rejected,—the envoy declaring that he must "again appeal to arms, leaving the result to the God of battles."

Humiliating conditions offered.

Some days elapsed without any important event; but the English were pressed continually closer. An important post was sacrificed through the cowardice of the garrison; and the scarcity of provisions approached to famine, being only relieved by precarious supplies from the Bala Hissar. On the 8th December, the general strongly recommended negotiation, as the only alternative left. On the 11th, Sir William had an interview with a number of chiefs, among whom the khans, Osman and Akbar took the lead. Their deportment was courteous; and it was finally agreed that the British should evacuate all Afghanistan, on being not only allowed to retire unmolested, but furnished with provisions and the means of transport. Shah Sujah was to be granted a pension, with the option of remaining at Cabul or accompanying the retreating army.

Accumulated disasters.

Satisfactory terms.

In pursuance of this treaty, the force in the Bala Hissar was on the 13th and 14th removed to the cantonment, not however without annoyance from the Afghans. Yielding to successive demands, the adjacent forts, hitherto maintained, were evacuated, and several English officers delivered as hostages. Yet the promised supplies indispensable to the march of the army were still, on various pretexts, withheld; and it became evident that, seeing the weak and desponding state of

Non-fulfilment of the treaty.

CHAP. XVI. A.D. 1841. the invaders, the barbarians had determined to treat them as entirely in their power.

Scheme of Akbar

Under these circumstances, Akbar formed the scheme which brought affairs to a fatal crisis. Captain Skinner, who happened to be in his power, was sent to the envoy with a proposal to unite with him in seizing Amenoollah Khan, the chief second in influence to himself. Shah Sujah was then to be acknowledged king, with Akbar as his vizier; the English would be allowed to remain till next spring, and then to depart under circumstances that would save their *honour*. Sir William caught with a fatal facility at this delusive proposition; his mind, owing to the late reverses, was in an excited state; and when warned by his officers of the danger, he declared that it appeared to present the only ray of hope, and that death would be preferable to the life he had lately led. He agreed to go out and meet the chiefs in an open space near the cantonment; and though a strong guard was ordered, it was very imperfectly furnished. About noon of the 23d, he proceeded thither, accompanied by Captains Lawrence, Mackenzie, and Trevor; and, on approaching the spot, he walked on with them, leaving the soldiers behind. The chiefs then came up, and opened the conference in the most friendly terms. It being remarked that numerous armed Afghans were coming up, and drawing a circle round them, Akbar said they were in the secret. Presently, however, he grasped the left hand of the envoy, while Sultan Jan seized his right; and a fierce struggle ensuing, the former chief drew out a pistol, and shot Sir William dead. This cruel action appears to have been prompted by the dread of his escape and the excitement of the moment, as it would have been better policy to have secured him as a hostage. The body, however, was instantly seized by the fanatic Ghazees, who cut it in pieces, and exposed the head to the people in the great bazaar. Captain Trevor also fell into their hands and was murdered on the spot; but other chiefs caused Lawrence and Mackenzie to mount on horseback, and conveyed them to Cabul, protecting them even at the hazard of their own lives. They were

Fatal imprudence of Sir William Macnaghten.

Treacherous assassination of the envoy.

there thrown into a fort, where the multitude made furious attempts to break in and put them to death.

Cowardly conduct of the British.

After this dreadful scene, it might have been expected that all the generous feelings of the troops would have been roused; that they would have been impelled to some deed of decisive and desperate valour; at all events, that they would have ceased to place any faith in Afghan promises, and hoped for a safe retreat only from their own efforts. It is mortifying, however, to think how much the highest qualities depend upon circumstances. That British spirit, which was elsewhere making such lofty displays, here entirely failed. Major Pottinger, now appointed envoy, alone urged vigorous measures; all the others insisted on yielding to the humiliating terms offered by the enemy. They were to leave behind most of their guns and treasure; bills were drawn on India for fourteen lacs of rupees (£140,000); and four additional officers were given as hostages.

Major Pottinger's measures rejected.

Commencement of the march.

Delays were still interposed till the 6th January, when the army at length began its inauspicious march. It consisted still of 690 Europeans, 2840 native infantry, and 970 cavalry; in all, 4500 fighting men. There were, besides, 12,000 camp followers, who rendered the preservation of order almost impossible. A straggling march, amid deep snow and many obstructions, prevented them from advancing more than five miles; and it was two in the morning before the last reached the place of encampment. The Ghazees, as soon as they saw the cantonment empty, rushed in, filled it with exulting shouts, and commenced a work at once of plunder and destruction. The troops during the night, being very ill supplied with clothes and shelter, suffered extremely from the cold, which to some proved fatal. Next day they resumed their march, forming a mingled mass of soldiers, followers, and beasts of burden. The enemy soon began to harass them with a fire of jezails; and though bravely repulsed at several points, obliged them to abandon some guns and much baggage. Captain Skinner, learning that Akbar was at hand, appealed to his sense of honour and hu-

Plunder of the camp.

CHAP. XVI. A.D. 1842. manity. The latter declared the attack to have been made against his will, but offered a safe conduct to Jellalabad, on condition of their stopping till the morning, and giving six other hostages. Next day, however, they were again assailed, and upon making a fresh appeal to the chief, were required to yield Major Pottinger and two more officers, before he would renew his promises of protection. In this way, no doubt, they obtained a respite, and reached the entrance of the tremendous pass of Koord Cabul; but the frost had so disabled even the strongest men, that only a few hundreds remained fit for service.

Successive concessions.

Pass of Koord Cabul.

They now entered the defile, five miles long, overhung by high cliffs, with a torrent dashing through it; and, contrary to every pledge, the Ghilzies crowned the heights, pouring down a destructive fire. The only safety lay in rushing rapidly through the pass, abandoning almost all their baggage and supplies. The females happily escaped unhurt, except Lady Sale, who was slightly wounded. They passed the night at Koord Cabul; but the snow was falling thick, and, from the loss of almost every equipment, their sufferings were much more severe than before.

Treachery of Akbar.

On the 9th, the army was about to renew its march, when Akbar, by plausible though treacherous promises, persuaded the general to halt. This step deeply discouraged the men, who conceived their only hope to be in the most expeditious movement; and the native troops began to desert in great numbers. About noon, Captain Skinner arrived with a proposal, that the ladies with their husbands should place themselves under the protection of the Afghan chief. The hardships endured by the former were indeed so excessive, that there appeared no other hope of saving their lives, and the general accordingly consented. The soldiers marched on, and spent another night of intense cold,—all the promises of food and fuel being unfulfilled.

Lady Sale and her companions left behind.

On the 10th, the army resumed its progress, though the fighting men were reduced now to a small number. They were unmolested for about two miles, when they came to a narrow gorge between two precipitous hills; but here the Afghans had occupied all the heights in great force, whence they directed a most murderous fire. The native troops, throwing away their arms and accoutrements, sought safety in flight, when the enemy rushed down, sword in hand, and commenced a general massacre. Nearly the whole force disappeared during this fearful march, at the end of which it was found that of the 4500 who had proceeded from Cabul, there survived only 270 Europeans, with indeed a considerable number of the 12,000 camp followers. Akbar, who now appeared in the neighbourhood, made an offer, that if the former would place themselves entirely under his protection, he would escort them safely to Jellalabad; but all the others must be left to their fate. The general humanely rejected such terms, and his people went on amid fresh losses, till they reached, at four o'clock, an encampment in the Tezeen valley. Another attempt was made to treat, but with the same result. Their only hope then appeared to be in making a night march of twenty-two miles to Jugduluk; when, under cover of the darkness, they might penetrate safely through that terrible pass. They eagerly pushed onward; but, through delays occasioned by the followers, when daylight had arrived they were still ten miles from their destination, while the enemy began to occupy the surrounding hills. They had now to encounter much suffering and loss, though Brigadier Shelton, redeeming somewhat his former errors, led them on with signal valour. At three in the afternoon, they were at Jugduluk, where the miserable remnant posted themselves in an enclosure, which afforded only imperfect shelter from the enemy's fire. Captain Bygrave, with fifteen brave men, drove the latter back, but they soon returned. The wretched resource was again tried of negotiating with Akbar, who demanded that General Elphinstone should come to a conference, while Shelton and Captain Johnson should be delivered as hostages. All was acceded to; the officers were courteously received, and refreshments supplied. At nine

Flight and massacre of native troops

Rejection of Akbar's terms.

Sufferings and renewed negotiation.

CHAP. XVI.
A.D. 1842.

next morning, a meeting was held, when a number of the chiefs inveighed bitterly against the English, while Akbar pretended to plead their cause; but in this discussion the day elapsed without any decisive arrangement. Brigadier Anquetil, who had been left in command, then saw no hope but to push in the dark through the next pass of two miles in length. Having taken the Afghans somewhat by surprise, the troops moved at first with little molestation; but at the summit found two barriers strongly formed of brushwood, which could not be removed without much difficulty and some delay. The enemy then came up, mixed with the fugitives, and committed a dreadful slaughter. Anquetil and eleven other officers fell; only about forty men, half of whom had lost their arms, advanced to Gundamuk, hoping there for security. They reached it about daybreak, but found themselves so beset, as to be obliged to leave the road, and take a defensive position on a height. An attempt was made to negotiate, but Major Griffiths and Mr Blewitt, who proceeded for the purpose, were detained. Hostilities were then renewed, and the little band, overpowered by numbers, were successively cut down, only Captain Souter and three men being made prisoners. A separate party of twelve, among whom were seven officers, pushed on for Jellalabad; but they fell successive victims to the fury and treachery of the inhabitants, except Dr Brydon, who reached that town, where he gave the first direful tidings of the fate of the army. Sergeant Lissant and four others, also seeking to escape individually, had been made prisoners. The captives on the whole were about seventy; an unknown proportion of the native troops and followers had gone over to the enemy; but by far the greater part of the 16,500 who left the cantonment at Cabul had miserably perished. This retreat may be considered without a parallel, if not in the extent, at least in the completeness of its calamity.*

Attempt to push through the pass.

Dreadful slaughter.

Tidings borne to Jellalabad

* This relation of events at Cabul, and during the retreat, has, in the absence of official documents, been drawn up chiefly on the authority of Lieutenant Eyre whose narrative of "Military Ope-

While this tragical drama was in progress, minor scenes were acting in different quarters, too much in accordance with its character. We have already related the adventures and narrow escape of Major Pottinger. In the same quarter, Lieutenants Maule and Wheeler, commanding a detachment about twenty miles north-west of Cabul, were deserted by their men and barbarously murdered.

Disastrous occurrences in other quarters.

Pesh Bolak, a fortress which commands the passes between Jellalabad and Peshawer, was held by Captain Ferris, with 250 native troops belonging to the shah; and there several officers halted, the roads in front being reported impracticable. On the 13th November, the piquets began to be attacked, and skirmishing parties to appear, who, though at first easily beaten off, gradually increased to 5000, when they surrounded the post, with wild yells and furious gestures. A gun placed in the centre bastion kept them at bay; but the sad discovery was soon made, that the ammunition was on the point of being exhausted, and moreover that there was treason within the walls. No hope then appeared but to cut their way through; and accordingly, on the night of the 16th, a column was formed, consisting of the armed force, in the centre of which were Mrs Ferris and her sister dressed in men's clothes, with all the civilians of the garrison. A brisk fire was kept up till the moment of departure, when they rushed forth. The enemy at once took the alarm, and made a furious attack; but some vigorous discharges of musketry obliged them to retire. The party hastened to Lallporah; but observing the sinister looks of the people, and hearing that the Khyber pass was closely guarded, they induced, by large gifts, one of the khans to lead them by a mountainous path to Peshawer. The ladies were obliged to travel about 150 miles, clambering a great part of the way on their hands and feet.

Pesh Bolak.

Desperate state of the garrison.

The great rising at Cabul was accompanied by one

rations" (London, Murray, 1843) appears intelligent and candid. The narratives of Dr Brydon and Sergeant Lissant have also been consulted.

CHAP. XVI. — A. D. 1842.

Rising at Ghizni.

equally determined at Ghizni. Captain Woodburn, with about 100 men, moving thence to the capital, was surrounded by a numerous body, and his little band almost entirely destroyed. The insurgents soon assembled in great force, and closely invested this celebrated fortress. Colonel Palmer, who commanded, not having quite 1000 men, was unable to prevent their entering the city, but maintained himself in the citadel, and in some outposts. Here he continued during the depth of winter; and hopes were entertained that he would be able to remain till relieved. In February, however, seemingly after the destruction of the Cabul army, the besieging force was greatly increased in numbers and courage. They are said on one occasion to have been repulsed with great loss; but his despatch of the 1st March states that they had established themselves under cover, within fifty yards of the fortress, and that the troops were exhausted by constant duty and the extreme cold,—the thermometer being 14° below the freezing point. Above all, water, which had long been scarce, was about to fail altogether, as the surrender of the outposts would, in forty-eight hours, enable the enemy to command the only well, and the whole garrison would in a few days inevitably perish. These reasons, if not exaggerated, appear sufficient; yet it is very curious to find him adding, as a further justification, that he had received a letter from General Elphinstone and Major Pottinger, desiring him to take this step on the arrival of Rohilla Khan, an Afghan chief; and he refers even to similar instructions from Sir W. Macnaghten. It would appear, indeed, that such a letter had been sent during the calamities of the army; but Generals Sale and Nott, who received similar ones, did not, under the circumstances, think themselves authorized to obey them. The governor-general, on receiving the intelligence, ordered a court-martial to be held as soon as convenient on the conduct of Palmer. He had obtained the promise of honourable treatment and a safe march to Cabul; but, in consequence of thousands of Ghazees being in the city, these terms were very imperfectly fulfilled.

Danger of the garrison.

Additional reasons for surrender.

Court-martial on Colonel Palmer.

General Nott, commanding at Candahar, on learning the crisis at Cabul, sent Colonel Maclaren, with a brigade, to support the British cause. That officer, however, on approaching Ghizni, found the snow so deep, and the animals with him perishing so fast, that he was obliged to retrace his steps. Candahar itself was threatened by a force of 5000 men under Mohammed Atta, a fanatical chief, and Prince Sufter Jung. The general marched with a strong corps, totally routed and dispersed them, with the loss on his own side of only three killed and between twenty and thirty wounded. By this seasonable success that important capital was for the present secured.

Attempt to send assistance to them.

Their triumph at Cabul, however, soon reanimated the insurgents in this quarter, who perhaps received reinforcements from the victorious army. In the beginning of March, they threatened Candahar with a larger force than before. Nott marched against them with the greater part of his troops, when they gradually retreated till they had drawn him to a considerable distance. Then, an imposing appearance being still preserved in his front, about 6000 of them wheeled round, and, by a circuitous route through a friendly country, came quite unexpectedly upon the capital. They immediately gained possession of the old town, and were penetrating into the new one, when 2700 British, who had been left for its defence, charged the assailants with such vigour, that they were totally dispersed, with great slaughter. This failure of a scheme, ingeniously planned and partially successful, seemed greatly to disconcert them; while the people became more friendly, and brought in supplies of provisions. The fall of Ghizni, however, seemed again to revive their spirits; and troops began to move from that quarter westward. On the 1st April, Colonel Wymer, having marched with about 1500 men to meet a force expected from Quetta, was furiously attacked by about 3000 of the enemy; but a few volleys from the infantry checked their ardour, and a charge of cavalry completely dispersed them.

Renewed attack on Candahar.

Failure of their schemes.

Candahar was well supplied with provisions, but the

CHAP. XVI. A.D. 1842.

public money was exhausted, and ammunition had become scarce. To supply these wants, General England was sent from Sinde with about 4000 men, escorting a numerous train of camels, with the requisite funds and stores. They marched in three divisions, of which two, on the 16th March, arrived at Quetta, 147 miles from Candahar; whence, as the country in front was occupied by insurgent bands, the commander advanced with a considerable force, to clear the way and obtain forage. He seems not to have been duly apprized of the enemy's strength, and hence his vanguard, on reaching the summit of a hill, were assailed by an ambuscade, and compelled to retreat, leaving Captain May and sixteen men dead on the field. The corps, in descending, were charged in the rear by a strong body of cavalry, when Major Apthorp of the 20th was mortally wounded; but, having formed themselves into a square, they repelled all farther attack, and fell back upon Quetta. Their loss is stated at 27 killed and 71 wounded. The Afghans had received large reinforcements from the north, under a resolute chief, Mohammed Sedeez, and became so strong, that General England was obliged to throw up intrenchments for the defence of the station he now occupied.

General England despatched with stores.

Attack by the enemy.

We have seen that General Sale at Jellalabad repulsed all attacks down to the 14th November; but it could not be expected that the triumphant operations at Cabul would not encourage the enemy to renew their assaults upon him. Accordingly, the tribes again began to muster, keeping up a fire which interrupted the defensive works, and they even threatened mining operations. It appeared necessary to drive them to a greater distance; with which view, on the 1st December 1841, a column was formed within the Cabul gate, which was then thrown open, and Colonel Dennie led out the troops with such impetuosity, that the enemy speedily took to flight. Our loss was trifling. They now retired about twelve miles, feeling that they could not make another attempt without a strong reinforcement of cavalry.

Renewed attack on Jellalabad.

Spirited repulse.

After the catastrophe of the Cabul army, however, they returned in increased numbers, commanded by Akbar in person, who had formerly, as we mentioned, been governor of Jellalabad. He made the most strenuous efforts to establish a rigorous blockade: the ravines, hollows, and remains of mud-forts, were filled with skirmishers, who kept up an incessant fire on the parapets. On the 10th March, operations were pressed with particular ardour on the north side, and a report was received, that they were driving a mine in that direction. It being highly important to ascertain this fact, Colonel Dennie next day, with 800 men, sallied out by the gate leading to Peshawer. Leaving Captain Oldfield with the cavalry to occupy the enemy's attention there, he swept round to the north quarter, which, beyond expectation, was found quite unoccupied. Only one picket held a spot of rising ground, from which it was soon driven by Captain Broadfoot. Full opportunity was thus given to ascertain whether any mining operation was going on, but neither shaft nor gallery was found to have been yet commenced. Akbar's camp was now seen in full movement, and masses of cavalry and infantry advancing: as, however, the object of the British was not to give battle, they returned in good order, and without loss, into the city. On the 1st April, General Sale, having observed some flocks of sheep grazing in the vicinity, sent out the cavalry and light infantry, who, driving off the covering parties, secured an opportune supply of 500 of these animals.

Attempted blockade.

Effective sally.

Opportune supply of provisions.

About this time various rumours began to thicken. General Pollock was said to have been repulsed in an attempt to penetrate the Kyber, and a *feu de joie* fired in the army of Akbar, was understood to celebrate that event. The latter chief was also reported to be about to despatch part of his force to assist in defending the pass, while other accounts bore, that he was preparing to retreat to Lughman, and even that a revolution had broken out at Cabul. Little reliance could be placed on any of these statements; but upon a general survey of affairs, General Sale concluded, that a victory over Akbar would at once relieve the pressure upon himself, and aid the

Rumours of British disasters.

CHAP. XVI. — A.D. 1842.

A general battle resolved upon.

operations of General Pollock; and though that chief commanded 6000 men, he hoped for success. He therefore formed his infantry, 1360 strong, into three columns, under Colonels Dennie and Monteath and Captain Havelock, while Captains Abbot and Oldfield led on the cavalry and artillery. On the 7th April, at daybreak, they issued forth by the Peshawer and Cabul gates, and saw the enemy drawn up in regular order to receive them, having their left resting on the river. Captain Havelock soon drove in the advance; while the central column attacked a strong fort, which covered that part of Akbar's line. They were repulsed, and in the attack Colonel Dennie received a mortal wound. They contrived, however, to pass this work on the left, and form the army on the opposite side. A grand general attack was then made, the artillery advancing at the gallop, and the three columns of infantry rushing on in concert. The enemy gave way immediately at all points, his left being dislodged from its posts on the river, and some men and horses pushed into it. Vigorous attempts were made to rally, particularly by masses of cavalry, while a battery, screened by a garden wall, was directed, it was supposed, by the sirdar himself. By seven in the morning, however, the whole army was in full retreat towards Lughman, the camp and tents were involved in a general conflagration, and their artillery captured, including four pieces taken from the Cabul army. The victory was complete, and only alloyed by the fall of Colonel Dennie, whose heroic exploits in this war we have repeatedly commemorated. General Sale, while deploring it as a public calamity, felt it must be a consolation to his friends, that he fell while most gallantly performing his duty.

Repulse of the enemy.

Their total rout.

Fresh troops sent into Afghanistan.

Meantime, as soon as the first disasters were known, all the troops that could be spared from the north of India were pushed forward into Afghanistan. Their rendezvous was at Peshawer, now belonging to the Seik government, who were ready to afford them every assistance. Early in January, several regiments had been mustered there; but the fort of Ali Musjid, about

20 miles in advance, and on the road to Jellalabad, was announced to be in great distress. Colonel Moseley was sent forward with two regiments, which, by a night-march, succeeded in reaching the place. Brigadier Wild, on the 19th, attempted to penetrate with two more; but he was repulsed, himself wounded, and the whole party obliged to retreat with considerable loss. In Ali Musjid, meantime, the provisions were so completely exhausted, that the colonel was obliged to quit it on the 25th, and push back to Jumrood, having suffered a loss of 175 killed and wounded, including several officers.

Ali Musjid abandoned.

Reinforcements, however, continued to arrive; and General Pollock, who has most fully justified the choice made of him, was appointed to command them and all the troops west of the Indus. He arrived in the end of January, but before attempting the formidable operation with which the campaign must open, he judged it necessary to await the accumulation of a considerable force. By the beginning of April, it had been raised to about 8000, and though this was scarcely adequate, and 4000 more were expected, the urgent state of affairs in Afghanistan made him determine to attempt the passage of the Khyber. This tremendous defile was defended by about 10,000 brave mountaineers, thoroughly skilled in this species of warfare. They had raised a strong breastwork to defend the narrow entrance, and their bands covered all the rocky and precipitous heights on the right and left, whence they could take sure aim against the small column, which alone could march on the road beneath. To have penetrated through this passage, exposed to so terrible a fire, would have been scarcely possible, and certainly not without dreadful carnage. The general saw that the only means of securing success was to send troops to scale the heights, and dislodge the enemy posted upon them. This was a most formidable operation; but British soldiers, when brought into close contact, had shown themselves able to vanquish the enemy under almost any circumstances. Two columns were therefore formed, of twelve companies

General Pollock appointed to the command.

Passage of the Khyber.

Difficulty of the passage.

CHAP. XVI. — A.D. 1842.

The enemy driven from the heights.

each, and placed, the one under Colonel Taylor and Major Anderson, the other under Colonel Moseley and Major Huish; while 400 of the native troops called Jezailchees, were led by Captain Ferris. Both columns, in the face of a determined opposition, which they overcame in the most gallant style, succeeded in expelling the enemy from the crest of the hill. In this achievement they were much aided by Captain Alexander of the artillery, who threw in shrapnell shells wherever opportunity offered. The assailants continued to drive the opposing force from height to height till they had cleared the whole range as far as Ali Musjid. At the view of this success, the barrier at the mouth of the pass was abandoned, and the body of the army, with treasure, ammunition, and baggage, marched through without opposition. This grand operation was accomplished with the incredibly small loss of 14 killed, 104 wounded, and 17 missing; the first including one and the second three officers.

The Khyber pass secured.

On the 6th, Ali Musjid was attacked, and possession taken, after a slight resistance. A full command was thus obtained of the Khyber Pass, and the route lay open to Jellalabad and into the interior of Cabul.

Operations at Candahar.

Meantime, active operations were proceeding in the west, where the enemy omitted no exertion to dislodge the force with which General Nott occupied Candahar. Prince Sufter Jung, a son of Shah Sujah, seconded the hostile chiefs in plundering the villages, and exciting the people to rise against the British. After continuing these movements during February, they began early in March to press close upon the city; when the general, finding it necessary to push them to a distance, left 2600 men under Major Lane for its defence, and with the main body dashed out against the marauders. Though possessing a strength of 12,000, of whom one half were cavalry, well mounted, they hastily retreated, passed the rivers Turnuk and Urghundab, and carefully shunned all contact with the pursuing infantry. On the 9th, General Nott approached so near that his artillery could open upon them with effect, when they were completely

Successful resistance of General Nott.

broken and dispersed, being only saved from destruction by his defect in horse. After accomplishing this object he returned, without sustaining the slightest loss in men, baggage, or camels.

Renewed attack on Candahar

While the commander was engaged in this expedition, a strong detachment of Afghans, making a wide circuit, and favoured by their knowledge of the country and affections of the people, came suddenly upon Candahar. Major Lane, seeing their assemblage in the forenoon of the 10th, caused every preparation to be made for resistance, and the gates to be secured by bags of grain piled inside. The enemy, however, about eight in the evening, when completely dark, succeeded, by combustibles secretly ignited, in setting fire to the Herat gate. The governor lost no time in reinforcing this post, and opening upon them a destructive fire; yet in the face of the havock thus made, dense masses kept up an incessant and heavy discharge, while eight or ten even tore down the burning fragments, and, scrambling over the bags, effected an entrance. They were soon despatched; and about midnight, after four hours of incessant attack, the assailants withdrew. A similar attempt to fire the Shikarpore gate entirely failed, as did a feebler one on that leading to Cabul. The enemy then retreated with such diligence, that when day broke not one of them was visible; but the ground was strewed with dead bodies, while the British had not sustained a single casualty.

Their total repulse.

Harassing proceedings of the enemy

Though the Afghans were thus severely checked at every point, they continued to lay waste the country, carrying away the forage, and turning aside the supplies of water. Colonel Wymer was sent out to check these movements and to collect supplies. On the banks of the Urghundab he saw large bodies of cavalry grazing their horses; and on emerging from a pass a considerable force was observed to be forming in his rear. He marched back and obliged them to retreat; while Colonel Maclaren dislodged another band from a village in front. But at the same time, an overwhelming body, which had collected on the right flank, gained a temporary advan-

CHAP. XVI. — A. D. 1842.

tage, several officers being wounded. The commander hastened to their aid; and the skirmish terminated in the enemy being driven in confusion across the Urghundab, while the convoy was completely secured.

Advance of General England.

We have already mentioned that General England, in the middle of March, had been repulsed in his attempt to convey stores to Candahar. Being reinforced, he advanced again in the end of April, and on the 28th found the enemy in considerable strength, strongly posted in front of the village of Hykulzie. He attacked them with such vigour, that, notwithstanding a spirited defence, they were soon broken and dispersed; his loss being only ten wounded. On the other side he found Colonel Wymer, who had come to aid him; and the united corps proceeded without opposition to Candahar. In the end of May, Sufter Jung, being joined by Auktur Khan with 3000 men, advanced upon the capital, where the force was weakened by Wymer having been sent with a detachment into the Ghilzie country. They took post on some steep rocky hills about a mile from the city, imagining the commander would not have strength enough to attack them in the field. Yet he without hesitation sallied out: all their positions were gallantly carried; and they were driven with great loss across the Urghundab. The strong fortress of Kelat-i-Ghilzie had been maintained with great difficulty during the winter, surrounded by a hostile people, who early in spring formed lines of circumvallation, and closely blockaded it. Unable to effect any impression, they retired; but now again, on the 21st May, made an attack, at four in the morning, in two columns, each of 2000 men, with thirty scaling ladders. After an hour's contest, they were completely beaten off.

Sufter Jung.

Compelled to retreat.

Dissensions at Cabul.

Meantime, Cabul itself, on the departure of the English, became the theatre of most violent dissensions and revolutions; but the train of these events, and the motives of the barbarous actors, are involved in much obscurity. Shah Sujah, having at that crisis remained behind unprotected, might have been expected to fall a

Conduct of Shah Sujah.

victim to the excited fury of the people. On the contrary, he retained possession of the Bala Hissar, exercised a powerful influence, and was even courted by the different parties. The odium attached to him, it thus appears, had been chiefly reflected from the foreign aid by which his cause was upheld. As all parties united in this sentiment, the shah evidently deemed it expedient to dissemble whatever attachment he might feel for the British; nor is there wanting ground to suspect, that he joined with apparent cordiality in schemes for their entire expulsion. One of the two factions into which the country was rent obtained, it is said, his consent to place himself at the head of a force levied for that purpose. On this destination he left the Bala Hissar; but the hostile party of the Baurikzehee sirdars, strongly attached to Dost Mohammed and Akbar, determined to seize so favourable an opportunity for gratifying their enmity. They placed in ambush a body of skilful musketeers, who, when they saw the monarch coming to the spot, sprung forth, and discharged against him a shower of balls. Two of them took effect in a vital part, when he fell down and expired almost immediately. Several of his attendants were also slain; his crown and jewels were seized; and he left his family in as distracted a state as his kingdom. We have seen his son Sufter Jung raising all the western tribes against the British power; while another, Futteh Jung, was understood to be animated by quite opposite sentiments. The latter, being on the spot, obtained possession of the Bala Hissar, and assumed the reins of sovereignty. Akbar, however, who had been absent during these transactions, and whose power was seemingly much reduced, now hastened to Cabul; and by his talents, influence, and address, regained the complete mastery of that capital. He then turned his arms against the Bala Hissar; and having effected a breach, compelled it to surrender. Yet he did not proceed to extremities against Futteh Jung, but acknowledged him as shah, upon the understanding that he himself, under the title of vizier, should exercise the whole authority. The prince at

His assassination.

Influence of Akbar.

CHAP. XVI. A. D. 1842.

first consented; but not brooking this mere shadow of royalty, and being in fact treated as a kind of state-prisoner, he made his escape, and presented himself in the camp of General Pollock, whom he urged to advance upon the capital. Akbar was thus left undisputed master of the country, and the only enemy with whom that commander had now to contend.

Futteh Jung.

Change of government at home.

The British counsels, at this era, underwent an important change; for in September 1841, Sir Robert Peel and his friends came into power, in no degree pledged to the Indian policy of their predecessors. They do not appear to have intended to recall Lord Auckland; but that nobleman, feeling himself in a delicate situation, and the usual term of his office being nearly expired, solicited permission to resign. This was granted; and, amid very opposite opinions as to the Afghan policy, his departure elicited a high tribute of regret and respect, on account of his strict attention to the duties of his office, generous patronage of merit, and zeal for the promotion of every object tending to the prosperity of the great country over which he had presided. In his room, the ministry appointed Lord Ellenborough, who had bestowed particular attention on the affairs of India, and had, in consequence, been placed at the head of the Board of Control. To this nomination the East India Company gave their cordial concurrence. His lordship having set out on the 8th November, arrived at Calcutta on the 28th February following; and after remaining there some weeks, he proceeded to Allahabad, and afterwards to Simla, the military headquarters in the west. He evidently came at once to the conclusion, that no attempt ought to be made to perpetuate the occupation of Afghanistan, or to control the people as to the choice of their government and ruler. After a correspondence, however, with General Pollock, it was finally settled that this commander from Jellalabad, and Nott from Candahar, should march upon Cabul, display the superiority of the British arms in open warfare, expel Mohammed Akbar, compel the restoration of the prisoners, and level with the ground all the strong for-

Resignation of Lord Auckland.

Appointment of Lord Ellenborough.

Change of policy.

tresses by which the country could be defended in case a future expedition should become necessary.

CHAP. XVI — A. D. 1842.

Junction of the armies.

Pollock having, in the manner above related, forced all the barriers opposed by the Khyber Pass, arrived on the 16th April at Jellalabad, where the two victorious armies united, and hailed each other with loud and enthusiastic cheers. Early in May they were reinforced by a brigade under Colonel Bolton, who was met on the way by Colonel Monteath. Captain Mackenzie, one of the prisoners, arrived from Akbar, followed soon afterwards by the dead body of General Elphinstone, who had fallen a victim to disease and anxiety. He bore also proposals from the Afghan ruler, understood to relate to the ransom of the captives and the release of Dost Mohammed; but he returned without being able to conclude any agreement. On the 13th July, Captain Troup, with several native chiefs, brought fresh proposals, and having returned to Cabul, came back on the 3d August; but all these negotiations proved fruitless. The English leader had proposed a general exchange of prisoners, which would have included Dost Mohammed, father to Akbar; but farther demands were made by the latter. The army, meantime, were somewhat straitened for provisions; the heat became intense; and dysentery with other diseases began to be prevalent. Bands of the enemy again hovered around, and rendered it impracticable to stir beyond cover of the fortifications, without the danger of being speared; the camels and other beasts of burden perished in great numbers, without the possibility of supplying their place, so that the means of conveyance became deficient. The army were depressed by seeing the summer months pass in a state of inaction, and without any prospect of avenging the injuries sustained by their countrymen.

Death of General Elphinstone.

Fruitless negotiations.

Sufferings in the British camp.

Proceedings against refractory chiefs.

Detachments were however sent out to keep open the passages, to overawe as well as punish refractory chiefs; and on these occasions, the most turbulent generally retreated without hazarding a combat. Some of the booty taken from the Cabul army being discovered in the village of Ali Baghan, the troops plundered and set the place on

CHAP. XVI — A. D. 1842.

fire, without any authority from their officers, by whom this conduct was much disapproved. On the 20th June, twenty-five forts of the Goolai tribe, a desperate race of freebooters, were found deserted, and a considerable supply of provisions procured. The Shinwarees, another fierce band, who boasted that no conqueror had ever entered their valley, refused tribute, and seized all opportunities of giving annoyance. On the 24th July, they attacked a detachment, and drove it with loss back into the camp; upon which Brigadier Monteath, commanding in this station, resolved to give them a serious lesson. On the 26th, leaving the baggage in camp, he pushed forward with his light troops into this supposed inaccessible valley. On his approach, a long range of forts were abandoned, and, to the number of thirty-five, were set on fire, filling the whole atmosphere with flame and smoke. All the men retreated to the castle of their principal chief, Secunder Khan, seated on a high mountain. Major Skinner, with the advance, obliged them to evacuate it, and drove them from successive posts in its vicinity. The British troops were then ordered to withdraw, when the enemy, who remained unbroken, followed them to the camp, but without being able to gain any advantage. Our loss was three killed and twenty-three wounded. They were supposed to have suffered severely, and their chief immediately afterwards intimated his willingness to pay the revenue.

Forts of the Goolai tribe deserted.

Attack on the Shinwarees.

Driven from the castle of Secunder Khan.

Renewed operations of General Pollock.

General Pollock remained at Jellalabad till nearly the end of August, apparently with the view of maturing his plans, and concerting with General Nott a joint movement on the capital. On the 20th, he left these quarters, and on the 23d reached Gundamuk: the enemy occupying the village and fort of Mammoo Khail, only two miles distant, with a strong body. To dislodge them, he marched on the 24th, and found them stationed in an orchard with some enclosures, having their front covered by field-works of loose stones. From these positions they were driven into the village, where they made a show of resistance; but on the British coming up, they abandoned it, retired into the fort, and barricaded the gates.

The assailants, by mounting on each other's shoulders, entered a shattered bastion eight feet high, when they saw the defenders going over the walls on the other side, but were unable from fatigue to pursue. The right wing, under General M'Caskill, advanced upon Kookhi Khail, another hamlet two miles distant, held also by hostile troops, who then abandoned it, but took post upon the adjacent peaks of the great range called Soofaid Koh. From several of these they were dislodged, but from others maintained a heavy fire with the long muskets called jezails, which obliged our men to retire from some of the points they had gained. General Pollock, not considering it an object to push farther, burned the remoter village, while in the nearer one he established his camp, lest the enemy should boast of having driven him thence. His loss amounted to seven killed and forty-nine wounded. The success had not been quite complete; yet it was sufficient to secure the British flank, and deter the barbarians from any further attempts to molest his position.

Partial success.

The general spent about a fortnight in this place collecting his troops, and making arrangements for their farther advance. On the 6th September, he began his final movement upon Cabul; next day reached Soorkab; and on the morning of the 8th, approached the terrible pass of Jugduluk. Here the enemy, nearly 5000 strong, under the standards of different chiefs, had crowned the amphitheatre of hills on the left of the road, whence they were separated by a deep ravine. They opened a formidable fire on the advancing column, when Captain Nugent, a highly promising young officer, was wounded, and died almost immediately. Our guns were well served, and shells burst among them with powerful effect, yet not so much as to shake their determination or slacken their fire. It was found that the heights must be scaled; for which purpose, Captain Broadfoot was directed to move on the extreme left, while Colonel Taylor, with the light infantry, should cross the ravine and attack the opposite hills, the key of the position, and where the principal chiefs were assembled. This force, in rushing up the steep, raised an animated and enthusiastic cheer.

Movement upon Cabul.

Pass of Jugduluk.

Scaling of the heights.

CHAP. XVI. A.D. 1842.

Panic and flight of the enemy.

on hearing which, the enemy, struck with panic, fled down the opposite declivities. Captain Lockwood, with the dragoons, nearly reached their cavalry, who, however, saved themselves by flight. Captain Broadfoot also completely succeeded on the left; but the fugitives from both points rallied on the top of a very lofty mountain, where they planted their standards, and seemed to consider themselves unapproachable. To dispel this idea, Captains Wilkinson and Broadfoot mounted in columns, covered by the guns of Captains Abbott and Backhouse. As soon as the Afghans saw them approach, they hastily took to flight, abandoning this last stronghold, and carrying off their standards. They included the most powerful of the hostile tribes—those among whom the insurrection had arisen—and who were led by numerous chiefs. But neither Akbar Khan nor any other of the first rank was present. Our loss amounted to six killed and fifty-eight wounded, among which last was General Sale.

Arrival at Tezeen.

Pollock now proceeded with the utmost diligence, and on the 11th arrived at Tezeen, where, finding the men and cattle much fatigued, he allowed them to repose on the 12th, before entering into the still more formidable passes which lay before him. The barbarians, imputing this pause to timidity, commenced an attack upon the outposts on the left, which it was necessary to send Colonel Taylor with 240 men to repel. The enemy then retired to the crests of the neighbouring hills, whence they kept up an obstinate fire; but the colonel, having made a circuit unperceived, took them in flank, and drove them down with severe loss. Soon after, however, they came suddenly upon a picket on the British right, under Lieutenant Montgomery, which was driven in, with the loss of four killed and seventeen wounded, before a reinforcement could arrive to strengthen the post. They continued similar attempts through the night, but found every point completely guarded. Major Skinner, who had been detached with a party in the evening, succeeded in dislodging a body of the enemy from the heights in front of the camp.

Renewed attacks on the outposts.

Pass of Tezeen.

On the morning of the 13th, the army entered the pass of Tezeen, and found mustered there the whole Cabul force, estimated at 16,000 men, under the personal command of Akbar, Ameenoolah, and other great chiefs attached to his cause. They had most carefully improved the naturally great strength of the position, and manifested a determination to defend it to the last extremity. When therefore the British troops ascended the heights, they found them, contrary to custom, advancing to the contest, which was maintained with desperation, and in many instances decided only by the bayonet. It was peculiarly obstinate before they were dislodged from the numerous positions on the lofty eminence of the Huft Kothul. The resistance was indeed protracted during a great part of the day; but at length British valour overcame every obstacle, and our troops, with three cheers, established themselves on this mighty summit. The enemy then fled in every direction, losing their guns and three standards. A strong body had attacked the rear-guard, with the view of hemming in the army on both sides, or at least of capturing the baggage; but they were gallantly repulsed by Colonel Richmond, who commanded in that quarter.

Obstinate defence of the heights.

Flight of the enemy

Pass of Koord Cabul.

The general now marched on to Koord Cabul. The dreadful pass of that name still lay before him, and troops were sent to crown its heights; but the enemy, dismayed and disorganized by their recent overthrow, had made no attempt to secure them. On the 14th, he arrived at Bootkhak, and next day encamped on the race-ground at Cabul. On the morning of the 16th, with his staff and a detachment, he entered the Bala Hissar, on whose summit, amid the anthem of "God save the Queen," the British colours were hoisted. Futteh Jung was allowed to accompany them, and placed himself on the throne, but without any co-operation or guarantee on our part. The strictest orders were issued to the officers and troops not to injure in any shape the city or its inhabitants, nor even to enter it without express permission.

British colours planted on Bala Hissar

Meantime, as early as the beginning of June, General

CHAP. XVI. A. D. 1842.

Evacuation of Candahar.

Nott had been making preparations to evacuate Candahar, after dismantling its fortified positions. Colonel Wymer, who had marched upon Kelat-i-Ghilzie, demolished its strongholds, and withdrew the garrison. A similar course was followed in respect to Ghirisk, long held by Bulwunt Sing, a steady adherent of England. All the stores in the capital which could not be carried off were destroyed; and on the 10th August, the city being evacuated, the army divided itself into two portions. One under General England, composed of the troops recently arrived from Bombay, and removing with them all the heavy baggage, commenced their return by Quetta and Dadur to the Lower Indus. On the 16th, he reached the entrance of the Kujuk Pass, where he had been informed that the Afghans were preparing to make a most desperate effort to intercept his artillery and supplies, including nearly 10,000 beasts of burden. He saw, however, that the highest mountain pinnacles were not yet occupied, and though the troops were fatigued by a night march of twenty-four miles, he lost no time in sending a light detachment to take possession of the most important ridge, and the peaks commanding the principal passes. This proved a most judicious precaution; for, next morning, the enemy began to appear in small bodies, their numbers continually increased, and repeated attacks were made, but rendered fruitless by the want of any commanding position. The loss sustained was only two killed and eight wounded. The army then marched in two columns by Quetta to Dadur, which it reached on the 9th October. In traversing the Bolan Pass, the heat was extremely severe, and some slight annoyance was experienced from the natives.

Kujuk Pass.

Principal heights secured.

The Bolan Pass.

Engagement of General Nott with Shumshoodeen Khan.

On the 10th August, also, General Nott quitted Candahar, leaving it to be occupied by Prince Sufter Jung and his adherents. On the general reaching Naunee, however, about twenty miles from Ghizni, Shumshoodeen Khan, governor of that capital, met him on the 30th with 12,000 men. He marched out with only a part of his force, when the enemy advanced boldly, opening a hot fire from small arms and two well-served guns.

The British columns, however, steadily advanced, and after a brisk but short contest, completely dispersed them. Their guns, tents, and ammunition fell into our hands, and the darkness alone saved them from being entirely cut up, their commander fleeing with a train of no more than thirty horsemen. Our loss, however, amounted to thirty-eight killed and sixty-six wounded.

Arrival at Ghizni.

On the morning of the 5th, the general arrived at Ghizni, which he found defended by strong bodies of troops, reinforced by Sultan Jan, one of the leading actors in the scene of assassination. They had occupied not only gardens and ravines in front of the walls, but a long range of mountains stretching to the north-east. The first object being to reconnoitre the place, and the party thus employed being briskly attacked, it was necessary to send additional companies to their support. It was judged requisite to begin by driving the Afghans from the heights, which the troops effected in gallant style, carrying successively every point. The village of Bullal was then chosen as a convenient site for erecting a battery; and before daybreak on the 6th, one of four eighteen pounders was constructed and advanced towards the walls. It was then, however, discovered that the enemy had evacuated the place; and arrangements were immediately made for the demolition of this celebrated citadel, as far as could be effected in two days. The loss in these operations consisted of three killed and forty-three wounded.

The heights carried.

Citadel of Ghizni demolished.

March on Cabul.

General Nott now marched directly northward upon Cabul; but in approaching Mydan, he again encountered Shumshoodeen and Sultan Jan, with a force as large as before, occupying a range of strong mountain-posts. The 14th and 15th September were spent in driving them successively from these eminences, which was done with the usual success, though not without a hard resistance, costing a loss of four killed and fifty-nine wounded. The army then proceeded to join General Pollock at Cabul.

An auspicious result now followed the triumph of the British arms. As soon as Akbar saw his victorious enemy

CHAP. XVI. — A.D. 1842.

Treatment of prisoners.

advancing, he despatched the prisoners under a strong guard to Khoolloom in Turkestan, where they were either to be thrown into dungeons or given as slaves to the principal chiefs. In this fearful predicament, they of course looked round for all means of deliverance. The escort was commanded by Salih Mohammed, who had deserted from the British cause, and might therefore not be incorruptible. A tender was repeatedly made to him of a lac of rupees (£10,000), on condition of enabling them to reach the English camp. He evaded these propositions, evidently doubtful which side would gain the ascendency. On their arrival at Bameean, however, he came and announced that orders had been received for their immediate departure for Khoolloom; but that General Pollock had intimated through another channel a readiness to bestow £2000 and a monthly pension of £100, in case of his effecting their deliverance. This he engaged to do, provided they should enter into a bond guaranteeing the offer just made. Four officers signed the obligation, the other prisoners engaging to pay such sums as might hereafter be demanded from them for fulfilling it. Salih then dismissed the escort, and changed the governor of the fort for one on whom he could rely. Dreading lest the Afghan army, even in its retreat, should take this direction, they made indefatigable efforts to put the stronghold in a state of defence. However, on learning the victory at Tezeen, and anticipating the entry of the British forces into Cabul, they conceived it possible to effect their deliverance by their own efforts, trusting to co-operation from that quarter. In fact, General Pollock, immediately on arriving there, had made arrangements for the departure of 700 Kuzzilbash horse, accompanied by Sir Richmond Shakespeare, to whom he advanced 10,000 rupees; and soon after General Sale followed, with a corps of 2000 men. The prisoners departed from Bameean on the 16th, and next day crossed the Kaloo mountain-range, 13,000 feet high, being little inferior to Mount Blanc. After descending, they were filled with joy by meeting with Sir Richmond and the Kuzzilbashes, and on the 19th with General Sale.

Negotiations for their ransom.

Terms accepted by Salih Mohammed.

Rescue of the prisoners.

The meeting of that officer with his heroic lady and daughter may be more easily conceived than described. His mission proved by no means superfluous, as Sultan Jan was in full pursuit, and would perhaps have been up in twenty-four hours. They arrived in camp on the evening of the 21st, when their arrival was celebrated by a royal salute and the most heartfelt rejoicings. They included General Shelton, Colonel Palmer, Majors Pottinger and Griffiths, twelve captains, three surgeons, nine lieutenants, three ensigns, twenty-eight non-commissioned officers and soldiers. The females were Ladies Macnaghten and Sale, besides the wives of five officers and of three privates. There remained only Captain Bygrave, who had been detained by Akbar; but he, too, arrived on the 27th, with a despatch from that chief.

Rejoicings on the arrival of the prisoners.

The Afghans, after so many disasters, retreated into the mountain-territory of Kohistan, immediately north of Cabul, where they hoped to find a present refuge and a point whence they might return upon the city. General Pollock, however, determined to dislodge them, and if he could not capture, at least drive them to a distance. The grand rallying point, to which most of the chiefs had conveyed their property and their wives, was Istalif. This town, with 15,000 inhabitants, consists of clusters of houses and forts built on the slope of a mountain, having in its rear still loftier eminences, that shut in a defile leading to Turkestan. It could be approached only across ranges of hills separated by dark ravines, and covered with gardens, vineyards, and orchards, enclosed by strong walls; all the heights being occupied by the Jezailchees, those formidable sharpshooters. After careful examination, it was determined to make the attack on the right, though the quarter naturally strongest; but from this very cause, the enemy had been induced to place on the left their guns and the most efficient of their force. The troops, formed into two columns, under Brigadiers Tulloch and Stacy, advanced in the face of a heavy fire from the gardens, and then united in a joint attack on the village Ismillah, considered the key of the position, which they stormed with distinguished gallantry. Press-

Retreat of the Afghans to Kohistan

Istalif.

Chosen point of attack.

Storming of Ismillah.

CHAP. XVI. — A.D. 1842.

ing on, and leaving the enemy not a moment to rally, they carried successively all the enclosures, forts, heights, suburbs, and finally the town. The singular spectacle was then presented of the women and children hastening up the mountain-side to effect their escape, which no attempt was made to intercept. As armed bodies, however, were seen rallying on some very lofty heights, guns were conveyed up by some narrow paths, and soon caused their dispersion. The British loss was six killed and forty-five wounded, considered very small in carrying so strong a position. The place was found filled with property conveyed thither for security, and in great part taken from our army in 1841. After removing every thing that could be useful, arrangements were made for the entire demolition of the fortress.

The fort and town carried.

Evacuation of the country resolved upon.

No further operations were undertaken against the enemy. Akbar and other chiefs, on whom it might have been desirable to let fall our resentment, had fled beyond the frontier, and sought refuge in Turkestan. The speedy approach of winter gave warning to lose no time in executing the resolution of evacuating a country which had been the scene of so much glory and disaster. Futteh Jung, as already mentioned, had seated himself on the throne, but without British sanction. It proved that the Kuzzilbashes, and other friendly chiefs, chose rather that it should be occupied by Shah Poora, his younger brother, a mere lad, hoping, it is probable, to govern in his name, and taking advantage of the respect with which his family were still regarded. General Pollock, who had resolved to refrain from dictating on this subject, not only acquiesced, but left uninjured the Bala Hissar, with a store of artillery for its defence. The elder brother accompanied our army to India. It was, however, considered indispensable that, before departing, a severe lesson should be given to the Afghans as to the hazards which must always attend a war with Britain. The great bazaar, erected under Aurengzebe, by the celebrated architect Ali Murdan Khan, was esteemed the most spacious edifice, and the chief seat of trade in Central Asia. It was 600 feet long,

Shah Poora seated on the throne.

Destruction of the great bazaar

and contained 2000 shops; and here had been exposed to public insult the remains of the late envoy. It was therefore determined to reduce it to ashes; and Colonel Richmond, with a party of sappers and miners, and a detachment of troops, were employed two days in completing its destruction.

Order of march.

The army marched on the 12th October in three divisions, commanded respectively by Generals Pollock, M'Caskill, and Nott. General Sale, with a light corps, went in advance to clear the right flank, and crown the heights of the Koord Cabul Pass. Through these good arrangements General Pollock's division arrived at Jugduluk on the 16th, without any serious attempt to molest it. The second, under General M'Caskill, suffered some annoyance and loss. General Nott's rear was much retarded by the exhaustion of the baggage-cattle, of which advantage was taken by large hordes of Ghilzies to make several brisk attacks. They were gallantly repulsed, yet with a loss on our side of twelve killed and forty-nine wounded. From Jugduluk, the divisions, for the convenience of march, proceeded separately, each at a day's interval. On the 22d, 23d, and 25th, they successively arrived at Jellalabad. Three days were employed in destroying the military works of that celebrated fortress. On the 27th, the first division left it, followed on the 29th by the others. They proceeded with all expedition through the passes, and though constantly harassed by the Khyberees, sustained no serious loss except on the 3d November, when General M'Caskill's division was attacked with great fury, and a contest ensued, in which two officers and a considerable number of men fell. Two guns were taken, but recovered next day. On the 6th, the last, under General Nott, emerged from the pass at Jumrood, and the whole were soon united in the vicinity of Peshawer. On the 10th, they marched in four brigades; on the 17th, crossed the Indus at Attock, and, proceeding through the Punjaub, on the 18th, passed the Sutledge to Ferozepore, where the governor and commander-in-chief joyfully received them. On the 25th October, Lord Ellenborough had

Attacks by the Ghilzies

Destruction of Jellalabad

Passage through the passes.

CHAP. XVI

A. D. 1842.

Captive Afghans set at liberty.

announced in a proclamation, that with a view to terminate as early as possible all the evils arising out of the war, the several Afghans now in the power of the British government would be set at liberty. In this number, Dost Mohammed, his wives and family, and also those of Akbar Khan, were included.

Result of the contest.

Such was the termination of this long contest diversified by so many events at once glorious and tragical. It was doubtless a subject of rather painful reflection that the only result should be, the restoration of all things to their previous state, and the renunciation of every object for which the war had been undertaken. Yet few, we think, will deny, that the resolution thus to close it, as announced by Lord Ellenborough, was highly judicious. The expedition had, as formerly shown, been projected by Lord Auckland, under the belief, that the deposed monarch would be welcomed by his former subjects, and that the secure possession of the throne in his hands would form a barrier to our Indian possessions. It has indeed appeared, that the people were not without some attachment to the ancient family, but as soon as it was proved that he could not be maintained in power except by a British force, all hope of holding this proud, brave, and turbulent people in willing subjection necessarily vanished. We might, indeed, by good management, have held a number of fortified positions in a besieged state, but could never have possessed the country. It must have been what Spain was to Napoleon, and what Algiers now is to France, a source of weakness, inasmuch as it would have proved a continual drain both of men and treasure.

Mistaken policy of Lord Auckland.

Wisdom of evacuating the country.

CHAPTER XVII.

The War in Sinde and Gwalior.

Rejoicings on the termination of the Afghan War—Desire for the consolidation of the British possessions in India—Disturbances in Sinde—Hostile manifestations of the Ameers—Sir Charles Napier assumes the command in Sinde—Faithless proceedings of the Ameers—Attack on the British Resident—Battle of Hyderabad—Defeat of the Sindian and Beloochee Forces—Important effects of the Victory—Battle of Dubba—Strong position of the Enemy—Decisive Victory—Insalubrity of the Climate—Disturbances on the Northern Frontiers—Disordered state of Afghanistan—Revolutions in the Punjaub—Army of Observation on the Sutledge—Disturbances at Gwalior—Battles of Maharajpoor and Punniar—Decisive effects of these Victories—Recall of Lord Ellenborough—Lord Hardinge appointed Governor-general—Change of Policy—Continued Disturbances in the Punjaub—Discussions which they gave rise to.

CHAP. XVII. A. D. 1842.

Disasters in Afghanistan.

THE year 1842 closed, both in India and at home, with gratulations and rejoicings for the successful termination of Eastern warfare. A succession of disasters had attended the British arms, such as had scarcely before been matched in its history. Dishonour, defeat, and flight, had disgraced the British standards beyond the Indus, and already boding prophets, both in England and on the Continent, were anticipating the overthrow of our whole Indian empire. Events the most tragical and disastrous had, however, been followed by triumphs no less glorious, and the temporary humiliation of British arms had only helped more thoroughly to show their superiority, in the long run, against any power that Asia can muster against them. All parties, however, were thoroughly convinced of the necessity imposed upon England, to accept of the

Final success.

CHAP. XVII. — A. D. 1842.

great natural barrier which the Indus appears to offer as the north-western boundary of her Eastern possessions; and the establishment of peace on a firm and lasting basis was confidently anticipated as the result of this definite line of policy. There remained, however, another enemy still bent on hostility.

Kingdom of Sinde.

The kingdom of Sinde which occupies both banks of the Great Delta of the Indus, immediately to the south of Afghanistan, altogether differs in climate and natural features from that rugged hill country which the British arms had so recently conquered, only to return into the hands of its turbulent native possessors. It was at the very close of 1842, that Lord Ellenborough completed the arrangements for the renunciation of Afghanistan, and restored to liberty the last of the Afghans still remaining in his power. Almost immediately thereafter, his attention was directed to various acts of the Ameers of Sinde in contravention of their existing engagements, as well as to decided manifestations of hostile intentions. During the temporary disasters in Afghanistan which threatened to destroy the prestige acquired by British valour in India, the Ameers had displayed an evident desire to avail themselves of the first favourable opportunity for setting at naught all existing treaties, and thereby almost as effectually favoured the Afghanistans as if they had raised an army to co-operate with them against the British. Decided symptoms of hostile intentions became speedily apparent. Early in August a letter describes the surrounding tribes as little better than in a state of insurrection. Chiefs were moving about with armed bands, endeavouring to enlist followers, and availing themselves of every opportunity to plunder. In the Bombay Gazetteer of 9th September. it is remarked:—"With regard to the Ameers of Sinde, we think there will be ample grounds for sending them to Benares." The movements of British troops speedily afforded indication that the governor-general was resolved to adopt summary measures for suppressing any hostile move-

Hostile manifestations of the Ameers of Sinde.

State of the surrounding tribes.

ments on the part of the Sindeans. The force under General England, amounting to about 3500, was ordered to move from Candahar, towards Sinde, and other bodies of troops soon followed them, increasing their number to above 5000 men. CHAP. XVII. A.D. 1843.

Sufferings in the Bolan Pass.

General England's forces experienced little interruption in their progress towards Sinde, excepting that which arose from the excessive heat. The temperature in the Bolan Pass is described as almost unbearable. Eight men died in the course of two days from its effects. The last portion of General England's forces left Quattah on the first of October, and proceeded without interruption for the first two marches into the Bolan Pass. But as they threaded a difficult portion of the defile on the 3d, an attack was made on the column, and skirmishing kept up for some hours, during which the rear-guard suffered considerably.

Sir Charles Napier assumes the command of the forces in Sinde.

On the 4th of October, Sir Charles Napier arrived at Sukker, and assumed the command of the forces in Sinde. On his way he had left with the Ameers Lord Ellenborough's ultimatum, and a few days after Major Outram was commissioned to demand an equally definite reply. It was then confidently anticipated that when they learned the complete success of the British arms in the North, there would be little difficulty in negotiating with them. In this, however, the governor-general was disappointed. Negotiations were indeed carried on for above four months, with considerable hopes of a satisfactory termination; and new provisions, which Lord Ellenborough deemed indispensable, in consequence not only of their manifestations of a hostile disposition, but of various acts in direct contravention of existing engagements, received the assent of the Ameers of Sinde. The usual difficulties, however, were experienced in dealing with native powers. It was obvious, notwithstanding their adoption of the prescribed terms, that no reliance could be placed on their good faith. Of this abundant evidence was speedily afforded. The new treaty which

Want of good faith in negotiating with the Ameers.

CHAP. XVII. A.D. 1843.

had been proposed and agreed to, received the signature of the Ameers on the 14th of February 1843, and on the very day thereafter, they made a sudden attack, at the head of a large force, on the residence of Major Outram, the British commissioner. Unexpectedly sudden and undisguised as this treacherous assault was, the commissioner had been warned to place little faith in their sincerity.

Assault of Major Outram.

On leaving the durbar the previous day, where the whole body of the Ameers had formally affixed their seals to the treaty, Major Outram and his companions were exposed to great peril, and were only rescued by the Ameers' guards from a hired band of assassins. But on the following morning, the Major's residence was attacked by a body of 8000 troops, headed by several of the Ameers and principal chiefs.

Attack of the British residency.

The small force under his command maintained their post with the utmost gallantry, and had it not been for the terror of the camp followers, who were employed to remove the property on board a steamer that lay in the river, the assailants would not have obtained possession of any portion of it.

Despatch of Major Outram.

Major Outram writes to Sir Charles Napier, on the 15th: "My despatches of the last few days will have led you to expect that my earnest endeavours to effect an amicable arrangement with the Ameers of Sinde would fail, and it is with much regret I have now to report that their highnesses have commenced hostilities by attacking my residence this morning, which, after four hours' most gallant defence by my honorary escort, the light company of Her Majesty's 22d regiment, commanded by Captain Conway, I was compelled to evacuate, in consequence of our ammunition running short. At nine A.M. this morning, a dense body of cavalry and infantry took post on three sides of the Agency compound, (the fourth being defended by the Planet steamer about 500 yards distant,) in the gardens and houses which immediately commanded the enclosure, and which it was impossible to hold with our limited numbers. A hot fire was opened by the enemy, and continued incessantly for four hours; but all their attempts to enter the Agency enclosure, although merely surrounded by a wall, varying from four to five feet high, were frustrated by Captain Conway's able distribution of his small band, and the admirable conduct of every individual soldier composing it under the gallant example of their commanding officer and his subalterns, Lieutenant Harding and Ensign Pennefather, Her Majesty's 22d regiment, also Captains Green of the 21st regiment native infantry, and Wells, of the 15th regiment, who volunteered their services, to each of whom was assigned the charge of a separate quarter, also to your aide-de camp Captain Brown, Bengal Engineers, who carried my orders to the steamer, and assisted in working her guns and directing her flanking fire. Our ammunition being limited to forty rounds per man, the officers directed their whole attention to reserving their fire, and keeping their men close under cover, never showing themselves or returning a shot, except when the enemy attempted to rush, or showed themselves in great numbers, consequently great execution was done with trifling expenditure of ammunition and with little loss." Major Outram had held out in the hope of obtaining reinforcements and a supply of ammunition from the Satellite steamer, which was hourly expected; but in this he was disappointed, and they were at length compelled to evacuate the place, which they did, says Major Outram, "covered by a few skirmishers, as deliberately as on parade." The commissioner joined Sir Charles Napier at Hala, and immediately on learning from him of the commencement of hostilities, he put the whole forces at his command in motion, to oppose the united armies of Upper and Lower Sinde, which were already in the field. On the 16th Sir Charles reached Muttaree, where he learned that the Ameers had taken up a position at Meeanee, about twelve miles distant, at the head of a force of 22,000 men, while the number then with him did not amount to 3000. At eight o'clock on the following morning, his advanced guard came in sight of their camp at

Slight defences of the residency.

Failure of ammunition.

Disappointed in expected supplies.

Sir Charles Napier puts his whole forces in motion.

CHAP. XVII. — A.D. 1843.

Position of the Sindeans at Meeanee.

Meeanee, within sight of the towers of Hyderabad. The position occupied by the Sindeans had been chosen with great skill, and their immense superiority in point of numbers allowed them to turn it to the utmost advantage. Both flanks were protected by thick woods, which seemed calculated to baffle any attempt to turn them, while the whole length of their front was effectually secured by the dry bed and steep banks of the river Fulaille, one of the branches of the Indus. So soon as the British forces came within range of the enemy's guns, a battery of fifteen pieces of artillery opened upon them with deadly effect. The whole artillery on the side of the British consisted of twelve small field-pieces, which Sir Charles posted on his right, while some skirmishers and a body of native cavalry were ordered to advance, in order to make the enemy show his force. The main body then advanced from the right in echellon of battalions, moving rapidly across the open plain, which was swept by the enemy's cannon. The British fire of musketry opened at about 100 yards from the bank of the river, and in a few minutes the engagement became general along the whole line. The Sindeans, however, made good use of their well chosen position, and for above three hours the combatants struggled for mastery along the banks of the river, fighting with the most deadly fury man to man. The Beloochees, who formed an important branch of the Sindean army, are celebrated as bold and skilful swordsmen, and they fought in this engagement with the most desperate fury. Rushing on to the top of the embankments, they discharged their matchlocks and pistols at their opponents, and then dashed into the midst of them sword in hand.

British artillery.

General engagement.

The Beloochees.

Difficulties arising from the strength of the Sindeans' position.

The nature of the ground almost completely precluded the ordinary manœuvres of a disciplined force, and from the vast superiority of the enemy in point of numbers, it appeared for a time impossible that the British could hold their ground. Fast as one wild band of desperate assailants fell before their cool and resolute defence, another band equally numerous and fearless sprung into their place. On seeing the perilous state in which the main body in his front was placed, after maintaining their ground for above three hours against a foe which seemed to spring up before them anew as fast as they were struck down or driven back, Sir Charles sent orders to his reserved cavalry to force the right wing of the enemy. This movement was most gallantly executed. In the first charge the 9th light cavalry took a standard and several pieces of artillery, and another body of native cavalry obtained possession of the enemy's camp, from whence a large body of their horse were slowly driven, fighting every inch of ground as they withdrew. They were pursued for upwards of two miles, until they were effectually broken and scattered in hopeless disorder. This gallant charge decided the fortunes of the day. Though the main body of the enemy did not immediately give way, their resistance slackened as soon as they saw their wing turned and the chief body of their cavalry driven from the field. The 22d, the 23d, and the 12th regiments then successively charged up the bank with muskets and fixed bayonets, which in the hands of British soldiers have rarely been withstood. They forced the line of the enemy at all points, the last regiment capturing several guns, while the Sindeans gave way in all directions and fled from the field, leaving the whole of their artillery, ammunition, standards, and camp, with considerable stores, and some treasure, in the hands of the victors. Not a single prisoner, however, was captured by the British, a fact to which Sir Charles Napier made special reference at a later period. In the barbarous system of warfare to which the Beloochees had been accustomed, no quarter is ever given to an enemy, and the consequence was, that, anticipating the same treatment from their British victors, the wounded refused all quarter, and continued to strike at every one that approached them, until they were bayoneted where they lay. On taking possession of Hyderabad, considerable

Successful charge of cavalry.

Its decisive effects.

The enemy's line broken.

Barbarous system of native warfare.

CHAP. XVII. A.D. 1843.

treasure fell into the hands of the British, and further discoveries afterwards greatly augmented this, so that a total amount of specie was ultimately reported in the hands of the victors, amounting to above three millions sterling.

Loss of the British.

This victory was not secured without considerable loss on the side of the British;—256 are reported in the despatch of the general as killed and wounded, including an unusual proportion of officers. But the loss of the enemy was immense, amounting, it is believed, to more than twenty times that of their opponents. In referring to the unavoidable absence of certain British officers, and the loss of others during the engagement, Sir Charles Napier remarks in his despatch to Lord Ellenborough:

Necessity for European officers for native troops.

"I hope your Lordship will pardon me for saying, that the want of European officers in the native regiment at one period endangered the success of the action. The sepoy is a brave and excellent soldier, but, like all soldiers, he expects to be led on in certain moments, and as he looks to his European officer, if he misses him, the greatest danger arises; three times I saw them retreat, evidently because the officers had fallen, and when another appeared and rallied them, they at once followed him boldly. This, my Lord, accounts for the great number of European officers killed and wounded in proportion to the whole." The policy indicated in this suggestion of the general, has since been acted upon by the government at home, and the staff of British officers for the Indian army, and especially for the native troops, has been permanently enlarged to a considerable extent.

Satisfaction at the victory.

Much satisfaction was naturally experienced at the news of a victory of so brilliant a character, gained under unexpected circumstances, and against such very considerable odds. Whatever doubts might have been entertained of the good faith or friendly intentions of the Ameers of Sinde, the British general might have been excused had he been found unprepared for so sudden and treacherous an attack as that which immediately followed

CHAP. XVII. A. D. 1843

the signing of the treaty. Still the disasters of the first Afghan war had not been entirely effaced from recollection, even by the decisive character of the victories of the second campaign. It was perhaps felt by some of the native powers, little inclined to appreciate any far-sighted course of policy, that the British had neither accomplished the object for which the war in Afghanistan was originally undertaken, nor had they enlarged their Indian empire by retaining possession of the conquered territory. Victory beneath the walls of Hyderabad might therefore be said to be indispensable to secure the prestige of British superiority, against whatever odds it had to be achieved. This the military skill of the leader, and the valour of the forces under his command, had accomplished, and their victory was welcomed with corresponding gratulations. By a despatch, dated from the palace of Agra, on the 5th of March, Lord Ellenborough conveys the thanks of the Government and people of India to their gallant defenders. In referring to the first act of hostility by the enemy, he remarks: "The governor-general cannot forgive a treacherous attack upon a representative of the British government, nor can he forgive hostile aggression prepared by those who were in the act of signing a treaty. It will be the first object of the governor-general to use the power victory has placed in his hands in the manner most conducive to the freedom of trade, and to the prosperity of the people of Sinde, so long misgoverned. To reward the fidelity of allies by substantial marks of favour, and so to punish the crime of treachery in princes as to deter all from its commission, are further objects which the governor-general will not fail to effect. To Major-general Sir Charles Napier, and to the brave troops he commanded, the governor-general offers the tribute of his own admiration, and of the gratitude of the government and people of India. The bravery of the enemy against whom they were engaged has enhanced their glory—the most decisive victory has been gained upon the best fought field. In perpetual commemoration of

Important effects of this victory.

Observations of the governor-general.

CHAP. XVII. A. D. 1843.

Honours awarded to the victors.

this brilliant achievement, the 2d company 2d battalion, and the 3d company 3d battalion, of Bombay artillery, and the company of the Madras sappers and miners, will bear upon their appointments, and the 9th regiment of Bengal light cavalry, the Poonah horse and the Sinde horse, upon their standards and appointments, and the 12th and 25th regiments of Bombay native infantry, upon their colours and appointments, the word 'Hyderabad, 1843.' The regiment of Sinde horse is on its present establishment permanently attached to the army of Bombay." The policy, however, which is indicated in the despatch of the governor-general, as to the use which was to be made of this important victory, was not yet to be carried out. The Ameers of Sinde must have been well aware that when they drew the sword under such circumstances they flung the scabbard away, as all further friendly treaty was vain with princes who had availed themselves of the very time of completing amicable negotiations to break through even the common courtesies of hostile nations.

Partial effects of this victory.

Superior numbers of the enemy.

Notwithstanding the very severe loss sustained by the enemy, they were still greatly the superior in point of numbers to their opponents, and were headed by chiefs who could not hope for any satisfactory terms from the conqueror. The foremost of these was Hoche Mohammed Seedee, one of the Beloochee chiefs, who, along with Meer Shere Mohammed, the chief of Meerpoor, was looked upon as the great promoter of the war. The deeply-rooted impression which had been left on the public mind by the disasters in Afghanistan, was manifest from the exaggerated and dubious rumours that speedily superceded the rejoicings with which the news of the defeat of the Sindean army under the walls of Hyderabad had been received, so that on the departure of the May mail from India, an ill-defined rumour was prevalent, that in a second engagement the British army under Sir Charles Napier had sustained a decided defeat.

Desperate position of their leaders.

Rumours of the defeat of the British.

The small number of the forces under Sir Charles's

command, amounting only to about 6000 men in all, prevented his occupying any extended positions beyond the walls of Hyderabad, which he had taken possession of immediately after the victory at Meeanee. The British commander, accordingly, learned, towards the middle of March, that the enemy were once more mustering in numbers not greatly inferior to the force he had already defeated after so arduous a struggle. On the 23d of March, the British General writes from the camp at Hyderabad, announcing to Lord Ellenborough the junction of Major Stack, on the previous day, with the 3d cavalry, the 8th native infantry, and Major Leslie's troop of horse artillery. This reinforcement sufficed to supply the losses sustained in the previous victory, and to restore confidence to the British army, in the prospect of again encountering the same determined foe. Sir Charles, accordingly, states in the same despatch to Lord Ellenborough, that the enemy then lay within six miles of his camp, in such force that they had already begun attacking his camels, and he was resolved to go in pursuit of them on the morrow, and attack them wherever they might be found.

Small numbers of the British forces.

Opportune reinforcement.

The Sindeans had posted themselves in a strong and well-selected position, little more than four miles distant from the British camp,—a strong evidence of the very restricted operations to which the British General had been reduced, in consequence of the small number of his available forces. The position of the enemy was nearly similar to that which had formerly proved so difficult to surmount. They had again posted themselves on the banks of the Fullalie, whose dry channel in the previous engagement afforded them such valuable protection. But they had improved not only on the experience acquired in the former defeat, but strengthened their position with a degree of skill never before manifested by them in their wars, and which was considered as affording undoubted indications of the presence of European councillors in their army.

Position of the Sindeans.

Skilful strengthening of their position.

CHAP. XVII. A. D. 1843.

Advance of the British forces.

Sir Charles put his forces in motion early in the morning, and by the time they had advanced about two miles, they descried the enemy about a mile and a half in advance. Approaching within twelve hundred yards of their position, the troops were drawn up in order of battle, and advanced in echellon of regiments to the attack.

Battle of Dubba.

About nine o'clock the British guns opened their fire on the enemy's position, producing considerable confusion in their centre, where considerable bodies were observed to move to the left, apparently unable to sustain the cross fire of the artillery. The position of the enemy was nearly a straight line. The nullah which formed its front consisted of two deep parallel ditches, one twenty feet wide and eight feet deep, the other forty-two feet wide and seventeen feet deep, further strengthened by banks and escarpments of the most formidable character. These skilful preparations, however, proved altogether ineffectual in arresting the victorious career of the British army, manned though they were by defenders immensely outnumbering them, and inferior in courage and daring to no native force which had yet attempted to withstand the British arms. When the centre of the enemy was seen to give way under the severe fire of the British artillery, Major Stack, at the head of the 3d cavalry, supported by a body of native horse, charged them on their left flank, crossing the nullah, and bearing down upon them with such determined valour, that they gave way before them, and were pursued for several miles with great slaughter.

Effect of the British artillery.

Sir Charles Napier's despatch.

Sir Charles Napier thus describes the action in the centre and on the left, at the period when the cavalry on his right charged the left flank of the enemy, and drove them from the field :—"While this was passing on the right, Her Majesty's 22d regiment, gallantly led by Major Poole, who commanded the brigade, and Captain George, who commanded the corps, attacked the nullah on the left with great gallantry, and, I regret to add, with considerable loss. This brave battalion marched up to the nullah under a heavy fire of matchlocks, without returning a shot till within forty paces of the intrenchment, and then stormed it like British soldiers. The intrepid Lieutenant Coote first mounted the rampart, seized one of the enemy's standards, and was severely wounded while waving it and cheering on his men. Meanwhile the Poonah horse, under Captain Tait, and the 9th cavalry, under Major Story, turned the enemy's right flank, pursuing and cutting down the fugitives for several miles. Her Majesty's 22d regiment was well supported by the batteries commanded by Captains Willoughby and Hutt, which crossed their fire with that of Major Leslie. Then came the 2d brigade, under command of Major Woodburn, bearing down into action with excellent coolness. It consisted of the 25th, 21st, and 12th regiments, under the command of Captains Jackson, Stevens, and Fisher, respectively. These regiments were strongly sustained by the fire of Captain Whitley's battery, on the right of which were the 8th and 1st regiments, under Majors Brown and Clibborne; these two corps advanced with the regularity of a review up to the intrenchments, their commanders, with considerable exertion, stopping their fire, on seeing that a portion of the Sinde horse and 3d cavalry in charging the enemy had got in front of the brigade. The battle was decided by the troop of horse artillery and Her Majesty's 22d regiment." The enemy stood their ground well, and defended themselves with the utmost bravery, in so much so that the victory has been pronounced by experienced officers, as perhaps the most sternly contested of any in which British troops have ever been engaged in India. The 22d regiment, which had to bear the brunt of the fight, alone lost six officers and 145 men, out of about 300 British killed and wounded. It is in the despatch, in which Sir Charles Napier announced this victory to the governor-general, that he refers to the capture of some prisoners (only eight in all) as a subject of congratulation, since it affords some indications of amelioration in the barbarous and exter-

Storming of the enemy's intrenchments.

Decisive charge.

Brave stand of the Sindean troops.

Capture of prisoners.

CHAP. XVII. A. D. 1843. minating mode of warfare which their enemies had forced upon them. The reference to this apparently trivial circumstance, in the flush of victory, is a pleasing and honourable trait in the gallant British leader. "It gives me," says he, "great satisfaction to say, that some prisoners have been taken, and though the number is small, it is still some advance towards a civilized mode of warfare; for I cannot help thinking that the desperate resistance generally made by wounded Beloochees has arisen from their own system of warfare, which admits of no quarter being given in action. We are at present employed in collecting the wounded Beloochees within our reach, in order to render them medical assistance."

Humanity of the British leader.

Bravery of the British officers.

Many acts of intrepid valour were displayed in this severe contest. The general exposed himself during the whole fight, moving with the utmost coolness where the enemy's shots were flying thickest, and his example was not lost on his officers. Eleven pieces of ordnance and nineteen standards were taken, Hoche Mohammed Seedee, and three other chiefs, fell in the battle, the Beloochee force was entirely routed and dispersed in every direction, and Meer Shere Mohammed fled into the desert, taking his family with him, and attended by only forty followers, whom he could attract to his service. The British commander is said to have been welcomed with joy by the inhabitants of the country, who had suffered so much from the fickle rule of the Ameers, that they testified the utmost anxiety to be assured that Sinde was to be annexed to the British possessions. By the 5th of April, Sir Charles Napier announced to Lord Ellenborough, that the important fortress of Oomercote had opened its gates to a British force sent against it.

Reception of the victors.

Policy of the Directory.

The termination of the Afghan war had been characterized by a practical manifestation of the policy repeatedly dictated to the governor-generals of India, by the Home Directory, to refrain from all further augmentation of the vast possessions of British India. The conquests in Sinde, however, which so speedily followed those in Afghanistan, originated under totally different circumstances, and showed how little reliance can be placed on theories of policy, however well grounded they may appear to be. The following is the opinion, expressed at the time, of this new acquisition, though longer experience has tended greatly to modify the first ideas of its value:—"It is a country without the possession of which our boundary of the Indus cannot be compact. Neither can the navigation of that river be considered safe while an independent, and now hostile power, keeps possession of either bank of the Delta. It is productive, and under our management, may be made more productive, and the troops required to keep possession of it, will cost us nothing; the country itself will maintain them with ease. It lies within a week's reach of our western capital. Its high roads do not run through impassable defiles like the Bolan and the Khyber and the Khoord Cabul; they consist of magnificent streams, which our steam flotilla may traverse with speed and safety. It lies open to the sea, and troops, ammunition, and supplies may be poured in with ease. It is a plain and may be defended with little difficulty, for there will soon be no enemy more formidable than the heat."

Inconsistency of the annexation of Sinde.

Ideas entertained of its value.

Considerable annoyance was experienced from the proceedings of such of the Ameers and Beloochee chiefs as were still at large, and especially from those of Shere Mohammed, who was making the most determined exertions to bring another army into the field. Meanwhile the conduct of the chiefs, who had been confided in as friendly to the British was even more alarming than the threatening position assumed by the defeated leaders. Ali Moorad, who had received repeated marks of favour from the British occupants of Sinde, when put in possession of Kyrpoor, appears to have concluded that whatever other territories the British wrested from the Ameers, would in like manner be transferred to him. As a further evidence of favour, the guns captured at

Continued opposition of the Ameers.

Alarming conduct of British allies.

CHAP. XVII. A. D. 1843.

All Moorad.

Meeanee had been made over to him, and so soon as he found that his extravagant expectations were not to be realized, he surrendered the artillery captured by our forces to Shere Mohammed.

Alarming rumours.

The near approach of the hot season, when Europeans are exposed to such severe sufferings if forced to take the field, led to much anxiety as to the movements of that chief. The most extravagant and contradictory rumours were afloat. Shere Mohammed was said to be already mus-

Shere Mohammed

tering a more numerous force, than either of those which had sustained such complete defeat; while great and well-grounded apprehensions of sickness were entertained within the camp at Hyderabad, where the troops were hemmed in by low marshy grounds and the river, in a situation in which any of the native epidemics could hardly fail to prove fearfully destructive if it should break

Extravagant reports of his forces.

out among them. By letters from the camp in the month of May, Shere Mohammed is said to be at Sukkurind, at the head of 40,000 men, and a large park of artillery; marauding parties of the Beloochees were moving about, and committing great depredations on the live stock, so that great fears were entertained of a scarcity of provisions. Most of these rumours, however, proved to be grossly exaggerated. A despatch of Sir Charles Napier's, dated 17th June 1843, announces an attack on Meer

Total rout of Shah Mohammed's force, and his capture.

Shah Mohammed at the head of 2000 men, in which that leader was captured, and his whole forces totally routed. So complete was their panic, that the British forces suffered much more from the heat than from any opposition offered by the enemy. In order to take them by surprise, Lieutenant-colonel Roberts, who commanded the detachment sent against the ameer, moved without any camp equipage, and the sufferings consequent on their exposure

Sufferings from the heat.

to the heat are described as very severe. "The heat," says Colonel Roberts, "after nine o'clock, became most awful, and the whole detachments were much distressed." Two European artillery-men died of *coup de soleil* while on the march. In a despatch, dated two days later, the commander refers to the sudden change to extraordinary heat, and reports the death of a lieutenant, five sergeants, and forty-four men, by the same sudden and terrible stroke.

Shere Mohammed.

While Lieutenant-colonel Roberts proceeded against Meer Shah Mohammed, other parties had been sent out to attempt to surround Shere Mohammed, where he kept the field at the head of a force of about 10,000 men. The ameer finding that several strong columns were advancing on him from different quarters, attempted to strike a sudden and decisive blow, by attacking Captain Jacob, who, at the head of a comparatively small force, had been sent to intercept him, in case of his attempting to retreat to the desert. The whole of the ameer's forces were totally routed and broken, dispersing in every direction, and leaving their guns and standards in the hands of the victors. Meer Shere Mohammed fled with only ten horsemen; but though intercepted in his attempt to gain the desert, he succeeded in effecting his escape.

His forces routed.

His escape.

Insalubrity of the climate.

The apprehensions as to the great danger to be dreaded from the effects of the climate, and position of the troops in Sinde, were speedily realized. Every account brought more alarming intelligence of the ravages of disease, in so much so that before the cold season began to set in, there was a period of about six weeks, during which it is doubtful if, out of a force of 10,000 men, 3000 could have taken the field had any sudden attack occurred; and the whole outposts in the country, exposed to the mountain Beloochees in front, and effectually cut off, by the Indus and the desert beyond it, from resources in the rear, were in such a condition, that a sudden and well-directed descent upon them by the scattered tribes of Beloochees, might have destroyed them to a man. Fortunately before this deadly enemy had prostrated for a time the conquerors of Sinde, the point of danger had been removed to an entirely different scene.

Critical position of the British.

News of general peace.

The letters brought home by the Indian mail of October 1843, announced the satisfactory intelligence that our

CHAP. XVII

A.D. 1843.

Eastern empire, which had been for many months the object of such lively and painful interest, had ceased to furnish any incidents worthy of comment or discussion. The Bombay Times, of 6th September, remarks:—"Letters are now received with as much punctuality from Sukkur and Hyderabad, as from any of the most tranquil quarters of our empire. The tidings brought by them are stale, flat, and unprofitable; no fighting, no adventure, no stir of any description, and even rumours of danger have died away. The chiefs, it is said, are daily coming in, and the country becoming pacified with most unexpected celerity." Accounts, however, from the north continued to indicate a very different state of things. Afghanistan furnished frequent reports of distraction and threatened outbreaks. Cabool was in the most disturbed state. Dost Mohammed Khan was stated to be exercising a most arbitrary and despotic sway, and directing his acts of oppression in an especial manner against such of the native chiefs as had manifested any friendly feeling towards the British during their occupation of that country. Ameenoollah Khan had been imprisoned and put in chains, and upwards of twenty of the chief men of Cabool were reported to be held in durance by the same chief. At Candahar, Sufter Jung was stated to be in close confinement with chains, while his adherents and advisers were every where seeking safety by flight. In all this, however, British interests were no further concerned than in so far as there might be any risk of the disturbances extending to the provinces under our control. The wise line of policy dictated to Lord Ellenborough, had happily freed Britain from the necessity of interfering in these intestine quarrels, though it could not but be felt that it was more difficult to throw off the responsibility of having to a great extent occasioned such division and strife among that brave but turbulent race.

Peaceful state of Sinde. — *Disturbed state of the northern frontier.* — *Disorders in Afghanistan.* — *Wise policy of abandoning Afghanistan.*

New source of apprehension.

Another country, beyond the northern boundaries of our Indian empire, was, however, already furnishing cause for apprehension. In the extensive regions comprehended between the Sutledge and the Indus, considerable symptoms of disturbance were already apparent, and we find official correspondents, early in the following year, giving expression to congratulations that the affairs of British India were in such a tranquil state, as to permit the attention of the governor-general and his council to be devoted to the crisis which seemed to be approaching both in the Punjaub and at Gwalior. So early as the month of August, the whole troops in the Agra district received orders to keep themselves in readiness to move at a moment's notice, and it was reported that an army of observation was to be immediately formed on the Sutledge, under the immediate command of Sir Hugh Gough. The causes which finally led to a sanguinary revolution in the Punjaub, may be thus briefly recapitulated. Upon the death of Runjeet Sing, in 1839, his favourite wife—after she had ascended the funeral pile, where, along with three others, she was burnt with his corpse—called to her Kurruck Sing, the deceased rajah's son and heir, along with Dhian Sing, his favourite minister, and placing the dead rajah's hand in that of his son, she required the latter to swear to protect and favour his father's minister, and by the like solemn oath bound the minister to be faithful to his new master. Kurruck Sing immediately ascended the throne. He was well-affected to the British government, but possessed none of the talent or energy requisite for so difficult a post. He had not occupied the throne four months when he died, as has been stated in a previous chapter, not without strong suspicions of poison, and his son and heir, Now Nehal Sing, who should have succeeded him, was killed by the falling of a beam, as he returned from the funeral pile on which his father's corpse was consumed. These successive deaths were both ascribed to the intrigues of Runjeet Sing's favourite minister; and, after some difficulty, chiefly arising from the opposition of one of the widows of the latter prince, he succeeded in his long-cherished project of placing Shere Sing on the throne. During the

CHAP. XVII. — A. D. 1843.

Disturbances in the Punjaub.

Army of observation on the Sutledge.

Causes of revolution.

Kurruck Sing.

Sudden death of Kurruck and Nehal Sing.

Shere Sing.

CHAP. XVII.

A. D. 1843.

frequent agitations and alarms that ensued, the British government continued to watch their proceedings with some anxiety; but after a time, the affairs of the kingdom, which chiefly owed its formation to the abilities of Runjeet Sing, seemed to acquire some degree of order and settlement, and ceased to attract special attention from the government of India, occupied as it soon was with objects of more pressing interest. Meanwhile causes of mutual difference and dislike were springing up between the new rajah and his ambitious minister. Various reasons are assigned for these. The Hon. Mr. Osborne, who describes Shere Sing as a fine, manly-looking fellow, adds that he had become especially obnoxious to his minister, in consequence of his attachment to European manners, and his friendly inclinations toward the British, whom Dhian regarded with rancorous hate. This, however, was probably only one of the causes of dissension, sufficing to indicate their disagreement on all questions of general policy. It is stated that the rajah had abandoned himself to the indolent and dissolute habits which have so frequently been the ruin of the native dynasties of India, and that during the frequent dissensions which prevailed between Shere Sing and his powerful minister, the latter went so far as to reproach him in open durbar with his dissipation and excesses.

Anxiety of the British government.

Internal sources of difference.

Accusations charged against the rajah.

Whatever might be the ostensible grounds of dispute, however, the previous character of the minister leaves little room to doubt, that the real ground of offence was the interference with his policy, and the curtailment of his power. He accordingly organized a conspiracy for the assassination of the rajah, in which he enlisted several of the chief sirdars of the court. His influence with the army is sufficiently apparent, from the time chosen for executing his base design. The rajah had appointed a general review of his troops, at the Dusserah festival, and Ajeet Sing, who is described as an effeminate-looking youth, was selected as the assassin. The Delhi Gazette thus describes the assassination and the fearful slaughter

Ambitious character of his minister.

Plots against the rajah.

that followed, in which the faithless originator of it perished, the victim of his own plot:—"Dhian Sing made the arrangement by proposing to the rajah to inspect Ajeet Sing's troops, which he said he would do the following morning, and orders were accordingly issued. On the rajah's arrival on the parade-ground, he found fault with the appearance and condition of some horsemen purposely placed to attract attention, when Ajeet Sing became saucy, words ran high, and, drawing a pistol from his bosom, he shot Shere Sing through the head, the ball having entered his right temple. General Ventura and his party attacked the murderer, but, being opposed by a powerful body of troops, were defeated. Ajeet Sing cut up the rajah's body, placed his head on a spear, and on entering the town met Prince Purtaub Sing's (Shere's son) suwarie, which was immediately attacked, and the prince killed; the palace was taken, and Dhulleep Sing, the only remaining son of Runjeet Sing, a lad ten years old, proclaimed to the throne. The treasury was thrown open, and the troops paid up their arrears. Troops were sent off to guard all the ghauts, and all the opposite party (except Ventura, who escaped) were made prisoners. Ajeet Sing, after having killed Shere Sing, was returning to the fort, and met Dhian; he told him he had done the deed, and asked him to return; he got into Dhian's carriage, and when they got near the gate of the fort, Ajeet Sing stabbed Dhian, and sent his body to his brother and son, Sookhet and Heera Sing. These two individuals surrounded the city with their troops, and the people within continued plundering all night. In the morning, Heera Sing having entered the fort, seized Ajeet Sing, Lena Sing, and others, and having put them to death, exposed their heads in the plain, and threw their bodies into the bazaar. Dhulleep Sing has been put on the guddee, and Heera Sing made vizeer. Six hundred men were slaughtered on both sides."

Assassination of Shere Sing.

Dhulleep Sing proclaimed rajah.

Assassination of Dhian Sing.

Consequent slaughter.

This barbarous deed was enacted on the 15th September 1843, and by means of it the nominal authority was

CHAP. XVII. — A. D. 1843.

Rajah Dhulleep Sing.

vested in Dhulleep Sing, a child of ten years old, while the real power, which the unprincipled minister destined for himself, had passed into the hands of Heera Sing, who was now both commander of the army and vizier, and was therefore actual ruler, so long as he could retain the fidelity of the army.

Disturbances at Gwalior.

Meanwhile the affairs of the court of Gwalior, which had so long occasioned anxiety and distrust, were at length brought to a crisis. Confusion and anarchy prevailed there, one party deposing another, and successive chiefs struggling for power, while the country was left at the mercy of licentious and undisciplined troops. The British government being bound by its treaties with the late rajah to protect his successor, and preserve his territories unviolated, the governor-general could no longer overlook the fact that the conduct of the authorities of Gwalior involved a virtual violation of the treaty. Lord Ellenborough accordingly immediately ordered the advance of troops, sufficient, as he said, "to obtain guarantees for the future security of its own subjects on the common frontier of the two states, to protect the person of the rajah, to quell disturbances within his highness's territories, and to chastise all who shall remain in disobedience." This was rendered the more imperative by the tender age and helpless position of the rajah, which exposed him to the double danger of being made a tool in the hands of his enemies, and the nominal source of wrongs to his friendly allies. Notwithstanding the preparations which had been made for such an emergency, the commander-in-chief, Sir Hugh Gough, was met by a much stronger and more determined opposition than he had anticipated.

Obligations of the British government.

Helpless position of the rajah.

Advance of the British army.

The army had left Agra betwixt the 12th and 18th December, and continued steadily to move on. On the 17th, General Valiant with the advance arrived at Dholpoor. On reaching the ghaut opposite Kentree, the Dholpoor Rajah paid a visit of ceremony to the governor-general, and his visit was returned by Lord Ellenborough and the commander-in-chief the following day. On the 22d they moved, with the head-quarters of the 4th brigade, on Kentree ghaut, and the advance, under Sir J. Thackwell, crossed to the right bank of the river. On the 23d the second division crossed the Chumbul, and proceeded seven miles in the direction of Hingonah, where the advance was encamped. The road was extremely difficult, winding through a steep ravine, scarcely more than twenty feet wide, which a determined enemy might for a time have obstructed almost with impunity. Here for five days the force halted to take rest and counsel. Bappoo Seetoleah had been despatched from Gwalior on the 22d, and on the following day had an audience with the governor-general, when it was believed in camp that every thing was settled—the Maharanee and the Sirdars having, it was said, agreed to the terms proposed. On the 24th, the Gwalior Vakeels had a further interview of some duration with the governor-general. Many of the more respectable inhabitants, who came from Gwalior on a visit to the camp, conceived the idea of resistance out of the question. Preparations were made to receive the Maharanee, who was expected in camp on the 28th, with sufficient pomp and circumstance for the rank she held, and audience to which she was about to be admitted. The governor-general, who had originally been moderate in his demands, requiring the restoration of the Mama Sahib and his friends—the surrender of the Khasjee Walla, and dismissal of his partisans—the exchange of certain portions of country, so as to improve the condition of the mutual frontier—and the disbanding of the mutinous portion of the troops—finally demanding the entire revision of the military establishment, and the surrender of the park of artillery, brought into existence about forty years since by Dowlut Rao Scindia, and regarded as the palladium of the state. This was looked upon as implying the entire destruction of the army, and surrender of the independence of the nation. There is every reason, however, to believe that, through-

Negotiations.

Rumours of agreement.

Increased demands of the governor-general.

Attachment of the natives to their artillery.

CHAP. XVII. A. D. 1843.

Insincerity of the durbar.

out, the professions of the Mahratta durbar were hollow and insincere—that so soon as it was found that their earlier and delusive propositions were insufficient to arrest our progress, it was resolved to offer the most determined resistance. Further negotiations appear to have been resorted to merely to gain time.

Difficulties of diplomatic intercourse with the natives.

It must always, indeed, form one of the greatest difficulties in the diplomatic intercourse between civilized and semi-barbarous nations, the difficulty of knowing what dependence can be placed on the most solemn asseverations, and professions of good faith. Among highly civilized nations the value of national credit and unblemished honour is so thoroughly appreciated, that it is rare indeed for the most unprincipled diplomatist to set it at defiance; but among the native princes of India such faithless proceedings as those of the Ameers of Scinde have been too frequent to excite very great surprise.

Formidable character of the Mahratta army.

The formidable character and position of the Mahratta army, however, had not been anticipated from the vacillating character of their councils. The country generally exhibits features offering great natural obstacles to the operations of disciplined forces, being intersected with

Difficulties of the country.

numerous deep and almost impassable ravines, and gullies, affording great facilities for the irregular tactics of an undisciplined army. It was only by the unceasing labours of the sappers, that a practicable passage was effected for the army under Sir H. Gough; and after passing the Koharee river in three columns, at points considerably distant from each other, the whole British

Position of the British army.

army took up their position by eight o'clock on the morning of the 29th of December 1843, about a mile in front of Maharajpoor. The Mahrattas had occupied the ground during the previous night, taking up their position with such skill as compelled the commander to alter the disposition of his forces. Seven regiments of Mah

Battle of Maharajpoor.

ratta infantry were ranged in front, each corps having four guns attached to it, which opened on the advanced forces of the British as they took up their ground. The

39th regiment of British infantry advanced gallantly to the charge, supported by the 56th native infantry. The Mahrattas stood their ground with great bravery, and the British forces sustained a severe loss, their guns doing great execution as they advanced. But no native force has ever been able to withstand the determined charge of the British bayonet. They drove them from their guns into the village, but there the Mahrattas again rallied, and a most sanguinary conflict ensued. After discharging their matchlocks, they flung them from them, and fought hand to hand with the most determined courage. Meanwhile General Valiant had led on his brigade, and succeeded in taking Maharajpoor in reverse. Twenty-eight guns were captured by this combined movement, but the Mahrattas still stood their ground; nor was their strong position taken till nearly every one of its defenders had been left dead on the spot. The same determined resistance was experienced at every point. They had thrown up entrenchments, and planted their guns with great skill, and in nearly every case the gunners were bayonetted at their posts, without attempting to fly. The consequence was, the loss of the British, both in officers and men, was unusually great. "I regret," says Sir H. Gough in his despatch to the governor-general, "I regret to say that our loss has been very severe, infinitely beyond what I calculated on; indeed, I did not do justice to the gallantry of my opponents. Their force, however, so greatly exceeded ours, particularly in artillery, the position of their guns was so commanding, they were so well served, and determinedly defended, both by their gunners and their infantry, and the peculiar difficulties of the country giving the defending force so great advantages, that it could not be otherwise." As usual, where the native forces have displayed peculiar steadiness and skill, it was found that they had had the benefit of more experienced assistance; though they required no aid to give effect to their undisciplined courage and gallant daring. There was found to have

Bravery of the Mahrattas.

Combined movement of the British.

Determined resistance.

Severe loss of the British.

Advantages of their opponents.

CHAP. XVII. A.D. 1843.

European deserters.

been a considerable number of the Company's discharged native infantry, as well as one or two European deserters among the Mahratta troops. One of the latter, it is stated, named Berry, from the 2d European regiment, had, when he fell, his lighted port-fire in his hand, and fired off his gun, sweeping away fifteen men.

Auxiliary force under Major-general Grey.

At the same time that the commander-in-chief crossed the Sindean frontiers, Major-general Grey led an auxiliary force, by order of the general, towards Punniar, twelve miles south-west of Gwalior, to co-operate with the main body, and place the Mahratta army between two forces, acting in concert. The immense excess of the Mahrattas in point of numbers over the British forces, however, was such as enabled them to counteract this plan of mutual co-operation. A body of 12,000 men, with a large complement of guns, &c. was detached to arrest the progress of Major-general Grey, whose whole force did not amount to a fourth of that number. The two armies met on the 29th of December, in the vicinity of the fortified village of Mangore, near Punniar, where the Mahrattas had taken up a strong position, and were able to begin the attack at considerable advantage, by assaulting the cumbrous baggage trains which necessarily accompany an Indian army. Towards four o'clock the commander observed the enemy taking up a strong position on a chain of hills to the east of his camp, and resolved on an immediate attack. By a judicious disposition of his forces, the enemy were assailed simultaneously on the centre and left, and completely broken. The whole guns, twenty-four in number, were captured, and all their ammunition, with a portion of treasure, were taken. The action did not close till nightfall, which prevented the pursuit of the enemy, and enabled them to carry off many of their killed and wounded. Their loss, however, had been very severe, and the occurrence of two such decisive victories on the same day, as those of Maharajpoor and Punniar, effectually put an end to further resistance.

Great disparity in point of numbers.

Battle of Punniar.

Capture of the Mahratta artillery.

CHAP. XVII.

A.D. 1843

Misconception of the Mahratta power.

Private accounts would lead to the idea, which the acknowledgments in the despatch of the commander-in-chief may seem in some degree to confirm, that little or no opposition had been anticipated either by the governor-general or the commander-in-chief, both of them probably conceiving that the presence of so large and effective a British force would have sufficed to overawe the rebellious Maharattas. The commander-in-chief's staff, with the ladies of his family, are said to have been quietly proceeding towards Maharajpoor when the Mahratta guns opened upon them. Lord Ellenborough was likewise present with the ladies of his family; nor was he forced to quit his dangerous and exposed position, until the well-served Mahratta guns gave proof that the elephants of the governor-general, towering over the rear of the 39th regiment, as it took up its position on the field, had become the objects towards which their fire was directed.

Surprise of the commander-in-chief, and governor-general.

Effects of the victories of Maharajpoor and Punniar.

The result of the two great battles of Maharajpoor and Punniar destroyed the hopes not only of the mutinous Mahrattas at Gwalior, but of numerous restless malcontents of Hindostan, and had the effect of diffusing tranquility throughout our whole Eastern empire, where the existence of so many races still very partially amalgamated, and curbed in their predatory habits and love of plunder only by the well-directed force of disciplined authority, renders the whole empire peculiarly sensitive to such indirect but powerful influences. The rajah was installed with great ceremony at Gwalior, in presence of the governor-general, the commander-in-chief, and an immense assemblage of native chiefs. An eye-witness of the imposing ceremonial describes the juvenile rajah as seated beneath a gorgeous canopy of gold, see-sawing his legs beneath his throne according to the fashion of listless schoolboys, seemingly altogether indifferent to the import of the stately proceedings in which he was made to bear so prominent a part.

Installation of the rajah.

Meanwhile, however, great and increasing dissatisfac-

CHAP. XVII.

A.D. 1844.

Dissatisfaction at Lord Ellenborough's government.

-tion was expressed in many quarters at the government of Lord Ellenborough. His fondness for military display, and for such pompous exhibitions of vice-regal grandeur as that which immediately followed the victories over the insurgent Mahratta forces, were occasionally manifested in a way that seemed somewhat inconsistent with the wonted gravity of British rule, and frequently led to the neglect of the civil service and the internal government of India, which were, in fact, his principal duties as governor-general. His whole course of procedure was erratic, and opposed to the definite policy by which the Directory had sought to avert a continued system of aggression on the surrounding native states, and to consolidate the vast possessions over which their rule was only very partially and imperfectly extended.

Motives for choosing him as governor-general.

In the choice of Lord Ellenborough as governor-general, they had calculated on the probable weight of his influence as a civilian, in carrying out measures in accordance with the peaceful line of policy they were anxious to see pursued; but the character of the proceedings of his successor suffice to show that the false glitter of military glory was more seductive to an inexperienced civilian than to a military veteran.

Contrast of the proceedings of his successor.

A writer, in the Indian Mail of December 1844, remarks of the latter: "The quiet, unostentatious demeanour of the governor-general has doubtless had its share in tranquilizing India. He has given no intimation, in public at least, of an intention to quit the Presidency, where he is employed in occupations which befit a man of peace." In addition,

Causes of the irritation of the Directory.

Lord Ellenborough had excited the indignation of the Directorship of the East India Company, by a line of conduct which seemed to imply that he was too well assured of the favour of the Duke of Wellington and the British Cabinet, to greatly concern himself as to the approval his proceedings might meet with from the Directory. Great, therefore, was the sensation created both in India and at home by the sudden recall of Lord Ellenborough, in consequence of the vote of the Court of

Directors, in the exercise of their legitimate power, not only without consulting with the government, but in direct opposition to its expressed opinions. The Duke of Wellington openly and severely censured their proceedings, and it was generally anticipated that an act so embarrassing, if not humiliating, to the government, and to one of its chief leaders, would have led to still more direct collision in the choice of a successor. Such anticipations, however, were not realized. Sir Henry Hardinge was selected to succeed to the important trust. On the 6th of May 1844, he was appointed by the Court of Directors to the office of Governor-general of India, and the Crown immediately confirmed the choice. This bold and decisive measure of the Court of Directors excited much discussion and considerable diversity of feeling for a time; but the contrast between the wonted proceedings of Lord Ellenborough, and the unobtrusive course adopted by Lord Hardinge, speedily reconciled all parties interested in the affairs of India to the change of its governor-general.

Threatened collision of the Government and Directory.

Sir Henry Hardinge appointed governor-general.

The country of the Mahrattas still continued in a disorderly and disturbed state, and required the presence of a considerable military force to hold the insurgents in check. Many of the difficulties unquestionably originated in the complicated system of Eastern policy, which has grown out of the circumstances by which a trading company gradually assumed the character of conquerors and rulers. The system of permitting independent or subsidiary princes or rajahs to sway their feeble sceptres within the British dominions has been again and again condemned, as leading to the very worst consequences. British rulers have thereby frequently been unwillingly made accessory to acts of which they could not approve, while such petty principalities become the centres of constant intrigue, and generally prove a barrier to any effectual measures for the improvement of the people.

Unsettled state of the Mahrattas.

Evils of subsidiary native rulers.

The Punjaub continued for many months to furnish the most novel and unexpected phases of intelligence.

State of the Punjaub.

CHAP. XVII.

A.D. 1844.

Influence of the unsettled state of its government.

Each successive Indian mail brought accounts of new revolutions, massacres, assassinations, and capricious plottings and schemings, leading to no definite settlement, and keeping up a feeling of anxiety and alarm throughout our whole Indian possessions, where so many elements exist ready to be excited into opposition and rebellion upon every new impediment or threat of danger to British supremacy in India. The army of observation was still maintained on the banks of the Sutledge. From time to time, skirmishes, assaults, and sorties, diversified the dull routine of their passive line of duty, and kept their leaders on the alert. Politicians meanwhile continued to discuss the propriety of the annexation of the Punjaub to our Indian empire to round its northern frontiers, and free it from the endless anxiety which must result from the proceedings of a barbarous people in a constant state of revolution, maintaining undisciplined hordes of fierce soldiery ready to take advantage of the first necessity that might induce us to recall the army on their frontier, to make aggressive inroads on our own possessions.

Schemes of annexation proposed.

CHAPTER XVIII.

War in the Punjaub.

Disturbed state of the Punjaub—Influence of British policy—Disparaging misconception of the Seiks—Their origin and singular character—Acts of aggression—War proclaimed by the British—The battle of Moodkee—Its uncertain results—Battle of Ferozeshah—Critical position of the British from insufficient supplies—Assault on their convoy—Victory of Aleewal—Its important results—General estimation of Indian policy—Battle of Sobraon—Passing of the Sutledge—Terms of peace—Proud bearing of the vanquished.

CHAP. XVIII. A.D. 1845.

Revolutionary state of the Punjaub.

FOR many months the news of each mail which brought to England information of the state of her vast Eastern possessions, consisted chiefly of confused and alarming rumours of revolutions, tumults, and assassinations, in the Punjaub. A large military force was concentrated on the banks of the Sutledge, and war was regarded as inevitable, however long circumstances might delay the commencement of hostilities. Very great misapprehension however existed, both in India and at home, as to the character of the Seiks, or the nature of the preparations requisite for meeting any aggressions on their part. So universal was the conviction of their disorderly and mutinous state, and of the want of any supreme power among them, calculated to secure that unanimity of action on which the success of great military movements so

CHAP. XVIII. — A.D. 1845.

Misapprehension of the Seik character.

greatly depends, that when at length the long-expected collision took place, both the governor-general and the commander-in-chief were found to have overlooked some of the most indispensable preparations for war. Considering the lengthened period during which war with the Seiks had been anticipated, and arrangements made for resisting their threatened aggressions, it may well astonish the reader to learn of the difficulties which impeded the first operations of Lord Gough, when hostilities were commenced by the Seik army crossing the Sutledge. Captain Cunningham, the impartial historian of the Seiks, seeks to show that, although the first aggressive movements were undoubtedly made by the Seiks, the English were guided rather by the selfish and short-sighted policy which guards against immediate danger, than by the wise and honourable foresight which should direct the councils of an enlightened nation when dealing with a people esteemed in every respect their inferiors. He accordingly conceives, that the open preparations for defensive, and, if necessary, for offensive measures, which marked the progress of the army of observation, appeared in the estimation of a rude people as so many acts of designed hostility deliberately marshalled for an attack on their country whenever a convenient opportunity offered. "The same defective apprehension," says this intelligent officer, "which saw no mark of hostility in collecting boats for bridges across a boundary river, and which paid no regard to the effect on a rude people, with more to fear than to hope, of displaying an army with no road before it except that to Lahore, also led the confident English to persevere in despising or misunderstanding the spirit of the disciples of Govind to an extent which almost proved fatal to the continuity of their triumphs. In 1842, the Seiks were held to be unequal to cope with the Afghans, and even to be inferior in martial qualities to the population of the Jummoo hills. In 1845, the Lahore soldiery was called a 'rabble' in sober official despatches, and although subsequent

Nature of English policy.

Misconstruction of their defensive preparations.

Presumed inferiority of the Seiks.

descriptions allowed the regiments to be composed of the yeomanry of the country, the army was still declared to be daily deteriorating as a military body. It is, indeed, certain that English officers and Indian Sepoys equally believed they were about to win battles by marching steadily and by the discharge of a few artillery shots, rather than by skilful dispositions, hard fighting, and a prolonged contest. The English not only undervalued their enemy, but they likewise mistook the form which the long-expected aggressions of the Seiks would assume. It was not thought that the ministry, or even that the army would have the courage to cross the river in force, and to court an equal contest; the known treasonable views of the chiefs, and the unity and depth of feeling which possessed the troops, were equally disregarded, and it continued to be believed that a desultory warfare would sooner or later ensue, which would require the British to interfere, but which would still enable them to do so at their own convenience. Thus boats for bridges, and regiments and guns, the provocatives to a war, were sufficiently numerous; but food and ammunition, and carriage and hospital stores, such as were necessary for a campaign, were all behind at Delhi or Agra, or still remained to be collected." Thus, at the very time when a soldier was at the head of the Indian government, distinguished for military experience as well as for courage and sound judgment, the army was allowed to take the field in every way worse provided and equipped than had been the case when an inexperienced and rash civilian held the office of governor-general.

Confidence of an easy victory.

Disregard of the unanimity of the Seik soldiers.

Inefficient provision of supplies.

Origin of the Seiks.

It is only now that the peculiar characteristics of the Seiks is coming to be rightly understood. Their origin is traced back to the sixteenth century, when Narruk and Govind, two Khutree prophets, obtained a few converts to a doctrine of religious and social reform, from among the peasants of Lahore and the southern banks of the Sutledge. It is not necessary here, however, to trace their history further than to remark, that by the time

CHAP. XVIII. — A. D. 1845.

the Seiks came into collision with the British empire in India, they had grown into a powerful nation, bound together not only by social and political ties, but by the still more stringent bonds of a common creed. The history of Mohammedanism furnishes sufficiently striking evidence of the remarkable effects that may result from such a source, and the Seiks, or "disciples," appear to be not a whit behind the zeal of the Arabian prophet's followers in their devotion to the "Khalsa," or chosen people. The powerful influence of such a bond of union can hardly be over-rated, though unfortunately the true character of the Seik nation was completely misunderstood previous to the war; and the source, as well as the spirit, of the continued revolutions which created such alarm on the northern frontiers of British India, entirely escaped the notice of the sagacious diplomatists who conducted our intercourse with that people. It would now seem, that so far from the revolutions and tumults being the evidences of disunion and revolt among that people, they originated in their devotion to the essential elements of their singular polity, while it was the successive rulers who struggled with them and sought alliances with the English that were in reality mutineers and rebels against the state. Ambition, and the desire for unlimited power, overcame in the minds of successive Seik rulers the earlier bonds of good faith as members of the Khalsa, but the very cause of alienation between the rulers and the people, supplied a stronger bond of union to the latter. The soldiery talked of themselves as pre-eminently the "Punt'h Khalsajee," or congregation of believers, and their leaders were awed into submission by the resolute spirit with which they were animated. It was by this united and resolute body that successive revolutions were brought about, and one ruler after another dethroned and put to death. Doubtless such a state of things was well calculated to excite uneasiness among neighbouring states, and might perhaps be justly enough characterized both as fanatic and revolutionary,

Points of resemblance to the Mohammedans.

Ignorance of the source of their revolutions.

Faithlessness of the Seik rulers.

Spirit of the Seik soldiers.

Just cause of anxiety.

according to more civilized notions of social and political compacts. Nevertheless, it was manifestly something altogether different from the mutinies and rebellions of an ordinary army of hireling soldiery, such as has most commonly opposed our arms in the East, where the only bond which secures the services of the soldiery is the prospect of pay and plunder. The aspect of the Seik army, indeed, is one altogether singular, and to a disinterested observer remarkably interesting. The soldiery are seen animated by a lofty spirit of patriotic daring, aided doubtless by the fierce fire of fanatic zeal, while the Seik leaders are frequently found secretly counteracting their brave efforts, and more effectually checking their success than the enemy by whom they are openly opposed. "The object of Lal Sing and Tej Sing," says Captain Cunningham, in describing some of the early proceedings of the Seiks, "was not to compromise themselves with the English by destroying an isolated division, but to get their own troops dispersed by the converging forces of their opponents. Their desire was to be upheld as the ministers of a dependent kingdom by grateful conquerors, and they thus deprecated an attack on Ferozepore, and assured the local British authorities of their secret and efficient good will. But these men had also to keep up an appearance of devotion to the interests of their country, and they urged the necessity of leaving the easy prey of a cantonment untouched, until the leaders of the English should be attacked, and the fame of the Khalsa exalted by the captivity or death of a governor-general. The Seik army itself understood the necessity of unity of counsel in the affairs of war, and the power of the regimental and other committees was temporarily suspended by an agreement with the executive heads of the state, which enabled these unworthy men to effect their base objects with comparative ease. Nevertheless, in the ordinary military arrangements of occupying positions and distributing infantry and cavalry, the generals and inferior commanders acted for themselves,

Singular aspect of the Seik army

Lal and Tej Sing.

Double dealing of the Seik leaders.

Wise policy of their army.

CHAP. XVIII.

A. D. 1845.

and all had to pay some respect to the spirit which animated the private soldiers in their readiness to do battle for the commonwealth of Govind. The effects of this enthusiastic unity of purpose in an army, headed by men not only ignorant of warfare, but studiously treacherous towards their followers, was conspicuously visible in the speediness with which numerous heavy guns and abundance of grain and ammunition were brought across a large river. Every Seik considered the cause as his own, and he would work as a labourer as well as carry a musket; he would drag guns, drive bullocks, lead camels, and load and unload boats with a cheerful alacrity, which contrasted strongly with the inapt and sluggish obedience of mere mercenaries, drilled, indeed, and fed with skill and care, but unwarmed by one generous feeling for their country or their foreign employers." Here, therefore, the Sepoy force, by which so much has been accomplished for British power in India, was opposed by native soldiers, actuated by all the inspiring influences of patriotic feeling, as well as by the wilder fire of fanatic zeal. It was doubly incumbent on British India to lean for safety on the indomitable energy and valour of her European troops, who could alone be safely entrusted to cope with such a foe.

Manifestations of enthusiastic zeal.

Ready co-operation of the Seiks.

Superiority to the Sepoys.

First acts of aggression.

The first acts of aggression were characteristic of the uncivilized race, with whom collision had become inevitable. Intelligence reached Ferozepore, on the 5th of December 1845, that a party of Seiks had crossed the river and carried off fifty of our camels, with which they had retraced their steps, in order to distribute the booty in their own camp. Several parties of their horse continuing on the left bank, it was deemed advisable, on the same day on which this information arrived, to send off a strong force for the purpose of protecting some military stores that were on their way from Dhurrumkote to Ferozepore. On the 6th, three days' supplies were ordered to be laid in by the different regiments, and it was supposed that operations against the Seiks would be

CHAP. XVIII.

A. D. 1845.

commenced without delay. This, however, was not the case, the measure being merely one of precaution. On the 8th, the Seik troops began to appear in large masses on the right bank of the Sutledge, and their numbers, on the two following days, greatly increased: they had a good deal of artillery with them, which they were constantly discharging. From opposite Ferozepore, they occupied the bank of the river as far as Hurreekee ghaut, some thirty-five miles distance, and considerable parties of their cavalry crossed to the left bank, within their own territory, however, and commenced cutting off supplies, in a manner which led to some apprehensions in Ferozepore that their store of firewood and bhoosa might run short. Between the 8th and 11th, thirty mor camels were carried off to the other side of the river, making a total of eighty. On the 9th or 10th, the main body that was opposite Ferozepore changed its position, and moved a little up the river towards the Hurreekee ghaut, and a rumour having found its way to Ferozepore on the night of the 10th, that the Seiks were crossing in numbers, the assistant quartermaster-general, Captain Egerton, was directed to reconnoitre early on the following morning. He went, escorted by a squadron of the 8th light cavalry, and on approaching the point at which he expected to find them, he left the escort behind and rode forward with two orderlies. The Seiks were seen to be busy collecting boats about eight miles from Ferozepore, a little beyond our boundary line, and they no sooner perceived Captain Egerton than they fired upon him. It would appear that the men who fired were on the left bank of the river, and only some 600 yards from Captain Egerton. Certain it is that the balls fell around him, and that the moment the firing commenced by the party, the alarm was given in the whole camp, the drums beat to arms, and the whole of the force turned out with great rapidity. It was now evident to all that a Punjaub campaign was inevitable. The whole of the ladies in the governor-general's camp took their depar-

Mustering of the Seiks on the Sutledge.

Harrassing manœuvres.

Preparation of the Seiks for passing the river

CHAP. XVIII. — A.D. 1845.

ture and returned to Umballah, while orders were issued to troops in all directions to move up with all practicable haste to the frontier. The governor-general paid a hurried visit to Loodiana on the 11th, and inspected the troops there, returning afterwards to Sirhind. The Seik vakeel at Loodiana received his *congé*, while the British agents at the Lahore court were ordered to withdraw themselves—a sure sign of coming hostilities. By the 12th, about 10,000 Seiks had crossed the river, with twenty-seven guns, at a place about twelve miles from Ferozepore, and on the 13th they were seven miles from that station, crossing, men and guns, by a bridge of boats, with great activity and expedition. The ladies at Ferozepore were now all sent into the fort for safety, and an immediate attack was expected." On the 13th, the governor-general issued a proclamation, setting forth the views and objects of the British government, and summoning all the chiefs and sirdars of the protected territories to render faithful service against the common enemy.

Signs of inevitable hostilities.

Proclamation of the governor-general.

Startling rumours of war.

The Indian mail of February 1846, which brought advices from Bombay up to the 3d of the previous month, startled all who sympathized in the fortunes of our Eastern empire, with the news that a great battle had been fought on the banks of the Sutledge, while it left the result in the utmost uncertainty. Rumour immensely exaggerated the number of the Seik forces, and the public mind, still agitated with the recollection of the early reverses in Afghanistan, was thrown anew into a state of feverish excitement by the nature of the information thus imperfectly conveyed.

Defence of Ferozepore.

Sir John Littler had been left with a body of 7000 men to defend the exposed post of Ferozepore. This was menaced by the overwhelming forces of the Seiks, but the British commander showed a resolute and undaunted front, and boldly led out his little force to give them battle. Had the Seik leaders been as resolutely bent on the defeat and extermination of their opponents as the faithful Khalsa were, it may be well doubted if all the heroism of this isolated division of the British army would have saved it from destruction. But Lal Sing and Tej Sing were both probably in greater dread of their Seik followers than of their British foes, and regarded the chances of victory with greater dread than the prospect of a defeat, which would disperse the enthusiastic Seiks, who, amid all their fickleness to their leaders, maintained an unimpeachable fidelity to their faith. A battle, however, had become inevitable, and the rumours which conveyed the first uncertain and contradictory reports, magnified the difficulties experienced by the British forces into renewed disasters, if not absolute defeat. Doubts and fears, however, were speedily dissipated by the arrival of well-authenticated news of victory, though purchased at a cost which served to temper the rejoicings at a partial triumph with many fears.

Vacillating policy of the Seik leaders.

The first battle fought with the Seiks took place on the 18th of December, between the Ambala and Loodiana divisions of the British army, which had been prudently united by order of Lord Hardinge, and a detachment of the Seik army under Lal Sing. The two armies met at Moodkee, twenty miles from Ferozepore, and the Seiks immediately begun the attack. The whole forces under Lord Gough amounted to about 11,000, while the Seiks were estimated at 30,000 men, with forty guns. This estimate, however, appears to have greatly exaggerated their number, and Captain Cunningham even inclines to doubt if they much exceeded the British in numbers. The Seiks were repulsed with severe loss, and seventeen of their guns were taken; but the British learned in the battle of Moodkee the valour of the enemy they had to contend with. The forces of Lord Gough, already too few, were reduced by a loss of 215 killed and 657 wounded; among the former of whom were Major-generals Sir Robert Sale and Sir John M'Caskill. The commander-in-chief remarks in his despatch: "The troops were in a state of great exhaustion, principally

Battle of Moodkee.

Relative numbers of the forces engaged.

Severe loss of the victors.

CHAP. XVIII. — A.D. 1845. from the want of water, which was not procurable on the road, when, about three P.M., information was received that the Seik army was advancing; and the troops had scarcely time to get under arms, and move to their positions, when the fact was ascertained. I immediately pushed forward the horse artilery and cavalry, directing the infantry, accompanied by the field batteries, to move forward in support. We had not proceeded beyond two miles when we found the enemy. They evidently had either just taken up this position, or were advancing in order of battle against us. To resist their attack, and to cover the formation of the infantry, I advanced the cavalry under Brigadiers White, Gough, and Mactier, rapidly to the front, in columns of squadrons, and occupied the plain. They were speedily followed by the five troops of horse artillery, under Brigadier Brooke, who took up a forward position, having the cavalry then on his flanks. The country is a dead flat, covered at short intervals with a low, but, in some places, thick jhow jungle, and dotted with sandy hillocks. The enemy screened their infantry and artillery behind this jungle, and such undulations as the ground afforded; and, whilst our twelve battalions formed from echellon of brigade into line, opened a very severe cannonade upon our advancing troops, which was vigorously replied to by the battery of horse artillery under Brigadier Brooke, which was soon joined by the two light field batteries. The rapid and well-directed fire of our artillery appeared soon to paralyse that of the enemy; and, as it was necessary to complete our infantry dispositions without advancing the artillery too near to the jungle, I directed the cavalry under Brigadiers White and Gough to make a flank movement on the enemy's left, with a view of threatening and turning that flank, if possible. With praiseworthy gallantry, the 3d light dragoons, with the 2d brigade of cavalry, consisting of the body guard and 5th light cavalry, with a portion of the 4th lancers, turned the left of the Seik army, and, sweeping along the whole

Meeting of the armies.

Character of the country.

Tactics of the British cavalry.

rear of its infantry and guns, silenced for a time the latter, and put their numerous cavalry to flight. Whilst this movement was taking place on the enemy's left, I directed the remainder of the 4th lancers, the 9th irregular cavalry, under Brigadier Mactier, with a light field battery, to threaten their right. This manœuvre was also successful. Had not the infantry and guns of the enemy been screened by the jungle, these brilliant charges of the cavalry would have been productive of greater effect. When the infantry advanced to the attack, Brigadier Brooke rapidly pushed on his horse artillery close to the jungle, and the cannonade was resumed on both sides. The infantry, under Major-generals Sir Harry Smith, Gilbert, and Sir John M'Caskill, attacked in echellon of lines the enemy's infantry, almost invisible amongst wood and the approaching darkness of night. The opposition of the enemy was such as might have been expected from troops who had every thing at stake, and who had long vaunted of being irresistible. Their ample and extended line, from their great superiority of numbers, far outflanked ours; but this was counteracted by the flank movements of our cavalry. The attack of the infantry now commenced, and the roll of fire from this powerful arm soon convinced the Seik army that they had met with a foe they little expected. Their whole force was driven from position after position with great slaughter, and the loss of seventeen pieces of artillery, some of them of heavy calibre; our infantry using that never-failing weapon, the bayonet, whenever the enemy stood. Night only saved them from worse disaster, for this stout conflict was maintained during an hour and a half of dim starlight, amidst a cloud of dust from the sandy plain which yet more obscured every object."

Formidable position of the Seik artillery.

Resolute opposition of the Seiks.

Driven from position with great loss.

The experience acquired by this victory taught the British leaders the necessity for bringing every available means to bear against their brave and resolute enemy. When it became evident that the Seiks were marching in force towards the Sutledge, bent on assuming the initia-

Experience acquired by the victory.

CHAP. XVIII. A. D. 1845.

Novel arrangement of the governor-general.

tive in the war, Lord Hardinge proceeded to the expected scene of contest, and made the somewhat novel arrangement of tendering his services as an officer to the commander-in-chief, and assuming the position of second in command under his own subordinate. By the arrangements which he effected the largest possible force was placed at the command of Lord Gough, to oppose the Seik invaders. According to the governor-general's despatch, the Seik army, which occupied the intrenched camp at Ferozeshah, amounted to 60,000 men, while the British forces opposed to them did not exceed 17,000 men. Captain Cunningham, however, in his history of the Seiks, altogether questions the evidence of this very great disparity. He states the forces of the enemy as amounting perhaps to 40,000; but he acknowledges that their numbers were further increased by numerous bodies of undisciplined horse, while their artillery included 150 pieces, served with the most desperate valour, as well as with great coolness and skill. "At Ferozeshah," says Captain Cunningham, "the larger calibre and greater weight of metal of the mass of the Seik artillery, and consequently the superiority of practice relatively to that of the field guns of the English, was markedly apparent in the condition of the two parks after the battle. The captured cannon showed scarcely any marks of round shot or shells, while nearly a third of the British guns were disabled in their carriages or tumbrils." Victory achieved against such a force, by an army composed in part of native mercenaries, and dependent for its sustaining energy and perseverance on the British officers and the European troops, composing a minority of its limited numbers, requires no exaggeration to stamp it with the character of a splendid achievement.

Estimates of the Seik forces.

Their great superiority in artillery.

New position taken up by the Seik army.

The Seik army encamped in the form of a horseshoe around the village of Ferozeshah, about ten miles from the scene of their partial defeat at Moodkee, and nearly at an equal distance from Ferozepore. On the 21st of December a junction was effected with Sir John

Littler's division, and an immediate attack on the enemy's position was resolved upon; but considerable delay occurred before the arrangements could be completed, and it was within an hour of sunset before the assault was commenced. Captain Cunningham, who fails not in his history to paint the evidences of bravery and military skill displayed by the Seiks, as well as to expose proceedings of their opponents not likely to be detailed in official gazettes, remarks of the proceedings on the evening of the 21st December:—"The confident English had at last got the field they wanted; they marched in even array, and their famed artillery opened its steady fire. But the guns of the Seiks were served with rapidity and precision, and the foot soldiers stood between and behind the batteries, firm in their order, and active with their muskets. The resistance met was wholly unexpected, and all started with astonishment. Guns were dismounted, and their ammunition was blown into the air; squadrons were checked in mid career; battalion after battalion was hurled back with shattered ranks, and it was not until after sunset that portions of the enemy's position were finally carried. Darkness, and the obstinacy of the contest, threw the English into confusion; men of all regiments and arms were mixed together; generals were doubtful of the fact or of the extent of their own success, and colonels knew not what had become of the regiments they commanded, or of the army of which they formed a part. Some portions of the enemy's line had not been broken, and the uncaptured guns were turned by the Seiks upon masses of soldiers oppressed with cold, thirst, and fatigue, and who attracted the attention of the watchful enemy by lighting fires of brushwood to warm their stiffened limbs. The position of the English was one of real danger and great perplexity; their mercenaries had proved themselves good soldiers in foreign countries as well as in India itself, when discipline was little known, or while success was continuous; but in a few hours the five

An attack resolved upon.

Unexpected resistance of the Seiks.

Confusion of the British forces.

Dangerous and critical position

CHAP. XVIII. — A.D. 1845.

thousand children of a distant land found that their art had been learnt, and that an emergency had arisen which would tax their energies to the utmost. On that memorable night the English were hardly masters of the ground on which they stood; they had no reserve at hand, while the enemy had fallen back upon a second army, and could renew the fight with increased numbers. The not imprudent thought occurred of retiring upon Ferozepore; but Lord Gough's dauntless spirit counselled otherwise, and his own and Lord Hardinge's personal intrepidity in storming batteries, at the head of troops of English gentlemen and bands of hardy yeomen, eventually achieved a partial success and a temporary repose."

Meditated retreat.

Causes assigned for the victory.

Even the victory of the following day, the candid historian of the Seiks ascribes fully as much to the faithless pusillanimity of their leaders, as to the skill and valour of the English. The latter were ill provisioned, and suffering from cold and thirst. They were led to the attack on the evening of the 21st, exhausted with fatigue, and unrelieved from hunger and thirst. When night put a temporary close to the action, there was still neither food nor drink to be had, and the exhausted soldiers had to lie down on their arms during that dreadful night, in a state that might well induce the bravest to despond. Even after they were involved in the fearful struggle of the morrow, they were exposed at one time to the most imminent risk from the failure of the artillery ammunition. With every acknowledgment which candour may induce the generous historian to concede, it cannot be questioned that the indomitable valour of British soldiers was never more strongly displayed than on the bloody field of Ferozeshah. Whatever amount of their success may have been really due to the infidelity of the Sikh leaders, the whole procedure of the British commanders was entirely independent, if not in ignorance of it. The most credulous, indeed, could attach little value to the co-operation of men who were

Disheartening condition of the British forces.

Indomitable force of British valour.

heading an overwhelming force against which victory had already been twice won with such difficulty and severe losses. During the battle, both on the 21st and 22d, the governor-general commanded the left wing of the army, while Lord Gough personally conducted the right.

Pause in the battle of Ferozeshah.

The night that intervened between the commencement and the close of the battle of Ferozeshah must have been one of the deepest anxiety to the British commanders; nor were even the exhausted troops allowed to slumber in peace, where they lay, with their arms at their side, ready with the dawn to renew the bloody struggle. "Night fell," says Lord Gough in his despatch, "while the conflict was everywhere raging. Although I now brought up Major-general Sir Harry Smith's division, and he captured and long retained another part of the position, and her Majesty's 3d light dragoons charged and took some of the most formidable batteries, yet the enemy remained in possession of a considerable portion of the great quadrangle, whilst our troops, intermingled with theirs, kept possession of the remainder, and finally bivouacked upon it, exhausted by their gallant efforts, greatly reduced in numbers, and suffering extremely from thirst, yet animated by an idomitable spirit. In this state of things the long night wore away. Near the middle of it, one of their heavy guns was advanced, and played with deadly effect upon our troops. Sir Henry Hardinge immediately formed her Majesty's 80th foot and the 1st European light infantry. They were led to the attack by their commanding officers, and animated in their exertions by Lieutenant-colonel Wood, who was wounded in the outset. The 80th captured the gun, and the enemy, dismayed by this counter-check, did not venture to press on further. During the whole night, however, they continued to harass our troops by fire of artillery, wherever moonlight discovered our position. But," adds the commander-in-chief, "with daylight came retribution. Our infantry formed in line, supported on both flanks by horse artillery whilst a fire was opened

Precarious position of the British.

Sufferings and losses.

Harrassing service during the night.

CHAP. XVIII.

A. D. 1845.

The battle resumed.

from our centre by such of our heavy guns as remained effective, aided by a flight of rockets. A masked battery played with great effect upon this point, dismounting our pieces, and blowing up our tumbrils. At this moment Lieutenant-general Sir Henry Hardinge placed himself at the head of the left, whilst I rode at the head of the right wing. Our line advanced, and, unchecked by the enemy's fire, drove them rapidly out of the village of Ferozeshah and their encampment; then, changing front to its left, on its centre, our force continued to sweep the camp, bearing down all opposition, and dislodged the enemy from their whole position. The line then halted, as if on a day of manœuvre, receiving its two leaders, as they rode along its front, with a gratifying cheer, and displaying the captured standards of the Khalsa army. We had taken upwards of seventy-three pieces of cannon, and were masters of the whole field."

Complete success of the British.

Capture of the enemy's cannon.

Opportune victory.

The victory was most opportune, and might well fill the minds of all with joy and gratitude. Nevertheless, though a complete, it was not a decisive victory. The Seiks had, indeed, been routed and driven from the field. "For twenty-four hours," says Lord Gough in his despatch, "not a Seik has appeared in our front. The remains of the Khalsa army are said to be in full retreat across the Sutledge, or marching up its left bank, towards Hurreekeeputhur, in the greatest confusion and dismay. Their camp is the scene of the most awful carnage, and they have abandoned large stores of grain, camp equipage, and ammunition." However satisfactory such evidences of flight might be, the narration of the commander-in-chief betrays the fact, that the exhausted victors had been unable to follow in pursuit of the retreating foe, and that the flying Seiks, who might have been scattered, and irretrievably broken by a timely pursuit, had been allowed to cross the Sutledge at their leisure, and to reform on the opposite bank. The loss of the British was very severe. The official despatches state 694 killed

Exhausted state of the victors.

and 1721 wounded, or 2415 in all, amounting to about a seventh of the whole British force in the field.

Reception of the news of victory.

When the details of the victory of Ferozeshah were reported to the British public through the official despatches, the news was received with gloomy forebodings rather than with the wonted exultations that follow in the train of victory. The commander-in-chief's conduct was made the subject of unsparing criticism. He was blamed alike for his ignorance of the formidable condition of the Seik army, and for the hardihood with which he had exposed his army to such fearful odds, and incurred the risk of defeat as well as the certainty of such severe loss as his despatches acknowledged. Even his tactics in the field were freely discussed and censured, and the excited critics seemed disposed to make the British general responsible alike for the bravery of the Seiks, and for his own inferiority in numbers and artillery. The want of proper supplies both of provisions and ammunition was unquestionably an oversight of the gravest nature, though not justly chargeable on the commander-in-chief. From the want of the latter, the British forces were compelled to remain inactive while the Seiks recrossed the Sutledge in great force, and proceeded to construct a bridge-head by which to secure the passage of the river. The commander-in-chief feared to oppose these proceedings of his beaten foe, lest an attack on his part should bring on another general engagement, while they were so deficient in ammunition that their artillery must have been nearly useless, and they were even prevented from attacking some petty forts which still overawed the neighbouring population, and checked the march of convoys and detachments whose approach was so indispensable to them.

Unreasonable censures.

Consequences of insufficient supplies.

Difficulties of the conquerors.

The battle of Ferozeshah threatened to prove a fruitless victory. By the capture of Dhurmkot, the safe transit of grain to the army was rendered more secure; but the march of the large convoy of guns, ammunition, and treasure, for want of which the British forces had been compelled to remain inactive, was not accomplished

CHAP. XVIII. A.D. 1845.

Partial triumph of the Seiks.

without a severe skirmish, in which 137 were killed or wounded, and, what was felt still more, several of the British were left prisoners in the hands of the Seiks. "Every beast of burden," says Captain Cunningham, "which had not got within sight of Loodiana, or which had not, timorously but prudently, been taken back to Jugraon, when the firing was heard, fell into the hands of the Seiks, and they were enabled boastfully to exhibit artillery store carts as if they had captured British cannon.

Relief of Loodiana.

"Loodiana was relieved; but an unsuccessful skirmish added to the belief, so pleasing to the prostrate princes of India, that the dreaded army of their foreign masters had at last been foiled by the skill and valour of the disciples of Govind, the kindred children of their own soil. The British sepoys glanced furtively at one another, or looked towards the east, their home; and the brows of Englishmen themselves grew darker as they thought of struggles rather than triumphs. The governor-general and commander-in-chief trembled for the safety of that siege train and convoy of ammunition, so necessary to the efficiency of an army which they had launched in haste against aggressors, and received back shattered by the shock of opposing arms. Sir Harry Smith, the leader of the beaten brigades, saw before him a tarnished name after the labours of a life, nor was he met by many encouraging hopes of rapid retribution. The Seiks on their side were correspondingly elated; the presence of European prisoners added to their triumph."

Critical position of the British forces.

Triumphant anticipations of the Seiks.

The Seiks seemed about to retrieve their losses, and march victorious into the British dominions. Golab Sing was chosen their leader, and with the unanimity and vigour of determined councils and a definite plan of action, the Khalsa forgot their previous losses and boasted that the British army should be annihilated, or driven in dishonour from the field. But the time was gone when unity in the councils of Seiks could secure their triumph over the conquerors of the East. Sir Harry Smith was the first to give the check to those who had momentarily tarnished his well-won reputation. With the reinforcements he had received, which raises the forces under his command to 11,000 men, he marched on the 28th of January 1846, determined to give the enemy battle. The commander-in-chief had reinforced him on the 26th both with cavalry and guns, and on the following day he occupied their deserted position. The Seiks retreated about ten miles, towards the banks of the Sutledge, where they were joined by a reinforcement, which raised their forces to fully 15,000 men, and they took up a position, with the village of Aleewal on their left, and threw up banks of earth to protect their line in front, and oppose additional impediments to their assailants. Sir Harry Smith's narrative of the battle which followed is characterised by singular coolness and precision "As I neared the enemy," he remarks in his despatch, "the ground became most favourable for the troops to manœuvre, being open and hard grass land. I ordered the cavalry to take ground to the right and left by brigades, thus displaying the heads of the infantry columns, and as they reached the hard ground I directed them to deploy into line. Brigadier Godby's brigade was in direct echellon to the rear of the right, the Shekawatte Infantry in like manner to the rear of my left. The cavalry in direct echellon on, and well to the rear of both flanks of the infantry. The artillery massed on the right, and centre and left. After deployment I observed the enemy's left to outflank me, I therefore broke into open columns and took ground to my right: when I had gained sufficient ground, the troops wheeled into line; there was no dust, the sun shone brightly. The manœuvres were performed with the celerity and precision of the most correct field-day. The glistening of the bayonets and swords of this order of battle was most imposing, and the line advanced. Scarcely had it moved forward 150 yards, when, at ten o'clock, the enemy opened a fierce canonade from his whole line. At first his balls fell short, but quickly reached

Operations of Sir Harry Smith.

Position of the Seiks at Aleewal.

Manœuvring of the British forces.

Coolness in presence of the enemy.

CHAP. XVIII. A. D. 1846.

us. Thus upon him, and capable of better ascertaining his position, I was compelled to halt the line, though under fire, for a few moments, until I ascertained that by bringing up my right and carrying the village of Aleewal, I could with great effect precipitate myself upon his left and centre."

Capture of the village.

The capture of the village proved an easier task than was anticipated. The holders of the post speedily gave way before the determined charge of the British brigades. The Seiks stood their ground on the field, however, with the most resolute valour, and even threatened at one time to out-flank the right wing of the British. "The enemy," says Sir Harry Smith, "fought with much resolution; they maintained frequent rencounters with our cavalry hand to hand. In one charge of infantry upon Her Majesty's 16th lancers, they threw away their muskets, and came on with their swords and targets against the lance." But their brave resistance proved unavailing. They made several ineffectual attempts to rally but at length were driven across the Sutledge, with immense loss, and in the utmost confusion and terror. The whole artillery of the enemy was either captured or destroyed, 52 guns remained in the hands of the victors. The whole of the Seik camp, baggage, stores of ammunition, grain, and nearly every thing brought into the field remained as the spoils of the conquerors, and the commander exultingly exclaims in his despatch, "I am unwont to praise when praise is not merited, and I here must avowedly express my firm opinion and conviction that no troops in any battle on record ever behaved more nobly."

Valour of the Seiks.

Their total defeat.

Importance of the victory of Alleewal.

The victory of Aleewal was one of the most important that has ever been gained by the British forces in India. The number engaged was indeed comparatively small. But the effect of this opportune defeat of the Seiks, at the very time when they were rejoicing in united councils and exulting in anticipated victory, completely overthrew their whole schemes. Golab Sing instead of attempting to rally his defeated forces upbraided them with the rashness and folly of hoping to overcome the conquerors of India, and immediately opened negotiations with the English commander. Another battle, however, had to be fought, and another victory won, before the British conquerors could dictate terms to the hardy and resolute race whom they encountered on the northern boundaries of British empire in the East. The terms offered by the British leaders in reply to the negotiations of Golab Sing were such as must be acknowledged to afford reasonable evidence of the integrity of their motives in entering on the contest. They disclaimed all desire of annexation or conquest, and intimated their readiness to acknowledge a Seik sovereignty in Lahore, so soon as the army should be disbanded. But, however reasonable and even generous such terms might appear to those that dictated them, they struck at the very root of the Khalsa's dreams of supremacy and integrity, and if the historian of the Seiks is to be relied upon, the battle of Sobraon, which followed these abortive negotiations, was fought with a perfect understanding with the faithless rajah, that in case of British arms being once more victorious, the Seik army should be openly abandoned by its own government, and that the victors should pass the Sutledge unchecked, and march without opposition to the capital. The conditional terms of a negotiation thus mutually agreed upon by belligerent leaders, preparatory to once more appealing to the arbitration of battle, are probably unparalleled in the history of ancient or modern warfare. They suffice, however, to show the singular footing on which our vast Eastern empire rests, and how difficult it is to judge of the proceedings of those to whom its conduct is committed, or by whom its progress is opposed, according to any standard of European policy.

Negotiations opened by Golab Sing.

Reasonable terms offered by the British.

Singular negotiations which preceded the battle of Sobraon.

The Seiks, meanwhile, were not wanting in preparation for renewing the contest. The brilliant achievement of Sir Harry Smith's division at Aleewal, had been conducted with an amount of boldness, caution, and military

Preparations of the Seiks.

CHAP. XVIII — A.D 1846.

skill, worthy of a brave and experienced commander, and it had been productive of the happiest effects on British interests in India, nevertheless it was only the victory of a division. Its moral effect in confirming the courage and high faith in the destiny of British arms of the one party, and in moving the opposite party to despondency and dread, was doubtless great. Fortune had deserted the Khalsa. Defeat and subjection already depended over them, and divided councils were hurrying on their fate. A decisive victory was, however, still needed, ere the British could force the passage of the Sutledge, and become masters of the Punjaub. Prompt measures were indispensably required. "To subjugate the Punjaub in one season, by force of arms, was a task of difficult achievement and full of imminent risks. The dominion of the English in India hinges mainly upon the number and efficiency of the troops of their own race which they can bring into the field. But besides this, it was felt that the minds of men throughout India were agitated, and that protracted hostilities would not only jeopardize the communications with the Jumna, but might disturb the whole of the north-western provinces, swarming with a military population which is ready to follow any standard affording pay or allowing plunder, and which already sighs for the end of a dull reign of peace. Bright visions of standing triumphant on the Indus and of numbering the remotest conquests of Alexander among the provinces of Britain, doubtless warmed the imagination of the governor-general; but the first object was to drive the Seiks across the Sutledge by force of arms, or to have them withdrawn to their own side of the river by the unconditional submission of the chiefs and the delegates of the army; for, until that were done, no progress could be said to have been made in the war, and every petty chief in Hindostan would have silently prepared for asserting his independence, or for enlarging his territory on the first opportunity." This critical state of things in our Indian empire has long been felt by the few earnest

Moral effect of Sir Harry Smith's victory.

Necessity for prompt measures.

The unconditional submission of the Seik chiefs indispensable to peace.

thinkers, on whom the false glare of military glory exercises no blinding influence. Even the short-sighted policy of self-interested motives has sufficed to awaken the Home Directory to a sense of it; and for many years each successive governor has been warned against any further aggressive movements, or the annexation of additional domains to the already unwieldly empire which owns our sway. It is easier, however, to dictate a theory of policy, than to control the events by which it must ultimately be modified. Some of the later wars have perhaps been justly characterized as aggressive, notwithstanding the necessity which frequently compelled the first movements which were thought to render the rest indispensable to the safety of our former possessions, but others of them were reluctantly begun, and only boldly and effectively carried on as the safest and swiftest means of preventing their recurrence.

General conviction of the necessity for consolidation in India.

Difficulty of carrying out this policy.

While Sir Harry Smith was manœuvring his division, and the indispensable reinforcements were being brought up from the rear, the main body of the Seiks had been no less active in their preparations for the final struggle. They had gradually brought the greater part of their available force into an intrenched camp formed on the left bank of the Sutledge, and which comprised within its irregular ramparts the whole possessions they still held by force of arms in the British dominions. Their force was estimated at 35,000 fighting men, though Captain Cunningham inclines to think that such an estimate greatly exceeds the truth. He adds, moreover, that their works exhibited marked evidence of a want of unity of design, the soldiers doing every thing and the leaders nothing. It is probable, however, that in this the candid historian of the Seiks ascribes to want of unity of purpose what should rather be ascribed only to imperfect knowledge and inferior skill. It was hardly to be expected that an experienced military engineer, as he is known to be, should find in the Seik intrenchments a satisfactory display of engineering skill, even although

Active preparations of the Seiks.

Number of the Seiks.

Defective nature of their works.

CHAP. XVIII. A.D. 1846.

there were European officers of acknowledged experience and great bravery in command of some of their divisions. But the defeat at Aleewal, which had proved so welcome and so important in its results to the British, had a corresponding depressive effect on the Seiks. Some of the older and more experienced Seik chiefs looked forward with sad forebodings to the approaching contest, and one favourite leader, Sham Sing, announced to the desponding Khalsa his resolution to meet death in the foremost ranks that engaged with the enemy, and so to offer himself up as a sacrifice on behalf of the sacred commonwealth, threatened with such impending danger.

Their despondency.

Confidence in the British camp.

Confidence and joyful anticipations of triumph prevailed throughout the British camp. The victory of Aleewal had restored the faith of the Sepoys in the fortune of British arms, while the European forces exulted in the anticipation of victory. Substantial grounds of confidence had meanwhile been supplied by the arrival of the heavy ordnance, with abundant ammunition and stores. The obstacles which had impeded their earlier operations, and made victory so difficult and so hardly won, no longer existed to check the bold advance of the British forces, or the daring impetuosity of the commander-in-chief. The 10th of February, only twelve days after the victory of Aleewal, was fixed for storming the Seik position, and driving them beyond the river. Through indifference or neglect, the British had allowed a post of observation of some importance to fall into the hands of the Seiks, and the surprising of this was determined upon as the first proceeding. Long before dawn, the whole British camp was in motion, and an advanced party was ordered to drive in the enemy's pickets. The additional gloom of a thick haze added to the darkness of the night, as the British forces silently advanced to assume the initiative in the contest, but the posts of observation, both at the Sobraon and in front of Koodeewalla, were found unoccupied, though held by a strong force on the previous day. The Seiks were every where

Arrival of heavy ordnance and abundant supplies.

Preparations for storming the Seik position.

taken by surprise, and beat loudly to arms throughout their wide intrenchments on both sides of the river. The English heavy ordnance had been arranged in masses on some of the most commanding points opposite the enemy's intrenchments, and at sunrise the batteries opened upon them. For three hours the deadly shower of iron hail poured down upon the Seik forces within their intrenchments, mingled with the more deadly shells, that scattered death on every side as they fell. But the Seik intrenchments bristled with the heavy ordnance which had told so effectively against the light fieldpieces that formed the sole British artillery in the earlier engagements, and the sun's level rays hardly pierced through the clouds of sulphurous smoke that loomed over the scene of deadly strife. "Our battery of nine-pounders," says the commander-in-chief in his despatch, "opened near the little Sobraon, with a brigade of howitzers formed from the light field batteries and troops of horse artillery, shortly after daybreak. But it was half-past six before the whole of our artillery fire was developed. It was most spirited and well directed; but notwithstanding the formidable calibre of our iron guns, mortars, and howitzers, and the admirable way in which they were served, and aided by a rocket battery, it would have been visionary to expect that they could, within any limited time, silence the fire of seventy pieces behind well-constructed batteries of earth, plank, and fascines, or dislodge troops covered either by redoubts or epaulements, or within a treble line of trenches. The effect of the cannonade was, as has since been proved by an inspection of the camp, most severely felt by the enemy; but it soon became evident that the issue of this struggle must be brought to the arbitrement of musketry and the bayonet. At nine o'clock, Brigadier Stacey's brigade, supported on either flank by Captains Horsford's and Fordyce's batteries, and Lieutenant-colonel Lane's troop of horse artillery, moved to the attack in admirable order. The infantry and guns aided each other correlatively.

Surprise of the Seiks.

Deadly effect of the heavy artillery.

Powerful batteries of the Seiks.

Charge of British brigades.

CHAP. XVIII. A. D. 1846.

The former marched steadily on in line, which they halted only to correct when necessary. The latter took up successive positions at the gallop, until at length they were within three hundred yards of the heavy batteries of the Seiks; but, notwithstanding the regularity, and coolness, and scientific character of this assault, which Brigadier Wilkinson well supported, so hot was the fire of cannon, musketry, and zumboorucks, kept up by the Khalsa troops, that it seemed for some moments impossible that the intrenchments could be won under it; but soon persevering gallantry triumphed, and the whole army had the satisfaction to see the gallant Brigadier Stacey's soldiers driving the Seiks in confusion before them within the area of their encampments." The resistance of the Seiks was terrible. The deadly fire of their muskets and well-served artillery, mowed down the advancing lines of the British, and compelled them to give way. The first assailants were repulsed, but they rallied and returned to the charge, and, supported by the advance of the second division, after a severe struggle, they obtained possession of some of the enemy's most important batteries in the front. Still the Seiks stood their ground. No panic seized these hardy enthusiasts, though thus assailed within their own intrenchments. One point after another was forced. The sappers levelled spaces sufficient for the cavalry to pour into their camp, and sustain the efforts of the infantry who had borne the brunt of the deadly struggle. But still the Seiks fought with all the wild fury of despair. Single batteries still held out, and hundreds fell in the attempt to arrest their persevering efforts to retrieve the hopeless fortunes of the Khalsa. "The interior," says Captain Cunningham, "was filled with courageous men, who took advantage of every obstacle, and fought fiercely for every spot of ground. The traitor, Tej Sing, indeed, instead of leading fresh men to sustain the failing strength of the troops on his right, fled on the first assault, and, either accidentally or by design, sank a boat in the middle of the bridge of com-

Coolness of their advance.

Their partial success.

Terrible resistance of the Seiks.

Desperate struggle for their position.

munication. But the ancient Sham Sing remembered his vow; he clothed himself in simple white attire, as one devoted to death, and calling on all around him to fight for the Gooroo, who had promised everlasting bliss to the brave, he repeatedly rallied his shattered ranks, and at last fell a martyr on a heap of his slain countrymen. Others might be seen standing on the ramparts amid showers of balls, waving defiance with their swords, or telling the gunners where the fair-haired English pressed thickest together. Along the stronger half of the battlements, and for the period of half an hour, the conflict raged sublime in all its terrors. The parapets were sprinkled with blood from end to end; the trenches were filled with the dead and the dying. Amid the deafening roar of cannon, and the multitudinous fire of musketry, the shouts of triumph or of scorn were yet heard, and the flashing of innumerable swords was yet visible; or from time to time exploding magazines of powder, threw bursting shells, beams of wood and banks of earth, high above the agitated sea of smoke and flame which enveloped the host of combatants, and for a moment arrested the attention amid all the din and tumult of the tremendous conflict. But gradually each defensible position was captured, and the enemy was pressed towards the scarcely fordable river. Yet, although assailed on either side by squadrons of horse and battalions of foot, no Seik offered to submit, and no disciple of Govind asked for quarter. They everywhere showed a front to the victors, and stalked slowly and sullenly away, while many rushed singly forth to meet assured death by contending with a multitude. The victors looked with stolid wonderment upon the indomitable courage of the vanquished, and forbore to strike when the helpless and the dying frowned unavailing hatred. But the warlike rage, or the calculating policy of the leaders, had yet to be satisfied, and, standing with the slain heaped on all sides around them, they urged troops of artillery almost into the waters of the Sutledge to more thoroughly destroy the army which had

Sham Sing sacrifice.

Bloody character of the conflict.

Desperate bravery of the Seiks.

Fierce policy of the victors

CHAP. XVIII. so long scorned their power. No deity of heroic fable
A. D. 1846. received the living within the oozy gulphs of the oppressed stream, and its current was choked with added numbers of the dead, and crimsoned with the blood of a fugitive multitude.

'Such is the lust of never-dying fame.'

Triumphant joy of the victors. But vengeance was complete; the troops, defiled with dust and smoke and carnage, stood mute indeed for a moment, until the glory of their success rushing upon their minds, they gave expression to their feelings, and hailed their victorious commanders with reiterated shouts of triumph and congratulation."

Determined nature of the struggle. Never before had British arms been opposed to such determined bravery and skill, as strove with them on that bloody plain. The deadly struggles which had hung disgrace for a time on the British banners in the passes of Afghanistan, owed their fatal terrors to the natural character of the country, far more than to the bravery of its hardy but undisciplined forces. But here Unexpected courage of the foe. they were withstood on a fair field by a foe that listened unappalled to the thunders of their cannon, and stood unmoved before the glittering points of their bayonets when laid to the charge. Even the brave Seiks, however, sustained by all the nerve that fanaticism can add to native valour, found British skill and daring more than a match for them on an equal field. "At one time," says the British commander, in his despatch from the field of battle, "the thunder of full 120 pieces of ord- Description of the battle. nance reverberated in this mighty combat through the valley of the Sutledge; and as it was soon seen that the weight of the whole force within the Seik camp was likely to be thrown upon the two brigades that had passed its trenches, it became necessary to convert into close and serious attacks the demonstrations with skirmishers and artillery of the centre and right; and the battle raged with inconceivable fury from right to left. The Seiks, even when at particular points their intrenchments were mastered with the bayonet, strove to regain them by the fiercest conflict sword in hand. Nor was it until the cavalry of the left, under Major-general Sir Joseph Thackwell, had moved forward, and ridden through the openings of the intrenchments made by our sappers, in single file, and reformed as they passed them, and the 3d dragoons, whom no obstacle usually held formidable by horse appears to check, had on this day, as at Ferozeshah, galloped over and cut down the obstinate defenders of batteries and field-works, and until the full weight of three divisions of infantry, with every field artillery gun which could be sent to their aid, had been cast into the scale, that victory finally declared for the British. The fire of the Seiks first slackened, and then nearly ceased, and the victors then pressing them on every side, precipitated them in masses over the bridge, and into the Sutledge, which a sudden rise had rendered hardly fordable. In their efforts to reach the right bank, through the deepened water, they suffered from our horse artillery a terrible carnage. Hundreds fell under this cannonade; hundreds upon hundreds were drowned in attempting the perilous passage. Their awful slaughter, confusion, and dismay, were such as would have excited compassion in the hearts of their generous conquerors, if the Khalsa troops had not, in the early part of the action, sullied their gallantry by slaughtering and barbarously mangling every wounded soldier whom, in the vicissitudes of attack, the fortune of war left at their mercy. 67 pieces of cannon, upwards of 200 camel swivels (zumboorucks), numerous standards, and vast munitions of war, captured by our troops, are the pledges and trophies of our victory. The battle was over by eleven in the morning, and in the forenoon I caused our engineers to burn a part and to sink a part of the vaunted bridge of the Khalsa army, across which they had boastfully come once more to defy us, and to threaten India with ruin and devastation."

Charge of British cavalry

Retreat of the Seiks.

Dreadful carnage of the vanquished.

Trophies of victory.

The victory was complete; but it was not purchased

CHAP. XVIII.

A. D. 1846.

without a severe loss on the part of the victors; 320 British soldiers lay dead on the field, including Major-general Sir Robert Dick, a veteran soldier, who had served with honour in the Peninsula and at Waterloo; Brigadier Taylor, and other distinguished officers, who fell while leading on their men, or recalling them to a sense of their duty, as they recoiled from the deadly fire of the enemy. In addition to these, the British had 2083 wounded, some of them fatally. But the loss of the Seiks did not amount to less than 8000, while they were irretrievably broken and scattered, without hope of again being able to take the field. "We have to deplore a severe loss," says the commander-in-chief, "but certainly not heavy when weighed in the balance against the obstacles overcome and the advantages gained." That same night several regiments were pushed across the Sutledge opposite Ferozepore, but no enemy appeared to resist their progress. On the 11th the British forces pushed on to Kussoor, and on the following day its fortress was occupied by them without opposition. On the 13th the British army encamped under the walls of that ancient town. They learned there that the Seiks had re-assembled to the amount of 20,000 men; but they were no longer formidable to the victorious invaders of the Punjaub. Their whole artillery and munitions of war were in the hands of the enemy. The power of the Khalsa was effectually broken, and no force of innate courage or fanatic zeal could replace to it the indefensible provisions for continuing the struggle, or even restoring the confidence which had before nerved them to the fight, and upheld them with the hope of victory even after repeated defeats.

Severe loss of the victors.

Passage of the Sutledge.

Occupation of Kussoor.

The power of the Seiks effectually broken.

Declaration of British policy.

The official proclamation of the governor-general, issued only four days after the victory of Sobraon, contains both a declaration and a defence of British policy. It thus proceeds to announce, and to justify the course pursued under the immediate surveillance of the governor-general, who had combined in so unwonted a manner the duties of the civilian and the soldier. "The British army has crossed the Sutledge, and entered the Punjaub. The governor-general announces by this proclamation that that measure has been adopted by the government of India, in accordance with the intentions expressed in the proclamation of the 13th of December last, as having been forced upon the governor-general for the purpose of 'effectually protecting the British provinces, for vindicating the authority of the British government, and for punishing the violators of treaties and the disturbers of the public peace.' These operations will be steadily persevered in and vigorously prosecuted, until the objects proposed to be accomplished are fully attained. The occupation of the Punjaub by the British forces will not be relinquished until ample atonement for the insult offered to the British government by the infraction of the treaty of 1809, and by the unprovoked invasion of the British provinces, shall have been exacted. These objects will include full indemnity for all expenses incurred during the war, and such arrangements for the future government of the Lahore territories as will give perfect security to the British government against similar acts of perfidy and aggression. Military operations against the government and army of the Lahore state have not been undertaken by the government of India from any desire of territorial aggrandizement. The governor-general, as already announced in the proclamation of the 13th of December, 'sincerely desired to see a strong Seik government re-established in the Punjaub, able to control its army, and to protect its subjects.' The sincerity of these professions is proved by the fact, that no preparations for hostilities had been made when the Lahore government suddenly, and without a pretext of complaint, invaded the British territories. The unprovoked aggression has compelled the British government to have recourse to arms, and to organize the means of offensive warfare, and whatever may now befall the Lahore state, the consequences can alone be attributed to the

Proclamation of the commander-in-chief.

Ample atonement required.

Defence of British policy.

Responsibility of the Seiks for the consequences of the war.

CHAP. XVIII. A.D. 1848.

misconduct of that government and its army. No extension of territory was desired by the government of India; the measures necessary for providing indemnity for the past and security for the future will, however, involve the retention by the British government of a portion of the country hitherto under the government of the Lahore state. The extent of territory which it may be deemed advisable to hold will be determined by the conduct of the durbar, and by considerations for the security of the British frontier. The government of India will, under any circumstances, annex to the British provinces the districts, hill and plain, situated between the rivers Sutledge and Beeas, the revenues thereof being appropriated as a part of the indemnity required from the Lahore state."

Forced extension of territory.

Limits of annexation.

From the sketch we have already drawn of the singular religious commonwealth of the Seiks, the reader will readily perceive that, however consistent with sound policy and the just claims of the victors the proposed terms might appear, they were dictated without any reference to the peculiar consistency of the Seik commonwealth, if not indeed in ignorance of the peculiar features on which it was based. For the British governor-general to dictate terms by which a government might be established in the Punjaub capable of controlling the Seik army, might not unreasonably be compared to the liberal offers of the English Edward to Baliol, on condition that he should control the patriot army of Scotland. The defence of British policy, however, lies in the fact that, whoever may be justly chargeable with the initiative in the war, the movements of the British was purely defensive. They desired no accession of territory, and did not seek to interfere in the control of the Seik soldiers, until their revolutionary movements menaced the British frontier, and endangered the peace and safety of the empire. In the conclusion of the same official proclamation, the governor-general thus confidently appeals to the integrity of purpose which had influenced the

Candid estimate of British policy

Its unsuitableness for the Seiks.

The truest defence of British policy

whole course of British policy. "The governor-general, at this moment of a most complete and decisive victory, cannot give a stronger proof of the forbearance and moderation of the British government than by making this declaration of his intentions, the terms and mode of the arrangement remaining for further adjustment. The governor-general, therefore, calls upon all those chiefs who are the well-wishers of the descendants of Runjeet Sing, and especially such chiefs as have not participated in the hostile proceedings against the British power, to act in concert with him in carrying into effect such arrangements as shall maintain a Seik government at Lahore, capable of controlling its army and protecting its subjects, and based upon principles that shall provide for the future tranquillity of the Seik states, shall secure the British frontier against a repetition of acts of aggression, and shall prove to the whole the moderation and justice of the paramount power of India. If this opportunity of rescuing the Seik nation from military anarchy and misrule be neglected, and hostile opposition to the British army be renewed, the government of India will make such other arrangements for the future government of the Punjaub as the interests and security of the British power may render just and expedient."

Appeal to native chiefs.

Alternative in case of renewed hostilities.

If the Seik soldiers did not acquiesce in the justice of British policy, which dictated the necessity for a supreme and independent power by which their future motions would be controlled and kept in check, they at least acknowledged the right of dictation which victory had placed in the conquerors of Sobraon. They agreed to authorize their chosen minister, Golab Sing, to treat with the British, and empowered him to concur in arrangements on the basis announced in the proclamation, of recognizing a Seik government in Lahore.

Submission of the Seik soldiers.

On the 15th of February, the governor-general was visited at Kussoor by the rajah and several of the most influential Seik chiefs, to whom he stated the terms upon which he was willing to conclude a peace. These in-

Interview of the Seik chiefs with the governor-general.

CHAP. XVIII — A.D. 1846.

Dhuleep Sing sovereign of Lahore.

cluded the recognition of Dhuleep Sing as sovereign of Lahore, but required the cession of the country between the Beeas and the Sutledge, as specified in the proclamation. They were likewise required to pay to the conquerors a million and a half sterling, as some indemnity for the expenses of the war. The governor-general was induced to dictate humiliating terms, in order that the full conviction of the supremacy and invincibility of British arms might be felt wherever rebellious thoughts had been cherished, among the allies or the dependents of our Indian empire. After vain endeavours to evade some of the most unpalatable requirements, the Seik chiefs reluctantly accepted the offered terms, and the young rajah personally tendered his submission. Still more effectually to demonstrate how effectually the Khalsa was humbled under the supremacy of their conquerors, the British army entered Lahore on the 20th February, and, two days afterwards, an English garrison occupied the citadel of the Seik capital.

Reasons for exacting humiliating terms.

Occupation of the citadel of Lahore.

Selfish policy of Golab Sing.

In the arrangements which followed, Golab Sing contrived that his own interests should be advanced, however those of the great body of the disciples of Govind might suffer. His influence with the Seik forces, and his own wealth both in treasure and munitions of war, rendered him still formidable, should he be driven, by the exacting demands of his conquerors, to fall back on the support of the Seiks. Captain Cunningham thus narrates this part of the transactions in the Punjaub:—"The low state of the Lahore treasury, and the anxiety of Lal Sing to get a dreaded rival out of the way, enabled the governor-general to appease Golab Sing in a manner sufficiently agreeable to the rajah himself, and which still further reduced the importance of the successor of Runjeet Sing. The rajah of Jummoo did not care to be simply the master of his native mountains; but as two-thirds of the pecuniary indemnity required from Lahore could not be made good, territory was taken instead of money, and Cashmeer and the hill states from the Beeas to the Indus

Impartial estimate of proceedings.

were cut off from the Punjaub Proper, and transferred to Golab Sing, as a separate sovereign, for a million of pounds sterling. The arrangement was a dexterous one, if reference be only had to the policy of reducing the power of the Seiks; but the transaction scarcely seems worthy of the British name and greatness, and the objections become stronger when it is considered that Golab Sing had agreed to pay sixty-eight lacs of rupees, (£680,000,) as a fine to his paramount, before the war broke out, and that the custom of the East as well as of the West requires the feudatory to aid his lord in foreign war and domestic strife. Golab Sing ought thus to have paid the deficient million of money as a Lahore subject, instead of being put in possession of Lahore provinces as an independent prince. The succession of the rajah was displeasing to the Seiks generally, and his separation was less in accordance with his own aspirations than the ministry of Runjeet Sing's empire; but his rise to sovereign power excited nevertheless the ambition of others, and Tej Sing, who knew his own wealth, and was fully persuaded of the potency of gold, offered twenty-five lacs of rupees for a princely crown and another dismembered province. He was chid for his presumptuous misinterpretation of English principles of action; the arrangement with Golab Sing was the only one of the kind which took place, and the new ally was formally invested with the title of Muharajah at Amritsir, on the 15th March 1846. But a portion of the territory at first proposed to be made over to him was reserved by his masters, the payments required from him were reduced by a fourth, and they were rendered still more easy of liquidation by considering him to be the heir to the money which his brother Soochet Sing had buried in Ferozepore." The author then describes this influential Seik chief, in a note which he appends to the previous narrative: "In the course of this history there has, more than once, been occasion to allude to the unscrupulous character of Rajah Golab Sing; but it must not therefore be

Nature of the transaction with Golab Sing.

Its unpopularity with the Seiks.

Golab Sing invested with the title Muharajah.

His character.

CHAP. XVIII

A. D. 1846.

supposed that he is a man malevolently evil. He will, indeed, deceive an enemy and take his life without hesitation, and in the accumulation of money he will exercise many oppressions; but he must be judged with reference to the morality of his age and race, and to the necessities of his own position. If these allowances be made, Golab Sing will be found an able and moderate man, who does little in an idle or wanton spirit, and who is not without some traits both of good humour and generosity of temper."

The standard by which to try him.

Spirit of the Seik soldiery.

The spirit of the Seik soldiery, however, was not broken by their reverses, though they had doubtless learned to acknowledge the superiority of British arms. But for such a formidable power to check this enthusiastic soldiery of the creed of Govind, it is difficult to conceive what might ultimately have proved the limits of their conquests. Their partial historian thus describes their deportment in the presence of their conquerors:—"While the governor-general and commander-in-chief remained at Lahore at the head of 20,000 men, portions of the Seik army came to the capital to be paid up and disbanded. The soldiers showed neither the despondency of mutinous rebels nor the effrontery and indifference of mercenaries, and their manly deportment added lustre to that valour which the victors had dearly felt and generously extolled. The men talked of their defeat as the chance of war, or they would say that *they* were mere imitators of unapproachable masters. But amid all their humiliation, they inwardly dwelt upon their future destiny with unabated confidence; and while gaily calling themselves inapt and youthful scholars, they would sometimes add, with a significant and sardonic smile, that the 'Khalsa' itself was yet a child, and that as the commonwealth of Seiks grew in stature, Govind would clothe his disciples with irresistible might and guide them with unequalled skill. Thus brave men sought consolation, and the spirit of progress which collectively animated them yielded with a murmur to the superior genius of England and civiliza-

Disbanding of the Seik army.

Confidence in their future destiny

tion, to be chastened by the rough hand of power, and perhaps to be moulded to noblest purposes by the informing touch of knowledge and philosophy." Such is the account furnished by the partial pen of a generous British soldier, of the hardy insurgents who assailed the north-western frontier of British India, and were thus hardly defeated, after repeated battles under the most undaunted of British generals. British arms were again triumphant. New additions were, temporarily or permanently, annexed to our Indian empire, forced on us by circumstances or necessity. New duties and cares helped to complicate the difficulties of our Indian policy, while sanguine politicians flattered themselves that the long-sought natural boundaries of Hindostan had at length been reached, and that the British soldier might now sheath his sword, unless as the weapon of defensive justice against aggression. What the final results of the first campaign in the Punjaub may yet prove to be, it is vain for the historian to speculate; but the view we have endeavoured to give of the singular race of armed zealots who constitute the Seik commonwealth, is alone sufficient to satisfy the reader that it would be folly to anticipate the reverses of a single campaign could suffice to reduce them to contented subjects, or peaceable and trustworthy allies. A much briefer experience than the least hopeful could have anticipated, served to show on how uncertain a tenure peace could be established with them.

Reflections on the issue of the war.

CHAPTER XIX.

War in Moultan and the Punjaub.

Confident anticipations of peace—Sudden outbreak at Moultan—Acquirement of the district by Runjeet Sing—Its original inhabitants—Succession of Lalla Moolraj—Sirdar Khan appointed governor—Assassination of British officers—Alarming conspiracy at Lahore—Prompt measures of Lieutenant Edwardes—Native allies—Siege of Moultan—Junction of General Whish—Fall of Moultan—Battle of Chillianwallah—Doubtful nature of the results—Decisive victory of Goojerat—Pursuit of the Afghans—Annexation of the Punjaub—Consideration of British policy.

CHAP. XIX.

A. D. 1848.

Confident anticipations of peace.

THE campaign of 1846 closed with the total rout of the Seiks, and their unequivocal submission to the supremacy of British arms. The ceded provinces were occupied by British forces, and early in 1848, Viscount Hardinge, who had returned from the scene of his civil and military triumphs, declared that all danger of insurrection or disturbance in the Punjaub was at an end. No combination of civil and military genius, however, could in so brief a period convert the wild Seiks of the Punjaub into peaceable subjects or faithful allies. The Indian Mail of June 1848, once more announced that the note of war had sounded on the north-western frontiers of British India.

Scene of renewed aggression.

The locality of renewed aggression and treachery was Moultan, the capital of a large tract of the same name, extending between the Indus and the Sutledge, to the south of Lahore. The city of Moultan is a place celebrated of old for its great strength. Its more recent history exhibits the Seik not as the patriot defending his native soil, but as the aggressor subjecting neighbouring districts by his sword. After various unsuccessful attempts, extending over a long period, Runjeet Sing succeeded in taking Moultan, though not without immense loss. Here, as in so many other instances in our Indian wars, Britain appears only as a new and stronger power superseding a previous conqueror, whose right of possession is of the sword. The inhabitants of the province of Moultan consist chiefly of Jats, the descendants of the Scythian invaders of India, who offered a fierce resistance to the Mohammedan invaders, and, since their conquest by Mahmood of Ghuzni in 1026, they have repeatedly asserted their independence. Towards the close of last century, this province was nominally dependent on the Afghan empire, between which and Runjeet Sing repeated struggles took place for its possession. After the Seik rajah had been again and again foiled by the Afghan governor, Mozuffer Khan, he at length succeeded, in 1818, more by good fortune than skill, in gaining possession of the long-coveted place of strength, and annexing the province to his kingdom. By the treaty of 1838, Moultan was finally ceded by Shah Sooja to the ruler of the Punjaub, who committed it to the care of Sawan Mull, a subordinate governor, who held it by a species of feudal tenure, administering its affairs as a dependent of the Seik state. Sawan, who is described as a ruler of great ability and moderation, perished by the hands of an assassin in a durbar affray, in September 1844. He was succeeded by his eldest son, Lalla Moolraj, whose name so frequently occurs in the narratives of recent events on the frontiers of British India. Differences occurred between Moolraj and Lall Sing. One of the districts of his government was violently snatched from him by the rajah. Subsequently he was summoned to Lahore to settle his accounts, at all times a complicated and reluc-

Capture of Moultan by Runjeet Sing.

Natives of the province.

Cession of Moultan to the Seiks.

Lalla Moolraj.

CHAP. XIX

A.D 1848.

tant proceeding in the East. He went under British guarantee, effected some sort of settlement, and returned in safety to Moultan; but negotiations were being still carried on, with the object chiefly of bringing the whole Seik kingdom under a uniform mode of government. These it was believed had, at length, been brought to a successful issue. Sirdar Khan Sing was appointed governor, and Mr Vans Agnew, assistant to the British resident at Lahore, was deputed to proceed, along with Lieutenant Anderson, to install the new governor in his office. No opposition was anticipated, and they were attended apparently by a force fit for little more than a guard of honour. The two British officers arrived at Moultan early in April 1848, and received from Lalla Moolraj the formal resignation of his fortress, &c. On the following day, while inspecting the fortress, Mr. Agnew was suddenly assaulted by assassins, and dangerously wounded. He was rescued by the new governor, and conveyed to a small fort outside the town. In the meantime, Lieutenant Anderson had been attacked in like manner, when riding in company with Lalla Moolraj, and was borne to the same fort, severely wounded. There a fire was opened upon them from Moultan, and three days after the Moultanese troops moved out to attack the fort in which they lay. The wounded officers resolved to hold out the fort in hope of relief. They sent out messengers to claim assistance from a neighbouring chief, of Bahawulpore, who retained his allegiance to the British. Had their garrison been faithful, these officers might have been able to maintain the fort till effectual aid reached them; but the Seik troops within joined the assailants without, and, flinging open the gates, both Lieutenant Anderson and Mr. Agnew were assassinated while vainly defending themselves against a host of assailants.

Sirdar Khan Sing appointed governor.

Reception by Moolraj.

The British representatives assaulted.

Attempts to maintain their position.

Their assassination.

It was believed for a time that this violent outbreak was entirely referrible to some temporary and accidental misunderstanding with the Seik soldiery, and was unconnected with any organized plan of opposition to established rule, or to any designed hostilities with the British. Long experience, however, suffices to prove that the more recent acquisitions of our Eastern empire resemble in their most quiescent state rather the stillness of a powder magazine than the calm of the unvexed sea. A single spark suffices for the explosion, and it is scarcely possible to calculate how far its effects may extend. Amid their most sanguine hopes this was not overlooked by those at the head of affairs in India; but the scene of danger was remote from means of defence or supply, the warm season was at hand, when active operations are scarcely possible, and rumours of the instability of affairs at Lahore, and of the equivocal fidelity of the Rajah Golaub Sing, furnished grounds for the deepest apprehension. The confidence expressed by Viscount Hardinge in the peace of the Punjaub was based doubtless to a considerable extent on the admirable military arrangements made by him previous to his departure. At Lahore these were rendered fully available by the vigilance of the British officers in charge. The troops all along the frontier were commanded to hold themselves in readiness for immediate action. Officers absent on leave were ordered to join their troops without delay, and every precaution was taken to guard against surprise. The wisdom of such precautions soon became apparent. The outbreak at Moultan was followed by the discovery of a conspiracy of the most alarming character at Lahore, having for its object the massacre of all the British officers, the expulsion of our whole troops from the Punjaub, and a revolution in the Seik government. Attempts had been made, not without some slight success, to seduce the Sepoys from their allegiance. On the discovery of this, the British resident, Sir Frederick Currie, directed certain native officers, whose fidelity could be relied upon, to fall in with the plans of the conspirators, by which means the whole plot was disclosed. Three native corps, it was found, had been tampered with, but only a small number of the men had yielded to the temptations by which they

Precarious peace of India.

Grounds for confident expectation of peace.

Precautions adopted.

Alarming conspiracy at Lahore.

Mode of its disclosure.

CHAP. XIX. A. D. 1848.

were assailed. Undoubted proofs, however, were discovered of persons of the highest rank being privy to the plot, by whom the fakeers had been employed to use their influence over the Sepoys in seducing them from their fidelity. It was at the very time that the Indian papers were filled with the accounts of this abortive conspiracy at Lahore, that the mail from England reported the speech of Viscount Hardinge, in which he stated "he had no apprehension for the tranquillity of the Punjaub!" So impossible is it for the most experienced statesman to anticipate the changes which a few months may effect on the state of our Eastern empire.

Extent of the plot.

False confidence of Lord Hardinge.

Lieutenant Edwardes.

The indomitable courage and skill of a British officer of youth and inexperience, sufficed at this critical juncture to do more for the safety of the British empire than all the experience and foresight of the civil and military rulers of India. It speedily became apparent that the zeal of Dewan Khan Sing, in the defence of the unfortunate British officers deputed to accompany him to his new government, was altogether assumed, and that he was in league with the conspirators in Lahore and elsewhere, by whom a scheme had been matured for overpowering the British, and expelling them from the country. In the neighbourhood of Lahore, a Gooroo, or priest, named Maharaj Sing, had raised the standard of revolt, and speedily collected a numerous force of the disbanded Seiks, among whom he enjoyed a reputation for great sanctity. By this means the British forces at Lahore were prevented attempting any movement upon Moultan, and every successive mail brought news of fresh difficulties or alarms, tending still further to confound the speculations of the most experienced politicians as to the extent, or probable issue, of this new revolution in the Punjaub. At this time Lieutenant Edwardes was stationed on the Indus with a force consisting only of one regiment of infantry and 300 sowars, with two guns. His duty was the collection of the land-tax due to Moolraj, and the occupation of Leiah, a town situated on the

Faithlessness of Dewan Khan Sing.

Maharaj Sing.

Lieutenant Edwardes on the Indus.

left bank of the Indus. "Hearing of the affair at Moultan, and finding himself exposed to risk, many of his Seik soldiers deserting him on learning the rumour of a general rising, he crossed the river into the Deerajat, whence he wrote to the Khan of Bhawulpore, to make a demonstration which should prevent Moolraj from executing any design against him or Colonel Cortlandt, who commanded the garrison of Dhera Ismael Khan. The Khan lost no time in making preparations to act. A party of 300 horse had been left by Lieutenant Edwardes to complete the collection of the revenue at Leiah, where they were attacked, on the 18th of May, by 400 Moultan horse, with ten zumbooruks (light field-guns), who were completely defeated, with the loss of their guns. Meanwhile, Colonel Cortlandt, with his force, amounting to about 4000 men, quitted Dhera Ismael Khan, and proceeded to the southward by the base of the mountains, being joined on his way by a Beloochee chief named Melah Khan, with 100 of his tribe, who were sent to take the fortress of Sunghur, a place to the west of Attock, which surrendered after six hours' fighting, the garrison retreating upon Moultan. Another Beloochee chief, named Kora Khan Khosa, soon after joined the colonel, who despatched him with 800 of his tribe, horse and foot, against the fort of Dhera Ghazee Khan, the second city in the province. The Beloochee chief seems to have executed his orders with great zeal, expedition, and success. He marched his men along the skirt of the hills, sending forward a messenger to the commandant of the fort with a summons to give it up. The Seiks, however, resolved to fight for the place. They went out to give battle, and were defeated; the fort was surrendered, and the karder slain. Colonel Cortlandt (who appears to have expected that the Beloochees would have only amused the garrison) found the business over when he came up. He occupied the town, where Lieutenant Edwardes joined him on the 20th of May, and on the morning of that day another engagement took place between the British forces and

Fidelity of the Khan of Bhawulpore.

Defeat of Moultan horse.

Native allies

Attack of the fort of Dhera Ghazee Khan.

Capture of the fort by the Beloochees.

CHAP. XIX. A. D. 1848. the Moultanese insurgents, who were routed with great slaughter, their chief, Chatur Mull, being killed, and another chief, Lunga Mull, taken prisoner."

Junction of Edwardes' and Cortlandt's forces. Lieutenant Edwardes effected a junction with Colonel Cortlandt's forces, by which a body of about 7000 men was placed under their joint command. With this force considerable success was achieved, and it was confidently anticipated for a time that these young officers, at the head of such a small and irregular force, were to bring the rebellion summarily to a close, and re-annex Moultan to the Punjaub, ere the British resident or the commander-in-chief could adopt any definite line of policy for the suppression of this unexpected outbreak. The Censures of the press. press as usual were as severe in their criticisms on the tardy operations of the commander-in-chief, as they afterwards were on his supposed rashness and indiscretion. The "Friend of India" censured in the severest terms "the tame conduct of the chief authorities," and predicted that there would be no Moultan laurels but for Anticipations of easy victory. Edwardes and Cortlandt. None more worthy indeed could be achieved. The gallant lieutenant, now advanced to the rank of a major, led the British troops and their allies under the very walls of Moultan, after twice defeating a force greatly superior to them in numbers. But Strength of Moultan. the fortifications of Moultan were such as bad defiance to the efforts of an irregular force, with no other artillery than a few light field-pieces. Major Edwardes at once perceived his inability to make the slightest impression on the fortress with the troops under his command, and he accordingly despatched a messenger to the British resident at Lahore, for reinforcements and heavy artillery. Meanwhile the position of the British force in the neighbourhood of Moultan was somewhat critical. The hold Influence of success on native alliance. he had upon his native allies had owed much of its force to his own tact and the success which had hitherto attended his operations; and to the latter cause also may be ascribed the successive junction of Shere Sing and other Seik chiefs, at the head of about 10,000 men.

Such allies, however, were a source of far more apprehension than confidence to Major Edwardes. Many of the Seiks were known to be disaffected, and he was obliged to watch their camp, situated about a mile from his own, with scarcely less jealousy than that of Moolraj. His suspicions of his Seik allies proved only too well founded. Their defection speedily turned the scale against him, and he was obliged to take up a new position, at a much greater distance from the stronghold of Moolraj. But though it was no longer to be hoped for that the gallantry of this British officer would prove sufficient to counteract the deep-laid plots and machinations of the Seiks, the check he had given at so critical a period was productive of the most important results. Much valuable time was gained. The cautious deliberations of those at the head of affairs were carried on while he held the enemy at bay, and by the time it became obvious that the most decisive measures were indispensable, they were ready to forward to his aid a force capable of coping with such difficulties. On the 21st December 1848, General Whish at length effected a junction with Major Edwardes, in the neighbourhood of Moultan, by which he found himself at the head of an efficient force, amounting to 15,000 British troops, and 17,000 allies, and with 150 pieces of ordnance, nearly half of which were of the largest calibre. The result became no longer doubtful. After one of the most obstinate and gallant defences on the part of the enemy ever recorded in the annals of Indian warfare, the city of Moultan was yielded to the British commander, and its citadel occupied by a British garrison, though not till the principal powder magazine of the defenders, containing nearly a million pounds of powder, had been blown into the air, and their principal granary and stores had been burned.

Faithlessness of the Seik allies.

Important results of Lieutenant Edwardes' gallant deeds.

Advance of a competent force for the siege.

When the citadel of Moultan had at length fallen into the hands of the British, one of the first acts of the victors was to pay a graceful though vain tribute to the remains of those who had been the first victims of Seik

Tribute to the assassinated British officers.

CHAP. XIX

A. D. 1849.

treachery. The proceeding is thus narrated by an officer who bore a part in the sad rites, with which the conquerors sought to repair the wrongs already so signally avenged:—"On the evening of the 26th, I joined in a very pleasing, though melancholy ceremony. The burial-place of Mr. Agnew and Lieutenant Anderson had been discovered, and it was determined to exhume the bodies, and move them to the fort. The grave was opened under the superintendance of one of their most intimate friends, and the bodies were found to be in a sufficient state of preservation to be identified. A carrying and funeral party, with the band of the fusiliers, to which regiment Lieutenant Anderson formerly belonged, attended, with a large portion of the officers in camp, and moved off from the Eedgah, near which the bodies had been found, at five o'clock, and, *entering the fort by the breach*, the coffins were deposited in a grave which had been prepared in the highest part of the fort. The chaplain was in attendance, and read the funeral service in a most impressive manner."

The burial.

Coincident operations in the field.

While the united forces under General Whish were breaching the walls of Moultan, and reducing Moolraj to the desperate position which at length compelled him to capitulate on the 21st of January 1849, and to yield up the ruined city and its shattered but still strong and formidable fortress to the British general, the commander-in-chief had to withstand a still more formidable resistance in the open field. Notwithstanding the dear-bought experience of the former Seik campaign, the commander-in-chief was found at this second outbreak of the turbulent soldiery of the Punjaub fully as unprepared as before. It was not indeed to be expected, that an establishment was to be kept along the banks of the Sutledge, ready to take the field at a moment's notice; still the knowledge acquired of the character and motives of the Seik revolutionists during the previous war, was such as showed the necessity of constant watchfulness and preparation for war, so long as British forces

Unprepared state of the British.

occupied any portion of the territory of the disciples of Govind. CHAP. XIX. A.D. 1849.

Rumours of a battle. After the lapse of a considerable period of painful suspense, the Indian Mail of February 1849, brought to England confused rumours of a decisive battle having been fought, which successive publications of demi-official information tended only more effectually to clothe with doubt and apprehension. During the interval between the arrival of the succeeding mails in March, the most painful anxiety prevailed. Reports of defeat. Reports were circulated that the British forces had sustained a total defeat, the most extravagant rumours were believed, and a state of feverish excitement prevailed, which required far more acceptable news than the most flattering narrative could convey of the doubtful victory gained by the British arms on the banks of the Jelum. "Our narrative of the sanguinary battle of Chillianwalla," says the Indian Mail of March 5, 1849, "which, though termed a victory, Dissatisfaction expressed at the result. might by a not very partial historian be described as a defeat, must be compiled from the details furnished by writers on the spot to the various public journals, which are unanimous in their condemnation of the general. 'Not, since the destruction of the garrison of Cabul,' says the Bombay Times, 'has so heavy a catalogue of blunders Blame attached to Lord Gough. and misfortunes been carried home from India as that which the present mail conveys; we have, for the first time since 1842, to give particulars of the annihilation of half regiments, from the sheer mismanagement of the commanding officer.' The Bombay Telegraph believes 'the opinion to be almost universal, that the terrible slaughter during the engagement is attributable, in a great measure, to the want of forethought, judgment, and tactical skill on the part of the commander.'"

Partiality of public opinion. Lord Hardinge was no longer present to control the impetuous hardihood of Lord Gough, and the public, however willing to overlook the rashest daring when it is successful, are little inclined to charity or even to reason, when it leads to loss or to defeat. Lord Gough had been

CHAP. XIX. A. D. 1849. compelled, as in his former campaign, to manœuvre instead of fight, from the want of an effective force and sufficient supplies. On the 5th of January, the British forces under his command lay encamped at Janiki, within a day's march of the Seik army, under Shere Sing, which had taken up a formidable position at Moong, on the left bank of the Jelum. Lord Gough had at one time intended to wait the fall of Moultan before he attacked the Seiks, but he found reason to dread the unfavourable effects which his inactivity was calculated to exert on that portion of the natives whose co-operation and neutrality depended solely on his success, while it afforded Shere Sing an opportunity of largely augmenting his army. Accordingly, on the 11th of January, the British forces left their encampment at Janiki, and marched in the direction of the Seik camp. Shere Sing's forces were found to be intrenched in a position of great natural strength, which they had still farther secured by works of formidable extent. The commander-in-chief is affirmed to have hastily changed his plan of operations, and to have perilled the safety of the whole British forces by ordering an attack on the enemy's camp about two hours after noon, when it had been previously resolved to defer all active operations till the following day. The ground was impeded with jungle, which concealed the Seik matchlock men, and afforded them an immense advantage. The British forces were compelled to storm batteries at the bayonet's point, most advantageously posted on steep heights, and still farther protected by artificial works. Darkness put an end to the engagement, leaving the British in possession of the field of battle. But their loss had been terrible. Nearly an hundred officers were killed or wounded; 2269 troops, including nearly 1000 Europeans, were disabled, or left dead on the field, while whole troops had been compelled to give way before the determined front of the enemy, and the deadly fire of their artillery. Such a questionable victory sufficed to overshadow the triumphs

Position of the Seik army.

Sudden change of plan by Lord Gough.

Formidable nature of the Seik camp.

Severe loss of the British.

at Moultan, and to increase the anxiety and apprehension with which the overland mail was anticipated in England. CHAP. XIX. — A.D. 1849.

Reinforcements consequent on the fall of Moultan.

Meanwhile the fall of Moultan had released a large body who were pressing forward to reinforce the army of Lord Gough, while the total inaction of Shere Sing proved that the bloody field of Chillianwallah had paralyzed the movements of the Seiks even more than it had crippled the available resources and damped the exulting anticipations of the British.

Victory of Goojerat

Victory, however, had not deserted the British arms in India. Another interval of feverish suspense elapsed, and then came the unofficial reports, followed after a comparatively brief interval by the despatches of the commander-in-chief, announcing the triumph of Goojerat. The Seik army estimated at 60,000 men, with fifty-nine pieces of artillery, and a powerful auxiliary force of Afghan cavalry, had been completely routed. "Their ranks broken; their position carried; their guns, ammunition, camp-equipage, and baggage, captured; and their flying masses driven before the victorious pursuers from mid-day to dusk." Fifty-three pieces of artillery left in the hands of the victors, along with the camp, baggage, magazines, and a vast store of ammunitions, abandoned by the flying Seiks, abundantly testified to the triumph which had at length dissipated the apprehensions of thousands, who waited with anxious dread the announcement of the first despatch that should narrate the proceedings subsequent to the dear-bought field of Chillianwallah.

Spoils of the victors.

Decisive character of the victory.

The victory of Goojerat proved to be complete and decisive. Once more the van of the British army had maintained its ground on this remote border of British India until reinforcements could be brought up, and supplies forwarded to the point of attack, and then trying the strength of the opposing power on a well-fought field, victory had unequivocally declared for the conquerors of the East. The fruits of this battle were the entire surrender of the Seik army, including their com-

CHAP. XIX. — A. D. 1849.

mander, Rajah Shere Sing, his father, Chuttur Sing, his brothers, and most of the principal Seik sirdars and chiefs. Forty-one pieces of artillery, the whole that remained uncaptured by the British, were at the same time unconditionally surrendered, and the remains of the conquered army, to the number of 16,000 Seik soldiers, laid down their arms in the presence of the British troops. The principal scene of this act of surrender by the vanquished was a place called Hoormuk, at one of the principal fords of the river, across which their broken ranks had fled in dismay before the final charge of the victors of Goojerat. At this spot the Seik soldiers crossed and delivered up their arms, passing through the lines of two native infantry regiments appointed for this duty. Each of the Seiks received a rupee to subsist him on his return home, in addition to which they were permitted to retain their horses.

Surrender of Seik artillery and arms.

Measures against the Afghans.

In the general order of the governor-general, with which he accompanied the welcome despatches announcing the result of the campaign, he adds: "But the war is not yet concluded; nor can there be any cessation of hostilities until Dost Mohammed Khan and the Afghan army are either driven from the province of Peshawur, or destroyed within it." The most determined measures were accordingly adopted against the Seik allies who still remained in arms. But the greatest apprehension of the victors was that they should escape them by flight, there being little reason to apprehend that any Afghan force would alone withstand the British arms on the open field. On the evening of the same day on which Major-general Sir Walter Gilbert superintended the disarming of Shere Sing's army, he pushed on by forced marches towards Attock, in hopes of overtaking the Afghans before they could succeed in crossing the Indus. In this, however, he failed. The Afghans were already across the great river, and the impatient general pushing on with his staff, and accompanied only by a small escort, beheld them from a neighbouring eminence

Pursuit of them by Walter Sir Gilbert.

busily engaged in the destruction of the bridge of boats by which they had effected their timely passage. The sight of the British staff filled the flying enemy with new apprehensions, as they had believed the British to be still two days' march behind. The artillery was speedily brought to bear upon them, and fifteen of the best boats forming the bridge were secured. By means of this the British troops were passed across the Indus, and negotiations were entered into with the Khyberries to obstruct the retreat of the Afghans through the dreaded defile of which they were the guardians. But the Indus was rising. Its deep and rapid flood retarded the passage of the cavalry and artillery indispensable for the pursuit, while fear urged on the retreat of the flying foe, who were struck with such panic at the sudden appearance of the British at the passage of the Indus, that they abandoned their baggage in order to accelerate their flight. By this means, Dost Mohammed Khan succeeded in reaching Dakka, on the western side of the Khyber Pass, and thereby escaping the vengeance he had provoked by his junction with the rebellious Seiks.

Passage of the Indus.

Impediments to the pursuit.

Escape of Dost Mohammed Khan.

With the flight of the Afghans beyond the Khyber Pass the war was at an end; but new measures were requisite to guard against the renewal of similar outbreaks of the restless and daring Khalsa. Within the brief period that had elapsed since the summary recall of Lord Ellenborough, experience and necessity had overthrown every theory of British policy in India. One critic, in summing up the record of events of the previous year, at the time when only the first steps in the new war beyond the Sutledge had transpired, remarks: "A year barren of events, although a tame and unattractive period to readers of history, is a propitious one to good rulers, especially rulers of such a country as India. The want of time, and opportunity, and political quiet, to digest plans of improvement, has been the ready and unanswerable excuse of every governor of India since the administration of its affairs has been transferred to our

Close of the war.

Difficulties of Indian rule.

CHAP. XIX. A.D. 1849.

Obstacles to permanent peace.

hands from those of the Moguls. The fault is not theirs; it is the vice, or rather a misfortune, inseparable from the circumstances of British rule in India in relation to the native powers, which clothe it with progressive (or, as some say, aggressive) attributes, that a stationary policy is not only irreconcileable with the security of our Indian empire, but impracticable, and the intervals of suspension of war and conquest are few and brief. The last three governors of India furnish examples which the next three may be compelled to follow.

Recent governor-generals.

"Lord Ellenborough, Sir Henry Hardinge, and Lord Dalhousie, proceeded to India with visions of peace, of prosperous revenues, and of the realization of benevolent schemes of social benefit for the people of India. The first was, upon his arrival, immersed in the perils and perplexities of the Cabul outbreak and the Mahratta campaign. The second was most unwillingly forced by a Seik invasion into a war, first of defence and then of conquest, beyond our frontiers. Lord Dalhousie, in like manner, has been compelled to desert the seat of government, where he was busied with plans of domestic improvement, and to enter upon projects which, from the magnitude of the preparations, appear to embrace the conquest of an extensive territory, the cost of which will exhaust the present and pledge the future revenues of India, postponing every scheme of local and general improvement and moral amelioration which demands an outlay of money. Should our presage be correct, and the British empire be extended to the Indus, that 'forbidden' river, conveniently termed the 'historical boundary of India,' will not be a final boundary any more than the Sutledge has been; the expansion of our line of frontiers, bringing us into contact with new neighbours, jealous of our greatness or alarmed at our proximity, will involve us in fresh quarrels, and we shall be led onward, until, as Baron Hugel predicts, we reach Herat. This is the condition of our existence as a ruling power in India; and critics of our administration there, instead of expos-

Overthrow of Lord Dalhousie's plans.

Questionable security of the Indus as a boundary.

ing its imperfections, and proclaiming the vast amount of what has not been done to ameliorate the people, would be more just if they compared what has been accomplished with the time and means at our command,—in snatches of repose, broken by sudden political explosions, which engross the attention and the energies of the government, amidst the financial incumbrances created by an increasing expenditure, which cannot be met, as in other countries, by increase of taxation." The result has proved the justice of these remarks. By a proclamation of the governor-general of India, dated March 30th 1849, the Punjaub is declared to be a portion of the British empire in India; and the same official document thus enters on the defence of British policy:—"For many years, in the time of Maharajah Runjeet Sing, peace and friendship prevailed between the British nation and the Seiks. When Runjeet Sing was dead, and his wisdom no longer guided the counsels of the state, the sirdars and the Khalsa army, without provocation and without cause, suddenly invaded the British territories. Their army was again and again defeated. They were driven with slaughter and in shame from the country they had invaded, and at the gates of Lahore the Maharajah Dhuleep Sing tendered to the governor-general the submission of himself and his chiefs, and solicited the clemency of the British government. The governor-general extended the clemency of his government to the state of Lahore; he generously spared the kingdom which he had acquired a just right to subvert; and, the maharajah having been replaced on the throne, treaties of friendship were formed between the states. The British have faithfully kept their word, and have scrupulously observed every obligation which the treaties imposed upon them. But the Seik people and their chiefs have, on their part, grossly and faithlessly violated the promises by which they were bound. Of their annual tribute, no portion whatever has at any time been paid, and large loans advanced to them by the government of Indis have never

Grounds of annexation of the Punjaub.

Clemency of the British.

Faithlessness of the Seiks.

CHAP. XIX. A.D. 1849.

been repaid. The control of the British government, to which they voluntarily submitted themselves, has been resisted by arms. Peace has been cast aside. British officers have been murdered when acting for the state; others engaged in the like employment have treacherously been thrown into captivity. Finally, the army of the state and the whole Seik people, joined by many of the sirdars in the Punjaub who signed the treaties, and led by a member of the regency itself, have risen in arms against us, and have waged a fierce and bloody war for the proclaimed purpose of destroying the British and their power. The government of India formerly declared that it desired no further conquest, and it proved by its acts the sincerity of its professions. The government of India has no desire for conquest now; but it is bound, in its duty, to provide fully for its own security, and to guard the interests of those committed to its charge. To that end, and as the only sure mode of protecting the state from the perpetual recurrence of unprovoked and wasting wars, the governor-general is compelled to resolve upon the entire subjection of a people whom their own government has long been unable to control, and whom (as events have now shown) no punishment can deter from violence, no acts of friendship can conciliate to peace. Wherefore the governor-general of India has declared, and hereby proclaims, that the kingdom of the Punjaub is at an end; and that all the territories of Maharajah Dhuleep Sing are now and henceforth a portion of the British empire in India."

Their final outbreak.

Honesty of British policy.

Necessity for abolishing Seik independence.

Justice of British rule.

The wonted justice of British rule tempered the policy thus forced upon it. The maharajah has been treated with due consideration of his rank, the property of all who had not forfeited their rights by their own conduct, has been respected, and the utmost care has been taken to preserve to all the free exercise of their religion. What the final results of this new annexation to our Indian empire may prove to be, it is vain to speculate. Whether the Indus, "the historical boundary of India," shall prove a barrier against foreign aggression and a limit to British acquisition, remains to be seen; but many years must elapse, even under the most peaceful sway, ere the diverse races and creeds of British India can be reconciled, and the vast peninsula consolidated into one kingdom, united by the safe bonds of mutual confidence and the sense of a wise, just, and benignant rule. Experience has heretofore overturned every speculation. The first campaign in the Punjaub was regarded by many, whose judgment was worthy of confidence, as final; few perhaps will venture to pronounce the same of the second, notwithstanding the apparent finality of its results.

Time indispensable to consolidation.

Such is the history of the latest and perhaps the most critical struggle which Britain has yet been compelled to engage in, in order to maintain the integrity of her Indian empire. The disastrous struggles in Afghanistan are altogether insignificant, when compared with a war thus waged on terms so nearly equal, and yet so hardly brought to a triumphant close. When we take into consideration all the circumstances of the former campaign, we can readily account for them. The real strength of the Afghans was shown in their final retreat from the Punjaub. They are indeed formidable in their native fastnesses; but this arises more from the natural features of the country, than from the skill of their brave but undisciplined bands. Even in their strongholds and amid their terrible passes, British arms, under proper and skillful leaders, found no difficulty in coping with them, and on a fair field they proved how little apprehension could be excited by them, even though greatly outnumbering their opponents. But the Seiks are altogether different. Their bravery is fully equal to that of their opponents. Their skill and discipline is not greatly inferior, and it can hardly be questioned, that under European leaders, and with the same unanimity which their patriotic devotion to the commonwealth of Govind inspired in their first contest with the British, the mercenaries of our

Reflections suggested by the war.

Comparison of the Afghans and Seiks

CHAP. XIX

A.D. 1349.

Earnest desire for peace in India.

native army could be little relied upon in a similar struggle. Britain, however, longs to lay aside the weapons of the conqueror, and to consolidate her Eastern empire by arts of peace. Time alone, however well employed, will bind the native Hindoo to the British sceptre by the only safe ties, those of mutual interest and the confidence of mutual justice. The necessity of this is acknowledged. All the efforts of British rulers are now directed to render our sway in India alike beneficent and just. Should they succeed in accomplishing such a purpose, it will be a more noble and lasting victory than the proudest triumph of British arms; and it is only by converting the devotion of the Seik foe into the patriotism of the British subject, that a safe, a lasting, and a beneficial peace shall be secured on the north-west frontiers, so long the source of anxiety and apprehension to the British rulers of India.

THE END.

1853.

NEW ILLUSTRATED WORKS.

BOOKS FOR PRESENTS. BOOKS FOR THE YOUNG.

SABBATH SCHOOL REWARDS,

&c. &c.

LONDON:
T. NELSON AND SONS, PATERNOSTER ROW;
AND EDINBURGH.

EDINBURGH CABINET LIBRARY.

New and Enlarged Editions.

HISTORY OF ARABIA AND ITS PEOPLE. By DR. CRICHTON. Post 8vo, handsomely bound in cloth, and beautifully illustrated, price 5s. Gilt leaves, 6s. Morocco elegant, 11s. 6d.

HISTORY OF BRITISH INDIA. By HUGH MURRAY, F.R.S.E. With Narrative of the Affghan War, The Conquest of Scinde and Gwalior, The War in the Punjaub. With Portrait of Sir Charles Napier. Post 8vo, price 5s. Gilt leaves, 6s. Morocco elegant, 11s. 6d.

POLYNESIA: or, the Island World of the South Sea and the Pacific. By the Right Rev. BISHOP RUSSELL, of St. John's College, Oxford. Post 8vo, with beautiful Steel Frontispiece and Vignette, price 4s. 6d. Gilt leaves, 5s. Morocco elegant, 11s. 6d.

CIRCUMNAVIGATION OF THE GLOBE—Narratives of Maritime Discovery and Adventure. Post 8vo, with fine Steel Frontispiece and Vignette, price 4s. 6d. Gilt leaves, 5s. Morocco elegant, 11s. 6d.

HISTORY OF EGYPT: HER TEMPLES AND MONUMENTS. By the Rev. BISHOP RUSSELL. With a Narrative of all the Recent Discoveries in Hieroglyphics. Post 8vo, handsomely bound in cloth, and beautifully illustrated, price 4s. 6d. Gilt leaves, 5s. Morocco elegant, 11s. 6d.

DISCOVERY AND ADVENTURE IN THE POLAR SEAS AND REGIONS. By SIR JOHN LESLIE, &c. With Steel Portrait of Sir John Franklin, and a Narrative of all the Recent Expeditions. Post 8vo, price 4s. 6d. Gilt leaves, 5s. Morocco elegant, 11s. 6d.

TRAVELS AND RESEARCHES OF ALEXANDER VON HUMBOLDT. With a Narrative of his most Recent Researches, including his Celebrated Journey to the Ural Mountains, Exploration of the Altaian Range, and the Caspian Sea, &c. &c. Price 4s. 6d. Gilt leaves, 5s. Morocco elegant, 11s. 6d.

PALESTINE: or, THE HOLY LAND. By the Right Rev. BISHOP RUSSELL, of St. John's College, Oxford. With a narrative of the Visits and Researches of recent Travellers, including an Account of the late American Expedition to the Dead Sea and the River Jordan, &c. &c. With Engravings, post 8vo, price 4s. 6d. Gilt leaves, 5s. Morocco elegant, 11s. 6d.

LIFE OF SIR WALTER RALEIGH. By P. FRASER TYTLER, Esq. Post 8vo, cloth, price 4s. 6d. Gilt leaves, 5s. Morocco elegant, 11s. 6d.

LIFE OF HENRY THE EIGHTH. By P. FRASER TYTLER, Esq. Post 8vo, cloth, price 4s. 6d. Gilt leaves, 5s. Morocco elegant, 11s. 6d.

NEW ILLUSTRATED WORKS FOR PRESENTS, &c.

THE SWISS FAMILY ROBINSON. Beautifully Illustrated. Foolscap 8vo, cloth, price 3s. 6d. Gilt leaves, 4s. 6d. Morocco elegant, 7s. 6d.

STORIES FROM SWITZERLAND AND THE TYROL. Beautifully Illustrated. Foolscap 8vo, cloth, price 3s. 6d. Gilt leaves, 4s. 6d. Morocco elegant, 7s. 6d.

THE ROMANCE OF NATURAL HISTORY. By C. WEBBER. Beautifully Illustrated. Foolscap 8vo, cloth, price 3s. 6d. Gilt leaves, 4s. 6d. Morocco elegant, 7s. 6d.

THE ISLAND HOME; or, THE YOUNG CASTAWAYS. By CHRISTOPHER ROMAUNT, Esq. Beautifully Illustrated. Foolscap 8vo, cloth, price 3s. 6d. Gilt leaves, 4s. 6d. Morocco elegant, 7s. 6d.

PICTURES OF TRAVEL AND ADVENTURE. Beautifully Illustrated. Foolscap 8vo, cloth, 3s. 6d. Gilt leaves, 4s. 6d. Morocco elegant, 7s. 6d.

ROBINSON CRUSOE. Beautiful edition, large type, foolscap 8vo, with fine Engravings from designs by GILBERT, price 3s. 6d. Gilt leaves, 4s. 6d. Morocco elegant, 7s. 6d.

THE PILGRIM'S PROGRESS. Foolscap 8vo, beautifully illustrated, price 3s. 6d. Gilt leaves, 4s. 6d. Morocco elegant, 7s. 6d.

GRACE HOWARD, AND THE FAMILY AT GLEN LUNA. By AMY LOTHROP. Fine Edition. Foolscap 8vo, beautifully bound in cloth, with Frontispiece, price 3s. 6d. Gilt leaves, price 4s. 6d. Morocco elegant, 7s. 6d.

MAURICE GRAY, AND OTHER STORIES. A Book for Boys. Foolscap 8vo, beautifully illustrated, price 3s. 6d. Gilt leaves, 4s. 6d. Morocco elegant, 7s. 6d.

AMY ROSE, AND OTHER STORIES. A Book for Girls. Foolscap 8vo, beautifully illustrated, price 3s. 6d. Gilt leaves, 4s. 6d. Morocco elegant, 7s. 6d.

THE SEASONS OF THE YEAR; or, The Hand of God as Manifested in His Works. With two beautiful Steel Engravings from designs by BIRKET FOSTER, Esq. Price 3s. 6d. Gilt leaves, 4s. 6d. Morocco elegant, 7s. 6d.

UNCLE TOM'S CABIN. Beautiful edition, large type. With Life of MRS. STOWE. Post 8vo, handsomely bound, price 3s. 6d.

SAME EDITION. Splendidly illustrated, and richly gilt, adapted for a Present Book. Price 5s. Morocco elegant, 11s. 6d.

THE WIDE WIDE WORLD. By ELIZABETH WETHERELL. Fine Edition. Foolscap 8vo, beautifully bound in cloth, with Frontispiece and Vignette, price 3s. 6d. Cloth extra, richly gilt, price 5s. Morocco elegant, 10s.

BOOKS FOR THE FAMILY LIBRARY.

HOME—a Book for Young Ladies. Foolscap 8vo, with beautiful Frontispiece and Vignette, cloth, 2s. Gilt leaves, 2s. 6d. Morocco elegant, 6s.

SEED-TIME AND HARVEST: or, Sow Well and Reap Well. A Book for the Young. By the Rev. W. K. TWEEDIE, D.D., Tolbooth Free Church, Edinburgh. Fcp. 8vo, cloth, 2s. Gilt leaves, 2s. 6d. Morocco elegant, 6s.

KIND WORDS AWAKEN KIND ECHOES. Foolscap 8vo, cloth, price 2s. Gilt leaves, 2s. 6d. Morocco elegant, 6s.

MINISTER AND PEOPLE: or, Lights and Shadows in the Pastor's Life. A Tale. With Preface by the Rev. Dr. MASSIE, London. Foolscap 8vo, cloth, price 2s. Gilt leaves, 2s. 6d. Morocco elegant, 6s.

THE CHRISTIAN MISSIONARY.—Incidents in the Life of the Rev. Dr. Judson, Missionary to Burmah. Foolscap 8vo, price 2s. Gilt leaves, 2s. 6d. Morocco elegant, 6s.

LIFE OF SARAH B. JUDSON. By FANNY FORESTER. Foolscap 8vo, price 2s. Gilt leaves, 2s. 6d. Morocco elegant, 6s.

THE YOUNG LADY'S COMPANION. By H. NEWCOMB. Foolscap 8vo, price 2s. Gilt leaves, 2s. 6d. Morocco elegant, 6s.

THE HAND OF GOD IN HISTORY. By the Rev. HOLLIS READ. Foolscap 8vo, cloth, price 2s. Gilt leaves, 2s. 6d. Morocco elegant, 7s.

THE PLANETARY AND STELLAR WORLDS; OR, THE DISCOVERIES OF MODERN ASTRONOMY. With numerous Telescopic Views. Foolscap 8vo, price 2s. Gilt leaves, 2s. 6d. Morocco elegant, 7s.

SUCCESS IN LIFE. A Book for Young Men. Foolscap 8vo, with Beautiful Engraved Title. Elegantly bound in cloth, price 3s. Gilt leaves, 3s. 6d. Morocco elegant, 7s.

MEMORIALS OF EARLY GENIUS, AND ACHIEVEMENTS IN THE PURSUIT OF KNOWLEDGE. With Engravings. Foolscap 8vo, cloth, price 2s. Cloth extra, richly gilt, 3s. 6d. Morocco elegant, 7s.

OLIVER CROMWELL. By DR. D. WILSON, F.S.A., Scot. With Engravings. Foolscap 8vo, handsomely bound in cloth, price 2s. Cloth extra, richly gilt, 3s. 6d. Morocco elegant, 7s.

MEMORIALS OF THE DAWN OF THE REFORMATION IN EUROPE. With Engravings. Foolscap 8vo, handsomely bound in cloth, price 2s. Cloth extra, richly gilt, 3s. 6d. Morocco elegant, 7s.

FRANCE AND HER RELIGIOUS HISTORY: With Sketches of her Martyrs and Reformers. Foolscap 8vo, handsomely bound in cloth, price 2s. Cloth extra, richly gilt, 3s. 6d. Morocco elegant, 7s.

BOOKS FOR SCHOOL PRIZES, &c.

SPLENDIDLY ILLUSTRATED.

Foolscap 8vo, handsomely bound in cloth, 2s. 6d.
Cloth extra, richly gilt, 3s. 6d.
Morocco elegant, 7s.

SCENES OF MODERN TRAVEL AND ADVENTURE. With Engravings.

PERILS AND ADVENTURES ON THE DEEP. With Engravings.

SCENES FROM THE HISTORY OF THE CHRISTIAN CHURCH. With Engravings.

INCIDENTS OF MISSIONARY ENTERPRISE. With Engravings.

STORIES FROM EUROPEAN HISTORY. With Engravings.

LAST DAYS OF EMINENT CHRISTIANS. With Frontispiece.

NATURAL HISTORY OF BEASTS, BIRDS, FISHES, &c. With One Hundred Engravings.

BOOKS FOR SCHOOL PRIZES, &c. 18mo.

THE WHALE AND ITS CAPTORS. By CHEEVER. 18mo, cloth plain, price 1s. 6d. Cloth, gilt leaves, 2s.

BIOGRAPHY OF SELF-TAUGHT MEN. 18mo, cloth plain, price 1s. 6d. Cloth, gilt leaves, 2s.

DANGERS OF THE DEEP. With Engravings, 18mo, cloth, gilt leaves, 2s.

SCENES OF TRAVEL AND ADVENTURE IN CENTRAL AFRICA. With Engravings, 18mo, cloth, gilt leaves, 2s.

LIFE OF NAPOLEON AND HISTORY OF FRANCE TO THE DEATH OF LOUIS PHILIPPE. With Engravings, 18mo, cloth plain, price 1s. 6d. Cloth, gilt leaves, 2s.

MRS. SIGOURNEY'S POETICAL WORKS. With Steel Portrait, 18mo, cloth, gilt leaves, 2s.

GOLDSMITH'S POETICAL WORKS, AND VICAR OF WAKEFIELD. With Engravings, 18mo, cloth, gilt leaves, 2s.

BOOK OF USEFUL AND ORNAMENTAL KNITTING AND NETTING WORK. Square 16mo, cloth, gilt leaves, price 2s., with Illustrations.

BOOK OF CROCHET WORK. Square 12mo, cloth, gilt leaves, price 2s. 6d. With Illustrations.

SUPERIOR PRESENT BOOKS,

Foolscap 8vo, cloth extra, richly gilt, 3s. 6d. Morocco elegant, 7s.

WAYSIDE FLOWERS. Tales and Pencillings by FANNY FORRESTER, (MRS. JUDSON.) Foolscap 8vo. With two beautiful Illuminated Plates.

THE SOUVENIR. A Gift for all Seasons. Containing Tales, Poetry, and Music. With two beautiful illuminated Plates.

THE KEEPSAKE: A Fireside Companion of Tales, Sketches, and Poetry. With two beautiful illuminated Plates.

EVENINGS AT DERLEY MANOR. Pencilings and Sketches of the English Poets, and their Favourite Scenes.

THE GIFT BOOK OF BIOGRAPHY FOR YOUNG LADIES. By MISS KENDRICK and MRS. MARIA L. CHILD. With Engravings.

BEAUTIES OF MODERN BRITISH POETRY. Systematically arranged by D. GRANT, Esq., with fine Steel Frontispiece.

BEAUTIES OF MODERN SACRED POETRY. Systematically arranged, with Preface; by W. M'COMBIE, Esq., Author of "Hours of Thought."

DAILY TEXT BOOKS, &c.

GREEN PASTURES: or, Daily Food for the Lord's Flock. By the Rev. JAMES SMITH. 32mo, cloth gilt, price 1s. Morocco, 2s.

STILL WATERS: or, Refreshment for the Lord's Flock at Eventide. By the Rev. JAMES SMITH. 32mo, gilt, price 1s. Morocco, 2s.

THE CHRISTIAN'S DAILY BREAD. A Text Book of Scripture Truth and Promises, for every day in the year. Square 48mo. Roan plain, price 6d. Roan gilt, 9d. With tuck, 1s.

BIBLE READINGS; or, The Christian's Daily Monitor, by the Rev. JAMES SMITH. Square 48mo. Roan plain, 6d. Roan gilt, 9d. With tuck, 1s.

A CHAPLET OF FLOWERS, comprising a Scripture Text, with a Gem of Thought illustrating its meaning, for every day in the year. Square 48mo. Roan plain, price 6d. Roan gilt, 9d. With tuck, 1s.

COMPANION BY THE WAY, FOR A CHRISTIAN PILGRIM. Square 48mo. Roan plain, price 6d. Roan gilt, 9d. With tuck. 1s.

THE SHEPHERD OF ISRAEL; or, "Faithful is He that calleth you." Square 48mo. Roan plain, price 6d. Roan gilt, 9d. With tuck, 1s.

THE FAITHFUL PROMISER. Square 48mo. Roan plain, price 6d. Roan gilt, 9d. With tuck, 1s.

VALUABLE RELIGIOUS WORKS.

GLAD TIDINGS; or, The Gospel of Peace—A Series of Daily Readings for Christian Disciples. By the Rev. Dr. TWEEDIE, author of "Seed Time and Harvest," &c. Fcp. 8vo, cloth, 2s. 6d. Gilt leaves, 3s. Morocco elegant, 7s.

DAILY BIBLE READINGS FOR THE LORD'S HOUSEHOLD. By the Rev. JAMES SMITH, 18mo, cloth gilt, 2s. Mor. plain, 3s. 6d. Mor. extra, 5s.

THE BOOK OF FAMILY WORSHIP AND HELPS TO DEVOTION. By the Rev. W. B. CLARK. Foolscap 8vo, cloth, price 2s. Gilt leaves, 2s. 6d. Morocco antique, 5s. 6d.

THE CONGREGATIONAL TUNE BOOK, Containing upwards of 270 of the most admired Psalm and Hymn Tunes, Chaunts, &c. arranged for four voices, by ADAM WRIGHT, Esq., Organist of Rev. J. Angell James' Chapel, Birmingham. Cloth, price 3s. 6d. Half morocco, 6s.

ELIJAH THE TISHBITE. New and elegant edition. Foolscap 8vo, cloth, price 2s. Gilt leaves, 2s. 6d. Morocco elegant, 7s.

ELISHA. By KRUMMACHER, with Preface by BICKERSTETH. Foolscap 8vo, cloth, price 2s. Gilt leaves, 2s. 6d. Morocco elegant, 7s.

BOGATSKY'S GOLDEN TREASURY. Foolscap 8vo, cloth, price 2s. Gilt leaves, 2s. 6d. Morocco elegant, 7s.

FAMILY PICTURES FROM THE BIBLE. 18mo, cloth, price 1s. 6d. Gilt leaves, 2s.

THE WORLD TO COME. By ISAAC WATTS. 18mo, cloth, price 1s. 6d. Gilt leaves, 2s.

JENKS' FAMILY AND PRIVATE DEVOTIONS. 18mo, cloth, price 1s. 6d. Gilt leaves, 2s.

ASLEEP IN JESUS; or, Words of Consolation for Bereaved Parents. 18mo, cloth, gilt edges, 1s. 6d.

CHRISTIAN BIOGRAPHY—Lives of Bunyan, Hall, and Henry. By the Rev. Dr. JAMES HAMILTON. 18mo, cloth, gilt leaves, 1s. 6d.

BARROW'S (DR. ISAAC) WHOLE WORKS, 3 volumes 8vo. With Life, by the Rev. JAMES HAMILTON, D.D., London. Cloth, price 23s.

BISHOP HALL'S CONTEMPLATIONS. With Life, by the Rev. JAMES HAMILTON, D.D., London. One handsome volume 8vo, price 7s. 6d.

BISHOP HORNE'S COMMENTARY ON THE PSALMS. One volume 8vo. price 6s.

LEIGHTON'S (ARCHBISHOP) WHOLE WORKS. With Life. Complete in one volume 8vo, price 7s. 6d.

MILNER'S HISTORY OF THE CHRISTIAN CHURCH. Complete in one volume 8vo, price 10s. 6d.

BOOKS OF TRAVEL, BIOGRAPHY, &c.

CHINA: Sketches of the Country, Religion, and Customs of the Chinese. Illustrated. Royal 32mo, cloth, price 1s. 3d. Cloth gilt, 1s. 6d.

THE ARCTIC REGIONS. Royal 32mo, cloth, price 1s. 3d. Cloth gilt, 1s. 6d.

THE ISLAND WORLD OF THE PACIFIC. By CHEEVER. Royal 32mo, cloth, price 1s. 3d. Cloth gilt, 1s. 6d.

WATTS' SCRIPTURE HISTORY, Complete. Royal 32mo, cloth, price 1s. 3d. Cloth gilt, 1s. 6d.

THE YOUNG LADY'S FRIEND. Royal 32mo, cloth, price 1s. 3d. Cloth gilt, 1s. 6d.

THE GIRL'S BOOK. By MRS. SIGOURNEY. Royal 32mo, cloth, price 1s. 3d. Cloth gilt, 1s. 6d.

THE BOY'S BOOK. By MRS. SIGOURNEY. Royal 32mo, cloth, price 1s. 3d. Cloth gilt, 1s. 6d.

STEPHEN'S TRAVELS IN THE HOLY LAND. Royal 32mo, cloth, price 1s. 3d. Cloth gilt, 1s. 6d.

THE BOOK OF NATURAL HISTORY. Royal 32mo, cloth, price 1s. 3d. Cloth gilt, 1s. 6d.

THE BOOK OF ENTERTAINING AND INSTRUCTIVE ANECDOTE. Royal 32mo, cloth, price 1s. 3d. Cloth gilt, 1s. 6d.

EVENINGS AT HOME. Royal 32mo, cloth, price 1s. 3d. Cloth gilt, 1s. 6d.

CURIOSITIES AND WONDERS OF NATURE AND ART. Royal 32mo, cloth, price 1s. 3d. Cloth gilt, 1s. 6d.

ADVENTURES OF ROBINSON CRUSOE. Royal 32mo, cloth, price 1s. 3d. Cloth gilt, 1s. 6d.

MILTON'S POETICAL WORKS. Paradise Lost and Regained. Royal 32mo, cloth, price 1s. 3d. Cloth gilt, 1s. 6d.

LONGFELLOW'S POETICAL WORKS. With Steel Portrait. Royal 32mo, cloth, price 1s. 3d. Cloth gilt, 1s. 6d.

HISTORY OF SANDFORD AND MERTON. Royal 32mo, cloth, price 1s. 3d. Cloth gilt, 1s. 6d.

FOXE'S BOOK OF MARTYRS. Royal 32mo, cloth, price 1s. 3d. Cloth gilt, 1s. 6d.

KIRKE WHITE'S POETICAL WORKS. With Life by SOUTHEY. Royal 32mo, cloth, price 1s. 3d. Cloth gilt, 1s. 6d.

CHEEVER'S MEMORIALS OF A YOUTHFUL CHRISTIAN. Royal 32mo, cloth, price 1s. 3d. Cloth gilt, 1s. 6d.

HOME LIBRARY FOR LITTLE READERS.

Price 6d. each, with beautiful gilt cover. Or 9d. each, fancy cloth, gilt leaves.

Jessie Graham; or, Friends Dear, but Truth Dearer.
Blind Alice; or, Do Right, if you wish to be Happy.
Grace and Clara; or, Be Just as well as Generous.
Florence Arnot; or, Is She Generous?
Ellen Leslie; or, The Reward of Self-Control.
Stories for Little Readers. Adorned with Pi tures. First Series.
Stories for Little Readers. Adorned with Pictures. Second Series.
Love Tok n for Children.
A Kiss for a Blow; or, Stories of Love and Kindness in the Young.
Little Clara.
Harry Burne.
Sunshine and Shade; or, The Denham Family.
Sister Mary's Stories.
Story of the Walter Family.
The Mother's Story, &c.
The Well-Spent Hour.
Ellen Carrol.
Cousin Clara.
Mary Ross.
The Little Poetry Book.
The Faithful Dog, &c.
The Play Hour, &c.
James Thornton.
Harry Sanford.
Wild Flowers.
Harry Edwards.
Stories for the Young. First Series.
Stories for the Young. Second Series.

SABBATH STORIES FOR LITTLE READERS.

Price One Farthing each.

Harriet and Edward, &c.
The Almond Blossom, &c.
James Simpson, &c.
The Golden Key.
The Way to be Happy
Story of Theodore.

And a variety of others.

Price One Halfpenny each.

Little Charles.
The Broken Flower.
Sarah Williams.
The Kind Little Boy, &c.
Edith and Charles, &c.
Stories on the Lord's Prayer.

And a variety of others.

Price One Penny each.

The Children and the Dove.
Little Frank and his Letter.
Sailor Boy and his Bible.
Who Directs our Steps?
The Lark's Nest.
Lucy Roberts.

And a variety of others.

Price Twopence each.

Robert, Margaret, and Maria.
Robert Ellis.
Honesty the Best Policy.
The Morning Walk, &c.
The Holidays; or, A Visit Home.
Jane Scott.

And a variety of others.